THE
CAMBRIDGE EDITION OF
THE LETTERS AND WORKS OF
D. H. LAWRENCE

THE WORKS OF D. H. LAWRENCE

EDITORIAL BOARD

STUDIES IN CLASSIC AMERICAN LITERATURE

D. H. LAWRENCE

EDITED BY

EZRA GREENSPAN
LINDETH VASEY

AND

JOHN WORTHEN

CAMBRIDGE
UNIVERSITY PRESS

PUBLISHED BY THE PRESS SYNDICATE OF THE UNIVERSITY OF CAMBRIDGE
The Pitt Building, Trumpington Street, Cambridge, United Kingdom

CAMBRIDGE UNIVERSITY PRESS
The Edinburgh Building, Cambridge CB2 2RU, UK
40 West 20th Street, New York, NY 10011-4211, USA
477 Williamstown Road, Port Melbourne, VIC 3207, Australia
Ruiz de Alarcón 13, 28014 Madrid, Spain
Dock House, The Waterfront, Cape Town 8001, South Africa

http://www.cambridge.org

First published 2003

Printed in India at TechBooks Electronic Services

Typeface Ehrhardt 10/12 pt   *System* LATEX 2ε   [TB]

A catalogue record for this book is available from the British Library

Library of Congress cataloguing in publication data

Lawrence, D. H. (David Herbert), 1885–1930.
Studies in Classic American Literature / D. H. Lawrence; edited by Ezra Greenspan,
Lindeth Vasey and John Worthen.
p.   cm. – (The works of D. H. Lawrence)
ISBN 0 521 55016 5
I. Greenspan, Ezra.   II. Vasey, Lindeth.   III. Worthen, John.
IV. Series: Lawrence, D. H. (David Herbert), 1885–1930. Works. 1979.
PR6023/A93A19   2003
882'.912 – dc21   98-8068 CIP

CONTENTS

GENERAL EDITOR'S PREFACE

D. H. Lawrence was one of the great writers of the twentieth century - yet the texts of his writings, whether published during his lifetime or since, are, for the most part, textually corrupt. The extent of the corruption is remarkable; it can derive from every stage of composition and publication. We know from study of his MSS that Lawrence was a careful writer, though not rigidly consistent in matters of minor convention. We know also that he revised at every possible stage. Yet he rarely if ever compared one stage with the previous one, and overlooked the errors of typists or copyists. He was forced to accept, as most authors are, the often inflexible house-styling of his printers, which overrode his punctuation and even his sentence-structure and paragraphing. He sometimes overlooked plausible printing errors. More important, as a professional author living by his pen, he had to accept, with more or less good will, stringent editing by a publisher's reader in his early days, and at all times the results of his publishers' timidity. So the fear of Grundyish disapproval, or actual legal action, led to bowdlerisation or censorship from the very beginning of his career. Threats of libel suits produced other changes. Sometimes a publisher made more changes than he admitted to Lawrence. On a number of occasions in dealing with American and British publishers Lawrence produced texts for both which were not identical. Then there were extraordinary lapses like the occasion when a typist turned over two pages of MS at once, and the result happened to make sense. This whole story can be reconstructed from the introductions to the volumes in this edition; cumulatively they form a history of Lawrence's writing career.

The Cambridge edition aims to provide texts which are as close as can now be determined to those he would have wished to see printed. They have been established by a rigorous collation of extant manuscripts and typescripts, proofs and early printed versions; they restore the words, sentences, even whole pages omitted or falsified by editors or compositors; they are freed from printing-house conventions which were imposed on Lawrence's style; and interference on the part of frightened publishers has been eliminated. Far from doing violence to the texts Lawrence would have wished to see published, editorial intervention is essential to recover them. Though we have to accept that some cannot now be recovered in their entirety because early states have not survived, we must be glad that so much evidence remains. Paradoxical as it may seem, the outcome of this recension will be texts which differ, often radically and certainly frequently, from those seen by the author himself.

Editors adopt the principle that the most authoritative form of the text is to be followed, even if this leads sometimes to a 'spoken' or a 'manuscript' rather than a 'printed' style. We have not wanted to strip off one house-styling in order to impose another. Editorial discretion has been allowed in order to regularise Lawrence's sometimes wayward spelling and punctuation in accordance with his most frequent practice in a particular text. A detailed record of these and other decisions on textual matters, together with the evidence on which they are based, will be found in the textual apparatus which records variant readings in manuscripts, typescripts and proofs; and printed variants in forms of the text published in Lawrence's lifetime. We do not record posthumous corruptions, except where first publication was posthumous. Significant MS readings may be found in the occasional explanatory note.

In each volume, the editor's introduction relates the contents to Lawrence's life and to his other writings; it gives the history of composition of the text in some detail, for its intrinsic interest, and because this history is essential to the statement of editorial principles followed. It provides an account of publication and reception which will be found to contain a good deal of hitherto unknown information. Where appropriate, appendixes make available extended draft manuscript readings of significance, or important material, sometimes unpublished, associated with a particular work.

Though Lawrence was a twentieth-century writer and in some respects remains our contemporary, the idiom of his day is not invariably intelligible now, especially to the many readers who are not native speakers of British English. His use of dialect forms is another difficulty, and further barriers to full understanding are created by now obscure literary, historical, political or other references and allusions. On these occasions explanatory notes are supplied by the editor; it is assumed that the reader has access to a good general dictionary and that the editor need not gloss words or expressions that may be found in it. Where Lawrence's letters are quoted in editorial matter, the reader should assume that his manuscript is alone the source of eccentricities of phrase or spelling.

ACKNOWLEDGEMENTS

We are grateful in particular to the following for their encouragement, advice and support: Michael Black, James T. Boulton, Andrew Brown and the late Warren Roberts.

We are also grateful to the staff of Cambridge University Press (especially to Linda Bree); to Harold Shapiro for pioneering work on this edition; to Cathy Henderson, Cliff Farrington, John Kirkpatrick and the staff of the Harry Ransom Humanities Research Center (HRHRC) of the University of Texas at Austin; to the Office of Sponsored Programs and Research at the University of South Carolina for a travel-to-collections grant; to the late Charles Harold Bennett Smith; to Hilary Laurie and Andrew Rosenheim at Penguin Books; to Gerald Pollinger; to Anthony Rota; and to the following individuals, libraries and institutions (together with their librarians and archivists) for making available materials for this edition: Victor A. Berch and Bucknell University, Anna Lou Ashby and the Pierpont Morgan Library, the University of Illinois, Dorothy Johnston and the University of Nottingham, Cynthia Andrews and the University of New Mexico, Lori N. Curtis and David Farmer at the University of Tulsa and Yale University.

We also wish to thank the following for their particular contributions: Harry Acton, Andrew Barker, Sam Dawson, David Ellis, Susan Gagg, Jane Gibson, Andrew Harrison, Paul Heapy, Michael Herbert, Judith Jesch, Bethan Jones, Mark Kinkead-Weekes, Dieter Mehl, Stefania Michelucci, Paul Poplawski, Peter Preston, Neil Reeve, Pat Roberts, Cornelia Rumpf-Worthen, Tatiana Rapatzikou, M. Wynn Thomas, John Turner, Ronald Vasey, Andrew Wawn, † Thomas Wiedemann, Sue Wilson, Dorothy Worthen, † F. M. Worthen, Jeremy Worthen, Peter Worthen.

July 2001   E.G.
                                                                             L.S.V.
                                                                             J.W.

Note

Early in 1978 the late Charles Harold Bennett Smith wrote to Gerald Pollinger (agent for the Estate of D. H. Lawrence) announcing that he possessed a number of Lawrence manuscripts. When Gerald Pollinger asked for some idea of what Smith might have, the latter replied (on 6 September 1978) with a list that included a great many unpublished *Studies* essays and over 300 previously unknown letters and postcards. As Gerald Pollinger made enquiries in Lawrence circles, it became clear that no-one had ever heard of Smith as a collector, let alone had any knowledge of him as the owner of such an extraordinary archive. Very little is in fact known of Smith; he had lived in New York for some years and in 1978 was residing in Bermuda. He explained that he had long been enthusiastic about Lawrence's writing and had seen the manuscript material for sale in a small bookshop; as he was not a man of means he had had to acquire his collection slowly, piece by piece.

What he possessed all turned out to be linked in one way or another with Lawrence's American agent of the early 1920s, Robert Mountsier. When Lawrence had originally broken with Mountsier in February 1923, he had asked him to 'Tell me what MSS you have. And if you would like to keep any of them' (*Letters*, iv. 400). In September 1924, however, he had asked Mountsier to hand over to his New York agent, Curtis Brown, 'all the manuscripts and papers I left in your keeping' (v. 127); the agency also wrote to Mountsier asking what manuscripts he still retained, so that they could 'arrange to have them collected' (v. 128 n. 2). Mountsier objected, and Lawrence wrote a good deal more strongly to him on 5 October 1924: 'I must once more ask you, therefore, to hand over to Mr Barmby all Manuscripts and papers of mine you have in your possession. They are not in any sense your property. And what name does one give to a man who deliberately detains property not his own?' (v. 145). Mountsier, however, kept his Lawrence manuscripts: as late as 1929, Lawrence was complaining 'I've lost so many MSS already – Seltzer has some – Mountsier – some have disappeared unaccountably – and it seems a shame' (vii. 204). When, some years later, the Harry Ransom Humanities Research Center in Austin, Texas, acquired Robert Mountsier's papers, it turned out that, although much of the material concerned Lawrence, none of Lawrence's letters or manuscripts – indeed, practically nothing in his handwriting – was included. Someone had carefully separated this material off from the rest and removed it; and it seems undeniable that this was what had now turned up in Smith's possession. How he acquired it we shall probably never know.

Gerald Pollinger invited Smith to the D. H. Lawrence Conference at the University of Southern Illinois at Carbondale in April 1979, and Smith brought with him photocopies of some of the letters he owned, and a photo-copy of a Seltzer contract for *Studies* dated 2 January 1923. Lawrentians who saw the materials agreed that they were genuine, that they were completely unknown, and that they would utterly alter our understanding of Mountsier's role in Lawrence's life. It was decided that the late Warren Roberts (then Director of the HRHRC, but also Lawrence's bibliographer and an eminent Lawrence scholar) would go to Bermuda to see exactly what Smith possessed. Warren Roberts and his wife Pat stayed in Smith's house, where they found large numbers of Lawrence manuscripts, typescripts and letters lying about. With Smith's permission, Warren Roberts began to photocopy the collection on a nearby machine, making two copies of everything, and ensuring that the photocopies were clear and complete – something which would turn out to be vital for the editors of this edition. Pat Roberts meanwhile attempted to en-tertain an increasingly impatient Smith, who may have been starting to realise how the value of his collection would be affected if copies were made available. Another example of the unexpected richness of Smith's collection came just as Warren and Pat Roberts were leaving for the airport. Warren spotted still further unpublished material – the carbon typescript of *The Lost Girl*, a not inconsiderable stack of 486 pages, and totally unexpected; it was something Smith had never previously mentioned. In January the following year, Lindeth Vasey went to Bermuda to photocopy this and any other material which she could find or Smith could turn up – and one item which emerged from this visit was the photograph of Robert Mountsier reproduced in *Letters*, iv. Smith died in the early 1980s and his collection was sold at auction by Sothebys in New York; much of it is now unlocated (see footnote 29 to the Introduction).

As can be seen by the large number of Smith items referred to in footnotes to the Introduction (their Roberts numbers taken from the manuscript section in the third edition of Roberts's *Bibliography*), this edition of *Studies* is hugely indebted to Smith's materials; without them it would not have been possi-ble to assemble very much more material than Armin Arnold had included in *The Symbolic Meaning* in 1962. Of the twenty manuscripts or groups of manuscripts used in this edition, no fewer than ten came from the Smith col-lection; to cite just two examples, not only the crucial final manuscript (E382q) of *Studies*, containing Lawrence's references to Whitman's naked peregrina-tions in senility, but the very earliest surviving example of that same essay, dating from 1919 (E382b), shocking and fascinating in quite a different way.

The first person to work on an edition of *Studies* for the Cambridge Edition, Harold Shapiro, abandoned his work on hearing of the Smith collection; it not only rendered what he had done up to that point incomplete but ensured that nearly all of his work would have to be done again. The history of the *Studies* manuscripts since 1980, however (and the fact that no scholarly or indeed any kind of access to them has been possible), means that the opportunity which Warren Roberts took to make photocopies of them in 1979 effectively rescued them for this edition, and their texts for posterity. The textual editors would therefore like to dedicate their work on this volume to the patience and generosity of Harold Smith, and the forethought and perspicacity of Warren Roberts.

Lindeth Vasey
John Worthen

CHRONOLOGY

11 September 1885	Born in Eastwood, Nottinghamshire
September 1898–July 1901	Pupil at Nottingham High School
1902–1908	Pupil teacher; student at University College, Nottingham
7 December 1907	First publication: 'A Prelude', in *Nottinghamshire Guardian*
October 1908	Appointed as teacher at Davidson Road School, Croydon
November 1909	Publishes five poems in *English Review*
9 December 1910	Death of his mother, Lydia Lawrence
19 January 1911	*The White Peacock* published in New York (20 January in London)
19 November 1911	Ill with pneumonia; resigns his teaching position 28 February 1912
March 1912	Meets Frieda Weekley; they leave for Germany on 3 May
23 May 1912	*The Trespasser*
February 1913	*Love Poems and Others*
29 May 1913	*Sons and Lovers*
13 July 1914	Marries Frieda Weekley in London
26 November 1914	*The Prussian Officer and Other Stories*
30 September 1915	*The Rainbow* published; suppressed by court order on 13 November
February 1916	Reading Melville's *Moby Dick*
May 1916	Reading Dana's *Two Years Before the Mast* (and wants to read Melville's *Typee* and *Omoo*); requests Everyman's Library catalogue
June 1916	*Twilight in Italy*
July 1916	*Amores*
summer 1916	Gives Murry copy of Crèvecoeur's *Letters From an American Farmer*

4 January 1917	Requests from Mountsier copies from Everyman's Library of works by Melville, Cooper, Whitman, Crèvecoeur, Hawthorne, Rousseau, Lincoln, Emerson, Franklin, Hamilton and Poe
February 1917	Planned visit to USA postponed when passport applications denied
August 1917	Begins work on *Studies*
15 October 1917	Composition interrupted when the Lawrences are expelled from Cornwall by authorities; DHL probably resumes only in January 1918
26 November 1917	*Look! We Have Come Through!*
mid-February 1918	At work on 'Poe' essay
June 1918	Writing 'a last essay on Whitman'
August 1918	Sends his agent James B. Pinker the first essay ('The Spirit of Place') for possible publication in the *English Review*
October 1918	*New Poems*
November 1918–June 1919	Publication of first eight essays from *Studies in Classic American Literature* in *English Review*: 'The Spirit of Place' (November), 'Benjamin Franklin' (December), 'Henry [*sic*] St. John de Crèvecoeur' (January), 'Fenimore Cooper's Anglo-American Novels' (February), 'Fenimore Cooper's Leatherstocking Novels' (March), 'Edgar Allan Poe' (April), 'Nathaniel Hawthorne' (May) and 'The Two Principles' (June)
February 1919	DHL tries to interest his American publisher, Benjamin Huebsch, in *Studies* by having first four essays from *English Review* sent to him
7 September 1919	Receives offer from Thomas Seltzer to act as American publisher of *Women in Love*

September 1919	Revises essays on Hawthorne (second part), Dana, Melville and Whitman
10 October 1919	Sends revised composite text of *Studies* to Huebsch; Huebsch remains indecisive well into mid 1920
November 1919	To Italy, then Capri and Sicily
20 November 1919	*Bay*
16 February 1920	Asks Robert Mountsier to act as his American agent (accepted on 26 March)
May 1920	*Touch and Go*
June 1920	Returns to work on *Studies* in anticipation of its book publication; negotiates with Martin Secker and Cecil Palmer for publication in England, with Huebsch and Seltzer for publication in USA
July 1920	Huebsch announces that he is ceding American publication of *Studies* to Seltzer
2 August 1920	DHL sends revised composite text of essays to Mountsier in New York
7 September 1920	Sends Mountsier new introduction to *Studies*, published as 'America, Listen to Your Own' in December 1920 *New Republic*
9 November 1920	*Women in Love* published in USA by Seltzer (in England by Secker on 10 June 1921)
25 November 1920	*The Lost Girl*
February 1921	*Movements in European History*
4 April 1921	Asks Curtis Brown to act as his English agent
10 May 1921	*Psychoanalysis and the Unconscious*
23 July 1921	'Whitman', shortened by Mountsier, in *Nation and Athenaeum* (reprinted in *New York Call* on 21 August 1921)
5 November 1921	Receives invitation from Mabel Dodge Sterne to stay in Taos, New Mexico
12 December 1921	*Sea and Sardinia*

9 December 1921	*Tortoises*
18 February 1922	Sends Curtis Brown text of *Studies* to offer to Jonathan Cape for publication in England; Cape declines
26 February 1922	Departs with Frieda for Ceylon from Naples, en route to Western Hemisphere
13 March 1922	Arrives in Ceylon; departs for Australia on 24 April and arrives in Perth on 4 May
14 April 1922	*Aaron's Rod*
11 August 1922	Sails out of Sydney for San Francisco on the *Tahiti*
4 September 1922	Arrives at San Francisco
11 September 1922	Reaches Taos, New Mexico
22 September 1922	Requests copy of text of *Studies* from Seltzer (and from Mountsier), as well as Raymond Weaver's Melville biography
11 October 1922	Asks Mountsier his opinion of 'Studies of the American Daimon' as an alternative title
23 October 1922	*Fantasia of the Unconscious*
24 October 1922	*England, My England and Other Stories*
by 11 November 1922	Starts rewriting *Studies* one final time
28 November 1922	Informs Mountsier that *Studies* is 'nearly done'
1 December 1922	Moves with Frieda to Del Monte Ranch north of Taos
3 December 1922	Sends Mountsier texts of rewritten essays up to 'Dana'
12 December 1922	Finishes rewriting *Studies* and prepares to send last four essays to Mountsier
late December 1922–early Jan. 1923	Visits of Seltzers and Mountsier at Del Monte Ranch
19 January 1923	Mails Seltzer text of *Studies*
3 February 1923	Severs connection with Mountsier
25 February 1923	Accepts Secker's terms for publication of *Studies* in England

March 1923	*The Ladybird, The Fox, The Captain's Doll*
March–April 1923	Leaves New Mexico and settles in Chapala, Mexico
1 May 1923	Second contract with Seltzer for *Studies*
May–June 1923	Reads proof of *Studies* and rewrites ending of 'Whitman'
7 June 1923	Returns contract for Secker edition of *Studies* to Curtis Brown
9 July 1923	Departs Mexico; arrives in New York on 19 July
20 July–21 August 1923	Stays with the Seltzers at a rented cottage in New Jersey; reads proofs of various works and meets New York literati
22 August 1923	Departs New York en route to return trip through south western USA and Mexico
27 August 1923	*Studies in Classic American Literature* published in USA by Seltzer
September 1923	*Kangaroo*
9 October 1923	*Birds, Beasts and Flowers*
December 1923–March 1924	In England, France and Germany
March 1924–September 1925	In New and Old Mexico
June 1924	*Studies in Classic American Literature* published in England by Secker
August 1924	*The Boy in the Bush* (with Mollie Skinner)
10 September 1924	Death of his father, Arthur John Lawrence
February 1925	Replaces Seltzer with Alfred A. Knopf as US publisher
14 May 1925	*St. Mawr and Other Stories*
7 December 1925	*Reflections on the Death of a Porcupine*
January 1926	*The Plumed Serpent*
June 1927	*Mornings in Mexico*
24 May 1928	*The Woman Who Rode Away and Other Stories*
June 1928–March 1930	In Switzerland and, principally, in France

CUE-TITLES

A. Manuscript locations

BucU   Bucknell University
Pierpont Morgan   Pierpont Morgan Library
Smith   The late Charles Harold Bennett Smith
UIll   University of Illinois
UN   University of Nottingham
UNM   University of New Mexico
UT   University of Texas at Austin
UTul   University of Tulsa
YU   Yale University

B. Printed works: American Literature

(The place of publication, here and throughout, is London unless otherwise stated.)

BFA   *Benjamin Franklin's Autobiography* (1791). Introduction by William Macdonald. J. M. Dent & Sons (Everyman's Library), 1908.

BR   Nathaniel Hawthorne. *The Blithedale Romance* (1852). Introduction by Ernest Rhys. J. M. Dent & Sons (Everyman's Library), 1912.

DS   James Fenimore Cooper. *The Deerslayer, or the First Warpath* (1841). Editor's Note anon. J. M. Dent & Sons (Everyman's Library), 1906.

HB   James Fenimore Cooper. *Homeward Bound* (1838). George Routledge & Sons, 1888.

LAF   Hector St Jean de Crèvecoeur [Michel-Guillaume Jean de Crèvecoeur]. *Letters From an American Farmer* (1783). Introduction by Warren Barton Blake. J. M. Dent & Sons (Everyman's Library), 1912.

xix

LG	Walt Whitman. *Leaves of Grass* (*1*) & *Democratic Vistas*. Introduction by Horace Traubel. J. M. Dent & Sons (Everyman's Library), 1912.
LOM	James Fenimore Cooper. *The Last of the Mohicans* (1826). Editor's Note anon. J. M. Dent & Sons (Everyman's Library), 1906.
MD	Herman Melville. *Moby Dick, or the White Whale* (1851). Editor's Note anon. J. M. Dent & Sons (Everyman's Library), 1907.
OMO	Herman Melville. *Omoo* (1847). Introduction anon. J. M. Dent & Sons (Everyman's Library), 1908.
PF	James Fenimore Cooper. *The Pathfinder, or the Inland Sea* (1840). Editor's Note anon. J. M. Dent & Sons (Everyman's Library), 1906.
PI	James Fenimore Cooper. *The Pioneers* (1823). Editor's Note anon. J. M. Dent & Sons (Everyman's Library), 1907.
PR	James Fenimore Cooper. *The Prairie* (1827). Editor's Note anon. J. M. Dent & Sons (Everyman's Library), 1907.
TMI	Edgar Allan Poe. *Tales of Mystery and Imagination*. Introduction by Pádraic Colum. J. M. Dent & Sons (Everyman's Library), 1908.
TSL	Nathaniel Hawthorne. *The Scarlet Letter* (1850). Introduction by Ernest Rhys. J. M. Dent & Sons (Everyman's Library), 1906.
TYB	Richard Henry Dana. *Two Years Before the Mast* (1840). Introduction anon. Nelson (Nelson's Classics), n.d. [1912].
TYP	Herman Melville. *Typee* (1846). Introduction anon. J. M. Dent & Sons (Everyman's Library), 1907.

C. Other works

FWL	D. H. Lawrence. *The First 'Women in Love'*. Ed. John Worthen and Lindeth Vasey. Cambridge: Cambridge University Press, 1998.

Hardy	D. H. Lawrence. *Study of Thomas Hardy and Other Essays*. Ed. Bruce Steele. Cambridge: Cambridge University Press, 1985.
KJB	*The Holy Bible Containing the Old and New Testaments (Authorised King James Version)*.
Letters, i.	James T. Boulton, ed. *The Letters of D. H. Lawrence*. Volume I. Cambridge: Cambridge University Press, 1979.
Letters, ii.	George J. Zytaruk and James T. Boulton, eds. *The Letters of D. H. Lawrence*. Volume II. Cambridge: Cambridge University Press, 1981.
Letters, iii.	James T. Boulton and Andrew Robertson, eds. *The Letters of D. H. Lawrence*. Volume III. Cambridge: Cambridge University Press, 1984.
Letters, iv.	Warren Roberts, James T. Boulton and Elizabeth Mansfield, eds. *The Letters of D. H. Lawrence*. Volume IV. Cambridge: Cambridge University Press, 1987.
Letters, viii.	James T. Boulton, ed. *The Letters of D. H. Lawrence*. Volume VIII. Cambridge: Cambridge University Press, 2000.
Movements	D. H. Lawrence. *Movements in European History*. Ed. Philip Crumpton. Cambridge: Cambridge University Press, 1988.
Nehls	Edward Nehls, ed. *D. H. Lawrence: A Composite Biography*. 3 volumes. Madison: University of Wisconsin Press, 1957–9.
OED2	*The Oxford English Dictionary*. Second edn. on Compact Disc. Oxford University Press, 1994.
Phoenix	Edward D. McDonald, ed. *Phoenix: The Posthumous Papers of D. H. Lawrence*. New York: Viking, 1936.
Reflections	D. H. Lawrence. *Reflections on the Death of a Porcupine and Other Essays*. Ed. Michael Herbert. Cambridge: Cambridge University Press, 1988.
Roberts	Warren Roberts and Paul Poplawski. *A Bibliography of D. H. Lawrence*. Third edn. Cambridge: Cambridge University Press, 2001.
Seltzer	Gerald M. Lacy, ed. *D. H. Lawrence: Letters to Thomas and Adele Seltzer*. Santa Barbara, California: Black Sparrow Press, 1976.

Studies   *Studies in Classic American Literature*
Symbolic Meaning   Armin Arnold, ed. *The Symbolic Meaning*. Arundel:
                       Centaur Press Limited, 1962.
VOA   Leo Frobenius. *The Voice of Africa*, tr. Rudolf Blind. 2
                       volumes. Hutchinson & Co., 1913.
WL   D. H. Lawrence. *Women in Love*. Ed. David Farmer,
                       Lindeth Vasey and John Worthen. Cambridge:
                       Cambridge University Press, 1987.

INTRODUCTION

Background

Judged even by the standards of the sometimes tortuous publishing history of Lawrence's work, *Studies* occupies a unique position. The essays span vastly different periods in his writing career; the esoteric subjects which interested him in the period 1917–19, for example, and which profoundly influenced the essays of that date, had almost no connection with the much brisker and hard-hitting concentration on America demonstrated in the final revision, which he wrote at the end of 1922. There were, at various times, fifteen separate items which belonged to or were designed for the book, all of them revised on different occasions, nearly all of them more than once, some of them four or five times, and each time corrected with the errors of their predecessors preserved or extended. Two items (a 'Foreword' drafted in 1920 and the essay called 'The Two Principles') were discarded before the final book was assembled; other essays grew so much in revision that they split into two separate items. Tracing a clear textual history is at times almost impossible, because so many of the significant artefacts of the various stages of revision are lost. The Textual Diagram may help to reveal at least some of the textual paths of the various items, but it also shows just how many individual items are missing.

It is convenient, however, to posit five main stages in the creation of the book. There was a first stage of preliminary reading and planning, which extended from early in 1916 into the first half of 1917. The second stage, of actual composition and revision, occurred during the years 1917–19, and culminated in eight of what were at that stage twelve essays being published in the *English Review*. The third stage involved Lawrence's continued revision of the essays not printed by the *English Review*, and his efforts in 1919 to get these revised forms into print, together with attempts to interest publishers in the idea of the book. The fourth stage of work came through his attempts between 1920 and 1921 to establish a new (though also frequently revised) text of the book, along with fresh attempts to get a new Foreword and versions of the last five essays published in magazines. Fifth came his creation of the final version of the book between October 1922 and June 1923, culminating in the

TEXTUAL

	'America, Listen to Your Own'	Foreword	The Spirit of Place	Benjamin Franklin	Crève-coeur	Cooper I White Novels	Cooper II Leather-stocking Novels
FIRST STAGE 1916–17: reading and making notes				?	?		?
SECOND STAGE 1917–19: MS and TS Essays			lost	lost	lost	lost	
English Review publication of the **First Version**			Nov. 1918	Dec. 1918	Jan. 1919	Feb. 1919	Mar. 1919
THIRD STAGE 1919: revision of unpublished MS and TS essays							
1919: Intermediate Version assembled and sent to Huebsch							
FOURTH STAGE 1920–1: revised text to RM	E382.5a E382.5c						
'Foreword' in the *New Republic*	**15 Dec. 1920**						
RM's							
attempts at							
periodical							
publication							
Version of 'Whitman' in the *Nation & Athenaeum*							
FIFTH STAGE 1922–4: Autumn 1922 TCC		E382p					
Autumn 1922 Final MS						E382q	
Lost duplicate Final MS		E382o	E382o	E382o			
1922–3 Final corrected TS						lost	
1923 Seltzer's proofs						lost	
'Whitman' extra revision MS							
'Whitman' extra revision TS							
American First edition: Final Version				New York, 1923: Thomas Seltzer			
English First edition				London, 1924: Martin Secker			

Texts in **bold** are printed in full in this volume: other surviving texts are recorded in the Textual apparatus. Shadings in column one show development from First to Fifth Stage.

DIAGRAM

Edgar Allan Poe	Hawthorne I	Hawthorne II *Scarlet Letter*	The Two Principles	Dana	Melville I	Melville II *Moby Dick*	Whitman	Textual apparatus
?		E382e	?	?		?	?	
lost		E382g	lost	E382r		E382s	lost	TS1
Apr. 1919	May 1919	Proofs	June 1919					Per
		E382f		E382n	E382l	E382i	E382b	MS2
		lost						
		lost						
								Per
		E382h						TS3
					E382m			TS4
						E382k/j		TS5/TCC5
							E382d	TCC6
							23 July 1921	Per
	E382p						E382p	TCC7
					E382q		E382q	MS8
lost					*lost*			
					lost			
					lost			
							E382a	MS9
							E382c	TS10
				New York, 1923: Thomas Seltzer				A1
				London, 1924: Martin Secker				E1

Diagonal hatchings represent versions which belong together. E nos. are those of manuscripts in Roberts. Per = periodical RM = Robert Mountsier

publication of the book on 27 August 1923 in the USA and in June 1924 in England.

First Stage 1916–17: reading and note-making

The idea of a study of the 'American classics' – the term so new in the second decade of the twentieth century that it was still an oxymoron to many of his contemporaries in the United States, no less than in Britain – seems to have come to Lawrence late in 1916–17. In a real sense, though, the seed of *Studies in Classic American Literature* lay buried deep in his sensibility and can be traced back to his childhood, when he first read James Fenimore Cooper's 'Leatherstocking' novels and absorbed their portrayal of the New World with a boy's wide-eyed fascination. When and to what extent he developed a further acquaintance with American writing is a matter of conjecture. He would have encountered, at home in Eastwood, extensive selections from various American writers in Richard Garnett's remarkable twenty-volume anthology, *The International Library of Famous Literature* (1899), a set of which had been purchased by his brother Ernest.[1] Of Walt Whitman, the central figure in his appreciation of American culture and society and the one to whom he was most often compared, Lawrence was certainly well aware (he quoted Whitman in *The White Peacock*[2]), as he was aware of Henry Wadsworth Longfellow and Jack London – writers all mentioned (and Whitman and Longfellow quoted) in his early letters. Of William James, especially on pragmatism, he was also cognisant, as he was of Henry James, although the former would probably have been the more compatible with Lawrence's thought and sensibility.[3] Two additional writers whom he had not only encountered by 1906 but also

---

[1] *Letters*, i. 4–6. (*Letters* hereafter usually cited in text and footnotes by volume and page number.) Garnett saw the literatures of Britain and the United States 'not as two great literatures regarding each other across the Atlantic, but one colossal literature bestriding that vast ocean' (*The International Library of Famous Literature*, i. xv). He was aided in the project by various critics and writers, including three Americans: Donald G. Mitchell ('Ik Marvel'), Henry James and Bret Harte. Volume xiv featured as its introduction James's 'The Future of the Novel' and contained numerous selections from nineteenth-century writers; volume xv, edited by Harte, consisted exclusively of works by American writers or about the United States. The set included extracts from Franklin's *Autobiography* (xv. 6860), Cooper's *The Pilot* (xiv. 6645) and *The Spy* (xv. 6994), complete texts of Poe's *The Fall of the House of Usher* (xii. 5789), *The Gold Bug* (xv. 7122) and *William Wilson* (xvii. 7944), extracts from Hawthorne's *The Scarlet Letter* (xv. 7088), Dana's *Two Years Before the Mast* (xiii. 6122) and Melville's *Moby-Dick* (xii. 5806), and complete texts of Whitman's 'O Captain! My Captain!' (xv. 7304), 'Death's Valley' (xviii. 8392) and 'Song of the Banner at Daybreak' (xix. 8826).

[2] *The White Peacock*, ed. Andrew Robertson (Cambridge, 1983), 171:5 ('uttering joyous leaves', from 'I saw in Louisiana a Live-Oak Growing' – *LG* 106). DHL's friend Jessie Chambers quoted the poem in February 1908, suggesting that they both knew it by then ('The Collected Letters of Jessie Chambers', *D. H. Lawrence Review*, xii, 1–2, Spring–Summer 1979, 2).

[3] John Worthen, *D. H. Lawrence: The Early Years, 1885–1912* (Cambridge, 1991), p. 180.

responded to enthusiastically were Ralph Waldo Emerson and Henry David Thoreau.[4] Frank Norris was still so much in Lawrence's mind that in the first published version of 'Fenimore Cooper's Leatherstocking Novels' he would refer to 'the late book of Frank Norris, the book about the wheat' (*The Octopus*, 1901); he had first encountered Norris's work back in 1909.[5] As for American writers in the flesh, he was to make the acquaintance in 1909 of one of the finest among the younger generation settled in Europe, Ezra Pound (i. 144–5, 147–8), who would have been capable of putting Lawrence through the ABCs of a schooling in American letters had his energies not then been generally directed elsewhere.

Lawrence's interest in American writers gradually became coupled during the next decade with a growing desire to see the New World with his own eyes. By the beginning of the First World War, matters personal, artistic and historical were combining to redirect his attention toward not just the physical reality of the New World but also its psycho/cultural status as an alternative location for a writer and thinker. Affected, like many of his European contemporaries, by the shadow cast by the war over Britain and the Continent, Lawrence came to see the New World during the war years, L. D. Clark has claimed, 'as a haven for the rebirth of self and society'.[6] Over the course of those years, it emerged as the nearest territorial approximation to several of Lawrence's most passionately held ideas about the life of the self, the spirit and the psyche.

As early as October 1915, he was making plans to travel to the New World.[7] What he then wrote to Harriet Monroe, a leading supporter of the Imagist movement in the United States and the founding editor of *Poetry*, he was to state many times in the years to come: 'I must see America. I think one can feel hope there. I think that there the life comes up from the roots, crude but vital. Here the whole tree of life is dying. It is like being dead: the underworld. I must see America. I believe it is beginning, not ending' (ii. 417). Such thoughts and wishes at times intersected, at times merged with, his desire to go away to the place which he had originally, in the English winter of 1914–15, called 'Rananim', but which by the winter of 1915 had become an unnamed retreat sometimes identified with Florida (ii. 444); by the still drearier winter of 1918 he would be thinking of his retreat as a place as far removed physically and spiritually as possible from 'Britannia's miserable shores' (iii. 215). With his

---

[4] E. T. [Jessie Chambers], *D. H. Lawrence: A Personal Record* (1935), p. 101.
[5] See Explanatory note on 60:40.
[6] Introduction, *The Plumed Serpent* (Cambridge, 1987), p. xix.
[7] On DHL's impassioned desire in autumn 1915 to leave Europe for the New World, see Mark Kinkead-Weekes, *D. H. Lawrence: Triumph to Exile, 1912–1922* (Cambridge, 1996), pp. 275–82.

career desperately set back by the banning of *The Rainbow* in 1915, and his own emotions about England, the war and the state of his career complicated in the extreme, he considered at various times the possibility of setting down his fantasia on the terra firma of such places as the Andes, California or a South Sea island inspired by Herman Melville's *Typee*. References to America, made often by way of contrast to Europe, and his own wish to take its measure in person, became common in Lawrence's letters during the latter years of the war. One of the strongest statements he made in this respect came late in 1916, when he stated his disgust with Europe and his hopefulness for America in a letter to his friend Catherine Carswell:

I *know* now, finally:

a. that I want to go away from England for ever.
b. That I want *ultimately* to go to a country of which I have hope, in which I feel the new unknown.

In short, I want, immediately or at length, to transfer all my life to America. (iii. 25)

The least formalist of writers and readers in his habits and temperament, Lawrence was no more inclined to separate his views of literature and culture from his ideas about history, society and psychology than he was given to detach his writing from his life. Over the course of 1916, by now occupying with Frieda a house in Cornwall – 'a sort of no-man's land . . . not England' (ii. 494) – his intensifying interest in the New World increasingly coincided with a fascination with American literature. Despite his prior general introduction to the subject of American writing, it was during 1916 that Lawrence entered for the first time into a more sustained, focused engagement both with the subject and with some of the writers who would figure in his American literary essays. In February, he was reading Melville's *Moby-Dick*[8] – 'a very odd, interesting book' – and wishing that he was 'going on a long voyage, far into the Pacific. I wish that very much' (ii. 528–9). Still in a sea-faring mood in June, he reported to his friend Barbara Low that he had recently read Richard Henry Dana's *Two Years Before the Mast* (*'very good'*), and enquired whether she had copies of either of Melville's first two novels, *Typee* and *Omoo* (ii. 614). Two days later, he expressed his enthusiasm for Cooper, whose *The Last of the Mohicans* and *The Deerslayer* he found 'lovely beyond words' (ii. 615); he and Frieda had been reading Cooper together.[9] Furthermore, he was then contemplating a

---

[8] DHL possibly recognised this phenomenon himself; a year later he referred to himself in a letter to the American novelist–critic Waldo Frank as 'hav[ing] *really* read your literature' (iii. 160). For DHL's references to *Moby-Dick* as *Moby Dick* see Explanatory note on 133:3.

[9] *Frieda Lawrence: The Memoirs and Correspondence*, ed. E. W. Tedlock (1961), p. 108.

more extensive immersion in American literature, since directly after stating his high valuation of Melville and Dana to Barbara Low he requested that she send him an Everyman's Library catalogue (ii. 614), which he probably knew contained the fullest list of American literary texts then available in Britain. In August 1916, Lawrence spoke warmly about his wish to come to the United States in a letter to the American poet Amy Lowell, whom he had first met in 1914 and who had made him a gift of the typewriter on which he was then typing out *Women in Love*. By August, too, his desire to make the journey was spilling over into a special appreciation of American writing, as he expressed it to her: 'Often I have longed to go to a country which has new, quite unknown flowers and birds. It would be such a joy to make their acquaintance. Have you still got humming birds, as in Crèvecoeur?' (ii. 645). At what stage he had first read *Letters From an American Farmer* we do not know (he liked it 'so much'), but some time in the late summer of 1916 he sent his friend John Middleton Murry a copy which must have been the Everyman reprint of 1912.[10] And both in his letter to Amy Lowell and in the first surviving version of *Women in Love*, written no later than August 1916 (and drafted in May), he stressed how 'splendid' (ii. 645) and 'astonishingly good' the writing of Melville was: 'It surprises me how much older, over-ripe and withering into abstraction, this American classic literature is, than English literature of the same time.'[11] He also praised Dana again, and ended: 'But your classic American Literature I find to my surprise, is *older* than our English. The tree did not become new, which was transplanted. It only ran more swiftly into age, impersonal, non-human almost. But how good these books are! Is the *English* tree in America almost dead? By the literature, I think it is' (ii. 645).

If his ambition to set down his thoughts about the United States and its culture in a formal study had not yet crystallised, it soon did. His letters during the last months of 1916 and early 1917 were filled with intensely stated feelings about the New World. In November 1916 he wrote to his friend S. S. Koteliansky ('Kot'), in London, to request that he send, among other works, copies of Melville's *Typee* or *Omoo* and of Cooper's *The Last of the Mohicans* and *The Pathfinder* (iii. 40). The next month he enjoyed a Christmas visit from an American friend (and later his US agent) Robert Mountsier, in the company of another American whom Lawrence found appealing, Esther

---

[10] John Middleton Murry, *Between Two Worlds* (1935), p. 424. Apart from an expensive edition published in 1908 by Chatto & Windus in London and by Duffield & Co. in New York, the only previous printing of the book in England had been in 1783. DHL's spellings and forms 'Henry', 'Henri' and 'Crêvecoeur' in all the versions of the essay he himself wrote are unaccountable; for the correct forms see Explanatory note on 32:3.

[11] *FWL* 135:21–3.

Andrews (iii. 64). As an immediate consequence of the visit, on 4 January 1917 Lawrence ordered a list of Everyman's Library books from Mountsier, now back in London, consisting of Melville's *Moby Dick* and *Omoo*, Cooper's *The Pioneers*, *The Prairie* and *The Deerslayer*, Whitman's *Leaves of Grass* (the edition also included Whitman's long essay 'Democratic Vistas'), Crèvecoeur's *Letters From an American Farmer*, Hawthorne's *Twice-Told Tales*, *The Scarlet Letter* and *The Blithedale Romance*, Jean-Jacques Rousseau's *Emile*, Abraham Lincoln's *Speeches*, three volumes of Emerson's essays, Franklin's *Autobiography*, Alexander Hamilton's *The Federalist* and Poe's *Tales of Mystery and Imagination* (iii. 65–6). That list already included seven of the eight writers destined for *Studies in Classic American Literature* – the eighth (Dana) in all likelihood omitted because Lawrence had kept his Nelson's Classics copy of *Two Years Before the Mast* after reading it the previous June (ii. 614–15).

Lawrence's list, even in this preliminary form, reflected as much as it departed from contemporary taste. It encompassed writers widely recognised at the time – Franklin, Hawthorne, Poe and Whitman – and also those generally ignored, or regarded as writers for children: Crèvecoeur, Cooper, Dana and – until his 'renaissance' in the early 1920s, heralded by Raymond Weaver's book – Melville.[12] It entirely passed over the still popular 'Fireside Poets' (Longfellow, William Cullen Bryant, James Russell Lowell, Oliver Wendell Holmes and John Greenleaf Whittier), as well as the New England Transcendentalist Thoreau, whose personal and fictional example of a self-reliant life, according to Jessie Chambers, had greatly appealed to Lawrence in the previous decade.[13] Lawrence had also admired Emerson as a 'great man' and 'great individual', but concluded that he was a narrow-minded romantic idealist out of touch with current reality: 'Emerson listened to one sort of message, and only one. To all others he was blank ... He was only connected on the Ideal 'phone.'[14] And Lawrence never included him in the project, in spite of his renewed reading of him in 1917.

Lawrence's list, characteristically for its time, included no women; but we need only compare this with the work of the prominent writer and critic John Macy (who would review the 1923 *Studies*), whose well-regarded, often-reprinted study of American literature (*The Spirit of American Literature*, 1908) consisted of seventeen chapters each titled after a male writer. Similarly, Lawrence's list followed current critical practice in excluding all writers of

---

[12] See footnote 62.   [13] *D. H. Lawrence: A Personal Record*, p. 101.
[14] 'Model Americans', *Dial*, lxxiv (May 1923), 506–7.

colour or ethnicity: Macy, for example, had chosen only white Anglo-Saxon Protestants as the major figures of his study. But the argument that equates Lawrence's practices with those of his contemporaries has only limited value, since he saw far more deeply into and cared more passionately about the aboriginal origins of Native American culture than did his contemporaries; his essays on Cooper and Hawthorne, in particular, are evidence of this.

The nonchalant manner in which Lawrence stated his request for the Everyman's Library books to Mountsier – 'I make a list of the books', followed immediately by their titles – demonstrates that he and Mountsier had already discussed the subject of American letters, Lawrence's need for books and no doubt also his projected essays. Within a couple of days of his request, Lawrence acknowledged the arrival of twelve of the eighteen books and thanked Mountsier for his help (iii. 67–8), and by the following day he had 'already begun to study'.[15]

Two days later, he expressed his mind openly to J. B. Pinker, his literary agent in Britain, about his twin American desires: 'I want to go to America. It is necessary now for me to address a new public. You must see that. It is no use my writing in England for the English any more. I want to go to New York and write a set of essays on American literature, and perhaps lecture . . . I have got in my head a set of essays, or lectures, on Classic American Literature' (iii. 73).

His planned visit was forestalled, however, when in February 1917 his passport applications for Frieda and himself were rejected. Despite that 'bitter blow' (iii. 92), his visceral fascination with his subject persisted, as did his resolve to make the journey, if only at some still unforeseeable date. Even America's entry into the war against Germany a couple of months later, on 6 April – his immediate reaction was that America was now 'a stink-pot in my nostrils, after having been the land of the future for me' (iii. 124) – could not completely destroy his belief in it. As Frieda had put it to Esther Andrews in February, it was 'America in our sense' which mattered, even more than the reality (viii. 20). In July 1917, feeling himself cooped up, he complained to Waldo Frank, using a significant metaphor, that he could see no 'Rainbow' in Europe but assumed one still reached across to the West. And he expressed his desire to see it in person: 'I want to come to America, bodily, as soon as the war stops and the gates are opened. I believe America is the New World.'

[15] One of the missing books he really wanted ('it is a book I like *very* much') was the Everyman *Moby Dick* and he was still asking for it on 16 January – as a result, by 12 March he had 'two copies' (iii. 77, 104); Louise Wright, 'Dear Montague: Letters from Esther Andrews to Robert Mountsier', *D. H. Lawrence Review*, xxvi (1995–6), 184.

He was not so sure, however, either then or later, that he was as eager to make the acquaintance of 'Uncle Samdom' (iii. 142–4).

Second Stage 1917–19: MS and TS essays

Within weeks of opening himself to Waldo Frank, Lawrence had launched himself into his American project.[16] In a letter written in late August 1917 to Amy Lowell, his benefactress on previous occasions, he indicated that he was at work on his set of essays, which he was then calling 'The Transcendental Element in American (Classic) Literature'.[17] Filled with the quick pride he took in his project, he described his work as 'very keen essays in criticism – cut your fingers if you don't handle them carefully . . . Tis a chef-d'oeuvre of soul-searching criticism' (iii. 156–7). Already thinking ahead to their publication, he went on to ask her help in placing them with an American periodical, such as the *Yale Review* or the *New Republic* ('or some such old fat coach'), both of which had recently published his work. The same day, he took the more practical step of stating his desire to publish what he was labelling 'this ten-barrelled pistol of essays of mine' to Pinker,[18] indicating

---

[16] It is not self-evident that DHL originally conceived of *Studies* as a book. In January 1917 he had referred to 'a set of essays, or lectures' (iii. 73), while in August and September 1917 he described it as 'a set of essays' (iii. 155, 156, 160, 163), a term he repeated as late as January 1918 (iii. 201). The following month, he noted that 'I don't think the American essays will be so impossible for the editors, if we let the poor puppies chop them up for puppy-meat, and take out all the bone and gristle' (iii. 206): he was still thinking primarily of magazine editors. The first reference to a 'book' of essays came from Frieda Lawrence in April (see next note) and not until June 1918 did DHL himself refer to the work as 'a book of American essays' (iii. 247), something he confirmed in September: 'they would make a decent little book – about 70,000 words' (iii. 287).

[17] *Letters*, iii. 156. At the time, the title was still uncertain: variants that he mentioned during late summer 1917 were 'The Transcendental Element in American Literature' (iii. 155), 'The Transcendent Element in Classic American Literature' (iii. 158) and – a probable title – 'Essays on The Mystic Import of American Literature' (iii. 163). Frieda Lawrence was still using the latter on 15 April 1918 when she said he was 'writing a book on "the mystic significance of American Classic Literature"' (*The Letters of D. H. Lawrence & Amy Lowell 1914–1925*, ed. E. Claire Healey and Keith Cushman, Santa Barbara, 1985, p. 133).

[18] Clearly a set of ten essays: probably 'Crèvecoeur', 'Franklin', 'Cooper I', 'Cooper II', 'Poe', 'Hawthorne', 'Dana', 'Melville', 'Whitman' and either 'The Spirit of Place' or 'The Two Principles'. If the Cooper essay were still planned as a single work, then probably both the non-author-based essays were included in the count; it is just possible that DHL was contemplating an essay on another author (e.g. Emerson). In January 1919, however, while the essays were coming out in the *English Review* but before either part of 'Cooper' had appeared (and before Harrison split the Hawthorne essay and only printed its first part), DHL referred to them as 'a dozen essays in all' (iii. 324) and then on 1 February as 'twelve essays in all' (iii. 325). 'The Spirit of Place' and 'The Two Principles' both existed by then and would have been included

that his wish to do so was 'in the hopes of relieving my ominous financial prospects' (iii. 155–6). That wish was so strong during this low point in his professional and financial affairs that it found its way repeatedly into his letters.[19]

He was already drafting the essays when, a few weeks later, in mid-September 1917, he informed Frank that he was writing a set of essays on American literature 'beginning with Crèvecoeur' (iii. 160). It sounds as if he may have initially been giving Crèvecoeur, Franklin's younger contemporary, a priority which would pass to Franklin by the time the essays began appearing in print the following year; he had probably not yet thought of starting with the more general essay 'The Spirit of Place'. One thing that did not change, however, was Lawrence's pioneering view of Crèvecoeur's formative position in American letters and of his stature as an 'artist' (36:9) equal to the American writers who had followed him. Lawrence's progress was interrupted in October 1917, however: the authorities expelled him and Frieda from Cornwall. This was a major disruption in their lives which left composition of the essays at a 'standstill', as he told his friend Cecil Gray on 23 October (iii. 172), and the 'standstill' stretched into mid-January, when he reported to Gray, 'I'm not writing anything' (iii. 197). He appears finally to have worked through that blockage toward the end of the month, by which time he and Frieda were installed at Chapel Farm Cottage, Hermitage, to which they had their possessions (probably including some at least of the texts from which he was working) forwarded from Cornwall.[20] In mid-February he was writing the essay on Poe, for which he requested from Kot a second copy of *Tales of Mystery and Imagination* to replace his lost original (iii. 212). By that point, he had probably reached the approximate midpoint of the work – if, as seems likely, he were composing the author-specific essays (with the exception of 'Franklin') from 'Crèvecoeur' onwards in the loosely chronologically

in the count, but the fact that DHL only split the Melville essay in two at a later date shows that – to reach the figure of twelve – DHL may himself have been responsible for the two-part form of the Cooper work.

[19] E.g. *Letters*, iii. 158, 160 and 163, although his statement in the last seems more nearly accurate than simple protestations about writing for money: 'These [essays] were begun in the hopes of making money: for money is a shy bird. – But I am afraid they have already passed beyond all price. It is a pity.'

[20] *Letters*, iii. 201, 205–6. Like Harriett and Somers in *Kangaroo*, when leaving in October they would probably have left 'the house as it was, the books on the shelves' (*Kangaroo*, ed. Bruce Steele, Cambridge, 1994, 245:20). The fact that the notebook containing DHL's reading notes for *The Scarlet Letter* remained in Cornwall and was never sent on (see 'Texts', p. lxix), and that DHL needed a replacement copy of Poe's stories (*Letters*, iii. 212), shows that by no means everything in Cornwall had been forwarded to Berkshire.

determined order in which they would be published in the *English Review*.[21]
By the end of that month, he felt confident enough about his progress to
think ahead toward the next stage of their preparation. Drawing on his close
friendship with Kot, on whom he had relied in 1914 for the typing of 'Study
of Thomas Hardy' (ii. 220), Lawrence sent him 'the first part of the essays'
for typing, no easy task given the many alterations in the manuscripts, and
warned him, 'there is much more to follow'. While declaring them 'a weariness to me', Lawrence also stated that he considered them 'really very good'
and hoped that they would bring him an infusion of money (iii. 214, 217–18).

The interrelated acts of enlisting Kot's help in preparing typescripts, and
of alerting Pinker early in February 1918 that he would be sending him the
essays 'in a little while' (iii. 205–6), did not take account of the amount of
writing and revision that lay ahead during the first half of 1918. Lawrence's
frustration with his slow progress showed in May when he described his daily
life to his friend Edith Eder: 'I set potatoes and mow the grass and write
my never-to-be-finished *Studies in Classic American Literature*' (iii. 242). The
work was still not completed in early June, when he reported that he was
writing 'a last essay on Whitman – then I have done my book of American
essays' (iii. 247). Later in June, he again alerted Pinker, to whom he had by
then mentioned the essays several times, that he meant to send them to him
'shortly' (iii. 255); it was not until 3 August, however, that Lawrence sent him
the first of the essays, which he identified as 'The Spirit of Place' (we do not
know when he had written this), and promised to send 'six or seven more' the
following week (iii. 270).

Why this delay between his statements to Pinker in February that he would
send the essays 'in a little while' and to Gray in mid-March that the essays
were 'in their last and final form' (iii. 224), and his mailing of the first essay to Pinker only in August? For one thing, Kot was not able to complete
more than a portion of the typing of the manuscript sent to him; as a result, the completion of the typing remained stalled for months.[22] For another,

---

[21] Scarcity of surviving early manuscripts and infrequency of references to individual essays
during 1917–18 makes reconstruction of the chronology of composition extremely difficult;
we only know of (1) an opening essay on Crèvecoeur (reported in September 1917), (2) an
essay on Poe (February 1918) and (3) a closing essay on Whitman (June 1918). Since DHL
halted composition from mid-October 1917 until late January 1918, he might well not have
got any further than midway by February 1918, when he was at work on 'Poe'.

[22] He returned a single typed essay to DHL in mid-March (*Letters*, iii. 228), but then apparently
made no further progress; his inactivity may well have provoked DHL's remark of 28 April
1918: 'stick pins or something into Kot – I believe he's getting into a state of gangrened inertia'
(iii. 240). In July DHL wrote to Gray: 'I sent the American Essays to a friend in London, who
was going to put them with a "safe" friend to have them typed. The friend collapsed, and they
are hung up' (iii. 261).

the frequent moves that Lawrence and Frieda were making up until 1 May, when they acquired a place of their own in Derbyshire, interrupted whatever progress he was making. But the primary reason for the delay may well be signalled by that mention of 'The Spirit of Place', the essay that had by then replaced 'Crèvecoeur' (or 'Franklin') as the opening piece in the projected book. In all likelihood, the originating impulse behind *Studies* had altered significantly as Lawrence worked through the essays during the first half of 1918. The most plausible explanation for the change of plan is that given by Mark Kinkead-Weekes, who infers a profound transformation experienced by Lawrence during the spring of 1918 as he read deeply in works of psychology and cosmic history that resonated with his revulsion from war-torn Europe. The result showed most graphically in his reconfigured work, which came that spring to include not only 'The Spirit of Place' and 'The Two Principles', but also what must have been texts of the author-specific essays rewritten to accord with the ideas about the psyche and world history expressed at length in those two new essays.[23] If so, the completion of the last essay, on Whitman, after the expense of so much time and energy over that half-year in the composition and revision of the essays, must have brought Lawrence to a point of deep release. Furthermore, it presumably served as the *Consummatum est* of the book, for in all versions of *Studies* known to arrive at a culminating essay on Whitman, the latter was to be the figure with whom Lawrence wrestled – to use the figure dear to both men to describe the engagement of the artist with the self and the universe.[24]

With the set of essays now complete, and his earlier fears about their unpublishable character having given way, at least for the moment, to excitement, Lawrence wrote to Pinker on 3 August 1918 to express as eager and optimistic a reading as he had yet voiced about the prospects of the work: 'I think we may really sell these essays, both in America and in England – and really make something with them.' His dependence on them was manifestly acute: 'Really, I place my hopes of the world on these essays' (iii. 270). As a practical measure, he suggested that Pinker send that first essay for initial publication to the *English Review*, whose editor Austin Harrison had been one of his steadiest patrons in recent years. In preparation for the possible publication of the whole

---

[23] Kinkead-Weekes, *Triumph to Exile*, pp. 438–40; it should be pointed out, however, that no MS evidence survives of such rewriting.

[24] As early as 1913, DHL had expressed his ambivalence about Whitman:
   But writing should come from a strong root of life: like a battle song after a battle. – And Whitman did this, more or less. But his battle was not a real battle . . . He never fought with another person – he was like a wrestler who only wrestles with his own shadow – he never came to grips. He chucked his body into the fight, and stood apart, saying 'Look how I am living'. He is really false as hell. – But he is fine too. (ii. 130)

series, Lawrence sent off his remaining essays to an unidentified person for typing, while also continuing to revise.[25] Having previously informed others of the project, he also solicited the opinions of his old friends Donald and Catherine Carswell, at whose house he had left copies of some of the essays (he mentioned 'Melville' specifically).[26]

English Review publication of the First Version

The process of revision continued into September as the last essays came back to him from the typist (iii. 286, 287), even while Pinker's negotiations with Harrison were continuing. Late that month, Harrison responded positively to Lawrence by offering him five guineas for the opening essay (iii. 286–7), the same sum the *English Review* had paid for each of the (considerably shorter) four parts of 'The Reality of Peace' which it had printed the previous year (iii. 159). That was a sum which Harrison had thought of in 1917 as charity to a needy author: six years earlier, as an almost unknown young author, Lawrence had been paid almost twice as much by the *English Review* for a rather briefer short story (i. 282 and n. 4). Lawrence wrote to Pinker on 25 September to ask him whether five guineas really constituted reasonable payment (iii. 286–7). Pinker must have urged Lawrence to accept it, and each subsequent essay appears to have earned the same (iii. 286–7, 310, 315, 319 and 327). 'The Spirit of Place' was printed as the lead article in the November 1918 issue; by 13 November Harrison had committed himself to publishing at least one additional essay beyond 'The Spirit of Place' (iii. 298), and by 23 November to at least two more (iii. 299). In succeeding issues he actually went on to publish seven more of the essays, each appearing in the *English Review* with its sequential series number as part of what Lawrence was by now definitively calling *Studies in Classic American Literature*: 'Benjamin Franklin' (December), 'Henry [*sic*] St. John de Crèvecoeur' (January), 'Fenimore

---

[25] *Letters*, iii. 276. Probably still anxious about the 'Whitman' essay, he remarked that he did not want them to go to 'the ordinary typist' (iii. 261). Kinkead-Weekes plausibly speculates that DHL found a typist through his new friend, Nancy Henry, a part-time editor for Oxford University Press to whom he was sending manuscript chapters of *Movements in European History* at roughly the same time that he was looking to have the *Studies* typed (*Triumph to Exile*, p. 464). DHL's remark to her on 23 August – 'I have got more typed MS. of the Essays' – suggests that *Studies* manuscripts had passed through her hands (iii. 276): he mentioned them again to her the following month (iii. 286). No *Movements* typescript survives for comparison.

[26] *Letters*, iii. 278, 279, 288. DHL remarked in his letter of 11 September to Donald Carswell, 'Glad you like "Moby Dick"' (iii. 279); it seems more likely that he was referring to an essay than to the novel, and – if so – he was referring to a version of 'Melville' which treats *Typee* and *Moby-Dick* together (Roberts E382s, UN).

Cooper's Anglo-American Novels' (February), 'Fenimore Cooper's Leather-stocking Novels' (March), 'Edgar Allan Poe' (April), 'Nathaniel Hawthorne' (May) and 'The Two Principles' (June).[27]

With the June 1919 publication of 'The Two Principles', the serialisation stopped. We do not know whether Harrison had ever actually agreed with Lawrence to publish the other essays, or – if he had – why he failed to carry through his intention. The nearest basis of comparison is Harrison's initial offer the previous year to publish only three of Lawrence's seven 'The Reality of Peace' essays, of which he actually printed four.[28] If Harrison had in fact initially planned to print all of the *Studies* essays, he might well have been persuaded by their length to end the run prematurely, since they typically constituted the longest pieces in their respective numbers of the journal. In at least one instance, length was unquestionably a problem. With the series progressing into its second half-year, Harrison chose to print only the first 60 per cent of the very long seventh essay, 'Hawthorne'. The remaining part, which had already gone into proof,[29] would remain unpublished for years; but the effective division of the essay into two would become the basis of the two-part strategy which Lawrence himself adopted when he revised it the following year. If Harrison had seen a copy of 'Melville', he would have known that that essay, too, ran even longer than the pieces already in print. But he would have had another reason to end the publication prematurely if he had ever seen the 'Whitman', which Lawrence himself considered in 1919 too controversial for a publisher to print (because, almost certainly, of its frank treatment of homosexuality); as late as September 1919 Lawrence would note that 'no one has seen the essay on Whitman – no one in the world'.[30] It may well have been the fact that he kept the 1918 essay to himself, and possibly never even sent it out for typing, which led to its being the only one of the original 1917–18 essays not to survive.

---

[27] There is no direct evidence to establish whether DHL or Harrison was responsible for the publication of 'Cooper' as a two-part sequence, but see footnote 18.

[28] From May to August 1917; for DHL's wavering hopes and expectations over their publishing prospects, see *Letters*, iii. 104, 106, 107, 108, 110–11 and 113–14.

[29] Roberts E382f (Smith). Once part of the collection of Charles Harold Bennett Smith of Bermuda, and deriving from the papers of Robert Mountsier, all the originals of the *Studies* essays (and of the other manuscripts and typescripts in his collection) were subsequently sold and are currently unlocated; the editors have had to rely upon photocopies made (with equal stamina and forethought) by Warren Roberts in 1979; see the 'Note' to the Acknowledgements for further details. The collection was auctioned again in 1990 by Sothebys in London; the buyer (using the bidding name of 'Beckett') paid £26,000. A letter from the volume editors to Sothebys for forwarding to the buyer brought no reply.

[30] *Letters*, iii. 400. The nearest surviving text is Roberts E382b (Smith), here printed in the Intermediate Version (1919) as 'Whitman'.

Whatever the formal understanding between Harrison and Pinker had been, it certainly seems plausible that Lawrence, for his part, harboured hopes, if not necessarily expectations, that Harrison might publish the work all or nearly all the way to its conclusion. In a letter of 27 January 1919, however, Lawrence remarked: 'There are a dozen essays in all: I don't know if he'll go patiently on to the end' (iii. 324), which suggests that he had reason to believe that Harrison was likely to baulk. Moreover, the last essay printed in the *English Review*, 'The Two Principles', was hardly a desirable place to conclude. As its opening paragraph indicates, it was meant to lead into the Dana and Melville essays that were to follow. For Harrison, by contrast, its broad philosophy might have made it seem suitable as a concluding bookend to match 'The Spirit of Place'. But – combined with the very small sum he had been paid for each essay – the result was that, rather than being grateful to a supporter at a difficult time, Lawrence felt considerable dissatisfaction with, even distrust of, Harrison. He expressed very guarded feelings to Kot about Harrison two months after the appearance of the eighth essay, and advised his friend to '*Manage* him about money', as a necessary negotiating strategy for getting selections from Kot's translation of Leo Shestov into the *English Review* (iii. 383). Harrison, it should be added, published nothing else of Lawrence's for a year.[31] He presumably felt that this act of charity – and the extensive space of each issue that the essays had occupied – was all that either Lawrence or the magazine's readers deserved for the moment. But at least a substantial part of the First Version of the *Studies* – Lawrence calculated it as 'about $^2/_3$ . . . not quite so much' (iii. 407) – had got into print.

Third Stage 1919: revision of unpublished MS and TS essays

Even while Lawrence was revising the proofs of the essays as they passed through the *English Review*, his main ambition for *Studies* by the autumn of 1918 was to see the essays published in America too. Like many of his British peers, he had previously pursued a two-coast publication strategy with regard to both book and periodical publication, if with only limited success. As early as November 1918, he had told Pinker that Harrison had informed him of the purchase by an American of twenty copies of the November *English Review* containing 'The Spirit of Place' for distribution in the United States (iii. 299). To advance his ultimate goal of the essays' publication as a book, too, Lawrence decided by early 1919 to give first preference for the essays to an American publisher (with English publication arrangements to be made subsequently).

---

[31] 'The Blind Man' appeared in July 1920 (xxxi, 22–41).

In order to expedite matters, he bypassed Pinker, whose competence in dealing with the American market he rightly doubted, and made his own appeal directly to the New York publisher Benjamin Huebsch[32] in late January 1919, informing him that Harrison would be sending him copies of the four essays already published. A few days later Lawrence alerted Harriet Monroe, in whose *Poetry* (the February issue) six of his poems were about to appear, that she, too, would be receiving copies of those essays from Harrison: 'I wish you would tell me if you liked them' (iii. 325 and n. 1). No record survives, however, of how (or whether) she replied; and Huebsch did not respond until April, when he wrote a friendly letter inviting Lawrence to come to America to visit and lecture. He also asked noncommittally to see, among other works, the complete *Studies* (iii. 356–7 n. 1).

Huebsch's caution was understandable. Although he admired Lawrence's writings, he hesitated about the wisdom of publishing his more controversial works in the uncertain, censorious climate enveloping the publishing industry following the United States's entrance into the war. On the other hand, he remained well-disposed to Lawrence and seriously considered paying a visit to England (and to Lawrence) in July, a plan which paralleled Lawrence's own thinking in June about travelling to the United States 'at once', provided that proper arrangements could be made for him there: 'I weary myself here' (iii. 364). In the event, however, neither man would make his planned journey in 1919. The extent of Lawrence's desire to write for America can, however, be gauged by a letter he sent to Amy Lowell in July 1919 when – in apparently a unique mention – he said he was considering writing a second series of essays 'on the Moderns, next' (iii. 369).

He was, however, also still harbouring reservations during the first half of 1919 about the current state of at least some of the essays' formulations. As a result of this dissatisfaction, he postponed responding to Huebsch's request to see the full text of the volume until the end of August 1919, when he claimed that after a period of inactivity on the essays he would 'do them' and send them on 'soon' (iii. 388). And within days he began an intensive revision of the unpublished essays, which continued throughout September 1919. Out of this effort came new or revised versions of four or five of the essays (he was obviously ignoring those essays which had already appeared in the *English Review*): perhaps a second 'Hawthorne' (though this may have

---

[32] *Letters*, iii. 324. Known throughout the industry simply as 'Ben', Huebsch was one of the dynamic figures in early twentieth-century American literary publishing. The first Jew to break through the nearly impermeable Protestant wall surrounding the industry, he also broke through barriers of taste by publishing such authors as Joyce (*Portrait of the Artist as a Young Man*), Sherwood Anderson (*Winesburg, Ohio*) and DHL (*The Rainbow*).

been written earlier),[33] 'Dana', 'Melville' (now also separated into two parts) and a 'Whitman'. The fact that this set of five manuscripts ended with a Whitman essay confirms that 'Whitman' had always been part of the whole project, and that the lack of a 1918–19 version is simply mischance. On 24 September 1919 Lawrence would ask Kot to make clean copies of three of these five essays – 'Your handwriting is so nice and plain' – on 'smallish' stationery, suitable in size to be incorporated with *English Review* pages (iii. 397 and n. 2, 399). He already had a fair copy of one essay, recently made for him by his friend and hostess for much of August, Rosalind Baynes, while he presumably made a fair copy of the fifth essay (probably the Whitman essay) himself. He obviously planned to incorporate the handwritten copies with pages removed from copies of the *English Review* of the first eight essays, so as to make two copies of the complete work to send to publishers.[34]

1919: Intermediate Version assembled and sent to Huebsch

He had thus for the second time – the first had been for Harrison in the autumn of 1918 – assembled a complete text; we can entitle this stage of the work the Intermediate Version, which at this stage was the volume he wanted published. Only a week after asking for Kot's help, Lawrence was therefore able to write to Huebsch that he would shortly send him the full text of the '*Classic American* essays', 'the result of five years of persistent work' (iii. 400). Before we dismiss this as understandable exaggeration, or simple inaccuracy, we should consider whether he might not have regarded his 'Study of Thomas Hardy' of late 1914 as the real start of the project he still sometimes thought of as his 'philosophy': he had told Harriet Monroe in February 1919 that he had worked at the essays 'for more than four years' (iii. 325), confirming that late 1914 was the date he was giving to the project's start.[35] He still had a lingering

---

33 The composition of 'Hawthorne II' might have begun shortly after DHL received page proofs from the *English Review* printer in April, several of whose pages he incorporated into MS2. It is just as plausible, however, that he retained the proofs and turned to 'Hawthorne II' only when he prepared to redraft the other unpublished essays.

34 *Letters*, iii. 399; see Kinkead-Weekes, *Triumph to Exile*, p. 522. If Rosalind Baynes, as seems likely, copied the first of the unpublished essays (on Hawthorne), then Kot would have been sent the Dana essay and the two Melville essays; DHL did not ask Kot to use carbon-paper between the 'smallish' sheets of paper on which he was writing, so presumably only two copies of the complete work were planned. (None of the copies made by Rosalind Baynes or Kot survives.)

35 See *Hardy* 7–128. He might even have considered his brief 'Foreword' to *Sons and Lovers* of January 1913 – see *Sons and Lovers*, ed. Carl Baron and Helen Baron (Cambridge, 1992), pp. 467–73 – as the start of that 'philosophy'.

unease, however, about the final – and, no doubt, most provocative – essay, the task of whose copying he had most likely reserved for himself: he told Huebsch 'The essay on Whitman you may find it politic not to publish – if so leave it out altogether – don't alter it' (iii. 400).

A rail strike prevented the operation of postal services for a few days, and it was not until 10 October 1919 that Lawrence informed Huebsch that he was that day posting him one of the new, complete sets of *Studies* – printed pages from the *English Review* supplemented with handwritten copies: 'I'm sorry I can't send you typed MS' (iii. 405). To cover all possibilities, he also sent along with the text for Huebsch the pages of the Whitman-centred essays on 'Democracy' that he had also written the previous month (iii. 405), thus giving Huebsch the option of using 'Democracy' as a substitute for the closing essay on Whitman.[36] He expressed no such hesitation about the only other pieces still unpublished in any form, the Dana and Melville essays, the latter of which (like the lengthy Hawthorne original) he had recently adapted into separate essays on *Typee/Omoo* and *Moby-Dick*.[37] He also asked Huebsch if he might try to place those unpublished essays with the *Atlantic Monthly*, a magazine of serious opinion long associated with the cultural elite but in recent years moving toward the journalistic mainstream: 'If you could get some of the essays in respectable sound periodicals, I'm sure it would help my reputation immensely, and simplify your job' (iii. 405). Six days later, he offered the complete work, whose length he was now estimating as about 80,000 words – a figure greater by 10,000 than the one he had given Pinker the previous autumn (iii. 287) – to Martin Secker, his English publisher (iii. 406–7), although he did not yet send it to him. He must have retained a complete duplicate copy himself.

Once the full text of *Studies* was finally in Huebsch's possession, it became the publisher's turn to waver. His reaction had been indecisive in April 1919 when he had seen the first four essays – 'I shall have to ask you for more patience before I reply with regard to your articles in The English Review' (iii. 356–7 n. 1) – and indecision remained his position, even with the full work at hand, through the remainder of 1919 and into 1920. That delay, not surprisingly, left Lawrence frustrated about a work he increasingly considered important to his career and reputation in the United States. He found himself inclined to wonder about Huebsch's intentions not only for this project but also for other works already offered to him. Letters from Lawrence first requesting,

---

[36] *Letters*, iii. 405. DHL was still so concerned over the Whitman essay in July 1920 that he instructed Seltzer, should he agree to publish the essays, to wait for a revised version before sending the work to press (iii. 565).

[37] Roberts E382i and E382l (Smith).

then demanding, a decision on *Studies* would obtain no definite response from New York (iii. 423, 430, 456, 493, 501).

In August 1919, however, Lawrence had received a cable from a second New York publisher, Thomas Seltzer, tendering him his publishing services, an offer which Lawrence – more accustomed in recent years to soliciting than being solicited by publishers – did nothing to discourage, despite his prior relationship with Huebsch. In many regards, Seltzer struck a publishing profile similar to that of Huebsch – young, enthusiastic, literary, cosmopolitan, Jewish – but with one significant difference: he was conspicuously less worried about possible legal entanglements arising from the publication of Lawrence's works.[38] Despite their differing assessments of the legal and financial risk of publishing his books, and of their willingness to take that risk, Huebsch and Seltzer each epitomised the kind of publisher most available to Lawrence and best able to bring his works before the contemporary reading public. As small, independent publishers specialising in belles lettres, their firms were part of a new sector in early twentieth-century American publishing which emerged alongside the larger, established houses and which successfully competed for the works of the most innovative writers of the current generation.

Fourth Stage 1920–1: revised text to Robert Mountsier

The period between the autumn of 1919 and the spring of 1920 was an especially complex time in Lawrence's writing career. With the war over and professional opportunities slowly opening up for him on both sides of the Atlantic, he had become involved not only with Huebsch and Seltzer in New York but also with Secker in London in a complicated conflict of interests over publishing priority for a variety of his works, new and old, but in particular *Women in Love*. What made the dealings of this publishing troika still more awkward was the fact that Lawrence (by this time living without a fixed residence on the Continent) no longer had an agent to serve him as a clearing house for his affairs, Pinker having been formally fired in the last days of 1919 but effectively dispensed with months before.[39] Feeling renewed confidence in his creative powers and hopeful about his career, yet unsure about the commercial chances of his works in the post-war economy, Lawrence had to try

---

[38] Seltzer was DHL's main American publisher from 1920 until 1925. Born in Tsarist Russia and brought to America as a child, he had graduated from the University of Pennsylvania, gained experience as a journalist, editor and translator, and eventually formed a connection with his nephew, Albert Boni, in the avant-garde publishing house of Boni and Liveright. He went into business on his own in 1920. See G. Thomas Tanselle, 'The Thomas Seltzer Imprint', *Papers of the Bibliographical Society of America*, lviii (1964), 380–448.
[39] On his firing, see *Letters*, iii. 439.

to keep his different prospective publishers happy with what he was able to offer them; and at times he fell back on ambiguous directives to them, as he attempted to ensure that someone ended up publishing his work. He had by this time not only multiple publishers with whom to deal but multiple works to offer (*Studies, Women in Love* and *The Rainbow* to be reissued, he hoped), not to mention various projects in progress including his new novel, *The Lost Girl*. He was now inclined to see the United States as his primary market not only for *Studies*, a logical deduction, but also for his works generally. This was the gist of his remark to his old friend Mountsier, a journalist by profession, in the February 1920 letter in which he invited Mountsier to become his American agent: 'I want to plant my stuff *first* in America, and let England take second chance every time' (iii. 476–7).

After moving around in Italy late in 1919, the Lawrences settled in Sicily for an extended period beginning in February 1920, where late that spring Lawrence undertook yet another thorough revision of the *Studies* essays. In June, he wrote to Mountsier to detail the state of his literary affairs, which were indeed so complicated as to require a lengthy explanation (iii. 544–8). Working presumably on the duplicate copy of the essays he had kept in his possession, he reported that he was at that moment 'finishing' the only 'complete MS.' (iii. 545, viii. 36) of the essays, one which would supersede the copy which he believed (correctly) still to be in Huebsch's possession.[40] His new text, he informed Mountsier, was the only one that could be used for printing, and would be sent for publication in New York once the issue of the competition between Huebsch and Seltzer was settled. He had presumably made changes to the *English Review* essays as well as to the five unpublished ones. Lawrence also spoke his mind freely about the worth of the project and of the two major novels he was also hoping to place with publishers:

The Rainbow, *Women in Love* and *Studies in C. A. Lit.* are all more or less 'dangerous.' I don't think a 'standard' publisher would handle them. Yet they are the works I set my heart on most – myself privately. My chief interest lies in them. I have to go softly and gently to get them properly published and established . . . Remember I am a *typo speciale*: you can't handle me like any other simple commercial proposition – J. M. Barrie or Hugh Walpole. I am different, and must approach the public rather differently. (iii. 546–7)[41]

---

[40] DHL's usage of the term is loose, as usual in the period; by 'MS.' he might mean holograph writing, typescript or composite; publishers continue to use 'manuscript' for author's copy, long after the introduction of typescript.

[41] James M. Barrie (1860–1937), dramatist and novelist, author of *Peter Pan* (1904), and Hugh Seymour Walpole (1884–1941), novelist and critic, were writers far more popular and better paid than DHL.

His letters during the surrounding weeks were full of references to Melville's South Sea idyll in *Typee*, a preoccupation no doubt intensified by the fantasy he had developed with his fellow writer Compton Mackenzie of chartering a boat for a cruise through southern waters. He was entirely business-like, though, in his attempt to place his revised work. In late June, he informed Cecil Palmer, a small-scale English publisher specialising in belles lettres who had expressed interest in 1917 in publishing *Women in Love* and who had 'recently' enquired about the essays, that he had completed their revision ten days before; and, what is more, he offered Palmer English publication rights.[42] Though eager to see the essays published, Lawrence added the forthright warning: 'publishers are a bit shy of the book' (iii. 556). When Palmer apparently responded with interest, Lawrence promptly sounded out Secker's intentions before sending the revised text to Palmer (iii. 563). In doing so, he seriously considered reversing his previous decision and allowing Palmer prior publication of *Studies* in England, even though Lawrence presumably knew that the work was more likely to make its mark – if at all – in the United States.

Briefly, then, Lawrence had twin suitors for the work on both sides of the Atlantic. He moved promptly, however, to force the issue. He had by now good reason to doubt whether Huebsch would ever issue the work, and in any case he had come to prefer Seltzer as its American publisher, as he explained to the latter early in July 1920 (iii. 565). Lawrence did not yet know that a letter from Huebsch of 8 July was already en route, announcing that he was ceding the book to Seltzer.[43] Meanwhile, for its English publication, Lawrence decided initially on 23 July to proceed with Palmer, though allowing Secker to retain the right of veto over any proposed deal. He informed Palmer that he was mailing him the 'complete MS.' (viii. 36), consisting of the first eight essays in their printed *English Review* form, but certainly revised, and the second Hawthorne, Dana, Melville and Whitman essays in manuscript and typescript. In addition, Lawrence bargained for royalties of 15% on the first thousand copies and 20% on all subsequent copies.[44]

But no sooner had he told Palmer that he would be putting the complete set in the post than he changed his mind, informing Mountsier, then in Paris

---

[42] 'Recently' refers to the date of reception; Palmer's letter, written on 31 December 1919, had reached DHL in Sicily only on 26 June 1920 (*Letters*, iii. 556).

[43] For Huebsch's letter, see *Letters*, iii. 544 n. 1. But DHL was apprised by the time of his 1 August letter to Seltzer: 'Huebsch wrote that he is handing you the MS. of *Studies* – and he more or less says goodbye to me' (viii. 36).

[44] *Letters*, iii. 577. The Whitman essay was still in holograph manuscript; DHL asked Palmer in his letter of 23 July to have it typed and then to forward it to Mountsier in New York (iii. 577–8).

and soon to sail for New York, that he would be sending the text previously earmarked for Palmer to him instead, for American publication: 'I would rather it came in America first. I mistrust England horribly' (iii. 582). That same day, he informed Seltzer of his decision: 'I am sending to Mountsier my complete MS. of *Studies in Classic American Literature*, which he is to give you when he lands – he sails on the *Rotterdam* from Boulogne – Aug 11th' (viii. 36). Palmer soon thereafter disappeared from Lawrence's calculations, probably because Lawrence saw him as a less desirable option than better-established London publishers; but above all because, as a priority, he wanted both the essays and the book published in America. On 2 August 1920, Lawrence posted to Mountsier what was almost certainly his *only* existing copy of the revised, 'complete' text.[45]

1920–1: 'Foreword' in the *New Republic*; Mountsier's attempts at periodical publication; version of 'Whitman' in the *Nation and Athenaeum*

A month later, from Italy, Lawrence posted to Mountsier the newly written text of an essay that he had written as a Foreword to *Studies*.[46] Drawing on its sarcastic, New World / Old World juxtapositioning of the Knights of Columbus and I Cavalieri di Colombo, Mountsier jokingly called it '"the Knights of Columbus" introduction to *Studies in Classic American Literature*' and – following Lawrence's suggestion that 'it might appear in a periodical' (iii. 591) – managed to place it with the *New Republic* (iii. 626–7 n. 2), which paid Lawrence $40 for it on 5 December and published it on 15 December as 'America, Listen to Your Own', followed by a response from Walter Lippmann.[47] No doubt encouraged by that placement, and already informed by Mountsier that he intended to shorten other essays in order to make them more commercially appealing (iii. 644 n. 1), Lawrence urged Mountsier to continue his initiative with American periodicals: 'Do try and get them to

---

45 Diary entry in E. W. Tedlock, *The Frieda Lawrence Collection of D. H. Lawrence Manuscripts: A Descriptive Bibliography* (Albuquerque, 1948), p. 91.

46 Roberts E382.5a (Smith).

47 Vol. xxv, pp. 68–70, followed immediately by Lippmann's 'The Crude Barbarian and the Noble Savage'. Lippmann criticised 'the distinguished author of *Sons and Lovers*' for misdiagnosing the current malaise in America: rather than being a nation of 'noble savages' needing, as DHL exhorted, to find its roots in native as opposed to European soil, America (Lippmann argued) was a nation of European rather than of American descent. Its most pressing need was to overcome the prevailing spirit of philistinism, one symptom of which was 'bureaucrats who will not permit Mr. Lawrence's novels to go unexpurgated through the mails' (pp. 70–1). Mountsier encouraged DHL to 'answer' Lippmann in a cut-down version of 'The Spirit of Place' (iii. 644 n. 1), but no such article has been found.

publish the *Studies* in the magazines – or parts of them' (iii. 653). Mountsier duly complied; typescripts of the essays on Melville's *Moby-Dick* and on Whitman survive in versions which he had shortened. It also seems probable that at some date late in 1920 or early in 1921 Mountsier had a new complete typescript prepared (probably with carbon copies) of the whole book; Lawrence would have wanted a copy for English publication, and by early in 1922 he had access to a complete copy which almost certainly originated with Mountsier.

Meanwhile, in England, Lawrence had taken on a new agent, Curtis Brown, who gradually centralised his hold on various unpublished Lawrence works, including the *Studies* essays. Brown succeeded in selling Mountsier's shortened version of 'Whitman',[48] which he had only received on 14 July 1921, to the *Nation and Athenaeum* for publication on 23 July 1921, from which it was reprinted in the *New York Call* on 21 August; but as Lawrence was only offered 'eight guineas' for the piece, the agency checked with Mountsier first: 'It isn't a very high price.'[49] As Mountsier had been trying to get periodical publication of the essays for nearly two years, however, he was unlikely to refuse. Just a few days after its London publication, nonetheless, Lawrence urged Brown to 'tell your magazine man to go slowly: not to send out anything unless it seems really likely to suit the miserable periodicals'.[50] In contrast to the United States, nine of the twelve essays had by now been published in magazines in England, and Lawrence had not only relatively little to gain from further periodical publication there but more personal dignity, as he stated, to lose from rejections.

1920–1: *Studies* volume not published

Progress in publication of the book version on either side of the Atlantic remained stalled until the end of 1921. Lawrence's best hope at that time was that Seltzer would choose to put into effect what must have been a nonbinding agreement between them that he would publish the book. But Seltzer

---

[48] Roberts E382d (Smith).

[49] Harry Leggett (Curtis Brown) to Robert Mountsier, 18 July 1921 (UT).

[50] *Letters*, iv. 55. It seems probable that Mountsier also succeeded with the *Blithedale Romance* essay on Hawthorne; in February 1922, DHL reminded Curtis Brown that 'the *Nation* published "Whitman", and some other little paper published "Blithedale Romance" ' (*Letters*, iv. 197). No trace of the latter publication has yet been found, but DHL is unlikely to have been mistaken; unfortunately, his diary of financial transactions contains no entries between 4 April and 26 October 1921 (see Tedlock, *Frieda Lawrence Collection of D. H. Lawrence Manuscripts*, p. 93).

was manifestly in no hurry to act, any more than Huebsch had been. For one thing he agreed with Mountsier's assessment of the book as 'dangerous' – the word Lawrence had himself used about it in June 1920 (iii. 546). Mountsier had reported Seltzer's opinion to Lawrence in September 1920:

He has suggested the possibility of publishing it in a limited edition to sell for possibly $12.00 or $15.00 and I think that such publication is highly desirable. Otherwise I fear that there would be trouble with it. Considering it purely from a point of view of money, I think the royalties would be just [*sic*] from such a publication as from general publication. If it is to be published for the general reader, as it might be after a limited edition is sold, certain parts would have to be eliminated.[51]

Seltzer was to publish his first Lawrence book, the limited edition of *Women in Love*, on 9 November 1920, charging $15.00 for it, so the subject (and an appropriate selling price – except that *Studies* was shorter than the novel) was clearly on his mind. We do not, however, know exactly what it was that *made* the book 'dangerous'; the Whitman chapter, almost for certain, but we can only speculate about which other parts led to such a judgement, and why.

Lawrence was inclined to agree with Seltzer's plans for a limited edition of *Studies*; it was, after all, still relatively early in his rehabilitation as a respectable author, and a book such as *The Lost Girl* – which he had written, in part, to further that rehabilitation – was still not in print, either in America or England; nor was *Women in Love*. He replied to Mountsier on 18 October 1920, 'Very well, let Seltzer do *Studies in Classic American Literature* in a limited edition, if he sees fit' (iii. 612). It seems likely, too, that Seltzer then (and no doubt later) thought the book likely to attract a limited readership and make little profit, so that – with more attractive Lawrence titles ready to be published – he had little incentive to give *Studies* priority.[52] For that matter, Lawrence gave him no particular encouragement. Whereas he had more than once complained to Huebsch during 1919–20 about his inaction with regard to *Studies*, Lawrence was silent during 1921; his surviving correspondence hardly mentions the work. Perhaps the sheer number and extent of the other projects with which he was then engaged distracted his attention. More plausibly, however, he might not have been eager to part with the work until he had had yet another chance to update the essays, some of them untouched since the spring of 1920. Since 1918 – and in one way of thinking, since the autumn of 1914 – his 'philosophical' writing had been a barometer of his innermost moods and

---

[51] Robert Mountsier to DHL, 24 September 1920 (UT).
[52] *Seltzer* 175–8. Business prospects in the United States in 1921 were so gloomy that Seltzer delayed his autumn list (ibid. p. 211). Word of Seltzer's difficulties reached DHL, who revealed his anxiety to Mountsier in December: 'I hope Seltzer isn't going to fail' (*Letters*, iv. 150).

concerns,[53] and the longer the book remained unpublished, the more likely it was that he was planning to revise at least parts of it.

In January 1922, when Lawrence was superintending a number of professional matters on the eve of making his break with the Old World, he informed Brown: 'I have made *no* arrangement for the publication of *Studies in Classic American Literature*, but Seltzer is booked to publish them in New York' (iv. 177). He chose, however, to direct Brown to try to arrange for their book publication in England with Jonathan Cape, who had written to Lawrence in November 1921 to enquire whether he 'had any book of short things' available (iv. 129). At the time, Lawrence had initially considered offering Cape a collection of the short fictions he was then working on, but in January belatedly decided to meet Cape's request with *Studies*, a proposition to which Cape at first responded with interest – as did Lawrence: 'I should rather like Cape to publish them.' This in turn made Lawrence consider the state of the text; he asked Curtis Brown, '*Is your MS. of these complete?*' (iv. 177). Mountsier may have sent Curtis Brown a copy of the complete set at the same time as he had prepared one for Lawrence, back in the winter of 1920–1. At all events, Lawrence was spurred to prepare a slightly modified version of the text then in his possession; he mailed it to Brown on 18 February (iv. 197) and sent yet another rewriting (and sanitising) of the 'Whitman' essay to Mountsier on the same day: 'I enclose the last three sheets of the "Whitman" essay. Please substitute them in the MS., and let these be printed. Then there will be nothing censurable also. And *this* is what I mean. You will see where it goes on' (iv. 198). No copy of this stage of revision survives, unfortunately. Lacking a copy of the second Melville essay ('Moby Dick') in his own text, Lawrence had instructed Mountsier the day before to send a duplicate from his complete copy to his English agent, though on 17 March it was still missing from the Curtis Brown set. Cape, however, was to turn down the work. Thus, even as Lawrence made his plans to leave Italy (and Europe altogether), book publication of the essays remained stalled by delays and rejections on both sides of the Atlantic.

Fifth Stage 1922–4: the publication of *Studies*

Over the course of the early months of 1922, Lawrence's twin ambitions to bring out the American essays in book form and to see America in person

---

53 When DHL completed 'At the Gates' in September 1917, he told Kot that it was the 'final form' (*Letters*, iii. 163) of his philosophy, 'which might be called mysticism or metaphysic' (iii. 143). This might seem to rule out *Studies* as another 'final' form; but the letter about 'At the Gates' went on 'Now I am doing a set of Essays on the Mystic Import of American Literature' and commented that they had 'already passed beyond all price' (iii. 163).

began to coalesce as one reality. His reasons for making the journey to America were undoubtedly mixed, but his desire to move on had become irresistible. For Lawrence in the autumn of 1921, as for Melville's Bulkington, 'the land seemed scorching to his feet'.[54] Despite trepidation about what he might actually encounter, he yearned to come into direct contact with the lands of his imagination. He had written to some American friends in September 1921 about his impending plans to circle the globe –'I will go east, intending ultimately to go west' (iv. 90) – although he was to waver several times in the following months over whether to reach the Western Hemisphere via an eastern or a western itinerary.

He had compelling professional as well as personal reasons to make the trip. With many of his works now circulating, professional doors opening and his reputation rising in the United States, he increasingly believed that he needed to be in closer touch with the primary market for his works. This was precisely the advice he had received from Mountsier in spring 1921 – 'Your chief publishing field is here, and the nearer you are to it the better' – and also from Seltzer who, seconded by his wife Adele, fervently wished the Lawrences to come to the United States and visit them.[55] More appealing yet was the enthusiastic invitation he had received in November 1921 from a new American supporter, Mabel Dodge Sterne, a leading social advocate and patroness of the arts, who was assembling an artists' colony around her in Taos, New Mexico (iv. 110–11). As the year 1921 neared its end, with spare money in his pocket, various works in his portfolio, *Women in Love* already in print and profitable, and Seltzer preparing to follow that up with other works, Lawrence was finally ready to make the venture, though not without his usual pre-departure vacillation. By the time he and Frieda embarked from Naples on 26 February 1922, their itinerary had expanded to include Ceylon (and, later, Australia), though Lawrence was still not entirely firm in his resolve to continue his easterly circuit; in the act of informing Mabel Sterne of his 'real desire to approach America from the west', he could not restrain himself from expressing his 'mistrust' of Taos and his 'opposition' to all the Americans he was encountering on the journey (iv. 225–6).

The Lawrences arrived in America in early September 1922 after crossing the Pacific and calling at Raratonga ('very lovely') and Tahiti ('such a lovely sea and land – but the town all spoilt' – iv. 284–5), Lawrence doubtless thinking of Melville in the South Seas. In San Francisco they passed through the majestic

---

54 Chapter 23 ('The Lee Shore'), *Moby-Dick* (Evanston, Ill.: Northwestern University Press, 1988; CEAA authorised edition), p. 106.
55 *Letters*, iii. 685 n. 1. Adele Szold Seltzer, the sister of the pioneering Zionist Henrietta Szold, was as much an enthusiast for DHL as was her husband: see, e.g., *Seltzer* 220.

harbour whose description as an unspoiled paradise in *Two Years Before the Mast* had been so powerfully etched in Lawrence's mind as he wrote his first version of 'Dana'.[56] Seltzer had hoped to meet their ship but proved unable to come, being successfully engaged in fending off the attempt of the New York Society for the Suppression of Vice to censor his editions of *Women in Love* and several other works.[57] Having accepted Mabel Sterne's invitation, the Lawrences proceeded straight to Taos where they settled into a small adobe house on her compound – 'Mabeltown', as he would later derisively call it.[58] There in Taos, and later in the northern New Mexico foothills, he and Frieda passed a memorable half-year during which they came into contact with a land of elemental beauty, broad vistas and exotic peoples which would prove far more appealing to Lawrence's sensibility and stimulating to his imagination[59] than did Mabel Sterne's imperious style of hospitality.

He also arrived with a sense of urgency about the *Studies* essays which had been missing for well over a year. Seltzer had already begun to make initial moves towards publication while Lawrence and Frieda were travelling across the Pacific, but this Lawrence was almost certainly unaware of. Perhaps stirred into action by Lawrence's mention of his plan to give the book to Cape for first publication, Seltzer had written to Mountsier on 12 June 1922 to 'send me MS of *Studies in Classic American Literature*. I have none of the essays in the office.' It is hard to imagine how this state of affairs could have come about unless – having discarded the 1919 set which at some stage had been passed to him by Huebsch, because he knew from both Lawrence and Mountsier that it was now out of date – Seltzer had never received from Mountsier the copy of the whole set of essays which Lawrence had charged Mountsier to deliver to him in August 1920. It is certainly possible that Mountsier had kept his set together to have it typed while he tried to interest magazines in publishing individual essays, but it is still odd to find Lawrence's American publisher determined on publishing a work which he did not actually possess in its most recent form. It might, however, help to explain Seltzer's failure to act during 1921 if he had actually been waiting to see a complete set of the essays. Nevertheless, by the end of June 1922 he presumably had a set from

56 After his own experience of America in 1922, DHL had changed his opinion: 'Think of it now, and the Presidio! The idiotic guns' (114:30).
57 The immediate effect of the legal case was greatly to improve sales of *Women in Love*, as well as to increase DHL's celebrity in the United States. On the Seltzer–Vice Society affair of 1922, see Tanselle, 'Thomas Seltzer Imprint', pp. 393–402, 406.
58 On 'Mabeltown', see David Ellis, *D. H. Lawrence: Dying Game, 1922–1930* (Cambridge, 1998), p. 70.
59 Cf. 'I think New Mexico was the greatest experience from the outside world that I have ever had. It certainly changed me for ever', 'New Mexico', *Phoenix*, p. 142.

Mountsier, and was resolved on publishing *Studies* 'early in the fall', at the same time as *Fantasia of the Unconscious*. He even seems to have advertised the book's forthcoming appearance.[60]

Fortunately, he did not pursue this course; the fact that Cape had after all turned the book down in England may have weakened his initial resolve and, as usual during this period of his publishing, Seltzer had on his hands other finished books by Lawrence which he admired and very much wanted to publish (and did so, in October 1922): *Fantasia* and *England, My England*. When he actually saw the text of *Studies*, too, his sense of its potentially problematic nature may well have returned to him; and by the beginning of September 1922 he had obviously postponed its publication. It is also possible that he realised (or Mountsier had informed him) that Lawrence might well want some actual experience of America before clearing the book for publication; and, as it turned out, Lawrence intended to put the essays through a final, thoroughgoing process of revision, in America, which perhaps lies behind his remark, made within a week of his arrival, about Seltzer: 'I don't mind if he defers *Studies* until Spring' (iv. 300).[61]

1922–3: Autumn 1922 TCC, Final MS, Final Corrected TS

With this goal in mind, Lawrence, who had evidently decided not to take any copy of *Studies* in the pile of trunks and suitcases which he and Frieda had carried halfway around the world, wrote to Seltzer just eleven days after his arrival in Taos to request a copy of the complete set of essays, as well as of Raymond Weaver's recent pioneering biography of Melville.[62] Understandably unsure whether the most recently revised set of the *Studies* was with his agent or his publisher, Lawrence requested Mountsier the same day to post him a copy of the text in his possession (iv. 307).

He was, however, for the moment prevented from 'going over' the essays (viii. 57) because he was busy working over his revision of his Australian novel *Kangaroo*; but when this was finished (around 16 October 1922) he turned to the *Studies* (Mountsier had forwarded a TS) and by the 18th was 'going over them' (viii. 57): 'Americanising them: much shorter', as he would later write to Mountsier (iv. 338). He tried out a new title on both Mountsier and Seltzer: '(shall we call this Studies of the American Daimon, Demon?)' he asked his

---

[60] *Seltzer* 225, 230; 'the book has already been announced' (Thomas Seltzer to DHL, 6 November 1922, UT). No copy of any advertisement has, however, been traced.

[61] See too *Seltzer* 239.

[62] *Letters*, iv. 306. Seltzer supplied Weaver's book, *Herman Melville, Mariner and Mystic* (New York, 1921); see Explanatory notes on 126:15, 128:16, 129:5, 131:3 and 131:8.

agent (iv. 324), while proposing to his publisher 'I think we'd better have a shorter title: "The American Demon" – or "The American Daimon" – and keep *Studies in C. A. Lit.* as a sub-title' (viii. 57). Seltzer was intrigued but determined: 'I like the title "The American Daimon", but am doubtful about the advisability of using it, as the book has already been announced under the old title and there may be some confusion.'[63] The title stayed unchanged.

Informing Mountsier on 18 November of his progress to date and his general publishing plans, Lawrence reported that he had already worked through the first five essays (iv. 341). Mountsier replied that he hoped to see the book published by Seltzer as soon as possible: 'I now have nightmares of you spending the rest of your life rewriting it!' (iv. 341 n. 1). Lawrence had, after all, apparently taken the best part of a month to revise less than half the book: but it was the most radical revision he had ever given it, and he had been doing many other things beside work on *Studies*.[64] Lawrence was, however, determined that Seltzer should bring out the book 'this spring' and mentioned the idea in letters to Mountsier on 18 October and 18 November (iv. 324, 341).

Lawrence also kept Seltzer informed as he moved through the essays, and insisted on their commercial potential: 'You'll like them much better, I think; much sharper, quicker' (iv. 342). On 28 November he reported to Mountsier in the heat of the revising process: 'you may think them too violent now, to print. Anyhow they are the first reaction on me of America itself'. The first eight essays were to go into the mail to Mountsier in New York the following day, to be freshly typed (iv. 343). That same day, he reported to Seltzer that the book was 'nearly done' and referred to it as 'the American Demon indeed. Lord knows what you'll think of them. But they'll make a nice little book: much shorter' (iv. 345). Work seems hardly to have been delayed by the Lawrences' moving house; in order to put greater distance between themselves and Mabel Sterne, on 1 December 1922 they and their new Danish artist friends Knud Merrild and Kai Götzsche moved up to the high-altitude Del Monte Ranch on Lobo mountain to the north of Taos. Early in December Lawrence finished work on the ninth *Studies* essay ('Dana') and, setting his sights on Melville, asked Seltzer to bring copies of *Mardi* and *Pierre* with him when he came down for his planned Christmas visit to New Mexico (iv. 345). Lawrence was working far too intensely, however, to postpone finishing his revision until the Seltzers arrived with the books. On 12 December, he reported to Mountsier that he had finished the revision of the last of the essays, and was sending him the second batch of text for typing: 'I hope you got the first

---

of the *Studies*. The rest are finished – tied up – when I can get them to the post office they'll come on: probably Thursday. They'll no doubt horrify you. But then you'll see their form is now final. Bed-rock' (iv. 358–9). He marked his completion of the essays in their new form, in the new place, with a celebratory 'Lobo, New Mexico' at the bottom of the final page of manuscript.

Lawrence had so thoroughly rewritten the work that little of the old TCC sent on by Mountsier in October had survived. In addition, he had left out 'The Two Principles', leaving the work as twelve essays introduced by a new, brief, high-spirited Foreword addressed to America, if not strictly to Americans. The result was a work not only 'sharper, quicker' in style but far more contentious in manner, which abandoned much of what Lawrence called its 'esotericism' in taking a more critical attitude towards the people and culture of the United States (iv. 342, 365). Lawrence planned, however, to 'go through' the book in yet another stage of revision when its typescript came back from Mountsier's typist in New York. On 4 January 1923 he was still waiting for the last four chapters of the typescript to arrive (iv. 367).

The timing of the book's completion was auspicious, preceding by just a couple of weeks the arrival of the Seltzers in Taos on Christmas Day. They spent the full week of their stay with the Lawrences up at Del Monte, and the visit proved a generally happy and encouraging one for the two men and the two women: the ranch with its sweeping vistas providing a fitting venue for a central week in what has been called 'Lawrence's honeymoon period with Seltzer'.[65] The days spent together certainly did nothing to curb the Seltzers' infatuation with Lawrence: Adele came away from their visit thinking him a 'Titan' and Frieda 'a Norse goddess', and Seltzer was perhaps even more impressed by Lawrence than was healthy for a publisher meeting one of his authors.[66] Mountsier arrived to join them on New Year's Day, the timing of his visit just the day before the Seltzers' departure designed, no doubt, to minimise the overlap between the two mistrustful men.[67] Nevertheless there was enough time for the three men to transact some accumulated business and to discuss the contracts for some of Lawrence's works, including one for

[65] John Worthen, *D. H. Lawrence: A Literary Life* (New York, 1989), p. 117.
[66] *Seltzer* 251.
[67] On their bad relations, see Ellis, *Dying Game*, pp. 87–90; the disappointing sales of Mountsier's *Our Eleven Billion Dollars: Europe's Debt to the United States*, which Seltzer had published earlier in 1922, was one source of tension between the two men. Seltzer had initially sent copies to President Warren Harding and other international leaders, but he reported more soberly to Mountsier in October: 'In the past six or eight weeks, we have hardly sold a single copy of *Our Eleven Billions*, and yet most favourable reviews still continue to be written' (*Seltzer* 226, 242).

Studies, dated 2 January 1923.[68] The three men also discussed the order and dates of publication of the next batch of Lawrence books, although Seltzer was not yet ready to commit himself to a definite timetable.

Seltzer returned home via Los Angeles, where, among the other business matters he attended to, he tried to capitalise on the publicity generated by the censorship trial to sell film rights of *Women in Love* to Warner Brothers. Several days after his departure from the ranch, Lawrence stated his intention to send him the new, complete copy of *Studies* once he had had the chance to revise its typescript, and also told Seltzer 'If you want to make any minor alterations, you are free to do so' (iv. 367). Two weeks later, Lawrence mailed a parcel of work to Seltzer in New York (iv. 369): it consisted of the corrected typescript of *Studies* (which does not survive), along with a corrected text of *The Ladybird* and a final request in a letter from Mountsier that *Studies* be published in the spring.[69] The timing was tight, but Lawrence still believed and would continue to believe as late as 8 March that Seltzer meant to issue *Studies* in April (iv. 399, 405). And such apparently was Seltzer's own intention as late as 17 February (viii. 63, 68).

By the end of January, Lawrence had also made an important professional decision. Having come to rely on Seltzer's publishing judgement and general helpfulness, and having grown intensely annoyed with Mountsier during his recent visit, Lawrence had decided to fire Mountsier (iv. 376, 377, 382). As he had done several years earlier, after dispensing with Pinker, he then proceeded to supervise his American literary affairs personally, despite the fact that his new success, recent productivity and regular changes of address rendered his literary affairs more complicated than for years past.

Meanwhile, he was also negotiating through Curtis Brown for the English publication of both *Studies* and other recently completed works. Early in January, Mountsier wrote to Curtis Brown announcing that the complete typescript of *Studies* would be ready 'shortly' and explaining that it had been 'delayed because of changes'; and, presumably at Lawrence's request, Mountsier asked Curtis Brown to 'arrange with another publisher than

---

[68] The 2 January 1923 contract for *Studies* was at one time in the possession of Charles Smith (see 'Note' to the Acknowledgements); DHL's letter to Seltzer of 16 January 1923 also mentions it (viii. 58). Seltzer apparently left it with Mountsier together with those for *Kangaroo* and *The Captain's Doll* and two Italian translations (ibid.). Another contract with Seltzer for *Studies* was signed by DHL in Mexico on 1 May 1923 (YU); as the 2 January contract is currently unavailable, however, no comparison between the two documents can be made.

[69] *Letters*, iv. 369. DHL requested that Seltzer simply write him the page and line of any alterations he wished made, since he had kept 'a third MS.' in his possession (presumably a carbon copy). The parcel also contained three book jackets by Knud Merrild which DHL hoped that Seltzer would accept, and a number of book contracts.

Secker' for their publication in England. However, despite his reservations about Secker – as in time about all his publishers – Lawrence remained in principle loyal to him. But he was always annoyed by timidity in publishers, something he felt Secker had shown over *Women in Love*: hence his injunction, now, that 'I'll stick to Secker if he will print all of me' (iv. 394). What was probably a carbon copy of the new typescript of *Studies* for Curtis Brown arrived on 12 February 1923 and went straight to Secker, Lawrence himself retaining a second carbon (iv. 369); and by late February, Lawrence was willing to accept Secker's offer to publish *Studies* on the basis of 10% royalties on the first 1,000 copies, 15% on the next 2,000 and 20% on sales beyond 3,000, apparently the best he could then get in either Britain or the United States for non-fiction.[70] With American publication now seemingly imminent, he also wished Secker to establish a date of publication.[71] He was surprised when Secker responded that with five Lawrence titles coming out that year – he actually published six – he had decided to delay the publication of *Studies* until 1924.[72] Seltzer, too, did after all delay publication until late August, but we know far less about his motives. He too may have been conscious of the sheer number of Lawrence books he was currently producing (seven original Lawrence titles and one translation between April 1922 and October 1923); but he may also have realised that he wanted to think about the essays more carefully than an April date would have allowed. The Whitman essay in its final form, which he might not have got around to reading by 17 February (when he reconfirmed April publication), would especially have worried him.

1923: Seltzer's proofs, 'Whitman' MS and TS extra revision

Their six-month tourist visas for the US were set to expire in March, so the Lawrences needed to make travel plans. With a growing number of his typescripts gathering in Seltzer's possession and no-one to represent him in New York City, Lawrence had good professional reasons for making a brief visit there to see to his affairs. But he and Frieda decided instead to head down to the warmth of Mexico for an indeterminate stay. There, in the small town of Chapala, they remained well into summer, as Lawrence poured himself into his new Mexican novel, eventually published as *The Plumed Serpent*.

---

[70] Seltzer offered him similar terms: 10% royalties on the first 5,000 copies and 15% on all additional copies sold in the United States (and half as much on copies sold in Canada).

[71] *Letters*, iv. 399; Tedlock, *The Frieda Lawrence Collection of D. H. Lawrence Manuscripts*, p. 96.

[72] On his decision to postpone publication of *Studies* from 1923 to 1924, see *Letters*, iv. 401 and n. 1. DHL returned Secker's contract for *Studies*, along with three others, on 7 June (*Letters*, iv. 454).

Though he had hoped to receive Seltzer's proofs of *Studies* before leaving New Mexico, they reached him only in Chapala; in early May he read, corrected and returned to New York the first batch, concluding with 'Poe' (iv. 441–2). He then waited impatiently for several weeks for the arrival of the second batch (iv. 445, 448), which he returned in June. In the course of doing his proof correction, Lawrence felt compelled to address Seltzer's reservations about the closing Whitman essay, as Seltzer probably anticipated that readers would object when they encountered Lawrence's commentary on Whitman's verse as masturbatory, and his descriptions of Whitman as a senile old man foolishly pursuing small girls, not to speak of Lawrence's remarks in the final pages about the Holy Ghost and Jesus ('only an intermediary god'). Lawrence's willing response was to excise the objectionable material and to rewrite the ending completely, substituting it with the part beginning, 'Whitman, the great poet, has meant so much to me.'[73] With that last serious revision, whose text he posted to Seltzer on or around 22 June – 'Sent you "Whitman" with piece added: hope you like it' (viii. 81) – the composition of *Studies in Classic American Literature* was finished. (See 'Texts' below for a discussion of editorial policy on these revisions.)

With Lawrence having already written much of his Mexican novel, he and Frieda began their delayed journey to New York on 9 July, travelling overland via New Orleans and Washington and arriving in New York City on the 19th. There they were the guests of the Seltzers, who took an out-of-the-way cottage in rural North Jersey for the two couples during the Lawrences' stay, which lasted about a month. Seltzer's primary motive for inviting Lawrence and Frieda was because he and Adele were so deeply impressed by them, but he could also reap the professional reward of showing off his literary lion in New York; an underlying purpose of the visit was to bring system and expediency to the publication of the various Lawrence works gathering in his office. He had already issued *The Captain's Doll* in April, and in the months immediately following Lawrence's stay, part of which Lawrence spent catching up with the reading of proofs, Seltzer was to issue in rapid sequence *Studies* (27 August), *Kangaroo* (17 September) and *Birds, Beasts and Flowers* (9 October).[74]

1923: American First Edition

The Seltzer edition of *Studies* (A1) was issued in a blue cloth binding with gold lettering, and priced at $3, a high price both by his standards for Lawrence's

---

[73] MS9 and TS10, Roberts E382a (Pierpont Morgan) and E382c (UTul); see 155:18.
[74] See Tanselle, 'Thomas Seltzer Imprint', pp. 429–31, and Roberts A24–A27.

works[75] and by general publishing standards for non-fiction. Its press run is unknown. Lawrence had solicited a dust jacket for the volume from the talented Knud Merrild, but Seltzer, who had found the drawing attractive upon receiving it in February, decided to reject it. Instead he chose a cream-coloured design,[76] which consisted primarily of the title written in two scripts and the author's name in a third: the final 'E' of the title avoids the symmetry of a rectangular design by spilling over into a line of its own; the author's name is framed by what might possibly be a stylised inkwell and a feather pen, but might just as well be broken architecture. As Keith Cushman has observed, the design has a certain wit: it 'suggests that the book's approach to the American literary classics (and to literature itself) will be less than reverential'.[77] Seltzer publicised the book, along with *Kangaroo*, in a full-page advertisement in *Publishers' Weekly* on 1 September 1923, calling Lawrence 'the greatest of modern writers' and describing the book as charting 'the spiritual history of America. This is a book that is less about writers than about America itself – a vital enquiry and criticism of the young nation which is cradling the new civilization.'[78]

The Lawrences' relationship had, however, been straining to breaking point, and had broken down completely when they separated on 18 August.[79] Frieda had embarked by ship for England and Lawrence was en route west when he wrote to Seltzer: 'Well, now we know one another, so we can go on with our mutual burden separately. I am glad to have stayed that month with you and Adele. I find a real reassurance in it' (iv. 492). For the time being, he was well satisfied with Seltzer as a publisher, literary adviser, paymaster and all-purpose aide. He could not have foreseen how in the months following the publication of *Studies* Seltzer would begin a financial decline that terminated in the virtual disbandment of his operations in 1926. He was already teetering on the verge of bankruptcy when Lawrence left America after his second and last visit, in 1925, by which time Lawrence had broken with him and moved on to the larger firm of Alfred Knopf. The Seltzers, he reported on the eve

---

75 In 1922–3, Seltzer priced the comparably long non-fictional *Fantasia of the Unconscious* at $2.50, and the fictional *Aaron's Rod, Kangaroo, The Captain's Doll* and *England, My England* all at $2.

76 *Seltzer* 259; *Letters*, iv. 345 n. 2, 369.

77 'Lawrence's Dust-Jackets: A Selection with Commentary', *D. H. Lawrence Review*, xxviii, no. 2 (1999), 45. The jacket appears as colour illustration no. 6 in Roberts (between pp. 328 and 329). DHL's own sketch of ideas for a cover, probably drawn in the winter of 1922–3, survives at UT: it shows objects as diverse as a cask of Amontillado, a witch on a broomstick, a cat, several whales, numerous letter 'A's, a large and ornate shoe, a house with seven gables, various ships, some wigwams and pine-trees, a distinctly seventeenth-century face and hat, some chemical apparatus, a Bible, and the word EI DO LONS, along with some unidentifiable objects (for reproduction see *Seltzer* [59]).

78 Vol. civ, 643.   79 Ellis, *Dying Game*, pp. 124–6.

of his latter departure from New York, 'had too many "feelings" '; Knopf, by contrast, he considered 'really sound and reliable'.[80]

1924: English First Edition

Lawrence had been a good deal less favourably disposed to Secker in the early 1920s, yet he chose in the end to work with him far longer than he did with any of his American publishers. Although Lawrence was well aware that the sales of his works in Britain had fallen well behind those in America, he continued to keep a watchful eye on the state of his literary properties there. During the early 1920s, Secker struggled to keep pace with the rapid-fire publication of Lawrence's works in the United States, but at the same time he was encouraged by the rise in Lawrence's reputation; as he wrote to Curtis Brown on 1 November 1923: 'Please tell Lawrence when you write that his position here was never more secure than it is now.'[81] But he continued to hope that Lawrence would one day 'produce a book which will give his work really popular recognition and place an entirely different complexion on his affairs and mine', and *Studies* was certainly not such a book; when he finally brought it out in June 1924, it was in an edition of 1,000 copies – far smaller, for instance, than the 4,000 copies of his edition of *England, My England* which he proudly announced himself ready to bring out that autumn.[82] He too priced his edition of *Studies* rather high for non-fiction at 10s 6d (half a guinea), a clear indication that he did not expect it to sell very well; it was bound in plain red cloth and set in a small type against broad margins, with its text running to 176 pages; he omitted the Foreword which Lawrence had composed especially for American publication, and which until now has never been published in Britain.

Mention should also be made of the 1962 publication *The Symbolic Meaning*, edited by Armin Arnold, which brought together the eight *English Review* essays and supplemented them with five extra essays ('Dana' from the 1923 first edition, Mountsier's shortened version of 'Whitman' from the *Nation and Athenaeum*, the other three from various typescript originals[83]). Arnold's edition, however, was in several ways unreliable. It was produced before the essays and sets of essays from the Smith collection and elsewhere had been located;[84] its dating of artefacts was speculative; and it was extremely opinionated (the introductory notes constantly repeat Arnold's contempt for the 1923 essays).

[80] *Letters*, v. 306: see too v. 78–9.   [81] Secker Letter-book, vol. 5, p. 158 (UIll).
[82] Ibid. and p. 433.
[83] See footnotes 112, 117, 119 and 122.   [84] See footnote 29.

Reception

During the ten-month interval between the book's publication in New York and in London, Lawrence travelled to the American West and Mexico, then to England and the Continent, and then back to America. Early news of the American reception of *Studies* had reached him first on the West Coast, and subsequent reviews followed him as he made his circuit. The critical reaction to *Studies* should be understood in terms not only of Lawrence's general reputation but also of the situation of American culture itself in the 1920s. To appreciate how Lawrence's analysis itself became – and rather quickly, too – a classic study of American culture, one needs first to grasp how problematic in Lawrence's day was the status of the subject itself.

The formal study of American letters was a relatively recent development when Lawrence wrote and published his essays. It was even then still meeting resistance from critics and scholars in the United States and Europe who denied the moral or aesthetic worth of American literature – or, in some cases, of America itself. Lawrence was himself well aware of this fact. In the Foreword to the American edition, he referred to himself as a 'midwife to the unborn homunculus'; no doubt, he enjoyed himself all the more for that privileged position.[85] At the time of his writing, the field of American literature was not yet part of the curriculum in most American universities, while the first professorship in American letters had not been established until 1919. Similarly, the founding of the American Literature Group of the Modern Language Association did not take place until 1921, and its journal, *American Literature*, began publication only in 1929.[86]

Of course, part of Lawrence's power as a critic and writer was precisely his own immunity to formalist and academic views. He had no hesitation about calling 'classic[s]' works of nineteenth-century American literature whose status as serious works of imagination had been disputed by many professional readers from the time of their composition right up to Lawrence's day. Many had been received by professional and lay readers alike as children's works, denigrated by other readers as a parody of true classics and treated by still others as a matter of obscenity (Twain, Whitman and other major American writers having met with censorship at various times). Almost predictably, therefore, the very title of Lawrence's work was certain to raise eyebrows, as

---

[85] 11:30 see, in this context, the analysis of David R. Shumway, *Creating American Civilization: A Genealogy of American Literature as an Academic Discipline* (Minneapolis, 1994), pp. 321–3.

[86] For a discussion of these developments, see Kermit Vanderbilt, *American Literature and the Academy: The Roots, Growth, and Maturity of a Profession* (Philadelphia, 1986), chaps. 13–15 *passim*. There had been a Professor of English Literature and History at King's College in the University of London as early as June 1840.

it did for example with Henry Irving Brock, the assistant editor of the *New York Times Book Review*; he centred his comments on 'what [Lawrence] calls classic American literature', while Kurt L. Daniels considered such a term 'a new phrase to most of us'.[87] By the time Lawrence was ready to publish his book with Seltzer, however, American letters were passing through a state of considerable flux. Following the war, a new self-consciousness about America accompanied a surge of nationalism, clear signs of which were discernible in recent critical works about the country by H. L. Mencken, Waldo Frank, Van Wyck Brooks and others. Similar signs were also present in new works of fiction: Sinclair Lewis's *Babbitt* had been issued the year before the appearance of *Studies*, and Willa Cather's *A Lost Lady* appeared just a few weeks after.

To say this is hardly to diminish the distinctiveness of Lawrence's *Studies* at the time of its appearance; the proof of its ability to call attention to itself was in the quick, vociferous reaction it prompted in the American literary press. Seltzer had deliberately introduced Lawrence to New York literary society during the weeks preceding its publication, walking him through the circles of the Algonquin Hotel and other New York literary gathering places. Perhaps he did so in part in order to reflect glory on himself, but no doubt his primary intent was to promote the fortunes of his prized leading author. Lawrence made the acquaintance of many of the city's leading literary journalists and editors, including Henry Seidel Canby of the *New York Evening Post Literary Review* (and soon to be founding editor of the *Saturday Review of Literature*) and Oswald Garrison Villard, owner of the *Nation*. He also met John Macy, the literary editor of the *Nation*, who, as both Seltzer and Lawrence presumably knew, was one of Lawrence's most ardent supporters in the United States; he had written a lavishly complimentary composite review in 1921 of *Women in Love* and *The Lost Girl*, and in 1922 had edited the Modern Library edition of *Sons and Lovers*.[88] Within weeks of their meeting, Macy wrote one of the earliest reviews of *Studies*, for which, however, he felt less than total admiration.

Lawrence was already widely known in America by the early 1920s; as a result, it is not surprising that a work by him on a topic of current interest was widely reviewed in many of the leading journals of the day: *Nation, New Republic, New York Times Book Review, New York Evening Post Literary Review* and

---

[87] 'D. H. Lawrence Strings Some American Literary Pearls', *New York Times Book Review*, 16 September 1923, p. 9; 'Mr. Lawrence on American Literature', *New Republic*, xxxvi (24 October 1923), 236.

[88] Macy concluded the earlier review as follows: 'No writer of this generation is more singular, more unmistakably individual, than Mr. Lawrence, and none is endowed with his unfairly great variety of gifts' (*New York Evening Post Literary Review*, 19 March 1921, p. 4; reprinted in R. P. Draper, ed., *D. H. Lawrence: The Critical Heritage*, New York, 1970, p. 160).

Dial, most of which were to come out with their reviews within the first months of the book's publication. Reactions were typically (and predictably) strong; few reviewers reacted mildly to Lawrence's powerfully expressed views, and many confessed their inability to respond impartially. To judge by what they wrote not one of the reviewers knew anything about the *English Review* versions of the essays published four years earlier; they restricted their comments exclusively to what Seltzer had published. What primarily mattered to them, in any case, was not any particular textual or formalistic concern but the crackling topicality of Lawrence's analysis. In addition to these reviews, Lawrence also received a number of informal critiques of the book from friends and acquaintances. In fact, the first critique he was to see was a letter of 'real generous appreciation' from Alfred Stieglitz that reached him in Los Angeles in advance of the more formal reviews (iv. 499).

At one end of the critical spectrum came the attack in *Current Opinion* within weeks of publication by an anonymous critic whose title indicated his attitude: 'D. H. Lawrence Bombs Our Literary Shrines'. Calling Lawrence the most 'thoroughgoing iconoclast since Nietzsche', this reviewer branded *Studies* a study in 'egotism': 'Mr. Lawrence is not so much concerned with the writers in themselves as he is with the opportunities they afford for the discussion and elucidation of his own philosophy.'[89] So, too, in another stiff-necked early review, Maurice Francis Egan attacked the author for writing 'a criticism of a life of which Lawrence knows nothing'.[90] Having denigrated Lawrence's authority to speak, he proceeded to quarrel with virtually every one of Lawrence's specific readings.

Such attacks launched from the defensive redoubt of offended patriotism were to be expected of a book that offered sweeping and controversial criticisms of American society and letters. There were, however, strongly opposing voices. At the other end of the spectrum came responses like those of Macy and H. J. Seligmann. Macy thought *Studies* 'honest, independent, and eccentric, a thousand miles, or a million light-days, away from most books of critical essays'.[91] But, for all his admiration for the book's pyrotechnical brilliance and flashing insights, Macy also expressed strong reservations. He had no patience for 'Lawrentian physics and anatomy': 'In what other physiology than Mr. Lawrence's is it written that "the poles of the will are the great ganglia of the voluntary nerve system, located beside the spinal column in the back."' More seriously, he attacked Lawrence broadly on matters of ideology and method, and, in doing so, anticipated the essentialist claim to be

[89] Vol. lxxv (September 1923), 305–7.
[90] 'On the Sin of Being an American', *Literary Digest International*, i (September 1923), 28.
[91] 'The American Spirit', *Nation*, cxvii (10 October 1923), 398.

made by future Lawrence analysts. Noting that 'his central theme seems to be an attempt to discover in a few American books and American history some characteristics peculiar to the inhabitants of These States', Macy challenged what he considered Lawrence's reductive, homogenising reading of the American past: 'One is tempted to fall back on Mark Twain's dictum that the only distinctly American peculiarity is a liking for ice-water.'[92]

More purely enthusiastic was Seligmann, who would be the author of the first book-length American critique of Lawrence, in which he pronounced *Studies* one of Lawrence's most important works to date and did not hesitate to call it the 'foundation for a new American critical literature'.[93] As it turned out, that statement would border on the prophetic. Seligmann, however, was far less a serious, independent-minded critic than an early Lawrence acolyte, which presumably explains Seltzer's motivation in publishing Seligmann's book.

A more measured initial assessment, and one more typically located between these extremes, was that written by Brock for the *New York Times Book Review*, a few weeks after the book's publication. He admired Lawrence's acumen but deplored his style. Lawrence's observations about American writers were 'arresting, illuminating, often the truth – or very near it'. On the other hand, his style was execrable: 'If upon the subject properly in hand he writes like a man of insight and a clever workman with the edged tools of language, the next sentence might often be composed by a gum-chewing Main Street soda-fountain cut-up or a blear-eyed, bar-room bum.'[94] Brock was also quick – may actually have been the very first – to note and comment formally on Lawrence's soon-to-be famous distinction between the tale and the teller. Brock then proceeded to apply that distinction ambivalently to Lawrence, deploring his personal style but applauding the critical insights of *Studies*.

A far more astute and sophisticated analysis was made by Stuart P. Sherman, a leading literary critic and academician who had himself been the subject of a recent book review by Lawrence.[95] In his own reading of Lawrence, Sherman foresaw that *Studies* would be received in the United States along the existing fault line separating 'the Party of Nature' from 'the Party of Culture'

[92] DHL was not pleased with this review, which Seltzer forwarded to him in Mexico and which prompted him to respond with 'a little letter' of his own (iv. 518). In 1926, DHL was kinder: 'I know John Macy, and like him very much, though I do think he lets the world use him badly' (v. 375 and n. 3).
[93] *D. H. Lawrence: An American Interpretation* (New York, 1924), p. 73.
[94] 'D. H. Lawrence Strings Some Literary Pearls', p. 9.
[95] 'Model Americans', *Dial*, lxxiv (May 1923), 503–10; DHL wrote his review between mid-December 1922 and 16 January 1923 (see Explanatory note on 15:20).

(an insight that was itself an anticipation of Philip Rahv's Lawrentian dichotomy a decade and a half later about American writers being either 'Paleface' or 'Redskin').[96] For Sherman, the book was a kind of adversarial agitator belonging to the Party of Nature, and Lawrence himself a kind of 'philosophic cave-man', by which he meant to emphasise both the naturalism and the brazen masculinity of Lawrence's ideology. Here is his image of Lawrence, the author as twentieth-century Neanderthal: 'Mr. Lawrence himself, glaring fuliginous from his cavern, and far more interested in winning male converts to his philosophy than silly women to hear his story.' Far from being repelled by Lawrence's caveman utterances, Sherman, who had made a reputation for himself the previous decade with his slashing assault on Theodore Dreiser for his 'jungle-motive', found them 'invigorating'.[97]

Two reviews as interesting for their authorship as for their content were those of Raymond Weaver and Newton Arvin. Weaver was the author of the Melville biography which Lawrence had read shortly before making his final revisions of *Studies*. Whatever Lawrence had thought of his work, Weaver thought very little of *Studies*, which he criticised harshly, or of Lawrence, about whom he declared, 'His ignorance of American literature is comprehensive and profound.'[98] Weaver expressed doubt whether Lawrence commanded a knowledge of American literature extending much beyond the texts treated in the book (although he did rightly assume Lawrence was familiar with his own Melville biography). All in all, he thought *Studies* an expression more of Lawrence's egotism than of insight into American society and culture. Arvin is an even more interesting case. Although then only in his early twenties, he was to distinguish himself over the next generation as one of the leading scholars not only of nineteenth-century American writing but of the very writers who most interested Lawrence (especially Melville and Whitman). To anticipate from him a deep engagement with and bold reading of the text, however, would lead to disappointment. Arvin was plainly put off by Lawrence's style, which he thought so overwrought and 'tedious' that the interpretative acuity of the essays needed to be saved, finally, from Lawrence himself. He also found it difficult to accept what he believed to be Lawrence's 'dualis[tic]' interpretation of American letters, although he was willing to follow Lawrence at least part of the way down this analytical line: 'One does

---

[96] Sherman, 'America is Discovered', *New York Evening Post Literary Review*, 20 October 1923, p. 144 (Draper, *D. H. Lawrence: The Critical Heritage*, p. 213); Rahv, 'Paleface and Redskin', *Kenyon Review*, i (Summer 1939), 251–6.

[97] 'The Naturalism of Mr. Dreiser', *Nation*, ci (2 December 1915), 648–50.

[98] 'Narcissus and Echo', *Bookman*, lviii (November 1923), 327. His book had commented on *Pierre*: 'for morbid unhealthy pathology, it has not been exceeded even by D. H. Lawrence' (*Herman Melville*, p. 342).

not need to see double, in a special sense, so fixedly as he does, in order to admit that the American mind has never been at peace with itself.'[99]

A comparably interesting reaction was that of the young literary critic and academic Robert Spiller, then an instructor at Swarthmore College and soon to emerge as one of the most influential scholars in the emerging discipline of American literature, with his oft-reprinted *Literary History of the United States*. Spiller was plainly put off by what he took to be Lawrence's substitution of psychoanalysis for Christianity but found his originality and verve more than ample compensation for his iconoclasm: 'As a point of view it is one of the most stimulating things that has come into literary criticism for a long time. Even Mencken or Macy seems like a pedant and an academician when Lawrence is making the sparks fly. The display of verbal fireworks is breathtaking.'[100]

For Kurt L. Daniels in the *New Republic*, 'one might feel that behind Studies in Classic American Literature there is Lawrence struggling with Lawrence and calling it a study of America'.[101] This view was common among reviewers, but Daniels took it more approvingly than did most, adding his relief to see such writers as Franklin, Cooper and Melville, who had previously been 'delivered over into the hands of the gift-book makers and the "juvenile" eight-to-thirteen lists', now taken in hand by a serious reader with powerful, original insights into their writings.[102] Still, like many others, Daniels had his reservations about the book, two of which were commonly made: that Lawrence's views were misogynist and that his style was unpleasing. In addition he accused Lawrence of making 'the argument fit the phrase'.

Most British reviews were tied to the Secker edition and therefore appeared only in 1924. As a group, reviewers in Britain typically read *Studies* in a different context from their American counterparts, having little or no direct vested interest in their content. The earliest review, however, was by the American poet–critic Conrad Aiken in the *Nation and Athenaeum*; he declared that *Studies* 'is probably without exception the most singular book ever written on American literature'.[103] But while appreciative of Lawrence's

---

[99] 'Mr. D. H. Lawrence's Criticism', *Freeman*, viii (31 October 1923), 190–1.

[100] 'Lawrence's Comparative Estimate of American Authors Found "Sane, Well Proportioned, Conservative" ', *Philadelphia Public Ledger*, 17 November 1923, p. 16.

[101] 'Mr. Lawrence on American Literature', p. 236.

[102] A related point was made a generation later by Edward Dahlberg: '[The *Studies*] are the first *Ecce Homo* book on American literature, which weaned us from the college presbyters on Whitman, Melville, Poe, Franklin' ('Lawrentian Analects', *Poetry*, lxxxiii, October 1953– March 1954, 349).

[103] 'Mr. Lawrence Sensationalist', xxix (12 July 1924), 616–18; reprinted in W. T. Andrews, ed., *Critics on D. H. Lawrence* (Coral Gables 1971), pp. 28–9.

flashes of brilliance, Aiken was plainly offended by what he disparaged as Lawrence's colloquial manner, pseudo-scientific jargon and psychologically unbalanced conclusions. Three years later, he stated his judgement bluntly: 'It is surely no exaggeration to say that in his *Studies in Classic American Literature* his literary "manners" are, to put it baldly, bad.'[104]

To Professor Ernest de Selincourt, the reviewer in *The Times Literary Supplement* in July, the key to the book was the temper of the author, who expressed himself 'less as a critic than as a moralist'.[105] De Selincourt's analogue to Lawrence, in this respect, was Ruskin. Although concentrating on the book as a study in morality and on Lawrence as the exponent of a subjectivist philosophy of 'wholeness', de Selincourt did make several good points, which would recur in later criticism on Lawrence and American writing. One was the observation that for Lawrence the 'greatest American work has been associated with an impulse of escape from human associations'. Another was de Selincourt's suggestion that Lawrence saw America 'as a nation of Puritans' and its great books as a ceaseless fight to come to terms with that ideological heritage. If the idea of America as a Puritan nation was widely taken by critics in the 1920s to be the equivalent of a national badge of shame, it would be taken more generously and probingly by scholars in succeeding decades, following the lead of the Harvard literary historian Perry Miller.

For J. F. H. the following month in the *New Statesman*, the fundamental issue was one of taste. His revulsion from what he had read was clear from his opening words: 'These essays show Mr. Lawrence's style at its worst', leaving him wondering how a single age could foster the criticism of writers as opposed in thought and sensibility as Lawrence and T. S. Eliot.[106] The answer to his quandary, he declared, was that twentieth-century England was a land living with a 'hybrid tradition' inherited from the previous century, which had absorbed the unhealthy incursion of a democratic sensibility into the province of civilised discourse. In recent times, those contrasting elements had separated themselves out, leaving England with both a civilised mode of discourse best exhibited in the works of Lytton Strachey, E. M. Forster and Aldous Huxley, and a vulgar one whose prime spokesmen were Lawrence and Joyce. So absorbed was the critic with this cultural situation that he had not a single critical word to say about *Studies*.

[104] 'Mr. Lawrence's Prose', *Dial*, lxxxiii (October 1927), 344.
[105] 'Mr. Lawrence's American Studies', 24 July 1924, p. 461.
[106] 'Mr. Lawrence's Criticism', xxiii (2 August 1924), 498. He went on to ask: 'Where is the link between Mr. Eliot's thirst for discipline, his insistence that literature, not life, nor religion, nor sociology, is the sole concern of the literary critic, and Mr. Lawrence's vatic and foam-flecked pronouncements on democracy, on religion, on sex, on the soul of America and the destiny of man?'

Edward Shanks, the assistant editor of the *London Mercury*, reviewed *Studies* in a brief joint review of a handful of literary critical works in his periodical, although he quickly pointed out that he considered it 'not strictly a work of literary criticism' but an excuse by Lawrence to use his purported topic to propound 'that peculiar dark philosophy of his which seems to be the theme of all his later works'.[107] Shanks confessedly did not understand that philosophy, which may explain why his review was little more than an exercise in bewilderment.

If *Studies* first appeared at a time when the field of American letters was undergoing a rapid transformation into an academic field of studies in the United States and, after the Second World War, in Europe, it quickly became a core constituent of that field. In 1951, with the book then out of print as a separate volume, Doubleday elected to issue a new edition in its distinguished line of Anchor Books, advertising *Studies* on its back cover as 'one of Lawrence's most important books' and 'one of the wisest books ever to have been written about the American mind'.[108] That list would also soon include a number of other 'classic' works in American literary, cultural and social history: Van Wyck Brooks's *America's Coming of Age* (1913), Constance Rourke's *American Humor* (1931), Lionel Trilling's *The Liberal Imagination* (1950), Perry Miller's *The American Transcendentalists: Their Prose and Poetry* (1957) and Richard Chase's *The American Novel and Its Tradition* (1957) – some of them also heavily influenced by the views of Lawrence. Little wonder that the academic critic Leo Marx, writing self-consciously in 1961 as part of the newly ascendant American Studies movement in the United States, noted that three of its leading recent works (*The American Novel and Its Tradition* by Richard Chase, *Symbolism and American Literature* by Charles Feidelson and *The American Adam* by R. W. B. Lewis) 'carry on where Lawrence left off'; he called them 'attempts to name more precisely the special attributes of the exciting voice' which Lawrence had heard.[109] By that time, for many readers such a voice could no longer be separated from the echo of Lawrence's own.

Texts

The earliest surviving manuscript for *Studies* is the set of notes (9 pages, unnumbered) on *The Scarlet Letter* which Lawrence made in a notebook some

---

[107] Vol. x (October 1924), 662.
[108] Edmund Wilson had paid *Studies* the compliment a decade earlier of reprinting its full text, except for the Foreword, in what he called his 'collection of literary documents' relating to the 'progress of literature in the United States as one finds it recorded by those who had some part in creating that literature' (*The Shock of Recognition*, New York, 1943, p. vii).
[109] 'Listen to the States!', *Critical Quarterly*, iii (1961), 82. The title, of course, comes from the opening sentence of *Studies*.

time in the first half of 1917, and which he left behind when he moved out of his Cornish cottage in October; it came into the possession of his neighbour Stanley Hocking. It is transcribed in quasi-facsimile in Appendix I.[110]

TS1

The original manuscripts – and with the exception of the *Scarlet Letter* notes all other draft materials – of the essays which the *English Review* published in 1918–19 are lost. Lawrence had had these manuscripts typed at various times and by various people in 1917 and 1918 before the essays were formally submitted to the *English Review*; the typescripts of three of them – 'Nathaniel Hawthorne', 'Dana' and 'Melville' (i.e. the essays which had not been published or not completely published) – have fortunately survived. In this edition they are called TS1,[111] as the first surviving stage of typescript materials. All were typed on the same machine, in a generally uniform fashion, on the same paper. All were heavily revised and were at some stage extensively cut, as can be seen from the various paginations: 'Nathaniel Hawthorne' had originally been at least 48 pages long (over 11,750 words), but was cut twice: to 33 pages and then to 28 (with misnumberings), about 8,225 words. But this shortened version was still considerably longer than the essays the *English Review* had already published (4,500–6,500 words, or 12–16 printed pages), and Harrison would only print the first part (about 60 per cent) of the essay. 'Dana' had originally been 28 pages (7,750 words), revised to 26; 'Herman Melville' 48 pages (11,550 words), revised to 42 and then to 29. The revision of the 'Nathaniel Hawthorne' typescript must have been completed by the end of March 1919, because TS1 was sent by the *English Review* to the printers, where it was date-stamped '4 April 1919'; the first part was published in the May issue.[112] The *English Review* editors must have decided against publishing the complete essay in one issue after the whole of TS1 had been set up in type; the proofs of the second part survive in MS2 (see below). It was almost certainly Lawrence himself who had divided his work on Cooper into two separate essays, both of which the magazine had published (in February and March),[113] and Harrison may initially have planned to publish the Hawthorne essay in two instalments as well, before it was decided to bring the *Studies* series to an end

---

[110] E382e (BucU). For the history of this notebook, along with photographic reproductions and transcriptions of the notes, see Charles W. Mann, 'D. H. Lawrence: Notes on Reading Hawthorne's *The Scarlet Letter*', *Nathaniel Hawthorne Journal* (1973), pp. 9–10, 13–25.

[111] Roberts E382g (UT), E382r (UN) and E382s.

[112] Richard Clay stamped the date on the verso of the first and last pages; a note on the typescript p. [17] indicates where the magazine publication ended. The second English edition (hereafter E2), *Symbolic Meaning* 134–58, used E382g as the source of its setting-copy.

[113] See footnote 18.

with 'The Two Principles' in the June number. Lawrence must have come to recognise that such essays were too long for publication even in specialised literary magazines, and he would divide his Melville essay in two in MS2.

Thus the three essays of TS1, together with the essays published in the *English Review*, in the editors' judgement make up the first extant version of *Studies*, and have been printed as First Version (1918–19) in this volume. (Only an essay on Whitman – and it seems certain that one was written in 1918 – is lacking.)

MS2

The next identifiable stage of composition consists of a set of five autograph manuscripts (here designated MS2), here printed for the first time and making up this volume's Intermediate Version (1919): essays on Hawthorne (second part), Dana, two on Melville, and Whitman.[114] MS2 almost certainly dates from the burst of attention which Lawrence gave to the project in September 1919. Turning his attention to the unpublished second part of the Hawthorne essay, Lawrence adapted the last few pages of the *English Review* proofs into a new analysis of *The Scarlet Letter* and *The Blithedale Romance*. He must have decided to use the proofs before he started work: the lined paper he used for all of MS2 is the same size as the proof sheets, and so, for 'Nathaniel Hawthorne (II.)', pp. 1–9 are autograph manuscript, pp. 10–13 the proofs. It is not possible to tell from the surviving photocopy whether all the revisions on the proofs were made at one time, or if Lawrence started to correct the proofs and later made further revisions.[115] He also redrafted the Dana essay (22 pages) and the Melville essays – 'Herman Melville (1)', 14 pages, 'Herman Melville (2)', 26 pages. With all these essays his minimal hope was periodical publication (iii. 405), but he was also preparing a complete set of the essays to post to America, and almost certainly used copies of the *English Review* printings to complete the set. By the end of September he had also finished work on the Whitman essay (20 pages), for which he had no expectation of periodical publication (iii. 400). That concluded his 1919 work; the whole set of essays (the second complete version of *Studies*) was posted to Huebsch on 10 October 1919.

On 2 August 1920, from Sicily, Lawrence posted to Mountsier the next complete version of *Studies* which we can be certain was assembled for volume publication. The text he sent (none of which survives) would presumably once

---

114 Roberts E382f, E382n, E382i, E382l and E382b (Smith).
115 The printer's reader marked a few corrections and queried readings, e.g. 'metamorphoses' at 318:5, which DHL corrected to 'metamorphosis'.

again have consisted of a mixture of manuscript and revised periodical pages, and was designed for eventual book publication in New York (iii. 582–3) with his new publisher Thomas Seltzer. This version of the complete set of essays was the result of the rewriting which Lawrence had done early in 1920, and was meant to replace the October 1919 set in Huebsch's possession. Lawrence also posted to Mountsier from Florence, on 7 September, a newly drafted 'Foreword', which was published in the December 1920 *New Republic* as an independent piece, there entitled 'America, Listen to Your Own' (printed in Appendix II).[116] Mountsier retained this complete August 1920 set of (probably thirteen) essays, and the new Foreword, until September 1922. It also seems probable that he had this set of essays typed, probably in two or three copies (one for American volume publication, one for his own use as he attempted to place individual essays with magazines, and possibly one for eventual English publication).

TS3, TS4, TS5, TCC5, TCC6

Following his success with placing the new Foreword, Mountsier tried to arrange for serial publication in the United States of other essays; he was still only trying to place the unpublished material, as is shown by the fact that he prepared three new typescripts (and one shortened carbon copy) of the Hawthorne and Melville essays.[117] They do not match the text of MS2, so they must either have been typed from Lawrence's August 1920 text or possibly from Mountsier's typed copy.[118] These typescripts are here called TS3 ('Nathaniel Hawthorne's "Blithedale Romance" ', 12 pp.),[119] TS4 ('Herman Melville's "Typee" and "Omoo" ', 13 pp.), and TS5 and TCC5 ('Herman Melville's "Moby Dick" ', 23 and 19 pp.). They were all typed in the same

---

[116] Mountsier had had typed (6 pages, unnumbered, E382.5c, Smith) the six-page MS (E382.5a) which DHL had sent him. The piece was reprinted in *The 'New Republic' Anthology 1915:1935*, ed. Groff Conklin (New York, 1936) and collected in *Phoenix* 87–91. E382.5b (Smith) has now been recognised as being part of E382g, and E382.5d (Smith) as part of E382p (Smith).

[117] Roberts E382h (UT), E382m (UT), E382k (UNM) and E382j (UT). *Symbolic Meaning* 219–50 (E2) used E382m (which has Mountsier's address on it) as the source of its setting-copy.

[118] It is unlikely that they were typed from the 1919 Huebsch text; there is no evidence that Mountsier ever handled this.

[119] On E382h (TS3) someone not identified (but perhaps Mountsier) deleted the title and replaced it with *The Scarlet Letter*, deleted the first sentence and altered the second, and copied a sentence later (without deleting the first occurrence). It has the Curtis Brown (London) stamp on it as well as Mountsier's address. There are minor typographical corrections, but no evidence exists that DHL at any stage saw TS3 or altered it. *Symbolic Meaning* 162–72 (E2) used E382h as the source of its setting-copy.

style, probably at about the same time and on the same machine for Mountsier, presumably late in 1920 or early in 1921; Mountsier later sent copies of them (with perhaps a complete set of the other essays) to Curtis Brown, who became Lawrence's London agent early in 1921: they carry Brown's business stamp and Mountsier's handwritten name and address towards the bottom of the first page.

TCC5 is not identical with TS5, but shows itself to have been shortened; Mountsier (as he told Lawrence) was cutting the essays for magazine publication.[120] The text of TS3 is sufficiently different from the other versions of the second Hawthorne essay for it to be given in full in Appendix IV. The variants of TS4 and TS5 (and TCC5) are given in the Textual apparatus for the corresponding essays in MS2.

Separate from, although probably roughly contemporaneous with these typescripts, was a shortened carbon copy of 8 single-spaced pages, here designated TCC6, of the essay on Whitman which Mountsier must have had produced by early 1921, for periodical publication: his annotation '*Magazine*' appears on its first page.[121] A corrected copy of TCC6 presumably served as the setting-copy for the *Nation and Athenaeum* (Per 1), while the text in the *New York Call* (Per 2) was set from Per 1.[122] The variants in TCC6 are recorded in the Textual apparatus. Mountsier later restored the passages cut from TCC6 when assembling TCC7, a full typescript (see below) of all the essays in their 1920–2 form; Lawrence himself had changed the ending of the Whitman essay (and sent a copy to Mountsier) as one of the very last tasks he did in Sicily in February 1922 before leaving Europe (iv. 197–8). Mountsier also ensured that Curtis Brown had a complete and updated typescript of *Studies* in the spring of 1922.

TCC7

Within days of his arrival in Taos, New Mexico, in September 1922, Lawrence signalled to Seltzer his intention to 'go over the *Studies in C A Literature* again' (iv. 306); and by mid-October he had received from Mountsier a copy (probably the ribbon copy) of a full typescript, here called TCC7. This consisted of an intermediate version of the Foreword (here printed as Appendix III), a text

---

[120] *Letters*, iii. 644 n. 1. TCC5 (E382j, which has both the Curtis Brown stamp and Mountsier's indication on it) seems, e.g., to have been planned as a cut version: an unusually large top margin was left on the first page (which corresponds to page [4] of TS5), so that the title and the opening three-line paragraph could be inserted later. At least one other cut copy must have been created at the same time, as the additional material is typed in carbon.

[121] Roberts E382d.

[122] XXIX (23 July 1921), 616–18; 21 August 1921, pp. 3–4. *Symbolic Meaning* 254–64 (E2) used Per 1 as the source of its setting-copy.

otherwise unknown – we do not know when Lawrence wrote it – and the full set of thirteen essays.[123] The importance of TCC7 in the evolution of the final text was small, as Lawrence revised it at the next stage virtually beyond recognition. But as a source of information about Mountsier's preparation of typescripts and about preceding versions, TCC7 is extremely important. Mountsier made minor corrections to TCC7 himself, e.g. adding underlining by hand, inserting omitted phrases and correcting typographical mistakes, but rarely altering punctuation or words unless they seemed wrong to him.[124]

The relationship of TS3, TS4 and TS5 to TCC7 seems to be that of independent typings from the same source. For example, TS3 (the second Hawthorne essay) differs from TCC7 in a few single words[125] and in small details, such as the capitalisation of initial letters (often a matter of debate for Lawrence's typists and compositors). TS4 and TS5 (the Melville essays) are less clear: some variants seem to indicate a separate typing from one source,[126] but TCC7 follows TS4 and TS5 in others[127] and also in accidentals. This may be because the sources of the Melville essays were different from those for the Hawthorne. For the Whitman essay, the TCC7 typist must have been working from one of Mountsier's shortened copies: in TCC7 the omitted material has been added in Mountsier's hand, inserted through additional typed pages[128] as well as typed directly into TCC7 (the later omitted ending, pp. 13–17). The TCC7 Whitman essay is very different from other states of the texts and is printed here in Appendix V: it is the only uncut source of the version published in periodicals in 1921.

MS8

Working from the copy of TCC7, Lawrence had finished revising the first five chapters by 18 November 1922 and was ready to send 'the first eight – out of twelve' on the 28th (iv. 343), i.e. including both Hawthorne essays. He had completed work on 'Dana' and the first 'Melville' by 5 December, but did not post them; the final four essays went off together to Mountsier around 14–16 December 1922 (iv. 358).

---

[123] Roberts E382p (see notes 46 and 116). The typist of TCC7 numbered the pages consecutively (with errors) from the Foreword down to the second Cooper essay; thereafter each chapter was numbered separately. On DHL's request for a complete copy, see *Letters*, iv. 177, 196–8.

[124] Mountsier did, for example, change the *English Review*'s 'inevitable' to 'inevitably' (168:38). TCC7 has been collated in full, but is only recorded in the Textual apparatus where its text was not superseded because DHL re-used pages from it in MS8 and its transcription errors thus carried through to the final text.

[125] 394:14, 395:36, 395:40.   [126] E.g. 335:25, 337:37, 339:38.   [127] E.g. 334:27, 342:15.

[128] Numbered with alphabet letters (2a, 8a–8e).

Lawrence's work had been so extensive that he had created what was virtually a new work: a surviving combined manuscript and typescript, here designated MS8, of 164 pages.[129] Few pages of the TCC7 typescript survive intact in MS8. Lawrence began by retyping, apparently in ribbon and carbon copies, the Foreword, 'The Spirit of Place', 'Franklin' and most of the Crèvecoeur essay, adding additional changes by hand, but four pages into the first Cooper essay he started writing by hand in a single copy, occasionally incorporating pages from his copy of TCC7 (34 in all), in particular where they contained long quotations which he was re-using.[130] He dropped the 'Two Principles' chapter (chapter numbering and pagination confirm that this was his choice). MS8 therefore consisted of the new Foreword and twelve essays rewritten in a radically altered style which expressed a more aggressively critical interpretation of the United States and its culture.

Lawrence received back from Mountsier's typist a typed copy of the Foreword and the first eight essays, either by post from New York or possibly by hand, when late in December 1922 Mountsier himself came to Taos. He had the first part of the typescript by 4 January 1923, but was still waiting for the last four essays; his intention was to 'go through' it all (iv. 367). By 19 January he had corrected the entire typescript and was ready to post it to Seltzer (iv. 369). None of this corrected typescript survives, so that for the most part we cannot know either in what ways its typist had departed from MS8, or what Lawrence changed, but some new small inaccuracies must have crept into the text, given the nature of Lawrence's handwriting and the amount of revision. We can however identify a few of the changes as Lawrence's own: at this late stage of revision he introduced several borrowings from Stuart P. Sherman's *Americans*, of which he had received a review copy sometime after 12 December 1922.[131]

---

129   Roberts E382q (Smith). An American Art Association catalogue dated 29–30 January 1936 offered for sale, as item. 379, a corrected typescript (E382o: now unlocated) of 23 pp. of the Foreword, 'The Spirit of Place' and 'Benjamin Franklin', with autograph corrections numbering about '375 words'. This may possibly have been a copy of the opening of MS8 (apparently typed in ribbon and carbon copies), in which these three items are numbered 1–23, but in which there are approximately 100 changes (in which case the level of correction in E382o would appear to be a sales catalogue exaggeration); it may, however, have been a differently corrected typescript, its source not now identifiable.

130   DHL also occasionally wrote his new text on the verso of a typed page, e.g. the last page of MS8's 'Fenimore Cooper's White Novels' (p. 47) is written on the verso of the last page of the equivalent chapter in TCC7 (p. 43). He had also used pp. 46–51 of his copy of TCC7 in his revision of the Crèvecoeur essay; see Explanatory note on 37:10.

131   *Letters*, iv. 355, 359, 369, viii. 59; and see Explanatory notes on 15:20, 81:18, 85:40, 100:8 and 149:21. We could also expect DHL to have made at this stage some of the changes apparent between MS8 and A1; e.g. those recorded in the Textual apparatus at 11:18 and 12:15.

This corrected typescript[132] probably served as the setting-copy for Seltzer's 1923 edition (A1). Lawrence read Seltzer's proofs while living in Chapala, Mexico, in the early summer of 1923; he had finished work on the proofs of the Foreword and essays I–VI by 9 May, making 'one or two serious alterations' to 'The Spirit of Place' (iv. 442). He was, however, still waiting for 'the balance of the *Studies* proofs' on 22 May, which presumably meant that essays VII–XII had not yet come; and he complained that there were still 'No *Studies* proofs yet' on 26 May (iv. 448). They must have arrived very shortly afterwards, however, there was time for him to finish work on them and return them to Seltzer, and for Seltzer to ask for further changes to the Whitman essay, all by 15 June (iv. 457). When Lawrence wrote to Seltzer on 27 June he did not mention the proofs, strongly suggesting that everything had been finished and posted off well before that date. The Final Version of this volume was thus almost complete.

MS9, TS10

We do not know what Lawrence did during proof-correction apart from correcting errors; we do not know, either, if Seltzer had made any particular requests for changes, nor can we tell whether Seltzer had altered or censored the typescript before it went to the printer for proofs to be made. But it is fairly clear that when he got the proofs back from Lawrence, Seltzer was still not happy with the Whitman essay (the ending in particular), which may suggest that he had not as yet done much to censor it. On 15 June, Lawrence wrote to him: 'All right, I'll go over the "Whitman" essay again. Wait for it' (iv. 457). Lawrence at this point probably censored the essay 'again', and certainly added a new handwritten ending of 7 pages (here called MS9) to replace the original ending. Seltzer had MS9 typed to create a setting-copy (TS10) of 9 pages,[133] and at some stage also slightly bowdlerised it. This revised version of the Whitman essay, added to the other eleven essays and the Foreword, made up the Final Version (1923) of this volume.

A1, E1

A1 consists of gatherings of 16 leaves, except for the last, which is of 10 leaves: this anomaly was probably due to Lawrence's extending the ending of the

---

[132] Or just possibly a retyping of it. Seltzer had had corrected typescripts of DHL's works retyped on at least two occasions in the past (*Women in Love* and *Aaron's Rod*: see *WL* xl, xlv and n. 62, and *Aaron's Rod*, ed. Mara Kalnins, Cambridge, 1988, pp. xxxiv–xxxvi), but it seems unlikely that the recently made typescript of *Studies* would have been so heavily corrected as to warrant complete retyping.

[133] Roberts E382a, E382c.

Whitman essay in MS9 while the book was in proof; the printer provided a short final gathering rather than putting in blank pages to make the final gathering up to 16 leaves.

The English edition (E1) was set from a copy of the American edition, which Secker had requested from Curtis Brown by 13 March 1923;[134] Secker's edition omitted the Foreword.

The Cambridge Text of the Final Version (1923)

For the Cambridge edition, the editors have turned to the earliest source wherever practicable for the correction of A1. In the first six chapters (up to and including Poe), the *English Review* (Per) is used to correct MS8; for the later chapters, TS1 and MS2 are used (these changes are recorded in the Textual apparatus). Involved are occasional punctuation errors or minor, unrevised mistypings, and in particular errors in quotations, because Lawrence as usual almost never returned to his sources but simply recopied his quotations, thus perpetuating errors in them. For example, Lawrence probably had no copy of Whitman's verse to hand when writing out MS8 – certainly not the copy he had used when composing MS2 (or its missing earlier version) – and accordingly the poetry in the Whitman quotations has been altered to read as MS2.[135]

There remains the thorny issue of censorship by Seltzer, and by Lawrence on Seltzer's behalf. We know that Seltzer (like all publishers at this date) objected to sexual and excremental language and reference, as well as to religious language used in non-religious contexts or blasphemously. He had cut out what he had seen as objectionable words and phrases from other Lawrence books, e.g. *The Lost Girl, Women in Love, Aaron's Rod* and *Sea and Sardinia*.[136] For *Studies*, the volume editors have borne several considerations in mind. Lawrence knew from 1918 that (in particular) his Whitman essay was likely to cause editors and publishers to baulk; there was also language both directly

---

[134] Secker Letter-book, vol. 4, p. 969 (UIll).

[135] Similarly MS8 is corrected to read as TS1 on the occasions where quotations from *The Scarlet Letter* first written into TS1 survive into MS8; i.e. 88:24–31. There are fewer than a dozen variants in punctuation and three words: TS1 has 'his' and MS2 'him' at 88:25, 'looked' and 'lookest' at 88:26, 'Then tell' and 'Tell' at 88:27.

[136] E.g. in *Sea and Sardinia*, in 1921, Seltzer had confronted the problem of the narrator and wife in Sorgono their first evening coming across a 'steep little lane' used as 'the public lavatory', and having to look out for an appropriate 'side-lane' for themselves the following morning. He began by trying to extract the objectionable words and phrases but ended up cutting the text completely; see *Sea and Sardinia*, ed. Mara Kalnins, (Cambridge, 1997) 94:18–25, 113:13–15 and Textual apparatus. See too *The Lost Girl*, ed. John Worthen (Cambridge, 1981), p. 396, Explanatory note 322:11; *WL* xlix and footnote 78; *Aaron's Rod*, ed. Kalnins, pp. xxxiii–xxxiv and footnotes 45 and 46.

sexual and excremental in several other essays. The crucial question is how far Lawrence was prepared to go to meet the anxieties which his work would provoke. His response at this (or indeed any) stage of his career was sometimes to comply with what a publisher wanted; he had, for example, at first refused to respond to Methuen's desire to bowdlerise 'passages and paragraphs' of *The Rainbow* back in 1915, but in the end had co-operated with toning some of them down.[137]

By the early 1920s, Lawrence was in general taking a rather more hostile attitude towards the censorship of his work; and was not, for example, prepared to cut phrases and passages from his fiction even when a publisher whom he liked and trusted, such as Seltzer, asked him to. The most recent example had been *Aaron's Rod* in January 1922, when Lawrence had rather angrily left it to Seltzer to make whatever cuts he wished to in passages which, after looking at them again, Lawrence had completely refused to change:

The essential scenes of Aaron and the Marchesa it is impossible to me to alter. With all the good-will towards you and the general public that I am capable of, I can no more alter those chapters than if they were cast iron. You can lift out whole chunks if you like. You can smash them if you like. But you can no more alter than you can alter cast iron.

There you are. It's your dilemma. You can now do what you like with the book . . . It is useless asking me to do any more. I shall return you the MS. On Monday. Then say no more to me. I am tired of this miserable, paltry, haffling and caffling world – dead sick of it. (iv. 167)

To Mountsier he had remarked: 'I sent back the type MS. of *Aaron* to Seltzer because it is just physically impossible to me to alter it. He may do as he likes now. I just won't alter it: can't, the alterations won't come: and the general public can go to hell in any way it likes' (iv. 168). His only solution was to suggest that the publisher should produce two editions: one, censored, for the open market ('leave out anything you like for a popular edition'), and a second, unaltered one for a private public (iv. 167). Interestingly, he himself attempted the same strategy in 1928, when he published – privately – his own uncensored edition of *Lady Chatterley's Lover*, but also attempted to create a self-censored version for publication in the normal way.[138]

137 See *Letters*, ii. 370. Mark Kinkead-Weekes, the editor of the 1989 Cambridge edition of *The Rainbow* – lacking any evidence about what DHL had done in the proofs, as none survive – felt that this often left him no choice except to treat the 'self-censorship' changes in the same way as changes made elsewhere in the first edition: where arguments were 'equally poised', he concluded that he was obliged to follow 'the same procedure as for cases left doubtful by the loss of the proofs', and so give 'the benefit of the doubt' to the first edition (*The Rainbow*, pp. lxii–lxix).
138 See *Lady Chatterley's Lover*, ed. Michael Squires (Cambridge, 1993), pp. xxiv, xliv and n. 59, and Ellis, *Dying Game*, pp. 399–400.

How he dealt with the 'dangerous' aspects of *Studies* was, however, rather different. During the period January–June 1923 he co-operated with Seltzer at all times and explicitly authorised him to go ahead and make 'minor alterations' (iv. 367); he was prepared to receive suggestions about other changes too, and also to make them himself (iv. 369). It is clear that he had different standards for discursive prose (or literary criticism) than for fiction; and in the case of *Studies* he may have been prepared to reflect rather differently, at a later stage, on what between October and December 1922 he had written fast and at times with gleeful joy, especially about Whitman: he was well aware that the book represented 'the first reaction on me of America itself' (iv. 343). We must not exaggerate: with the exception of the Whitman essay and its extensive changes, there are fewer than thirty occurrences of words and phrases in 'The Spirit of Place', 'Poe', the two 'Hawthorne' and the 'Dana' essays which might arguably have been subject to censorship.

There was one occasion when it seems probable that Lawrence did indeed engage in self-censorship, as some evidence for it survives: as described above, Seltzer asked Lawrence to 'go over the Whitman essay again' in June 1923. Lawrence agreed to do so: 'Wait for it.' But there were three other periods during which Lawrence *may* have engaged in self-censorship. (1) During his revision of the typescript of MS8 between December 1922 and January 1923 (Seltzer might even have made suggestions while staying with the Lawrences over New Year); (2) while waiting for Seltzer to set the book up in type between January and May 1923 (he explicitly told Seltzer in January that he had kept 'a third MS.' in his possession – presumably a second carbon copy – so that Seltzer could send him 'the page and line' of places where he wanted 'anything altered or eliminated' (iv. 369), which certainly sounds as if he were expecting such requests); (3) while correcting proofs in Chapala during May–June 1923. It seems likely that Seltzer had cut words and perhaps even phrases – in Lawrence's words, making 'minor alterations' – from the text of *Studies* before Lawrence saw the proofs, and it is also possible – though this does not seem to have been his usual practice – that the publisher had marked in the proofs what he wanted Lawrence to tone down. At any stage, of course, Seltzer may have written letters of the kind which, back in January 1923, Lawrence seemed to expect, and made suggestions about what should be deleted, although no such letters survive for this or (indeed) any other book.

The editors therefore accept that some censorship and some self-censorship are incorporated in the text of A1. The question is how (or whether) such censorship can be identified, isolated and reversed.

While Seltzer would certainly not have been prepared to make on his own the kind of major textual changes which were eventually made to the Whitman essay, what he did with *Sea and Sardinia* indicates how prepared he was to patch together an acceptable sentence from an unacceptable Lawrentian original.[139] In this way he was rather different from a publisher like Secker, who was quite prepared to make extensive textual changes without consulting Lawrence.[140] Furthermore, the fact that some of the examples of censorship in the Whitman essay were accompanied by, replaced by or exist in close proximity to substitutions clearly made by Lawrence himself demonstrates that such cuts were either made (or at least known about) by Lawrence. What, however, makes the Whitman essay especially problematic is that it is in many cases impossible to justify returning to the earlier state of the text, as what Lawrence frequently did was not simply to bowdlerise but to *rethink*. Given Lawrence's acceptance that some such changes might need to be made before publication, and his obvious preparedness to listen to Seltzer's requests for changes, it becomes impossible to argue that his acquiescence and co-operation should be entirely ignored.

The editors have, with some reluctance, therefore decided that, rather than trying to pick and choose in the Whitman essay among changes which *may* have been wholly authorial, which may have been asked for, which may have been imposed and which may have been a collaboration of some kind – and all of which were made at some unknown point between MS8 and A1 – they must select one state as the Whitman essay's base-text, and record all variants of the other state.

1. Taking MS8 as base-text would produce an entirely authorial text, but one which would exclude the changes that Lawrence introduced into his text during revision of the typescript as well as ignoring changes which he made during revision of the proofs.
2. Taking MS8 and MS9 together would apparently produce an entirely authorial base-text, but MS9 was written to be added on to a state of text (surviving only in A1) which had already superseded MS8.
3. Taking A1 as base-text would mean including all that the author did at various stages, but at the expense of including the censorship, whether imposed by Seltzer or agreed to by Lawrence.

We have, therefore, chosen A1 as our base-text for the bulk of the 1922–3 version of the Whitman essay, although we know that it was subject to serious censorship. With one specific exception, the revised ending, where we can tell exactly what Lawrence expected to see printed (because he sent it to

[139] E.g. *Sea and Sardinia*, ed. Kalnins, Textual apparatus for 94:22.
[140] See, e.g., *WL* xlviii.

Seltzer in MS9) – and where we can precisely evade the effects of Seltzer's further censorship – A1 is unquestionably closer to what in the summer of 1923 Lawrence expected to see printed as his Whitman essay. The uncensored readings of MS9 have, however, been preferred to those of TS10 and A1; in these five cases we need be in no doubt about what Lawrence expected to see printed.[141] The edited text for the Whitman essay thus consists of A1 emended from MS9. The reader who wishes to see in detail what was revised, censored or developed in the Whitman essay between MS8 and A1 can consult both the Textual apparatus and Appendix VI, where the whole of the MS8 text is reproduced.

The cases of censorship in the first part of the book are, however, of arguably a rather different kind. They bowdlerise particular words or phrases, and nearly all of them consist either of omissions or of tiny rewritings made in order to make omissions possible. On a number of occasions Lawrence used words such as 'coition', 'act', 'intercourse' and 'phallic'; but in the Poe essay, for example, where MS8 reads 'into flaming frictional contact, the merest film intervening. That is coition', A1 reads 'into contact, the merest film intervening'. Elsewhere in the same essay, Lawrence's 'through the act of coition' was cut, 'Coition' was replaced by 'The embrace of love', and 'as the act of coition' was also omitted. MS8's phrase 'sex intercourse' was changed to 'love-making', 'had intercourse' was changed to 'lived', and 'in the act' was omitted; the word 'phallic' was also removed.[142] Lawrence may have been consulted about these alterations, and in two cases may possibly have been involved in the rephrasing required by them, but there can be no doubt that such alterations had been provoked or demanded by Seltzer, and – in a very different way from what happened in the Whitman essay – none of them resulted in any significant rethinking or rewriting of Lawrence's text. Similarly, a series of comic references to Adam's 'appendage' (and 'what Eve has got to match') in the *Scarlet Letter* essay were all removed before A1 appeared. Furthermore, two obviously blasphemous references – to God on the WC (170:27) and to the dead Christ – 'by this time he stinketh' (161:24) – were also removed in A1.

If we were to maintain the censorship, we would indeed exclude words which Lawrence himself acknowledged were perhaps 'too violent now, to print' (iv. 343); and we would ensure that a text which Lawrence had worked on with his publisher remained as the final and approved text. However,

---

[141] Textual apparatus entries recording where the readings of MS9 have been preferred to censored readings in A1 are at 156:18, 156:20, 160:15, 160:19, 161:5.

[142] Seltzer had, e.g., refused to print the word 'phallus' in 1920: see *The Lost Girl*, ed. Worthen, 322:11.

to retain the censorship would also be to impose the particular fears and susceptibilities of a mid-1920s publisher upon a text which Lawrence had written (and rewritten) well aware of Seltzer's sensitivity, yet without limiting himself to the demands for decorum which he knew Seltzer would make. We have – with some hesitation – concluded that on these eighteen occasions we should engage in a conservative restoration of Lawrence's text, and should revert to the readings of MS8.[143]

In other cases, however – a potential lesbian reference which might have made Seltzer anxious, bad language and violent language – it is a good deal less easy to be certain whether the omissions, changes and rewritings in A1 were the result of Lawrence's response to Seltzer's sensitivity. In such cases, we have allowed the readings of A1 to stand.[144]

Lawrence worked on the contents of *Studies* for longer than for any other of his published books, with the exception of *Women in Love*; it is also rare to have surviving evidence of so many stages of his composition and revision. Accordingly, the Cambridge edition has incorporated all states of the texts, including all revisions in the manuscripts and typescripts (listed in a separate Variorum apparatus).[145] The choices of base-texts and emendations are listed in the Notes on the Texts. This volume thus enables its reader to consult the almost complete set of the 1918–19 essays (both those published in the *English Review* and those never before printed), an intermediate, partial version and the very different 1922–3 version, as well as a number of individual essays in different states; the volume offers the richest compilation of Lawrence's essay materials ever published. *Studies in Classic American Literature*, with its long and immensely complicated development from initial planning to book publication, not only documents and reveals the history of a crucial seven-year period in Lawrence's own writing career, but illuminates the subject area of American Literature studies in which the book would eventually be recognised as a pioneer, and where it remains a seminal text.

---

[143] The Textual apparatus entries recording such reversion to the readings of MS8 are: 67:4(1), 67:4(2), 70:37, 75:18, 75:20, 75:21, 82:10, 82:11, 82:24(1), 82:24(2), 82:24(3), 82:25, 82:35, 83:36, 91:24, 91:27, 103:29, 109:8.

[144] Textual apparatus entries recording where the readings of A1 have been allowed to stand are, for example, at 13:33, 69:25, 84:23, 90:20 and 134:6(1).

[145] The only exceptions are variants in TCC7 which did not affect MS8, as noted above.

STUDIES IN
CLASSIC AMERICAN
LITERATURE

NOTE ON THE TEXTS

Final Version

The base-text for this edition is the first American edition (A1) published by Thomas Seltzer on 27 August 1923. Emendations have been accepted from DHL's final manuscript (MS8) completed in December 1922, and, where words, phrases and quotations had been mistranscribed in the course of the revision of the essays, from earlier versions of a number of the essays. MS8 is now unlocated but was in the Smith collection (see Introduction note 29); for it and all other materials from this collection the editors have had to rely upon photocopies. The first English edition, published by Martin Secker in 1924, which was set from a copy of A1, has been collated and its variants recorded.

First Version

For the essays originally published in the *English Review* (with the exception of 'Nathaniel Hawthorne'), Per is the only source and therefore is the base-text. For 'Nathaniel Hawthorne', 'Dana' and 'Herman Melville', TSI is the base-text, and the 'Nathaniel Hawthorne' essay has been emended by reference to Per. A number of these essays were published in *Symbolic Meaning* (E2), and its variants have been recorded.

Intermediate Version

MS2 is the only surviving state of the texts for these versions of the essays, and is the base-text. Occasional editorial emendation has been recorded.

In addition to the standard Textual apparatus the editors have included in the Variorum apparatus (manuscript and typescript variants) a complete record of all additions, deletions and revisions in all manuscripts and typescripts, except for the texts reproduced in Appendix I (a quasi-facsimile) and Appendix VI (a diplomatic transcription). The Textual apparatus and – where applicable – the Variorum apparatus record all variants except for the following ten categories of silent emendations; if, however, what would normally be a silent

3

emendation occurs in the process of recording another variant, it is recorded exactly.

1. Clearly inadvertent spelling and typesetting errors have been corrected, but potentially significant errors in manuscript by DHL (e.g. 'cultivate' for 'cultivated') have been included (see Textual apparatus at 26:7). Misreadings of substantives and accidentals by typists, corrected back to the original before publication, are not recorded.

2. Inadvertent omissions (e.g. incomplete quotation marks, accents and full stops omitted at the end of sentences where no other punctuation exists) have been supplied, no matter what their origin. Lower-case letters at the beginning of sentences have been silently corrected to capital letters.

3. DHL's variants of the name Hector St. John de Crèvecoeur as Henri and Henry St. John de Crèvecoeur in Per and MS8 have been adopted; see Explanatory note on 32:3.

4. DHL frequently inscribed colloquial contractions without joining them up (e.g. 'did n't' and 'would n't'). Typists and compositors usually presented these as 'didn't' and 'wouldn't'; these normalisations have been adopted and are not recorded. DHL also sometimes used the ampersand '&' or the symbol '+': these have also been normalised as 'and', and are not recorded.

5. Variants in the lengths of spacing and of dashes in typescripts and printed texts (e.g. en, em or two-em dashes) have not been recorded in the Textual apparatus except where they form part of another variant. This edition has some essay titles (and the *Studies* title in Appendix III) on two lines whereas DHL wrote them on one, and in the Intermediate Version DHL had the essay number immediately following the *Studies* title; these are not recorded DHL often followed a full stop, comma, question mark or exclamation mark with a dash, before beginning the next sentence with a capital letter; typists and compositors often omitted the dash, but it has been silently restored in this edition.

6. DHL usually wrote 'Mrs', 'Mr' and 'Dr' without a full stop; his typists and compositors often supplied one. DHL usually wrote words such as 'realise' and 'recognise' (and their derivative forms) with an 's'; typists and compositors often changed these forms to 'realize', 'recognize', etc. He also usually wrote words having potentially variant inscriptions ('today', 'colour', 'neighbour' and 'centre') in that form rather than as 'to-day', 'color', 'neighbor' and 'center'. DHL's practice has been preserved where appropriate manuscripts survive, but the habits of typists and compositors have not been recorded.

7. Printed texts regularly applied period conventions and set poetry in smaller-sized type; this edition sets it in text-sized type. Where DHL in MS8 showed emphasis by writing capitals and occasionally very large letters, A1 used full caps. and E1 used a combination of large and small caps.; these variants are not recorded, but this edition records such effects with larger capitals. Variations in the conventions of printed texts such as depth of indentation and centring have not been recorded. Punctuation following an italicised or underlined word or phrase was, in A1 and E1, usually printed as italic; this is not recorded unless it forms part of another variant.

8. Manuscript idiosyncrasies (e.g. the placing of punctuation in relationship to closing quotation marks) are inconsistent and (except in the Variorum apparatus) we have normalised so that the punctuation precedes the closing quotation marks (e.g.,").

9. The titles and numbers of DHL's individual essays were written and typed by him and others in various styles; these have been normalised to his most frequent usage. DHL wrote and typed book titles sometimes in italics and sometimes within quotation marks; typesetters were also inconsistent in these matters. The titles have been standardised to italics throughout.

10. It is often unclear whether initial letters (e.g. 'w', 's' and 'c') in DHL's handwriting are capitals or not. Editorial decisions about these have not been recorded. Some editorial angst may nevertheless be assumed.

FINAL VERSION (1923)

CONTENTS

Foreword.

Listen to the States asserting: "The hour has struck! Americans shall be American. The U. S. A. is now grown up, artistically. It is time we ceased to hang on to the skirts of Europe, or to behave like schoolboys let loose from European schoolmasters—" 5

All right, Americans, let's see you set about it. Go on then, let the precious cat out of the bag.* If you're sure he's in.

> *Et interrogatum est ab omnibus:*
> *"Ubi est ille Toad-in-the-Hole?"*
> *Et iteratum est ab omnibus:* 10
> *"Non est inventus!"**

Is he or isn't he inventus?

If he is, of course, he must be somewhere inside you, Oh American. No good chasing him over all the old continents, of course. But equally no good *asserting* him merely. Where *is* this new bird called the true 15 American? Show us the homunculus of the new era. Go on, show us him. Because all that is visible to the naked European eye, in America, is a sort of recreant European. We want to see this missing link* of the next era.

Well, we still don't get him. So the only thing to do is to have a look for him under the American bushes. The old American literature, to 20 start with.

"The old American literature! Franklin, Cooper, Hawthorne & Co? All that mass of words! all so unreal!" cries the live American.

Heaven knows what we mean by reality. Telephones, tinned meat, Charlie Chaplin, water-taps, and World-Salvation,* presumably. Some 25 insisting on the plumbing, and some on saving the world: these being the two great American specialties. Why not? Only, what about the young homunculus of the new era, meanwhile? You can't save yourself before you are born.

Look at me trying to be midwife to the unborn homunculus! 30

Two bodies of modern literature seem to me to have come to a real verge: the Russian and the American. Let us leave aside the more brittle bits of French or Marinetti or Irish* production, which are perhaps

11

over the verge. Russian and American. And by American I do not mean
Sherwood Anderson,* who is so Russian. I mean the old people, little thin volumes of Hawthorne, Poe, Dana, Melville, Whitman. These
seem to me to have reached a verge, as the more voluminous Tolstoi,
5   Dostoevsky, Tchekov, Artzibashev* reached a limit on the other side.
The furthest frenzies of French modernism or futurism* have not
yet reached the pitch of extreme consciousness that Poe, Melville,
Hawthorne, Whitman reached. The European moderns are all *trying*
to be extreme. The great Americans I mention just were it. Which is
10 why the world has funked them, and funks them today.

The great difference between the extreme Russians and the extreme Americans lies in the fact that the Russians are explicit and hate
eloquence and symbols, seeing in these only subterfuge, whereas the
Americans refuse everything explicit and always put up a sort of dou-
15 ble meaning. They revel in subterfuge. They prefer their truth safely
swaddled in an ark of bulrushes, and deposited among the reeds until
some friendly Egyptian princess comes to rescue the babe.*

Well, it's high time now that someone came to lift out the swaddled
infant of truth that America spawned some time back. The child must
20 be getting pretty thin, from neglect.

I.

The Spirit of Place.

We like to think of the old-fashioned American classics as children's books.* Just childishness, on our part.

The old American art-speech contains an alien quality, which belongs to the American continent and to nowhere else. But of course, so long as we insist on reading the books as children's tales, we miss all that.

One wonders what the proper high-brow Romans of the Third and Fourth or later centuries read into the strange utterances of Lucretius or Apuleius or Tertullian, Augustine or Athanasius.* The uncanny voice of Iberian Spain, the weirdness of old Carthage, the passion of Libya and North Africa: you may bet the proper old Romans never heard these at all. They read old Latin inference over the top of it, as we read old European inference over the top of Poe or Hawthorne.*

It is hard to hear a new voice, as hard as it is to listen to an unknown language. We just don't listen. There is a new voice in the old American classics. The world has declined to hear it, and has blabbed about children's stories.

Why?—Out of fear. The world fears the new experience more than it fears anything. Because a new experience displaces so many old experiences. And it is like trying to use muscles that have perhaps never been used, or that have been going stiff for ages. It hurts horribly.

The world doesn't fear a new idea. It can pigeon-hole any idea. But it can't pigeon-hole a real new experience. It can only dodge. The world is a great dodger, and the Americans the greatest. Because they dodge their own very selves.

There is a new feeling in the old American books, far more than there is in the modern American books, which are pretty empty of any feeling, and proud of it. There is a "different" feeling in the old American classics. It is the shifting over from the old psyche to something new, a displacement. And displacements hurt. This hurts. So we try to tie it up, like a cut finger. Put a rag round it.

It is a cut, too. Cutting away the old emotions and consciousness. Don't ask what is left.

13

Art-speech is the only truth. An artist is usually a damned liar, but his art, if it be art, will tell you the truth of his day. And that is all that matters. Away with eternal truth. Truth lives from day to day, and the marvellous Plato* of yesterday is chiefly bosh today.

5   The old American artists were hopeless liars. But they were artists, in spite of themselves. Which is more than you can say of most living practitioners.

And you can please yourself, when you read the *Scarlet Letter*,* whether you accept what that sugary, blue-eyed little darling of a
10   Hawthorne has to say for himself, false as all darlings are, or whether you read the impeccable truth of his art speech.

The curious thing about art speech is that it prevaricates so terribly, I mean it tells such lies. I suppose because we always all the time tell ourselves lies. And out of a pattern of lies art weaves the truth. Like
15   Dostoevsky posing as a sort of Jesus, but most truthfully revealing himself all the while as a little horror.*

Truly art is a sort of subterfuge. But thank God for it, we can see through the subterfuge if we choose. Art has two great functions. First, it provides an emotional experience. And then, if we have the courage of
20   our own feelings, it becomes a mine of practical truth. We have had the feelings *ad nauseam*. But we've never dared dig the actual truth out of them, the truth that concerns us, whether it concerns our grandchildren or not.

The artist usually sets out—or used to—to point a moral and adorn
25   a tale.* The tail, however, points the other way, as a rule. Two blankly opposing morals, the artist's and the tale's. Never trust the artist. Trust the tale. The proper function of a critic is to save the tale from the artist who created it.

Now we know our business in these studies; saving the American tale
30   from the American artist.

Let us look at this American artist first. How did he ever get to America, to start with? Why isn't he a European still, like his father before him?

Now listen to me, don't listen to him. He'll tell you the lie you expect.
35   Which is partly your fault for expecting it.

He didn't come in search of freedom of worship.* England had more freedom of worship in the year 1700 than America had. Won by Englishmen who wanted freedom, and so stopped at home and fought for it.* And got it. Freedom of worship? Read the history of New
40   England during the first century of its existence.

Freedom anyhow? The land of the free!* This the land of the free! Why, if I say anything that displeases them, the free mob will lynch me, and that's my freedom. Free? Why I have never been in any country where the individual has such an abject fear of his fellow countrymen. Because, as I say, they are free to lynch him the moment he shows he is   5 not one of them.

No no, if you're so fond of the truth about Queen Victoria,* try a little about yourself.

Those Pilgrim Fathers and their successors never came here for freedom of worship. What did they set up when they got here? Freedom   10 would you call it?

They didn't come for freedom. Or if they did, they sadly went back on themselves.

All right then, what did they come for? For lots of reasons. Perhaps least of all in search of freedom of any sort: positive freedom, that is.   15

They came largely to get *away*—that most simple of motives. To get away. Away from what? In the long run, away from themselves. Away from everything. That's why most people have come to America, and still do come. To get away from everything they are and have been.

"Henceforth be masterless."*   20

Which is all very well, but it isn't freedom. Rather the reverse. A hopeless sort of constraint. It is never freedom till you find something you really *positively want to be.* And people in America have always been shouting about the things they are *not.* Unless of course they are millionaires, made or in the making.   25

And after all there is a positive side to the movement. All that vast flood of human life that has flowed over the Atlantic in ships from Europe to America has not flowed over simply on a tide of revulsion from Europe and from the confinements of the European ways of life. This revulsion was, and still is, I believe, the prime motive in emigration.   30 But there was some cause, even for the revulsion.

It seems as if at times man had a frenzy for getting away from any control of any sort. In Europe the old Christianity was the real master. The Church and the true aristocracy bore the responsibility for the working out of the Christian ideals: a little irregularly, maybe, but responsible   35 nevertheless.

Mastery, kingship, fatherhood had their power destroyed at the time of the Renaissance.

And it was precisely at this moment that the great drift over the Atlantic started. What were men drifting away from? The old authority   40 of Europe? Were they breaking the bonds of authority, and escaping to a new more absolute unrestrainedness? Maybe. But there was more to it. Liberty is all very well, but men cannot live without masters. There is always a master. And men either live in glad obedience to the master they

5   believe in, or they live in a frictional opposition to the master they wish to undermine. In America this frictional opposition has been the vital factor. It has given the Yankee his kick. Only the continual influx of more servile Europeans has provided America with an obedient labouring class. The true obedience never outlasting the first generation.

10 But there sits the old master, over in Europe. Like a parent. Somewhere deep in every American heart lies a rebellion against the old parenthood of Europe. Yet no American feels he has completely escaped its mastery. Hence the slow, smouldering patience of American opposition. The slow, smouldering, corrosive obedience to the old master Europe,

15 the unwilling subject, the unremitting opposition.
Whatever else you are, be masterless.

    "Ca Ca Caliban
    Get a new master, be a new man.."*

Escaped slaves, we might say, people the republics of Liberia or Haiti.*

20 Liberia enough! Are we to look at America in the same way? A vast republic of escaped slaves. When you consider the hordes from eastern Europe, you might well say it: a vast republic of escaped slaves. But one dare not say this of the Pilgrim Fathers, and the great old body of idealist Americans, the modern Americans tortured with thought. A

25 vast republic of escaped slaves. Look out, America! And a minority of earnest, self-tortured people.
The masterless.

    "Ca Ca Caliban
    Get a new master, be a new man.."

30 What did the Pilgrim Fathers come for, then, when they came so gruesomely over the black sea? Oh, it was in a black spirit. A black revulsion from Europe, from the old authority of Europe, from kings and bishops and popes. And more. When you look into it, more. They were black, masterful men, they wanted something else. No kings, no

35 bishops maybe. Even no God Almighty. But also, no more of this new "humanity" which followed the Renaissance. None of this new liberty which was to be so pretty in Europe. Something grimmer, by no means free-and-easy.

America has never been easy, and is not easy today. Americans have always been at a certain tension. Their liberty is a thing of sheer will, sheer tension: a liberty of THOU SHALT NOT. And it has been so from the first. The land of THOU SHALT NOT. Only the first commandment is: THOU SHALT NOT PRESUME TO BE   5
A MASTER. Hence democracy.

"We are the masterless." That is what the American Eagle* shrieks. It's a Hen-Eagle.

The Spaniards refused the post-Renaissance liberty of Europe. And the Spaniards filled most of America.* The Yankees too refused, re-   10
futed the post-Renaissance humanism of Europe. First and foremost, they hated masters. But under that, they hated the flowing ease of humour in Europe. At the bottom of the American soul was always a dark suspense, at the bottom of the Spanish-American soul the same. And this dark suspense hated and hates the old European spontaneity,   15
watches it collapse with satisfaction.

Every continent has its own great spirit of place. Every people is polarised in some particular locality, which is home, the homeland. Different places on the face of the earth have different vital effluence, different vibration, different chemical exhalation, different polarity with differ-   20
ent stars: call it what you like. But the spirit of place is a great reality. The Nile valley produced not only the corn, but the terrific religions of Egypt.* China produces the Chinese, and will go on doing so. The Chinese in San Francisco will in time cease to be Chinese, for America is a great melting pot.   25

There was a tremendous polarity in Italy, in the city of Rome. And this seems to have died. For even places die. The Island of Great Britain had a wonderful terrestial magnetism or polarity of its own, which made the British people. For the moment, this polarity seems to be breaking. Can England die? And what if England died?   30

Men are less free than they imagine; ah, far less free. The freest are perhaps least free.

Men are free when they are in a living homeland, not when they are straying and breaking away. Men are free when they are obeying some deep, inward voice of religious belief. Obeying from within. Men are free   35
when they belong to a living, organic, *believing* community, active in fulfilling some unfulfilled, perhaps unrealised purpose. Not when they are escaping to some wild west. The most unfree souls go west, and shout of freedom. Men are freest when they are most unconscious of freedom. The shout is a rattling of chains, always was.   40

Men are not free when they are doing just what they like. The moment you can do just what you like, there is nothing you care about doing. Men are only free when they are doing what the deepest self likes.

And there is getting down to the deepest self! It takes some diving.

5   Because the deepest self is way down, and the conscious self is an obstinate monkey. But of one thing we may be sure. If one wants to be free, one has to give up the illusion of doing what one likes, and seek what IT wishes done.

But before you can do what IT likes, you must first break the spell
10 of the old mastery, the old IT.

Perhaps at the Renaissance, when kingship and fatherhood fell, Europe drifted into a very dangerous half-truth: of liberty and equality. Perhaps the men who went to America felt this, and so repudiated the old world altogether. Went one better than Europe. Liberty in America has
15 meant so far the breaking away from *all* dominion. The true liberty will only begin when Americans discover IT, and proceed possibly to fulfil IT. IT being the deepest *whole* self of man, the self in its wholeness, not idealistic halfness.

That's why the Pilgrim Fathers came to America, then: and that's
20 why we come. Driven by IT. We cannot see that invisible winds carry us, as they carry swarms of locusts, that invisible magnetism brings us as it brings the migrating birds to their unforeknown goal.* But it is so. We are not the marvellous choosers and deciders we think we are. IT chooses for us, and decides for us. Unless of course we are just escaped
25 slaves, vulgarly cocksure of our ready-made destiny. But if we are living people, in touch with the source, IT drives us and decides us. We are free only so long as we obey. When we run counter, and think we will do as we like, we just flee round like Orestes pursued by the Eumenides.*

And still, when the great day begins, when Americans have at last
30 discovered America and their own wholeness, still there will be the vast number of escaped slaves to reckon with, those who have no cocksure, ready-made destinies.

Which will win in America, the escaped slaves, or the new whole men?

35   The real American day hasn't begun yet. Or at least, not yet sunrise. So far it has been the false dawn. That is, in the progressive American consciousness there has been the one dominant desire, to do away with the old thing. Do away with masters, exalt the will of the people. The will of the people being nothing but a figment, the exalting doesn't count
40 for much. So, in the name of the will of the people, get rid of masters.

When you have got rid of masters, you are left with this mere phrase of the will of the people. Then you pause and bethink yourself, and try to recover your own wholeness.

So much for the conscious American motive, and for democracy over here. Democracy in America is just the tool with which the old mastery of Europe, the European spirit, is undermined. Europe destroyed, potentially, American democracy will evaporate. America will begin.

American consciousness has so far been a false dawn. The negative ideal of democracy. But underneath, and contrary to this open ideal, the first hints and revelations of IT. IT, the American whole soul.

You have got to pull the democratic and idealistic clothes off American utterance, and see what you can of the dusky body of IT underneath.

"Henceforth be masterless."

Henceforth be mastered.

II.

Benjamin Franklin.*

The Perfectibility Of Man! Ah heaven, what a dreary theme! The perfectibility of the Ford car!* The perfectibility of which man? I am many
5   men. Which of them are you going to perfect? I am not a mechanical contrivance.

Education! Which of the various me's do you propose to educate, and which do you propose to suppress?

Anyhow I defy you. I defy you, oh society, to educate me or to suppress
10   me, according to your dummy standards.*

The ideal man! And which is he, if you please? Benjamin Franklin or Abraham Lincoln? The ideal man! Roosevelt or Porfirio Diaz?*

There are other men in me, besides this patient ass who sits here in a tweed jacket. What am I doing, playing the patient ass in a tweed jacket?
15   Who am I talking to? Who are you, at the other end of this patience?

Who are you? How many selves have you? And which of these selves do you want to be?

Is Yale College going to educate the self that is in the dark of you, or Harvard College?*
20   The ideal self! Oh, but I have a strange and fugitive self shut out and howling like a wolf or a coyote under the ideal windows. See his red eyes in the dark? This is the self who is coming into his own.

The perfectibility of man, dear God! When every man as long as he remains alive is in himself a multitude of conflicting men. Which of
25   these do you choose to perfect, at the expense of every other?

Old Daddy Franklin will tell you. He'll rig him up for you, the pattern American. Oh, Franklin was the first downright American. He knew what he was about, the sharp little man. He set up the first dummy American.
30   At the beginning of his career this cunning little Benjamin drew up for himself a creed that should "satisfy the professors of every religion, but shock none."*

Now wasn't that a real American thing to do?

"That there is One God, who made all things."
35   (But Benjamin made Him.)

"That He governs the world by His Providence."
(Benjamin knowing all about Providence.)
"That He ought to be worshipped with adoration, prayer, and thanks-giving."
(Which cost nothing.)	5
"But——
(But me no buts,* Benjamin, saith the Lord.)
"But that the most acceptable service of God is doing good to man."
(God having no choice in the matter.)
"That the soul is immortal."	10
(You'll see why, in the next clause.)
"And that God will certainly reward virtue and punish vice, either here or hereafter."
Now if Mr Andrew Carnegie,* or any other millionaire had wished to invent a God to suit his ends, he could not have done better. Benjamin	15
did it for him in the eighteenth century. God is the supreme servant of men who want to get on, to *produce*. Providence. The provider. The heavenly store-keeper. The everlasting Wanamaker.
And this is all the God the grandsons of the Pilgrim Fathers had left. Aloft on a pillar of dollars.*	20
"That the soul is immortal."
The trite way Benjamin says it!
But man has a soul, though you can't locate it either in his purse or his pocket-book or his heart or his stomach or his head. The *wholeness* of a man is his soul. Not merely that nice little comfortable bit which	25
Benjamin marks out.
It's a queer thing, is a man's soul. It is the whole of him. Which means it is the unknown him, as well as the known. It seems to me just funny, professors and Benjamins fixing the functions of the soul. Why the soul of man is a vast forest, and all Benjamin intended was a neat	30
back garden. And we've all got to fit in to his kitchen garden scheme of things. Hail Columbia!*
The soul of man is a dark forest. The Hercynian Wood that scared the Romans so,* and out of which came the white-skinned hordes of the next civilisation.	35
Who knows what will come out of the soul of man! The soul of man is a dark vast forest, with wild life in it. Think of Benjamin fencing it off!
Oh, but Benjamin fenced a little tract that he called the soul of man, and proceeded to get it into cultivation. Providence, forsooth! And they	40

think that bit of barbed wire is going to keep us in bounds* forever? More fools them.

This is Benjamin's barbed wire fence.* He made himself a list of virtues, which he trotted inside like a grey nag in a paddock.

1
TEMPERANCE
Eat not to fulness: drink not to elevation.

2
SILENCE
Speak not but what may benefit others or yourself; avoid trifling conversation.

3
ORDER
Let all your things have their places; let each part of your business have its time.

4
RESOLUTION
Resolve to perform what you ought; perform without fail what you resolve.

5
FRUGALITY
Make no expense but to do good to others or yourself—i.e. waste nothing.

6
INDUSTRY
Lose no time, be always employed in something useful; cut off all unnecessary action.

7
SINCERITY
Use no hurtful deceit; think innocently and justly, and, if you speak, speak accordingly.

8
JUSTICE
Wrong none by doing injuries, or omitting the benefits that are your duty.

9
MODERATION
Avoid extremes, forbear resenting injuries as much as you think they deserve.

10
CLEANLINESS
Tolerate no uncleanliness in body, clothes, or habitation.

11
TRANQUILLITY
Be not disturbed at trifles, or at accidents common or unavoidable.

12
CHASTITY
Rarely use venery but for health and offspring, never to dulness, weakness, or the injury of your own or another's peace or reputation.

13
HUMILITY
Imitate Jesus and Socrates.*

A Quaker friend told Franklin that he, Benjamin, was generally considered proud, so Benjamin put in the Humility touch as an afterthought. The amusing part is the sort of humility it displays. "Imitate Jesus and Socrates," and mind you don't outshine either of these two. One can just imagine Socrates and Alcibiades* roaring in their cups over Philadelphian Benjamin, and Jesus looking at him a little puzzled, and murmuring: "Aren't you wise in your own conceit,* Ben?"

"Henceforth be masterless," retorts Ben. "Be ye each one his own master unto himself, and don't let even the Lord put his spoke in."*
"Each man his own master" is but a puffing up of masterlessness.

Well, the first of Americans* practised this enticing list with assiduity, setting a national example. He had the virtues in columns, and gave himself good and bad marks according as he thought his behaviour deserved. Pity these conduct charts are lost to us. He only remarks that Order was his stumbling block.* He could *not* learn to be neat and tidy.

Isn't it nice to have nothing worse to confess?

He was a little model, was Benjamin. Doctor Franklin. Snuff-coloured
little man!* Immortal soul and all!

The immortal soul part was a sort of cheap insurance policy.

Benjamin had no concern, really, with the immortal soul. He was too
5 busy with social man.

1. He swept and lighted the streets of young Philadelphia.*
2. He invented electrical appliances.*
3. He was the centre of a moralising club in Philadelphia,* and he wrote
    the moral humorisms of Poor Richard.
10 4. He was a member of all the important councils of Philadelphia, and
    then of the American Colonies.*
5. He won the cause of American Independence at the French Court,
    and was the economic father of the United States.*

Now what more can you want of a man? And yet he is *infra dig*,* even
15 in Philadelphia.

I admire him. I admire his sturdy courage first of all, then his sagacity,
then his glimpsing into the thunders of electricity,* then his common-
sense humour. All the qualities of a great man, and never more than
a great citizen. Middle-sized, sturdy, snuff-coloured Doctor Franklin,
20 one of the soundest citizens that ever trod or "used venery."

I do not like him.

And, by the way, I always thought books of Venery were about hunting
deer.*

There is a certain earnest naiveté about him. Like a child. And like a
25 little old man. He has become again as a little child,* always as wise as
his grandfather, or wiser.

Perhaps, as I say, the most complete citizen that ever "used venery."

Printer, philosopher, scientist, author and patriot, impeccable husband* and citizen, why isn't he an archetype?

30 Pioneer, Oh Pioneers!* Benjamin was one of the greatest pioneers of
the United States. Yet we just can't do with him.

What's wrong with him then? Or what's wrong with us?

I can remember, when I was a little boy, my father used to buy a
scrubby yearly almanack* with the sun and moon and stars on the cover.
35 And it used to prophesy bloodshed and famine. But also crammed in
corners it had little anecdotes and humorisms, with a moral tag. And
I used to have my little priggish laugh at the woman who counted her
chickens before they were hatched, and so forth, and I was convinced
that honesty was the best policy, also a little priggishly. The author of

these bits was Poor Richard, and Poor Richard was Benjamin Franklin, writing in Philadelphia well over a hundred years before.

And probably I haven't got over those Poor Richard tags yet. I rankle still with them. They are thorns in young flesh.*

Because although I still believe that honesty is the best policy, I dislike policy altogether; though it is just as well not to count your chickens before they are hatched, it's still more hateful to count them with gloating when they *are* hatched. It has taken me many years and countless smarts to get out of that barbed wire moral enclosure that Poor Richard rigged up. Here am I now in tatters and scratched to ribbons, sitting in the middle of Benjamin's America looking at the barbed wire, and the fat sheep crawling under the fence to get fat outside, and the watchdogs yelling at the gate lest by chance anyone should get out by the proper exit. Oh America! Oh Benjamin! And I just utter a long loud curse against Benjamin and the American corral.

Moral America! Most moral Benjamin! Sound, satisfied Ben!

He had to go to the frontiers of his State, to settle some disturbance among the Indians.* On this occasion he writes:—

"We found that they had made a great bonfire in the middle of the square; they were all drunk, men and women quarrelling and fighting. Their dark-coloured bodies, half naked, seen only by the gloomy light of the bonfire, running after and beating one another with fire-brands, accompanied by their horrid yellings, formed a scene the most resembling our ideas of hell that could be well imagined. There was no appeasing the tumult, and we retired to our lodging. At midnight a number of them came thundering at our door, demanding more rum, of which we took no notice.

"The next day, sensible they had misbehaved in giving us that disturbance, they sent three of their counsellors to make their apology. The orator acknowledged the fault, but laid it upon the rum, and then endeavoured to excuse the rum by saying: 'The Great Spirit, who made all things, made everything for some use; and whatever he designed anything for, that use it should always be put to. Now, when he made* rum, he said: "Let this be for the Indians to get drunk with." And it must be so.'

"And, indeed, if it be the design of Providence to extirpate these savages in order to make room for the cultivators of the earth, it seems not improbable that rum may be the appointed means. It has already annihilated all the tribes who formerly inhabited all the sea coast—— "

This, from the good doctor, with such suave complacency, is a little disenchanting. Almost too good to be true.

But there you are! The barbed wire fence. "Extirpate these savages in order to make room for the cultivators of the earth." Oh Benjamin
5   Benjamin! He even "used venery" as a cultivator of seed.

Cultivate the earth, ye gods! The Indians did that, as much as they needed. And they left off there. Who built Chicago? Who cultivated the earth until it spawned Pittsburgh, Pa.?*

The moral issue! Just look at it! Cultivation included. If it's a mere
10 choice of Kultur* or cultivation, I give it up.

Which brings us right back to our question, what's wrong with Benjamin, that we can't stand him? Or else, what's wrong with us, that we find fault with such a paragon?

Man is a moral animal. All right. I am a moral animal. And I'm
15 going to remain such. I'm not going to be turned into a virtuous little automaton as Benjamin would have me. "This is good, that is bad. Turn the little handle and let the good tap flow," saith Benjamin and all America with him. "But first of all extirpate those savages who are always turning on the bad tap."

20   I am a moral animal. But I am not a moral machine. I don't work with a little set of handles or levers. The Temperance-silence-order-resolution-frugality-industry-sincerity-justice-moderation-cleanliness-tranquillity-chastity-humility keyboard is not going to get me going. I'm really not just an automatic piano* with a moral Benjamin getting tunes
25 out of me.

Here's my creed, against Benjamin's. This is what I believe.

"That I am I."

"That my soul is a dark forest."

"That my known self will never be more than a little clearing in the
30   forest."

"That gods, strange gods come forth from the forest into the clearing
of my known self, and then go back."

"That I must have the courage to let them come and go."

"That I will never let mankind put anything over me, but that I will
35   try always to recognise and submit to the gods in me and the
gods in other men and women."

There is my creed. He who runs may read.* He who prefers to crawl, or to go by gasoline, can call it rot.

Then for a "list." It is rather fun to play at Benjamin.

1
TEMPERANCE
Eat and carouse with Bacchus,* or munch dry bread with Jesus,
but don't sit down without one of the gods.

2
SILENCE
Be still when you have nothing to say; when genuine passion
moves you, say what you've got to say, and say it hot.

3
ORDER
Know that you are responsible to the gods inside you and to the
men in whom the gods are manifest. Recognise your superiors and
your inferiors, according to the gods. This is the root of all order.

4
RESOLUTION
Resolve to abide by your own deepest promptings, and to sacrifice the smaller thing to the greater. Kill when you must, and be
killed the same: the *must* coming from the gods inside you, or from
the men in whom you recognise the Holy Ghost.

5
FRUGALITY
Demand nothing; accept what you see fit. Don't waste your
pride or squander your emotion.

6
INDUSTRY
Lose no time with ideals; serve the Holy Ghost; never serve
mankind.

7
SINCERITY
To be sincere is to remember that I am I; and that the other man
is not me.

8
JUSTICE
The only justice is to follow the sincere intuition of the soul,
angry or gentle. Anger is just, and pity is just, but judgment is
never just.

5

10

15

20

25

30

35

9
MODERATION
Beware of absolutes. There are many gods.

10
CLEANLINESS
Don't be too clean. It impoverishes the blood.

11
TRANQUILLITY
The soul has many motions, many gods come and go. Try and find your deepest issue, in every confusion, and abide by that. Obey the man in whom you recognise the Holy Ghost; command when your honour comes to command.

12
CHASTITY
Never "use" venery at all. Follow your passional impulse, if it be answered in the other being; but never have any motive in mind, neither offspring nor health nor even pleasure, nor even service. Only know that "venery" is of the great gods. An offering-up of yourself to the very great gods, the dark ones, and nothing else.

13
HUMILITY
See all men and women according to the Holy Ghost that is within them. Never yield before the barren.

There's my list. I have been trying dimly to realise it for a long time, and only America and old Benjamin have at last goaded me into trying to formulate it.

And now I, at least, know why I can't stand Benjamin. He tries to take away my wholeness and my dark forest, my freedom. For how can any man be free, without an illimitable background? And Benjamin tries to shove me into a barbed-wire paddock and make me grow potatoes or Chicagoes.

And how can I be free, without gods that come and go? But Benjamin won't let anything exist except my useful fellow-men, and I'm sick of them; as for his Godhead, his Providence, He is Head of nothing except a vast heavenly store that keeps every imaginable line of goods, from victrolas to cat-o-nine-tails.*

And how can any man be free without a soul of his own, that he believes in and won't sell at any price? But Benjamin doesn't let me have a soul of my own. He says I am nothing but a servant of mankind— galley-slave I call it—and if I don't get my wages here below—that is, if Mr Pierpont Morgan or Mr Nosey Hebrew* or the grand United States Government, the great US, US or SOMEOFUS, manages to scoop in my bit along with their lump—why, never mind, I shall get my wages HEREAFTER.

Oh Benjamin! Oh Binjum! You do NOT suck me in any longer.

And why oh why should the snuff-coloured little trap have wanted to take us all in? Why did he do it?

Out of sheer human cussedness, in the first place. We do all like to get things inside a barb-wire corral. Especially our fellow-men. We love to round them up inside the barb-wire enclosure of FREEDOM, and make 'em work. *Work, you free jewel, WORK*! shouts the liberator, cracking his whip. Benjamin, I will not work. I do not choose to be a free democrat. I am absolutely a servant of my own Holy Ghost.

Sheer cussedness! But there was as well the salt of a subtler purpose. Benjamin was just in his eyeholes—to use an English vulgarism meaning he was just delighted—when he was at Paris judiciously milking money out of the French monarchy* for the overthrow of all monarchy. If you want to ride your horse to somewhere you must put a bit in his mouth. And Benjamin wanted to ride his horse so that it would upset the whole apple-cart of the old masters. He wanted the whole European apple-cart upset. So he had to put a strong bit in the mouth of his ass.

"Henceforth be masterless."

That is, he had to break-in the human ass completely, so that much more might be broken, in the long run. For the moment it was the British government that had to have a hole knocked in it. The first real hole it ever had: the breach of the American rebellion.

Benjamin, in his sagacity, knew that the breaking of the old world was a long process. In the depths of his own under-consciousness he hated England, he hated Europe, he hated the whole corpus of the European being. He wanted to be American. But you can't change your nature and mode of consciousness like changing your shoes. It is a gradual shedding. Years must go by, and centuries must elapse before you have finished. Like a son escaping from the domination of his parents. The escape is not just one rupture. It is a long and half-secret process.

So with the American. He was a European when he first went over the Atlantic. He is in the main a recreant European still. From Benjamin

Franklin to Woodrow Wilson* may be a long stride, but it is a stride along the same road. There is no new road. The same old road, become dreary and futile. Theoretic and materialistic.

Why then did Benjamin set up this dummy of a perfect citizen as a
5   pattern to America? Of course he did it in perfect good faith, as far as he knew. He thought it simply was the true ideal. But what we *think* we do is not very important. We never really know what we are doing. Either we are materialistic instruments, like Benjamin or we move in the gesture of creation, from our deepest self, usually unconscious. We are only the
10 actors, we are never wholly the authors of our own deeds or works. IT is the author, the unknown inside us or outside us. The best we can do is to try to hold ourselves in unison with the deeps which are inside us. And the worst we can do is to try to have things our own way, when we run counter to IT, and in the long run get our knuckles rapped for our
15 presumption.

So Benjamin contriving money out of the Court of France. He was contriving the first steps of the overthrow of all Europe, France included. You can never have a new thing without breaking an old. Europe happens to be the old thing. America, unless the people in America assert
20 themselves too much in opposition to the inner gods, should be the new thing. The new thing is the death of the old. But you can't cut the throat of an epoch. You've got to steal the life from it through several centuries.

And Benjamin worked for this both directly and indirectly. Directly, at the Court of France, making a small but very dangerous hole in the
25 side of England, through which hole Europe has by now almost bled to death. And indirectly in Philadelphia, setting up this unlovely, snuff-coloured little ideal, or automaton, of a pattern American. The pattern American, this dry, moral, utilitarian little democrat, has done more to ruin the old Europe than any Russian nihilist.* He has done it by a slow
30 attrition, like a son who has stayed at home and obeyed his parents, all the while silently hating their authority, and silently, in his soul, destroying not only their authority but their whole existence. For the American spiritually stayed at home in Europe. The spiritual home of America was and still is Europe. This is the galling bondage, in spite of
35 several billions of heaped-up gold. Your heaps of gold are only so many muck-heaps, America, and will remain so till you become a reality to yourselves.

All this Americanising and mechanising has been for the purpose of overthrowing the past. And now look at America, tangled in her
40 own barbed wire, and mastered by her own machines. Absolutely got

down by her own barbed wire of shalt-nots, and shut up fast in her own "productive" machines like millions of squirrels running in millions of cages.* It is just a farce.

Now is your chance, Europe. Now let Hell loose and get your own back, and paddle your own canoe on a new sea, while clever America lies on her muck-heaps of gold, strangled in her own barb-wire of shalt-not ideals and shalt-not moralisms. While she goes out to work like millions of squirrels in millions of cages. Production!

Let Hell loose, and get your own back, Europe!

5

III.
Henry St. John de Crêvecoeur.

Crêvecoeur was born in France, at Caen, in the year 1735.* As a boy
he was sent over to England and received part of his education there.
5 He went to Canada as a young man, served for a time with Montcalm
in the war against the English, and later passed over into the United
States, to become an exuberant American. He married a New England
girl, and settled on the frontier. During the period of his "cultivating
the earth" he wrote the *Letters from an American Farmer*, which enjoyed
10 great vogue in their day, in England especially, among the new reformers
like Godwin and Tom Payne.*
    But Crêvecoeur was not a mere cultivator of the earth. That was
his best stunt,* shall we say. He himself was more concerned with a
perfect society and his own manipulation thereof, than with growing
15 carrots. Behold him then trotting off importantly and idealistically to
France, leaving his farm in the wilds to be burnt by the Indians, and
his wife to shift as best she might. This was during the American War
of Independence, when the Noble Red Man took to behaving like his
own old self. On his return to America, the American Farmer entered
20 into public affairs and into commerce. Again tripping to France, he
enjoyed himself as a littérateur Child-of-Nature-sweet-and-pure, was
a friend of old Benjamin Franklin in Paris, and quite a favourite with
Jean Jacques Rousseau's Madame d'Houdetot,* that literary soul.
    Hazlitt, Godwin, Shelley, Coleridge, the English romanticists, were
25 of course thrilled by the *Letters from an American Farmer*. A new world, a
world of the Noble Savage and Pristine Nature and Paradisal Simplicity
and all that gorgeousness that flows out of the unsullied fount of the
ink-bottle. Lucky Coleridge, who got no farther than Bristol.* Some of
us have gone all the way.*
30   I think this wild and noble America is the thing that I have pined for
most ever since I read Fenimore Cooper, as a boy. Now I've got it.
    Franklin is the real *practical* prototype of the American. Crêvecoeur
is the emotional. To the European, the American is first and foremost a
dollar-fiend. We tend to forget the emotional heritage of Henri St. Joan
35 de Crêvecoeur. We tend to disbelieve, for example, in Woodrow Wilson's

wrung heart and wet hanky.* Yet surely these are real enough. Aren't they?

It wasn't to be expected that the dry little snuff-coloured Doctor should have it all his own way. The new Americans might use venery for health or offspring, and their time for cultivating potatoes and Chicagoes, but they had got *some* sap in their veins after all. They had got to get a bit of luscious emotion somewhere.

NATURE.

I wish I could write it larger than that.

NATURE.

Benjamin overlooked NATURE. But the French Crêvecoeur spotted it, long before Thoreau and Emerson worked it up.* Absolutely the safest thing to get your emotional reactions over, is NATURE.

Crêvecoeur's *Letters* are written in a spirit of touching simplicity, almost better than Chateaubriand.* You'd think neither of them would ever know how many beans make five. This American Farmer tells of the joys of creating a home in the wilderness, and of cultivating the virgin soil. Poor virgin, prostituted from the very start.

The Farmer had an Amiable Spouse and an Infant Son, his progeny. He took the Infant Son—who enjoys no other name than this—

> "What is thy name?
> I have no name.
> I am the Infant Son—"

to the fields with him, and seated the same I.S. on the shafts of the plough whilst he, the American Farmer, ploughed the potato patch.* He also, the A.F., helped his Neighbours, whom no doubt he loved as himself, to build a barn,* and they laboured together in the Innocent Simplicity of one of Nature's Communities.* Meanwhile the Amiable Spouse, who likewise in Blakean simplicity has No Name, cooked the dough-nuts or the pie, though these are not mentioned. No doubt she was a deep-breasted daughter of America,* though she may equally well have been a flat-bosomed methodist. She would have been an Amiable Spouse in either case, and the American Farmer asked no more. I don't know whether her name was Lizzie or Ahoolibah,* and probably Crêvecoeur didn't. Spouse was enough for him. "Spouse, hand me the carving knife."

The Infant Son developed into Healthy Offspring as more appeared: no doubt Crêvecoeur had used venery as directed. And so these Children of Nature toiled in the Wilds at Simple Toil with a little Honest Sweat*

now and then. You have the complete picture, dear reader. The American
Farmer made his own Family Picture, and it is still on view. Of course
the Healthy Offspring had their faces washed for the occasion, and the
Amiable Spouse put on her best apron to be *Im Bild*,* for all the world
5   to see and admire.

I used to admire my head off: before I tiptoed into the Wilds and saw
the shacks of the Homesteaders. Particularly the Amiable Spouse, poor
thing. No wonder *she* never sang the song of Simple Toil in the Innocent
Wilds. Poor haggard drudge, like a ghost wailing in the wilderness, nine
10 times out of ten.

Henri St. Jean you have lied to me. You lied even more scurrilously
to yourself. Henri St. Jean, you are an emotional liar.

Jean Jacques, Bernadin de St. Pierre, Chateaubriand, exquisite
François Le Vaillant,* you lying little lot, with your Nature Sweet and
15 Pure! Marie Antoinette* got her head off for playing dairy-maid, and
nobody even dusted the seats of your pants, till now, for all the lies you
put over us.

But Crèvecoeur was an artist as well as a liar, otherwise we would not
have bothered with him. He wanted to put N A T U R E in his pocket, as
20 Benjamin put the human being. Between them, they wanted the whole
scheme of things in their pockets, and the things themselves as well.
Once you've got the scheme of things in your pocket, you can do as you
like with it, even make money out of it, if you can't find in your heart
to destroy it, as was your first intention. So H. St. J. de C. tried to put
25 Nature-Sweet-and-Pure in his pocket. But nature wasn't having any,
she poked her head out and baa-ed.

This Nature-sweet-and-pure business is only another effort at intel-
lectualising. Just an attempt to make all nature succumb to a few laws
of the human mind. The sweet-and-pure sort of laws. Nature seemed
30 to be behaving quite nicely, for a while. She has left off.

That's why you get the purest intellectuals in a Garden Suburb or a
Brook Farm* experiment. You bet, Robinson Crusoe was a high-brow
of high-brows.*

You can idealise or intellectualise. Or, on the contrary, you can let the
35 dark soul in you see for itself. An artist usually intellectualises on top, and
his dark under-consciousness goes on contradicting him beneath. This
is almost laughably the case with most American artists. Crèvecoeur is
the first example. He is something of an artist, Franklin isn't anything.

Crèvecoeur the idealist puts over us a lot of stuff about Nature and the
40 noble savage and the innocence of toil etc. etc. Blarney! But Crèvecoeur
the artist gives us glimpses of actual nature, not writ large.

Curious that his vision sees only the lowest forms of natural life. Insects, snakes and birds he glimpses in their own mystery, their own pristine being. And straightway gives the lie to Innocent Nature.

"I am astonished to see," he writes quite early in the *Letters*, "that nothing exists but what has its enemy, one species pursue and live upon 5 another: unfortunately our king-birds are the destroyers of those industrious insects (the bees); but on the other hand, these birds preserve our fields from the depredations of the crows, which they pursue on the wing with great vigilance and astonishing dexterity."*

This is a sad blow to the sweet-and-pureness of Nature. But it is 10 the voice of the artist in contrast to the voice of the ideal turtle.* It is the rudimentary American vision. The glimpsing of the king-birds in winged hostility and pride is no doubt the aboriginal Indian vision carrying over. The Eagle symbol in human consciousness. Dark, swinging wings of hawk-beaked destiny, that one cannot help but feel, beating here 15 above the wild centre of America. You look round in vain for the "One being Who made all things, and governs the world by His providence."

"One species pursue and live upon another."

Reconcile the two statements if you like. But, in America, act on Crêvecoeur's observation. 20

The horse, however, says Henry, is the friend of man, and man is the friend of the horse. But then we leave the horse no choice. And I don't see much *friend*, exactly, in my sly old Indian pony,* though he is quite a decent old bird.

Man too, says Henry, is the friend of man.* Whereupon the Indians 25 burnt his farm; so he refrains from mentioning it in the *Letters*, for fear of invalidating his premises.

Some great hornets have fixed their nest on the ceiling of the living-room of the American Farmer, and these tiger-striped animals fly round the heads of the Healthy Offspring and the Amiable Spouse, to the 30 gratification of the American Farmer. He liked their buzz and their tiger waspishness. Also, on the utilitarian plane, they kept the house free of flies. So Henri says. Therefore Benjamin would have approved. But of the feelings of the Amiable S. on this matter, we are not told. And after all, it was she who had to make the jam. 35

Another anecdote. Swallows built their nest on the verandah of the American Farm. Wrens took a fancy to the nest of the swallows. They pugnaciously (I like the word pugnaciously, it is so American*) attacked the harbingers of spring, and drove them away from their nice adobe nest. The swallows returned upon opportunity. But the wrens, coming 40 home, violently drove them forth again. Which continued until the

gentle swallows patiently set about to build another nest, while the wrens
sat in triumph, in the usurped home. The American Farmer watched
this contest with delight, and no doubt loudly applauded those little
rascals of wrens.* For in the Land of the Free, the greatest delight of
5   every man is in getting the better of the other man.

Crêvecoeur says he shot a kingbird that had been devouring his bees.
He opened the craw and took out a vast number of bees, which little
democrats, after they had lain a minute or two stunned, in the sun
roused, revived, preened their wings and walked off debonair, like Jonah
10   up the seashore;* or like true Yanks escaped from the craw of the kingbird
of Europe.

I don't care whether it's true or not. I like the picture, and see in it a
parable of the American resurrection.

The humming-bird.

15   "Its bill is as long and as sharp as a coarse sewing needle; like the bee,
Nature has taught it to find out in the calyx of flowers and blossoms
those mellifluous particles that can serve it for sufficient food; and yet it
seems to leave them untouched, undeprived of anything that the eye can
possibly distinguish. When it feeds it appears as if immovable, though
20   continually on the wing: and sometimes, from what motives I know not,
it will tear and lacerate flowers into a hundred pieces; for, strange to tell,
they are the most irascible of the feathered tribe. Where do passions find
room in so diminutive a body? They often fight with the fury of lions,
until one of the combatants falls a sacrifice and dies. When fatigued,
25   it has often perched within a few feet of me, and on such favourable
opportunities I have surveyed it with the most minute attention. Its little
eyes appear like diamonds, reflecting light on every side; most elegantly
finished in all parts, it is a miniature work of our Great Parent, who
seems to have formed it smallest, and at the same time most beautiful,
30   of the winged species.—"

A regular little tartar, too. Lions no bigger than ink spots! I have
read about humming birds elsewhere, in Bates and W.H.Hudson,* for
example. But it is left to the American Farmer to show me the real little
raging lion.

35   Birds are evidently no angels in America, or to the true American. He
sees how they start and flash their wings like little devils, and stab each
other with egoistic sharp bills. But he sees also the reserved, tender shy-
ness of the wild creature, upon occasion. Quails in winter, for instance.

"Often, in the angles of the fences, where the motion of the wind
40   prevents the snow from settling, I carry them both chaff and grain; the

one to feed them, the other to prevent their tender feet from freezing fast to the earth, as I have frequently observed them to do."

This is beautiful, and blood-knowledge. Crêvecoeur knows the touch of birds' feet, as if they had stood with their vibrating, sharp, cold-cleaving balance, naked-footed on his naked hand. It is a beautiful, barbaric tenderness of the blood. He doesn't after all turn them into "little sisters of the air," like St. Francis,* or start preaching to them. He knows them as strange, shy, hot-blooded concentrations of bird-presence.

The *Letter* about snakes and humming-birds* is a fine essay, in its primal, dark veracity. The description of the fight between two snakes, a great water-snake and a large black serpent, follows the description of the humming-bird: "Strange was this to behold; two great snakes strongly adhering to the ground, mutually fastened together by means of the writhings which lashed them to each other, and stretched at their full length, they pulled but pulled in vain; and in the moments of greatest exertions that part of their bodies which was entwined seemed extremely small, while the rest appeared inflated, and now and then convulsed with strong undulations, rapidly following each other. Their eyes seemed on fire, and ready to start out of their heads; at one time the conflict seemed decided; the water-snake bent itself into two great folds, and by that operation rendered the other more than commonly outstretched. The next minute the new struggles of the black one gained an unexpected superiority; it acquired two great folds likewise, which necessarily extended the body of its adversary in proportion as it had contracted its own."

This fight, which Crêvecoeur describes to a finish, he calls a sight "uncommon and beautiful." He forgets the sweet-and-pureness of Nature, and is for the time a sheer ophiolater, and his chapter is as handsome a piece of ophiolatry,* perhaps, as that coiled Aztec rattlesnake carved in stone.*

And yet the real Crêvecoeur is, in the issue, neither farmer, nor child of Nature, nor ophiolater. He goes back to France, and figures in the literary salons, and is a friend of Rousseau's Madame d'Houdetot. Also he is a good business man, and arranges a line of shipping between France and America. It all ends in materialism, really. But the *Letters* tell us nothing about this.

We are left to imagine him retiring in grief to dwell with his Red Brothers under the wigwams.* For the War of Independence has broken out, and the Indians are armed by the adversaries; they do dreadful

work on the frontiers. While Crêvecoeur is away in France his farm is
destroyed, his family rendered homeless. So that the last letter laments
bitterly over the war, and man's folly and inhumanity to man.

But Crêvecoeur ends his lament on a note of resolution. With his
5 amiable spouse, and his healthy offspring, now rising in stature, he will
leave the civilised coasts, where man is sophisticated and therefore inclined to be vile,* and he will go to live with the Children of Nature, the
Red Men, under the wigwam. No doubt, in actual life, Crêvecoeur made
some distinction between the Indian, who drank rum *à la* Franklin, and
10 who burnt homesteads and massacred families, and those Indians, the
noble Children of Nature, who peopled his own pre-determined fancy.
Whatever he did in actual life, in his innermost self he would not give up
this self-made world, where the natural man was an object of undefiled
brotherliness. Touchingly and vividly he describes his tented home near
15 the Indian village, how he breaks the aboriginal earth to produce a little
maize, while his wife weaves within the wigwam.* And his imaginary
efforts to save his tender offspring from the brutishness of unchristian
darkness are touching and puzzling, for how can Nature, so sweet and
pure under the greenwood tree,* how can it have any contaminating
20 effect?

But it is all a swindle. Crêvecoeur was off to France in high-heeled
shoes and embroidered waistcoat, to pose as a literary man, and to
prosper in the world. We, however, must perforce follow him into the
backwoods, where the simple natural life shall be perfected, near the
25 tented village of the Red Man.

He wanted, of course, to imagine the dark, savage way of life, to get
it all off pat in his head. He wanted to know as the Indians and savages
know, darkly, and in terms of otherness. He was simply crazy, as the
Americans say, for this.* Crazy enough! For at the same time he was
30 absolutely determined that Nature is sweet and pure, that all men are
brothers, and equal, and that they love one another like so many cooing
doves. He was determined to have life according to his own prescription.
Therefore, he wisely kept away from any too close contact with Nature,
and took refuge in commerce and the material world. But yet, he was
35 determined to know the savage way of life, to his own *mind's* satisfaction.
So he just faked us the last *Letters*. A sort of wish-fulfilment.

For the animals and savages are isolate each one in its own pristine self.
The animal lifts its head, sniffs, and knows within the dark, passionate
belly. It knows at once, in dark mindlessness. And at once it flees in
40 immediate recoil; or it crouches predatory, in the mysterious storm

of exultant anticipation of seizing a victim; or it lowers its head in blank indifference again; or it advances in the insatiable wild curiosity, insatiable passion to approach that which is unspeakably strange and incalculable; or it draws near in the slow trust of wild, sensual love.

Crèvecoeur wanted this kind of knowledge. But comfortably, in his head, along with his other ideas and ideals. He didn't go too near the wigwam. Because he must have suspected that the moment he saw as the savages saw, all his fraternity and equality would go up in smoke, and his ideal world of pure sweet goodness along with it. And still worse than this, he would have to give up his own will, which insists that the world is so, because it would be nicest if it were so. Therefore he trotted back to France in high-heeled shoes, and imagined America in Paris.

He wanted his ideal state. At the same time he wanted to *know* the other state, the dark, savage mind. He wanted both.

Can't be done, Henry. The one is the death of the other.

Best turn to commerce, where you may get things your own way.

He hates the dark, pre-mental life, really. He hates the true sensual mystery. But he wants to "know." To K N O W. Oh insatiable American curiosity!

He's a liar.

But if he won't risk knowing in flesh and blood, he'll risk all the imagination you like.

It is amusing to see him staying away and calculating the dangers of the step which he take so luxuriously, in his fancy alone. He tickles his palate with a taste of true wildness, as men are so fond nowadays of tickling their palates with a taste of imaginary wickedness—just self-provoked.

"I must tell you," he says, "that there is something in the proximity of the woods which is very singular. It is with men as it is with the plants and animals that live in the forests; they are entirely different from those that live in the plains. I will candidly tell you all my thoughts, but you are not to expect that I shall advance any reasons. By living in or near the woods, their actions are regulated by the wildness of the neighbourhood. The deer often come to eat their grain, the wolves destroy their sheep, the bears kill their hogs, the foxes catch their poultry. This surrounding hostility immediately puts the gun into their hands; they watch these animals, they kill some; and thus by defending their property they soon become professed hunters; this is the progress; once hunters, farewell to the plough. The chase renders them ferocious, gloomy, unsociable; a hunter wants no neighbours, he rather hates them, because he dreads the competition.... Eating of wild meat, whatever you may think, tends to alter their temper...."

Crêvecoeur, of course, had never intended to return as a *hunter* to the bosom of Nature, only as a husbandman. The hunter is a killer. The husbandman, on the other hand, brings about the birth and increase. But even the husbandman strains in dark mastery over the unwilling earth and beast; he struggles to win forth substance, he must master the soil and the strong cattle, he must have the heavy blood-knowledge, and the slow, but deep, mastery. There is no equality or selfless humility. The toiling blood swamps the ideal, inevitably. For this reason the most idealist nations invent most machines. America simply teems with mechanical inventions, because nobody in America ever wants to *do* anything. They are idealists. Let a machine do the doing.

Again, Crêvecoeur dwells on "the apprehension lest my younger children should be caught by that singular charm, so dangerous to their tender years"—meaning the charm of savage life. So he goes on: "By what power does it come to pass that children who have been adopted when young among these people (the Indians) can never be prevailed upon to readopt European manners? Many an anxious parent have I seen last war who, at the return of peace, went to the Indian villages where they knew their children to have been carried in captivity, when to their inexpressible sorrow they found them so perfectly Indianised that many knew them no longer, and those whose more advanced ages permitted them to recollect their fathers and mothers, absolutely refused to follow them, and ran to their adopted parents to protect them against the effusions of love their unhappy real parents lavished on them! Incredible as this may appear, I have heard it asserted in a thousand instances, among persons of credit.

"There must be something in their (the Indians') social bond singularly captivating, and far superior to anything to be boasted of among us; for thousands of Europeans are Indians, and we have no examples of even one of those aborigines having from choice become Europeans...."

Our cat and another,* Henry.

I like the picture of thousands of obdurate offspring, with faces averted from their natural white father and mother, turning resolutely to the Indians of their adoption.

I have seen some Indians whom you really couldn't tell from white men. And I have never seen a white man who looked really like an Indian. So Henry is again a liar.

But Crêvecoeur wanted to be an *intellectual* savage, like a great many more we have met. Sweet children of Nature. Savage and bloodthirsty children of Nature.

White Americans do try hard to intellectualise themselves. Especially white women Americans. And the latest stunt is this "savage" stunt again.

White savages, with motor-cars, telephones, incomes and ideals! Savages fast inside the machine;* yet savage enough, ye gods!

IV.

Fenimore Cooper's* White Novels.

Benjamin Franklin had a specious little equation in providential mathematics:

5   Rum + Savage = 0.

Awfully nice! You might add up the universe to nought, if you kept on.
Rum plus Savage may equal a dead savage. But is a dead savage
nought? Can you make a land virgin by killing off its aborigines?
The Aztec is gone, and the Incas. The Red Indian, the Esquimo, the
10 Patagonian* are reduced to negligible numbers.
*Où sont les neiges d'antan?**
My dear, wherever they are, they will come down again next winter,
sure as houses.
Not that the Red Indian will ever possess the broad lands of America
15 again. At least I presume not. But his ghost will.
The Red Man died hating the white man. What remnant of him lives,
lives hating the white man. Go near the Indians, and you just feel it.
As far as we are concerned, the Red Man is subtly and unremittingly
diabolic. Even when he doesn't know it. He is dispossessed in life, and
20 unforgiving. He doesn't believe in us and our civilisation, and so is our
mystic enemy, for we push him off the face of the earth.
Belief is a mysterious thing. It is the only healer of the soul's wounds.
There is no belief in the world.
The Red Man is dead, disbelieving in us. He is dead and unappeased.
25 Do not imagine him happy in his Happy Hunting Ground.* No. Only
those that die in belief die happy. Those that are pushed out of life in
chagrin come back unappeased, for revenge.
A curious thing about the Spirit of Place is the fact that no place
exerts its full influence upon a new-comer until the old inhabitant is
30 dead or absorbed. So America. While the Red Indian existed in fairly
large numbers the new colonials were in a great measure immune from
the daimon, or demon of America. The moment the last nuclei of Red
life break up in America, then the white men will have to reckon with
the full force of the demon of the continent. At present the demon of

the place and the unappeased ghosts of the dead Indians act within the unconscious or under-conscious soul of the white American, causing the great American grouch, the Orestes-like frenzy of restlessness in the Yankee soul, the inner malaise which amounts almost to madness, sometimes. The Mexican is macabre and disintegrated in his own way. Up till   5
now, the unexpressed spirit of America has worked covertly in the American, the white American soul. But within the present generation the surviving Red Indians are due to merge in the great white swamp. Then the Daimon of America will work overtly, and we shall see real changes.

There has been all the time, in the white American soul, a dual   10
feeling about the Indian. First was Franklin's feeling, that a wise Providence no doubt intended the extirpation of these savages. Then came Crèvecoeur's contradictory feeling about the noble Red Man and the innocent life of the wigwam. Now we hate to subscribe to Benjamin's belief in a Providence that wisely extirpates the Indian to make room   15
for "cultivators of the soil." In Crèvecoeur we meet a sentimental desire for the glorification of the savages. Absolutely sentimental. Henri pops over to Paris to enthuse about the wigwam.

The desire to extirpate the Indian. And the contradictory desire to glorify him. Both are rampant still, today.   20

The bulk of the white people who live in contact with the Indian today would like to see this Red brother exterminated; not only for the sake of grabbing his land, but because of the silent, invisible, but deadly hostility between the spirit of the two races. The minority of whites intellectualise the Red man and laud him to the skies. But this minority   25
of whites is mostly a high-brow minority with a big grouch against its own whiteness. So there you are.

I doubt if there is possible any real reconciliation, in the flesh, between the white and the red. For instance, a Red Indian girl who is servant in the white man's home, if she is treated with natural consideration will   30
probably serve well, even happily. She is happy with the new power over the white woman's kitchen. The white world makes her feel prouder, so long as she is free to go back to her own people at the given times. But she is happy because she is playing at being a white woman.—There are other Indian women who would never serve the white people, and   35
who would rather die than have a white man for a lover.

In either case, there is no reconciliation. There is no mystic conjunction between the spirit of the two races. The Indian girl who happily serves white people leaves out her own race-consideration, for the time being.   40

Supposing a white man goes out hunting in the mountains with an Indian. The two will probably get on like brothers. But let the same white man go alone with two Indians, and there will start a most subtle persecution of the unsuspecting white. If they, the Indians, discover
5 that he has a natural fear of steep places, then over every precipice in the country will the trail lead. And so on.—Malice!* That is the basic feeling in the Indian heart, towards the white. It may even be purely unconscious.

Supposing an Indian loves a white woman, and lives with her.* He
10 will probably be very proud of it, for he will be a big man among his own people, especially if the white mistress has money. He will never get over the feeling of pride at dining in a white dining-room and smoking in a white drawing-room. But at the same time he will subtly jeer at his white mistress, try to destroy her white pride. He will submit to her,
15 if he is forced to, with a kind of false, unwilling childishness, and even love her with the same childlike gentleness, sometimes beautiful. But at the bottom of his heart he is gibing, gibing, gibing at her. Not only is it the sex resistance, but the race resistance as well.

There seems to be no reconciliation in the flesh.
20 That leaves us only expiation, and then reconciliation in the soul. Some strange atonement: expiation and oneing.*

Fenimore Cooper has probably done more than any writer to present the Red man to the white man. But Cooper's presentment is indeed a wish-fulfilment. That is why Fenimore is such a success, still.
25 Modern critics begrudge Cooper his success.* I think I resent it a little myself. This popular wish-fulfilment stuff makes it so hard for the real thing to come through, later.

Cooper was a rich American of good family. His father founded Coopers-Town, by Lake Champlain. And Fenimore was a gentleman
30 of culture. No denying it.

It is amazing how cultured these Americans of the first half of the eighteenth century were. Most intensely so. Austin Dobson and Andrew Lang* are fleabites in comparison. Volumes of very *raffiné* light verse and finely-drawn familiar literature will prove it to anyone who cares to
35 commit himself to these elderly books. The English and French writers of the same period were clumsy and hoydenish,* judged by the same standards.

Truly, European decadence was anticipated in America; and American influence passed over to Europe, was assimilated there, and then re-
40 turned to this land of innocence as something purplish in its modernity

and a little wicked. So absurd things are. Cooper quotes a Frenchman, who says, *"L'Amérique est pourrie avant d'être mûre."** And there is a great deal in it. America was not taught by France—by Baudelaire, for example. Baudelaire learned his lesson from America.*

Cooper's novels fall into two classes: his white novels, such as *Homeward Bound, Eve Effingham, The Spy, The Pilot,* and then the Leatherstocking Series.* Let us look at the white novels first.

The Effinghams are three extremely refined, genteel Americans who are *Homeward Bound* from England to the States. Their party consists of father, daughter, and uncle,* and faithful nurse. The daughter has just finished her education in Europe. She has, indeed, skimmed the cream off Europe. England, France, Italy, and Germany have nothing more to teach her. She is a bright and charming, admirable creature; a real modern heroine; intrepid, calm, and self-collected, yet admirably impulsive, always in perfectly good taste; clever and assured in her speech, like a man, but withal charmingly deferential and modest before the stronger sex. It is the perfection of the ideal female—We have learned to shudder at her, but Cooper still admired.

On board is the other type of American, the parvenu, the demagogue,* who has *done* Europe and put it in his breeches pocket, in a month. Oh Septimus Dodge, if a European had drawn you, that European would never have been forgiven by America. But an American drew you, so Americans wisely ignore you.

Septimus is the American self-made man. God had no hand in his make-up. He made himself. He has been to Europe, no doubt seen everything, including the Venus de Milo.* "What, is *that* the Venus de Milo?" And he turns his back on the lady. He's seen her. He's got her. She's a fish he has hooked, and he's off to America with her, leaving the scum of a statue standing in the Louvre.

That is one American way of Vandalism. The original Vandals* would have given the complacent dame a knock with a battle-axe, and ended her. The insatiable American looks at her. "Is *that* the Venus de Milo?— Come on!" And the Venus de Milo stands there like a naked slave in a market-place, whom someone has spat on. Spat on!

I have often thought, hearing American tourists in Europe—in the Bargello in Florence, for example, or in the Piazza di San Marco* in Venice—exclaiming "Isn't that just too cunning!" or else "Aren't you perfectly crazy about Saint Mark's! Don't you think those cupolas are like the loveliest *turnips* upside down, you know—" as if the beautiful things of Europe were just having their guts pulled out by these

American admirers. They admire so wholesale. Sometimes they even
seem to grovel. But the golden cupolas of St. Marks in Venice are turnips
upside down in a stale stew, after enough American tourists have looked
at them. Turnips upside down in a stale stew. Poor Europe!

5   And there you are. When a few German bombs fell upon Rheims
cathedral* up went a howl of execration. But there are more ways than
one, of vandalism. I should think the American admiration of five-
minute tourists has done more to kill the sacredness of old European
beauty and aspiration than multitudes of bombs would have done.

10   But there you are. Europe has got to fall, and peace hath her victories.*

Behold then Mr Septimus Dodge returning to Dodge-town* victorious. Not crowned with laurel, it is true, but wreathed in lists of things
he had seen and sucked dry. Seen and sucked dry, you know: Venus de
Milo, the Rhine, or the Coliseum:* swallowed like so many clams, and

15   left the shells.

Now the aristocratic Effinghams, Homeward Bound from Europe
to America, are at the mercy of Mr Dodge: Septimus. He is their
compatriot, so they may not disown him. Had they been English,
of course, they would never once have let themselves become aware

20   of his existence. But no. They are American democrats, and therefore, if Mr Dodge marches up and says: "Mr Effingham? Pleased to
meet you, Mr Effingham"—why, then Mr Effingham is *forced* to reply: "Pleased to meet you, Mr Dodge."* If he didn't, he would have
the terrible hounds of democracy on his heels and at his throat, the

25   moment he landed in the Land of the Free. An Englishman is free to
continue unaware of the existence of a fellow-countryman, if the looks
of that fellow-countryman are distasteful. But every American citizen
is free to force his presence upon you, no matter how unwilling you
may be.

30   Freedom!

The Effinghams detest Mr Dodge. They abhor him. They loathe and
despise him. They have an unmitigated contempt for him. Everything
he is, says, and does seems to them too vulgar, too despicable. Yet they
are forced to answer, when he presents himself: "Pleased to meet you,

35   Mr Dodge."

Freedom!

Mr Dodge, of Dodgetown, alternately fawns and intrudes, cringes
and bullies. And the Effinghams, terribly "superior" in a land of equality,
writhe helpless. They would fain snub Septimus out of existence. But

40   Septimus is not to be snubbed. As a true democrat, he is unsnubbable.
As a true democrat, he has right on his side. And right is might.*

Right is might. It is the old struggle for power.

Septimus, as a true democrat, is the equal of any man. As a true democrat with a full pocket, he is, by the amount that fills his pocket, so much the superior of the democrats with empty pockets. Because, though all men are born equal and die equal, you will not get anybody 5
to admit that ten dollars equal ten thousand dollars. No no, there's a difference there, however far you may push equality.

Septimus has the Effinghams on the hip.* He has them fast, and they will not escape. What tortures await them at home, in the Land of the Free, at the hands of the hideously affable Dodge, we do not care to 10
disclose. What was the persecution of a haughty Lord or a marauding Baron or an inquisitorial Abbot compared to the persecution of a million Dodges. The proud Effinghams are like men buried naked to the chin in ant-heaps, to be bitten into extinction by a myriad ants. Stoically, as good democrats and idealists, they writhe and endure, without making 15
too much moan.

They writhe and endure. There is no escape. Not from that time to this. No escape. They writhed on the horns of the Dodge dilemma.* Since then Ford has gone one worse.

Through these white novels of Cooper runs this acid of ant-bites, 20
the formic acid of democratic poisoning. The Effinghams feel superior. Cooper felt superior. Mrs Cooper felt superior too. And bitten.

For they were democrats. They didn't believe in kings, or lords, or masters, or real superiority of any sort. Before God, of course. In the sight of God, of course, all men were equal. This they believed. And 25
therefore, though they *felt* terribly superior to Mr Dodge, yet, since they were his equals in the sight of God, they could not feel free to say to him: "Mr Dodge, please go to the devil." They had to say: "Pleased to meet you."

What a lie to tell! Democratic lies. 30

What a dilemma! To feel so superior. To *know* you are superior. And yet to believe that, in the sight of God, you are equal. Can't help yourself.

Why couldn't they let the Lord Almighty look after the equality, since it seems to happen specifically in His Sight, and stick themselves to their own superiority? Why couldn't they? 35

Somehow, they daren't.

They were Americans, idealists. How dare they balance a mere intense feeling against an IDEA and an IDEAL?

Ideally—i. e., in the sight of God, Mr Dodge was their equal.

What a low opinion they held of the Almighty's faculty for discrim- 40
ination.

But it was so. The IDEAL of EQUALITY.

Pleased to meet you, Mr Dodge.

We are equal in the sight of God, of course. But er—

Very glad to meet you, Miss Effingham. Did you say—*er?* Well now,

5 I think my bank balance will bear it.

Poor Eve Effingham.

Eve!

Think of it. Eve! And birds of paradise. And apples!*

And Mr Dodge.

10 This is where apples of knowledge get you, Miss Eve. You should leave 'em alone.

"Mr Dodge, you are a hopeless and insufferable inferior."

Why couldn't she say it? She felt it. And she was a heroine.

Alas, she was an American heroine. She was an EDUCATED

15 WOMAN. She KNEW all about IDEALS. She swallowed the IDEAL of EQUALITY with her first mouthful of KNOWLEDGE. Alas for her and that apple of Sodom* that looked so rosy. Alas for all her knowing.

Mr Dodge (in check knickerbockers): Well, feeling a little uncom-

20 fortable below the belt, are you, Miss Effingham?

Miss Effingham (with difficulty withdrawing her gaze from the INFINITE OCEAN): Good morning, Mr Dodge. I was admiring the dark blue distance.

Mr Dodge: Say, couldn't you admire something a bit nearer.*

25 Think how easy it would have been for her to say "Go away!"—or "Leave me, varlet!"—or "Hence, base-born knave!" Or just to turn her back on him.

But then he would simply have marched round to the other side of her. Was she his superior, or wasn't she?

30 Why surely, intrinsically, she *was.* Intrinsically Fenimore Cooper was the superior of the Dodges of his day. He felt it. But he felt he ought not to feel it. And he never had it out with himself.

That is why one rather gets impatient with him. He feels he is superior, and feels he ought *not* to feel so, and is therefore rather snobbish,

35 and at the same time a little apologetic. Which is surely tiresome.

If a man feels superior, he should have it out with himself. "Do I feel superior because I *am* superior? Or is it just the snobbishness of class, or education, or money?"

Class, education, money won't make a man superior. But if he's just

40 *born* superior, in himself, there it is. Why deny it?

It is a nasty sight to see the Effinghams putting themselves at the mercy of a Dodge, just because of a mere idea or ideal. Fools. They ruin more than they know. Because at the same time they are snobbish.

Septimus at the Court of King Arthur.*

Septimus: Hello Arthur! Pleased to meet you. By the way, what's all   5
      that great long sword about?

Arthur: This is Excalibur, the sword of my knighthood and my
      kingship.*

Septimus: That so! We're all equal in the sight of God, you know,
      Arthur.   10

Arthur: Yes.

Septimus: Then I guess it's about time I had that yard-and-a-half of
      Excalibur to play with. Don't you think so? We're equal in
      the sight of God, and you've had it for quite a while.

Arthur: Yes, I agree. (Hands him Excalibur).   15

Septimus (prodding Arthur with Excalibur): Say, Art, which is your
      fifth rib?*

Superiority is a sword. Hand it over to Septimus, and you'll get it back between your ribs.—The whole moral of democracy.

But there you are. Eve Effingham had pinned herself down on the   20
Contrat Social,* and she was prouder of that pin through her body than of any mortal thing else. Her IDEAL. Her IDEAL of DEMOCRACY.

When America set out to destroy Kings and Lords and Masters, and the whole paraphernalia of European superiority, it pushed a pin right through its own body, and on that pin it still flaps* and buzzes and twists   25
in misery. The pin of democratic equality. Freedom.

There'll never be any life in America till you pull the pin out and admit natural inequality. Natural superiority, natural inferiority. Till such time, Americans just buzz round like various sorts of propellers, pinned down by their freedom and equality.   30

That's why these white novels of Fenimore Cooper are only historically and sardonically interesting. The people are all pinned down by some social pin, and buzzing away in social importance or friction, round and round on the pin. Never real human beings. Always things pinned down, choosing to be pinned down, transfixed by the idea or   35
ideal of equality and democracy, on which they turn loudly and importantly, like propellers propelling These States.* Humanly, it is boring. As a historic phenomenon, it is amazing, ludicrous, and irritating.

If you don't pull the pin out in time, you'll never be able to pull it out. You must turn on it forever, or bleed to death.   40

"Naked to the waist was I
And deep within my breast did lie,
Though no man any blood could spy,
The truncheon of a spear—"*

5   Is it already too late?
Oh God, the democratic pin!
Freedom, Equality, Equal Opportunity, Education, Rights of Man.*
The pin! The pin!
Well, there buzzes Eve Effingham, snobbishly, impaled. She is a per-
10   fect American heroine, and I'm sure she wore the first smartly-tailored
"suit," that ever woman wore.* I'm sure she spoke several languages.
I'm sure she was hopelessly competent. I'm sure she "adored" her hus-
band, and spent masses of his money, and divorced him because he
didn't understand L O V E.
15   American women in their perfect "suits." American men in their
imperfect coats and skirts!
I feel I'm the superior of most men I meet. Not in birth, because I
never had a great-grandfather.* Not in money, because I've got none.
Not in education, because I'm merely scrappy.* And certainly not in
20   beauty or in manly strength.
Well what then?
Just in myself.
When I'm challenged, I do feel myself superior to most of the men I
meet. Just a natural superiority.
25   But not till there enters an element of challenge.
When I meet another man, and he is just himself—even if he is an
ignorant Mexican pitted with small-pox—then there is no question
between us of superiority or inferiority. He is a man and I am a man.
We are ourselves. There is no question between us.
30   But let a question arise, let there be a challenge, and then I feel he
should do reverence to the gods in me, because they are more than the
gods in him. And he should give reverence to the very me, because it is
more at one with the gods than is his very self.
If this is conceit, I am sorry. But it's the gods in me that matter. And
35   in other men.
As for me, I am so glad to salute the brave, reckless gods in another
man, so glad to meet a man who will abide by his very self.
Ideas! Ideals! All this paper between us. What a weariness.

If only people would meet in their very selves, without wanting to put some idea over one another, or some ideal.

Damn all ideas and all ideals. Damn all the false stress, and the pins.

I am I. Here am I. Where are you?

Ah, there you are! Now, damn the consequences, we have met.

That's my idea of democracy, if you can call it an idea.

V.

Fenimore Cooper's
Leatherstocking Novels.

In his Leatherstocking books, Fenimore is off on another track. He is
no longer concerned with social white Americans that buzz with pins
through them, buzz loudly against every mortal thing except the pin
itself. The pin of the Great Ideal.

One gets irritated with Cooper because he never for once snarls at
the Great Ideal Pin which transfixes him. No indeed. Rather he tries to
push it through the very heart of the Continent.

But I have loved the Leatherstocking books so dearly. Wish-fulfilment!

Anyhow one is not supposed to take LOVE seriously, in these books.
Eve Effingham, impaled on the social pin, conscious all the time of her
own ego and of nothing else, suddenly fluttering in throes of love: no, it
makes me sick. Love is never LOVE until it has a pin pushed through
it and becomes an IDEAL. The ego turning on a pin is wildly IN
LOVE, always. Because that's the thing to be.

Cooper was a GENTLEMAN, in the worst sense of the word. In
the Nineteenth Century sense of the word. A correct, clock-work man.
Not altogether, of course.

The great National Grouch was grinding inside him. Probably he
called it COSMIC URGE. Americans usually do: in capital letters.

Best stick to National Grouch. The great American grouch.

Cooper had it, gentleman as he was. That is why he flitted round
Europe so uneasily.* Of course in Europe he could be, and was, a gentleman to his heart's content.

"In short," he says in one of his letters, "we were at table two counts,
one monsignore, an English Lord, an Ambassador, and my humble
self."*

Were we really!

How nice it must have been to know that one self, at least, was humble.

And he felt the democratic American tomahawk wheeling over his
uncomfortable scalp all the time.

The great American Grouch.

Two monsters loomed on Cooper's horizon.

MRS COOPER	MY WORK.
MY WORK	MY WIFE
MY WIFE	MY WORK

THE DEAR CHILDREN   5

MY WORK!!!

There you have the essential keyboard of Cooper's soul.

If there is one thing that annoys me more than a business man and his BUSINESS, it is an artist, a writer, painter, musician, and MY WORK. When an artist says MY WORK, the flesh goes tired on my   10
bones.* When he says MY WIFE, I want to hit him.

Cooper grizzled about his work. Oh heaven, he cared so much whether it was good or bad, and what the French thought, and what Mr Snippy Knowall* said, and how Mrs Cooper took it. The pin, the pin!

But he was truly an artist: then an American: then a gentleman.   15
And the grouch grouched inside him, through all.

They seemed to have been specially fertile in imagining themselves "under the wigwam," do these Americans, just when their knees were comfortably under the mahogany, in Paris, along with the knees of

4 Counts
2 Cardinals   20
1 Milord
5 Cocottes
1 Humble self.

You bet, though, that when the cocottes were being raffled off, Fen-   25
imore went home to his WIFE.

	THE WIGWAM	versus MY HÔTEL	
wish-fulfilment	CHINGACHGOOK	versus MY WIFE	ACTUALITY
	NATTY BUMPPO	versus MY HUMBLE SELF	

Fenimore lying in his Louis Quatorze hôtel in Paris,* passionately   30
musing about Natty Bumppo and the pathless forest, and mixing his imagination with the Cupids and butterflies on the painted ceiling, while Mrs Cooper was struggling with her latest gown in the next room, and déjeûner was with the Countess at eleven....

Men live by lies.   35

In actuality, Fenimore loved the genteel continent of Europe, and waited gasping for the newspapers to praise his WORK.

In another actuality, he loved the tomahawking continent of America, and imagined himself Natty Bumppo.

His actual desire was to be: Monsieur Fenimore Cooper, le grand écrivain américain.

5   His innermost wish was to be: Natty Bumppo.

Now Natty and Fenimore arm-in-arm are an odd couple.

You can see Fenimore: blue coat, silver buttons, silver-and-diamond buckle shoes, ruffles.

You see Natty Bumppo: a grizzled, uncouth old renegade, with gaps
10   in his old teeth and a drop on the end of his nose.

But Natty was Fenimore's great Wish: his wish-fulfilment.

"It was a matter of course," says Mrs Cooper, "that he should dwell on the better traits of the picture rather than on the coarser and more revolting, though more common points. Like West, he could see Apollo
15   in the young Mohawk."*

The coarser and more revolting, though more common points.

You see now why he depended so absolutely on MY WIFE. She had to look things in the face for him. The coarser and more revolting, and certainly more common points, she had to see.

20   He himself did so love seeing pretty-pretty, with the thrill of a red scalp now and then.

Fenimore, in his imagination, wanted to be Natty Bumppo, who, I am sure, belched after he had eaten his dinner. At the same time Mr Cooper was nothing if not a gentleman. So he decided to stay in France and
25   have it all his own way.

In France, Natty would not belch after eating, and Chingachgook could be all the Apollo he liked.

As if ever any Indian was like Apollo. The Indians, with their curious female quality, their archaic figures, with high shoulders and deep, ar-
30   chaic waists, like a sort of woman! And their natural devilishness, their natural insidiousness.

But men see what they want to see: especially if they look from a long distance, across the ocean, for example.

Yet the Leatherstocking books are lovely. Lovely half-lies.

35   They form a sort of American Odyssey, with Natty Bumppo for Odysseus.

Only, in the original Odyssey, there is plenty of devil, Circes and swine and all. And Ithacus* is devil enough to outwit the devils. But Natty is a saint with a gun, and the Indians are gentlemen through and
40   through, though they may take an occasional scalp.

There are five Leatherstocking novels: a *decrescendo* of reality, and a crescendo of beauty.

1. *Pioneers*: A raw frontier-village on Lake Champlain, at the end of the eighteenth century. Must be a picture of Cooper's home, as he knew it when a boy. A very lovely book. Natty Bumppo   5
an old man, an old hunter half civilised.

2. *The Last of The Mohicans*:* A historical fight between the British and the French, with Indians on both sides, at a Fort by Lake Champlain. Romantic flight of the British general's two daughters, conducted by the Scout, Natty, who is in the   10
prime of life; romantic death of the last of the Delawares.

3. *The Prairie*: A wagon of some huge, sinister Kentuckians trekking west into the unbroken prairie. Prairie Indians, and Natty, an old, old man; he dies seated in a chair on* the Rocky Mountains, looking east.   15

4. *Pathfinder*: The Great Lakes. Natty, a man of about thirty-five, makes an abortive proposal to a bouncing damsel, daughter of the sergeant at the Fort.

5. *Deerslayer*: Natty and Hurry Harry, both quite young, are hunting in the virgin wild. They meet two white women. Lake   20
Champlain again.

There are the five Leatherstocking books: Natty Bumppo being Leatherstocking, Pathfinder, Deer-slayer, according to his ages.

Now let me put aside my impatience at the unreality of this vision, and accept it as a wish-fulfilment vision, a kind of yearning myth. Because it   25
seems to me that the things in Cooper that make one so savage, when one compares them with actuality, are perhaps, when one considers them as presentations of a deep subjective desire, real in their way, and almost prophetic.

The passionate love for America, for the soil of America, for example.   30
As I say, it is perhaps easier to love America passionately, when you look at it through the wrong end of the telescope, across all the Atlantic water, as Cooper did so often, than when you are right there. When you are actually *in* America, America hurts, because it has a powerful disintegrative influence upon the white psyche. It is full of girning,*   35
unappeased aboriginal demons, too, ghosts, and it persecutes the white men like some Eumenides, until the white men give up their absolute whiteness. America is tense with latent violence and resistance. The very common-sense of white Americans has a tinge of helplessness in it, and deep fear of what might be if they were not common-sensical.   40

Yet one day the demons of America must be placated, the ghosts must be appeased, the Spirit of Place atoned for. Then the true passionate love for American soil will appear. As yet, there is too much menace in the landscape.

5   But probably, one day America will be as beautiful in actuality as it is in Cooper. Not yet, however. When the factories have fallen down again.

And again, this perpetual blood-brother theme of the Leatherstocking novels, Natty and Chingachgook, the Great Serpent.* At present it is a sheer myth. The Red Man and the White Man are not blood-
10   brothers: even when they are most friendly. When they are most friendly, it is as a rule the one betraying his race-spirit to the other. In the white man—rather highbrow—who "loves" the Indian, one feels the white man betraying his own race. There is something unproud, underhand in it. Renegade. The same with the Americanised Indian who believes
15   absolutely in the white mode. It is a betrayal. Renegade again.

In the actual flesh, it seems to me the white man and the red man cause a feeling of oppression, the one to the other, no matter what the good will. The red life flows in a different direction from the white life. You can't make two streams that flow in opposite directions meet and
20   mingle soothingly.

Certainly, if Cooper had had to spend his whole life in the backwoods, side by side with a Noble Red Brother, he would have screamed with the oppression of suffocation. He had to have Mrs Cooper, a straight strong pillar of society, to hang on to. And he had to have the culture of
25   France to turn back to, or he would just have been stifled. The Noble Red Brother would have smothered him and driven him mad.

So that the Natty and Chingachgook myth must remain a myth. It is a wish-fulfilment, an evasion of actuality. As we have said before, the folds of the Great Serpent would have been heavy, very heavy, too heavy,
30   on any white man. Unless the white man were a true renegade, hating himself and his own race spirit, as sometimes happens.

It seems there can be no fusion in the flesh. But the spirit can change. The white man's spirit can never become as the red man's spirit. It doesn't want to. But it can cease to be the opposite and the negative of
35   the red man's spirit. It can open out a new great area of consciousness, in which there is room for the red spirit too.

To open out a new wide area of consciousness means to slough the old consciousness. The old consciousness has become a tight-fitting prison to us, in which we are going rotten.

40   You can't have a new, easy skin before you have sloughed the old, tight skin.

You can't.

And you just can't, so you may as well leave off pretending.

Now the essential history of the people of the United States seems to me just this. At the Renaissance the old consciousness was becoming a little tight. Europe sloughed her last skin, and started a new, final phase. 5

But some Europeans recoiled from the last final phase. They wouldn't enter the *cul de sac* of post-Renaissance, "liberal" Europe. They came to America.

They came to America for two reasons:

1. To slough the old European consciousness completely. 10

2. To grow a new skin underneath, a new form. This second is a hidden process.

The two processes go on, of course, simultaneously. The slow forming of the new skin underneath is the slow sloughing of the old skin. And sometimes this immortal serpent feels very happy, feeling a new golden 15 glow of a strangely-patterned skin envelop him: and sometimes he feels very sick, as if his very entrails were being torn out of him, as he wrenches once more at his old skin, to get out of it.

Out! Out! he cries, in all kinds of euphemisms.

He's got to have his new skin on him before ever he can get out. 20

And he's got to get out before his new skin can ever be his own skin.

So there he is, a torn, divided monster.

The true American, who writhes and writhes like a snake that is long in sloughing.

Sometimes snakes can't slough. They can't burst their old skin. Then 25 they go sick and die inside the old skin, and nobody ever sees the new pattern.

It needs a real desperate recklessness to burst your old skin at last. You simply don't care what happens to you, if you rip yourself in two, so long as you do get out. 30

It also needs a real belief in the new skin. Otherwise you are likely never to make the effort. Then you gradually sicken and go rotten and die in the old skin.

Now Fenimore stayed very safe inside the old skin: a gentleman, almost a European, as proper as proper can be. And, safe inside the old 35 skin, he *imagined* the gorgeous American pattern of a new skin.

He hated democracy. So he evaded it, and had a nice dream of something beyond democracy. But he belonged to democracy all the while.

Evasion!—Yet even that doesn't make the dream worthless.

Democracy in America was never the same as Liberty in Europe. 40 In Europe Liberty was a great life-throb. But in America Democracy

was always something anti-life. The greatest democrats, like Abraham
Lincoln, had always a sacrificial, self-murdering note* in their voices.
American Democracy was a form of self-murder, always. Or of murder-
ing somebody else.

5   Necessarily. It was a *pis aller.** It was the *pis aller* to European Liberty.
It was a cruel form of sloughing. Men murdered themselves into this
democracy. Democracy is the utter hardening of the old skin, the old
form, the old psyche. It hardens till it is tight and fixed and inorganic.
Then it *must* burst, like a chrysalis shell. And out must come the soft

10   grub, or the soft damp butterfly of the American-at-last.

America has gone the *pis-aller* of her democracy. Now she must slough
even that. Chiefly that, indeed.

What did Cooper dream beyond democracy? Why, in his immortal
friendship of Chingachgook and Natty Bumppo he dreamed the nucleus

15   of a new society. That is, he dreamed a new human relationship. A stark,
stripped human relationship of two men, deeper than the deeps of sex.
Deeper than property, deeper than fatherhood, deeper than marriage,
deeper than love. So deep that it is loveless. The stark, loveless, wordless
unison of two men who have come to the bottom of themselves. This is

20   the new nucleus of a new society, the clue to a new world-epoch. It asks
for a great and cruel sloughing first of all. Then it finds a great release
into a new world, a new moral, a new landscape.

Natty and The Great Serpent are neither equals nor unequals. Each
obeys the other when the moment arrives. And each is stark and dumb

25   in the other's presence, starkly himself, without illusion created. Each is
just the crude pillar of a man, the crude living column of his own manhood. And each knows the godhead of this crude column of manhood.
A new relationship.

The Leatherstocking novels create the myth of this new relation. And

30   they go backwards, from old age to golden youth. That is the true myth
of America. She starts old, old, wrinkled and writhing in an old skin.
And there is a gradual sloughing of the old skin, towards a new youth.
It is the myth of America.

You start with actuality. *Pioneers* is no doubt Cooperstown, when

35   Cooperstown was in the stage of inception: a village of one wild street
of log cabins under the forest hills by Lake Champlain: a village of
crude, wild frontiersmen, reacting against civilisation.

Towards this frontier-village, in the winter time, a negro slave drives
a sledge through the mountains, over deep snow. In the sledge sits a fair

40   damsel, Miss Temple, with her handsome pioneer father, Judge Temple.

They hear a shot in the trees. It is the old hunter and backwoodsman, Natty Bumppo, long and lean and uncouth, with a long rifle and gaps in his teeth.

Judge Temple is "squire" of the village, and he has a ridiculous, commodious "hall" for his residence. It is still the old English form. Miss Temple is a pattern young lady, like Eve Effingham: in fact she gets a young and very genteel but impoverished Effingham for a husband.* The old world holding its own on the edge of the wild. A bit tiresomely, too, with rather more prunes and prisms* than one can digest. Too romantic.

Against the "hall" and the gentry, the real frontiers-folk, the rebels. The two groups meet at the village inn, and at the frozen church, and at the Christmas sports, and on the ice of the lake, and at the great pigeon shoot. It is a beautiful, resplendent picture of life. Fenimore puts in only the glamour.

Perhaps my taste is childish, but these scenes in *Pioneers* seem to me marvellously beautiful. The raw village street, with wood-fires blinking through the unglazed window-chinks, on a winter's night. The inn, with the rough woodsmen and the drunken Indian John; the church, with the snowy congregation crowding to the fire. Then the lavish abundance of Christmas cheer, and turkey-shooting in the snow. Spring coming, forests all green, maple-sugar taken from the trees: and clouds of pigeons flying from the south, myriads of pigeons, shot in heaps; and night-fishing on the teeming, virgin lake; and deer-hunting.

Pictures! Some of the loveliest, most glamorous pictures in all literature.

Alas, without the cruel iron of reality. It is all real enough. Except that one realises that Fenimore was writing from a safe distance, where he could idealise and have his wish-fulfilment.

Because, when one comes to America, one finds that there is always a certain slightly devilish resistance in the American landscape, and a certain slightly bitter resistance in the white man's heart. Hawthorne gives this. But Cooper glosses it over.

The American landscape has never been at one with the white man. Never. And white men have probably never felt so bitter anywhere, as here in America, where the very landscape, in its very beauty, seems a bit devilish and grinning, opposed to us.

Cooper however glosses over this resistance, which in actuality can never quite be glossed over. He *wants* the landscape to be at one with him. So he goes away to Europe and sees it as such. It is a sort of evasion.*

And nevertheless the oneing will surely take place—some day.

The myth is the story of Natty. The old, lean hunter and backwoods-man lives with his friend, the grey-haired Indian John, and old Delaware chief, in a hut within reach of the village. The Delaware is christianised
5 and bears the Christian name of John. He is tribeless and lost. He hu-miliates his grey hairs in drunkenness, and dies, thankful to be dead, in a forest fire, passing back to the fire whence he derived.

And this is Chingachgook, the splendid Great Serpent of the later novels.

10 No doubt Cooper, as a boy, knew both Natty and the Indian John. No doubt they fired his imagination even then. When he is a man, crys-tallised in society and sheltering behind the safe pillar of Mrs Cooper, these two old fellows become a myth to his soul. He traces himself to a new youth in them.

15 As for the story: Judge Temple has just been instrumental in passing the wise game laws. But Natty has lived by his gun all his life in the wild woods, and simply childishly cannot understand how he can be poaching on the Judge's land among the pine trees. He shoots a deer in the close season.

20 The Judge is all sympathy, but the law *must* be enforced. Bewildered Natty, an old man of seventy, is put in stocks and in prison. They release him as soon as possible. But the thing was done.

The letter killeth.*

Natty's last connection with his own race is broken. John, the Indian,
25 is dead. The old hunter disappears, lonely and severed into the forest, away, away from his race.

In the new epoch that is coming, there will be no Letter of the Law.

Chronologically, *The Last of the Mohicans* follows *Pioneers*. But in the myth, *The Prairie* comes next.

30 Cooper of course knew his own America. He travelled west and saw the prairies,* and camped with the Indians of the prairie.

The Prairie, like *Pioneers*, bears a good deal the stamp of actuality. It is a strange, splendid book, full of a sense of doom. The figures of the great Kentuckian men, with their wolf-women,* loom colossal on
35 the vast prairie, as they camp with their wagons. These are different pioneers from Judge Temple. Lurid, brutal, tinged with the sinisterness of crime, these are the gaunt white men who push west, push on and on against the natural opposition of the continent. On towards a doom. Great wings of vengeful doom seem spread over the west, grim against
40 the intruder. You feel them again in Frank Norris' novel, *The Octopus.**

While in the West of Bret Harte* there is a very devil in the air, and beneath him are sentimental self-conscious people being wicked and goody by evasion.

In *The Prairie* there is a shadow of violence and dark cruelty flickering in the air. It is the aboriginal demon hovering over the core of the continent. It hovers still, and the dread is still there.

Into such a prairie enters the huge figure of Ishmael, ponderous, pariah-like Ishmael and his huge sons and his were-wolf wife.* With their wagons they roll on from the frontiers of Kentucky, like Cyclops* into the savage wilderness. Day after day they seem to force their way into oblivion. But their force of penetration ebbs. They are brought to a stop. They recoil in the throes of murder and entrench themselves in isolation on a hillock in the midst of the prairie. There they hold out like demi-gods against the elements and the subtle Indian.

The pioneering brute invasion of the west, crime-tinged!

And into this setting, as a sort of minister of peace, enters the old, old hunter Natty, and his suave, horse-riding Sioux Indians. But he seems like a shadow.

The hills rise softly west, to the Rockies. There seems a new peace: or is it only suspense, abstraction, waiting? Is it only a sort of beyond?

Natty lives in these hills, in a village of the suave, horse-riding Sioux. They revere him as an old wise father.

In these hills he dies, sitting in his chair and looking far east, to the forest and great sweet waters, whence he came. He dies gently, in physical peace with the land and the Indians. He is an old, old man.

Cooper could see no further than the foothills where Natty died, beyond the prairie.

The other novels bring us back east.

The Last of the Mohicans is divided between real historical narrative and true "romance." For myself, I prefer the romance. It has a myth-meaning, whereas the narrative is chiefly record.

For the first time, we get actual women: the dark, handsome Cora and her frail sister, the White Lily. The good old division, the dark sensual woman and the clinging, submissive little blonde, who is so "pure."

These sisters are fugitives through the forest, under the protection of a Major Heyward, a young American officer and Englishman. He is just a "white" man, very good and brave and generous, etc., but limited, most definitely *borné*.* He would probably love Cora, if he dared, but he finds it safer to adore the clinging White Lily of a younger sister.

This trio is escorted by Natty, now Leatherstocking, a hunter and scout in the prime of life, accompanied by his inseparable friend Chingachgook, and the Delaware's beautiful son—Adonis rather than Apollo*—Uncas, the Last of the Mohicans.

5   There is also a "wicked" Indian, Magua, handsome and injured incarnation of evil.

Cora is the scarlet flower of womanhood, fierce, passionate offspring of some mysterious union between the British officer and a Creole woman in the West Indies. Cora loves Uncas, Uncas loves Cora. But
10   Magua also desires Cora, violently desires her. A lurid little circle of sensual fire. So Fenimore kills thems all off, Cora, Uncas, and Magua, and leaves the white lily to carry on the race. She will breed plenty of white children to Major Heyward. These tiresome "lilies that fester,"* of our day.

15   Evidently Cooper—or the artist in him—has decided that there can be no blood-mixing of the two races, white and red. He kills 'em off.

Beyond all this heart-beating stand the figures of Natty and Chingachgook: the two childless, womanless men of opposite races. They are the abiding thing. Each of them is alone, and final in his race. And
20   they stand side by side, stark, abstract, beyond emotion, yet eternally together. All the other loves seem frivolous. This is the new great thing, the clue, the inception of a new humanity.

And Natty, what sort of a white man is he? Why, he is a man with a gun. He is a killer, a slayer. Patient and gentle as he is, he is a slayer.
25   Self-effacing, self-forgetting, still he is a killer.

Twice, in the book, he brings an enemy down hurling in death through the air, downwards. Once it is the beautiful, wicked Magua—shot from a height, and hurtling down ghastly through space, into death.

This is Natty, the white forerunner. A killer. As in *Deerslayer* he
30   shoots the bird that flies in the high, high sky,* so that the bird falls out of the invisible into the visible, dead, he symbolises himself. He will bring the bird of the spirit out of the high air. He is the stoic American killer of the old great life. But he kills, as he says, only to live.

Pathfinder takes us to the Great Lakes, and the glamour and beauty
35   of sailing the great sweet waters. Natty is now called Pathfinder. He is about thirty-five years old, and he falls in love. The damsel is Mabel Dunham, daughter of Sergeant Dunham of the Fort garrison. She is blond and in all things admirable. No doubt Mrs Cooper was very much like Mabel.

40   And Pathfinder doesn't marry her. She won't have him. She wisely prefers a more comfortable Jasper.* So Natty goes off to grouch, and

to end by thanking his stars. When he had got right clear, and sat by the camp-fire with Chingachgook, in the forest, didn't he just thank his stars! A lucky escape!

Men of an uncertain age are liable to these infatuations. They aren't always lucky enough to be rejected.

What ever would poor Mabel have done, had she been Mrs Bumppo? Natty had no business marrying. His mission was elsewhere.

The most fascinating Leatherstocking book is the last, *Deerslayer.* Natty is now a fresh youth, called Deerslayer. But the kind of silent prim youth who is never quite young, but reserves himself for different things.

It is a gem of a book. Or a bit of perfect paste.* And myself, I like a bit of perfect paste in a perfect setting, so long as I am not fooled by pretense of reality. And the setting of *Deerslayer could* not be more exquisite. Lake Champlain again.

Of course it never rains: it is never cold and muddy and dreary: no one ever has wet feet or toothache: no one ever feels filthy, when they can't wash for a week. God knows what the women would really have looked like, for they fled through the wilds without soap, comb, or towel. They breakfasted off a chunk of meat, or nothing, lunched the same, and supped the same.

Yet at every moment they are elegant, perfect ladies, in correct toilet.

Which isn't quite fair. You need only go camping for a week, and you'll see.

But it is a myth, not a realistic tale. Read it as a lovely myth. Lake Glimmerglass.

Deerslayer, the youth with the long rifle, is found in the woods with a big, handsome, blond-bearded backwoodsman called Hurry Harry. Deerslayer seems to have been born under a hemlock-tree, out of a pine-cone: a young man of the woods. He is silent, simple, philosophic, moralistic, and an unerring shot. His simplicity is the simplicity of age rather than of youth. He is race-old. All his reactions and impulses are fixed, static. Almost he is sexless, so race-old. Yet intelligent, hardy, dauntless.

Hurry Harry is a big blusterer, just the opposite of Deerslayer. Deerslayer keeps the centre of his own consciousness steady and unperturbed. Hurry Harry is one of those floundering people who bluster from one emotion to another, very self-conscious, without any centre to them.

These two young men are making their way to a lovely, smallish lake, Lake Glimmerglass. On this water the Hutter family has established itself. Old Hutter, it is suggested, has a criminal, coarse, buccaneering

past, and is a sort of fugitive from justice. But he is a good enough father to his two grown-up girls. The family lives in a log hut "castle," built on piles in the water, and the old man has also constructed an "ark," a sort of house-boat, in which he can take his daughters when he goes
5 on his rounds to trap the beaver.

The two girls are the inevitable dark and light. Judith, dark, fearless, passionate, a little lurid with sin, is the scarlet-and-black blossom. Hetty, the younger, blond, frail and innocent, is the white lily again. But alas, the lily has begun to fester. She is slightly imbecile.
10 The two hunters arrive at the lake among the woods just as war has been declared.* The Hutters are unaware of the fact. And hostile Indians are on the lake already. So, the story of thrills and perils.

Thomas Hardy's inevitable division of women into dark and fair, sinful and innocent, sensual and pure,* is Cooper's division too. It is
15 indicative of the desire in the man. He wants sensuality and sin, and he wants purity and "innocence." If the innocence goes a little rotten, slightly imbecile, bad luck!

Hurry Harry, of course, like a handsome impetuous meat-fly, at once wants Judith, the lurid poppy-blossom. Judith rejects him with scorn.
20 Judith, the sensual woman, at once wants the quiet, reserved, un-mastered Deerslayer. She wants to master him. And Deerslayer is half tempted, but never more than half. He is not going to be mastered. A philosophic, old soul, he does not give much for the temptations of sex. Probably he dies virgin.
25 And he is right of it. Rather than be dragged into a false heat of deliberate sensuality, he will remain alone. His soul is alone, forever alone. So he will preserve his integrity, and remain alone in the flesh. It is a stoicism which is honest and fearless, and from which Deerslayer never lapses, except when, approaching middle age, he proposes to the
30 buxom Mabel.

He lets his consciousness penetrate in loneliness into the new continent. His contacts are not human. He wrestles with the spirits of the forest and the American wild, as a hermit wrestles with God and Satan. His one meeting is with Chingachgook, and this meeting is silent,
35 reserved, across an unpassable distance.

Hetty, the White Lily, being imbecile, although full of vaporous religion and the dear, good God "who governs all things by his providence,"* is hopelessly infatuated with Hurry Harry. Being innocence gone imbecile, like Dostoevsky's Idiot,* she longs to give herself to the handsome
40 meat-fly. Of course he doesn't want her.

And so nothing happens: in that direction.—Deerslayer goes off to meet Chingachgook, and help him woo an Indian maid. Vicarious.

It is the miserable story of the collapse of the white psyche. The white man's mind and soul are divided between these two things: innocence and lust, the Spirit and Sensuality. Sensuality always carries a stigma, and is therefore more deeply desired, or lusted after. But spirituality alone gives the sense of uplift, exaltation, and "winged life": with the inevitable reaction into sin and spite. So the white man is divided against himself. He plays off one side of himself against the other side, till it is really a tale told by an idiot,* and nauseating.

Against this, one is forced to admire the stark, enduring figure of Deerslayer. He is neither spiritual nor sensual. He is a moraliser, but he always tries to moralise from actual experience, not from theory. He says: "Hurt nothing unless you're forced to."* Yet he gets his deepest thrill of gratification, perhaps, when he puts a bullet through the heart of a beautiful buck,* as it stoops to drink at the lake. Or when he brings the invisible bird fluttering down in death, out of the high blue. "Hurt nothing unless you're forced to." And yet he lives by death, by killing the wild things of the air and earth.

It's not good enough.

But you have there the myth of the essential white American. All the other stuff, the love, the democracy, the floundering into lust, is a sort of by-play. The essential American soul is hard, isolate, stoic, and a killer. It has never yet melted.

Of course the soul often breaks down into disintegration, and you have lurid sin and Judith, imbecile innocence lusting, in Hetty, and bluster, bragging, and self-conscious strength, in Harry. But these are the disintegration products.

What true myth concerns itself with is not the disintegration product. True myth concerns itself centrally with the onward adventure of the integral soul. And this, for America, is Deerslayer. A man who turns his back on white society. A man who keeps his moral integrity hard and intact. An isolate, almost selfless, stoic enduring man, who lives by death, by killing, but who is pure white.

This is the very intrinsic-most American. He is at the core of all the other flux and fluff. And when *this* man breaks from his static isolation, and makes a new move, then look out, something will be happening.

VI.

Edgar Allan Poe.*

Poe has no truck with Indians or Nature. He makes no bones about Red Brothers and Wigwams.

5   He is absolutely concerned with the disintegration-processes of his own psyche. As we have said, the rhythm of American art-activity is dual:

1. A disintegrating and sloughing of the old consciousness.
2. The forming of a new consciousness underneath.

10   Fenimore Cooper has the two vibrations going on together. Poe has only one, only the disintegrative vibration. This makes him almost more a scientist than an artist.

    Moralists have always wondered helplessly why Poe's "morbid" tales need have been written. They need to be written because old things need to die and disintegrate, because the old white psyche has to be gradually broken down before anything else can come to pass.

    Man must be stripped even of himself. And it is a painful, sometimes a ghastly process.

    Poe had a pretty bitter doom. Doomed to seethe down his soul in
20   a great, continuous convulsion of disintegration, and doomed to register the process. And then doomed to be abused for it, when he had performed some of the bitterest tasks of human experience, that can be asked of a man. Necessary tasks, too. For the human soul must suffer its own disintegration, *consciously*, if ever it is to survive.

25   But Poe is rather a scientist than an artist. He is reducing his own self as a scientist reduces a salt in a crucible. It is an almost chemical analysis of the soul and consciousness. Whereas in true art there is always the double rhythm of creating and destroying.

    This is why Poe calls his things "tales." They are a concatenation of
30   cause and effect.

    His best pieces, however, are not tales. They are more. They are ghastly stories of the human soul in its disruptive throes.

    Moreover, they are "love" stories.

    Ligeia and *The Fall of the House of Usher** are really love stories.

66

Love is the mysterious vital attraction which draws things together, closer, closer together. For this reason sex is the actual crisis of love. For in sex the two blood-systems, in the male and female, concentrate and come into flaming, frictional contact, the merest film intervening. That is coition. Yet if the intervening film breaks down, it is death.

So there you are. There is a limit to everything. There is a limit to love.

The central law of all organic life is that each organism is intrinsically isolate and single in itself.

The moment its isolation breaks down, and there comes an actual mixing and confusion, death sets in.

This is true of every individual organism, from man to amœba.

But the secondary law of all organic life, is that each organism only lives through contact with other matter, assimilation, and contact with other life, which means assimilation of new vibrations, non-material. Each individual organism is vivified by intimate contact with fellow organisms: up to a certain point.

So man. He breathes the air into him, he swallows food and water. But more than this. He takes into him the life of his fellow men, with whom he comes into contact, and he gives back life to them. This contact draws nearer and nearer, as the intimacy increases. When it is a whole contact, we call it love. Men live by food, but die if they eat too much. Men live by love, but die, or cause death, if they love too much.

There are two loves: sacred and profane, spiritual and sensual.

In sensual love, it is the two blood-systems, the man's and the woman's, which sweep up into pure contact, and *almost* fuse. Almost mingle. Never quite. There is always the finest imaginable wall between the two blood-waves, through which pass unknown vibrations, forces, but through which the blood itself must never break, or it means bleeding.

In spiritual love, the contact is purely nervous. The nerves in the lovers are set vibrating in unison like two instruments. The pitch can rise higher and higher. But carry this too far, and the nerves begin to break, to bleed, as it were, and a form of death sets in.

The trouble about man is that he insists on being master of his own fate,* and he insists on *oneness*. For instance, having discovered the ecstasy of spiritual love, he insists that he shall have this all the time, and nothing but this, for this is life. It is what he calls "heightening" life. He wants his nerves to be set vibrating in the intense and exhilarating unison with the nerves of another being, and by this means he acquires an ecstasy of vision, he finds himself in glowing unison with all the universe.

But as a matter of fact this glowing unison is only a temporary thing, because the first law of life is that each organism is isolate in itself, it must return to its own isolation.

Yet man has tried the glow of unison, called love, and he *likes* it. It
5 gives him his highest gratification. He wants it. He wants it all the time. He wants it and he will have it. He doesn't want to return to his own isolation. Or if he must, it is only as a prowling beast returns to its lair to rest and set out again.

This brings us to Edgar Allan Poe. The clue to him lies in the motto
10 he chose for *Ligeia*, a quotation from the mystic Joseph Glanville: "And the will therein lieth, which dieth not. Who knoweth the mysteries of the will, with its vigour? For God is but a great will pervading all things by nature of its intentness. Man doth not yield himself to the angels, nor unto death utterly, save only through the weakness of his feeble will."*
15 It is a profound saying: and a deadly one.

Because if God is a great will, then the universe is but an instrument.

I don't know what God is. But He is not simply a will. That is too simple. Too anthropomorphic. Because a man wants his own will, and nothing but his will, he needn't say that God is the same will, magnified
20 *ad infinitum.*

For me, there may be one god, but he is nameless and unknowable.

For me, there are also many gods, that come into me and leave me again. And they have very various wills, I must say.

But the point is Poe.
25 Poe had experienced the ecstasies of extreme spiritual love. And he wanted those ecstasies and nothing but those ecstasies. He wanted that great gratification, the sense of flowing, the sense of unison, the sense of heightening of life. He had experienced this gratification. He was told on every hand that this ecstasy of spiritual, nervous love was the
30 greatest thing in life, was life itself. And he had tried it for himself, he knew that for him it *was* life itself. So he wanted it. And he *would have* it. He set up his will against the whole of the limitations of nature.

This is a brave man, acting on his own belief, and his own experience. But it is also an arrogant man, and a fool.
35 Poe was going to get the ecstasy and the heightening, cost what it might. He went on in a frenzy, as characteristic American *women* nowadays go on in a frenzy, after the very same thing: the heightening, the flow, the ecstasy. Poe tried alcohol, and any drug he could lay his hand on.* He also tried any human being he could lay his hands on.
40 His grand attempt and achievement was with his wife: his cousin: a girl with a singing voice.* With her he went in for the intensest flow,

the heightening, the prismatic shades of ecstasy. It was the intensest
nervous vibration of unison, pressed higher and higher in pitch, till the
blood-vessels of the girl broke, and the blood began to flow out loose. It
was love. If you call it love.

Love can be terribly obscene.

It is love that causes the neuroticism of the day. It is love that is the
prime cause of tuberculosis.

The nerves that vibrate most intensely in spiritual unisons are the
sympathetic ganglia* of the breast, of the throat, and the hind brain.
Drive this vibration over-intensely, and you weaken the sympathetic
tissues of the chest—the lungs—or of the throat, or of the lower brain,
and the tubercles are given a ripe field.

But Poe drove the vibrations beyond any human pitch of endurance.
Being his cousin, she was more easily keyed to him.

Ligeia is the chief story. Ligeia! A mental-derived name.* To him
the woman, his wife, was not Lucy. She was Ligeia. No doubt she even
preferred it thus.

Ligeia is Poe's love-story, and its very fantasy makes it more truly his
own story.

It is a tale of love pushed over a verge. And love pushed to extremes
is a battle of wills between the lovers.

Love is become a battle of wills.

Which shall first destroy the other, of the lovers? Which can hold out
longest, against the other?

Ligeia is still the old-fashioned woman. Her will is still to submit.
She wills to submit to the vampire of her husband's consciousness. Even
death.

"In stature she was tall, somewhat slender, and, in her later days, even
emaciated. I would in vain attempt to portray the majesty, the quiet ease,
of her demeanour, or the incomprehensible lightness and elasticity of
her footfall. I was never made aware of her entrance into my closed
study save by the dear music of her low, sweet voice as she placed her
marble hand on my shoulder."

Poe has been so praised for his style. But it seems to me a meretricious
affair. "Her marble hand" and "the elasticity of her footfall" seem more
like chair-springs and mantel-pieces than a human creature. She never
was quite a human creature to him. She was an instrument, from which
he got his extremes of sensation. His *machine à plaisir*, as somebody
says.*

All Poe's style, moreover, has this mechanical quality, as his poetry
has a mechanical rhythm. He never sees anything in terms of life, almost

always in terms of matter—jewels, marble, etc.*—or in terms of force, scientific. And his cadences are all managed mechanically. This is what is called "having a style."

What he wants to do with Ligeia is to analyse her, till he knows all
5 her component parts, till he has got her all in his consciousness. She is some strange chemical salt which he must analyse out in the test-tubes of his brain, and then—when he's finished the analysis—*È finita la commedia*!*

But she won't be quite analysed out. There is something, something
10 he can't get. Writing of her eyes, he says: "They were, I must believe, far larger than the ordinary eyes of our race"—as if anybody would want eyes "far larger" than other folks'—"They were even fuller than the fullest of the gazelle eyes of the tribe of Nourjahad— — —" Which is blarney. "The hue of the orbs was the most brilliant of black, and,
15 far over them, hung jetty lashes of great length"—suggests a whip-lash.—"The brows, slightly irregular in outline, had the same tint. The *strangeness*, however, which I found in the eyes was of a nature distinct from the formation, or the colour, or the brilliancy of the features, and must, after all, be referred to the *expression*."—Sounds like an anatomist
20 anatomising a cat.— "Ah, word of no meaning! behind whose vast latitude of sound we intrench our ignorance of so much of the spiritual. The expression of the eyes of Ligeia! How for long hours have I pondered upon it! How have I, through the whole of a midsummer night, struggled to fathom it! What was it—that something more profound
25 than the well of Democritus—which lay far within the pupils of my beloved? What *was* it? I was possessed with a passion to discover. . . . "*

It is easy to see why each man kills the thing he loves.* To *know* a living thing is to kill it. You have to kill a thing to know it satisfactorily. For this reason, the desirous consciousness, the S P I R I T, is a vampire.
30 One should be sufficiently intelligent and interested to know a good deal *about* any person one comes into close contact with. *About* her. Or *about* him.

But to try to *know* any living being is to try to suck the life out of that being.
35 Above all things, with the woman one loves. Every sacred instinct teaches one that one must leave her unknown. You know your woman darkly, in the blood, through the act of coition. To try to *know* her mentally is to try to kill her. Beware, oh woman, of the man who wants to *find out what you are*. And oh men, beware a thousand times more of
40 the woman who wants to *know* you, to *get* you, what you are.

It is the temptation of a vampire fiend, is this Knowledge.

Man does so horribly want to master the secret of life and of individuality *with his mind*. It is like the analysis of protoplasm. You can only analyse *dead* protoplasm, and know its constituents. It is a death process.

Keep KNOWLEDGE for the world of matter, force, and function. It has got nothing to do with being.

But Poe wanted to know—wanted to know what was the strangeness in the eyes of Ligeia. She might have told him it was horror at his probing, horror at being vamped* by his consciousness.

But she wanted to be vamped. She wanted to be probed by his consciousness, to be KNOWN. She paid for wanting it, too.

Nowadays it is usually the man who wants to be vamped, to be KNOWN.

Edgar Allan probed and probed. So often he seemed on the verge. But she went over the verge of death before he came over the verge of knowledge. And it is always so.

He decided, therefore, that the clue to the strangeness lay in the mystery of will. "And the will therein lieth, which dieth not . . ."

Ligeia had a "gigantic volition." . . . "An intensity in thought, action, or speech was possibly, in her, a result, or at least an index" (he really meant indication)* "of that gigantic volition which, during our long intercourse, failed to give other and more immediate evidence of its existence."

I should have thought her long submission to him was chief and ample "other evidence."

"Of all the women whom I have ever known, she, the outwardly calm, the ever-placid Ligeia, was the most violently a prey to the tumultuous vultures of stern passion. And of such passion I could form no estimate, save by the miraculous expansion of those eyes which at once so delighted and appalled me—by the almost magical melody, modulation, distinctness, and placidity of her very low voice—and by the fierce energy (rendered doubly effective by contrast with her manner of utterance) of the wild words which she habitually uttered."

Poor Poe, he had caught a bird of the same feather as himself. One of those terrible cravers, who crave the further sensation. Crave to madness or death. "Vultures of stern passion" indeed! Condors!*

But having recognised that the clue was in her gigantic volition, he should have realised that the process of this loving, this craving, this knowing, was a struggle of wills. But Ligeia, true to the great tradition and mode of womanly love, by her will kept herself submissive, recipient. She is the passive body who is explored and analysed into death. And yet, at times, her great female will must have revolted. "Vultures of stern passion!" With a convulsion of desire she desired his further probing 5 and exploring. To any lengths. But then "tumultuous vultures of stern passion." She had to fight with herself.

But Ligeia wanted to go on and on with the craving, with the love, with the sensation, with the probing, with the knowing, on and on to the end.

10 There is no end. There is only the rupture of death. That's where men, and women, are "had."* Man is always sold, in his search for final KNOWLEDGE.

"That she loved me I should not have doubted; and I might have been easily aware that, in a bosom such as hers, love would have reigned 15 no ordinary passion. But in death only was I fully impressed with the strength of her affection. For long hours, detaining my hand, would she pour out before me the overflowing of a heart whose more than passionate devotion amounted to idolatry." (Oh the indecency of all this endless intimate talk!) "How had I deserved to be blessed by such 20 confessions?" (Another man would have felt himself cursed). "How had I deserved to be cursed with the removal of my beloved in the hour of her making them? But upon this subject I cannot bear to dilate. Let me say only that in Ligeia's more than womanly abandonment to a love, alas! unmerited, all unworthily bestowed, I at length recognised the principle 25 of her longing with so wildly earnest a desire for the life which was now fleeing so rapidly away. It is this wild longing—it is this vehement desire for life—*but* for life—that I have no power to portray—no utterance capable of expressing."

Well, that is ghastly enough, in all conscience.

30 "And from them that have not shall be taken away even that which they have."

"To him that have life shall be given life, and from him that hath not life shall be taken away even that life which he hath."*

Or her either.

35 These terribly conscious birds like Poe and his Ligeia deny the very life that is in them, they want to turn it all into talk, into *knowing*. And so life, which will *not* be known, leaves them.

But poor Ligeia, how could she help it. It was her doom. All the centuries of the SPIRIT, all the years of American rebellion against 40 the Holy Ghost, had done it to her.

She dies, when she would rather do anything than die. And when she dies the clue, which he only lived to grasp, dies with her.

Foiled!

Fooled!

No wonder she shrieks with her last breath.

On the last day Ligeia dictates to her husband a poem. As poems go, it is rather false, meretricious. But put yourself in Ligeia's place, and it is real enough, and ghastly beyond bearing.

> "Out, out are all the lights—out all!
> And over each quivering form
> The curtain, a funeral pall,
> Comes down with the rush of a storm,
> And the angels, all pallid and wan,
> Uprising, unveiling, affirm
> That the play is the tragedy 'Man,'
> And its hero the Conqueror Worm."

Which is the American equivalent for a William Blake poem.* For Blake too was one of these ghastly, obscene "knowers."

" 'Oh God!' half shrieked Ligeia, leaping to her feet and extending her arms aloft with a spasmodic movement, as I made an end of these lines. 'O God! O Divine Father!—shall these things be undeviatingly so? Shall this Conqueror be not once conquered? Are we not part and parcel in Thee? Who—who knoweth the mysteries of the will and its vigour? Man doth not yield him to the angels, *nor unto death utterly*, save only through the weakness of his feeble will.' "

So Ligeia dies. And yields to death at least partly. Anche troppo.*

As for her cry to God—has not God said that those who sin against the Holy Ghost shall not be forgiven?*

And the Holy Ghost is within us. It is the thing that prompts us to be real, not to push our own cravings too far, not to submit to stunts and high falutin, above all not to be too egoistic and wilful in our conscious self, but to change as the spirit inside us bids us change, and leave off when it bids us leave off, and laugh when we must laugh, particularly at ourselves, for in deadly earnestness there is always something a bit ridiculous. The Holy Ghost bids us never be too deadly in our earnestness, always to laugh in time, at ourselves and everything. Particularly at our sublimities. Everything has its hour of ridicule—everything.

Now Poe and Ligeia, alas, couldn't laugh. They were frenziedly earnest. And frenziedly they pushed on this vibration of consciousness and unison in consciousness. They sinned against the Holy Ghost that bids us all laugh and forget, bids us know our own limits. And they weren't forgiven.

Ligeia needn't blame God. She had only her own will, her "gigantic
5   volition" to thank, lusting after more consciousness, more beastly KNOWING.

Ligeia dies. The husband goes to England,* vulgarly buys or rents a gloomy, grand old abbey, puts it into some sort of repair, and furnishes it with exotic, mysterious, theatrical splendour. Never anything open and
10 real. This theatrical "volition" of his. The bad taste of sensationalism.

Then he marries the fair-haired, blue-eyed Lady Rowena Trevanion, of Tremaine.* That is, she would be a sort of Saxon-Cornish blue-blood damsel. Poor Poe!

"In halls such as these—in a bridal chamber such as this—I passed,
15 with the Lady of Tremaine, the unhallowed hours of the first month of our marriage—passed them with but little disquietude. That my wife dreaded the fierce moodiness of my temper—that she shunned me and loved me but little—I could not help perceiving, but it gave me rather pleasure than otherwise. I loathed her with a hatred belonging rather to
20 a demon than a man. My memory flew back (Oh, with what intensity of regret!) to Ligeia, the beloved, the august, the entombed. I revelled in recollections of her purity.—" etc.

Now the vampire lust is consciously such.

In the second month of the marriage the Lady Rowena fell ill. It is
25 the shadow of Ligeia hangs over her. It is the ghostly Ligeia who pours poison into Rowena's cup.* It is the spirit of Ligeia, leagued with the spirit of the husband, that now lusts in the slow destruction of Rowena. The two vampires, dead wife and living husband.

For Ligeia has not yielded unto death *utterly*. Her fixed, frustrated
30 will comes back in vindictiveness. She could not have her way in life. So she too will find victims in life. And the husband, all the time, only uses Rowena as a living body on which to wreak his vengeance for his being thwarted with Ligeia. Thwarted from the final KNOWING her.

35 And at last from the corpse of Rowena Ligeia rises. Out of her death, through the door of a corpse they have destroyed between them, re-appears Ligeia, still trying to have her will, to have more love and knowledge, the final gratification which is never final, with her husband.

For it is true, as William James and Conan Doyle and the rest* allow,
40 that a spirit can persist in the after-death. Persist by its own volition. But

usually, the evil persistence of a thwarted will, returning for vengeance on life. Lemures,* vampires.

It is a ghastly story of the assertion of the human will, the will-to-love and the will-to-consciousness, asserted against death itself. The pride of human conceit in KNOWLEDGE.

There are terrible spirits, ghosts, in the air of America.

Eleonora, the next story, is a fantasy revealing the sensational delights of the man in his early marriage with the young and tender bride. They dwelt, he, his cousin and her mother, in the sequestered Valley of Many-coloured Grass, the valley of prismatic sensation, where everything seems spectrum-coloured. They looked down at their *own images* in the River of Silence, and drew the god Eros* from that wave: out of their own self-consciousness, that is. This is a description of the life of introspection and of the love which is begotten by the self in the self, the self-made love. The trees are like serpents worshipping the sun. That is, they represent the phallic passion in its poisonous or mental activity. Everything runs to consciousness: serpents worshipping the sun. Coition, which should bring darkness and oblivion, would with these lovers be a daytime thing bringing more heightened consciousness, visions, spectrum-visions, prismatic. The evil thing that daytime sex-intercourse is, and daytime sex-palaver.

In *Berenice* the man must go down to the sepulchre of his beloved and pull out her thirty-two small white teeth, which he carries in a box with him. It is repulsive and gloating. The teeth are the instruments of biting, of resistance, of antagonism. They often become symbols of opposition, little instruments or entities of crushing and destroying. Hence the dragon's teeth in the myth. Hence the man in *Berenice* must take possession of the irreducible part of his mistress. "Toutes ses dents étaient des idées," he says. Then they are little fixed ideas of mordant hate, of which he possesses himself.

The other great story linking up with this group is *The Fall of the House of Usher*. Here the love is between brother and sister. When the self is broken, and the mystery of the recognition of *otherness* fails, then the longing for identification with the beloved becomes a lust. And it is this longing for identification, utter merging, which is at the base of the incest problem. In psychoanalysis almost every trouble in the psyche is traced to an incest-desire.* But it won't do. Incest-desire is only one of the modes by which men strive to get their gratification of the intensest vibration of the spiritual nerves, without any resistance. In the family, the natural vibration is most nearly in unison. With a stranger, there is greater resistance. Incest is the getting of gratification and the avoiding of resistance.

The root of all evil* is that we all want this spiritual gratification, this flow, this apparent heightening of life, this knowledge, this valley of
5   many-coloured grass, even grass and light prismatically decomposed, giving ecstasy.* We want all this *without resistance*. We want it continually. And this is the root of all evil in us.

We ought to pray to be resisted and resisted to the bitter end. We ought to decide to have done at last with craving.
10   The motto to *The Fall of the House of Usher* is a couple of lines from Béranger.

> "Son cœur est un luth suspendu;
> Sitôt qu'on le touche il résonne."*

We have all the trappings of Poe's rather overdone, vulgar fantasy.
15 "I reined my horse to the precipitous brink of a black and lurid tarn that lay in unruffled lustre by the dwelling, and gazed down—but with a shudder even more thrilling than before—upon the remodelled and inverted images of the grey sedge, and the ghastly tree-stems, and the vacant and eye-like windows." The House of Usher, both dwelling and
20 family, was very old. Minute fungi overspread the exterior of the house, hanging in festoons from the eaves. Gothic archways, a valet of stealthy step, sombre tapestries, ebon black floors, a profusion of tattered and antique furniture, feeble gleams of encrimsoned light through latticed panes, and over all "an air of stern, deep, irredeemable gloom"—this
25 makes up the interior.

The inmates of the house, Roderick and Madeline Usher, are the last remnants of their incomparably ancient and decayed race. Roderick has the same large, luminous eye, the same slightly arched nose of delicate Hebrew model, as characterised Ligeia. He is ill with the nervous malady
30 of his family. It is he whose nerves are so strung that they vibrate to the unknown quiverings of the ether. He, too, has lost his self, his living soul, and become a sensitised instrument of the external influences; his nerves are verily like an æolian harp which must vibrate. He lives in "some struggle with the grim phantasm, Fear," for he is only the
35 physical, post-mortem reality of a living being.

It is a question how much, once the true centrality of the self is broken, the instrumental consciousness of man can register. When man becomes self-less, wafting instrumental like a harp in an open window,* how much can his elemental consciousness express? The blood as it runs has its own sympathies and responses to the material world, quite apart from seeing. And the nerves we know vibrate all the while to unseen presences, unseen forces. So Roderick Usher quivers on the edge of material existence.

It is this mechanical consciousness which gives "the fervid facility of 5 his impromptus." It is the same thing that gives Poe his extraordinary facility in versification. The absence of real central or impulsive being in himself leaves him inordinately mechanically sensitive to sounds and effects, associations of sounds, associations of rhyme, for example— mechanical, facile, having no root in any passion. It is all a secondary, 10 meretricious process. So we get Roderick Usher's poem, *The Haunted Palace*, with its swift yet mechanical subtleties of rhyme and rhythm, its vulgarity of epithet. It is all a sort of dream-process, where the association between parts is mechanical, accidental as far as passional meaning goes. 15

Usher thought that all vegetable things had sentience. Surely all material things have a *form* of sentience, even the inorganic: surely they all exist in some subtle and complicated tension of vibration which makes them sensitive to external influence and causes them to have an influence on other external objects, irrespective of contact. It is of this vibration 20 or inorganic consciousness that Poe is master: the sleep-consciousness. Thus Roderick Usher was convinced that his whole surroundings, the stones of the house, the fungi, the water in the tarn, the very reflected image of the whole, was woven into a physical oneness with the family, condensed, as it were, into one atmosphere—the special atmosphere in 25 which alone the Ushers could live. And it was this atmosphere which had moulded the destinies of his family.

But while ever the soul remains alive, it is the moulder and not the moulded. It is the souls of living men that subtly impregnate stones, houses, mountains, continents, and give these their subtlest form. People 30 only become subject to stones after having lost their integral souls.

In the human realm, Roderick had one connection: his sister Madeline. She, too, was dying of a mysterious disorder, nervous, cataleptic.* The brother and sister loved each other passionately and exclusively. They were twins,* almost identical in looks. It was the same absorb- 35 ing love between them, this process of unison in nerve-vibration, resulting in more and more extreme exaltation and a sort of consciousness, and a gradual break-down into death. The exquisitely sensitive Roger,* vibrating without resistance with his sister Madeline, more and more exquisitely, and gradually devouring her, sucking her life 40 like a vampire in this anguish of extreme love. And she asking to be sucked.

Madeline died and was carried down by her brother into the deep vaults of the house. But she was not dead. Her brother roamed about in
5 incipient madness—a madness of unspeakable terror and guilt.* After eight days they were suddenly startled by a clash of metal, then a distinct, hollow, metallic, and clangorous, yet apparently muffled, reverberation. Then Roderick Usher, gibbering, began to express himself: *"We have put her living into the tomb!* Said I not that my senses were acute? I *now*
10 tell you that I heard her first feeble movements in the hollow coffin. I heard them—many, many days ago—yet I dared not—*I dared not speak."*

It is the same old theme of "each man kills the thing he loves." He knew his love had killed her. He knew she died at last, like Ligeia,
15 unwilling and unappeased. So, she rose again upon him. "But then without those doors there *did* stand the lofty and enshrouded figure of the Lady Madeline of Usher. There was blood upon her white robes, and the evidence of some bitter struggle upon every portion of her emaciated frame. For a moment she remained trembling and reeling to
20 and fro upon the threshold, then, with a low moaning cry, fell heavily inward upon the person of her brother, and in her violent and now final death-agonies bore him to the floor a corpse, and a victim to the terrors he had anticipated."

It is lurid and melodramatic, but it is true. It is a ghastly psychological
25 truth of what happens in the last stages of this beloved love, which cannot be separate, cannot be isolate, cannot listen in isolation to the isolate Holy Ghost. For it is the Holy Ghost we must live by. The next era is the era of the Holy Ghost. And the Holy Ghost speaks individually inside each individual: always, forever a Ghost. There is no manifestation to
30 the general world. Each isolate individual listening in isolation to the Holy Ghost within him.

The Ushers, brother and sister, betrayed the Holy Ghost in themselves. They would love, love, love, without resistance. They would love, they would merge,* they would be as one thing. So they dragged each
35 other down into death. For the Holy Ghost says you must *not* be as one thing with another being. Each must abide by itself, and correspond only within certain limits.

The best tales all have the same burden. Hate is as inordinate as love, and as slowly consuming, as secret, as underground, as subtle. All this
40 underground vault business in Poe only symbolises that which takes

place *beneath* the consciousness. On top, all is fair-spoken. Beneath, there is the awful murderous extremity of burying alive. Fortunato, in *The Cask of Amontillado*, is buried alive out of perfect hatred,* as the Lady Madeline of Usher is buried alive out of love. The lust of hate is the inordinate desire to consume and unspeakably possess the soul   5
of the hated one, just as the lust of love is the desire to possess, or to be possessed by, the beloved, utterly. But in either case the result is the dissolution of both souls, each losing itself in transgressing its own bounds.

The lust of Montresor is to devour utterly the soul of Fortunato. It   10
would be no use killing him outright. If a man is killed outright his soul remains integral, free to return into the bosom of some beloved, where it can enact itself. In walling-up his enemy in the vault, Montresor seeks to bring about the indescribable capitulation of the man's soul, so that he, the victor, can possess himself of the very being of the vanquished.   15
Perhaps this can actually be done. Perhaps, in the attempt, the victor breaks the bounds of his own identity, and collapses into nothingness, or into the infinite. Becomes a monster.

What holds good for inordinate hate holds good for inordinate love. The motto, *Nemo me impune lacessit*, might just as well be *Nemo me*   20
impune amat.*

In *William Wilson* we are given a rather unsubtle account of the attempt of a man to kill his own soul. William Wilson, the mechanical, lustful ego succeeds in killing William Wilson, the living self. The lustful ego lives on, gradually reducing itself towards the dust of the infinite.   25

In the *Murders in the Rue Morgue* and *The Gold Bug* we have those mechanical tales where the interest lies in following out a subtle chain of cause and effect. The interest is scientific rather than artistic, a study in psychologic reactions.

The fascination of murder itself is curious. Murder is not just killing.   30
Murder is a lust to get at the very quick of life itself, and kill it—hence the stealth and the frequent morbid dismemberment of the corpse, the attempt to get at the very quick of the murdered being, to find the quick and to possess it. It is curious that the two men fascinated by the art of murder, though in different ways, should have been De Quincey* and   35
Poe, men so different in ways of life, yet perhaps not so widely different in nature. In each of them is traceable that strange lust for extreme love and extreme hate, possession by mystic violence of the other soul, or violent deathly surrender of the soul in the self: an absence of manly virtue, which stands alone and accepts limits.   40

Inquisition and torture are akin to murder: the same lust. It is a
combat between inquisitor and victim as to whether the inquisitor shall
get at the quick of life itself, and pierce it. Pierce the very quick of
the soul. The evil will of man tries to do this. The brave soul of man
5   refuses to have the life-quick pierced in him. It is strange: but just as
the thwarted will can persist evilly, after death, so can the brave spirit
preserve, even through torture and death, the quick of life and truth.
Nowadays society is evil. It finds subtle ways of torture, to destroy the
life-quick, to get at the life-quick in a man. Every possible form. And
10 still a man can hold out, if he can laugh and listen to the Holy Ghost.—
But society is evil, evil. And Love is evil. And evil breeds evil, more and
more.

So the mystery goes on. La Bruyère says that all our human unhappinesses *viennent de ne pouvoir être seuls.** As long as man lives he will
15 be subject to the yearning of love or the burning of hate, which is only
inverted love.

But he is subject to something more than this. If we do not live to
eat,* we do not live to love either.

We live to stand alone, and listen to the Holy Ghost. The Holy Ghost,
20 who is inside us, and who is many gods. Many gods come and go, some
say one thing and some say another, and we have to obey the God of
the innermost hour. It is the multiplicity of gods within us make up the
Holy Ghost.

But Poe knew only love, love, love, intense vibrations and heightened
25 consciousness. Drugs, women, self-destruction, but anyhow the prismatic ecstasy of heightened consciousness and sense of love, of flow.
The human soul in him was beside itself. But it was not lost. He told us
plainly how it was, so that we should know.

He was an adventurer into vaults and cellars and horrible under-
30 ground passages of the human soul. He sounded the horror and the
warning of his own doom.

Doomed he was. He died wanting more love, and love killed him.* A
ghastly disease, love. Poe telling us of his disease: trying even to make
his disease fair and attractive. Even succeeding.
35 Which is the inevitable falseness, duplicity of art, American art in
particular.

VII.

Nathaniel Hawthorne and
*The Scarlet Letter.**

Nathaniel Hawthorne writes romance.

And what's romance? Usually, a nice little tale where you have every-   5
thing As You Like It, where rain never wets your jacket and gnats never
bite your nose and it's always daisy-time. *As You Like It* and *Forest
Lovers*, etc. *Morte D'Arthur.**

Hawthorne obviously isn't this kind of romanticist: though nobody
has muddy boots in the *Scarlet Letter,* either.   10

But there is more to it. *The Scarlet Letter* isn't a pleasant, pretty
romance. It is a sort of parable, an earthly story with a hellish meaning.*

All the time there is this split in the American art and art-conscious-
ness. On the top it is as nice as pie, goody-goody and lovey-dovey. Like
Hawthorne being such a blue-eyed darling, in life, and Longfellow* and   15
the rest such sucking doves. Hawthorne's wife said she "never saw him
in time." Which doesn't mean she saw him too late. But always in the
"frail effulgence of eternity."*

Serpents they were. Look at the inner meaning of their art and see
what demons they were.   20

You *must* look through the surface of American art, and see the inner
diabolism of the symbolic meaning. Otherwise it is all mere childishness.

That blue-eyed darling Nathaniel knew disagreeable things in his
inner soul. He was careful to send them out in disguise.

Always the same. The deliberate consciousness of Americans so fair   25
and smooth-spoken, and the under-consciousness so devilish. *Destroy!
destroy! destroy!* hums the under-consciousness. *Love and produce! Love
and produce!* cackles the upper consciousness. And the world hears only
the Love-and-produce cackle. Refuses to hear the hum of destruction
underneath. Until such time as it will *have* to hear.   30

The American has got to destroy. It is his destiny. It is his destiny to
destroy the whole corpus of the white psyche, the white consciousness.
And he's got to do it secretly. As the growing of a dragon-fly inside a
chrysalis or cocoon destroys the larva grub, secretly.

81

Though many a dragon-fly never gets out of the chrysalis case; dies inside. As America might.

So the secret chrysalis of the *Scarlet Letter*, diabolically destroying the old psyche inside.

5 *Be good! Be good!* warbles Nathaniel. *Be good, and never sin! Be sure your sins will find you out.*

So convincingly that his wife never saw him "as in time."

Then listen to the diabolic undertone of *The Scarlet Letter*.

Man ate of the tree of Knowledge, and became ashamed of himself.

10 Do you imagine Adam had never had intercourse with Eve before that apple episode? Many a time. As a wild animal with his mate.

It didn't become "sin" till the Knowledge-poison entered. That apple of Sodom.

We are divided in ourselves, against ourselves. And that is the meaning of the Cross symbol.*

15 In the first place, Adam knew Eve as a wild animal knows its mate, momentaneously, but vitally, in blood knowledge. Blood-knowledge, not mind knowledge. Blood knowledge, that seems utterly to forget, but doesn't. Blood knowledge, instinct, intuition, all the vast vital flux of knowing that goes on in the dark, antecedent to the mind.

20 Then came that beastly apple, and the other sort of knowledge started. Adam began to look at himself. "My hat!" he said. "What's this appendage? My Lord, just look at it behaving! What the deuce!—I wonder what Eve has got to match."

25 Thus starts KNOWING. Which shortly runs to UNDERSTANDING, when the devil gets his own.

When Adam went and took Eve, *after* the apple, he didn't do any more than he had done many a time before, in act. But in consciousness he did something very different. So did Eve. Each of them kept an eye on what they were doing, they watched what was happening to them. They wanted to KNOW. And that was the birth of sin. Not *doing* it, but KNOWING about it. Before the apple, they had shut their eyes and their minds had gone dark. Now, they peeped and pryed and imagined. They watched themselves in the act. And they felt uncomfortable after. They felt self-conscious. So they said "The *act* is sin. Let's hide, we've sinned."

No wonder the Lord kicked them out of the Garden. Dirty hypocrites.

40 The sin was the self-watching self-consciousness. The sin, and the doom. Dirty UNDERSTANDING.

Nowadays men do hate the idea of dualism. It's no good, dual we are. The Cross. If we accept the symbol, then, virtually, we accept the fact. We are divided against ourselves.

For instance, the blood *hates* being KNOWN by the mind. It feels itself destroyed when it is KNOWN. Hence the profound instinct of privacy.

And on the other hand, the mind and the spiritual consciousness of man simply *hates* the dark potency of blood-acts: hates the genuine dark sensual orgasms, which do, for the time being, actually obliterate the mind and the spiritual consciousness, plunge them in a suffocating flood of darkness.

You can't get away from this.

Blood-consciousness overwhelms, obliterates, and annuls mind-consciousness.

Mind-consciousness extinguishes blood-consciousness, and consumes the blood.

We are all of us conscious in both ways. And the two ways are antagonistic in us.

They will always remain so.

That is our cross.

The antagonism is so obvious, and so far-reaching, that it extends to the smallest thing. The cultured, highly-conscious person of today *loathes* any form of physical, "menial" work: such as washing dishes or sweeping a floor or chopping wood. This menial work is an insult to the spirit. "When I see men carrying heavy loads, doing brutal work, it always makes me want to cry," said a beautiful, cultured woman to me.

"When you say that, it makes me want to beat you," said I in reply. "When I see you with your beautiful head pondering heavy thoughts, I just want to hit you. It outrages me."*

My father hated books, hated the sight of anyone reading or writing.

My mother hated the thought that any of her sons should be condemned to manual labour. Her sons must have something higher than that.

She won. But she died first.*

He laughs longest who laughs last.

There is a basic hostility in all of us between the physical and the mental, the blood and the spirit. The mind is "ashamed" of the blood: as the act of coition. And the blood is destroyed by the mind, actually. Hence pale-faces.

At present the mind-consciousness and the so-called spirit triumphs. In America supremely. In America, nobody does anything from the blood. Always from the nerves, if not from the mind. The blood is chemically reduced by the nerves, in American activity.

When an Italian laborer labours, his mind and nerves sleep, his blood acts, ponderously.

5 Americans, when they are *doing* things, never seem really to be doing them. They are "busy about" it. They are always busy "about" something. But truly *immersed* in *doing* something, with the deep blood-consciousness active, that they never are.

They *admire* the blood-conscious spontaneity. And they want to get 10 it in their heads. "Live from the body," they shriek. It is their last mental shriek. *Co-ordinate!* *

It is a further attempt still to rationalise the body and the blood. "Think about such and such a muscle," they say, "and relax there." And every time you "conquer" the body with the mind (you can say 15 "heal" it, if you like) you cause a deeper, more dangerous complex or tension somewhere else.

Ghastly Americans, with their blood no longer blood. A yellow spiritual fluid.

The Fall!

20 There have been lots of Falls.

We *fell* into *knowledge* when Eve bit the apple. Self-conscious knowledge. For the first time the mind put up a fight against the blood. Wanting to UNDERSTAND. That is to intellectualise the blood.

25 The blood must be *shed*, says Jesus.*

Shed on the cross of our own divided psyche.

Shed the blood, and you become mind-conscious. Eat the body and drink the blood, self-cannibalising, and you become extremely extremely conscious, like Americans and some Hindus. Devour your- 30 self, and God knows what a lot you'll know, what a lot you'll be conscious of.

Mind you don't choke yourself.

For a long time men *believed* that they could be perfected through the mind, through the spirit. They believed, passionately. They had their 35 ecstasy in pure consciousness. They *believed* in purity, chastity, and the wings of the spirit.

America soon plucked the bird of the spirit. America soon killed the *belief* in the spirit. But not the practice. The practice continued with a sarcastic vehemence. America, with a perfect inner contempt for the 40 spirit and the consciousness of man, practises the same spirituality and universal love and KNOWING all the time, incessantly, like a drug

habit. And inwardly gives not a fig for it. Only for the *sensation*. The pretty-pretty *sensation* of love, loving all the world. And the nice fluttery aeroplane *sensation** of knowing, knowing, knowing. Then the prettiest of all sensations, the sensation of UNDERSTANDING. Oh, what a lot they understand, the darlings! *So* good at the trick, they are, Just   5
a trick of self-conceit.

The Scarlet Letter *gives the show away.*

You have your pure-pure young parson Dimmesdale.

You have the beautiful Puritan Hester at his feet.

And the first thing she does is to seduce him.*   10

And the *first* thing he does is to be seduced.

And the second thing they do is to hug their sin in secret, and gloat over it, and try to understand.

Which is the myth of New England.

Deerslayer refused to be seduced by Judith Hutter. At least the Sodom   15
apple of Sin didn't fetch him.

But Dimmesdale was seduced gloatingly. Oh luscious Sin!

He was such a pure young man.

That he had to make a fool of purity.

The American psyche.   20

Of course the best part of the game lay in keeping up pure appearances.

The greatest triumph a woman can have, especially an American woman, is the triumph of seducing a man: especially if he is pure.

And he gets the greatest thrill of all, in falling.—"Seduce me,   25
Mrs Hercules."*

And the pair of them share the subtlest delight in keeping up pure appearances, when everybody knows all the while. But the power of pure appearances is something to exult in. All America gives in to it. *Look* pure!   30

To seduce a man. To have everybody know. To keep up appearances of purity. Pure!

This is the great triumph of woman.

A. The Scarlet Letter. Adulteress! The great Alpha. Alpha! Adulteress! The new Adam and Adama!* American!   35

A. Adulteress! Stitched with gold thread, glittering upon the bosom. The proudest insignia.

Put her upon the scaffold* and worship her there. Worship her there. The Woman, the Magna Mater. A. Adulteress! Abel!*

Abel! Abel! Able! Admirable!*   40

It becomes a farce.

The fiery heart. A. Mary of the Bleeding Heart. Mater Adolorata!*
A. Capital A. Adulteress. Glittering with gold thread. Abel! Adultery.
Admirable!

It is perhaps the most colossal satire ever penned, The Scarlet Letter.
5   And by a blue-eyed darling of a Nathaniel.

Not Bumppo, however.

The human spirit, fixed in a lie, adhering to a lie, giving itself perpetually the lie.

All begins with A.

10   Adultress. Alpha. Abel. Adam. A. America.

The Scarlet Letter.

"Had there been a Papist among the crowd of Puritans, he might have seen in this beautiful woman, so picturesque in her attire and mien, and with the infant at her bosom, an object to remind him of the image of
15   Divine Maternity, which so many illustrious painters have vied with one another to represent; something which should remind him, indeed, but only by contrast, of that sacred image of Sinless Motherhood, whose infant was to redeem the world."

Whose infant was to redeem the world indeed! It will be a startling
20   redemption the world will get from the American infant.

"Here was a taint of deepest sin in the most sacred quality of human life, working such effect, that the world was only the darker for this woman's beauty, and more lost for the infant she had borne."

Just listen to the darling. Isn't he a master of apology?
25   Of symbols too.

His pious blame is a chuckle of praise all the while.

Oh Hester, you are a demon. A man *must* be pure, just that you can seduce him to a fall. Because the greatest thrill in life is to bring down the sacred saint with a flop into the mud. Then when you've
30   brought him down, humbly wipe off the mud with your hair, another Magdalen.* And then go home and dance a witches jig of triumph, and stitch yourself a Scarlet Letter with gold thread, as duchesses used to stitch themselves coronets.* And then stand meek on the scaffold and fool the world. Who will all be envying you your sin, and beating you
35   because you've stolen an advantage over them.

Hester Prynne is the great nemesis of woman. She is the KNOWING Ligeia risen diabolic from the grave. Having her own back. UNDERSTANDING.

This time it is Mr Dimmesdale who dies. She lives on and is Abel.

His spiritual love was a lie. And prostituting the woman to his spiritual love, as popular clergymen do, in his preachings and loftiness, was a tall white lie. Which came flop.
We are so pure in spirit. Hi-tiddly-i-ty!
Till she tickled him in the right place, and he fell.   5
Flop.
Flop goes spiritual love.
But keep up the game. Keep up appearances. Pure are the pure. To the pure all things etc.*
Look out, Mister, for the Female Devotee. Whatever you do, don't let   10
her start tickling you. She knows your weak spot. Mind your Purity.
When Hester Prynne seduced Arthur Dimmesdale it was the beginning of the end. But from the beginning of the end to the end of the end is a hundred years or two.   15
Mr Dimmesdale also wasn't at the end of his resources. Previously, he had lived by governing his body, ruling it, in the interests of his spirit. Now he has a good time all by himself torturing his body, whipping it, piercing it with thorns, macerating himself.* It's a form of masturbation. He wants to get a mental grip on his body. And since he can't quite   20
manage it with the mind,—witness his fall—he will give it what for,* with whips. His will shall *lash* his body. And he enjoys his pains. Wallows in them. To the pure all things are pure.
It is the old self-mutilation process, gone rotten. The mind wanting to set its teeth in the blood and flesh. The ego exulting in the tortures of   25
the mutinous flesh. I, the ego, I *will* triumph over my own flesh. Lash! Lash! I am a grand free spirit *Lash!* I am the master of my soul! *Lash!* *Lash!* I am the Captain of my soul. *Lash!* Hurray! "In the fell clutch of circumstance," etc., etc.*
Goodbye Arthur. He depended on women for his Spiritual Devotees,   30
spiritual brides. So the woman just touched him in his weak spot, his Achilles Heel* of the flesh. Look out for the spiritual bride. She's after the weak spot.
It is the battle of wills.
"For the will therein lieth, which dieth not— —" *   35
The Scarlet Woman becomes a Sister of Mercy. Didn't she just, in the late war.* Oh prophet Nathaniel!
Hester urges Dimmesdale to go away with her, to a new country, to a new life. He isn't having any.*

He knows there is no new country, no new life on the globe today. It is the same old thing, in different degrees, everywhere. *Plus ça change, plus c'est la même chose.**

Hester thinks, with Dimmesdale for her husband, and Pearl for her 5 child, in Australia, maybe, she'd have been perfect.

But she wouldn't. Dimmesdale had already fallen from his integrity as a minister of the Gospel of the Spirit. He had lost his manliness. He didn't see the point of just leaving himself between the hands of a woman, and going away to a "new country," to be her thing entirely. 10 She'd only have despised him more, as every woman despises a man who has "fallen" to her: despises him with her tenderest lust.

He stood for nothing any more. So let him stay where he was and dree out his weird.*

She had dished him and his spirituality, so he hated her. As Angel 15 Clare was dished, and hated Tess. As Jude in the end hated Sue:* or should have done. The women make fools of them, the spiritual men. And when, as men, they've gone flop in their spirituality, they can't pick themselves up whole any more. So they just crawl, and die detesting the female, or the females who made them fall.

20   The saintly minister gets a bit of his own back, at the last minute, by making public confession from the very scaffold where she was exposed. Then he dodges into death. But he's had a bit of his own back, on everybody.

' "Shall we not meet again?" whispered she, bending her face down 25 close to him. "Shall we not spend our immortal life together? Surely, surely we have ransomed one another, with all this woe! Thou looked far into eternity with those bright dying eyes. Then tell me what thou seest!" '

' "Hush, Hester—hush," said he, with tremulous solemnity. "The 30 law we broke!—the sin here so awfully revealed!—let these alone be in thy thoughts. I fear! I fear!" '

So he dies, throwing the "sin" in her teeth, and escaping into death. The law we broke, indeed. You bet! Whose law?

35   But it is truly a law, that man must either stick to the belief he has grounded himself on, and obey the laws of that belief. Or he must admit the belief itself to be inadequate, and prepare himself for a new thing.

There was no change in belief, either in Hester or in Dimmesdale or in Hawthorne or in America. The same old treacherous belief, which 40 was really cunning disbelief, in the Spirit, in Purity, in Selfless Love, and in Pure Consciousness. They would go on following this belief, for the sake of the sensationalism of it. But they would make a fool of it all the time. Like Woodrow Wilson, and the rest of modern Believers. The rest of modern Saviours.

If you meet a Saviour, today, be sure he is trying to make an innermost   5
fool of you. Especially if the saviour be an UNDERSTANDING WOMAN, offering her love.

Hester lives on, pious as pie, being a public nurse.* She becomes at last an acknowledged saint, Abel of the Scarlet Letter.

She would, being a woman. She has had her triumph over the indi-   10
vidual man, so she quite loves subscribing to the whole spiritual lie of society. She will make herself as false as hell, for society's sake, once she's had her real triumph over Saint Arthur.

Blossoms out into a Sister of Mercy saint.

But it's a long time before she really takes anybody in. People kept   15
on thinking her a witch. Which she was.

As a matter of fact, unless a woman is held, by man, safe within the bounds of belief, she becomes inevitably a destructive force. She can't help herself. A woman is almost always vulnerable to pity. She can't bear to see anything *physically* hurt. But let a woman loose from the bounds   20
and restraints of man's fierce belief, in his gods and in himself, and she becomes a gentle devil. She becomes subtly diabolic. The colossal evil of the united spirit of Woman, WOMAN, German woman or American woman or every other sort of woman, in the last war, was something frightening. As every *man* knows.   25

Woman becomes a helpless, would-be-loving demon. She is helpless. Her very love is a subtle poison.

Unless a man believes in himself and his gods, *genuinely*; unless he fiercely obeys his own Holy Ghost; his woman will destroy him. Woman is the nemesis of doubting man. She can't help it.   30

And with Hester, after Ligeia, woman becomes a nemesis to man. She bolsters him up from the outside, she destroys him from the inside. And he dies hating her, as Dimmesdale did.

Dimmesdale's spirituality had gone on too long, too far. It had become a false thing. He found his nemesis in woman. And he was done for.   35

Woman is a strange and rather terrible phenomenon, to man. When the subconscious soul of woman recoils from its creative union with man, it becomes a destructive force. It exerts, willy nilly, an invisi-ble destructive influence. The woman herself may be as nice as milk, to all appearance, like Ligeia. But she is sending out waves of silent   40

destruction of the faltering spirit in men, all the same. She doesn't
know it. She can't even help it. But she does it. The devil is in her.

The very women who are most busy saving the bodies of men, and
saving the children: these women-doctors, these nurses, these educa-
5   tionalists, these public-spirited women, these female saviours: they are
all, from the inside, sending out waves of destructive malevolence which
eat out the inner life of a man, like a cancer. It is so, it will be so, till men
realise it and react to save themselves.

God won't save us. The women are so devilish godly. Men must save
10 themselves in this strait, and by no sugary means either.

A woman can use her sex in sheer malevolence and poison, while
she is *behaving* as meek and good as gold. Dear darling, she is really
snow-white in her blamelessness. And all the while she is using her sex
as a she-devil, for the endless hurt of her man. She doesn't know it.
15 She will never believe it if you tell her. And if you give her a slap in the
face for her fiendishness, she will rush to the first magistrate, in indig-
nation. She is so *absolutely* blameless, the she-devil, the dear, dutiful
creature.

Give her the great slap, just the same, just when she is being most
20 angelic. Just when she is bearing her cross most meekly.

Oh, woman out of bounds is a devil. But it is man's fault. Woman
never *asked*, in the first place, to be cast out of her bit of an Eden of
belief and trust. It is man's business to bear the responsibility of belief.
If he becomes a spiritual fornicator and liar, like Ligeia's husband and
25 Arthur Dimmesdale, how *can* a woman believe in him? Belief doesn't
go by choice. And if a woman doesn't believe in a *man*, she believes,
essentially, in nothing. She becomes, willy nilly, a devil.

A devil she is, and a devil she will be. And most men will succumb
to her devilishness.

30 Hester Prynne was a devil. Even when she was so meekly going round
as a sick-nurse. Poor Hester. Part of her wanted to be saved from her own
devilishness. And another part wanted to go on and on in devilishness,
for revenge. Revenge! REVENGE! It is this that fills the unconscious
spirit of woman today. Revenge against man, and against the spirit of
35 man, which has betrayed her into unbelief. Even when she is most sweet
and a salvationist, she is her most devilish, is woman. She gives her man
the sugar-plum of her own submissive sweetness. And when he's taken
this sugar-plum in his mouth, a scorpion* comes out of it. After he's
taken this Eve to his bosom, oh so loving, she destroys him inch by
40 inch. Woman and her revenge! She will have it, and go on having it, for

decades and decades, unless she's stopped. And to stop her you've got
to believe in yourself and your gods, your own Holy Ghost, Sir Man;
and then you've got to fight her, and never give in. She's a devil. But in
the long run she is conquerable. And just a tiny bit of her wants to be
conquered. You've got to fight three-quarters of her, in absolute hell, to   5
get at the final quarter of her that wants a release, at last, from the hell
of her own revenge. But it's a long last. And not yet.

"She had in her nature a rich voluptuous oriental characteristic—a
taste for the gorgeously beautiful." This is Hester. This is American.
But she repressed her nature in the above direction. She would not   10
even allow herself the luxury of laboring at fine, delicate stitchery. Only
she dressed her little sin-child Pearl vividly, and the scarlet letter was
gorgeously embroidered. Her Hecate* and Astarte insignia.

"A voluptuous, oriental characteristic—" That lies waiting in American women. It is probable that the Mormons* are the forerunners of the   15
coming real America. It is probable that men will have more than one
wife, in the coming America. That you will have again a half-oriental
womanhood, and a polygamy.

The grey nurse,* Hester. The Hecate, the hell-cat. The slowly-
evolving voluptuous female of the new era, with a whole new sub-   20
missiveness to the dark, phallic principle.

But it takes time. Generation after generation of nurses and political women and salvationists. And in the end, the dark erection of the
ithyphallic images* once more, and the newly submissive women. That
kind of depth. Deep women in that respect. When we have at last broken   25
this insanity of mental-spiritual consciousness. And the women *choose*
to experience again the great phallic submission.

"The poor, whom she sought out to be the objects of her bounty,
often reviled the hand that was stretched to succour them."

Naturally. The poor hate a salvationist. They smell the devil under-   30
neath.

"She was patient—a martyr indeed—but she forbore to pray for her
enemies, lest, in spite of her forgiving aspirations, the words of the
blessing should stubbornly twist themselves into a curse."

So much honesty, at least. No wonder the old witch-lady Mistress   35
Hibbins claimed her for another witch.

"She grew to have a dread of children; for they had imbibed from
their parents a vague idea of something horrible in this dreary woman
gliding silently through the town, with never any companion but only
one child."   40

"A vague idea!"—Can't you see her "gliding silently"? It's not a question of a vague idea imbibed, but of a definite feeling directly received.

"But sometimes, once in many days, or perchance in many months, she felt an eye—a human eye—upon the ignominious brand, that
5   seemed to give a momentary relief, as if half her agony were shared. The next instant, back it all rushed again, with a still deeper throb of pain; for in that brief interval she had sinned again. Had Hester sinned alone?"

Of course not. As for sinning again, she would go on all her life silently,
10   changelessly "sinning." She never repented. Not she. Why should she? She had brought down Arthur Dimmesdale, that too-too snow-white bird, and that was her life-work.

As for sinning again when she met two dark eyes in a crowd: why of course. Somebody who understood as she understood.
15   I always remember meeting the eyes of a gipsy woman, for one moment, in a crowd, in England. She knew, and I knew. What did we know? I was not able to make out. But we knew.

Probably the same fathomless hate of this spiritual-conscious society in which the outcast woman and I both roamed like meek-looking
20   wolves. Tame wolves waiting to shake off their tameness. Never able to.

And again, that "voluptuous, oriental" characteristic that knows the mystery of the ithyphallic gods. She would not betray the ithyphallic gods to this white, leprous-white society of "lovers." Neither will I, if I can help it. These leprous-white, seducing, spiritual women, who "un-
25   derstand" so much. One has been too often seduced, and "understood." "I can read him like a book," said my first lover,* of me. The book is in several vols., dear. And more and more comes back to me the gulf of dark hate and *other* understanding, in the eyes of the gipsy woman. So different from the hateful white light of understanding which floats like
30   scum on the eyes of white, oh so white English and American women, with their understanding voices and their deep, sad words, and their profound, *good* spirits. Pfui!

Hester was scared only of one result of her sin: Pearl. Pearl, the scarlet letter incarnate. The little girl. When women bear children, they
35   produce either devils or sons with gods in them. And it is an evolutionary process. The devil in Hester produced a purer devil in Pearl. And the devil in Pearl will produce—she married an Italian Count*—a piece of purer devilishness still.

And so from hour to hour we ripe and ripe,
40   And then from hour to hour we rot and rot.*

There was that in the child "which often impelled Hester to ask in bitterness of heart, whether it were for good or ill that the poor little creature had been born at all."

For ill, Hester. But don't worry. Ill is as necessary as good. Malevolence is as necessary as benevolence. If you have brought forth, spawned, a young malevolence, be sure there is a rampant falseness in the world against which this malevolence must be turned. Falseness has to be bitten and bitten, till it is bitten to death. Hence Pearl.

Pearl. Her own mother compares her to the demon of plague, or scarlet fever,* in her red dress. But then plague is necessary to destroy a rotten, false humanity.

Pearl, the devilish girl-child, who can be so tender and loving and *understanding*,* and then when she has understood, will give you a hit across the mouth,* and turn on you with a grin of sheer diabolical jeering.

Serves you right, you shouldn't be *understood*. That is your vice. You shouldn't want to be loved, and then you'd not get hit across the mouth. Pearl will love you: marvellously. And she'll hit you across the mouth: oh so neatly. And serve you right.

Pearl is perhaps the most modern child in all literature.

Old-fashioned Nathaniel, with his little-boy charm, he'll tell you what's what. But he'll cover it with smarm.*

Hester simply *hates* her child, from one part of herself. And from another, she cherishes her child as her one precious treasure. For Pearl is the continuing of her female revenge on life. But female revenge hits both ways. Hits back at its own mother. The female revenge in Pearl hits back at Hester, the mother, and Hester is simply livid with fury and "sadness." Which is rather amusing.

"The child could not be made amenable to rules. In giving her existence a great law had been broken; and the result was a being whose elements were perhaps beautiful and brilliant, but all in disorder, or with an order peculiar to themselves, amidst which the point of variety and arrangement was difficult or impossible to discover."

Of course the order is peculiar to themselves. But the point of variety is this: "Draw out the loving, sweet soul, draw it out with marvellous understanding; and then spit in its eye."

Hester of course didn't at all like it when her sweet child drew out her motherly soul, with yearning and deep understanding: and then spit in the motherly eye, with a grin. But it was a process the mother had started.

Pearl had a peculiar look in her eyes: "a look so intelligent, yet so inexplicable, so perverse, sometimes so malicious, but generally accompanied by a wild flow of spirits, that Hester could not help questioning at such moments whether Pearl was a human child."

5 A little demon! But her mother, and the saintly Dimmesdale, had borne her. And Pearl, by the very openness of her perversity, was more straightforward than her parents. She flatly refuses any Heavenly Father, seeing the earthly one such a fraud. And she has the pietistic Dimmesdale on toast, spits right in his eye: in both his eyes.

10 Poor, brave, tormented little soul, always in a state of recoil, she'll be a devil to men when she grows up. But the men deserve it. If they'll let themselves be "drawn," by her loving understanding, they deserve that she shall slap them across the mouth the moment they *are* drawn. The chickens! Drawn and trussed.

15 Poor little phenomenon of a modern child, she'll grow up into the devil of a modern woman. The nemesis of weak-kneed modern men, craving to be love-drawn.

The third person in the diabolic trinity, or triangle, of the scarlet letter, is Hester's first husband, Roger Chillingworth. He is an old Eliza-
20 bethan physician with a grey beard and a long-furred coat and a twisted shoulder. Another healer. But something of an alchemist, a magician. He is a magician on the verge of modern science, like Francis Bacon.

Roger Chillingworth is of the old order of intellect, in direct line from the mediaeval Roger Bacon* alchemists. He has an old, intellectual belief
25 in the dark sciences, the Hermetic philosophies.* He is no christian, no selfless aspirer. He is not an aspirer. He is the old authoritarian in man. The old male authority. But without passional belief. Only intellectual belief in himself and his male authority.

Shakspere's whole tragic wail* is because of the downfall of the true
30 male authority, the ithyphallic authority and masterhood. It fell with Elizabeth. It was trodden underfoot with Victoria.

But Chillingworth keeps on the *intellectual* tradition. He hates the new spiritual aspirers, like Dimmesdale, with a black, crippled hate. He is the old male authority, in intellectual tradition.

35 You can't keep a wife by force of an intellectual tradition. So Hester took to seducing Dimmesdale.

Yet her only marriage, and her last oath,* is with the old Roger. He and she are accomplices in pulling down the spiritual saint.

' "Why dost thou smile so at me— —" she says to her old, vengeful
40 husband. "Art thou not like the Black Man that haunts the forest round

us? Hast thou not enticed me into a bond which will prove the ruin of
my soul?" '
    ' "Not thy soul!" he answered with another smile. "No, not thy soul!" '
It is the soul of the pure preacher, that false thing, which they are
after. And the crippled physician—this other healer—blackly vengeful   5
in his old, distorted male authority, and the "loving" woman, they bring
down the Saint between them.
    A black and complementary hatred, akin to love, is what Chilling-
worth feels for the young, saintly parson. And Dimmesdale responds, in
a hideous kind of love. Slowly the saint's life is poisoned. But the black   10
old physician smiles, and tries to keep him alive. Dimmesdale goes in for
self-torture, self-lashing, lashing his own white, thin, spiritual saviour's
body. The dark old Chillingworth listens outside the door and laughs,
and prepares another medicine, so that the game can go on longer. And
the saint's very soul goes rotten. Which is the supreme triumph. Yet he   15
keeps up appearances still.
    The black, vengeful soul of the crippled, masterful male, still dark
in his authority: and the white ghastliness of the fallen saint! The two
halves of manhood mutually destroying one another.
    Dimmesdale has a "coup" in the very end. He gives the whole show   20
away by confessing publicly on the scaffold, and dodging into death,
leaving Hester dished, and Roger as it were doubly cuckolded. It is a
neat last revenge.
    Down comes the curtain, like in Ligeia's poem.
    But the child Pearl will be on in the next act, with her Italian Count   25
and a new brood of vipers. And Hester greyly Abelling, in the shadows,
after her rebelling.
    It is a marvellous allegory. It is to me one of the greatest allegories in
all literature, *The Scarlet Letter*. Its marvellous under-meaning! And its
perfect duplicity.   30
    The absolute duplicity of that blue-eyed *Wunderkind* of a Nathaniel.
The American wonder-child, with his magical allegorical insight.
    But even wonder-children have to grow up in a generation or two.
And even SIN becomes stale.

VIII.

Hawthorne's *Blithedale Romance*.*

No other book of Nathaniel Hawthorne is so deep, so dual, and so complete as *The Scarlet Letter*: this great allegory of the triumph
5   of Sin.

Sin is a queer thing. It isn't the breaking of divine Commandments. It is the breaking of one's own integrity.

For instance, the sin in Hester and Arthur Dimmesdale's case was a
10   sin because they did what they *thought* it *wrong* to do. If they had really *wanted* to be lovers, and if they had had the honest courage of their own passion, there would have been no sin: even had the desire been only momentary.

But if there had been no sin, they would have lost half the fun, or
15   more, of the game.

It was this very doing of the thing that *they themselves* believed to be wrong, that constituted the chief charm of the act. Man invents sin, in order to enjoy the feeling of being naughty. Also, in order to shift the responsibility for his own acts. A Divine Father tells him what to do.
20   And Man is naughty and doesn't obey. And then shiveringly, ignoble man lets down his pants for a flogging.

If the Divine Father doesn't bring on the flogging, in this life, then Sinful Man shiveringly awaits his whipping in the afterlife.

Bah, the Divine Father, like so many other Crowned Heads, has
25   abdicated his authority.* Man can sin as much as he likes.

There is only one penalty: the loss of his own integrity. Man should *never* do the thing he believes to be wrong. Because if he does, he loses his own singleness, wholeness, natural honour.

If you want to do a thing, you've either got to believe, sincerely,
30   that it's your true nature to do this thing: or else you've got to let it alone.

Believe in your own Holy Ghost. Or else, if you doubt, abstain.

A thing that you sincerely believe in, cannot be wrong. Because belief does not come at will. It comes only from the Holy Ghost within.
35   Therefore a thing you truly believe in, cannot be wrong.

96

But there is such a thing as spurious belief. There is such a thing as *evil* belief: a belief that one *cannot* do wrong. There is also such a thing as a half-spurious belief. And this is rottenest of all. The devil lurking behind the cross.

So there you are. Between genuine belief, and spurious belief, and   5
half-genuine belief, you're as likely as not to be in a pickle.* And the half-genuine belief is much the dirtiest, and most deceptive thing in life.

Hester and Dimmesdale believed in the Divine Father, and almost gloatingly sinned against Him. The Allegory of Sin.

Pearl no longer believes in the Divine Father. She says so. She has no   10
Divine Father. Disowns Papa both big and little.

So she can't sin against him.

What will she do, then, if she's got no god to sin against? Why, of course, she'll not be able to sin at all. She'll go her own way gaily, and do as she likes, and she'll say, afterwards, when she's made a mess: "Yes,   15
I did it. But I acted for the best, and therefore I am blameless. It's the other person's fault. Or else it's Its fault."

She will be blameless, will Pearl, come what may.

And the world is simply a string of Pearls, today. And America is a whole rope of these absolutely immaculate Pearls, who can't sin, let   20
them do what they may. Because they've no god to sin against. Mere men, one after another. Men with no ghost to their name.

Pearls!

Oh the irony, the bitter, bitter irony of the name! Oh Nathaniel, you great man! Oh America, you Pearl, you Pearl without a blemish.   25

How *can* Pearl have a blemish, when there's no one but herself to judge Herself? Of course she'll be immaculate, even if, like Cleopatra, she drowns a lover a night in her dirty Nile. The Nilus Flux of her love. Candida!*

By Hawthorne's day it was already Pearl. Before swine, of course.   30
There never yet was a Pearl that wasn't cast before swine.*

It's part of her game, part of her pearldom.

Because when Circe lies with a man, *he's* a swine after it,* if he wasn't one before. Not *she*. Circe is the great white impeccable Pearl.

And yet, oh Pearl, there's a Nemesis even for you.   35

There's a Doom, Pearl.

Doom! What a beautiful northern word.* Doom.

The Doom of the Pearl.

Who will write that Allegory?*

Here's what the Doom is, anyhow.   40

When you don't have a Divine Father to sin against: and when you don't sin against the Son; which the Pearls don't, decause they all are very strong on LOVE, stronger on LOVE than on anything: then there's nothing left for you to sin against except the Holy Ghost.

5   Now Pearl, come, let's drop you in the vinegar.*

And it's a ticklish thing sinning against the Holy Ghost. "*It shall not be forgiven him.*"*

Didn't I tell you there was Doom.

It shall not be forgiven her.

10   The Father forgives: the Son forgives:* but the Holy Ghost does *not* forgive. So take that.

The Holy Ghost doesn't forgive because the Holy Ghost is within you. The Holy Ghost *is* you:* your very YOU. So if, in your conceit of your ego, you make a breach in your own YOU, in your own

15   integrity, how can you be forgiven? You might as well make a rip in your own bowels. You *know* if you rip your own bowels they will go rotten and *you* will go rotten. And there's an end of you: in the body.

The same if you make a breach with your own Holy Ghost. You go

20   soul-rotten. Like the Pearls.

These dear Pearls, they do anything they like, and remain pure. Oh purity!

But they can't stop themselves from going rotten inside. Rotten Pearls, fair outside. Their *souls* smell, because their souls are putrefying

25   inside them.

The sin against the Holy Ghost.

And gradually, from within outwards, they rot. Some form of dementia. A thing disintegrating. A decomposing psyche. Dementia.

Quos vult perdere Deus, dementat prius. *

30   Watch these Pearls, these Pearls of modern women. Particularly American women. Battening on* love. And fluttering in the first bat-like throes of dementia.

You *can* have your cake and eat it. But my god, it will go rotten inside you.

35   Hawthorne's other books are nothing compared to *Scarlet Letter.*

But there are good parables, and wonderful dark glimpses of early Puritan America, in *Twice Told Tales.*

*The House of the Seven Gables** has "atmosphere." The passing of the old order of the proud, bearded, black-browed Father: an order

40   which is slowly ousted from life, and lingeringly haunts the old dark

places. But comes a new generation to sweep out even the ghosts, with these new vacuum cleaners.* No ghost could stand up against a vacuum cleaner.

The new generation is having no ghosts or cobwebs. It is setting up in the photography line, and is just going to make a sound financial thing out of it. For this purpose all old hates and old glooms, that belong to the antique order of Haughty Fathers, all these are swept up in the vacuum cleaner, and the vendetta-born young couple effect a perfect understanding under the black cloth of a camera* and prosperity. Vivat industria!*

Oh Nathaniel, you savage ironist. Ugh, how you'd have *hated* it if you'd had nothing but the prosperous, "dear" young couple to write about! If you'd lived to the day when America was nothing but a Main Street.*

The Dark Old Fathers.

The Beloved Wishy-Washy Sons.

The Photography Business.

? ? ?

Hawthorne came nearest to actuality in *The Blithedale Romance.* This novel is a sort of picture of the notorious Brook Farm experiment.* There the famous idealists and transcendentalists of America met to till the soil and hew the timber in the sweat of their own brows, thinking high thoughts the while, and breathing an atmosphere of communal love, and tingling in tune with the Oversoul,* like so many strings of a super-celestial harp. An old twang of the Crèvecoeur instrument.

Of course they fell out like cats and dogs. Couldn't stand one another. And all the music they made was the music of their quarreling.

You *can't* idealise hard work. Which is why America invents so many machines and contrivances of all sort: so that they need do no physical work.

And that's why the idealists left off brookfarming, and took to book-farming.

You *can't* idealise the essential brute blood-activity, the brute blood desires, the basic, sardonic blood knowledge.

This you *can't* idealise.

And you can't eliminate it.

So there's the end of ideal man.

Man is made up of a dual consciousness, of which the two halves are most of the time in opposition to one another. And will be so as long as time lasts.

You've got to learn to change from one consciousness to the other, turn and about. Not to try to make either absolute, or dominant. The Holy Ghost tells you the how and when.

5 Never did Nathaniel feel himself more spectral—of course he went brookfarming—than when he was winding the horn* in the morning to summon the transcendental laborers to their tasks, or than when marching off with a hoe ideally to hoe the turnips. "Never did I feel more spectral,"* says Nathaniel.

Never did I feel such a fool, would have been more to the point.

10 Farcical fools, trying to idealise labour. You'll never succeed in idealising hard work. Before you can dig mother earth you've got to take off your ideal jacket. The harder a man works, at brute labour, the thinner becomes his idealism, the darker his mind. And the harder a man works at mental labour, at idealism, at transcendental occupations, the thinner

15 becomes his blood, and the more brittle his nerves.

Oh the brittle-nerved brookfarmers!

You've got to be able to do both: the mental work, and the brute work. But be prepared to step from one pair of shoes into another. Don't try and make it all one pair of shoes.

20 The attempt to idealise the blood!

Nathaniel knew he was a fool, attempting it.

He went home to his amiable spouse and his sanctum sanctorum* of a study.

Nathaniel!

25 But the *Blithedale Romance.*—It has a beautiful, wintry-evening farm-kitchen sort of opening.

Dramatis Personae.

1. *I.* The narrator: whom we will call Nathaniel.* A wisp of a sensitive, withal deep, literary young man no longer so very young.

30 2. *Zenobia.* A dark, proudly voluptuous clever woman with a tropical flower in her hair. Said to be sketched from Margaret Fuller,* in whom Hawthorne saw some "evil nature." Nathaniel was more aware of Zenobia's voluptuousness than of her "mind."

3. *Hollingsworth*: a black-bearded blacksmith with a deep-voiced lust

35 for saving criminals. Wants to build a great Home for these unfortunates.

4. *Priscilla*: a sort of White Lily, a clinging little mediumistic sempstress who has been made use of in public séances. A sort of prostitute soul.

5. *Zenobia's Husband*: an unpleasant decayed person with magnetic

40 powers and teeth full of gold—or set in gold. It is he who has given

public spiritualist demonstrations, with Priscilla for the medium. He is of the dark, sensual, decayed-handsome sort, and comes in unexpectedly by the back door.*

Plot I. I, Nathaniel, at once catch cold and have to be put to bed. Am nursed with inordinate tenderness by the blacksmith, whose great hands are gentler than a woman's, etc.

The two men love one another with a love surpassing the love of women,* so long as the healing-and-salvation business lasts. When Nathaniel wants to get well and have a soul of his own, he turns with hate on this black-bearded, booming salvationist, Hephaestos of the underworld.* Hates him for a tryrannous monomaniac.

Plot II. Zenobia, that clever lustrous woman, is fascinated by the criminal-saving blacksmith, and would have him at any price. Meanwhile she has the subtlest current of understanding with the frail but deep Nathaniel. And she takes the White Lily half-pityingly, half contemptuously, under a rich and glossy dark wing.

Plot III. The blacksmith is after Zenobia, to get her money for his criminal asylum: of which of course he will be the first inmate.

Plot IV. Nathaniel also feels his mouth watering for the dark-luscious Zenobia.

Plot V. The White Lily, Priscilla, vapourously festering, turns out to be the famous Veiled Lady of public spiritualist shows: she whom the undesirable Husband, called the Professor, has used as a medium. Also she is Zenobia's half-sister.

Débâcle.

Nobody wants Zenobia in the end. She goes off without her flower.* The blacksmith marries Priscilla. Nathaniel dribblingly confesses that he too has loved Prissy all the while.* Boo-hoo!

Conclusion.

A few years after, Nathaniel meets the blacksmith in a country lane near a humble cottage, leaning totteringly on the arm of the frail but fervent Priscilla. Gone are all dreams of asylums,* and the saviour of criminals can't even save himself from his own Veiled Lady.

There you have a nice little bunch of idealists, transcendentalists, brookfarmers, and disintegrated gentry. All going slightly rotten.

Two Pearls: a white Pearl and a black Pearl: the latter more expensive, lurid with money.

The white Pearl, the little medium, Priscilla, the imitation pearl, has truly some "supernormal" powers. She could drain the blacksmith of his blackness and his smith-strength.

Priscilla, the little psychic prostitute. The degenerate descendant of Ligeia. The absolutely yielding, "loving" woman, who abandons herself utterly to her lover. Or even to a gold-toothed "professor" of spiritualism.

Is it all bunkum, this spiritualism? Is it just rot, this Veiled Lady?

Not quite. Apart even from telepathy, the apparatus of human consciousness is the most wonderful message-receiver in existence. Beats a wireless station to nothing.

Put Prissy under the tablecloth then. Miaow!

What happens? Prissy under the table cloth, like a canary when you cover his cage, goes into a "sleep", a trance.

A trance, not a sleep. A trance means that all her *individual*, personal intelligence goes to sleep, like a hen with her head under her wing. But the *apparatus* of consciousness remains working. Without a soul in it.

And what can this apparatus of consciousness do, when it works? Why surely something. A wireless apparatus goes tick-tick-tick, taking down messages.* So does your human apparatus. All kinds of messages. Only the soul, or the under-conciousness deals with these messages in the dark, in the underconscious. Which is the natural course of events.

But what sorts of messages? All sorts. Vibrations from the stars, vibrations from unknown magnetos,* vibrations from unknown people, unknown passions. The human apparatus receives them all, and they are all dealt with in the underconscious.

There are also vibrations of thought, many, many. Necessary to get the two human instruments in key.

There may even be vibrations of ghosts in the air. Ghosts being dead *wills*, mind you, not dead souls. The soul has nothing to do with these dodges.

But some unit of force may persist for a time, after the death of an individual—some associations of vibrations may linger like little clouds in the etheric atmosphere after the death of a human being, or an animal. And these little clots of vibration may transfer themselves to the conscious-apparatus of the medium. So that the dead son of the disconsolate widow may send a message to his mourning mother to tell her that he owes Bill Jackson seven dollars: or that Uncle Sam's will is in the back of the bureau: and cheer up, Mother, I'm all right.

There is never much worth in these "messages." Because they are never more than fragmentary items of dead, disintegrated consciousnesses. And the medium has and always will have a hopeless job, trying to disentangle the muddle of messages.

Again, coming events *may* cast their shadow before. The oracle may   5
receive on her conscious-apparatus material vibrations to say that the next great war will break out in 1925. And in so far as the realm of cause-and-effect is master of the living soul, in so far as events are mechanically mustering, the forecast may be true.

But the living souls of men may upset the *mechanical* march of events   10
at any moment.

Rien de certain.*

Vibrations of subtlest matter. Concatenations of vibrations and shocks! Spiritualism.

And what then? It is all just materialistic, and a good deal is and   15
always will be charlatanry.

Because the real human soul, the Holy Ghost, has its own deep prescience, which will not be put into figures, but flows on dark, a stream of prescience.

And the real human soul is too proud, and too sincere in its belief   20
in the Holy Ghost that is within, to stoop to the practices of these spiritualist and other psychic tricks of material vibrations.

Because the first part of reverence is the acceptance of the fact that the Holy Ghost will never materialise: will never be anything but a ghost.

And the second part of reverence is the watchful observance of the   25
motions, the comings and goings within us, of the Holy Ghost, and of the many gods that make up the Holy Ghost.

The Father had his day, and fell.

The Son has had his day, and by this time he stinketh.*

It is the day of the Holy Ghost.   30

But when souls fall corrupt, into disintegration, they have no more day. They have sinned against the Holy Ghost.

These people in *Blithedale Romance* have sinned against the Holy Ghost, and corruption has set in.

All, perhaps, except the I, Nathaniel. He is still a sad, integral con-   35
sciousness.

But not excepting Zenobia. The Black Pearl is rotting down. Fast. The cleverer she is, the faster she rots.

And they are all disintegrating, so they take to psychic tricks. It is a certain sign of the disintegration of the psyche in man, and much more   40 so in a woman, when she takes to spiritualism, and table-rapping, and occult messages, or witchcraft and supernatural powers of that sort. When men want to be supernatural, be sure that something has gone wrong in their natural stuff. More so even, with a woman.

5   And yet the soul has its own profound subtleties of knowing. And the blood has its strange omniscience.

But this isn't impudent and materialistic, like spiritualism and magic and all that range of pretentious supernaturalism.

IX.

Dana's *Two Years Before The Mast.**

You can't idealise brute labour.

That is to say, you can't idealise brute labour, without coming undone, as an idealist.

The soil! The great ideal of the soil. Novels like Thomas Hardy's and pictures like the Frenchman Millet's.* The soil.

What happens when you idealise the soil, the mother-earth, and really go back to it? Then with overwhelming conviction it is borne in upon you, as it was upon Thomas Hardy, that the whole scheme of things is against you. The whole massive rolling of natural fate is coming down on you like a slow glacier, to crush you to extinction. As an idealist.

Thomas Hardy's pessimism* is an absolutely true finding. It is the absolutely true statement of the idealist's last realisation, as he wrestles with the bitter soil of beloved mother-earth. He loves her, loves her, loves her. And she just entangles and crushes him like a slow Laocoön snake.* The idealist must perish, says mother earth. Then let him perish.

The great imaginative love of the soil itself! Tolstoi had it,* and Thomas Hardy. And both are driven to a kind of fanatic denial of life, as a result.

You can't idealise mother earth. You can try. You can even succeed. But succeeding, you succumb. She will have no pure idealist sons. None.

If you are a child of mother earth, you must learn to discard your ideal self, in season, as you discard your clothes at night.

Americans have never loved the soil of America as Europeans have loved the soil of Europe. America has never been a blood-home-land. Only an ideal home-land. The home-land of the idea, of the *spirit*. And of the pocket. Not of the blood.

That has yet to come, when the idea and the spirit have collapsed from their false tyranny.

Europe has been loved with a blood love. That has made it beautiful.

In America, you have Fenimore Cooper's beautiful landscape: but that is wish-fulfilment, done from a distance. And you have Thoreau in Concord. But Thoreau sort of isolated his own bit of locality and put it under a lens, to examine it. He almost anatomised it, with his admiration.

America isn't a blood-home-land. For every American, the blood-home-land is Europe. The spirit home-land is America.

5   Transcendentalism.* Transcend this home-land business, exalt the idea of These States till you have made it a universal idea, says the true American. The oversoul is a world-soul, not a local thing.

So, in the next great move of imaginative conquest, Americans turned to the sea. Not to the land. Earth is too specific, too particular. Besides, 10 the blood of white men is wine of no American soil. No no.

But the blood of all men is ocean-born. We have our material universality, our blood-oneness, in the sea. The salt water.

You can't idealise the soil. But you've got to try. And trying, you reap a great imaginative reward. And the greatest reward is failure. To know 15 you have failed, that you *must* fail. That is the greatest comfort of all, at last.

Tolstoi failed with the soil: Thomas Hardy too: and Giovanni Verga;* the three greatest.

The further extreme, the greatest mother, is the sea. Love the great 20 mother of the sea, the Magna Mater. And see how bitter it is. And see how you must fail to win her to your ideal: forever fail. Absolutely fail.

Swinburne tried, in England.* But the Americans made the greatest trial. The most vivid failure.

At a certain point, human life becomes uninteresting to men. What 25 then? They turn to some universal.

The greatest material mother of us all is the sea.

Dana's eyes failed him when he was studying at Harvard.* And suddenly, he turned to the sea, the naked Mother. He went to sea as a common sailor before the mast.

30   You can't idealise brute labour. Yet you can. You can go through with brute labour, and *know* what it means. You can even meet and match the sea, and KNOW her.

This is what Dana wanted: a naked fighting experience with the sea. KNOW THYSELF.* That means, know the earth that is in your 35 blood. Know the sea that is in your blood. The great elementals.

But we must repeat: KNOWING and BEING are opposite, antagonistic states. The more you KNOW, exactly, the less you *are*. The more you *are*, in being, the less you KNOW.

This is the great cross of man, his dualism. The blood-self, and the 40 nerve-brain self.

Knowing, then, is the slow death of being. Man has his epochs of being, his epochs of knowing. It will always be a great oscillation. The goal is to know how not to know.

Dana took another great step in knowing: knowing the mother sea. But it was a step also in his own undoing. It was a new phase of dissolution   5
of his own being. Afterwards, he would be a less human thing. He would be a knower: but more near to mechanism than before. That is our cross, our doom.

And so he writes, in his first days at sea, in winter, on the Atlantic: "Nothing can compare with the *early breaking of day* upon the wide, sad   10
ocean. There is something in the first grey streaks stretching along the eastern horizon, and throwing an indistinct light upon the face of the deep, which creates a feeling of loneliness, of dread, and of melancholy foreboding, which nothing else in nature can give." So he ventures wakeful and alone into the great naked watery universe of the end of life,   15
the twilighty place where integral being lapses, and warm life begins to give out. It is man moving on into the face of death, the great adventure, the great undoing, the strange extension of the consciousness. The same in his vision of the albatross. "—But one of the finest sights that I have ever seen was an albatross asleep upon the water, during a calm, off   20
Cape Horn, when a heavy sea was running. There being no breeze, the surface of the water was unbroken, but a long, heavy swell was rolling, and we saw the fellow, all white, directly ahead of us, asleep upon the waves, with his head under his wing; now rising upon the top of a huge billow, and then falling slowly until he was lost in the hollow between.   25
He was undisturbed for some time, until the noise of our bows, gradually approaching, roused him, when, lifting his head, he stared upon us for a moment, and then spread his wide wings, and took his flight."

We must give Dana credit for a profound mystic vision. The best Americans are mystics by instinct. Simple and bare as his narrative is,   30
it is deep with profound emotion and stark comprehension. He sees the last light-loving incarnation of life exposed upon the eternal waters: a speck, solitary upon the verge of the two naked principles, aerial and watery. And his own soul is as the soul of the albatross.

It is a storm-bird. And so is Dana. He has gone down to fight with   35
the sea. It is a metaphysical, actual struggle of an integral soul with the vast, non-living, yet potent element. Dana never forgets, never ceases to watch. If Hawthorne was a spectre on the land, how much more is Dana a spectre at sea. But he must watch, he must know, he must conquer the sea in his consciousness. This is the poignant difference between him   40

and the common sailor. The common sailor lapses from consciousness, becomes elemental like a seal, a creature. Tiny and alone, Dana watches the great seas mount round his own small body. If he is swept away, some other man will have to take up what he has begun. For the sea
5 must be mastered by the human consciousness, in the great fight of the human soul for mastery over life and death, in KNOWLEDGE. It is the last bitter necessity of the Tree. The Cross.* Impartial, Dana beholds himself among the elements, calm and fatal. His style is great and hopeless, the style of a perfect tragic recorder.

10 "Between five and six the cry of 'All starbowlines ahoy!' summoned our watch on deck, and immediately all hands were called. A great cloud of a dark slate-colour was driving on us from the south-west; and we did our best to take in sail before we were in the midst of it. We had got the light sails furled, the courses hauled up, and the top-sail reef
15 tackles hauled out, and were just mounting the fore-rigging when the storm struck us. In an instant the sea, which had been comparatively quiet, was running higher and higher; and it became almost as dark as night. The hail and sleet were harder than I had yet felt them, seeming almost to pin us down to the rigging."

20 It is in the dispassionate statement of plain material facts that Dana achieves his greatness. Dana writes from the remoter, non-emotional centres of being—not from the passional-emotional self.

So the ship battles on, round Cape Horn, then out into quieter seas. The island of Juan Fernandez, Crusoe's island,* rises like a dream from
25 the sea, like a green cloud, and like a ghost Dana watches it, feeling only a faint, ghostly pang of regret for the life that was.

But the strain of the long sea-voyage begins to tell. The sea is a great disintegrative force. Its tonic quality is its disintegrative quality. It burns down the tissue, liberates energy. And after a long time, this
30 burning-down is destructive. The pysche becomes destroyed, irritable, frayed, almost dehumanised.

So there is trouble on board the ship, irritating discontent, friction unbearable, and at last a flogging. This flogging rouses Dana for the first and last time to human and ideal passion.

35 "Sam was by this time seized up—that is, placed against the shrouds, with his wrists made fast to the shrouds, his jacket off, and his back exposed. The captain stood on the break of the deck, a few feet from him, and a little raised, so as to have a good swing at him, and held in his hand a light, thick rope. The officers stood round, and the crew
40 grouped together in the waist. All these preparations made me feel

sick and faint, angry and excited as I was. A man—a human being made in God's likeness—fastened up and flogged like a beast! The first and almost uncontrollable impulse was resistance. But what could be done?—The time for it had gone by—"

So Mr Dana couldn't act. He could only lean over the side of the ship 5 and spue.

Whatever made him vomit?

Why shall man not be whipped? Because a man is "made in God's image?"* If so, then God himself must upon occasion unbutton his pants and sit on the seat of a W. C. The other sort of throne. And wipe 10 his own behind.

Isn't it so?

And why not? If I worship a god, it shall be a god who also must go to stool. None of your posteriorless Cherubim for me. The Lord Almighty has a bottom. 15

And this is not blasphemy.

And as long as man has a bottom, he must surely be whipped. It is as if the Lord intended it so.

Why? For lots of reasons.

Man doth not live by bread alone,* to absorb it and to evacuate it. 20

What is the breath of life? My dear, it is the strange current of interchange that flows between men and men, and men and women, and men and things. A constant current of interflow, a constant vibrating interchange. That is the breath of life.

And this interflow, this electric vibration is polarised. There is a 25 positive and a negative polarity. This is a law of life, of vitalism.

Only ideas are final, finite, static, and single.

All life interchange is a polarised communication. A circuit.

There are lots of circuits. Male and female, for example, and master and servant. The idea, the IDEA, that fixed gorgon* monster, and the 30 IDEAL, that great stationary engine, these two Gods-of-the-machine have been busy destroying all *natural* reciprocity and *natural* circuits, for centuries. IDEAS have played the very old Harry with* sex relationship, that is, the great circuit of man and woman. Turned the thing into a wheel on which the human being in both is broken. And the 35 IDEAL has mangled the blood-reciprocity of master and servant into an abstract horror.

Master and servant—or master and man relationship is, essentially, a polarised flow, like love. It is a circuit of vitalism which flows between master and man and forms a very precious nourishment to each, and 40

keeps both in a state of subtle, quivering, vital equilibrium. Deny it as you like, it is so. But once you *abstract* both master and man, and make them both serve an *idea*: production, wage, efficiency, and so on: so that each looks on himself as an instrument performing a certain repeated
5   evolution, then you have changed the vital, quivering circuit of master and man into a mechanical machine unison. Just another way of life: or anti-life.

You could never quite do this on a sailing ship. A master had to be master, or it was hell. That is, there had to be this strange interflow of
10 master-and-man, the strange reciprocity of command and obedience.

The reciprocity of command and obedience is a state of unstable, vital equilibrium. Everything vital, or natural, is unstable, thank God.

The ship had been at sea many weeks. A great strain on master and men. An increasing callous indifference in the men, an increasing
15 irritability in the master.

And then what?

A storm.

Don't expect me to say *why* storms must be. They just are. Storms in the air, storms in the water, storms of thunder, storms of anger. Storms
20 just are.

Storms are a sort of violent readjustment in some polarised flow. You have a polarised circuit, a circuit of unstable equilibrium. The instability increases till there is a crash. Everything seems to break down. Thunder roars, lightning flashes. The master roars, the whip
25 whizzes. The sky sends down sweet rain. The ship knows a new strange stillness, a readjustment, a re-finding of equilibrium.

Ask the Lord Almighty why it is so. I don't know. I know it is so.

But flogging? Why flogging? Why not use reason or take away jam for tea?*
30 Why not? Why not ask the thunder please to abstain from this physical violence of crashing and thumping, please to swale away* like thawing snow.

Sometimes the thunder *does* swale away like thawing snow, and then you hate it. Muggy, sluggish, inert, dreary sky.
35 Flogging.

You have a Sam, a fat slow fellow, who has got slower and more slovenly as the weeks wear on. You have a master who has grown more irritable in his authority. Till Sam becomes simply wallowing in his slackness, makes your gorge rise. And the master is on red hot iron.

Now these two men, Captain and Sam, are there in a very unsteady equilibrium of command and obedience. A polarised flow. Definitely polarised.

The poles of will are the great ganglia of the voluntary nerve system, located beside the spinal column, in the back. From the poles of will   5 in the backbone of the Captain, to the ganglia of will in the back of the sloucher Sam, runs a frazzled, jagged current, a staggering circuit of vital electricity. This circuit gets one jolt too many, and there is an explosion.

"Tie up that lousy swine!" roars the enraged Captain.   10

And whack! whack! down on the bare back of that sloucher Sam comes the cat.

What does it do? By Jove, it goes like ice-cold water into his spine. Down those lashes runs the current of the captain's rage, right into the blood and into the toneless ganglia of Sam's voluntary system.   15 Crash! Crash! runs the lightning flame, right into the cores of the living nerves.

And the living nerves respond. They start to vibrate. They brace up. The blood begins to go quicker. The nerves begin to recover their vividness. It is their tonic. The man Sam has a new clear day of intelli-   20 gence, and a smarting back. The captain has a new relief, a new ease in his authority, and a sore heart.

There is a new equilibrium, and a fresh start. The *physical* intelligence of a Sam is restored, the turgidity is relieved from the veins of the Captain.   25

It is a natural form of human coition, interchange.

It is good for Sam to be flogged. It is good, on this occassion, for the Captain to have Sam flogged. I say so. Because they were both in that physical condition.

Spare the rod and spoil the *physical* child.   30

Use the rod and spoil the *ideal* child.*

There you are.

Dana, as an idealist, refusing the blood-contact of life, leaned over the side of the ship powerless, and vomited: or wanted to. His solar plexus was getting a bit of its own back. To him, Sam was an "ideal" being,   35 who should have been approached through the mind, the reason, and the spirit. That lump of a Sam!

But there was another idealist on board, the seaman John, a Swede. He wasn't named John for nothing, this Jack-tar of the Logos. John

felt himself called upon to play Mediator, Interceder, Saviour, on this
occasion. The popular Paraclete.*

"Why are you whipping this man, Sir?"

But the Captain had got his dander up.* He wasn't going to have
5   his natural passion judged and interfered-with by these long-nosed
salvationist Johannuses.* So he had nosey John hauled up and whipped
as well.

For which I am very glad.

Alas, however, the captain got the worst of it in the end. He smirks
10 longest who smirks lasts. The Captain wasn't wary enough. Natural
anger, natural passion has its unremitting enemy in the idealist. And the
ship was already tainted with idealism. A good deal more so, apparently,
than Herman Melville's ships* were.

Which reminds us that Melville was once going to be flogged. In
15 *White Jacket.** And he too would have taken it as the last insult.

In my opinion, there are worse insults than floggings. I would rather
be flogged than have most people "like" me.

Melville too had an Interceder: a quiet, self-respecting man, not a
Saviour. The man spoke in the name of Justice. Melville was to be
20 unjustly whipped. The man spoke honestly and quietly. Not in any
salvationist spirit. And the whipping did not take place.

Justice is a great and manly thing. Saviourism* is a despicable thing.

Sam was justly whipped. It was a passional justice.

But Melville's whipping would have been a cold, disciplinary in-
25 justice. A foul thing. Mechanical *justice* even is a foul thing. For true
justice makes the heart's fibres quiver. You can't be cold in a matter of
real justice.

Already in those days it was no fun to be a captain. You had to learn
already to abstract yourself into a machine-part, exerting machine-
30 control. And it is a good deal bitterer to exert machine-control, selfless,
ideal control, than it is to have to obey, mechanically. Because the idealists who mechanically obey almost always hate the *man* who must give
the orders. Their idealism rarely allows them to exonerate the man for
the office.

35   Dana's captain was one of the real old-fashioned sort. He gave himself
away terribly. He should have been more wary, knowing he confronted a
shipful of enemies and at least two cold and deadly idealists, who hated
all "masters" on principle.

"As he went on, his passion increased, and he danced about on the
40 deck, calling out as he swung the rope, 'If you want to know what I flog

you for, I'll tell you. It's because I like to do it!—because I like to do
it!—It suits me. That's what I do it for!'

"The man writhed under the pain. My blood ran cold, I could look
no longer. Disgusted, sick, and horror-struck, I turned away and leaned
over the rail and looked down in the water. A few rapid thoughts of my   5
own situation, and the prospect of future revenge, crossed my mind;
but the falling of the blows, and the cries of the man called me back at
once. At length they ceased, and, turning round, I found that the Mate,
at a signal from the Captain, had cut him down—"

After all, it was not so terrible. The captain evidently did not exceed   10
the ordinary measure. Sam got no more than he asked for. It was a
natural event. All would have been well, save for the *moral* verdict. And
this came from theoretic idealists like Dana and the seaman John, rather
than from the sailors themselves. The sailors understood spontaneous
passional morality, not the artificial ethical. They respected the violent   15
readjustments of the naked force, in man as in nature.

"The flogging was seldom, if ever alluded to by us in the forecastle.
If anyone was inclined to talk about it, the other, with a delicacy which
I hardly expected to find among them, always stopped him, or turned
the subject—"   20

Two men had been flogged: the second and elder, John, for interfering
and asking the captain why he flogged Sam. It is whilst flogging John
that the Captain shouts "If you want to know what I flog you for, I'll
tell you—"

"But the behaviour of the two men who were flogged," Dana con-   25
tinues, "toward one another, showed a delicacy and a sense of honour
which would have been worthy of admiration in the highest walks of
life. Sam knew that the other had suffered solely on his account, and in
all his complaints he said that if he alone had been flogged it would have
been nothing, but that he could never see that man without thinking that   30
he had been the means of bringing that disgrace upon him; and John
never, by word or deed, let anything escape him to remind the other
that it was by interfering to save his ship-mate that he had suffered.—"

As a matter of fact, it was John who ought to have been ashamed
for bringing confusion and false feeling into a clear issue. Conventional   35
morality apart, John is the reprehensible party, not Sam or the captain.
The case was one of passional re-adjustment, nothing abnormal. And
who was the sententious Johannus, that he should interfere in this? And
if Mr Dana had a weak stomach as well as weak eyes, let him have it.
But let this pair of idealists abstain from making all the other men feel   40

uncomfortable and fuzzy about a thing they would have left to its natural course, if they had been allowed. No, your Johannuses and your Danas have to be creating "public opinion," and mugging up the life-issues with their sententiousness. Oh idealism!

5   The vessel arrives at the Pacific coast, and the swell of the rollers falls in our blood—the dreary coast stretches wonderful, on the brink of the unknown.

"Not a human being but ourselves for miles—the steep hill rising like a wall, and cutting us off from all the world—but the 'world of waters.'
10   I separated myself from the rest, and sat down on a rock, just where the sea ran in and formed a fine spouting-horn. Compared with the dull, plain sand-beach of the rest of the coast this grandeur was as refreshing as a great rock in a weary land. It was almost the first time I had been positively alone— — —My better nature returned strong upon me.—
15   I experienced a glow of pleasure at finding that what of poetry and romance I had ever had in me had not been entirely deadened in the laborious life I had been lately leading. Nearly an hour did I sit, almost lost in the luxury of this entire new scene of the play in which I was acting, when I was aroused by the distant shouts of my companions."
20   So Dana sits and Hamletises* by the Pacific—chief actor in the play of his own existence. But in him, self-consciousness is almost nearing the mark of scientific indifference to self.—He gives us a pretty picture of the then wild, unknown bay of San Francisco.—"The tide leaving us, we came to anchor near the mouth of the bay, under a high and
25   beautifully sloping hill, upon which herds of hundreds of red deer, and the stag, with his high-branching antlers were bounding about, looking at us for a moment, and then starting off affrighted at the noises we made for the purpose of seeing the variety of their beautiful attitudes and motions—"
30   Think of it now, and the Presidio!* The idiotic guns.

Two moments of strong human emotion Dana experiences: one moment of strong but impotent hate for the Captain, one strong impulse of pitying love for the Kanaka boy, Hope—a beautiful South Sea Islander sick of a white man's disease, phthisis or syphilis.* Of him Dana
35   writes "—but the other, who was my friend, and aikane—Hope—was the most dreadful object I had ever seen in my life; his eyes sunken and dead, his cheeks fallen in against his teeth, his hands looking like claws; a dreadful cough, which seemed to rack his whole shattered system; a hollow, whispering voice, and an entire inability to move himself.
40   There he lay, upon a mat on the ground, which was the only floor of

the oven, with no medicine, no comforts, and no-one to care for or help him but a few kanakas, who were willing enough, but could do nothing. The sight of him made me sick and faint. Poor fellow! During the four months that I lived upon the beach we were continually together, both in work and in our excursions in the woods and upon the water. I really felt a strong affection for him, and preferred him to any of my own countrymen there. When I came into the oven he looked at me, held out his hand and said in a low voice, but with a delightful smile, 'Aloha, Aikane! Aloha nui!' I comforted him as well as I could, and promised to ask the Captain to help him from the medicine chest.—"

We have felt the pulse of hate for the Captain—now the pulse of saviour-like love for the bright-eyed man of the Pacific, a real child of the ocean, full of the mystery-being of that great sea. Hope is for a moment to Dana what Chingachgook is to Cooper—the hearts-brother, the answerer. But only for an ephemeral moment. And even then his love was largely pity, tinged with philanthropy. The inevitable saviourism. The ideal being.

Dana was mad to leave the Californian coast, to be back in the civilised east. Yet he feels the poignancy of departure when at last the ship draws off. The Pacific is his glamour-world: the eastern States his world of actuality, scientific, materially real. He is a servant of civilisation, an idealist, a democrat, a hater of masters, a KNOWER. Conscious and self-conscious, without ever forgetting.

"When all sail had been set and the decks cleared up the *California* was a speck in the horizon, and the coast lay like a low cloud along the north-east. At sunset they were both out of sight, and we were once more upon the ocean, where sky and water meet."

The description of the voyage home is wonderful. It is as if the seas rose up to prevent the escape of this subtle explorer. Dana seems to pass into another world, another life, not of this earth. There is first the sense of apprehension, then the passing right into the black deeps. Then the waters almost swallow him up, with his triumphant consciousness.

"The days became shorter and shorter, the sun running lower in its course each day, and giving less and less heat, and the nights so cold as to prevent our sleeping on deck; the Magellan Clouds in sight of a clear night; the skies looking cold and angry; and at times a long, heavy, ugly sea, setting in from the Southward, told us what we were coming to—"

They were approaching Cape Horn, in the southern winter, passing into the strange, dread regions of the violent waters.

"And there lay, floating in the ocean, several miles off, an immense irregular mass, its top and points covered with snow, its centre a deep indigo. This was an iceberg, and of the largest size. As far as the eye could reach the sea in every direction was of a deep blue colour, the
5   waves running high and fresh, and sparkling in the light; and in the midst lay this immense mountain-island, its cavities and valleys thrown into deep shade, and its points and pinnacles glittering in the sun. But no description can give any idea of the strangeness, splendour, and, really, the sublimity of the sight. Its great size—for it must have been two
10   to three miles in circumference, and several hundred feet in height; its slow motion, as its base rose and sank in the water and its points nodded against the clouds; the dashing of the waves upon it, which, breaking high with foam, lined its base with a white crust; and the thundering sound of the cracking of the mass, and the breaking and the tumbling
15   down of huge pieces; together with its nearness and approach, which added a slight element of fear—all combined to give it the character of true sublimity—"
       But as the ship ran further and further into trouble, Dana became ill. First it is a slight toothache. Ice and exposure cause the pain to take hold
20   of all his head and face. And then the face so swelled, that he could not open his mouth to eat, and was in danger of lock-jaw.* In this state he was forced to keep his bunk for three or four days. — "At the end of the third day, the ice was very thick; a complete fog-bank covered the ship. It blew a tremendous gale from the eastward, with sleet and snow, and
25   there was every promise of a dangerous and fatiguing night. At dark, the Captain called all hands aft, and told them that not a man was to leave the deck that night; that the ship was in the greatest danger; any cake of ice might knock a hole in her, or she might run on an island and go to pieces. The look-outs were then set, and every man was put in his
30   station. When I heard what was the state of things, I began to put on my things, to stand it out with the rest of them, when the mate came below, and looking at my face ordered me back to my berth, saying if we went down we should all go down together, but if I went on deck I might lay myself up for life.—In obedience to the mate's orders, I went
35   back to my berth; but a more miserable night I never wish to spend—."
       It is the story of a man pitted in conflict against the sea, the vast, almost omnipotent element. In contest with this cosmic enemy, man finds his further ratification, his further ideal vindication. He comes out victorious, but not till the sea has tortured his living, integral body,
40   and made him pay something for his triumph in consciousness.

The horrific struggle round Cape Horn, homewards,* is the crisis of the Dana history. It is an entry into chaos, a heaven of sleet and black ice-rain, a sea of ice and iron-like water. Man fights the element in all its roused, mystic hostility to conscious life. This fight is the inward crisis and triumph of Dana's soul. He goes through it all consciously,   5
enduring, *knowing*. It is not a mere overcoming of obstacles. It is a pitting of the deliberate consciousness against all the roused, hostile, anti-life waters of the Pole.

After this fight, Dana has achieved his success. He KNOWS. He knows what the sea is. He knows what the Cape Horn is. He knows   10
what work is, work before the mast. He knows, he knows a great deal. He has carried his consciousness open-eyed through it all.* He has won through. The ideal being.

And from his book, we know too. He has lived this great experience for us, we owe him homage.   15

The ship passes through the strait, skirts the polar death-mystery, and turns northward, home. She seems to fly with new strong plumage, free. "Every rope-yarn seemed stretched to the utmost, and every thread of the canvas; and with this sail added to her the ship sprang through the water like a thing possessed. The sail being nearly all forward, it   20
lifted her out of the water, and she seemed actually to jump from sea to sea."

Beautifully the sailing-ship nodalises* the forces of sea and wind, converting them to her purpose. There is no violation, as in a steam-ship, only a winged centrality. It is this perfect adjusting of ourselves to   25
the elements, the perfect equipoise between them and us, which gives us a great part of our life-joy. The more we intervene machinery between us and the naked forces, the more we numb and atrophy our own senses. Every time we turn on a tap to have water, every time we turn a handle to have fire or light, we deny ourselves and annul our being. The great   30
elements, the earth, air, fire, water, are there like some great mistresses whom we woo and struggle with, whom we heave and wrestle with. And all our appliances do but deny us these fine embraces, take the miracle of life away from us. The machine is the great Neuter. It is the eunuch of eunuchs. In the end it emasculates us all. When we balance the sticks and   35
kindle a fire, we partake of the mysteries. But when we turn on an electric tap there is as it were a wad* between us and the dynamic universe. We do not know what we lose by all our labour-saving appliances. Of the two evils it would be much the lesser to lose all machinery, every bit, rather than to have, as we have, hopelessly too much.   40

When we study the pagan Gods, we find they have now one meaning, now another. Now they belong to the creative essence, and now to the material-dynamic world. First they have one aspect, then another. The greatest god has both aspects. First he is the source of life. Then he is
5 mystic dynamic lord of the elemental physical forces. So Zeus is Father, and Thunderer.*

Nations that worship the material-dynamic world, as all nations do in their decadence, seem to come inevitably to worship the Thunderer. He is Ammon, Zeus, Wotan and Thor, Shango* of the West Africans.
10 As the creator of man himself, the Father, is greatest in the creative world, the Thunderer is greatest in the material world. He is the god of force and of earthly blessing, the god of the bolt and of sweet rain.

So that electricity seems to be the first, intrinsic principle among the Forces. It has a mystic power of readjustment. It seems to be the
15 overlord of the two naked elements, fire and water, capable of mysteriously enchaining them, and of mysteriously sundering them from their connections. When the two great elements become hopelessly clogged, entangled, the sword of the lightning can separate them. The crash of thunder is really not the clapping together of waves of air. Thunder
20 is the noise of the explosion which takes place when the waters are loosed from the elemental fire, when old vapours are suddenly decomposed in the upper air by the electric force. Then fire flies fluid, and the waters roll off in purity. It is the liberation of the elements from hopeless conjunction. Thunder, the electric force, is the counterpart in
25 the material-dynamic world of the life-force, the creative mystery itself, in the creative world.

Dana gives a wonderful description of a tropical thunderstorm.

"When our watch came on deck at twelve o'clock it was as black as Erebus; not a breath was stirring; the sails hung heavy and motion-
30 less from the yards; and the perfect stillness, and the darkness, which was almost palpable, were truly appalling. Not a word was spoken, but everyone stood as though waiting for something to happen. In a few minutes the mate came forward, and in a low tone which was almost a whisper, gave the command to haul down the jib— —When we got
35 down we found all hands looking aloft, and then, directly over where we had been standing, upon the main top-gallant masthead, was a ball of light, which the sailors name a corposant (*corpus sancti*). They were all watching it carefully, for sailors have a notion that if the corposant rises in the rigging, it is a sign of fair weather, but if it comes lower
40 down, there will be a storm. Unfortunately, as an omen, it came down and showed itself on the top-gallant yard.

"In a few minutes it disappeared and showed itself again on the fore top-gallant-yard, and, after playing about for some time, disappeared again, when the man on the forecastle pointed to it upon the flying-jib-boom end. But our attention was drawn from watching this by the falling of some drops of rain. In a few minutes low growling thunder was heard, and some random flashes of lightning came from the south-west. Every sail was taken in but the top-sail. A few puffs lifted the topsails, but they fell again to the mast, and all was as still as ever. A minute more, and a terrific flash and peal broke simultaneously upon us, and a cloud appeared to open directly over our heads and let down the water in one body like a falling ocean. We stood motionless and almost stupified, yet nothing had been struck. Peal after peal rattled over our heads with a sound which actually seemed to stop the breath in the body. The violent fall of the rain lasted but a few minutes, and was succeeded by occasional drops and showers; but the lightning continued incessant for several hours, breaking the midnight darkness with irregular and blinding flashes.

"During all this time hardly a word was spoken, no bell was struck, and the wheel was silently relieved. The rain fell at intervals in heavy showers, and we stood drenched through, and blinded by the flashes, which broke the Egyptian darkness with a brightness which seemed almost malignant, while the thunder rolled in peals, the concussion of which appeared to shake the very ocean. A ship is not often injured by lightning, for the electricity is separated by the great number of points she presents, and the quantity of iron which she has scattered in various parts. The electric fluid ran over our anchors, topsail-sheets and ties; yet no harm was done to us. We went below at four o'clock, leaving things in the same state."*

Dana is wonderful at relating these mechanical, or dynamic-physical events. He could not tell about the being of men: only about the *forces*. He gives another curious instance of the process of de-creation, as it takes place within the very corpuscles of the blood. It is *salt* this time which arrests the life-activity, causing a static arrest in Matter, after a certain sundering of water from the fire of the warm-substantial body.

"The scurvy had begun to show itself on board. One man had it so badly as to be disabled and off duty; and the English lad, Ben, was in a dreadful state, and was gradually growing worse. His legs swelled and pained him so that he could not walk; his flesh lost its elasticity, so that if it were pressed in, it would not return to its shape; and his gums swelled until he could not open his mouth. His breath, too, became very offensive; he lost all strength and spirit; could eat nothing; grew worse

every day; and, in fact, unless something was done for him, would be a
dead man in a week at the rate at which he was sinking. The medicines
were all gone, or nearly all gone; and if we had had a chest-full, they
would have been of no use; for nothing but fresh provisions and terra
5   firma has any effect upon the scurvy."*

However, a boat-load of potatoes and onions was obtained from a
passing ship. These the men ate raw. "The freshness and crispness of
the raw onion, with the earthy state, gave it a great relish to one who
has been a long time on salt provisions. We were perfectly ravenous
10 after them. We ate them at every meal, by the dozen; and filled our
pockets with them, to eat in the watch on deck. The chief use, however,
of the fresh provisions was for the men with the scurvy. One was able
to eat, and he soon brought himself to by gnawing upon raw potatoes;
but the other, by this time, was hardly able to open his mouth; and the
15 cook took the potatoes raw, pounded them in a mortar, and gave him
the juice to drink. The strong earthy taste and smell of this extract
of the raw potatoes at first produced a shuddering through his whole
frame, and after drinking it, an acute pain, which ran through all parts
of his body; but knowing by this time that it was taking strong hold, he
20 persevered, drinking a spoonful every hour or so, until, by the effect of
this drink, and of his own restored hope, he became so well as to be able
to move about, and open his mouth enough to eat the raw potatoes and
onions pounded into a soft pulp. This course soon restored his appetite
and strength; and ten days after we spoke the Solon, so rapid was his
25 recovery that, from lying helpless and almost hopeless in his berth, he
was at the mast-head, furling a royal."*

This is the strange result of the disintegrating effect of the sea, and
of salt in food. We are all sea-born, science tells us. The moon, and the
sea, and salt, and phosphorus,* and us: it is a long chain of connection.
30 And then the earth: mother-earth. Dana talks of the relish which the
earthy taste of the onion gives. The taste of created juice, the living milk
of Gea.* And limes, which taste of the sun.

How much stranger is the interplay of *life* among the elements,
than any chemical interplay among the elements themselves. Life—
35 and salt—and phosphorus—and the sea—and the moon. Life—and
sulphur—and carbon—and volcanoes—and the sun. The way up, and
the way down.* The strange ways of life.

But Dana went home, to be a lawyer, and a rather dull and
distinguished citizen. He was once almost an ambassador.* And pre-
40 eminently respectable.

He had been. He KNEW. He had even told us. It is a great achievement.

And then what?—Why, nothing. The old vulgar hum-drum. That's the worst of knowledge. It leaves one only the more lifeless. Dana lived his bit in two years, and knew, and drummed out the rest. Dreary lawyer's   5
years, afterwards.

We know enough. We know too much. We know nothing.

Let us smash something. Ourselves included. But the machine above all.

Dana's small book* is a very great book: contains a great extreme of   10
knowledge, knowledge of the great element.

And after all, we have to know all before we can know that knowing is nothing.

Imaginatively, we have to know all: even the elemental waters. And know and know on, until knowledge suddenly shrivels and we know   15
that forever we don't know.

Then there is a sort of peace, and we can start afresh, knowing we don't know.

X.

Herman Melville's *Typee* and *Omoo*.*

The greatest seer and poet of the sea for me is Melville. His vision is more
5   real than Swinburne's, because he doesn't personify the sea, and far
sounder than Joseph Conrad's, because Melville doesn't sentimentalise
the ocean and the sea's unfortunates. Snivel in a wet hanky like Lord
Jim.*

Melville has the strange, uncanny magic of sea-creatures, and some
10   of their repulsiveness. He isn't quite a land animal. There is something
slithery about him. Something always half-seas-over.* In his life they
said he was mad—or crazy. He was neither mad nor crazy. But he was
over the border. He was half a water animal, like those terrible yellow-
bearded Vikings who broke out of the waves in beaked ships.*
15   He was a modern viking. There is something curious about real blue-
eyed people. They are never quite human, in the good classic sense,
human as brown-eyed people are human: the human of the living humus. About a real blue-eyed person there is usually something abstract,
elemental. Brown-eyed people are, as it were, like the earth, which is tis-
20   sue of bygone life, organic, compound. In brown* eyes there is sun and
earth and shadow and soaked water. But in blue eyes there is principally
the abstract, uncreate element, water, ice, air, space, but not humanity.
Brown-eyed people are people of the old, old world: *allzu menschlich*.*
Blue-eyed people tend to be too keen and abstract.
25   Melville is like a Viking* going home to the sea, encumbered with
age and memories, and a sort of accomplished despair, almost madness.
For he cannot accept humanity. He can't belong to humanity. Cannot.

The great Northern cycle of which he is the returning unit has almost completed its round, accomplished itself. Balder the beautiful is
30   mystically dead,* and by this time he stinketh. Forget-me-nots and sea-
poppies* fall into water. The man who came from the sea to live among
men can stand it no longer. He hears the horror of the cracked church-
bell, and goes back down the shore, back into the ocean again, home,
into the salt water. Human life won't do. He turns back to the element.

And all the vast sun-and-wheat consciousness of his day he plunges back into the deeps, burying the flame in the deep, self-conscious and deliberate. Like blue flax and sea-poppies fall into the waters and give back their created sun-stuff to the dissolution of the flood.

The sea-born people, who can meet and mingle no longer: who turn away from life, to the abstract, to the elements: the sea receives her own. Let life come asunder, they say. Let water conceive no more with fire.* Let mating finish. Let the elements leave off kissing, and turn their backs on one another. Let the merman turn away from his human wife and children,* let the seal-woman forget the world of men,* remembering only the waters.

So they go down to the sea, the sea-born people. The Vikings are wandering again. Homes are broken up. Cross the seas, cross the seas, urges the heart. Leave love and home. Leave love and home. Love and home are a deadly illusion. Woman, what have I to do with thee? It is finished. *Consummatum est.** The crucifixion into humanity is over. Let us go back to the fierce, uncanny elements: the corrosive vast sea. Or fire.

Basta!* It is enough. It is enough of life. Let us have the vast elements. Let us get out of this loathsome complication of living humanly with humans. Let the sea wash us clean of the leprosy of our humanity: our humanness.

Melville was a northerner, sea-born. So the sea claimed him. We are most of us, who use the English language, water-people, sea-derived.

Melville went back to the oldest of all the oceans, to the Pacific. *Der Grosse oder Stille Ozean.**

Without doubt the Pacific Ocean is aeons older than the Atlantic or the Indian Oceans. When we say older, we mean it has not come to any modern consciousness. Strange convulsions have convulsed the Atlantic and Mediterranean peoples into phase after phase of consciousness, while the Pacific and the Pacific peoples have slept. To sleep is to dream:* you can't stay unconscious. And oh heaven, for how many thousands of years has the true Pacific been dreaming, turning over in its sleep and dreaming again. Dreams: idylls: nightmares.

The Maoris, the Tongans, the Marquesans, the Fijians, the Polynesians:* holy God, how long have they been turning over in the same sleep, with varying dreams. Perhaps, to a sensitive imagination, those islands in the middle of the Pacific are the most unbearable places on earth. It simply stops the heart, to be translated there, unknown ages back, back into that life, that pulse, that rhythm. The scientists say the South Sea Islanders belong to the Stone Age.* It seems absurd to class people

according to their implements. And yet there is something in it. The heart of the Pacific is still the Stone Age: in spite of steamers. The heart of the Pacific seems like a vast vacuum, in which, mirage-like, continues the life of myriads of ages back. It is a phantom-persistence of human
5   beings who should have died, by our chronology, in the Stone Age. It is a phantom, illusion-like trick of reality: the glamorous South Seas.

Even Japan and China have been turning over in their sleep for countless centuries. Their blood is the old blood, their tissue the old soft tissue. Their busy day was myriads of years ago, when the world was a softer
10 place, more moisture in the air, more warm mud on the face of the earth, and the lotus was always in flower. The great bygone world, before Egypt.* And Japan and China have been turning over in their sleep, while we have "advanced." And now they are starting up into nightmare. The world isn't what it seems.

15 The Pacific Ocean holds the dream of immemorial centuries. It is the great blue twilight of the vastest of all evenings: perhaps of the most wonderful of all dawns. Who knows.

It must once have been a vast basin of soft, lotus-warm civilisation, the Pacific. Never was such a huge man-day swung down into slow
20 disintegration, as here. And now the waters are blue and ghostly with the end of immemorial peoples. And phantom-like the islands rise out of it, illusions of the glamorous Stone Age.

To this phantom Melville returned. Back, back, away from life. Never man instinctly hated human life, our human life, as we have it, more
25 than Melville did. And never was a man so passionately filled with the sense of the vastness and mystery of life which is non-human. He was mad to look over our horizons. Anywhere, anywhere out of *our* world. To get away. To get out, out!

To get away, out of our life. To cross a horizon into another life. No
30 matter what life, so long as it is another life.

Away, away from humanity. To the sea. The naked, salt, elemental sea. To go to sea, to escape humanity.

The human heart gets into a frenzy at last, in its desire to dehumanise itself.

35 So he finds himself in the middle of the Pacific. Truly over a horizon. In another world. In another epoch. Back, far back, in the days of palm trees and lizards and stone implements. The sunny Stone Age.

Samoa, Tahiti, Raratonga, Nukuheva:* the very names are a sleep and a forgetting. The sleep-forgotten past magnificence of human history.
40 "Trailing clouds of glory."*

Melville hated the world: was born hating it. But he was looking for heaven. That is, choosingly. Choosingly, he was looking for paradise. Unchoosingly, he was mad with hatred of the world.

Well, the world is hateful. It is as hateful as Melville found it. He was not wrong in hating the world. Delenda est Chicago.* He hated it to a 5 pitch of madness, and not without reason.

But it's no good *persisting* in looking for paradise "regained."*

Melville at his best invariably wrote from a sort of dream-self, so that events which he relates as actual fact have indeed a far deeper reference to his own soul, his own inner life. 10

So in *Typee* when he tells of his entry into the valley of the dreaded cannibals of Nukuheva. Down this narrow, steep, horrible dark gorge he slides and struggles as we struggle in a dream, or in the act of birth, to emerge in the green Eden of the Golden Age, the valley of the cannibal savages. This is a bit of birth-myth, or re-birth myth, on Melville's 15 part—unconscious, no doubt, because his running underconsciousness was always mystical and symbolical. He wasn't aware that he was being mystical.

There he is then, in Typee, among the dreaded cannibal savages. And they are gentle and generous with him, and he is *truly* in a sort of Eden. 20

Here at last is Rousseau's Child of Nature and Châteaubriand's Noble Savage* called upon and found at home. Yes, Melville loves his savage hosts. He finds them gentle, laughing lambs compared to the ravening wolves of his white brothers, left behind in America and on an American whale-ship. 25

The ugliest beast on earth is the white man, says Melville.

In short, Herman found in Typee the paradise he was looking for. It is true, the Marquesans were "immoral,"* but he rather liked that. Morality was too white a trick to take him in. Then again, they were cannibals. And it filled him with horror even to think of this. But the 30 savages were very private and even fiercely reserved in their cannibalism, and he might have spared himself his shudder. No doubt he had partaken of the Christian Sacraments many a time: "This is my body, take and eat. This is my blood. Drink it in remembrance of me."* And if the savages liked to partake of their sacrament without raising the transubstantiation 35 quibble, and if they liked to say, directly: "This is thy body, which I take from thee and eat. This is thy blood, which I sip in annihilation of thee," why surely their sacred ceremony was as awe-inspiring as the one Jesus substituted. But Herman chose to be horrified.* I confess, I am not horrified. Though of course I am not on the spot. But the savage 40 sacrament seems to me more valid than the Christian: less side-tracking about it.—Thirdly he was shocked by their wild methods of warfare.* He died before the great European war, so his shock was comfortable.

Three little quibbles: morality, cannibal sacrament, and stone axes.
5   You must have a fly even in Paradisal ointment. And the first was a ladybird.*

But Paradise. He insists on it, Paradise. He could even go stark naked, like before the Apple episode. And his Fayaway, a laughing little Eve, naked with him, and hankering after no apple of knowledge, so long as
10 he would just love her when he felt like it. Plenty to eat, needing no clothes to wear, sunny, happy people, sweet water to swim in: everything a man can want. Then why wasn't he happy along with the savages?

Because he wasn't.

He grizzled in secret, and wanted to escape.
15 He even pined for Home and Mother,* the two things he had run away from as fast as ships would carry him. HOME and MOTHER. The two things that were his damnation.

There on the island, where the golden-green great palm-trees chinked in the sun, and the elegant reed houses let the sea-breeze through, and
20 people went naked and laughed a great deal, and Fayaway put flowers on his hair for him—great red hibiscus flowers, and frangipani*—Oh God, why wasn't he happy? Why wasn't he?

Because he wasn't.

Well, it's hard to make a man happy.
25 But I should not have been happy either. One's soul seems under a vacuum, in the South Seas.*

The truth of the matter is, one cannot go back. Some men can: renegade. But Melville couldn't go back: and Gauguin couldn't really go back:* and I know now that I could never go back. Back towards the
30 past, savage life. One cannot go back. It is one's destiny inside one.

There are these peoples, these "savages." One does not despise them. One does not feel superior. But there is a gulf. There is a gulf in time and being. I cannot commingle my being with theirs.

There they are, these South Sea Islanders, beautiful big men with
35 their golden limbs and their laughing, graceful laziness. And they will call you brother, choose you as a brother. But why cannot one truly be brother?

There is an invisible hand grasps my heart and prevents it opening too much to these strangers. They are beautiful, they are like children,
40 they are generous: but they are more than this. They are far off, and

in their eyes is an easy darkness of the soft, uncreate past. In a way, they are uncreate. Far be it from me to assume any "white" superiority. But they are savages. They are gentle and laughing and physically very handsome. But it seems to me, that in living so far, through all our bitter centuries of civilisation, we have still been living onwards, forwards. God 5 knows it looks like a *cul de sac* now. But turn to the first negro, and then listen to your own soul. And your own soul will tell you that however false and foul our forms and systems now are, still, through the many centuries since Egypt, we have been living and struggling forwards along some road that is no road, and yet is a great life development. We have 10 struggled on in life-development. And our own soul says inside us that on we must still go. We may have to smash things. Then let us smash. And our road may have to take a great swerve, that seems a retrogression.

But we can't go back. Whatever else the South Sea Islander is, he is centuries and centuries behind us in the life struggle, the consciousness- 15 struggle, the struggle of the soul into fulness. There is his woman, with her knotted hair and her dark, inchoate, slightly sardonic eyes. I like her, she is nice. But I would never want to touch her. I could not go back on myself so far. Back to their uncreate condition.

She has soft warm flesh, like warm mud.* Nearer the reptile, the 20 Saurian age. *Noli me tangere.**

We can't go back. We can't go back to the savages: not a stride. We can be in sympathy with them. We can take a great curve in their direction, onwards. But we cannot turn the current of our life backwards, back towards their soft warm twilight and uncreate mud. Not for a moment. 25 If we do it for a moment, it makes us sick.

We can only do it when we are renegade. The renegade hates life itself. He wants the death of life. So these many "reformers" and "idealists" who glorify the savages in America.* They are death-birds, life-haters. Renegades. 30

We can't go back. And Melville couldn't. Much as he hated the civilised humanity he knew. He couldn't go back to the savages. He wanted to. He tried to. And he couldn't.

Because, in the first place, it made him sick. It made him physically ill. He had something wrong with his leg, and this would not heal.* It 35 got worse and worse, during his four months on the island. When he escaped, he was in a deplorable condition. Sick and miserable. Ill, very ill.

Paradise!

But there you are. Try to go back to the savages, and you feel as if your very soul was decomposing inside you. That is what you feel in the 40

South Seas, anyhow: as if your soul was decomposing inside you. And with any savages the same, if you try to go their way, take their current of sympathy.

Yet, as I say, we must make a great swerve in our onward-going life-course now, to gather up again the savage mysteries. But this does not mean going back on ourselves.

Going back to the Savages made Melville sicker than anything. It made him feel as if he were decomposing. Worse even than Home and Mother.

And that is what really happens. If you prostitute your psyche by returning to the savages, you gradually go to pieces. Before you can go back, you *have* to decompose. And a white man decomposing is a ghastly sight. Even Melville in Typee.

We have to go on, on, on, even if we must smash a way ahead.

So Melville escaped. And threw a boat-hook full in the throat of one of his dearest savage friends, and sank him,* because that savage was swimming in pursuit. That's how he felt about the savages when they wanted to detain him. He'd have murdered them one and all, vividly, rather than be kept from escaping. Away from them—he must get away from them—at any price.

And once he had escaped, immediately he begins to sigh and pine for the "Paradise." Home and Mother being at the other end even of a whaling voyage.

When he really was Home with Mother, he found it Purgatory.* But Typee must have been even worse than Purgatory, a soft hell, judging from the murderous frenzy which possessed him, to escape.

But once aboard the whaler that carried him off from Nukuheva, he looked back and sighed for the Paradise he had just escaped from in such a fever.

Poor Melville! He was determined Paradise existed. So he was always in Purgatory.

He was born for Purgatory. Some souls are purgatorial by destiny.

The very freedom of his Typee was a torture to him. Its ease was slowly horrible to him. This time *he* was the fly in the odorous tropical ointment.

He needed to fight. It was no good to him, the relaxation of the non-moral tropics. He didn't really want Eden. He wanted to fight. Like every American. To fight. But with weapons of the spirit, not the flesh.

That was the top and bottom of it. His soul was in revolt, writhing forever in revolt. When he had something definite to rebel against—like the bad conditions on a whaling ship—then he was much happier in his miseries. The mills of God were grinding inside him,* and they needed something to grind on.

When they could grind on the injustice and folly of missionaries, or of brutal sea-captains, or of governments,* he was easier. The mills of   5
God were grinding inside him.

They are grinding inside every American. And they grind exceeding small.

Why? Heaven knows. But we've got to grind down our old forms, our old selves, grind them very very small, to nothingness. Whether a new   10
somethingness will ever start, who knows. Meanwhile the mills of God ground on, in American Melville, and it was himself he ground small: himself and his wife, when he was married. For the present, the South Seas.

He escapes on to the craziest, most impossible of whaling ships.*   15
Lucky for us Melville makes it fantastic. It must have been pretty sordid.

And anyhow, on the crazy *Julia* his leg, that would never heal in the paradise of Typee, began quickly to get well. His life was falling into its normal pulse. The drain back into past centuries was over.

Yet oh, as he sails away from Nukuheva, on the voyage that will   20
ultimately take him to America, oh the acute and intolerable nostalgia he feels for the island he has left.

The past. The Golden Age of the past. What a nostalgia we all feel for it. Yet we don't want it when we get it. Try the South Seas.

Melville had to fight, fight against the existing world, against his   25
own very self. Only he would never quite put the knife in the heart of his paradisal ideal. Somehow, somewhere, somewhen, love should be a fulfilment, and life should be a thing of bliss. That was his fixed ideal. Fata Morgana.*

That was the pin he tortured himself on, like a pinned-down butterfly.   30

Love is never a fulfilment. Life is never a thing of continuous bliss. There is no paradise. Fight and laugh and feel bitter and feel bliss: and fight again. Fight, fight. That is life.

Why pin ourselves down on a paradisal ideal? It is only ourselves we torture.   35

Melville did have one great experience, getting away from humanity: the experience of the sea.

The South Sea Islands were not his great experience. They were a glamorous world outside New England. Outside. But it was the sea that was both outside and inside: the universal experience.   40

The book that follows on from *Typee* is *Omoo.*

Omoo is a fascinating book: picaresque, rascally, roving. Melville as a bit of a beach comber.* The crazy ship *Julia* sails to Tahiti, and the mutinous crew are put ashore. Put in the Tahitian prison. It is good
5   reading.

Perhaps Melville is at his best, his happiest, in *Omoo.* For once he is really reckless. For once he takes life as it comes. For once he is the gallant rascally epicurean, eating the world like a snipe,* dirt and all baked into one *bonne bouche.**
10   For once he is really careless, roving with that scamp, Doctor Long Ghost.* For once he is careless of his actions, careless of his morals, careless of his ideals: ironic, as the epicurean must be. The deep irony of your real scamp: your real epicurean of the moment.

But it was under the influence of the Long Doctor. This long and
15   bony Scotsman was not a mere neer-do-well. He was a man of humorous desperation, throwing his life ironically away. Not a mere loose-kneed loafer, such as the South Seas seem to attract.

That is good about Melville: he never repents. Whatever he did, in Typee or in Doctor Long Ghost's wicked society, he never repented. If
20   he ate his snipe dirt and all, and enjoyed it at the time, he didn't have bilious bouts afterwards. Which is good.

But it wasn't enough. The Long Doctor was really knocking about in a sort of despair. He let his ship drift rudderless.

Melville couldn't do this. For a time, yes. For a time, in the Long
25   Doctor's company, he was rudderless and reckless. Good as an experience. But a man who will not abandon himself to despair or indifference cannot keep it up.

Melville would never abandon himself either to despair or indifference. He always cared. He always cared enough to hate missionaries,
30   and to be touched by a real act of kindness. He always cared.

When he saw a white man really "gone savage," a white man with a blue shark tatooed over his brow,* gone over to the savages, then Herman's whole being revolted. He couldn't bear it. He could not bear a renegade.
35   He enlisted at last on an American man-of-war. You have the record in *White Jacket.** He was back in civilisation, but still at sea. He was in America, yet loose in the seas. Good regular days, after Doctor Long Ghost and the *Julia.*

As a matter of fact, a long thin chain was round Melville's ankle all
40   the time, binding him to America, to civilisation, to democracy, to the ideal world. It was a long chain: and it never broke. It pulled him back.

By the time he was twenty-five his wild oats were sown; his reckless wanderings were over. At the age of twenty-five he came back to Home and Mother,* to fight it out at close quarters. For you can't fight it out by running away. When you have run a long way from Home and Mother, then you realise that the earth is round, and if you keep on running you'll be back on the same old doorstep. Like a fatality.

Melville came home to face out the long rest of his life. He married and had an ecstasy of a courtship and fifty years of disillusion.*

He just furnished his home with disillusions. No more Typees. No more paradises. No more Fayaways. A mother: a gorgon. A home: a torture box. A wife: a thing with clay feet. Life: a sort of disgrace. Fame: another disgrace, being patronised by common snobs who just know how to read.

The whole shameful business just making a man writhe.

Melville writhed for eighty years.

In his soul he was proud and savage.

But in his mind and will, he wanted the perfect fulfilment of love. He wanted the lovey-doveyness* of perfect mutual understanding.

A proud savage-souled man doesn't really want any perfect lovey-dovey fulfilment in love. No such nonsense. A mountain-lion doesn't mate with a Persian cat. And when a grizzly bear roars after a mate, it is a she-grizzly he roars after. Not after a silky sheep.

But Melville stuck to his ideal. He wrote *Pierre** to show that the more you try to be good the more you make a mess of things: that following righteousness is just disastrous. The better you are, the worse things turn out with you. The better you try to be, the bigger mess you make. Your very striving after righteousness only causes your own slow degeneration.

Well, it is true. No men are so evil today as the idealists: and no women half so evil as your earnest woman, who feels herself a power for good.

It is inevitable. After a certain point, the ideal goes dead and rotten. The old pure ideal becomes in itself an impure thing of evil. Charity becomes pernicious, the spirit itself becomes foul. The meek are evil. The pure in heart have base, subtle revulsions: like Dostoevsky's Idiot. The whole Sermon on the Mount becomes a litany of white vice.*

What then?

It's our own fault. It was *me* who set up the ideals. And if we are such fools, that we aren't able to kick over our ideals in time, the worse for us.

Look at Melville's eighty long years of writhing. And to the end he writhed on the ideal pin.

From the "perfect woman lover" he passed on to the "perfect friend."
He looked and looked for the perfect man friend.

Couldn't find him.

Marriage was a ghastly disillusion to him, because he looked for
5   perfect marriage.

Friendship never even made a real start in him—save perhaps his
half-sentimental love for Jack Chase, in *White Jacket.**

Yet to the end he pined for this: a perfect relationship: perfect mating:
perfect mutual understanding. A perfect friend.

10   Right to the end he could never accept the fact that *perfect* relationships cannot be. Each soul is alone, and the aloneness of each soul is a
double barrier to perfect relationship between two beings.

Each soul *should* be alone. And in the end the desire for a "perfect
relationship" is just a vicious, unmanly craving. *"Tous nos malheurs
15   viennent de ne pouvoir être seuls."*

Melville however refused to draw this conclusion. *Life* was wrong, he
said. He refused Life. But he stuck to his ideal of perfect relationship,
possible perfect love. The world *ought* to be a harmonious loving place.
And it *can't* be. So Life itself is wrong.

20   It is silly arguing. Because after all, only temporary man sets up the
"oughts."

The world ought *not* to be a harmonious loving place. It ought to be
a place of fierce discord and intermittent harmonies: which it is.

Love ought *not* to be perfect. It ought to have perfect moments, and
25   wildernesses of thorn bushes. Which it has.

A "perfect" relationship ought *not* to be possible. Every relationship
should have its absolute limits, its absolute reserves, essential to the
singleness of the soul in each person. A truly perfect relationship is one
in which each party leaves great tracts unknown in the other party.

30   No two persons can meet at more than a few points, consciously. If
two people can just be together fairly often, so that the presence of each
is a sort of balance to the other, that is the basis of perfect relationship.
There must be true separatenesses as well.

Melville was, at the core, a mystic and an idealist.

35   Perhaps, so am I.

And he stuck to his ideal guns.

I abandon mine.

He was a mystic who raved because the old ideal guns shot havoc.
The guns of the "noble spirit." Of "ideal love."

40   I say, let the old guns rot.

Get new ones, and shoot straight.

XI.

Herman Melville's *Moby Dick*.

*Moby Dick, or the White Whale.**
A hunt. The last great hunt.
For what?   5
For Moby Dick, the huge white sperm whale: who is old, hoary,
monstrous, and swims alone; who is unspeakably terrible in his wrath,
having so often been attacked; and snow-white.
Of course he is a symbol.
Of what?   10
I doubt if even Melville knew exactly. That's the best of it.
He is warm-blooded, he is lovable. He is lonely Leviathan, not a
Hobbes sort.* Or is he?
But he is warm-blooded, and lovable. The South Sea Islanders, and
Polynesians, and Malays, who worship shark, or crocodile, or weave   15
endless frigate-bird distortions,* why did they never worship the whale?
So big!
Because the whale is not wicked. He doesn't bite. And their gods had
to bite.
He's not a dragon. He is Leviathan. He never coils like the Chinese   20
dragon of the sun.* He's not a serpent of the waters. He is warm-
blooded, a mammal. And hunted, hunted down.
It is a great book.
At first you are put off by the style. It reads like journalese. It seems
spurious. You feel Melville is trying to put something over you. It won't   25
do.
And Melville really is a bit sententious: aware of himself, self-
conscious, putting something over even himself. But then it's not easy
to get into the swing of a piece of deep mysticism when you just set out
with a story.   30
Nobody can be more clownish, more clumsy and sententiously in
bad taste, than Herman Melville, even in a great book like *Moby Dick*.
He preaches and holds forth because he's not sure of himself. And he
holds forth, often, so amateurishly.*

133

The artist was so *much* greater than the man. The man is rather a
tiresome New Englander of the ethical-mystical-transcendentalist sort:
Emerson, Longfellow, Hawthorne etc. So unrelieved, the solemn ass
even in humour. So hopelessly *au grand sérieux*.* You feel like saying:
5   Good God, what does it matter? If life is a tragedy, or a farce, or a
disaster, or anything else, what do I care! Let Life be what it likes. Give
me a drink, that's what I want just now.

For my part, life is so many things I don't care what it is. It's not
my affair to sum it up. Just now it's a cup of tea. This morning it was
10 wormwood and gall.* Hand me the sugar.

One wearies of the *grand sérieux*. There's something false about it.
And that's Melville. Oh dear, when the solemn ass brays! brays! brays!

But he was a deep, great artist, even if he was rather a sententious
man. He was a real American in that he always felt his audience in
15 front of him. But when he ceases to be American, when he forgets all
audience, and gives us his sheer apprehension of the world, then he is
wonderful, his book commands a stillness in the soul, an awe.

In his "human" self, Melville is almost dead. That is, he hardly reacts
to human contacts any more: or only ideally: or just for a moment. His
20 human-emotional self is almost played out. He is abstract, self-analytical
and abstracted. And he is more spell-bound by the strange slidings and
collidings of Matter than by the things men do. In this he is like Dana.
It is the material elements he really has to do with. His drama is with
them. He was a futurist long before futurism found paint.* The sheer
25 naked slidings of the elements. And the human soul experiencing it all.
So often, it is almost over the border: psychiatry.* Almost spurious. Yet
so great.

It is the same old thing as in all Americans. They keep their old-
fashioned ideal frock-coat on, and an old-fashioned silk hat, while they
30 do the most impossible things. There you are: you see Melville hugged
in bed by a huge tatooed South Sea Islander, and solemnly offering
burnt offering to the savage's little idol,* and his ideal frock coat just
hides his shirt-tails and prevents us from seeing his bare posterior as
he salaams, while his ethical silk hat sits correctly over his brow the
35 while. That is so typically American: doing the most impossible things
without taking off their spiritual get-up. Their ideals are like armour
which has rusted in, and will never more come off. And meanwhile in
Melville his bodily knowledge moves naked, a living quick among the
stark elements. In sheer physical, vibrational sensitiveness, like a mar-
40 vellous wireless-station, he registers the effects of the outer world. And
he records also, almost beyond pain or pleasure, the extreme transitions

of the isolated, far-driven soul, the soul which is now alone, without any real human contact.

The first days in New Bedford* introduce the only human being who really enters into the book, namely Ishmael, the "I" of the book.* And then the moment's hearts-brother, Queequeg, the tatooed, powerful South Sea harpooneer,* whom Melville loves as Dana loves "Hope." The advent of Ishmael's bed-mate is amusing and unforgettable. But later the two swear "marriage," in the language of the savages. For Queequeg has opened again the flood-gates of love and human connection in Ishmael.

"As I sat there in that now lonely room; the fire burning low, in that mild stage when, after its first intensity has warmed the air, it then only glows to be looked at; the evening shades and phantoms gathering round the casements, and peering in upon us silent, solitary twain; I began to be sensible of strange feelings. I felt a melting in me. No more my splintered hand and maddened heart was turned against the wolfish world. This soothing savage had redeemed it. There he sat, his very indifference speaking a nature in which there lurked no civilised hypocrisies and bland deceits. Wild he was; a very sight of sights to see; yet I began to feel myself mysteriously drawn towards him."—So they smoke together, and are clasped in each other's arms. The friendship is finally sealed when Ishmael offers sacrifice to Queequeg's little idol, Gogo.

"I was a good Christian, born and bred in the bosom of the infallible Presbyterian Church. How then could I unite with the idolater in worshipping his piece of wood? But what is worship?— thought I. But what is worship?—to do the will of God—*that* is worship. And what is the will of God?—to do to my fellow-man what I would have my fellow-man do to me—*that* is the will of God.—"* Which sounds like Benjamin Franklin, and is hopelessly bad theology. But it is real American logic.—"Now Queequeg is my fellow-man. And what do I wish that this Queequeg would do to me? Why, unite with me in my particular Presbyterian form of worship. Consequently, I must then unite with him; ergo, I must turn idolater. So I kindled the shavings; helped prop up the innocent little idol; offered him burnt biscuit with Queequeg; salaamed before him twice or thrice; kissed his nose; and that done, we undressed and went to bed, at peace with our own consciences and all the world. But we did not go to sleep without some little chat. How it is I know not; but there is no place like bed for confidential disclosures between friends. Man and wife, they say, open the very bottom of their souls to each other; and some old couples often lie and chat over old times till nearly morning. Thus, then, lay I and Queequeg—a cosy, loving pair—"

You would think this relation with Queequeg meant something to Ishmael. But no. Queequeg is forgotten like yesterday's newspaper. Human things are only momentary excitements or amusements to the American Ishmael. Ishmael, the hunted. But much more, Ishmael the

5 hunter. What's a Queequeg? What's a wife? The white whale must be hunted down. Queequeg must be just "KNOWN," then dropped into oblivion.

And what in the name of fortune is the white whale?

Elsewhere Ishmael says he loved Queequeg's eyes: "large, deep eyes,

10 fiery black and bold." No doubt, like Poe, he wanted to get the "clue" to them. That was all.

The two men go over from New Bedford to Nantucket, and there sign on to the Quaker whaling-ship, the *Pequod*.* It is all strangely fantastic, phantasmagoric. The voyage of the soul. Yet curiously a real whaling-

15 voyage too. We pass on into the midst of the sea with this strange ship and its incredible crew. The Argonauts were mild lambs in comparison. And Ulysses went *defeating* the Circes and overcoming the wicked hussies of the isles.* But the *Pequod*'s crew is a collection of maniacs fanatically hunting down a lonely, harmless white whale.

20 As a soul-history, it makes one angry. As a sea-yarn, it is marvellous: there is always something a bit over the mark, in sea-yarns. Should be. Then again the masking up of actual sea-man's experience with sonorous mysticism sometimes gets on one's nerves. And again, as a revelation of destiny the book is too deep even for sorrow. Profound

25 beyond feeling.

You are some time before you are allowed to see the captain, Ahab: the mysterious Quaker.* Oh, it is a god-fearing Quaker ship.

Ahab, the captain. The captain of the soul.

"I am the master of my fate.
30   I am the captain of my soul!"

Ahab!

"Oh captain, my captain, our fearful trip is done."*

The gaunt Ahab, Quaker, mysterious person, only shows himself after some days at sea. There's a secret about him? What?

35 Oh he's a portentous person. He stumps about on an ivory stump, made from sea-ivory. Moby Dick, the great white whale, tore off Ahab's leg at the knee, when Ahab was attacking him.

Quite right too. Should have torn off both his legs, and a bit more besides.

But Ahab doesn't think so. Ahab is now a monomaniac. Moby Dick is his monomania. Moby Dick must DIE, or Ahab can't live any longer. Ahab is atheist by this.

All right.

This *Pequod*, ship of the American soul, has three mates.

1. Starbuck:*   Quaker, Nantucketer, a good responsible man of reason, forethought, intrepidity, what is called a dependable man. At the bottom, *afraid*.

2. Stubb: "Fearless as fire, and as mechanical."* Insists on being reckless and jolly on every occasion. Must be afraid too, really.

3. Flask: Stubborn, obstinate, without imagination. To him "the wondrous whale was but a species of magnified mouse, or water-rat— —"

There you have them: a maniac captain and his three mates, three splendid sea-men, admirable whale-men, first class men at their job. America!

It is rather like Mr Wilson and his admirable, "efficient" crew, at the Peace Conference. Except that none of the Pequodders took their wives along.*

A maniac captain of the soul, and three eminently practical mates. America!

Then such a crew. Renegades, castaways, cannibals: Ishmael, Quakers. America!

Three giant harpooneers, to spear the great white whale.

1. Queequeg, the South Sea Islander, all tatooed, big and powerful.

2. Tashtego, the Red Indian of the sea-coast, where the Indian meets the sea.

3. Daggoo, the huge black negro.

There you have them, three savage races, under the American flag, the maniac captain, with their great keen harpoons ready to spear the *white* whale.

And only after many days at sea does Ahab's own boat-crew appear on deck. Strange, silent, secret, black-garbed Malays, fireworshipping Parsees. These are to man Ahab's boat, when it leaps in pursuit of that whale.

What do you think of the ship *Pequod*, the ship of the soul of an American.

Many races, many peoples, many nations, under the Stars and Stripes.
Beaten with many stripes.*
Seeing stars sometimes.
And in a mad ship, under a mad captain, in a mad, fanatic's hunt.
5   For what?
For Moby Dick, the great White Whale.
But splendidly handled. Three splendid mates. The whole thing
practical, eminently practical in its working. American industry!
And all this practicality in the service of a mad, mad chase.
10   Melville manages to keep it a real whaling ship, on a real cruise, in
spite of all fantastics. A wonderful, wonderful voyage. And a beauty
that is so surpassing only because of the author's awful flounderings
in mystical waters. He wanted to get metaphysically deep. And he got
deeper than metaphysics. It is a surpassingly beautiful book. With an
15   awful meaning. And bad jolts.
It is interesting to compare Melville with Dana, about the albatross.*
Melville a bit sententious.—"I remember the first albatross I ever saw.
It was during a prolonged gale, in waters hard upon the Antarctic seas.
From my forenoon watch below I ascended to the overclouded deck;
20   and there, lashed upon the main hatches, I saw a regal, feathery thing
of unspotted whiteness, and with a hooked, Roman bill sublime. At intervals it arched forth its vast, archangel wings— —. Wondrous throbbings and flutterings shook it. Though bodily unharmed, it uttered
cries, as some king's ghost in supernatural distress. Through its in-
25   expressible, strange eyes methought I peeped to secrets not below the
heavens— —the white thing was so white, its wings so wide, and in
those for ever exiled waters, I had lost the miserable warping memories
of traditions and of towns.—I assert then, that in the wondrous bodily
whiteness of the bird chiefly lurks the secret of the spell—"
30   Melville's albatross is a prisoner, caught by a bait on a hook.*
Well, I have seen an albatross too: following us in waters hard upon
the Antarctic, too, south of Australia. And in the southern winter. And
the ship, a P. and O. boat, nearly empty. And the lascar crew* shivering.
The bird with its long, long wings following, then leaving us. No one
35   knows till they have tried how lost, how lonely those southern waters
are. And glimpses of the Australian coast.
It makes one feel that our day is only a day. That in the dark of the
night ahead other days stir fecund, when we have lapsed from existence.
One knows how utterly we shall lapse.

But Melville keeps up his disquisition about "whiteness." The great abstract fascinated him. The abstract where we end, and cease to be. White or black. Our white, abstract end! Then again it is lovely to be at sea on the *Pequod*, with never a grain of earth to us. 5

"It was a cloudy, sultry afternoon; the seamen were lazily lounging about the decks, or vacantly gazing over into the lead-coloured waters. Queequeg and I were mildly employed weaving what is called a sword-mat, for an additional lashing to our boat. So still and subdued and yet somehow preluding was all the scene, and such an incantation of reverie 10 lurked in the air, that each silent sailor seemed resolved into his own invisible self—"

In the midst of this preluding silence came the first cry: "There she blows! there! there! there! She blows! She blows!"—And then comes the first chase, a marvellous piece of true sea-writing, the sea, and sheer 15 sea-beings on the chase, sea-creatures chased. There is scarcely a taint of earth—pure sea-motion.

'"Give way men," whispered Starbuck, drawing still further aft the sheet of his sail; "there is time to kill fish yet before the squall comes. There's white water again!—Close to!—Spring!" Soon after, two cries 20 in quick succession on each side of us denoted that the other boats had got fast; but hardly were they overheard, when with a lightning-like hurtling whisper Starbuck said: "Stand up!" and Queequeg, harpoon in hand, sprang to his feet.— Though not one of the oarsmen was then facing the life and death peril so close to them ahead, yet with their eyes 25 on the intense countenance of the mate in the stern of the boat, they knew that the imminent instant had come; they heard, too, an enormous wallowing sound, as of fifty elephants stirring in their litter. Meanwhile the boat was still booming through the mist, the waves curling and hissing around us like the erected crests of enraged serpents. 30

'"That's his hump. *There! there*, give it to him!" whispered Starbuck. —A short rushing sound leapt out of the boat; it was the darted iron of Queequeg. Then all in one welded motion came a push from astern, while forward the boat seemed striking on a ledge; the sail collapsed and exploded; a gush of scalding vapour shot up near by; something 35 rolled and tumbled like an earthquake beneath us. The whole crew were half suffocated as they were tossed helter-skelter into the white curdling cream of the squall. Squall, whale, and harpoon had all blended together; and the whale, merely grazed by the iron, escaped—'

Melville is a master of violent, chaotic physical motion, he can keep up a whole wild chase without a flaw. He is as perfect at creating stillness. The ship is cruising on the Carrol Ground, south of St Helena.—"It was while gliding through these latter waters that one serene and moonlight
5   night, when all the waves rolled by like scrolls of silver; and by their soft, suffusing seethings, made what seemed a silvery silence, not a solitude; on such a silent night a silvery jet was seen far in advance of the white bubbles at the bow.—"

Then there is the description of Brit. "Steering north-eastward from
10 the Crozetts, we fell in with vast meadows of brit, the minute, yellow substance upon which the Right whale largely feeds. For leagues and leagues it undulated round us, so that we seemed to be sailing through boundless fields of ripe and golden wheat. On the second day, numbers of Right whales were seen, secure from the attack of a Sperm whaler like
15 the *Pequod*, with open jaws sluggishly swam through the brit, which, adhering to the fringed fibres of that wondrous Venetian blind in their mouths, was in that manner separated from the water that escaped at the lip. As morning mowers who side by side slowly and seethingly advance their scythes through the long wet grass of the marshy meads; even
20 so these monsters swam, making a strange, grassy, cutting sound; and leaving behind them endless swaths of blue on the yellow sea. But it was only the sound they made as they parted the brit which at all reminded one of mowers. Seen from the mast-heads, especially when they paused and were stationary for a while, their vast black forms looked more like
25 masses of rock than anything else—"

This beautiful passage brings us to the apparition of the squid.

"Slowly wading through the meadows of brit; the *Pequod* still held her way north-eastward towards the island of Java; a gentle air impelling her keel, so that in the surrounding serenity her three tall, tapering masts
30 mildly waved to that languid breeze, as three mild palms on a plain. And still, at wide intervals in the silvery night, that lonely, alluring jet would be seen.

"But one transparent blue morning, when a stillness almost preter-natural spread over the sea, however unattended with any stagnant calm;
35 when the long burnished sunglade on the waters seemed a golden finger laid across them, enjoining secrecy; when all the slippered waves whis-pered together as they softly ran on; in this profound hush of the visible sphere a strange spectre was seen by Daggoo from the mainmast head.

"In the distance, a great white mass lazily rose, and rising higher and
40 higher, and disentangling itself from the azure, at last gleamed before our

prow like a snow-slide, new slid from the hills. Thus glistening for a moment, as slowly it subsided, and sank. Then once more arose, and silently
gleamed. It seemed not a whale; and yet, is this Moby Dick? thought
Daggoo— —"
The boats were lowered and pulled to the scene.   5
"In the same spot where it sank, once more it slowly rose. Almost
forgetting for the moment all thoughts of Moby Dick, we now gazed
at the most wondrous phenomenon which the secret seas have hitherto
revealed to mankind. A vast pulpy mass, furlongs in length and breadth,
of a glancing cream-colour, lay floating on the water, innumerable long   10
arms radiating from its centre, and curling and twisting like a nest of
anacondas, as if blindly to clutch at any hapless object within reach.
No perceptible face or front did it have; no conceivable token of either
sensation or instinct; but undulated there on the billows, an unearthly,
formless, chance-like apparition of life. And with a low sucking sound   15
it slowly disappeared again. "
The following chapters, with their account of whale-hunts, the killing,
the stripping, the cutting up, are magnificent records of actual happening. Then comes the queer tale of the meeting of the *Jereboam*, a whaler
met at sea, all of whose men were under the domination of a religious   20
maniac, one of the ship's hands. There are detailed descriptions of the
actual taking of the sperm oil from a whale's head. Dilating on the smallness of the brain of a sperm whale, Melville significantly remarks—"for
I believe that much of a man's character will be found betokened in
his back-bone. I would rather feel your spine than your skull, who-   25
ever you are—." And of the whale, he adds—"For, viewed in this light,
the wonderful comparative smallness of his brain proper is more than
compensated by the wonderful comparative magnitude of his spinal
cord."
In among the rush of terrible, awful hunts come touches of pure   30
beauty.
"As the three boats lay there on that gently rolling sea, gazing down
into its eternal blue noon; and as not a single groan or cry of any sort,
nay not so much as a ripple or a thought, came up from its depths;
what landsman would have thought, that beneath all that silence and   35
placidity the utmost monster of the seas was writhing and wrenching
in agony!—"*
Perhaps the most stupendous chapter is the one called "The Grand
Armada," at the beginning of Volume III. The *Peqoud* was drawing
through the Sunda Straits towards Java* when she came upon a vast host   40

of sperm whales. "Broad on both bows, at a distance of two or three miles,
and forming a great semi-circle embracing one-half of the level horizon,
a continuous chain of whale-jets were up-playing and sparkling in the
noonday air—"—Chasing this great herd, past the Straits of Sunda,
5   themselves chased by Javan pirates, the whalers race on. Then the boats
are lowered. At last that curious state of inert irresolution came over the
whales, when they were, as the seamen say, gallied.* Instead of forging
ahead in huge martial array, they swam violently hither and thither, a
surging sea of whales, no longer moving on. Starbuck's boat, made fast
10   to a whale, is towed in amongst this howling Leviathan chaos. In mad
career it cockles through the boiling surge of monsters, till it is brought
into a clear lagoon in the very centre of the vast, mad, terrified herd.
There, a sleek,* pure calm reigns. There the females swam in peace,
and the young whales came snuffing tamely at the boat, like dogs. And
15   there the astonished sea-men watched the love-making of these amazing
monsters, mammals, now in rut far down in the sea.— "But far beneath
this wondrous world upon the surface, another and still stranger world
met our eyes as we gazed over the side. For, suspended in these watery
vaults, floated the forms of the nursing-mothers of the whales, and
20   those that by their enormous girth seemed shortly to become mothers.
The lake, as I have hinted, was to a considerable depth exceedingly
transparent; and as human infants while sucking will calmly and fixedly
gaze away from the breast, as if leading two different lives at a time; and
while yet drawing mortal nourishment, be still spiritually feasting upon
25   some unearthly reminiscence, even so did the young of these whales
seem looking up towards us, but not at us, as if we were but a bit of gulf-
weed in their newborn sight. Floating on their sides, the mothers also
seemed quietly eyeing us.———Some of the subtlest secrets of the seas
seemed divulged to us in this enchanted pond. We saw young Leviathan
30   amours in the deep. And thus, though surrounded by circle upon circle
of consternation and affrights, did these inscrutable creatures at the
centre freely and fearlessly indulge in all peaceful concernments; yea,
serenely revelled in dalliance and delight.—"

    There is something really overwhelming in these whale-hunts, almost
35   superhuman or inhuman, bigger than life, more terrific than human
activity. The same with the chapter on ambergris: it is so curious, so
real, yet so unearthly. And again in the chapter called "The Cassock"—
surely the oddest piece of phallicism in all the world's literature.

    After this comes the amazing account of the Try-works, when the
40   ship is turned into a sooty, oily factory in mid-ocean, and the oil is

extracted from the blubber. In the night of the red furnace burning on deck, at sea, Melville has his startling experience of reversion. He is at the helm, but has turned to watch the fire: when suddenly he feels the ship rushing backward from him, in mystic reversion.— "Uppermost was the impression, that whatever swift, rushing thing I stood on was not so much bound to any haven ahead, as rushing from all havens astern. A stark, bewildered feeling, as of death, came over me. Convulsively my hands grasped the tiller, but with the crazy conceit that the tiller was, somehow, in some enchanted way, inverted. 'My God! What is the matter with me!' thought I!—"*

This dream-experience is a real soul-experience. He ends with an injunction to all men, not to gaze on the red fire when its redness makes all things look ghastly. It seems to him that his gazing on fire had evoked this horror of reversion, undoing.

Perhaps it had. He was water-born.

After some unhealthy work on the ship, Queequeg caught a fever and was like to die.*—"How he wasted and wasted in those few, long-lingering days, till there seemed but little left of him but his frame and tatooing. But as all else in him thinned, and his check-bones grew sharper, his eyes, nevertheless, seemed growing fuller and fuller; they took on a strangeness of lustre; and mildly but deeply looked out at you there from his sickness, a wondrous testimony to that immortal health in him which could not die, or be weakened. And like circles on the water, which, as they grow fainter, expand; so his eyes seemed rounding and rounding, like the circles of Eternity. An awe that cannot be named would steal over you as you sat by the side of this waning savage—"

But Queequeg did not die—and the *Pequod* emerges from the Eastern Straits, into the full Pacific. "To my meditative Magian rover, this serene Pacific once beheld, must ever after be the sea of his adoption. It rolls the midmost waters of the world—"

In this Pacific the fights go on.—"It was far down the afternoon; and when all the spearings of the crimson fight were done; and floating in the lovely sunset sea and sky, sun and whale both died stilly together; then, such a sweetness and such a plaintiveness, such inwreathing orisons curled up in that rosy air, that it almost seemed as if far over from the deep green convent valleys of the Manila isles, the Spanish land-breeze had gone to sea, freighted with these vesper hymns.—Soothed again, but only soothed to deeper gloom, Ahab, who had sterned off from the whale, sat intently watching his final wanings from the now tranquil boat. For that strange spectacle observable in all sperm whales

dying—the turning of the head sunwards, and so expiring—that strange
spectacle, beheld of such a placid evening, somehow to Ahab conveyed
a wondrousness unknown before. 'He turns and turns him to it;—how
slowly, but how steadfastly, his homage-rendering* and invoking brow,
5   with his last dying motions. He too worships fire';——— "

     So Ahab soliloquises: and so the warm-blooded whale turns for the
last time to the sun, which begot him in the waters.

     But as we see in the next chapter, it is the Thunder-fire which Ahab
really worships: that livid sundering* fire of which he bears the brand,
10   from head to foot.—It is storm, the electric storm on the *Pequod*, when
the corposants burn in high, tapering flames of supernatural pallor
upon the mast-heads, and when the compass is reversed. After this all is
fatality. Life itself seems mystically reversed. In these hunters of Moby
Dick there is nothing but madness and possession. The captain Ahab
15   moves hand in hand with the poor imbecile negro boy, Pip, who has
been so cruelly demented, left swimming alone in the vast sea. It is the
imbecile child of the sun hand in hand with the northern monomaniac,
captain and master.

     The voyage surges on. They meet one ship, then another. It is all
20   ordinary day-routine, and yet all is a tension of pure madness and horror, the approaching horror of the last fight. "Hither and thither, on
high, glided the snow-white wings of small, unspeckled birds; these
were the gentle thoughts of the feminine air; but to and fro in the deeps,
far down in the bottomless blue, rushed mighty leviathans, sword-fish
25   and sharks; and these were the strong, troubled, murderous thinkings
of the masculine sea—" —On this day Ahab confesses his weariness,
the weariness of his burden. "—But do I look very old, so very, very
old, Starbuck? I feel deadly faint, and bowed, and humped, as though
I were Adam staggering beneath the piled centuries since Paradise—"
30   It is the Gethsemane* of Ahab, before the last fight: the Gethsemane
of the human soul seeking the last self-conquest, the last attainment of
extended consciousness—infinite consciousness.

     At last they sight the whale. Ahab sees him from his hoisted perch at
the mast-head.—"From this height the whale was now seen some mile
35   or so ahead, at every roll of the sea revealing his high, sparkling hump,
and regularly jetting his silent spout into the air.—"

     The boats are lowered, to draw near the white whale. "At length
the breathless hunter came so nigh his seemingly unsuspecting prey
that his entire dazzling hump was distinctly visible, sliding along the
40   sea as if an isolated thing, and continually set in a revolving ring of

finest, fleecy, greenish foam. He saw the vast involved wrinkles of the slightly projecting head, beyond. Before it, far out on the soft, Turkish-rugged waters, went the glistening white shadow from his broad, milky forehead, a musical rippling playfully accompanying the shade; and behind, the blue waters interchangeably flowed over the moving valley 5 of his steady wake; and on either side bright bubbles arose and danced by his side. But these were broken again by the light toes of hundreds of gay fowl softly feathering the sea, alternate with their fitful flight; and like to some flagstaff rising from the pointed hull of an argosy, the tall but shattered pole of a recent lance projected from the white whale's 10 back; and at intervals one of the clouds of soft-toed fowls hovering, and to and fro shimmering like a canopy over the fish, silently perched and rocked on this pole, the long tail-feathers streaming like pennons.

"A gentle joyousness—a mighty mildness of repose in swiftness, in-vested the gliding whale— —" 15

The fight with the whale is too wonderful, and too awful, to be quoted apart from the book. It lasted three days. The fearful sight, on the third day, of the torn body of the Parsee harpooneer, lost on the previous day, now seen lashed on to the flanks of the white whale by the tangle of harpoon-lines, has a mystic dream-horror. The awful and infuriated 20 whale turns upon the ship, symbol of this civilised world of ours. He smites her with a fearful shock. And a few minutes later, from the last of the fighting whale-boats comes the cry " 'The Ship! Great God, where is the ship?' —Soon they through the dim, bewildering medi-ums saw her sidelong fading phantom, as in the gaseous Fata Morgana; 25 only the uppermost masts out of the water; while fixed by infatuation, or fidelity, or fate, to their once lofty perches, the pagan harpooneers still maintained their sinking look-outs on the sea. And now, concentric circles seized the lone boat itself, and all its crew, and each floating oar, and every lance-pole, and spinning, animate and inanimate, all round 30 and round in one vortex, carried the smallest chip of the *Pequod* out of sight—"

The bird of heaven, the eagle, St. John's bird, the Red Indian bird, the American,* goes down with the ship, nailed by Tashtego's hammer, the hammer of the American Indian. The eagle of the Spirit. Sunk! 35

"Now small fowls flew screaming over the yet yawning gulf; a sullen white surf beat against its steep sides; then all collapsed; and then the great shroud of the sea rolled on as it rolled five thousand years ago."

So ends one of the strangest and most wonderful books in the world, closing up its mystery and its tortured symbolism. It is an epic of the 40 sea such as no man has equalled; and it is a book of esoteric symbolism of profound significance, and of considerable tiresomeness.

But it is a great book, a very great book, the greatest book of the sea ever written. It moves awe in the soul.

5   The terrible fatality.

Fatality.

Doom.

Doom! Doom! Doom! Something seems to whisper it in the very dark trees of America. Doom!

10   Doom of what?

Doom of our white day. We are doomed, doomed. And the doom is in America. The doom of our white day.

Ah well, if my day is doomed, and I am doomed with my day, it is something greater than I which dooms me, so I accept my doom as a

15   sign of the greatness which is more than I am.

Melville knew. He knew his race was doomed. His white soul, doomed. His great white epoch, doomed. Himself, doomed. The idealist, doomed. The Spirit, doomed.

The reversion. "Not so much bound to any haven ahead, as rushing

20   from all havens astern."

That great horror of ours! It is our civilisation rushing from all havens astern.

The last ghastly hunt. The White Whale.

What then is Moby Dick?—He is the deepest blood-being of the

25   white race. He is our deepest blood-nature.

And he is hunted, hunted, hunted by the maniacal fanaticism of our white mental consciousness. We want to hunt him down. To subject him to our will. And in this maniacal conscious hunt of ourselves we get dark races and pale to help us, red, yellow, and black, east and west,

30   Quaker and fire-worshipper, we get them all to help us in this ghastly maniacal hunt which is our doom and our suicide.

The last phallic being of the white man. Hunted into the death of upper consciousness and the ideal will. Our blood-self subjected to our own will. Our blood-consciousness sapped by a parasitic mental or ideal

35   consciousness.

Hot-blooded sea-born Moby Dick. Hunted by monomaniacs of the idea.

Oh god, oh god, what next, when the *Pequod* has sunk?

She sank in the war, and we are all flotsam.*

40   Now what next?

Who knows? Quien sabe? Quien sabe, señor?*
Neither Spanish nor Saxon America has any answer.
The *Pequod* went down. And the *Pequod* was the ship of the white
American soul. She sank, taking with her negro and Indian and Polyne-
sian, Asiatic and Quaker and good, business-like Yankees and Ishmael: 5
she sank all the lot of them.

Boom! as Vachel Lindsay would say.*

To use the words of Jesus, IT IS FINISHED.

Consummatum est!

But *Moby Dick* was first published in 1851. If the Great White Whale   10
sank the ship of the Great White Soul in 1851, what's been happening
ever since?

Post mortem effects,* presumably.

Because, in the first centuries, Jesus was Cetus, the Whale.* And
the Christians were the little fishes. Jesus, the Redeemer, was Cetus,   15
Leviathan. And all the Christians all his little fishes.

XII.

Whitman.*

Post mortem effects?
But what of Walt Whitman?
5   The "good gray poet."*
Was he a ghost, with all his physicality?
The good gray poet.
Post mortem effects. Ghosts.
A certain ghoulish insistency. A certain horrible pottage of human
10   parts. A certain stridency and portentousness. A luridness about his
beatitudes.*
DEMOCRACY! THESE STATES! EIDOLONS!
LOVERS, ENDLESS LOVERS!*
ONE IDENTITY!*
15   ONE IDENTITY!
I AM HE THAT ACHES WITH AMOROUS LOVE.*
Do you believe me, when I say post mortem effects?
When the *Pequod* went down, she left many a rank and dirty steam-
boat still fussing in the seas. The *Pequod* sinks with all her souls, but
20   their bodies rise again to man innumerable tramp steamers, and ocean-
crossing liners. Corpses.
What we mean is that people may go on, keep on, and rush on,
without souls. They have their ego and their will, that is enough to keep
them going.
25   So that you see, the sinking of the *Pequod* was only a metaphysical tragedy after all. The world goes on just the same. The ship of
the *soul* is sunk. But the machine-manipulating body works just the
same: digests, chews gum, admires Botticelli* and aches with amorous
love.
30   I AM HE THAT ACHES WITH AMOROUS LOVE.
What do you make of that? I AM HE THAT ACHES. First
generalisation. First uncomfortable universalisation. WITH AMO-
ROUS LOVE! Oh god! Better a belly-ache. A belly-ache is at least
specific. But the ACHE of AMOROUS LOVE!

Think of having that under your skin. All that!
I AM HE THAT ACHES WITH AMOROUS LOVE.
Walter, leave off. You are not HE. You are just a limited Walter.
And your ache doesn't include all Amorous Love, by any means. If you
ache you only ache with a small bit of amorous love, and there's so much   5
more stays outside the cover of your ache, that you might be a bit milder
about it.
I AM HE THAT ACHES WITH AMOROUS LOVE.
CHUFF! CHUFF! CHUFF!
CHU—CHU—CHU—CHU—CHUFFFF!   10
Reminds one of a steam-engine. A locomotive. They're the only
things that seem to me to ache with amorous love. All that steam inside
them. Forty million foot-pounds pressure.* The ache of AMOROUS
LOVE. Steam-pressure. CHUFF!
An ordinary man aches with love for Belinda, or his Native Land,*   15
or the Ocean, or the Stars, or the Oversoul: if he feels that an ache is in
the fashion.
It takes a steam-engine to ache with AMOROUS LOVE. All of it.
Walt was really too superhuman. The danger of the superman* is
that he is mechanical.   20
They talk of his "splendid animality."* Well, he'd got it on the brain,
if that's the place for animality.

"I am he that aches with amorous love;
   Does the earth gravitate? does not all matter, aching, attract
      all matter?   25
   So the body of me to all I meet or know."

What can be more mechanical? The difference between life and matter is that life, living things, living creatures, have the instinct of turning
right away from *some* matter, and of blissfully ignoring the bulk of most
matter, and of turning towards only some certain bits of specially se-   30
lected matter. As for living creatures all helplessly hurtling together into
one great snowball, why, most very living creatures spend the greater
part of their time getting out of the sight, smell or sound of the rest
of living creatures. Even bees only cluster on their own queen.* And
that is sickening enough. Fancy all white humanity clustering on one   35
another like a lump of bees.
No Walt, you give your self away. Matter *does* gravitate, helplessly.
But men are tricky-tricksy,* and they shy all sorts of ways.

Matter gravitates because it *is* helpless and mechanical.

And if you gravitate the same, if the body of you gravitates to all you meet or know, why, something must have gone seriously wrong with you. You must have broken your main-spring.

5   You must have fallen also into mechanisation.

Your Moby Dick must be really dead. That lonely phallic monster of the individual you. Dead mentalised.

I only know that my body doesn't by any means gravitate to all I meet or know. I find I can shake hands with a few people. But most I wouldn't
10   touch with a long prop.*

Your mainspring is broken, Walt Whitman. The mainspring of your own individuality. And so you run down with a great whirr, merging with everything.

You have killed your isolate Moby Dick. You have mentalised your
15   deep sensual body, and that's the death of it.

I am everything and everything is me and so we're all One in One Identity, like the Mundane Egg,* which has been addled quite a while.

"Whoever you are, to endless announcements— — — —"
20   "And of these one and all I weave the song of myself."

Do you? Well then it just shows you haven't *got* any self. It's a mush, not a woven thing. A hotch-potch, not a tissue. Your Self.

Oh Walter Walter,* what have you done with it? What have you done with yourself? With your own individual self? For it sounds as if it had
25   all leaked out of you, leaked into the universe.

Post-mortem effects. The individuality had leaked out of him.

No no, don't lay this down to poetry. These are post mortem effects. And Walt's great poems are really huge fat tomb-plants, great rank grave-yard growths.

30   All that false exuberance. All those lists of things boiled in one pudding-cloth!* No no!

I don't want all those things inside me, thank you.

"I reject nothing,"* says Walt.

If that is so, one must be a pipe open at both ends, so everything runs
35   through.

Post mortem effects.

"I embrace ALL," says Whitman. "I weave all things into myself."*

Do you really! There can't be much left of *you* when you've done. When you've cooked the awful pudding of One Identity.

"And whoever walks a furlong without sympathy walks to his own funeral dressed in his own shroud."*

Take off your hat then, my funeral procession of one is passing.

This awful Whitman. This post mortem poet. This poet with the private soul leaking out of him all the time. All his privacy leaking out in a sort of dribble, oozing into the universe.

Walt becomes in his own person the whole world, the whole universe, the whole eternity of time. As far as his rather sketchy knowledge of history will carry him, that is. Because to *be* a thing he had to know it. In order to assume the identity of a thing, he had to know that thing. He was not able to assume one identity with Charlie Chaplin, for example, because Walt didn't know Charlie. What a pity! He'd have done poems, paeans and what not, Chants, Songs of Cinematernity.

"Oh Charlie my Charlie, another film is done—"*

As soon as Walt *knew* a thing, he assumed a One Identity with it. If he knew that an Esquimo sat in a kyak,* immediately there was Walt being little and yellow and greasy, sitting in a kyak.

Now will you tell me exactly what a kyak is?

Who is he that demands petty definition? Let him behold me *sitting in a kyak*.

I behold no such thing. I behold a rather fat old man full of a rather senile, self-conscious sensuosity.

DEMOCRACY. EN MASSE.* ONE IDENTITY.

The universe, in short, adds up to ONE.

ONE.

1.

Which is Walt.

His poems, Democracy, En Masse, One Identity,* they are long sums in addition and multiplication, of which the answer is invariably MYSELF.

He reaches the state of ALLNESS.

And what then? It's all empty. Just an empty Allness. An addled egg.

Walt wasn't an Esquimo. A little, yellow, sly, cunning, greasy little Esquimo. And when Walt blandly assumed Allness, including Esquimoness, unto himself, he was just sucking the wind out of a blown eggshell, no more. Esquimos are not minor little Walts. They are something that I am not, I know that. Outside the egg of my Allness chuckles the greasy little Esquimo. Outside the egg of Whitman's Allness too.

But Walt wouldn't have it. He was everything and everything was in him. He drove an automobile with a very fierce headlight, along the track of a fixed idea, through the darkness of this world. And he saw Everything that way. Just as a motorist does in the night.

5   I, who happen to be asleep under the bushes in the dark, hoping a snake won't crawl into my neck; I, seeing Walt go by in his great fierce poetic machine, think to myself: What a funny world that fellow sees!

ONE DIRECTION! toots Walt in the car, whizzing along it.

10 Whereas there are myriads of ways in the dark, not to mention track-less wildernesses. As anyone will know who cares to come off the road, even the Open Road.

ONE DIRECTION! whoops America, and sets off also in an automobile.

15 ALLNESS! shrieks Walt at a cross-road, going whizz over an un-wary Red Indian.

ONE IDENTITY! chants democratic En Masse, pelting behind in motorcars, oblivious of the corpses under the wheels.

God save me, I feel like creeping down a rabbit-hole, to get away from

20 all these automobiles rushing down the ONE IDENTITY track to the goal of ALLNESS.

"A woman waits for me—"

He might as well have said: "The femaleness waits for my maleness." Oh beautiful generalisation and abstraction! Oh biological function.

25 "Athletic mothers of these States—"* Muscles and wombs. They needn't have had faces at all.

"As I see my soul reflected in Nature
As I see through a mist, One with inexpressible completeness,
    sanity, beauty,
30 See the bent head, and arms folded over the breast, the Female
    I see."

Everything was female to him: even himself. Nature just one great function.

"This is the nucleus—after the child is born of woman, man
35   is born of woman,
    This is the bath of birth, the merge of small and large, and
        the outlet again—"

"The Female I see—"

If I'd been one of his women, I'd have given him Female. With a flea in his ear.

Always wanting to merge himself into the womb of something or other.

"The Female I see—" 5

Anything, so long as he could merge himself.

Just a horror. A sort of white flux.

Post mortem effects.

He found, like all men find, that you can't really merge in a woman, though you may go a long way. You can't manage the last bit. So you 10 have to give it up, and try elsewhere. If you *insist* on merging.*

In *Calamus** he changes his tune. He doesn't shout and thump and exult any more. He begins to hesitate, reluctant, wistful.

The strange calamus has its pink-tinged root by the pond, and it sends up its leaves of comradeship, comrades from one root, without 15 the intervention of woman, the female.

So he sings of the mystery of manly love, the love of comrades.* Over and over he says the same thing: the new world will be built on the love of comrades, the new great dynamic of life will be manly love. Out of this manly love will come the inspiration for the future. 20

Will it though? Will it?

Comradeship! Comrades! This is to be the new Democracy: of Comrades. This is the new cohering principle in the world: comradeship.

Is it? Are you sure?

It is the cohering principle of true solidiery, we are told in *Drum-* 25 *Taps.** It is the cohering principle in the new unison for creative activity. And it is extreme and alone, touching the confines of death. Something terrible to bear, terrible to be responsible for. Even Walt Whitman felt it. The soul's last and most poignant responsibility, the responsibility of comradeship, of manly love. 30

"Yet you are beautiful to me, you faint-tinged roots, you make
  me think of death,
Death is beautiful from you (what indeed is finally beautiful
  except death and love?)
I think it is not for life I am chanting here my chant of lovers, 35
  I think it must be for death,
For how calm, how solemn it grows to ascend to the atmosphere
  of lovers,
Death or life, I am then indifferent, my soul declines to prefer,

(I am not sure but the high soul of lovers welcomes death most)
Indeed, O death, I think now these leaves mean precisely the same
    as you mean— "

This is strange, from the exultant Walt.
5   Death!
Death is now his chant! Death!
Merging! And Death! Which is the final merge.
The great merge into the womb. Woman.
And after that, the merge of comrades: man-for-man love.
10 And almost immediately with this, death, the final merge of death.
There you have the progression of merging. For the great mergers,
woman at last becomes inadequate. For those who love to extremes.
Woman is inadequate for the last merging. So the next step, is the
merging of man-for-man love. And this is on the brink of death. It
15 slides over into death.
David and Jonathan. And the death of Jonathan.*
It always slides into death.
The love of comrades.
Merging.
20 So that if the new Democracy is to be based on the love of Comrades,
it will be based on death too. It will slip so soon into death.
The last merging. The last Democracy. The last love. The love of
comrades.
Fatality. And fatality.
25 Whitman would not have been the great poet he is if he had not taken
the last steps and looked over into death. Death, the last merging, that
was the goal of his manhood.
To the mergers, there remains the brief love of comrades, and then
Death.

30 "Whereto answering, the sea
Delaying not, hurrying not,
Whisper'd me through the night, and very plainly before day-break,
Lisp'd to me the low and delicious word death,
And again death, death, death, death,
35 Hissing melodious, neither like the bird nor like my arous'd child's
    heart,
But edging near as privately for me rustling at my feet,
Creeping thence steadily up to my ears and laving me softly all over,
Death, death, death, death, death—"

Whitman is a very great poet, of the end of life. A very great post mortem poet, of the transitions of the soul as it loses its integrity. The poet of the soul's last shout and shriek, on the confines of death. *Après moi le déluge.**
But we have all got to die, and disintegrate.   5
We have got to die in life, too, and disintegrate while we live.
But even then the goal is not death.
Something else will come.
"Out of the cradle endlessly rocking — "
We've got to die first, anyhow. And disintegrate while we still live.   10
Only we know this much. Death is not the *goal*. And Love, and merging, are now only part of the death-process. Comradeship—part of the death process. Democracy—part of the death-process. The new Democracy—the brink of death. One Identity—death itself.
We have died, and we are still disintegrating.   15
But IT is finished.
Consummatum est.

Whitman, the great poet, has meant so much to me. Whitman, the one man breaking a way ahead. Whitman, the one pioneer. And only Whitman. No English pioneers, no French. No European pioneer- 20
poets. In Europe the would-be pioneers are mere innovators. The same in America. Ahead of Whitman, nothing. Ahead of all poets, pioneering into the wilderness of unopened life, Whitman. Beyond him, none. His wide, strange camp at the end of the great high-road. And lots of new little poets camping on Whitman's camping ground now. But none 25
going really beyond. Because Whitman's camp is at the end of the road, and on the edge of a great precipice. Over the precipice, blue distances, and the blue hollow of the future. But there is no way down. It is a dead end.

Pisgah. Pisgah sights. And Death. Whitman like a strange, modern, 30
American Moses.* Fearfully mistaken. And yet the great leader.

The essential function of art is moral. Not aesthetic, not decorative, not pastime and recreation. But moral. The essential function of art is moral.

But a passionate, implicit morality, not didactic. A morality which 35
changes the blood, rather than the mind. Changes the blood first. The mind follows later, in the wake.

Now Whitman was a great moralist. He was a great leader. He was a great changer of the blood in the veins of men.

Surely it is especially true of American art, that it is all essentially moral. Hawthorne, Poe, Longfellow, Emerson, Melville: it is the moral issue which engages them. They all feel uneasy about the old morality. Sensuously, passionally, they all attack the old morality. But they know
5   nothing better, mentally. Therefore they give tight mental allegiance to a morality which all their passion goes to destroy. Hence the duplicity which is the fatal flaw in them: most fatal in the most perfect American work of art, *The Scarlet Letter.* Tight mental allegiance given to a morality which the passional self repudiates.
10   Whitman was the first to break the mental allegiance. He was the first to smash the old moral conception, that the soul of man is something "superior" and "above" the flesh. Even Emerson still maintained this tiresome "superiority" of the soul.* Even Melville could not get over it. Whitman was the first heroic seer to seize the soul by the scruff of her
15   neck and plant her down among the potsherds.*
"There!" he said to the soul. "Stay there!"
Stay there. Stay in the flesh. Stay in the limbs and lips and in the belly. Stay in the breast and womb and the phallus. Stay there, oh soul, where you belong.
20   Stay in the dark limbs of negroes. Stay in the vagina of the prostitute. Stay in the sick flesh of the syphilitic. Stay in the marsh where the Calamus grows. Stay there, Soul, where you belong.
The Open Road.* The great home of the soul is the open road. Not heaven, not paradise. Not "above." Not even "within." The soul is
25   neither "above" nor "within." It is a wayfarer down the open road.
Not by meditating. Not by fasting. Not by exploring heaven after heaven, inwardly, in the manner of the great mystics. Not by exaltation. Not by ecstasy. Not by any of these ways does the soul come into her own.
30   Only by taking the open road.
Not through Charity. Not through sacrifice. Not even through Love. Nor through Good Works. Not through these does the soul accomplish herself.
Only through the journey down the open road.
35   The journey itself, down the open road. Exposed to full contact. On two slow feet. Meeting whatever comes down the open road. In company with those that drift in the same measure along the same way. Towards no goal. Always the open road.
Having no known direction, even. Only the soul remaining true to
40   herself in her going.

Meeting all the other wayfarers along the road. And how? How meet them, and how pass? With sympathy,* says Whitman. Sympathy. He does not say Love. He says sympathy. Feeling with. Feel with them as they feel with themselves. Catching the vibration of their soul and flesh as we pass.

It is a new great doctrine. A doctrine of life. A new great morality. A morality of actual living, not of Salvation. Europe has never got beyond the morality of salvation. America to this day is deathly sick with saviourism. But Whitman, the greatest and the first and the only American teacher, was no saviour. His morality was no morality of salvation. His was a morality of the soul living her life, not saving herself. Accepting the contact with other souls along the open way, as they lived their lives. Never trying to save them. As leave* try to arrest them and throw them in gaol. The soul living her life along the incarnate mystery of the open road.

This was Whitman. And the true rhythm of the American continent speaking out in him. He is the first white aboriginal.

"In my Father's house are many mansions."*

"No," said Whitman. "Keep out of mansions. A mansion may be heaven on earth, but you might as well be dead. Strictly avoid mansions. The soul is herself when she is going on foot down the open road."

It is the American heroic message. The soul is not to pile up defences round herself. She is not to withdraw and seek her heavens inwardly, in mystical ecstasies. She is not to cry to some God beyond, for salvation. She is to go down the open road, as the road opens into the unknown, keeping company with those whose soul draws them near to her, accomplishing nothing save the journey, and the works incident to the journey, in the long life-travel into the unknown, the soul in her subtle sympathies accomplishing herself by the way.

This is Whitman's essential message. The heroic message of the American future. It is the inspiration of thousands of Americans today, the best souls of today, men and women. And it is a message that only in America can be fully understood, finally accepted.

Then Whitman's mistake. The mistake of his interpretation of his watchword: Sympathy. The mystery of SYMPATHY. He still confounded it with Jesus' LOVE, and with Paul's CHARITY.* Whitman, like all the rest of us, was at the end of the great emotional highway of Love. And because he couldn't help himself, he carried on his Open Road as a prolongation of the emotional highway of Love, beyond Calvary.* The highway of Love ends at the foot of the Cross. There is no beyond. It was a hopeless attempt, to prolong the highway of love.

He didn't follow his Sympathy. Try as he might, he kept on automatically interpreting it as Love, as Charity. Merging!

5   This merging, en masse, One Identity, Myself monomania was a carry-over from the old Love idea. It was carrying the idea of love to its logical physical conclusion. Like Flaubert and the leper.* The decree of unqualified Charity, as the soul's one means of salvation, still in force.

Now Whitman wanted his soul to save itself, *he* didn't want to save
10 it. Therefore he did not need the great Christian receipt for saving the soul. He needed to supersede the Christian Charity, the Christian Love, within himself, in order to give his soul her last freedom. The highroad of Love is no Open Road. It is a narrow, tight way, where the soul walks hemmed in between compulsions.

15 Whitman wanted to take his soul down the open road. And he failed in so far as he failed to get out of the old rut of salvation. He forced his soul to the edge of a cliff, and he looked down into death. And then he camped, powerless. He had carried out his Sympathy as an extension of Love and Charity. And it had brought him almost to madness and
20 soul-death. It gave him his forced, unhealthy, post-mortem quality.

His message was really the opposite of Henley's rant:

"I am the master of my fate
I am the captain of my soul."

Whitman's essential message was the Open Road. The leaving of the
25 soul free unto herself, the leaving of his fate to her and to the loom of the open road. Which is the bravest doctrine man has ever proposed to himself.

Alas, he didn't quite carry it out. He couldn't quite break the old maddening bond of the love-compulsion, he couldn't quite get out of
30 the rut of the charity habit. For Love and Charity have degenerated now into habit: a bad habit.

Whitman said Sympathy. If only he had stuck to it! Because Sympathy means feeling with, not feeling for. He kept on having a passionate feeling *for* the negro slave, or the prostitute, or the syphilitic.* Which is
35 merging. A sinking of Walt Whitman's soul in the souls of these others.

He wasn't keeping to his open road. He was forcing his soul down an old rut. He wasn't leaving her free. He was forcing her into other peoples' circumstances.

Supposing he had felt true sympathy with the negro slave? He would have felt *with* the negro slave. Sympathy—compassion—which is partaking of the passion which was in the soul of the negro slave.

What was the feeling in the negro's soul?

"Ah, I am a slave! Ah, it is bad to be a slave! I must free myself. My soul will die unless she frees herself. My soul says I must free myself."

Whitman came along, and saw the slave, and said to himself: "That negro slave is a man like myself. We share the same identity. And he is bleeding with wounds. Oh, oh, is it not myself who am also bleeding with wounds?"

This was not *sympathy*. It was merging, and self-sacrifice. "Bear ye one another's burdens." — "Love thy neighbour as thyself." — "Whatsoever ye do unto him, ye do unto me."*

If Whitman had truly *sympathised*, he would have said: "That negro slave suffers from slavery. He wants to free himself. His soul wants to free him. He has wounds, but they are the price of freedom. The soul has a long journey from a slavery to freedom. If I can help him I will: I will not take over his wounds and his slavery to myself. But I will help him fight the power that enslaves him when he wants to be free, if he wants my help. Since I see in his face that he needs to be free. But even when he is free, his soul has many journeys down the open road, before it is a free soul."

And of the prostitute Whitman would have said:

"Look at that prostitute! Her nature has turned evil under her mental lust for prostitution. She has lost her soul. She knows it herself. She likes to make men lose their souls. If she tried to make me lose my soul, I would kill her. I wish she may die."

But of another prostitute he would have said:

"Look! She is fascinated by the Priapic mysteries.* Look, she will soon be worn to death by the Priapic usage. It is the way of her soul. She wishes it so."

Of the syphilitic he would say:

"Look! She wants to infect all men with syphilis. We ought to kill her."

And of still another syphilitic:

"Look! She has a horror of her syphilis. If she looks my way I will help her to get cured."

This is sympathy. The soul judging for herself, and preserving her own integrity.

But when, in Flaubert, the man takes the leper to his naked body: when Bubi de Montparnasse* takes the girl because he knows she's got syphilis: when Whitman embraces an evil prostitute: that is not sympathy. The evil prostitute has no desire to be embraced with love, so if you sympathise with her, you won't try to embrace her with love. The leper loathes his leprosy, so if you sympathise with him, you'll loathe it too. The evil woman who wishes to infect all men with her syphilis hates you if you haven't got syphilis. If you sympathise, you'll feel her hatred, and you'll hate too, you'll hate her. Her feeling is hate, and you'll share it. Only your soul will choose the direction of its own hatred.

The soul is a very perfect judge of her own motions, if your mind doesn't dictate to her. Because the mind says Charity! Charity!, you don't have to force your soul into kissing lepers or embracing syphilitics. Your lips are the lips of your soul, your body is your soul's body, your phallus, your vagina are the vagina and phallus of your soul; your own single, individual soul. That is Whitman's message. And your soul hates syphilis and leprosy. Because it *is* a soul, it hates these things, which are against the soul. And therefore to force the lips or phallus of your soul into contact with uncleanness is a great violation of your soul. The soul wishes to keep clean and whole. The soul's deepest will is to preserve its own integrity, against the mind and the whole mass of disintegrating forces.

Soul sympathises with soul. And that which tries to kill my soul, my soul hates. My soul and my body are one. Soul and body wish to keep clean and whole. Only the mind is capable of great perversion. Only the mind tries to drive my soul and body into uncleanness and unwholesomeness.

What my soul loves, I love.

What my soul hates, I hate.

When my soul is stirred with compassion, I am compassionate.

What my soul turns away from, I turn away from.

That is the *true* interpretation of Whitman's creed: the true revelation of his Sympathy.

And my soul takes the open road. She meets the souls that are passing, she goes along with the souls that are going her way. And for one and all, she has sympathy. The sympathy of love, the sympathy of hate, the sympathy of simple proximity: all the subtle sympathisings of the incalculable soul, from bitterest hate to passionate love.

It is not I who guide my soul to heaven. It is I who am guided by my own soul along the open road, where all men tread. Therefore I must accept her deep motions of love, or hate, or compassion, or dislike, or indifference. And I must go where she takes me. For my feet and my lips and my phallus are my soul. It is I who must submit to her.

This is Whitman's message of American democracy.

The true democracy, where soul meets soul, in the open road. Democracy. American democracy where all journey down the open road. And where a soul is known at once in its going. Not by its clothes or appearance. Whitman did away with that. Not by its family name. Not even by its reputation. Whitman and Melville both discounted that. Not by a progression of piety, or by works of charity. Not by works at all. Not by anything but just itself. The soul passing unenhanced, passing on foot and being no more than itself. And recognised, and passed by or greeted according to the soul's dictate. If it be a great soul, it will be worshipped in the road.

The love of man and woman: a recognition of souls, and a communion of worship. The love of comrades: a recognition of souls, and a communion of worship. Democracy: a recognition of souls, all down the open road, and a great soul seen in its greatness, as it travels on foot among the rest, down the common way of the living. A glad recognition of souls, and a gladder worship of great and greater souls, because they are the only riches.

Love, and Merging, brought Whitman to the edge of Death! Death! Death!

But the exultance of his message still remains. Purified of MERGING, purified of MYSELF, the exultant message of American Democracy, of souls in the Open Road, full of glad recognition, full of fierce readiness, full of the joy of worship, when one soul sees a greater soul.

The only riches, the great souls.

Chapala. 1923*

FIRST VERSION (1918-19)

CONTENTS

Studies in Classic
American Literature

I.

The Spirit of Place.

It is natural that we should regard American literature as a small branch   5
or province of English literature. None the less there is another view
to be taken. The American art-speech contains a quality that we have
not calculated. It has a suggestive force which is not relative to us, not
inherent in the English race. This alien quality belongs to the American
continent itself.   10
　　All art partakes of the Spirit of Place in which it is produced. The
provincial Latin literature ferments with a foreign stimulus. It is Africa,
and the mysterious religious passion of Libya, which, voicing itself in
Latin, utters the infant cry of Tertullian, Augustine, Athanasius,* the
great saints of the African Church. These are not Romans. They are   15
the prelude to a new era. It is not only that they utter the *ideas* which
made Europe. Chiefly in them is felt the first throb of the great mystic
passion of mediæval life. And in Apuleius, decadent and sensuous, we
feel the last throb of the old way of sensuality, Babylon, Tyre, Carthage.
Africa, seething in Roman veins, produces these strange pulses of new   20
experience, incipient newness within the old decadence.
　　In the same way America, the new continent, seething in English
veins, has produced us the familiar American classics, of Hawthorne,
Poe, Whitman, or Fenimore Cooper, for example. We read the English
utterance without getting the alien American implication. We listen to   25
our own speech in American mouths, but our ears have been shut to
the strange reverberation of that speech. We have not wanted to hear
the undertone, the curious foreign, uncouth suggestion, which is in the
over-cultured Hawthorne and Poe or Whitman. Augustine and Apuleius
are both writers of the Roman decadence. The orthodox Romans, no   30
doubt, saw mainly the decadence, and objected to it. They could not
see that the qualities which *they* called decadence, judging from the
standards of Virgil and Cicero and Tacitus,* were perhaps the incipient
realities of a whole new era of experience.
　　It is time now, for us, who have always looked with indulgence on   35
the decadent or uncouth or provincial American literature, to open new
eyes, and look with respect, if not with fear. It is time for us now to

see that our great race experience is surpassed and exceeded. Our race *idea* may apparently hold good in the American mind. What we have to realise is that our way of feeling is superseded, just as Cicero's way of feeling was superseded in Apuleius. It is the quality of life-experience,

5 of emotion and passion and desire, which has changed in the Romans of Africa, and in the English-speaking Americans. Life itself takes on a new reality, a new motion, even while the idea remains ostensibly the same.

    And it is this change in the way of experience, a change in being,

10 which we should now study in the American books. We have thought and spoken till now in terms of likeness and oneness. Now we must learn to think in terms of difference and otherness. There is a stranger on the face of the earth, and it is no use our trying any further to gull ourselves that he is one of us, and just as we are. There is an unthinkable gulf between

15 us and America, and across the space we see, not our own folk signalling to us, but strangers, incomprehensible beings, simulacra perhaps of ourselves, but *other*, creatures of an other-world. The connection holds good historically, for the past. In the pure present and in futurity it is not valid. The present reality is a reality of untranslatable otherness,

20 parallel to that which lay between St. Augustine and an orthodox senator in Rome of the same day. The oneness is historic only.

    The knowledge that we are no longer one, that there is this inconceivable difference in *being* between us, the difference of an epoch, is difficult and painful to acquiesce in. Yet our only hope of freedom lies

25 in acquiescing. The change has taken place in reality. And unless it take place also in our consciousness, we maintain ourselves all the time in a state of confusion. We must get clear of the old oneness that imprisons our real divergence.

    It is the genuine American literature which affords the best approach

30 to the knowledge of this othering. Only art-utterance reveals the whole truth of a people. And the American art-speech reveals what the American plain speech almost deliberately conceals. What Hawthorne deliberately says in *The Scarlet Letter* is on the whole a falsification of what he unconsciously says in his art-language. And this, again, is one of the

35 outstanding qualities of American literature: that the deliberate ideas of the man veil, conceal, obscure that which the artist has to reveal. This quality of duplicity which runs through so much of the art of the modern world is almost inevitable in an American book. The author is unconscious of it himself. He is sincere in his own intention. And yet, all

40 the time, the artist, who writes as a somnambulist, in the spell of pure

truth as in a dream, is contravened and contradicted by the wakeful man and moralist who sits at the desk.

The occultists say that once there was a universal mystic language,* known to the initiated, or to the adept, or to the priesthood of the whole world, whether Chinese or Atlantean or Maya or Druid—a language 5 that was universal over the globe at some period, perhaps before the Flood. This must have been a written rather than a spoken language, and must have consisted in symbols or ideographs. It is conceivable, perhaps even probable, that at one time the priesthoods of all the world—Asiatic, African, European, American, Polynesian—held some common idea of 10 the creation of the Cosmic universe, and expressed this idea in the same symbols or graphs. It is quite easy to conceive that the circle should be a universal symbol for the All, and the rosy cross, and the ankh, the Egyptian so-called symbol of life, may have been used by all the wise men on the earth to express certain cosmological ideas. 15 And it may be possible, as the scientists of the subtler psychic activities desire and need to do, to discover a universal system of symbology: for practically the whole of psychometry and psycho-analysis* depends on the understanding of symbols.

But art-speech, art-utterance, is, and always will be, the greatest 20 universal language of mankind, greater than any esoteric symbolism. Art-speech is also a language of pure symbols. But whereas the authorised symbol stands always for a thought or an idea, some mental *concept*, the art-symbol or art-term stands for a pure experience, emotional and passional, spiritual and perceptual, all at once. The intel- 25 lectual idea remains implicit, latent and nascent. Art communicates a state of being—whereas the symbol at best only communicates a whole thought, an emotional idea. Art-speech is a use of symbols which are pulsations on the blood and seizures upon the nerves, and at the same time pure percepts of the mind and pure terms of spiritual aspiration. 30

Therefore, when we reduce and diminish any work of art to its didactic capacity—as we reduce a man to his mere physical-functional capacity in the science of medicine—then we find that that work of art is a subtle and complex *idea* expressed in symbols. It is more or less necessary to view man as a thing of various functions and organs. And in the same 35 way, for certain purposes, it is necessary to degrade a work of art into a thing of meanings and reasoned exposition. This process of reduction is part of the science of criticism.

But before we can undertake to criticise American books, to discover their symbolic meaning, we must first trace the development of the 40

orthodox European idea on American soil; because there is always a dual import in these works of art: first, the didactic import given by the author from his own moral consciousness; and then the profound symbolic import which proceeds from his unconscious or subconscious soul, as
5 he works in a state of creation which is something like somnambulism or dreaming. Also we must wake and sharpen in ourselves the subtle faculty for perceiving the greater inhuman forces that control us. It is our fatal limitation, at the present time, that we can only understand in terms of personal and conscious choice. We cannot see that great
10 motions carry us and bring us to our place before we can even begin to know. We cannot see that invisible great winds carry us unwitting, as they carry the locust swarms, and direct us before our knowledge, as they direct the migrating birds.

We ask ourselves, How was it that America became peopled by white
15 men at all? How, in the first place, did Europeans ever get across the great blank ocean? The Greeks and Romans turned their backs on space, and kept their breasts landwards as if magnetised. How was it, then, that fifteenth-century Europe looked space-wards? Was it just the attraction of space? Or was it that Spanish and Venetian sailors*
20 were determined to fill in the great blank of the Atlantic Ocean which confronted them?

It was something more positive. Every people is polarised in some particular locality, some home or homeland. And every great era of civil-isation seems to be the expression of a particular continent or continent
25 region, as well as of the people concerned. There is, no doubt, some peculiar potentiality attaching to every distinct region of the earth's surface, over and above the indisputable facts of climate and geological condition. There is some subtle magnetic or vital influence inherent in every specific locality, and it is this influence which keeps the inhabitant
30 stable. Thus race is ultimately as much a question of place as of heredity. It is the island of Great Britain which has really determined the English race, the genius of Place has made us one people. The place attracts its own human element, and the race drifts inevitably to its own psychic geographical pole.
35 We see this in Roman history. We see the city of Rome gradually losing its psychic-magnetic polarity, the Roman individuals gradually loosed from the old stay, and drifting like particles absolved from the original influence, falling imperceptibly into two currents—one set-ting northwards towards Milan and Gaul, one setting east towards
40 Constantinople* and Asia. Africa had always been connected with Rome

herself—Rome and Carthage were the positive and negative poles of a stable, vital current, as were Athens and Sardis or Ecbatana.

After the removal of the Empire to the east a new circuit began, the circuit of Rome and Treves,* or, better, of Italy and Germany. There is, and has been since the break of the old Roman-African circuit, a natural 5 and inevitable balance between Rome and Germany.

England, France, and even Spain lay within the great German-Italian circuit of vital magnetism, which subsisted all through the Middle Ages. We can see Spain caught in another influence, from Africa again, and Germany influenced from the great Slavonic field. But the main polarity 10 of Europe, from the time of Diocletian* to the Renaissance, lay between Italy and Germany.

About the time of the Renaissance, however, this circuit exhausted itself, as the Italian-African circuit had been exhausted a thousand years before. Italy suddenly scintillated, and was finished in her polar poten- 15 tiality. The old stability of Europe was gone, the old circle of vital flow was broken. It was then that Europe fell directly into polar unison with America. Europe and America became the great poles of negative and positive vitalism.

And it was on the wings of this new attraction that Europe discovered 20 America. When the great magnetic sway of the mediæval polarity broke, then those units which were liberated fell under the sway of new vital currents in the air, and they were borne helplessly as birds migrate, without knowing or willing, down the great magnetic wind towards America, towards the centrality in the New World. So the first indi- 25 viduals were caught up and swept overseas in the setting of the great current. They had no choice, because the influence which was upon them was prior to all knowledge and all option.

Some races of Europe, moreover, seem never to have been included in the great Latin-Germanic circuit of cultural vitalism. Among these 30 are the Iberian and the Celtic. The strange early flowering of Celtic Christianity would be found, on examination, to be quite apart from the whole Italian-Germanic Christianity* which has prevailed in Europe. Its first principle was individualistic, separatist, almost anti-social, a recoil of the individual into a mystic isolation, quite the contrary of the 35 European religious principle, which was the fusing into a whole.

And these separate races located themselves on the sea-board, under the influence of the Atlantic Ocean; Spain, Ireland, Scotland, England, Brittany, these have lain from the beginning under the spell of the great western sea. And the people of Spain, dissociated from the circle of 40

Italian-German culture, felt most distinctly the pull of the American
magnetism. And they answered the pull as the needle answers the pull of
the magnetic north. Spain moved across-seas in one great blind impulse,
which was not primarily a desire for wealth. Desire for wealth never
5   shifted a nation which was attached to its home, or vital in its own
home-life.

If we are to understand the Celtic and Iberian races at all, we must
realise that they have always remained outside of the European circuit
of life—that they have always been excluded and subjected, never in-
10 corporated; and that their principle has been one of mystic opposition,
even hatred, of the civilising principle of the rest of Europe. These
races have remained true to some principle which was contained in the
African and the Druid realities, but which has had no place in the
European Christian-social scheme. Therefore they placed themselves
15 in a polarity with the great invisible force of America, they looked to
their positive pole into the west, the land of the setting sun, over the
great sea to the unknown America. Their heaven was the land under
the western wave, the Celtic Tir na Og.*

They knew of no America. And yet, in the most immediate sense,
20 they knew America. They existed in the spell of the vital magnetism of
the unknown continent. The same is more or less true of Spain and of
Scandinavia. These great sea-board countries are inevitably controlled
by the pull of America. It is inevitable that the Vikings should sail to
Greenland and Labrador.*

25 This unconscious reaction to the vital magnetism of the far-off unknown world is perhaps sufficient to have given rise to the Atlantis myth.
If it gave rise to the land of Tir na Og, which lies under the western
wave, why not to Atlantis? If the great magnetic pole of the Celtic and
Iberian psyche was away in the west, would it not follow that, as in
30 a dream, the myth should interpret the unconscious experience? The
same would be true of the Norse myths—their polarity is westwards,
towards America.

It follows, also, that if the Atlantic sea-board of Europe lies under
the spell of the far-off American vital magnetism, the Atlantic sea-
35 board of America must lie under the spell of Europe. And so, when
Cortes lands in Mexico, he finds the subtle and pathetic Montezuma,
the priest-emperor, who receives him with mystic sympathy, mystic
desire. In America a similar break in the circuit of vitalism, a similar
shifting of the great mystic-magnetic polarity must have taken place,
40 in the fifteenth century, as it took place in Europe. And as Europe fell

under the spell of America, America fell under the spell of Europe. So Montezuma embraced the Spanish* as the fulfilment of the legend of the white, bearded strangers, who should come as gods across the east. Legend is supposed to be race-memory. But surely it is just as likely to be a kind of race-clairvoyance. Montezuma, a priest, a decadent and   5
sensitive character, was filled with mystic apprehension. The Aztecs, subject to the fine vibrations in the ether, given off by vital Europe, highly religious and mystical in their natures, only expressed in their legend of the coming of the white stranger that which their innermost, sensitised souls knew beforehand as a fact. If we can understand the   10
sending of wireless messages from continent to continent, can we not much more readily understand that the unthinkably sensitive substance of the human intelligence could receive the fine waves of vital effluence transmitted across the intervening space, could receive, and, as in a dream, plainly comprehend? It was not even in symbols that the Aztecs   15
knew the future; but in plain, direct prescience. They knew the white, bearded strangers hundreds of years before they could see them. And they knew so perfectly because, in their semi-barbaric state, their consciousness was fluid, not mechanically fixed, and the rarest impressions upon the physical soul, from the invisible ether, could pass on occasion-   20
ally into uninterrupted consciousness.

Prophecy, the mystery of prophecy, is no absurdity. It is no more absurd than the sending of a wireless message. A people, or an individual, need only most delicately submit to the message which is being received all the time upon its own finest tissue, and it will be able to prophesy.   25
But it is easier for us to invent sensitive machines than to avail ourselves of our own extreme and marvellous sensibilities.

We may see, then, how Spain was called across the Atlantic, in the spell of the positive magnetism of the great western continent. And we may understand better the departure of the Pilgrim Fathers. It is   30
not enough, it is never enough, upon an important occasion to accept the plausible explanation offered by the protagonist. The protagonist will always assert that he moves of his own intention. The Pilgrim Fathers sailed off in an enthusiastic, stern vigour of desire for religious freedom. They sailed to find freedom of worship—so they say. But it is a   35
palpable fiction. Because at once they instigated the most cruel religious tyranny in America, equivalent to the Spanish-American Inquisition. Nay, it even seems as if the impulse to religious cruelty *came* to the Spaniards from America, and was exercised secondarily by them in Europe.   40

The Pilgrim Fathers did not sail to America in search of religious freedom. The Pilgrim Fathers, if they had wanted this freedom, would have stayed and fought for it, with Cromwell. Religious liberty was with them a phrase that covered complex motives. For the deepest human soul all the while offers specious reasons for her own movement, covering beyond all knowledge the true motive. The Pilgrim Fathers sternly believed themselves that they sailed in search of purer Christian worship and the liberty to that worship. It was the innermost soul offering a sufficient pretext to their stubborn, self-righteous minds.

For, if we consider the early American colonies, the Pilgrim Fathers were not Christians at all—not in any reasonable sense of the word. They were no more Christians than the dark and violent Spaniards of the Inquisition* were Christian. At the close of the fifteenth century Spain fell back from Christian Europe and became a thing apart. In the same way the first Americans departed from the Christian and the European vital mystery. They became dark, sinister, repellent. They seemed to seek, not liberty, but a gloomy and tyrannical sense of power. They wanted to have power over all immediate life. They had a gloomy passion, similar to that of some of the African sects of the Early Christian Church, to destroy or mutilate life at its very quick,* lusting in their dark power to annihilate all living impulses, both their own and those of their neighbour. For all of which the Christian religion served as a word, a weapon, an instrument: the instrument of their dark lust for power over the immediate life itself, as it stirred to motion in the breasts and bowels of the living.

This lust is latent in all religious passion. So long as a people is living and generous, it fulfils its religious passion in setting free the deep desires which are latent in all human souls. Bernard of Clairvaux, St. Francis of Assisi, Martin Luther,* these were liberators. They made it possible for every man to be more himself, more whole, more full and spontaneous than ever man had been before.

But into Puritanism and Calvinism* had already entered the dangerous *negative* religious passion of repression, this passion which so easily becomes a lust, a deep lust for vindictive power over the life-issue. It was on the hard recoil of this destructive religious passion that the Pilgrim Fathers left Europe. America, dark, violent, aboriginal, would lend them force to satisfy their lust of anti-life.

It is absolutely necessary to realise once and for all that every enthusiasm, every passion, has a dual motion: first a motion of liberation, of setting free; and secondly a motion of vindictive repression of the living impulse, the utter subjection of the living, spontaneous being to the fixed, mechanical, ultimately insane *will*.

When at the Renaissance the great religious impulse of Europe broke, these two motions became separate. We see the Calvinists, the Puritans, the Spaniards of the Inquisition, all filled with a wild lust for cruelty, the lust for the power to torture, to dominate and destroy the mysterious body of life. It is the will of man rising frenzied against the mystery of life itself, and struggling insanely to *dominate*, to have the life-issue in unutterable control, to squeeze the mystic thing, life, within the violent hands of possession, grasp it, squeeze it, have it, have unspeakable power over it.

Whereas, if we have one spark of sanity, we know that we can never possess and direct the life-mystery. The utmost of our power is to possess and destroy. The life-mystery precedes us. Our simplest spontaneous movement *precedes* all knowing and willing. Secondly, and afterwards, we are conscious, we have voluntary control. Our knowing is always secondary and subsequent to our being, which is an issue of the creative unknown. And our volition is always subsidiary to our spontaneous arrival.

But there lies latent in the soul of man, at all times, the desire to reverse this order. In every man lies latent the passion to control and compel the issue of creation, by force of the self-conscious will. We have a latent craving to control from our deliberate will the very springing and welling up of the life-impulse itself. This craving, once admitted, becomes a lust. This lust, once established and dominant, carries mankind to unthinkable lengths in the frenzied, insane purpose of having the life-issue utterly under human compulsion.

The Jews of old became established in this lust: hence their endless purifications, their assertion of control over the natural functions; hence also the rite of circumcision, the setting of the seal of self-conscious will upon the very quick of bodily impulse. The frenzied, self-mutilating Christians, the fakir-like saints, such as St. Simeon Stylites, the St. Anthony frenzied in celibacy,* these men do but assert the utter tyranny of deliberate will over every spontaneous, uncontrollable motion. There must be a measure of control, that every deep desire may be fulfilled in its own fulness and proportion. But there must never be control for control's sake.

The great field for the lust of control in the modern world is America. Whether we read the history of Spanish America or of English-speaking America, it is the same, a disheartening, painful record of the lusting

triumph of the deliberate will. On the one hand, the Spaniards in America, following the Spaniards of the Inquisition, lusted in the overweening sensual desire for repression of freedom in the spiritual self, whereas the North Americans lusted spiritually for utter repression in
5   the sensual or passional self.

The New Englanders, wielding the sword of the spirit backwards, struck down the primal impulsive being in every man, leaving only a mechanical, automatic unit. In so doing they cut and destroyed the living bond between men, the rich passional contact. And for this passional
10 contact gradually was substituted the mechanical bond of purposive utility. The spontaneous passion of social union once destroyed, then it was possible to establish the perfect mechanical concord, the concord of a number of parts to a vast whole, a stupendous productive mechanism. And this, this vast mechanical concord of innumerable machine-parts,
15 each performing its own motion in the intricate complexity of material production, this is the clue to the western democracy.

It has taken more than three hundred years to build this vast living machine. It has taken just as long to produce the modern Mexican, a creature of incomprehensible sensual reactions, barely human any longer.
20 But North America has proceeded in one line wonderfully. After only two generations in New England the first Yankees* noticed that their stock had changed. The sturdy, ruddy, lusty English yeoman had disappeared, the long-jawed, sallow American took his place, with a pale, nervous womenfolk such as England has only lately begun to reckon
25 with.

Uprooted from the native soil, planted in strong aboriginal earth, this thing happened to the English stock. The natural impulsive being withered, the deliberate, self-determined being appeared in his place. There was soon no more need to militate directly against the impulsive
30 body. This once dispatched, man could attend to the deliberate perfection in mechanised existence. This is what makes good business men. And in this the American is like the Jew: in that, having conquered and destroyed the instinctive, impulsive being in himself, he is free to be always deliberate, always calculated, rapid, swift, and single in prac-
35 tical execution as a machine. The perfection of machine triumph, of deliberate self-determined motion, is to be found in the Americans and the Jews.* Hence the race talent for acting. In other races the impulsive mystery of being interferes with the deliberate intention of the individual. In these not. Only, Americans and Jews suffer from a torturing
40 frictional unease, an incapacity to rest. They must run on, like machines,

or go mad. The only difference between a human machine and an iron machine is that the latter can come to an utter state of rest, the former cannot. No living thing can lapse into static inertia, as a machine at rest lapses. And this is where life is indomitable. It will be mechanised, but it will never allow mechanical inertia. Hence the Orestes-like flight of 5 unrest of Americans and Jews.

And yet it cannot be for this alone that the millions have crossed the ocean. This thing, this mechanical democracy, new and monstrous on the face of the earth, cannot be an end in itself. It is only a vast intervention, a marking-time, a mechanical life-pause. It is the tremendous 10 statement in negation of our European being.

This sheer and monstrous reflection of Europe, Europe in negative reality, reflected to enormity on the American continent, will surely vanish swiftly, like one of the horrifying dreams. This is not the reality of America. It is only the reality of our own negation that the vast aboriginal 15 continent reflects back at us. There will come an America which we cannot foretell, a new creation on the face of the earth, a world beyond us. The early Christianity produced monstrous growths, monstrous reflections of the world then dying, distorted and made huge by the new spirit. These monstrosities, like enormous horrifying phantoms 20 that men do not care to remember, disappeared, leaving the new era to roll slowly on to the European summer. So the mechanical monstrosity of the west will presently disappear.

It was not for this that myriads crossed the seas, magnetically carried like birds in migration, without knowing why or whither, yet conducted 25 along lines of pure magnetic attraction, to a goal. Spaniards, Puritans, Jews, Celts, they went in recoil of negation from Europe. They went in the lust for deliberate control of the living issues: lust for sensual gratification in pride or power or slave-tyranny on the part of the Spaniards and perhaps the Celts; lust for spiritual gratification in the ethical con- 30 trol of all life on the part of Jews and Puritans. But this was not the final motive for departure. This was the negative impulse. The positive is more unsearchable.

They went like birds down the great electric direction of the west, lifted like migrating birds on a magnetic current. They went in subtle 35 vibration of response to the new earth, as animals travel far distances vibrating to the salt-licks.*

They walked a new earth, were seized by a new electricity, and laid in line differently. Their bones, their nerves, their sinews took on a new molecular disposition in the new vibration. 40

They breathed a savage air, and their blood was suffused and burnt. A new fierce salt of the earth, in their mouths, penetrated and altered the substance of their bones. Meat of wild creatures, corn of the aboriginal earth, filled and impregnated them with the unknown America. Their subtlest plasm was changed under the radiation of new skies, new influence of light, their first and rarest life-stuff transmuted.

Thus, through hundreds of years, new races are made, people slowly smelted down and re-cast. There is the slow and terrible process of transubstantiation.* Who can tell what will come at the negative crisis of this reduction? What monstrosity? And, much more, who can tell what will come when the new world sets in?

For every great locality has its own pure daimon, and is conveyed at last into perfected life. We have seen Asia, and North Africa, and a good deal of Europe. We know the white abstraction of the Arctic and Antarctic continents, the unspeakable immortality of the ice, where existence is and being is not. There remains America, and, beyond, the even farther-off Australia.

Every great locality expresses itself perfectly, in its own flowers, its own birds and beasts, lastly its own men, with their perfected works. Mountains convey themselves in unutterable expressed perfection in the blue gentian flower and in the edelweiss flower, so soft, yet shaped like snow-crystals.* The very strata of the earth come to a point of perfect, unutterable concentration in the inherent sapphires and emeralds. It is so with all worlds and all places of the world. We may take it as a law.

So now we wait for the fulfilment of the law in the west, the inception of a new era of living. At present there is a vast myriad-branched human engine, the very thought of which is death. But in the winter even a tree looks like iron. Seeing the great trunk of dark iron and the swaying steel flails of boughs, we cannot help being afraid. What we see of buds looks like sharp bronze stud-points. The whole thing hums elastic and sinister and fatally metallic, like some confused scourge of swinging steel throngs. Yet the lovely cloud of green and summer lustre is within it.

We wait for the miracle, for the new soft wind. Even the buds of iron break into soft little flames of issue. So will people change. So will the machine-parts open like buds and the great machines break into leaf. Even we can expect our iron ships to put forth vine and tendril and bunches of grapes, like the ship of Dionysos* in full sail upon the ocean.

It only wants the miracle, the new, soft, creative wind: which does not blow yet. Meanwhile we can only stand and wait, knowing that what is, is not. And we can listen to the sad, weird utterance of this classic America, watch the transmutation from men into machines and ghosts, hear the last metallic sounds. Perhaps we can see as well glimpses of the mystic transubstantiation. 5

II.

Benjamin Franklin.

The idea of the perfectibility of man, which was such an inspiration in Europe, to Rousseau and Godwin and Shelley, all those idealists of 5 the eighteenth and early nineteenth century, was actually fulfilled in America before the ideal was promulgated in Europe. If we sift the descriptions of the "Perfect Man," and accept the chief features of this ideal being, keeping only to what is possible, we shall find we have the abstract of a character such as Benjamin Franklin's.

10 A man whose passions are the obedient servants of his mind, a man whose sole ambition is to live for the bettering and advancement of his fellows, a man of such complete natural benevolence that the interests of self never obtrude in his works or his desires—such was to be the Perfect Man of the future, in the Millennium of the world.* And such 15 a man was Benjamin Franklin, in the actual America.

Therefore it is necessary to look very closely at the character of this Franklin. The magicians knew, at least imaginatively, what it was to create a being out of the intense *will* of the soul.* And Mary Shelley, in the midst of the idealists, gives the dark side to the ideal being, showing 20 us Frankenstein's monster.*

The ideal being was man created by man. And so was the supreme monster. For man is not a creator. According to the early creed, the only power that the Almighty Creator could *not* confer upon His created being, not even upon the Son, was this same power of creation.* Man 25 by his own presence conveys the mystery and magnificence of creation. But yet man has no power over the creative mystery. He cannot *make* life—and he never will.

This we must accept, as one of the terms of our being. We know we cannot make and unmake the stars or the sun in heaven. We can only be 30 at one, or at variance with them. And we should have the dignity of our own nature, and know that we cannot ordain the creative issues, neither in ourselves nor beyond ourselves. The ultimate choice is not ours. The creative mystery precedes us.

This has been the fallacy of our age—the assumption that we, of our 35 own will, and by our own precept and prescription, can create the perfect

180

being and the perfect age. The truth is, that we *have* the faculty to form
and distort even our own natures, and the natures of our fellow men. But
we can *create* nothing. And the thing we can make of our own natures,
by our own will, is at the most a pure mechanism, an automaton. So
that if on the one hand Benjamin Franklin is the perfect human being of 5
Godwin, on the other hand he is a monster, not exactly as the monster in
Frankenstein, but for the same reason, viz., that he is the production or
fabrication of the human will, which projects itself upon a living being,
and automatises that being according to a given precept.

It is necessary to insist for ever that the source of creation is central 10
within the human soul, and the issue from that source proceeds without
any choice or knowledge on our part. The creative gesture, or emanation,
for ever precedes the conscious realisation of this gesture. We are moved,
we *are*, and then, thirdly, we *know*. Afterwards, fourthly, after we know,
then we can *will*. And when we *will*, then we can proceed to make 15
or construct or fabricate—even our own characters. But we can never
construct or fabricate or even change our own *being*, because we have
our being in the central creative mystery, which is the pure present,
and the pure Presence, of the soul—present beyond all knowing or
willing. Knowing and willing are external, they are as it were the reflex 20
or *afterwards* of being.

Fairly early in life Franklin drew up a creed, which, he intended,
"should satisfy the professors of every religion, but which should shock
none." It has six articles.

"That there is One God, who made all things." 25

"That He governs the world by His Providence."

"That He ought to be worshipped with adoration, prayer, and thanks-
giving."

"But that the most acceptable service of God is doing good to man."

"That the Soul is immortal." 30

"And that God will certainly reward virtue and punish vice, either
here or hereafter."

Here we have a God who is a maker and an employer, whose one
business is to look after the smooth running of the established creation,
particularly the human part of it—Benjamin is not afraid to "but" 35
the Lord his impertinent "buts"—who makes each man responsible
for the working of the established system; and who reserves for Himself
the right of granting a kind of immortal pension, in the after-life, to His
praiseworthy mechanics of creation, or of condemning the unworthy to
a kind of eternal workhouse. 40

Such a God is, of course, only the inventor and director of the universe, and not a God at all. In order to shock none of the professors of any religion, Benjamin left out all the qualities of the Godhead, utterly dispensed with the mystery of creation. The universe once set up, it has
5   only to be kept running. For this purpose it has an efficient manager in Providence. Providence sees that the business of the universe—that great and complicated factory of revolving worlds—is kept profitably going. The output of human life increases with each generation, and there is a corresponding increase in the necessities of life. Providence is
10 then entirely successful, and the earthly business is a paying concern.

Such is the open, flagrant statement which America makes, a hundred and fifty years after the religious arrival of the Pilgrim Fathers. The process of the will-to-control has worked so swiftly, in its activity of mystic destructive metabolism, that in a hundred and fifty years it has
15 reduced the living being to this automatic entity.

The religious truth is the same now as it ever has been: that preceding all our knowledge or will or effort is the central creative mystery, out of which issues the strange and for ever unaccountable emanation of creation: that the universe is a bush which burns for ever with the
20 Presence, consuming itself and yet never consumed;* it burns with new flowers and with crumpling leaves that fall to ash; for ever new flowers on the way out of the mystic centre of creation which is within the bush—central and omnipresent; for ever old leaves falling. We cannot know where the quick of next year's roses lies, within the tree. In what
25 part, root or stem or branch, is to be found the presence of next year's apples? We cannot answer. And yet we know that they are within the living body of the tree, nowhere and everywhere.

So, within the living body of the universe, and within the living soul of man, central and omnipresent, in the fingers and lips and eyes and
30 feet, as in the heart and bowels, and in the marshes as in the stars, lies the Presence, never to be located, yet never to be doubted, because it is *always* evident to our living soul, the Presence from which issues the first fine-shaken impulse and prompting of new being, eternal creation which is always Now.* All time is central within this ever-present creative Now.
35 Central is the mystery of Now, the creative mystery, what we have called the Godhead. It pulses for ever, in the motion of creation, drawing all things towards itself. And the running waves, as they travel towards the perfect centre of the revealed, now are buds, and infants, and children; further back, they are seed-scales and moving seed-leaves, and
40 caterpillars; and further back, they are sun and water and the elements

moving towards the centre of pure Now, of perfect creative Presence.
And in the outflow, the waves travel back. And the first waves are the
people with hair tinged with grey, and flowers passing into fruit, and
leaves passing into water and fire and mould, and the elements ebbing
asunder into the great chaos, and further than the great chaos into the   5
infinite. The reality of realities is the rose in flower, the man and woman
in maturity, the bird in song, the snake in brindled colour, the tiger
in his stripes.* In these, past and present and future are at one, the
perfect Now. This is wholeness and pure creation. So there is a ripple
and shimmer of the universe, ripples of futurity running towards the   10
Now, out of the infinite, and ripples of age and the autumn, glimmering back towards the infinite. And rocking at all times on the shimmer
are the perfect lotus flowers of immanent Now, the lovely beings of
consummation.

The quick of wholeness lies in this gleaming Now. But the whole of   15
wholeness lies in the ebbing haste of child-faced futurity, the consummation of presence, and the lapse of sunset-coloured old age. This is
completeness, the childish haste towards the consummation, the perfect
revelation, the pure Presence, when we are fully a flower and present,
the great *adsum** of our being, and then the slow retreat of becoming   20
old.

There is, however, the false Now, as well as the mystic Now. Perpetual
youth, or perpetual maturity, this is the false Now—as roses that never
fall are false roses. The remaining steady, fixed, this is the false Now.
And as the consummation into the whole infinite is the antithesis of   25
pure Presence, so is Eternity the antithesis of the mystic Present, the
great Now. For eternity is but the sum of the whole past and the whole
future, the complete *outside* or negation of being.

In Europe the desire to become infinite, one with the All, was the
adolescent desire to know everything and to be everything. The mystic   30
passion for infinitude is the ultimate of all our passion for love, oneness,
equality. It is all an adolescent process. It is a process which comes to
a conclusion, and out of which mankind must issue, as the individual
man issues from his period of loving and seeking, into the assured
magnificence of maturity. This experience of infinitude, oneness with   35
the all, is the ultimate communion wherein the individual is merged into
wholeness with all things, through love. But it is no goal. The individual
must emerge from this bath of love, as from the baths of blood in the old
religions, initiated, fulfilled, entering on the great state of independent
maturity.   40

In America, however, the state of oneness was soon reached. The Pilgrim Fathers soon killed off in their people the spontaneous impulses and appetites of the self. By a stern discipline and a fanatic system of repression, they subdued every passion into rigid control. And they did it quickly. England lapsed again into exuberance and self-indulgence. She produced her Congreves and Addisons and Smolletts, and Robert Burns.* But America moved on in one line of inexorable repression.

Now there are two kinds of oneness among mankind. First there is that ecstatic sense, religious and mystic, of uplifting into union with all men, through love. This experience we all know, more or less. But, secondly, there is the hard, practical state of being at one with all men, through suppression and elimination of those things which make differences—passions, prides, impulses of the self which cause disparity between one being and another. Now it seems as if, in America, this negative, destructive form of oneness predominated from the first, a oneness attained by destroying all incompatible elements in each individual, leaving the pattern or standard man.

So that whilst Europe was still impulsively struggling on towards a consummation of love, expressed in Shelley or Verlaine or Swinburne or Tolstoi,* a struggle for the mystic state of communion in being, America, much quicker and more decisive, was cutting down every human being towards a common standard, aiming at a homogeneous oneness through elimination of incommutable factors or elements, establishing a standardised humanity, machine-perfect.

This process of strangling off the impulses took place in Europe as in America. Spontaneous movement distinguishes one individual from another. If we remove the spontaneous or impulsive factor, and substitute deliberate purposiveness, we can have a homogeneous humanity, acting in unison. Hence the ideal Reason of the eighteenth century.

So man has a great satisfaction, at a certain period in his development, in seizing control of his own life-motion, and making himself master of his own fate. The desire is so strong it tends to become a lust. It became a lust in the French and in the American. Jean Jacques Rousseau had a fundamental lust for fingering and knowing and directing every impulse, as it was born. He intercepted every one of his feelings as it arose, caught it with his consciousness and his will, then liberated it again, so that he might watch it act within the narrow field of his own observation and permission.

All this was part of the process of oneing, the process of forming a deliberate, self-conscious, self-determined humanity which, in the acceptance of a common idea of equality and fraternity, should be quite homogeneous, unified, ultimately dispassionate, rational, utilitarian. The only difference was that whilst the European ideal remained one of mystic, exalted consciousness of oneness, the ideal in America was a practical unison for the producing of the means of life.

Rousseau analysed his feelings, got them into control in order to luxu- 5 riate in their workings. He enjoyed a mental voluptuousness in watching and following the turn of his self-permitted sensations and emotions, as one might watch a wild creature tamed and entrapped and confined in a small space. Franklin, on the other hand, had his voluptuous pleasure in subduing and reducing all his feelings and emotions and desires to 10 the material benefit of mankind.

To seize life within his own will, and control it by precept from his own consciousness, made him as happy as it now makes us sick. With us it is a sick, helpless process. We perceive at last that if we cannot act direct and spontaneous from the centre of creative mystery which is in 15 us, we are nothing. It is no good any more giving us choice—our free will is of no use to us if we no longer have anything to choose. It only remains for us now, in the purest sense, to choose not-to-choose.

Franklin, however, proceeded with joy to seize the life-issues, to get everything into his own choice and will. His God was no longer a creative 20 mystery—He was a reasonable Providence or Producer. And man, being made in the image of God, he too is at his highest a little Providence or Producer of the means of life. Production is the criterion of Godliness, which leads us to the plausible, self-righteous, altruistic materialism of our modern world. The difference between production and creation 25 is the difference between existence and being, function and flowering, mechanical force and life itself.

Franklin proceeded to automatise himself, to subdue life so that it should work automatically to his will. Like Rousseau, he makes a con-fession of his life. But he is purely self-congratulatory. He tells us in 30 detail how he worked out the process of reducing himself to a deliber-ate entity. This deliberate entity, this self-determined man, is the very Son of Man, man made by the power of the human will, a virtuous Frankenstein monster.

Almost scientifically, Franklin broke the impulses in himself. He 35 drew up a list of virtues, established a set of fixed Principles—strictly machine-principles—and by these he proceeded to control his every motion. The modern virtue is machine-principle, meaning the endless repetition of certain sanctioned motions. The old *virtus** meant just the opposite, the very impulse itself, the creative gesture, drifting out 40 incalculable from human hands.

Franklin's list of virtues is as follows:—

1.
TEMPERANCE.
Eat not to fulness; drink not to elevation.

5

2.
SILENCE.
Speak not but what may benefit others or yourself; avoid trifling conversation.

3.
10   ### ORDER.
Let all your things have their places; let each part of your business have its time.

4.
RESOLUTION.
15   Resolve to perform what you ought; perform without fail what you resolve.

5.
FRUGALITY.
Make no expense but to do good to others or yourself—*i.e.*,
20   waste nothing.

6.
INDUSTRY.
Lose no time, be always employed in something useful; cut off all unnecessary action.

25

7.
SINCERITY.
Use no hurtful deceit; think innocently and justly, and, if you speak, speak accordingly.

8.
30   ### JUSTICE.
Wrong none by doing injuries, or omitting the benefits that are your duty.

9.
MODERATION.
35   Avoid extremes, forbear resenting injuries so much as you think they deserve.

10.
CLEANLINESS.
Tolerate no uncleanliness in body, clothes, or habitation.

11.
TRANQUILLITY.
Be not disturbed at trifles, or at accident common or unavoidable.

12.
CHASTITY.
Rarely use venery but for health and offspring, never to dullness, weakness, or the injury of your own or another's peace or
reputation.

13.
HUMILITY.
Imitate Jesus and Socrates.

The last clause or item, of humility, Franklin added because a Quaker
friend told him he was generally considered proud. Truly he had something to be proud of.

He practised these virtues with ardour and diligence. He drew up a
table, giving each of the virtues a column to itself, and having the date,
like a calendar, down the side. And every day he put a mark against
himself for every lapse of virtue. Unfortunately, he does not give us his
marked chart—we might have an even closer view of his character had
he done so. He only tells us that the black column was that of "Order."*
In every other virtue he had considerable proficiency. But he *could not*
make himself tidy and neat in his business and in his surroundings, not
even to the end of his days. So he tells us.

This is his one weakness, his Achilles heel. Had he not had this harmless failing, he would have been the very Frankenstein of virtue. There
is something slightly pathetic, slightly ridiculous, and, if we look closer,
a little monstrous, about the snuff-coloured doctor. He worked so dili-
gently and seriously. He was so alive, full of inquisitive interest and eager
activity. He had his club for discussing philosophic questions, he made
his printing business prosper, he had the streets of Philadelphia swept
and lighted, he invented his electric appliances, he was such a straight-
principled member of all the important Councils of Philadelphia—then
of the American Colonies themselves. He defended himself with such

sturdy, snuff-coloured honesty in England, and against his enemies in
America, and in France. He wrestled with such indomitable integrity
with the French Court, a little, indomitable, amazingly clever and astute,
and at the same time amazingly disingenuous, virtuous man, winning
5   from the fine and decadent French such respect, and such huge sums of
money to help the Americans in their struggle for Independence. It is
a wonderful little snuff-coloured figure, so admirable, so *clever*, a little
pathetic, and, somewhere, ridiculous and detestable.

He is like a child, so serious and earnest. And he is like a little old
10   man, even when he is young, so deliberate and reasoned. It is difficult to
say which he is—a child or a little old man. But when we come to grips
he is neither. In his actuality he is a dreadful automaton, a mechanism.
He is a printer, and a philosopher, and an inventor, and a scientist, and a
patriot, and a writer of "Poor Richard" jokes for the calendar, and he is
15   virtuous and scrupulous and of perfect integrity. But he is never a man.
It did not seem to matter at all to him that he himself was an intrinsic
being. He saw himself as a little unit in the vast total of society. All he
wanted was to run well, as a perfect little wheel within the whole.

The beauty of incomparable *being* was nothing to him. The ines-
20   timable splendidness of a man who is purely himself, distinct and incommutable, a thing of pure, present reality, this meant nothing to
Benjamin. He liked comeliness, cleanliness, healthiness, and profusion
of the means of life. He could never see that the only riches of the earth
is in free, whole, incomparable beings, each man mystically himself,
25   and distinct, mystically distinguished. To him, men were like coin to
be counted up, coin interchangeable.

He was, perhaps, the most admirable little automaton the world has
ever seen, the invention of the human will, working according to good
principles. So far as affairs went, he was admirable. As far as life goes,
30   he is monstrous.

If we look in the little almanacks or booklets that are printed in
England, in out-of-the-way corners, even to-day, we shall find humorous,
trite paragraphs, where "Poor Richard" is the speaker, and which are
little object-lessons to one or another of the "virtues"—economy, or
35   frugality, or modesty. Franklin wrote these almanacks when he was still
a young man—more than a hundred and fifty years ago—and they are
still printed, now as then, for the poor and vulgar to profit by. They
are always trite and, in a measure, humorous, and always shrewd, and
always flagrantly material. Franklin had his humour, but it was always
40   of the "don't-put-all-your-eggs-in-one-basket" sort. It always derided

the spontaneous, impulsive, or extravagant element in man, and showed
the triumph of cautious, calculated, virtuous behaviour. Whatever else
man must be, he must be deliberate. He must live entirely from his
consciousness and his will. Once he lives from his consciousness and
his will, it will follow as a matter of course that he lives according to the   5
given precepts, because that is both easiest and most profitable.

We do, perhaps, get a glimpse of a really wondering young Franklin,
where he has still the living faculty for beholding with instinct the world
around him—when he was a printer's workman, in London, for a short
time.* But the glimpse is soon over. He is back in America, and is all   10
American, a very model of a man, as if a machine had made him.

He was so dreadfully all-of-a-piece, his attitude is always so consistent
and urbane. He has to go to the frontiers of his State, to settle some
disturbance among the Indians. And on this occasion he writes:—

"We found they had made a great bonfire in the middle of the square;   15
they were all drunk, men and women quarrelling and fighting. Their
dark-coloured bodies, half naked, seen only by the gloomy light of the
bonfire, running after and beating one another with fire-brands, accompanied by their horrid yellings, formed a scene the most resembling our
ideas of hell that could be well imagined. There was no appeasing the   20
tumult, and we retired to our lodging. At midnight a number of them
came thundering at our door, demanding more rum, of which we took
no notice.

"The next day, sensible they had misbehaved in giving us that disturbance, they sent three of their counsellors to make their apology.   25
The orator acknowledged the fault, but laid it upon the rum, and then
endeavoured to excuse the rum by saying: 'The Great Spirit, who made
all things, made everything for some use; and whatever he designed
anything for, that use it should always be put to. Now, when he made
rum, he said: "Let this be for the Indians to get drunk with." And it   30
must be so.'

"And, indeed, if it be the design of Providence to extirpate these
savages in order to make room for the cultivators of the earth, it seems
not improbable that rum may be the appointed means. It has already
annihilated all the tribes who formerly inhabited all the sea coast——"   35

This, from the good doctor, with such suave complacency, is a little
disenchanting. But this is what a Providence must lead to. A Providence
is a Provider for the universe, and the business of the provider is to get
rid of every waster, even if this waster happen to be part of the self-same
created universe. When man sets out to have all things his own way he   40

is bound to run up against a great many men. Even to establish the ideal of equality he has to reckon with the men who do really feel the force of inequality. And then equality sharpens his axe. He becomes a great leveller, cutting off all tall men's heads. For no man must be taller than
5   Franklin, who is middle-sized.

Nevertheless, this process of attaining to unison by conquering and subduing all impulses, this removing of all those individual traits which make for separateness and diversity, had to be achieved and accomplished. It is not until man has utterly seized power over himself, and
10 gained complete knowledge of himself, down to the most minute and shameful of his desires and sensations, that he can really begin to be free. Then, when man knows *all*, both shameful and good, that is in man; and when he has control over every impulse, both good and bad; then, and only then, having utterly bound and fettered himself in his
15 own will and his own self-conscious knowledge, will he learn to make the great choice, the choice between automatic self-determining, and mystic, spontaneous freedom.

When the great Greek-Christian will-to-knowledge* is fulfilled; and when the great barbaric will-to-power is also satisfied; then, perhaps,
20 man can recognise that neither power nor knowledge is the ultimate man's attainment, but only *being*; that the pure reality lies not in any infinitude, but in the mystery of the perfect *unique* self, incommutable; not in any eternity, but in the sheer Now.

The quick and issue of our being stands previous to any control, prior
25 to all knowledge. The centre of creative mystery is primal and central in every man, but in each man it is unique and incommutable. When we know *all things* about ourselves we shall know this, know, and enter upon our being. But first we must know all things, both bad and good. For this, the great liberating truth, is the last to be realised, the very
30 last.

When we know that the unique, incommutable creative mystery of the Self is within us and precedes us, then we shall be able to take our full being from this mystery. We shall at last learn the pure lesson of knowing not-to-know. We shall know so perfectly that in fulness of
35 knowledge we shall yield to the mystery, and become spontaneous in full consciousness. Our will will be so strong that we can simply, through sheer strength, defer from willing, accepting the spontaneous mystery, and saving it in its issue from the mechanical lusts of righteousness or power.

III.

Henry St. John de Crèvecœur.

Crèvecœur was born in France in the middle of the eighteenth century. As a boy he came over to England and received part of his education here. He went to Canada, served for a time there with the French in their 5 war against the English, and later passed over into the United States, to become an exuberant American. He married a New England girl, and established himself as a farmer. In this period he wrote his *Letters from an American Farmer*, a series of delightful egoistic accounts of his own ideal existence as an American citizen. He came to France, and 10 whilst he was there his far-off home was burnt and his wife a fugitive in the American War of Independence. Returning to America, he entered into public and commercial life. Again in France, he was known as a *littérateur*, he frequented the literary *salons*, he was acquainted with Benjamin Franklin. 15

The *Letters* were very popular in England among the Romanticists, such as Shelley, Coleridge, Godwin. They are quaint and effusive and affected, according to the Jean Jacques Rousseau affectation of "natural simplicity" and "pristine emotion." To us they are often tiresome and foolish, mere effusions of romantic egoism. But Crèvecœur had in him 20 some of the stern stuff of an artist.

Franklin was the Son of Man, as we have produced him after two thousand years of effort, from the Archetype. Crèvecœur also is a Son of Man. That is, his whole character has been produced by the human will, through the course of Christian ages, produced according to a 25 given idea. For two thousand years mankind was breeding the ideal type, the selfless and yet practical type. In the end we have the admirable little monster of a Franklin, produced by the Christian-ethical impulse, and we have Crèvecœur, produced by the Christian-emotional impulse. They are the last two instances of ethical England and emotional France, 30 and together they make the complete American.

Two thousand years of breeding to type bred us our Shelley in England, our Rousseau in France, our Franklin and our Crèvecœur in America. Shelley and Rousseau, Franklin and Crèvecœur, these are the two halves of the one whole. The whole duality, of body and soul, matter and spirit, is here again exemplified. Shelley and Franklin conceive of themselves in terms of pure abstraction, pure spirit, pure mathematical reality. But Rousseau and Crêvecœur exist in terms of emotion and 5 sensation. And surely this is the duality of spiritual and sensual being, spirit and senses, soul and body, mind and matter.

As a matter of fact, this duality does exist, in all our living, in all our experience. Before thought takes place, before the brain is awake in the small infant, the body is awake and alive, and in the body the great 10 nerve centres are active, active both in knowing and in asserting. This knowledge is not mental, it is what we may call first-consciousness. Now our first consciousness is seated, not in the brain, but in the great nerve centres of the breast and the bowels, the cardiac plexus and the solar plexus. Here life first seethes into active impulse and consciousness, the 15 mental understanding comes later. In the infant, life is wildly active. Yet we cannot say it is mentally so. The great nerve centres of the upper part of the body, and the great nerve centres of the lower part of the body, these are awake first, these send out the first impulses and gestures, these contain the first-knowledge, the root-knowledge. Mental consciousness 20 is only resultant from this. From this duality in first-consciousness, this duality in root-knowledge, arises the subsequent oneness and wholeness of full mental consciousness.

But all the time, and all through life, we are primarily creatures of dual consciousness, the duality of the upper and lower nerve centres, active in 25 first-consciousness; and then, subsequently, we are single and whole in full mental consciousness. As long as we live our first-knowledge is dual, of the upper and lower body. The strange consummation into oneness, of the final understanding, which consummates the upper and the lower knowledge into one third pure state of wholeness, whole understanding, 30 this only comes from a fulfilment in the duality.

We state the duality as the duality of our upper and lower body. The great nerve centre in the breast—called by the ancients the heart—this is the centre of our dynamic spiritual consciousness, our spiritual being; and the great plexus in the bowels is the centre of our dynamic sensual 35 consciousness.

We know, if we but think for a moment of our own immediate experience, that the breast is the dynamic centre of the great, passionate, selfless spiritual love; and that in the bowels lies the dark and unfathomable vortex of our sensual passion, sensual love.

We are creatures of duality, in the first place. Our oneness is subsequent. As creatures of duality we issue from the unknown, the creative unknown which precedes us, and must for ever precede us. Beginning with the tiny infant, like a flower that opens, the breast and the eyes unfurl to the earth and the sky, to enter into a selfless communion. The 5 breast opens day by day, and the life goes forth from it, the mysterious emanation, to be at one with the sky and the world; then the eyes also open, and the spirit goes forth through them, seeing and beholding, till the I, the self, has passed into the living universe to be at one with it, one and whole. And then this body, this breast, is but a socket or cup 10 for the unfolded flower of the infinite cosmos.

This is the process of my upper, or spiritual, consummation. It begins in the tiny child as it lies against its mother, or waves its arms from the wonder-centre of the breast. And it culminates in us all, in every man according to his degree: in the great love of humanity, in the love of 15 landscape, in the love of light itself.

Correspondingly, within the bowels lies the burning source of the sensual consciousness. Here the Self is positive and centripetal. Here I am I,* darkly and fiercely sentient. Here I am dark-centric, all that is not me roams outside, looming, wonderful, imminent, perilous—but 20 wonderful and unknown. And from this centre I draw all things into me, that they enter in passional communion into my self, become one with me, an increase and a magnificence in my self. This is the process of my sensual becoming, which culminates at last in the great dark glory of real almightiness, all things being added unto me for my power and 25 perfection, wherein I am whole and infinite, that infinite which has been symbolised as a point.

The process of this sensual fulfilment begins in the tiny infant, when instinctively it carries everything to its mouth, to absorb the mysterious mouth and abdominal knowledge of the unknown thing, carry this 30 unknown in a communion of most intimate contact, into the self; and when the child stirs mysteriously, as it hears new sounds, again receiving new impressions in the dark, sensual self, untranslatable; and when it quivers so delicately to a new touch. This is the beginning of the process of sensual fulfilment, which ends only in that strange, supreme 35 passion, when the "I" is singly consummate and almighty, in supreme possession of the All.

This every man experiences, according to his degree, in the dark magnificence of sensual love, and in the single, rich splendour of the positive

"I," the self paramount, that moves undiminished in a contributed universe. Every man, according to his degree, knows this consummation,
the consummation which he lives for: for this, as well as for the other,
spiritual consummation.

5   The third and last state is when I am fulfilled in both the great
dynamic ways of consciousness, and am free, a free being. Then I need
not compel myself in either of the two directions, I need not strive
after either consummation, but can accept the profound impulse, as it
issues from the incalculable soul, act upon it spontaneously; and can,
10   moreover, speak and know and be, uttering myself as a tree in full
flower utters itself. There is no real self-expression till there is a whole
consummation.

Shelley sought for the pure spiritual consummation,* that alone. It
is probable the Egyptians once knew the pure sensual consummation,
15   that alone. Franklin, however, had reached the point where he wished
to translate what is really a passional culmination into an established
state, what is a great dynamic condition, into a static condition. He
wanted to establish the laws of the spiritual state, as a fixed, mechanical
thing. This can only be done, at last, by destroying the impulsive being,
20   and a substituting of the laws of the mechanical universe. For we must
draw the great distinction between the life-mystery, in which is the
creative or God-mystery, and the mystery of Force and Matter. The
creative mystery, which is in life, is utterly beyond control, beyond us,
and before us. It is also beyond and before the whole material universe,
25   beyond and before the great Forces. Life is not a Force. It is, and will ever
remain, a mystery, a limit to our presumption. All attempt to subject
life, and its inherent creative mystery, to the will of man, and to the laws
of Force, is materialism and ultimate death.

Crêvecœur and Franklin, however, both asserted the triumph of
30   this materialism, the triumph of the will of man and of the laws of
the mechanical universe, over the creative mystery itself. But whereas
Franklin's satisfaction was in selfless working for the good of mankind,
Crêvecœur had his satisfaction in his own emotional triumph in concord and production. Franklin lived in the breast, in so far as he had
35   an impulsive or passionate life, Crêvecœur in the bowels. Both were
under the control of the same idea, the same mental prescription. But
Crêvecœur had his dynamic being in the sensual consciousness, whilst
Franklin's dynamic being—such as it was—was in the spiritual consciousness. Crêvecœur was an emotional idealist, the idea or ideal being
40   the same as Franklin's.

Thus the *Letters from an American Farmer*, affecting a naïve simplicity, are in reality most sophisticated. They tell of Crèvecœur's struggles to establish his farm in the wilderness, of the beneficent help of his "amiable spouse," the joy of seating his infant son on the shafts of the plough, the happiness of helping a neighbour build a barn, the supreme   5
satisfaction of finding himself a worthy and innocent member of a free community. But none of it is spontaneous emotion. It is all dictated from the head. "Now," says Crèvecœur to himself, "I am a pure child of Nature, Nature sweet and pure." So he proceeds to luxuriate in his *rôle*, to find everything sweet and pure. "That is my spouse," he   10
says, "amiable, sweet, and pure, a deep-breasted daughter of Nature, fountain of life."* Thus she is a kind of living image of Crèvecœur's own intention. That she was a woman, an individual, a being by herself could never occur to the American Farmer. She was an "amiable spouse," just as an oaken cupboard is an oaken cupboard. Likewise a little boy is a   15
healthy offspring, and when this same healthy offspring is seated on his father's plough, the whole picture represents the children of Nature—sweet and pure—toiling innocence and joy.

All this, as we see, is exactly according to prescription, it is life according to Man, not man according to Life. French romantic idealists   20
prescribe this life, and American farmers proceed to exemplify it—not only American farmers, but Châteaubriand* and Bernadin de St. Pierre and the most ridiculous François le Vaillant and even the Queen Marie Antoinette herself, playing dairymaid. The prescription still holds good: we still have Arcadians,* simple life, and garden suburb. It is all a most   25
artificial business of living according to prescription, keeping every impulse strangled, and ending where it begins, in materialism pure and simple. For this subjecting life to a prescription, according to the will of man, is materialism itself. It is a subjecting of the creative or life-mystery to the material or mechanical, psychic-mechanical law.   30

Crèvecœur, however, is an artist as well as an emotional idealist. And an artist is never, in being an artist, an idealist. The artist lives and sees and knows direct from the life-mystery itself. He sees the creative unencompassable mystery in all its nakedness of impulse and gesture. And living, as he does, from the ego-centric centres, as an idealist,   35
Crèvecœur as an artist lives from the great sensual centres, his art is in terms of the great sensual understanding, dark and rich and of that reserved, pagan tenderness to which we have almost lost the key.

In the sensual vision there is always the pause of fear, dark wonder, and glamour. The creature beheld is seen in its quality of *otherness*,   40 a term of the vivid, imminent unknown. And the new knowledge enters in rich, dark thrills into the soul. In the thrill and pulse within the bowels I gather the new creature into myself, into blood knowledge, I encompass the unknown within the dominion of myself.

5   Thus all wild creatures are shy—even the fiercest. They are reluctant to let themselves be seen. This is not fear of physical hurt, but fear of being *known*. No free thing can bear to be encompassed by the psyche of another being, save, perhaps, in sheer fright or in sensual love. Thus Dmitri Karamazov, when he is exposed naked, is virtually killed.* It is
10 the encompassing and overthrow of the immune sensual being which he is. Thus it is hard to catch weasels, or any wild creatures, at play. No free creature willingly yields itself to the *touch* of another being. It cannot bear to be sensually encompassed. The true self is like a star which must preserve the circumambient darkness which gives to it its
15 distinction and uniqueness. It must keep the splendid, vivid loneliness. Dawn only removes the gulf from between the stars, and makes them as nothing in the great one web of light, the universal sun-consciousness, the selfless spiritual being.

None the less, in the sensual mystery there is that impulse to trust
20 or love which leads to lordship and empire. There is the impulse of the lesser sensual psyche to yield itself, where it trusts and believes, to the greater psyche, yielding in the great culminating process which unifies all life in one gesture of magnificence. In this way we have acquired the domestic animals, which have yielded their psyche to us implicitly. In
25 the same way the Egyptian pyramids were built, symbolic of the culminating process, the lesser life yielding and culminating, step by step, towards the apex of the God-King.* In this same spirit of yielding and culminating, through dark faith, or trust, our mediæval cathedrals were erected: otherwise they never would have been erected. In the same
30 way Napoleon, the last great leader; attained his brief ascendancy.* It is necessary, before men can unite in one great living gesture, that this impulse towards the mystic sensual yielding and culminating shall find expression. In the modern spirit of equality, we can get tremendous concerted action, really machine action, but no culminating living oneness,
35 no great gesture of a creative people. Hence we have no architecture: we have only machines.

Crêvecœur the artist, however, glimpsed some of the passional dark mystery which Crêvecœur the idealist completely ignores. The artist is no longer European. Some little salt of the aboriginal America has
40 entered into his blood. And this aboriginal Crêvecœur sees as the savage

see, knows as they know, in the dark mystery of division, difference, culmination, and contest. It is true his vision is rudimentary. He can only see insects, birds, and snakes in their own pristine being. Above this level, all life should be innocent and pure and loving, merging in oneness. But so far as insects, birds, and serpents are concerned, he sees the pride, the recoil, the jewel-like isolation of the vivid self, the pure, tender trust which leads to culmination, and the frantic struggles for the enforcing of this culmination. If he had been an Aztec, confirmed in blood-sacrifice and wearing the dark-lustrous mantle of the feathers of birds,* he would have had the same way of knowledge.

"I am astonished to see," he writes quite early in the *Letters*, "that nothing exists but what has its enemy, one species pursue and live upon another: unfortunately our king-birds are the destroyers of those industrious insects (the bees); but on the other hand, these birds preserve our fields from the depredations of the crows, which they pursue on the wing with great vigilance and astonishing dexterity."

This is a strange admission from the Child of Nature, sweet and pure, a sad blow in the midst of romantic, pastoral, idyllic idealism. But the glimpsing of the king-birds is still more striking, the strength of Crèvecoeur's vision in winged hostility and pride, the swinging of the dark wings of the sensual ascendancy. We begin to look round for the "One Being Who made all things and governs the world by His providence."

He saves himself, however, when he proceeds further in the animal kingdom. The horse is the friend of man, man is the friend of the horse: and as for men, why, by Nature they all love one another innocently, but sometimes they lapse into atrocities, by some miscarriage in the womb of the events.

Some great hornets have fixed their nest on the ceiling of the living-room of the American Farmer, and these big, fierce, tiger-striped insects fly above the pastoral family, healthy offspring, and amiable spouse, apparently doing them no harm, though we are sure the amiable spouse had no say in the matter. The Farmer himself loved the creatures. There must have existed between him and the little winged tigers that mysterious *rapport*, the sensual sympathy and confidence that balanced man and wasps, and enriched both. This magic immediacy between Crèvecoeur and other life is the real beauty of the *Letters*. Again, on the useful plane, the hornets kept the house free of flies, we are told.

There is also an anecdote of wrens and swallows, that built in the verandah of the house. The wrens took a fancy to the nest of the swallows,

and determined to occupy it. They pugnaciously attacked the larger, swift birds, attacked them and drove them from the nest. The swallows returned upon opportunity. But the wrens, coming home, violently drove them forth again. Which continued until the swallows patiently
5   set about to build another nest, whilst the wrens installed themselves in triumph.

This event Crêvecœur watches with full delight. He takes no sides and feels no pangs. We can imagine Franklin, in a similar case, applying justice. But Crêvecœur only delights in the little living drama,
10 watching the mysterious nature of birds asserting itself in arrogance and pugnacity.

Again, he has some doubtful stories. One is, that he shot a kingbird which had been devouring his bees. He opened its craw, and took out a vast number of bees, which little creatures, after they had lain a
15 minute or two in the sun, roused, revived, preened themselves, walked off debonair, as Jonah up the seashore when the whale had spewed him out.

This story is considered improbable. It may be true. And even if not, it has a kind of mythical or legendary quality, which attracts us. It is like
20 Herodotus. Herodotus sees with the dark sensual eyes, in the reality of division of otherness. But his haste in asserting his own self dominant and cognisant over the being of the strangers makes him invent or repeat fables.* He assumes a victory in sensual cognition which he has not actually won. So with Crêvecœur. He too easily leaps at authority,
25 and invents from his own ego, instead of comprehending.

Again he describes the humming bird:

"Its bill is as long and as sharp as a coarse sewing needle; like the bee, Nature has taught it to find out in the calyx of flowers and blossoms those mellifluous particles that serve it for sufficient food; and yet it
30 seems to leave them untouched, undeprived of anything that the eye can possibly distinguish. When it feeds, it appears as if immovable, though continually on the wing; and sometimes, from what motives I know not, it will tear and lacerate flowers into a hundred pieces; for, strange to tell, they are the most irascible of the feathered tribe. Where
35 do passions find room in so diminutive a body? They often fight with the fury of lions, until one of the combatants falls a sacrifice and dies. When fatigued, it has often perched within a few feet of me, and on such favourable opportunities I have surveyed it with the most minute attention. Its little eyes appear like diamonds, reflecting light on every
40 side; most elegantly finished in all parts, it is a miniature work of our

Great Parent, who seems to have formed it the smallest, and at the same time the most beautiful, of the winged species."

He might have remembered, in his peroration, "the most irascible." We have read various descriptions of humming birds. W. H. Hudson has a good one. But this one gives a curiously sharp, hard bit of realisation, something surely intrinsic, a jewel-sharpness and refraction inherent in the little soul of the creature.

Indeed, Crêvecœur sees birds, not in their "little singing angel" aspect of modern sentiment. He has the more ancient vision. He sees their dark, primitive, weapon-like souls. He sees how they start and flash their wings darkly, in the spontaneous wonder of the retraction into isolation, or in a kind of vindictive self-arrogance. But he sees, also, that they come in the breath of the first creation, the breath of love. They issue on the spirit of tender confidence, the mute, shy, reserved love of the wild creature.

He is very beautiful about the quails. "Often," he writes, in a paragraph about quails in winter, "in the angles of the fences, when the motion of the wind prevents the snow from settling, I carry them both chaff and grain; the one to feed them, the other to prevent their tender feet from freezing fast to the earth, as I have frequently observed them to do."

The pure beauty of the sentiment here lies, not in a selfless or self-abandoning or spiritual love, but in the deep, tender recognition of the life-reality of the *other*, the other creature which exists not in union with the immediate self, but in dark juxtaposition. It is the tenderness of blood-knowledge, knowledge in separation. Crêvecœur knows the touch of the birds' feet, as if they had stood, with their vibrating, sharp, cold, cleaving balance, naked-footed on his naked hand. He knows there is no selfless oneing. They are they and he is he. And over the mysterious, dark gulf reaches his tenderness and the wild confidence of the quails, leaving their two natures uncommingled, yet strangely in contact. This is the barbaric tenderness and love.

Crêvecœur makes no attempt to identify himself with the birds. To him they are no "little sisters of the air." He knows them as strange, hot-blooded concentrations of dark presence. He could never have preached to them, as St. Francis preached. For to him they existed in the unutterable retraction of otherness, as all creatures exist to the barbarian. And he felt the blood-sympathy which allows and accepts this otherness as an enrichening, a joy. Accepting the quails into the spell of himself, he is enriched with the glamour of their contact, filled with passionate, tender joy.

This is the glamour and richness of the sensual, barbarian way. For if we reduce all things to terms of spirit and oneness, we impoverish life at last beyond bearing.

The *Letter* about snakes and humming-birds is a marvellous essay,
5   in its primal, dark veracity. The description of the fight between two snakes, a great water-snake and a large black serpent, follows the description of the humming-bird: "Strange was this to behold; two great snakes strongly adhering to the ground, mutually fastened together by means of the writhings which lashed them to each other, and stretched
10 at their full length, they pulled but pulled in vain; and in the moments of greatest exertions that part of their bodies which was entwined seemed extremely small, while the rest appeared inflated, and now and then convulsed with strong undulations, rapidly following each other. Their eyes seemed on fire, and ready to start out of their heads; at one time
15 the conflict seemed decided; the water-snake bent itself into two great folds, and by that operation rendered the other more than commonly outstretched. The next minute the new struggles of the black one gained an unexpected superiority; it acquired two great folds likewise, which necessarily extended the body of its adversary in proportion as it had
20 contracted its own."

This fight, which Crèvecœur describes to a finish, he calls a sight "uncommon and beautiful." He forgets the benevolence of Nature, and is for the time a sheer ophiolater, and his chapter is as handsome a piece of ophiolatory, perhaps, as that coiled Aztec rattlesnake carved in stone.
25   And yet the real Crèvecœur is, in the issue, neither farmer, nor child of Nature, nor ophiolater. He goes back to France, and figures in the literary salons, and is a friend of Rousseau's Madame d'Houdetot. Also he is a good business man, and arranges a line of shipping between France and America. It all ends in materialism, really. But the *Letters*
30 tell us nothing about this.

We are left to imagine him retiring in grief to dwell with his Red Brothers under the wigwams. For the War of Independence has broken out, and the Indians are armed by the adversaries; they do dreadful work on the frontiers. While Crèvecœur is away in France his farm is
35 destroyed his family rendered homeless. So that the last letter laments bitterly over the war, and man's folly and inhumanity to man.

But Crèvecœur ends his lament on a note of resolution. With his amiable spouse, and his healthy offspring, now rising in stature, he will leave the civilised coasts, where man is sophisticated, and, therefore,
40 inclined to be vile, and he will go to live with the Children of Nature, the Red Men, under the wigwam. No doubt, in actual life, Crèvecœur made

some distinction between the Indian, who drank rum *à la* Franklin, and who burnt homesteads and massacred families, and those Indians, the noble Children of Nature, who peopled his own pre-determined fancy. Whatever he did in actual life, in his innermost self he would not give up this self-made world, where the natural man was an object of undefiled 5 brotherliness. Touchingly and vividly he describes his tented home near the Indian village, how he breaks the aboriginal earth to produce a little maize, while his wife weaves within the wigwam. And his imaginary efforts to save his tender offspring from the brutishness of unchristian darkness are touching and puzzling, for how can Nature, so sweet and 10 pure under the greenwood tree, how can it have any contaminating effect?

But it is all a swindle. Crêvecoeur was off to France in high-heeled shoes and embroidered waistcoat, to pose as a literary man, and to prosper in the world. We, however, must perforce follow him into the 15 backwoods, where the simple natural life shall be perfected, near the tented village of the Red Man.

He wanted, of course, to know the dark, savage way of life, within the unlimited sensual impulse. He wanted to know as the Indians and savages know, darkly, and in terms of otherness. But this desire in him 20 was very strictly kept down by a fixed will. For he was absolutely determined that Nature is sweet and pure, that all men are brothers, and equal, and that they love one another like so many cooing doves. He was determined to have life according to his own prescription. Therefore, he wisely kept away from any too close contact with Nature, and took 25 refuge in commerce and the material world.

For the animals and savages are isolate each one in its own pristine self. The animal lifts its head, sniffs, and knows within the dark, passionate belly. It knows at once, in dark mindlessness. And at once it flees in immediate recoil; or it crouches predatory, in the mysterious storm 30 of exultant anticipation of seizing a victim; or it lowers its head in blank indifference again; or it advances in the insatiable wild curiosity, insatiable passion to approach that which is unspeakably strange and incalculable; or it draws near in the slow trust of wild, sensual love.

Crêvecoeur wanted this kind of knowledge. But to have it he must 35 forfeit all his fraternity and equality, his belief in a world of pure, sweet goodness, in the oneness of all things, and, above all, he must forfeit his own *will*, which insists that the world shall be so, because it is easiest so. And he will die rather than forfeit his fixed will and his fixed intention. He *will* have life according to his own prescription, come what may. And 40 life actually *is not* according to his prescription. So he eschews life, and

goes off into sentimental, idyllic fancy, and into practical commerce, both of which he *can* have as he likes it. For though he has a hankering after the wild, sensual life, he so hates the true, sensual mystery of otherness, and of proud culmination, that he will do anything to deny
5   this mystery, and to down it. So he is divided against himself, which makes for madness.

It is amusing to see him calculating the dangers of the step which he take so luxuriously, in his fancy alone. He tickles his palate with a taste of true wildness, as men are so fond nowadays of tickling their palates
10 with a taste of imaginary wickedness—just a taste.

"I must tell you," he says, "that there is something in the proximity of the woods which is very singular. It is with men as it is with the plants and animals that live in the forests; they are entirely different from those that live in the plains. I will candidly tell you all my thoughts, but you
15 are not to expect that I shall advance any reasons. By living in or near the woods, their actions are regulated by the wildness of the neighbourhood. The deer often come to eat their grain, the wolves destroy their sheep, the bears kill their hogs, the foxes catch their poultry. This surrounding hostility immediately puts the gun into their hands; they watch these
20 animals, they kill some; and thus by defending their property they soon become professed hunters; this is the progress; once hunters, farewell to the plough. The chase renders them ferocious, gloomy, unsociable; a hunter wants no neighbours, he rather, hates them, because he dreads the competition.... Eating of wild meat, whatever you may think, tends
25 to alter their temper...."

Crêvecœur of course, had never intended to return as a *hunter* to the bosom of Nature, only as a husbandman. The hunter, like the soldier, is engaged in the effort to win the fatal ascendancy, the last, over the enemy or the prey. This is the sensual passion in its overweening, destructive
30 activity, the terrible consummation in death. The husbandman, on the other hand, brings about the sensual birth and increase. But even the husbandman strains in dark mastery over the unwilling earth and beast; he struggles to win forth substance, he must master the soil and the strong cattle, he must have the strange blood-knowledge, and the slow,
35 but deep, mastery. There is no equality or selfless humility, no ecstasy of selfless communing in oneness. It is the dark reality of blood-mastery and blood-sympathy.

Again, Crêvecœur dwells on "the apprehension lest my younger children should be caught by that singular charm, so dangerous to
40 their tender years"—meaning the charm of savage life. So he goes

on: "By what power does it come to pass that children who have been adopted when young among these people (the Indians) can never be prevailed upon to readopt European manners? Many an anxious parent have I seen last war who, at the return of peace, went to the Indian villages where they knew their children to have been carried in captivity, 5 when to their inexpressible sorrow they found them so perfectly Indianised that many knew them no longer, and those whose more advanced ages permitted them to recollect their fathers and mothers, absolutely refused to follow them, and ran to their adopted parents to protect them against the effusions of love their unhappy real parents lavished 10 on them! Incredible as this may appear, I have heard it asserted in a thousand instances, among persons of credit.

"There must be something in their (the Indians) social bond singularly captivating, and far superior to anything to be boasted of among us; for thousands of Europeans are Indians, and we have no examples of even 15 one of those aborigines having from choice become Europeans...."

Crêvecœur's thousands of instances against not even one instance remind us of our cat and another. Some children may have refused to return to their European parents—but the thought of thousands of these obdurate offspring, with faces averted from their natural father 20 and mother, is too good a picture to be true. Also we know that some Indian brides of white men became very good civilised matrons.

The truth remains the same, as another century has proved it—it is easier to turn white men into Indians than Indians into white men. Crêvecœur exulted in the thought. He disliked civilisation even whilst 25 he continued one of the most civilised of all beings. He knew the awful barrenness even of emotional self-gratification. He knew the dreariness of living from the pre-determined will, admitting no otherness, only the mechanical oneness, as of two buttons from the same machine. He wanted equality and fraternity, and he would allow nothing else. At 30 the same time he wanted to know the mystery of the sensual being. He wanted to know the thing which he determinedly excluded from knowledge. Which cannot be done. He wanted to have his cake and eat it—the very nice cake of the human free-will, and the human ego self-determined; the creed of the ultimate oneness of all things, in a union 35 of love. He had his cake—kept it whole. Only he nibbled the corners. He opened the dark eyes of his blood to the presence of bees, birds, and serpents. He saw them in their magnificent struggling division, and their wonderful co-existence in luminous strangeness.

IV.

Fenimore Cooper's Anglo-American Novels.

We have seen that, when we try to trace our consciousness to its source
5 and fountain-head, we must approach the great nerve-centres of the
sympathetic and voluntary system. We have seen further that the moment we enter this field of primal or pre-cerebral consciousness we
enter the field of duality. Science has of late asserted the universal law
of polarity*—a law of dual poles. This law applies as much to the human
10 psyche as to the cosmic forces.

From the sympathetic centres in the abdomen rush out the vital vibrations of our first-being, our first-consciousness. In the solar plexus,
and the other centres of the lower body, we have the inscrutable well-
heads whence the living self bubbles up and enters into creation. What
15 lies before is a mystery, and must ever remain a mystery. When we
follow the mystery to its gates we find it entering by the great sympathetic plexuses of the body, entering and appearing in spontaneous
motion and spontaneous consciousness. And we find that at its very entry this motion, this being, this consciousness, is dual. What we know
20 as sensual consciousness has its fountain-head in the plexus of the abdomen; what we know as spiritual consciousness has its issue in the
cardiac plexus, the great sympathetic centre within the thorax. Our
mental consciousness is a third thing, resultant from this duality in
pre-cerebral cognition. But connected with the lower or sensual sys-
25 tem we have the mouth, which tastes and embraces, the nostrils which
smell, and the ears which hear. Connected with the spiritual system
of the upper body we have the eyes which see, and the hands which
touch.

This knowledge, which is the very beginning of psychology—the
30 psyche comprising our whole consciousness, physical, sensual, spiritual,
pre-cerebral as well as cerebral—seems to have been familiar to the
pagan priesthoods and to the esoteric mystics of the past. We can only
begin to understand the initiation into the religious mysteries, such as
the Eleusinian mysteries,* when we can grasp the rise of pre-cerebral
35 consciousness in the great plexuses, and the movement of passional or

204

dynamic cognition from one centre to another, towards culmination
or consummation in what we may call whole-experience, or whole-
consciousness.

It is quite certain that the pre-Christian priesthoods understood the
processes of *dynamic* consciousness, which is pre-cerebral conscious-   5
ness. It is certain that St. John gives us in the Apocalypse a cypher-
account of the process of the conquest of the lower or sensual dynamic
centres by the upper or spiritual dynamic consciousness,* a conquest
affected centre by centre, towards a culmination in the *actual* experience of spiritual infinitude. This account is of scientific exactitude.   10
But the cypher of symbols and number-valuation is exceedingly complicated. None the less it can be solved. And then we realise that the
old, immense religions were established upon a scientific knowledge so
immediate and profound that we cannot grasp it. They understood—
at least, those initiated understood—the rise and movement of the   15
dynamic consciousness in the individual, that which we might call our
unconsciousness or sub-consciousness, but which is more than these,
and which, though in very fact the bulk of our being and knowing, is
regarded from our mental standpoint as *nothing*, or nothingness. That
which we regard as nothing, that which is our pre-cerebral cognition,   20
this the priests understood as the great dynamic human consciousness,
the mind being no more than an abstract from it. And this profound
priestly understanding was scientific in its exactitude. It was of necessity symbolic in its expression—as when, in the Eleusinian mysteries, a
golden snake was crowded into the bosom of the postulant, and drawn   25
forth from the lowest part of the body—because there are perhaps no
mental terms to express, at least dynamically, that which takes place.
But in fact of *process* the initiation was a piece of most profound scientific exposition, perfectly expressing the secret and vital movement of
the psyche in its pre-cerebral activities.   30

This priestly knowledge, however, was inevitably sensual. The sensual understanding was the living field of the ancient world. The one-
sidedness of exclusively sensual understanding caused the downfall of
the old systems. The Greeks seem to have discovered the process of the
conquest of the sensual centres by the spiritual consciousness. They   35
worked this into an esoteric system, quite scientific, and much more
profound, nearer the quick, than anything we have since known in psychology. But their knowledge still was based upon the sensual activities,
even though it were but the knowledge of the process of conquest of
these activities. And if we were ever to escape into spiritual freedom,   40

into pure spiritual or upper understanding, what we have called freedom itself, then all idea of duality would have to be wiped out, the sensual understanding would have to be blanked out, as if it did not exist.

Which is what the early Christian world proceeded to do, by amazing
5 instinct. The Gnostics, the Manicheans, all those strange and obscure sects which really derived their understanding from the Greek esotericism, or from the Persian,* were destroyed by the new rising instinct, the instinctive passionate longing to be freed from the sensual self altogether, and from the whole body of ancient understanding. For the
10 sensual consciousness, hopelessly dominant, had become destructive and tyrannical in the human psyche. Hence the strange wild rage of Byzantine—or Greek—Christianity, the frenzy of destruction that possessed it. Hence a world gone mad over the intricacies, to us nonsensical, of the Homoousion.* Slaves were as mad as priests over these mystical
15 absurdities. But it was not absurd. It was a subtle, amazing process of displacing utterly, even destroying, one body of knowledge, one way of dynamic cognition, and giving all the scope to the other body. The curious decisions of the early Councils, the Council of Nice, and the General Councils,* only show us how perfect the instinct was which
20 rejected every trace of the old true science—every trace save, perhaps, the unreadable riddle of the Apocalypse.*

Now, after two thousand years of effort, we have so subjected the centres of sensual cognition that they depend automatically on the upper centres. Now, after two thousand years, having established our knowl-
25 edge and even our experience all in one sort, a halfness, we find ourself in a prison. We reach the condition when we are so imprisoned in the cul de sac of our mutilated psyche that we are in the first stages of that madness and self-destruction into which the ancients fell when they were imprisoned and driven mad within the cul de sac of the sensual
30 body. *Quos vult perdere Jupiter, dementat prius.*

What lies before us is either escape or death. We choose death. But is that any escape? We are always faced with the problem of the immortality of the soul. We elude it by imagining that souls can dissolve into an infinite, evaporate away as liquids can evaporate into space. But since
35 the very definition of a soul is that it is a unique entity, how can that which is a unique entity remain itself by merging into the infinite? It can only lose itself by so doing. And the soul does not lose itself in death.

We can no longer believe in angels, though we try. And all our efforts will not win from our souls a belief in disembodied spirits which cluster
40 innumerable in the invisible ether. What we believe we believe without

knowing it, first of all. In the first place, my belief lies in my active breast and in my active belly, potent there. I have to find the mental idea which will correspond.

The only thing to do is for each man to remember his own dead. Do we imagine our dead lying in some distant grave?—our own dead? We do not. Do we imagine them merged into some infinite? For my part, I find this impossible. When I hush my soul perfectly, to attend, as it were, to the dead I have loved and love, then I find that it is nonsense to try to project my attention in any outward direction, either upward or downward, or into universal space. My dead is neither above nor below, nor everywhere. My own dead, whom I have loved and love, is with me, within me, here, now, at one with me, and not elsewhere.

Those that die return to the most beloved, enter in, and at last live in peace; gladly, at one with the most beloved. So that the living are always living. The present is one and unbreakable. The present is not a fleeting, moment. Moments may flee, but I am here. And with me is one who is dead and who yet lives in me. So that all life is always living, and the Present is one and unbroken. The Present is always present, as the sun is always present. It is eternity that is an abstraction, an inference reached by negation of the present. My immortality lies in being present in life. And the dead have presence in the living. So that the dead are always present in life, here, in the flesh, always. It is inexplicable *how* they are present in us, but it is a physical fact that they are. So are the unborn which issue from us. Here, in our tissue, we know it, lie the unborn. And as surely, here, in our tissue, live the dead, present, and always present.

The great problem of the survival of the soul is not the same, however, as that of the survival of the will after death. The human self is not the same as the individual will. The self is the inexplicable, the mystery. The will is the dynamic force which belongs to the self, but which is subject to the consciousness, the mental consciousness. So that the mental ego can fix the will and use it in contravention to the primal spontaneous self. Which very often happens.

When, through the fixing of the will, a deadlock ensues in the soul, our living becomes an automatic process. And then the soul is frustrated, coiled, angry. Will death release this deadlock, save the soul from frustration? It will not. Only living will fulfil a frustrated soul.

Now, many of our dead have died in the misery of this frustration; automatised and unable to live, they have even sought death as an escape, only to find it no escape. Souls frustrated in life are not fulfilled by death,

save they die in a passionate consummation. Souls that find in death
itself a passionate consummation return to us appeased, and add the
beauty and richness of their presence to us. But what of the souls that
are caught out of life unliberated and unappeased? They return to
5   us unfree and girning, terrible ghosts. They enter into us angrily and
fill us with their destructive presence. There is no peace in death to
those who die in the terrible deadlock of frustration. And if there is no
peace for them, there is none for us. They return home to us. They are
the angry, unappeased shades that come darkly home to us, thronging
10   home to us from over the seas, entering our souls and filling us with
madness, ever more and more madness, unless we, by our active living,
shall give them the life that they demand, the living motions that were
frustrated in them now liberated and made free.

This explains the futility of sacrifice. What use is it to me if a man
15   sacrifice and murder his living desires for me, only to return in death and
demand this sacrifice again of me, tenfold? What is the use of a mother's
sacrificing herself for her children if after death her unappeased soul
shall perforce return upon the child and exact from it all the fulfilment
that should have been attained in the living flesh, and was not? We
20   cannot help this returning of our soul back into the living. What we
can help is its returning unappeased and destructive. We have now the
hosts of weary, clamorous, unsatisfied dead to appease by our living. If
we cannot appease them we shall go on dying until somewhere, in some
unknown people, life can start afresh.

25   Which brings us to Fenimore Cooper and the Red Indians. Franklin
had an equation in providential mathematics:—

$$\text{Rum} + \text{Savage} = 0.$$

It is a specious little equation. Proceeding like that we might add up the
universe to nought.

30   Rum plus Savage may equal a dead savage. But is a dead savage
nought? Bullet plus Yankee may equal a dead Yankee. But is a dead
Yankee nought, either?

The Aztec is gone, the Red Indian, the Esquimo, the Incas, the
Patagonian—and whither? *Où sont les neiges d'antan?* They are not far
35   to seek. They are no further off than the coming snows.

Do we imagine that the Aztecs are installed within the souls of the
present Mexicans? And are the Red Men at home within the breasts of
the Yankees of to-day? Assuredly the dead Indians have their place in
the souls of present-day Americans, but whether they are at peace there

is another question. It is said that Americans begin to show obvious Red Indian qualities. But they show no signs of peace in themselves.

It is plain that the American is not at one with the Red Man whom he has perforce lodged into his own soul. It is a dangerous thing to destroy any vital existence out of life. For then the destroyer becomes 5 responsible, in his own living body, for the destroyed. Upon the destroyer devolves the necessity of continuing the nature and being of the destroyed. This is an axiom. It follows from the law of polarity. If we destroy one pole, the other collapses, or becomes doubly responsible. The tiger destroys deer. If all deer are destroyed, the tiger collapses. 10 Similarly, if all tigers are destroyed, deer will collapse, for then there is no equipoise to keep them vivid in their being. Between the beast predative and the beast ruminative is a balance in polarity, and the destruction of either pole is a destruction of both in the long run.

With humanity it is not quite so simple. When the White American 15 destroys the Red Indian, he either ultimately brings about his own destruction or he takes upon himself the responsibility for the continuing and perfecting of the passional soul of the destroyed. This is true of any creatures, balanced either in a true polarity of love or of enmity. The Aztec lives unappeased and destructive within the Mexican, the Red 20 Indian lives unappeased and inwardly destructive in the American.

It is presumable, however, that at length the soul of the dead red man will be at one with the soul of the living white man. And then we shall have a new race. Meanwhile, the will is fixed in the white man; he works his automatic conclusions. How different is the deep, 25 unexpressed passion in the American, from the automatic spiritual ego which he demonstrates to the world, this is a matter for the world to discover later on.

Fenimore Cooper very beautifully gives the myth of the atonement, the communion between the soul of the white man and the soul of 30 the Indian. He also gives the frenzied, weary running-on of the self-determined ego, the mechanical spiritual being of America. Here are two classes of books—the famous Leatherstocking Series, and what we will call the Anglo-American Series, such as *Homeward Bound, Eve Effingham, The Spy, The Pilot*, and others, stories concerning white 35 Americans only. These last are now almost forgotten. They are thin and bloodless. But they are not by any means without point, for Cooper was a profound and clever man.

Cooper himself was rich and of good family. His father founded Cooperstown, in the Eastern States. Fenimore was a gentleman of culture. 40

He shows in *Homeward Bound* how bound he was, hand and foot, to the European culture tradition.

It should not be forgotten how intensely cultured these Americans of the early nineteenth century were. It is only necessary to read their
5   familiar literature, the light verse, to know that they were much more *raffiné* than Englishmen have ever been. In this matter of refined material culture, external and disillusioned, the Americans were ahead even of the French. Cooper quotes a Frenchman, who says, *"L'Amérique est pourrie avant d'être mûre."* And there is a great deal in it. America was
10 not taught by France—by Baudelaire, for example. Baudelaire learned his lesson from America.

The Effinghams are three extremely refined, genteel Americans who are homeward bound from England to the States. Their party consists of father, daughter, and uncle, and faithful nurse. The daughter has
15 just finished her education in Europe. She has, indeed, skimmed the cream off Europe. England, France, Italy, and Germany have nothing more to teach her. She is a bright and charming, admirable creature; a real modern heroine; intrepid, calm, and self-collected, yet admirably impulsive, always in perfectly good taste; clever and as-
20 sured in her speech, like a man, but withal charmingly deferential and modest before the stronger sex. It is the perfection of the public female,—a dreadful, self-determined thing, cold and mechanical and factitious.

On board is the other type of American, the parvenu, the demagogue,
25 who has *done* Europe and put it in his breeches pocket, in a month. No European writer has ever given us such a completely detestable picture of an American as did the American Cooper. Septimus Dodge is the object of loathing and contempt to the Effinghams. Yet they cannot get away from him—neither on ship-board nor even when they reach their
30 own estates. He is the bugbear of their lives—but he is the inevitable negative pole of their Americanism.

Mr. Dodge, the democrat, of Dodgetown, alternately fawns and intrudes, cringes and bullies. For the Effinghams are most terribly "superior" in a land of equality. No foreign count was ever as icily
35 superior to his lowest peasant as are the Effinghams to their successful, democratic compatriot, Septimus. Mr. Dodge cringes like the inferior he really is. But he is an American, and by asserting his democratic equality he gets the haughty Effinghams on the hip. They writhe— but Septimus has them fast. They will not escape. What tortures await
40 them in the free land of America, at the hands of the persecuting Dodge!

There, all their superiority writhes transfixed on the horns of the Dodge dilemma, the acute dilemma of democratic equality.

Through these American-social books of Fenimore Cooper—at least, through the most significant—runs this same helpless struggle with a false position. People are not free to be people. They are all of them 5 all the while impaled on a false social assumption, and all their passion and movement works back to this social assumption. They are never full, spontaneous human beings. All the while they are mere social units, social conscious, never passionately individual. For this reason the books are empty of life, while they are full of sharp social observation. 10

Miss Effingham never confronts Mr. Dodge as a real individual confronts another. She is a social unit confronting another social unit. She is a democrat—or at least a republican—confronting her fellow-democrat. And no matter how she despises and detests Mr. Dodge, the individual, she has in some degree to accept an equality with him as an 15 American citizen. All her patrician nature rebels. But it is mercilessly impaled. She pushes a pin through her haughty, winged soul, and pins it down on the *Contrat Social.* There it writhes and flaps ignominious. All her loves and adventures move us not at all. How can they? What do pursuits at sea, fleeing scoundrels, lords in disguise, shipwrecks, fero- 20 cious savages of the Sahara*—what do these amount to to a soul which is pinned down on the *Contrat Social?* Nothing at all. Nothing matters, save the pin which holds down Eve Effingham on the same card with Septimus Dodge.

Yet Eve Effingham will die rather than pull out the pin. She will 25 die rather than simply dismiss Septimus as a hopeless inferior—a natural inferior. He is the thorn in the proud Effingham flesh. But the Effinghams love their thorn. They believe in the equality of men and in the Rights of Man. They believe tremendously in social freedom. This is why they have impaled their souls. First, they are republican, American 30 citizens. And then, a long way behind, they are living individuals.

Which is nonsense. A man is, and can be, no more than himself: his own single, starry self, which has its place inscrutably in the firmament of existence. But if a man is to be himself he must be free. That is, by general consent all men must be free to be themselves. Nothing could 35 be more just or wise.

But to go on from this, and declare that all men are equal, and even, ultimately, identical, is nonsense. When men are most truly themselves, then the difference is most real and most evident. And it is not only a difference in kind, it is a difference in degree. Eve Effingham is not only 40 a finer being than Septimus Dodge, she is by nature a superior being. Septimus should yield her the reverence and respect due to a higher type from a lower. And she should implicitly command that reverence and respect.

5   Instead of which, Septimus, having money in his pocket, presumes that the difference between him and the Effinghams is a mere impertinence on their part, which ought to be done away with. And they feel a little guilty and confused by their own instinctive superiority. If this is not the ruin of all high things, and the triumph of all base things, what

10 is? It is like the Buddhists who bless the lice that eat them, because all life is sacred.

Democracy as we have it is mere falsity. It is true that the aristocratic system of the past is arbitrary and false. But it is not so arbitrary and false as our present democratic system. Every man knows that intrinsically

15 men are not equal. Intrinsically, in his true self which issues from the mystery and is a term of the Godhead, one man is either greater or less than another man, or perhaps approximately equal. But the deepest social truth about men is that some are higher, some lower, some greater, some less, some highest, and some lowest, even in the sight of the

20 everlasting God. To pretend anything else is mere sophistry. Some men are born from the mystery of creation, to know, to lead, and to command. And some are born to listen, to follow, to obey. Each man has his beauty and his wholeness in fulfilling his own true nature, whether it be the fulfilment of command or of service. And all that democracy needs to

25 do is to arrange the material world so that each man can be intrinsically himself, yielding service where he must instinctively yield respect or reverence, and taking command where instinctively he feels his own authority.

The old aristocratic system at least recognised this prime reality of the

30 intrinsic and holy disquality* between men. It was wrong in establishing an artificial distinction of mere birth. If we are to recognise true beauty and superiority it must be from the inmost sincere soul; we cannot proceed on accidents of heredity. But the aristocratic system was not so wrong as the democratic, which refuses, theoretically, to recognise any

35 intrinsic difference at all, and asserts that, since no man is higher than another, since we are all leaves of grass, no man shall presume to put the grass in the shade. No man is any higher than another man; no soul has any intrinsic right to command another soul. So says democracy. And if this is not far more arbitrary, far more sweeping, and far more

40 deadly than any arbitrary aristocratic system, then there is no reality in

living whatsoever. All men must be mown level with the grass, because most men, the average, are leaves of grass, and therefore it would be impertinent and arrogant to rise above the grass. So we mow life down.

Worse still. Though no man is higher than any other man, intrinsically, still, some men are superior mechanically. Some men are more productive materially than others. They know how to combine the mechanical forces of the universe to bring forth material produce. Those that can most successfully subject living and being to the mechanical forces, destroy the intrinsic self and substitute the machine unit, thereby increasing material production, let them be lords of material production. Let money rule.

Which is the inevitable outcome of democracy—Liberty, Equality, and Fraternity. And as long as we believe in Equality, so long shall we grind mechanically till, like most Jews, we have no living soul, no living self, but only a super-machine faculty which will coin money. Then no doubt we shall all be satisfied, negative, anti-life.

How dreary we are, putting up the social and political self as a first reality, dwindling the true self into a nothingness. So we all turn ourselves into ridiculous little political gramophones, all wound up and braying together, without a notion of the foolish and despicable sight we offer to the gods above. A man is either himself, or he is nothing. A braying little political gramophone is worse than nothing. We should teach our children a new prayer: "Dear God, let me not be wound up."*

Let every man get back to himself, and let the world at large sink down to its true perspective as the world at little, which it really is. Let every man learn to be himself, and in so being to give reverence and obedience where such is due, and to take command and authority where these are due. Let this be done spontaneously, from the living, real self. Otherwise we shall wind ourselves up till the spring breaks.

And let us recognise secondarily that truth of duality or polarity which is within us and without us, and which makes of equality a mechanical round-about at the very outset. St. Francis falling down before the embarrassed and astonished peasant,* what was he doing? He was doing the same as Father Zosimus, who falls down prostrate before Dmitri Karamazov.* He, the spiritual saint, a creature of the one half, fell in recognition before the pure sensual being, the creature of the other half of life. Already, where is equality between beings established in such opposite mysteries, so utterly different both of them, but so utterly real?

But the duality is within us, as well as outside us. It is the duality of life itself, the polarity of the living. The social units such as

Miss Effingham, impaled, whirl round on their pivot of negation like little machines, depolarised. When we depolarise ourselves we cease to live, as even St. Francis shows us. We must return to the great polarity of the life motion.

5 The tiger was a terrible problem to Shelley, who wanted life in terms of the lamb.* I should think the lamb must have been a puzzler, say, to Sennacherib, who wanted life all in terms of the winged and burning lion.* We must admit life in its duality.

We must admit that only the juxtaposition of the tiger keeps the 10 lamb a quivering, vivid, beautiful fleet thing. Take away the tiger and we get the sheep of our pasture, just clods of meat. If there were no hawks in the sky the larks would lose their song. It is the fanning of fear which makes the song flicker up, as well as the expansion of love. The soft, rolling sound of the dove among the leaves, her silken iridescence, 15 depends on the hawk that hangs on sultry wings like a storm in bird-life. The one concentrates the other. From the soft, loving principle there is a tendency to expand into disintegrate formlessness. The sharp compulsion of the fierce sensual principle drives back the soul from its looseness, concentrates it into the jewel-isolation of a perfected self. 20 Fear and suffering are great formative principles.

The full eye of the deer or the rabbit or the horse would stagnate and lose its lustre, save for the keen, strange eye of the wolf and the weasel, and of man. The electric, almost magical, flash of a rabbit's mysterious passion depends entirely on the existence of the stoat. Destroy the mys-25 terious circuit, teach the stoat to eat dandelion leaves, and life crumbles into dross and nullity. We must live in a world of perilous, pure freedom, having always the tincture of fear, danger, and exultance. Nothing else will keep us living. As jewels are crushed between the valves of the earth, and driven, through unutterable resistance, into their own clear 30 perfection, leaving the matrix exempt; so must the human soul be purified in unspeakable resistance to the mass. We wear the ruby and the sapphire as symbols of our splendid pride in singleness, our jewel-like self.

V.

Fenimore Cooper's Leatherstocking Novels.

In Cooper's Leatherstocking series we broach another world of reality. Here there are mystery and passion and the further progress into the unknown. We are not involved in the mechanical workings of the will, as it works itself into automatic self-determination.

It is the search for his own consummation, for the mystical "next step" which Cooper records in the Leatherstocking books. In the Anglo-American novels, the so-called love theme is the predominant interest. But it is not interesting. One does not care who marries Eve Effingham, because there is no vital marriage possible. There are only the intricacies of the self-determined psyche to record.

Cooper symbolises his own actual, mechanical, self-determined life in the Effinghams. But in Leatherstocking he symbolises his own last being, strange and wrought to a conclusion, seeking its consummation in the American woods and the Indian race, his pure complement in the Chief Chingachgook. As an American citizen he lived correct, impeccable—a clock-work man. Yet his living soul moved on in passional progress.

It is amazing the subjection a human being can suffer. A fakir can live buried up to the chin in earth, asserting the mechanical will and annulling the creative substantial bonds. And Cooper lived buried even over the head in the old concept—the European convention.

And still he had his vital reaction, his progressive mystery. He had still a last communion to make, a last consummation to effect. He describes this in his Indian novels.

He tells one of the last tales of the Odyssey of the white soul, as it vanishes into the unknown. The Odyssey of Homer is the story of the unfolding of the pristine soul of a race, in the potency and wonder of the surrounding unknown, until it consummates and perfects itself like a flower in spring. The novels of Leatherstocking give us the opposite story, of the passing of the final race-soul into the unknown, towards a surpassing of the old race being. This is the strange autumn-flowering, as

pallid crocuses flower in autumn, the last flame on the brink of darkness.
It is a consummation on the brink of oblivion, seeding in oblivion.
It is the mystery of conjunction in finality, when at last the soul in the
conqueror embraces and is at one with the ghost of the conquered. It
5   is the passing of Orpheus into hell,* whence he has not yet returned.
The new birth is the birth of a new race, risen from the inscrutable
consummation of two past races.

Crêvecœur imagines himself under the wigwam. Cooper goes much
further. He spends a whole lifetime, imaginatively, in the backwoods. He
10   has a passion for the aboriginal life, the aboriginal scene, and the native
savage. His innermost desire is polarised all the time by the primitive
America of the Red Man and the Red Man's way of life. His whole soul
embraces the dark aboriginal soul with unceasing, fertile love.

It is singular that the refined, cultured, nervous, snobbish Fenimore
15   Cooper should choose as his real hero, the symbol of his own innermost
man, Natty Bumppo, or Leatherstocking, Pathfinder, Deerslayer, as he
is severally called. We have Cooper, living in a Louis Quatorze *hotêl* in
Paris, lying looking up at the painted ceiling, dreaming passionately of
the naked savages, yearning for them; or Cooper walking down the long
20   *salon*, a gentleman in every thread, a finished social product, with his
soul courting the bloodthirsty Indian of his own American backwoods.

Natty is an unæsthetic figure, especially as we see him first, when he
is an old man, uncouth, ungainly, even ugly, with his wide mouth and
unlovely manner of speech, and with gaps in his old teeth. Yet he is
25   the innermost man of this Parisian-American. He is uneducated, and,
in the cultured sense, stupid, offensive. Yet he is Cooper's very self of
selves, the quick of his being. He is the twin, the "little man" of the
American's soul, the passional, so-called phallic dual or Doppelgänger*
which figures so often in the myths. In social reality, Cooper is an Eff-
30   ingham. In *passional* reality he is Natty Bumppo. And this is symbolic
of the American, who is at once so over-cultured and so crude or naïve
or child-like.

"It was a matter of course," says Mrs. Cooper, speaking of her
husband, "that he should dwell on the better traits of the picture rather
35   than on the coarser and more revolting, though more common points.
Like West, he could see the Apollo in the young Mohawk."

This tiny speech shows us Mrs. Cooper's attitude. She was impatient
of her husband's Indian passion. To her the coarse and revolting traits
of the savage were most in evidence—as they were to Franklin. She was
40   an Eve Effingham, fixed in the will of the old idea. Natty Bumppo to
her would be just a vulgar nonentity, almost a renegade of the great

white civilisation, and Chingachgook a disgusting old drunkard. In face of the great demon of the aboriginal Spirit of Place, she became only more cultured, more Parisian, and more self-determined. Her husband and herself were associated in the old culture and the old will. It was a strong, though external, association. In passionate reality they were mutually exclusive of one another. In passional being they were alien, even opposed.

To Fenimore Cooper himself there was one beloved, whom he loved ceaselessly. It was the aboriginal American, beloved in the same way by Longfellow and Prescott,* though not so passionately. The great demon, the vast Spirit of Place in the New World, drew him, polarised the whole of his living psyche. Europe was the fixed pole of his cultured ego, his finished self. But she was the extreme negative pole of repulsion to his vital, innermost being. He yearned mystically to the soul of his Red brother; he brooded over him and asked for him with superlative desire.

And he dreamed his true marriage with the aboriginal psyche. All futurity for him lay latent, not in the white woman, but in the dark, magnificent presence of American warriors, with whom he would be at one in the ultimate atonement between races.

In *Pioneers*, the first of the Indian series, Leatherstocking is old and paltry-looking, as Odysseus in the eyes of Ithacans on his return. This is no doubt something of a picture from Cooper's own life. Without doubt he draws the scene of his childhood and the actual people of his knowledge. For *Pioneers* is half-way between Europe and aboriginal America. It is a story of the early settlement of Cooperstown, as Cooper knew it, no doubt, when a boy, at the close of the eighteenth century. It is the story of the return of Leatherstocking to the European shores, the outposts of the white settlement of America.

There is a mixture of the Anglo-American novel and the Leatherstocking novel in *Pioneers*. We have a set of white people, social units; performing their necessary evolutions in the form of a plot; a Judge Temple and a favourite and only fair daughter of the admirable type, just home from school, from the finishing of her education in the eastern cities; also a mysterious Major Effingham and a young Edward Effingham in disguise. Half in contrast to these, half in the same world, are Leatherstocking, an uncouth old hunter, and Chingachgook, Christianised and christened John, a degenerate chief of the Delawares; also various frontier types, the prototypes of Hurry Harry and Hetty Hutter* and other later-developed characters. There is a wrong done by Judge Temple to old Major Effingham, to be put right by the inevitable but somewhat complicated love-match of Miss Temple with the young

Effingham—just a favourite bit of old social machinery—a satisfactory restitution of property through a love-match.

The book exists, really, as a wonderful and beautiful picture of an outpost village. It is England—but England lost on the edge of the
5   unknown; England more English and characteristic than England ever was, asserting itself in the toils of the great dark spirit of the Continent.

There is the actual village itself—the long, raw street of wooden houses, with wood-fires blinking and flashing through the uncurtained windows, in the winter nights. There is the curious, amusing "Hall"
10 of the village, Judge Temple's somewhat fantastic replica of a squire's residence. The inn, with the drunken Indian; the church, with the snowy congregation crowding to the fire; the astounding Christmas abundance of the tables, that groaned as English tables never groaned, with weight of good things, splendid things to eat; the turkey-shooting,
15 on the snow; the sports of the rough people; then summer coming, with heavy clouds of pigeons, myriads of pigeons, destroyed in heaps; the night fishing on the teeming, virgin lake; the deer-hunting, the forests all green, the maple sugar taken from the trees—all this is given with a beauty and a magnificence unsurpassable. It is rich with that
20 pristine magic of futurity, like the Odyssey. There is a glamour and an extravagance about the white men as they move, so very English, on this strange landscape; a mystery of the Red life as they pass in shadow against the glow of the burning night-fires.

No man could sufficiently praise the beauty and glamorous magnif-
25 icence of Cooper's presentation of the aboriginal American landscape, the New World. We cannot think of the opening of *Pioneers*, as the sledge drives over the snow, the negro guiding the horses through the wild, precipitous forest roads, the Judge and his daughter folding themselves in furs as the twilight advances over the pine-dusky winter, without ex-
30 periencing that strange, almost unbearable leap of enchantment such as we get only from the Odyssey. It is the magnificence of futurity flooding the heart.

Then there is the story of pain. The old, lean, uncouth huntsman, Natty Bumppo, a figure rather pathetic than attractive, lives in a hut
35 on the verge of civilisation with his grey-haired friend, the Delaware chief, christened John since he is converted to Christianity. The Great Serpent, the splendid Chingachgook of the later novels, is here a mere degraded John, who humiliates his grey hairs in drunkenness, and dies, thankful to be dead, in a forest fire, passing back into fire, whence he
40 derived.

Meanwhile Natty also is humiliated. The game laws have just been passed, partly owing to Judge Temple's wise provision. But Natty has shot through all the wild woods since he was a child and cannot understand that he is poaching on the Judge's land. He has lived all his life by his gun; so how can he hold back his bullet in the close season? He 5 must shoot to live.

Judge Temple is kind, but the laws must be enforced to prevent the wasting of all the natural supplies. Natty is convicted of shooting a deer in the close season. He is shut up in the village prison for a short term. He is an old man of seventy, simple almost as a wild animal, gentle and 10 natural. Yet, in the interest of humanity, he must be put in stocks and in prison.

This drives him off. The Indian chief is broken by shame in drink. He perishes. Natty goes west. He leaves the woods and waters where he has hunted all his life with the Red Men, and goes west, in his lonely 15 age, departing before the advance of civilisation. A strange, lonely, aged man, he advances into the void of the prairie.

It is the same bitter tale of the horrid advance of civilisation that subjects all life to its mechanisation of laws and penalties and benevolent Providence. Over the whole world we hear the great wail of natural life 20 under the triumph of civilisation. But the violated Spirits of Place will avenge themselves. How long will such a civilisation sterilise the creative world? Not long. The Spirits of Place take a slow, implacable revenge.

Chronologically, *The Last of the Mohicans* follows *Pioneers* in the list of books. But, according to internal chronology, *The Prairie* is second. 25 Here we follow the old hunter to his last place, to his last outlook on the hills of the Far West, and to his grave out there.

The Prairie is different from the other books of the series. It is the story of the recoil and death of the white element in the force of the native daimon. It is strange, and almost mythical, with a sense of vast, 30 inordinate doom. Great wings of vengeful doom seem spread over the western prairie, vengeful against the white men. We find them there still in the late book of Frank Norris, the novel about the wheat. There is a shadow of violence and dark cruelty flickering in the air. It is the last stronghold of the aboriginal Daimon. 35

Upon this scene enters the huge figure of Ishmael. The ponderous, pariah-like Ishmael and his huge sons and his great were-wolf of a wife roll lonely and inevitably forward from the frontiers of Kentucky into the vast, void prairie. They are primitive as the Cyclops themselves, and shadowed with a sense and a reality of crime. Huge, violent, barbarous 40

figures, they roll impassively on, with their few wagons, surrounded by the immensity of land space. Day after day they pass west into the vast oblivion. But their force of penetration ebbs. They are brought to a stop. They recoil in the throes of murder and entrench themselves in
5   isolation on a hillock in the midst of the prairie. There they hold out like rude demi-gods against the elements and the subtle Indian.

The plot is nothing—a mere excuse for the presentation. The presentation itself is marvellous, huge, vast, mythical, almost super-human in its import, like the story of the Sons of Anak.*
10 The old hunter and the suave, dark, horse-riding western Indians seem almost like shadows temporarily passing across the landscape. They do not inhabit the place; they are seen in a state of evanescent transit, and their settled habitations seem more like camps of invaders than homes of an established people. There is a difference between the
15 Indians of the west and of the east. The brutal spirit of the prairie, the brutal recoil of Ishmael, these are the place-reality. But as the hills rise softly west we come to a region of suspended abstraction, a borderland that has no force of its own, only an outlook.

The Indians of these hills have some sensuous, soft, Asiatic or Poly-
20 nesian quality,* according to Cooper's vision. They have a suave, swift beauty, physical and sensuous, and utterly dependent on horses. They seem to lie under the last spell of the Pacific influence; they have the grace and physical voluptuousness, as well as the subtlety and sudden ferocity, of the lands of the Great Ocean. It is quite a different Indian from
25 the stern, hard warrior of the east, whose sensual activity is all in death. And it is in these western Sioux, the despised nations, that one sees, if anywhere, the touch of Apollo in the young Indian. They have beautiful limbs, that cleave close to their horses, almost in one flesh. They are not abstracted, as the great nations of the east, in sensual intensity.
30 Among these men the old hunter dies, gently, in physical peace and soft affection, there west, in his chair on the western hills, under the heavens that are the limits of the world, looking far eastward, where his soul's land lies, among the forests and darkness of the trees and the great sweet waters. He had gone beyond himself, there in the west, in
35 the village of his last days.

The Last of the Mohicans brings us back to the trees and the lakes, the Delawares, and the white men. But in this book Cooper again seeks a pretext for his plot. He must describe actual historical events, and, hanging on to the skirts of history, hamper and spoil his natural move-
40 ment. Perhaps *The Last of the Mohicans* is the most imperfect of all

the Leatherstocking books, the most broken, hesitating as it does between historical narrative, desire for verity, and the true impulse of pure imaginative, creative revelation. It is not till the book passes away from contact with history and white man's settlement and enters the confines of the Red Man that it expands into sheer significance.   5

Natty is now Leatherstocking, a man in the prime of life. So we move backwards, from the old age of the *Pioneers*, and the death in the *Prairie*, successively backwards, to the lovely pristine youth of Deerslayer. It is the reverse of the ordinary course of biography. But this is not historical biography, record of the past as it approaches towards the present. This   10 is biography in futurity, record of the race-individual as he moves from the present old age of the race into re-birth and the new youth which lies ahead. It is the story of the return of the aged Ithacus and of his rejuvenation.

As far as the narrative concerns the actual struggle of the Red race   15 with the White race, it is not the object of our present interest. The real story lies in the flight and adventure of the two sisters, daughters of the British officer, with their young guard, Major Heyward, all under the care of Leatherstocking, with whom is associated the Indian chief, Chingachgook, and the chief's beautiful young son—a young Dionysos   20 rather than an Apollo of the west—Uncas, the last of the Mohicans.

For the first time, in the two sisters—the dark, handsome Cora and the fair, frail creature, the White Lily—Cooper gives us the vital presence of women. Cora is the passionate, fierce nature, child of some mysterious union between the British officer and a Creole of the West Indies. She   25 is the scarlet flower of womanhood; and she loves, and is loved by, the young Uncas. Magua also, the subtle and wicked Indian who causes the destruction of the young pair, loves her violently.

Magua, Uncas, and Cora all die a violent death. There is to be no marriage between the last fiery slips of the Red and the White race—no   30 marriage in the flesh. So we read the art-symbology. In the passionate physical reality both races die. Even the vivid and wicked Magua is shot in mid-air, and his beautiful if destructive body falls extinct like a meteorite. It is strange and appalling in this book that twice the hostile Indians are shot from overhead, and plunge down almost as from the   35 skies into death,* struck by the bullet of the inevitable white-hunter. They are the destroyed sun-children. Natty, in his fearful and unerring aim, is the mystic destroyer of the Red Man out of life.

The gentle sister of Cora, however, the timorous, will-less White Lily, she so frail and fainting, lives through all peril, beloved of the sturdy and   40 straightforward young Major. Later, we know, she marries and brings up her family of children. She is the woman of the white race, as she fades out of positive being and becomes just the medium of the man. She lives in the old idea, the old will. The governing principle of the young Major is the same as the governing principle of Franklin. Duty is his first call. He is the brave and manly social unit; he has no single, separate existence. In the woods and in danger he shows a manly, if unsubtle, slightly uninteresting figure. In civilised life he would be an open-handed, but unoriginal, citizen and officer. To Cora, however she might esteem him, he would appear, we imagine, another of the innumerable meaningless figures of social life. The White Lily is his counterpart. She is unutterably passive and subject to the will of the man. She is the passive instrument of the will of the man, as he seeks his ideal self-ratification. And of her the children of the next generation are born.

　　And over and above all this turmoil of loving and fighting and killing and dying we have the two impressive figures of the middle-aged men, Natty and Chingachgook. They are the dual centre of all the whirl of life. All the tides of death and marriage and birth seem to turn about their stable polarity. Two mature, silent, expressionless men, they stand on opposite shores of being, and their love, the inexpressible conjunction between them, is the bridge over the chasm.

　　Each of them is alone, and, since the death of Uncas, conclusive, concluded in himself. They are isolated, final instances of their race: two strangers, from opposite ends of the earth, meeting now, beholding each other, and balanced in unspeakable conjunction—a love so profound, or so abstract, that it is unexpressed; it has no word or gesture of intercommunion. It is communicated by pure presence alone, without contact of word or touch. This perfect relationship, this last abstract love, exists between the two isolated instances of opposite race.

　　And this is the inception of a new race. Beyond all expression, save the pure communion of *presence*, the abstract love of these two beings consummates itself in an unimaginable coalescence, the inception of a new psyche, a new race-soul that rises out of the last and first unknowable intercommunion of two untranslatable souls. That which Chingachgook was, Natty was not; nor could he ever know. In the same way, Natty himself was the untranslatable unknown to Chingachgook. Yet across this insuperable gulf in being there passed some strange communion between the two instances, invisible, intangible, unknowable—a quality of pure unknowable embrace. And out of this embrace arises the strange wing-covered scraph* of new race-being. From this communion is procreated a new race-soul, which henceforth gestates within the living humanity of the West.

The birth in flesh continues *almost* automatically. Physical population goes on in the intervals of being, like a mechanical marking-time of the creative presence. Until, from some perfect communion between living souls or some perfect passing of a soul through the extremes of spiritual and sensual experience, both, there arises a new soul-unit, a first term of creation, a potential anima,* which henceforth informs the fit souls of the children of men. So all new being comes into existence: first, in the consummation within the perfected soul of a mature creature; then in the translation of this consummated *new term* of creation into the fresh soil of the succeeding life. It is the flower that generates the seed in the first instance,* not the seed the flower. This is the process of creation: the rose itself appears in triumph out of chaos, and leaves behind it the seed of its own perpetuity. It is not in children that the new takes place: it is in the mature, consummated men and women.

The book that follows *The Last of the Mohicans* is *Pathfinder*. This is a beautiful and finished work, but it has not the passional profundity of its predecessors. What it gains in finish and harmony and unified beauty it loses, perhaps, in depth of significance. We are given Natty's abortive love story. But the splendour lies in the revelation of the spirit of place, the pristine beauty of the Great Lakes, the insuperable glamour of sailing the sweet-water seas in the early days when the continent was still virgin to white man, the lakes ringed round with forest and Indians.

Natty is now called Pathfinder. He is a man of thirty-four or thirty-five, a scout attached to a British outpost garrison on one of the Great Lakes. At the beginning of the story he is found in the woods with Chingachgook, escorting Sergeant Dunham and the sergeant's handsome and admirable daughter, Mabel Dunham, to the garrison on the lake. The life at the outpost is well given, almost in the same spirit as *Pioneers*. The action and climax of the story are removed far down the waters to an island in the narrows. The sense of wide, glimmering expanses of shiny water; the ship with her sails all spread, inland, footing the new, sweet waves; the tiny and furtive Indian canoe, venturing so fearlessly into space; the steep hills, the wild, high, virgin shores; then the lonely log-house on the island, hidden with trees in the narrow passage, garrisoned with outpost souls, uneasy and adventurous—all this makes up a magnificent American epic.

But the love of Pathfinder for Mabel Dunham leaves us cold. It is a
love which proceeds from the head and the will of the hunter. He finds
himself perilously departing from the season of youth into the rigidity of
age. And he experiences the inevitable misgiving. He is alone, without
5   kith or kin or place of abode. He trembles on the edge of space. And
the inevitable fear seizes him—the necessity for some fixed place, some
fixed condition, something which shall *determine* his existence, give
him a sense of stability, even of perpetuity. He must have a sheet-anchor
somewhere. And the orthodox sheet-anchor is marriage and children.
10 Most men would rather have a home which is misery and torment than
suffer from the sense of exposure to the winds of fate. They must have
children to give them the sense of perpetuity. It is one of the deepest
characteristics of the human nature, this craving for a sense of external
support, of fixity, even if the fixity be but a chain and an imprisonment.
15   Pathfinder falls, as all men are inclined to fall. His love for the admirable Mabel is dictated from ulterior purpose; he has, perhaps unknown to himself, an ulterior motive. It is not the love of a man for a
woman, in sheer impulse. It is the uneasy ego providing for itself. It is a
shrinking from the sheer communion in isolation, which lies ahead, the
20 mystic consummating of the White soul with the Red. It is the inevitable
denial of the extreme mystic impulse. When he is refused, Pathfinder
has one horrible struggle with his *amour propre,** then he has recovered.
He has got back to the right track. The passion for the young woman,
which in him has been somewhat ugly—a quality of roused function
25 and of *fear* rather than of deep desire—is gone in one breath as soon
as his *amour propre* is really struck by her rejection of him. We see him
writhe in humiliation of a man who has been foiled in making a bargain
advantageous to himself—then we draw a free breath. It is all over.
       Mabel Dunham is another Eve Effingham, or a Miss Tempest from
30 *Pioneers*, or the Ellen of the *Prairie*, or the admirable young female of
*Oak Openings.** She rejects Pathfinder quite decently, for she loves the
young Jasper, the half-French master-mariner of the inland waters. He
is an admirable character, who will die at his duty like Major Heyward,
and who will never do anything that he should not do. Their love is
35 just the continuing of the ordinary colonial population and purpose,
without profound significance.
       Cooper's last book of the Leatherstocking series *Deerslayer*, is the
loveliest and best. It has the purity of achievement of *Pathfinder* and
the passional depth of the earlier works. *Deerslayer* is, indeed, one of the
40 most beautiful and most perfect books in the world: flawless as a jewel

and of gem-like concentration. From the first words we pass straight into the world of sheer creation, with so perfect a transit that we are unconscious of our translation.

The world—the pristine world of Glimmerglass—is, perhaps, love-lier than any place created in language: lovelier than Hardy or Turgenev,   5
lovelier than the lands in ancient poetry or in Irish verse.* And the spell must lie in the luminous futurity which glimmers as a plasm in all the landscape.

Deerslayer is now a young man—little more than a youth. He is illiter-ate, and yet by nature thoughtful, of philosophic temperament. Having   10
been brought up all his life among the Indians and in the backwoods, he has a quality of virginity, and at the same time he has the terrible oldness, the old man's deliberateness, of his race. He is race-old; racially, he is an old man. Sensually, he is an infant. And then there is a new, suspended quality in him: the strange blankness that precedes a dawn: 15
He is found in the woods with a great, blonde-bearded, handsome back-woodsman, called Hurry Harry. The two young men direct their steps to the smallish lake, Glimmerglass.

On this water the Hutter family is established. It is suggested that the coarse old man, Hutter, has been a buccaneer, and that he has retired   20
beyond the reach of the law. He has been married to a woman of superior station, who had fallen into shame, and was given to this coarse scoundrel to cover her fall.

This is the element of sin which has a fascination for Cooper, and which he must introduce to justify any dark, sensual type—such as   25
Cora in *The Last of The Mohicans*. The flower of sin is Judith Hutter, daughter of the buccaneer—dark, handsome, fearless, and passionate, a scarlet-and-black blossom. She is juxtaposed by the fair Hetty Hutter, her sister, another White Lily, of almost angelic innocence, but, alas! touched with idiocy. She is weak in her mind.   30

Hutter, the brutal old scoundrel, is none the less an ingenious char-acter and a good father to the two girls—or young women, as they are now. On the remote Glimmerglass, away from all white men, he has constructed his castle and his ark, and has made a fair living by trap-ping the furred animals. His castle is a heavy log-house, built away in   35
the water on piles driven deep into the bed of the lake. It is surrounded by a palisade, and is thus almost impregnable: inaccessible save to the canoes of the Indians, and secure against these when the heavy water-gate is fast. His ark is a clumsy kind of boat-house, a square cabin built on a sort of raft. This can be slowly rowed from place to place, and   40

the family transported to whatever spot is most favourable to the old trapper's business. Meanwhile the castle is locked up.

So the two young hunters find it when they arrive on Glimmerglass. The ark is moored and hidden at the mouth of a stream which enters the
5   lake. But war has broken out, and, unrevealed, the Indians are on the shores of the lake, hostile. The story of peril and conflict begins at once in the midst of the marvellous peace and beauty of the wooded lake.

Cooper, like Hardy, has an inevitable break between fair and dark. He has only three types: the dark and sensual, the blonde and spiritual, and
10 the mechanical, material, conventional type. In Cooper it is Cora and the White Lily and Miss Tempest. In Hardy, the division is obvious.

This division into duality, and the conflict in dualism in the self, and the inevitable ensuing tragedy, is Hardy's theme as well as Cooper's. Hardy had no way out. He throws his approbation in the spiritual scale,
15 his passion in the sensual scale, and the balance is so equal and opposite that the scales themselves, the human life, can only break into death. Cooper has the same division, the same tragedy. But he has two ways out: either the material-social successfulness into which his admirable Mabels betake themselves, or the strange, blank reality of Deerslayer.
20   Hurry Harry, the big, blustering backwoodsman, has come to woo Judith Hutter. His deepest quality is a cowardice in the soul: not physical cowardice, but soul cowardice. He loves Judith, not with any intensity or real discrimination, but with prostituting appetite. Judith is the sensual flower of womanhood, a dark blossom, yet a pure blossom: whereas
25 Hurry Harry can conceive of no blossoming. He is in the vulgar sense a sensualist, greedy, full of appetite, but without true passion: a bully, established on an innate sense of his own insufficiency and weakness, giant as he is. There is a cringing, craven deficiency in his soul, so he becomes an outward blusterer. All of him is handsome except the very
30 core, the middle of the pupil of his eye, where there is a mongrel fear.

Judith rejects him with scorn. She is a flower of sin; for in her race the sensual mystery is the sin mystery. But she has a real magnificence and pathos. She loves Deerslayer, loves him profoundly; for he is as pure a spiritual type as she is a sensual type. If she could possess him,
35 sensually, she would yield to him utterly, in the rest of life.

But Deerslayer will not be sensually possessed by any woman. He is the spiritual type. He would melt like wax in the hot, possessive passion of Judith; she would absorb him, envelop him utterly. He would become an inclusive part of herself, flowing into her down the vivid current of
40 his negative sensuality, like some sheer fire she had drunk. She would

be fulfilled and suffused with him, and he would be gone, merged, consumed into the woman, having no being of his own apart from her. And she, possessing him utterly, as if he were enveloped in her own womb, would worship him.

This Deerslayer will never have. He sticks to his own singleness. A race falls when men begin to worship the Great Mother, when they are enveloped within the woman, as a child in the womb. And Deerslayer represents the heroic spirit of his race passing in singleness and perfection beyond his own race, into the pure unknown of the future. For him there is no slipping back into the womb. He is young, perhaps a little priggish, but candid, even candescent:* a delicate hero, frail like, an autumn crocus, and as deathly, but perfect.

Hetty Hutter, the fair child of God, falls in love with Hurry Harry. This is the horror of her imbecility, which, like a scotched snake,* turns back and bites itself, envenoms itself with its own poison. Wandering with her Bible into the hostile and dangerous camp of the Red men, she lisps to them, in her childish innocence, of the God of immaculate love, the beauty of holiness and humility. The chiefs listen and slowly, sadly smile. They see she is imbecile; and they see the fatality of her message. She is one of God's fools, the White Lily already festering at the quick.

For she falls violently and helplessly in love with Hurry Harry. This is the malignant mockery of imbecility. She herself longs to defile that which she most purely is. The child of immaculate love, she longs to prostitute herself to the mongrel embrace of Hurry Harry. This is the cunning of imbecility, which malignantly betrays that which it most purely worships. This fatal and hideous division of the self against the self, helpless, malignant, is the horror of imbecility.

The book ends sadly. Judith goes her way, to shame, as it seems. There has been killing and violence. Hetty is dead; so is old Hutter. The castle, the ark, the wonderful lake, are abandoned. Deerslayer goes his way into the woods with the young Indians.

And even he is really a slayer, as his name says. He, the last exponent of the Christian race in the West, whose God is symbolised as the Lamb, has the name of Deerslayer—Slayer of the Lamb. This is the paradox, almost as paradoxical as imbecility itself. Deerslayer remains true to the Christian tenet of humility, mercy, selflessness. A great deal of the Sermon on the Mount would apply to him. He lives for others.

And yet he can only live in presence of danger and death. He is the most perfect shot in the backwoods. He brings the highest bird dead from mid-heaven. He loves poignantly to see the deer stoop and drink

at the edge of the lake. And perhaps he has an even more poignant thrill of pleasure as he sends a bullet clean to the heart of that deer—but only, of course, if it be necessary for food. He has a passion for the experiences of danger and death. No woman could give him the sheer
5   flame of sensation he feels when the hand of a hostile Indian is laid on him as he lies in his canoe believing himself to be far out on the water.*

But Deerslayer is at the end of his race-journey. In him there is no succumbing to the woman, the Magna Mater of his shame. Nor is there any break into imbecility. He has come to the end of his journey, and
10 before him lies the leap into space, into oblivion, into death. And he will take it.

But now, at the end, he sees beyond him, in face of him, that which he has been journeying away from. Beyond him and in front of him he sees the Red Man, the sensual being which for ages he has been destroying
15 or fleeing from. And that which he has most perfectly destroyed he now most perfectly accepts across the gulf.

This is the beauty of Deerslayer, that he knows at last that there are two ways, two mysteries—the Red Man's and his own. He must remain true to his own way, his own mystery. But now at last he acknowledges
20 perfectly and in full the opposite mystery—the mystery of the other.

Still, there is no physical mating for him—only the passage and consummation into death. And this is why Deerslayer must live in peril and conflict, live by his death-dealing rifle. For him the physical consummation is a consummation into death. Ecstasy after ecstasy of keen
25 peril and terrible death-dealing passes through his frame, gradually, mystically reducing him, dissolving out his animate tissue, the tissue of his oldness, into death as a pearl dissolves in wine. This is his slow, perfect, sensual consummation, his ultimate mystic consummation into death. For as an individual and as a race unit he must pass utterly into
30 death—dissolve out.

But even this is a process of futurity. It is the flower which burns down to mould, to liberate the new seed. And the lovely American landscape is the pure landscape of futurity: not of our present factory-smoked futurity, but of the true future of the as yet unborn, or scarcely born,
35 race of Americans.

VI.

Edgar Allan Poe.

It seems a long way from Fenimore Cooper to Poe. But in fact it is only a step. Leatherstocking is the last instance of the integral, progressive soul of the white man in America. In the last conjunction between Leatherstocking and Chingachgook we see the passing out into the darkness of the interim, as a seed falls into the dark interval of winter. What remains is the old tree withering and seething down* to the crisis of winter-death, the great white race in America keenly disintegrating, seething back in electric decomposition, back to that crisis where the old soul, the old era, perishes in the denuded frame of man, and the first throb of a new year sets in.

The process of the decomposition of the body after death is slow and mysterious, a life process of post-mortem activity. In the same way, the great psyche, which we have evolved through two thousand years of effort, must die, and not only die, must be reduced back to its elements by a long, slow process of disintegration, living disintegration.

This is the clue to Edgar Allan Poe, and to the art that succeeds him, in America. When a tree withers, at the end of a year, then the whole life of the year is gradually driven out until the tissue remains elemental and almost null. Yet it is only reduced to that crisis of perfect quiescence which *must* intervene between life-cycle and life-cycle. Poe shows us the first vivid, seething reduction of the psyche, the first convulsive spasm that sets-in in the human soul, when the last impulse of creative love, creative conjunction, is finished. It is like a tree whose fruits are perfected, writhing now in the grip of the first frost.

For men who are born at the end of a great era or epoch nothing remains but the seething reduction back to the elements; just as for a tree in autumn nothing remains but the strangling-off of the leaves and the strange decomposition and arrest of the sap. It is useless to ask for perpetual spring and summer. Poe had to lead on to that winter-crisis when the soul is, as it were, denuded of itself, reduced back to the elemental state of a naked, arrested tree in midwinter. Man must be stripped of himself. And the process is slow and bitter and beautiful, too. But the beauty has its spark in anguish; it is the strange, expiring cry, the phosphorescence of decay.*

Poe is a man writhing in the mystery of his own undoing. He is a great dead soul, progressing terribly down the long process of post-
5   mortem activity in disintegration. This is how the dead bury their dead.* This is how man must bury his own dead self: in pang after pang of vital, explosive self-reduction, back to the elements. This is how the seed must fall into the ground and perish before it can bring forth new life.* For Poe the process was one of perishing in
10   the old body, the old psyche, the old self. He leads us back, through pang after pang of disintegrative sensation, back towards the end of all things, where the beginning is: just as the year begins where the year is utterly dead. It is only perfect courage which can carry us through the extremity of death, through the crisis of our own nullification,
15   the midwinter which is the end of the end and the beginning of the beginning.

Yet Poe is hardly an artist. He is rather a supreme scientist. Art displays the movements of the pristine self, the living conjunction or communion between the self and its context. Even in tragedy self meets
20   self in supreme conjunction, a communion of passionate or creative death. But in Poe the self is finished, already stark. It would be true to say that Poe had no soul. He lives in the post-mortem reality, a living dead.* He reveals the after-effects of life, the processes of organic disintegration. Arrested in himself, he cannot realise self or soul in any
25   other human being. For him, the vital world is the sensational world. He is not sensual, he is sensational. The difference between these two is a difference between growth and decay. In Poe, sensationalism is a process of explosive disintegration, phosphorescent, electric, refracted. In him, sensation is that momentaneous state of consciousness which
30   concurs with the sudden combustion and reduction of vital tissue. The combustion of his own most vital plasm liberates the white gleam of his sensational consciousness. Hence his addiction to alcohol and drugs, which are the common agents of reductive combustion.

It is for this reason that we would class the "tales" as science rather
35   than art: because they reveal the workings of the great inorganic forces, disruptive within the organic psyche. The central soul or self is in arrest. And for this reason we cannot speak of the tales as stories or novels. A tale is a concatenation of scientific cause and effect. But in a story the movement depends on the sudden appearance of spontaneous emotion
40   or gesture, causeless, arising out of the living self.

Yet the chief of Poe's tales depend upon the passion of love. The central stories, *Ligeia* and *The Fall of the House of Usher*, are almost stories; there is in these almost a relation of soul to soul. These are the two stories where love is still recognisable as the driving force.

Love is the mysterious force which brings beings together in creative 5 conjunction or communion. But it is also the force which brings them together in frictional disruption. Love is the great force which causes disintegration as well as new life, and corruption as well as procreation. It brings life together with life, either for production or for destruction, down to the last extremes of existence. 10

And in Poe, love is purely a frictional, destructive force. In him, the mystic, spontaneous self is replaced by the self-determined ego. He is a unit of will rather than a unit of being. And the force of love acts in him almost as an electric attraction rather than as a communion between self and self. He is a lodestone, the woman is the soft metal.* Each draws 15 the other mechanically. Such attraction, increasing and intensifying in conjunction, does not set up a cycle of rest and creation. The one life draws the other life with a terrible pressure. Each presses on the other intolerably till one is bound to disappear: one or both.

The story of this process of magnetic, self-less pressure of love is 20 told in the story of *Ligeia*, and this story we may take to be the clue to Poe's own love-tragedy. The motto to the tale is a quotation from Joseph Glanville: "And the will therein lieth, which dieth not. Who knoweth the mysteries of the will, with its vigour? For God is but a great will pervading all things by nature of its intentness. Man doth not 25 yield himself to the angels, nor unto death utterly, save only through the weakness of his feeble will."

If God is a great will, then the universe is a great machine, for the will is a fixed principle. But God is not a will. God is a mystery, from which creation mysteriously proceeds. So is the self a unit of creative 30 mystery. But the will is the greatest of all control-principles, the greatest machine-principle.

So Poe establishes himself in the will, self-less and determined. Then he enters the great process of destructive love, which in the end works out to be a battle of wills as to which can hold out longest. 35

The story is told in a slow method of musing abstraction, most subtle yet most accurate. Ligeia is never a free person. She is just a phenomenon with which Poe strives in ill-omened love. She is not a woman. She is just a re-agent, a re-acting force, chimerical almost. "In stature she was tall, somewhat slender, and, in her later days, even emaciated. I would 40

in vain attempt to portray the majesty, the quiet ease, of her demeanour, or the incomprehensible lightness and elasticity of her footfall. I was never made aware of her entrance into my closed study save by the dear music of her low, sweet voice as she placed her marble hand upon my
5 shoulder."

Perhaps it is hardly fair to quote fragments of Poe's prose, for the careful style shows up a little meretricious. It is for their scientific progress in sensation that the tales should be studied, not as art.

When Poe comes to the clue of Ligeia he leaves a blank. He paints her
10 portrait till he comes to the very look in her eyes. This he never meets, never knows. His soul never goes out to her in that strange conjunction where self greets self, beautiful and unspeakable. He only analyses her till he come to the unanalysable, the very quick of her.

Speaking of her eyes, he goes on: "They were, I must believe, far
15 larger than the ordinary eyes of our own race. They were even fuller than the fullest of the gazelle eyes of the tribe of Nourjahad. . . . The hue of the orbs was the most brilliant of black, and, far over them, hung pretty lashes of great length. The brows, slightly irregular in outline had the same tint. The *strangeness*, however, which I found in the eyes was
20 of a nature distinct from the formation, or the colour, or the brilliancy of the features, and must, after all, be referred to the *expression*. Ah, word of no meaning! behind whose vast latitude of sound we intrench our ignorance of so much of the spiritual. The expression of the eyes of Ligeia! How for long hours have I pondered upon it ! How have I,
25 through the whole of a midsummer night, struggled to fathom it! What was it— that something more profound than the well of Democritus— which lay far within the pupils of my beloved? What *was* it? I was possessed with a passion to discover. . . . "

This is the same old effort, to analyse and possess and know the
30 secret of the soul, the living self. It is the supreme lust of possession. But the soul can never be analysed any more than living protoplasm can be analysed. The moment we start we have dead protoplasm. We may, with our own soul, behold and know the soul of the other. Look can meet look in pure recognition and communion. And this communion
35 can be conveyed again in speech. But ever didactically. It is a motion of the whole soul in its entirety, whereas scientific knowledge is never more than a post-mortem residuum.

Of a piece with this craving to analyse the being of the beloved, to be scientifically master of the mystery of the other being, is the whole
40 passion for knowledge which fills these two. The learning of Ligeia was

immense, we are told, such as has never before been known in woman. It shows the unspeakable craving of those whose souls are arrested, to gain mastery over the world through knowledge. This is one of the temptations of Christ, when Satan offers him the world.* To possess the world in deliberate, scientific knowledge, this is one of the cravings 5 of the unrebuked human heart. It cannot be done. We can only know in full when we *are* in full. In the fulness of our own being we are at one with the mystery; in the deepest and most beautiful sense we know it. But as creatures of exact knowledge and deliberate will we exist in the world of post-mortem reality. Life is beyond us for ever, even as 10 the strangeness of the eyes of Ligeia was beyond the man's probing and fathoming. He seemed so often *on the verge*, thrillingly, awfully. But that was all.

He decided that the clue to the strangeness was in the mystery of will. "And the will therein lieth, which dieth not.... " Ligeia had a "gigantic 15 volition." ... "An *intensity* in thought, action, or speech was possibly, in her, a result, or at least an index, of that gigantic volition which, during our long intercourse, failed to give other and more immediate evidence of its existence. Of all the women whom I have ever known, she, the outwardly calm, the ever-placid Ligeia, was the most violently a prey to 20 the tumultuous vultures of stern passion. And of such passion I could form no estimate, save by the miraculous expansion of those eyes which at once so delighted and appalled me—by the almost magical melody, modulation, distinctness, and placidity of her very low voice—and by the fierce energy (rendered doubly effective by contrast with her manner 25 of utterance) of the wild words which she habitually uttered."

Having recognised the clue to Ligeia in her gigantic volition, there must inevitably ensue the struggle of wills. But Ligeia, true to the great traditions, remains passive or submissive, womanly, to the man; he is the active agent, she the recipient. To this her gigantic volition fixes her 30 also. Hence, moreover, her conquest of the stern vultures of passion.

The stress of inordinate love goes on, the consuming into a oneness. And it is Ligeia who is consumed. The process of such love is inevitable consumption. In creative love there is a recognition of each soul by the other, a mutual kiss, and then the balance in equilibrium which is 35 the peace and beauty of love. But in Poe and Ligeia such balance is impossible. Each is possessed with the craving to search out and *know* the other, entirely; to know, to have, to possess, to be identified with the other. They are two units madly urging together towards a fusion which must break down the very being of one or both of them. Ligeia 40

craves to be identified with her husband, he with her. And not until too
late does she realise that such identification is death.

"That she loved me I should not have doubted; and I might have
been easily aware that, in a bosom such as hers, love would have reigned
5   no ordinary passion. But in death only was I fully impressed with the
strength of her affection. For long hours, detaining my hand, would
she pour out before me the overflowing of a heart whose more than
passionate devotion amounted to idolatry. How had I deserved to be
blessed by such confessions? How had I deserved to be cursed with the
10   removal of my beloved in the hour of her making them? But upon this
subject I cannot bear to dilate. Let me say only that in Ligeia's more
than womanly abandonment to a love, alas! all unmerited, all unworthily
bestowed, I at length recognised the principle of her longing with so
wildly earnest a desire for the life which was now fleeing so rapidly away.
15   It is this wild longing—it is this vehement desire for life—*but* for life—
that I have no power to portray—no utterance capable of expressing."

Thus Ligeia is defeated in her terrible desire to be identified with her
husband, and live, just as he is defeated in his desire, living, to grasp
the clue of her in his own hand.

20   On the last day of her existence Ligeia dictates to her husband the
memorable poem, which concludes:—

"Out—out are all the lights—out all!
And over each quivering form
The curtain, a funeral pall,
25   Comes down with the rush of a storm,
And the angels, all pallid and wan,
Uprising, unveiling, affirm
That the play is the tragedy 'Man,'
And its hero the Conqueror Worm."

30   "'O God!' half shrieked Ligeia, leaping to her feet and extending
her arms aloft with a spasmodic movement, as I made an end of these
lines, 'O God! O Divine Father!—shall these things be undeviatingly
so? Shall this Conqueror be not once conquered? Are we not part and
parcel in Thee? Who—who knoweth the mysteries of the will with its
35   vigour? Man doth not yield him to the angels, *nor unto death utterly*,
save only through the weakness of his feeble will.'"

So Ligeia dies. Herself a creature of will and finished consciousness,
she sees everything collapse before the devouring worm. But shall her
will collapse?

The husband comes to ancient England, takes a gloomy, grand old abbey, puts it into some sort of repair, and, converting it into a dwelling, furnishes it with exotic, mysterious splendour. As an artist Poe is unfailingly in bad taste—always in bad taste. He seeks a sensation from every phrase or object, and the effect is vulgar. 5

In the story the man marries the fair-haired, blue-eyed Lady Rowena Trevanion, of Tremaine.

"In halls such as these—in a bridal chamber such as this—I passed, with the Lady of Tremaine, the unhallowed hours of the first month of our marriage—passed them with but little disquietude. That my wife 10 dreaded the fierce moodiness of my temper—that she shunned me and loved me but little—I could not help perceiving; but it gave me rather pleasure than otherwise. I loathed her with a hatred belonging rather to a demon than to a man. My memory flew back (Oh, with what intensity of regret!) to Ligeia, the beloved, the august, the entombed. I revelled 15 in recollections of her purity," etc.

The love which had been a wild craving for identification with Ligeia, a love inevitably deadly and consuming, now in the man has become definitely destructive, devouring, subtly murderous. He will slowly and subtly consume the life of the fated Rowena. It is his vampire lust. 20

In the second month of the marriage the Lady Rowena fell ill. It is Ligeia whose presence hangs destructive over her; it is the ghostly Ligeia who pours poison into Rowena's cup. It is Ligeia, active and unsatisfied within the soul of her husband, who destroys the other woman. The will of Ligeia is not yet broken. She wants to live. And she wants to live to 25 finish her process, to satisfy her unbearable craving to be identified with the man. All the time, in his marriage with Rowena, the husband is only using the new bride as a substitute for Ligeia. As a substitute for Ligeia he possesses her. And at last from the corpse of Rowena Ligeia rises fulfilled. When the corpse opens its eyes, at last the two are identified, 30 Ligeia with the man she so loved. Henceforth the two are one, and neither exists. They are consumed into an inscrutable oneness.

Eleonora, the next story, is a fantasy revealing the sensational delights of the man in his early marriage with the young and tender bride. They dwelt, he, his cousin and her mother, in the sequestered Valley of Many- 35 coloured Grass, the valley of prismatic sensation, where everything seems spectrum-coloured. They looked down at their own images in the River of Silence, and drew the god Eros from that wave. This is a description of the life of introspection and of the love which is begotten by the self in the self, the self-made love. The trees are like serpents 40

worshipping the sun. That is, they represent the phallic passion in its
poisonous or destructive activity. The symbolism of Poe's parables is
easy, too easy, almost mechanical.

  In *Berenice* the man must go down to the sepulchre of his beloved
5 and take her thirty-two small white teeth which he carries in a box
with him. It is repulsive and gloating. The teeth are the instruments
of biting, of resistance, of antagonism. They often become symbols of
opposition, little instruments or entities of crushing and destroying.
Hence the dragon's teeth in the myth. Hence the man in *Berenice* must
10 take possession of the irreducible part of his mistress. "Toutes ses dents
étaient des idées," he says. Then they are little fixed ideas of mordant
hate, of which he possesses himself.

  The other great story somewhat connected with this group is *The
Fall of the House of Usher*. Here the love is between brother and sister.
15 When the self is broken, and the mystery of the recognition of *otherness*
fails, then the longing for identification with the beloved becomes a
lust. And it is this longing for identification, utter merging, which is at
the base of the incest problem. In psychoanalysis almost every trouble
in the psyche is traced to an incest-desire. But this will not do. The
20 incest-desire is only one of the manifestations of the self-less desire
for merging. It is obvious that this desire, for merging, or unification,
or identification of the man with the woman, or the woman with the
man, finds its gratification most readily in the merging of those things
which are already near—mother with son, brother with sister, father
25 with daughter. But it is not enough to say, as Jung does, that all life is a
matter of lapsing towards, or struggling away from, mother-incest.* It
is necessary to see what lies at the back of this helpless craving for utter
merging or identification with a beloved.

  The motto to *The Fall of the House of Usher* is a couple of lines from
30 De Béranger.

> "Son cœur est un luth suspendu;
> Sitôt qu'on le touche il résonne."

We have all the trappings of Poe's rather overdone vulgar fantasy.
"I reined my horse to the precipitous brink of a black and lurid tarn
35 that lay in unruffled lustre by the dwelling, and gazed down—but with
a shudder even more thrilling than before—upon the remodelled and
inverted images of the grey sedge, and the ghastly tree-stems, and the
vacant and eye-like windows." The House of Usher, both dwelling and
family, was very old. Minute fungi overspread the exterior of the house,

hanging in festoons from the eaves. Gothic archways, a valet of stealthy step, sombre tapestries, ebon black floors, a profusion of tattered and antique furniture, feeble gleams of encrimsoned light through latticed panes, and over all "an air of stern, deep, irredeemable gloom"—this makes up the interior. 5

The inmates of the house, Roderick and Madeline Usher, are the last remnants of their incomparably ancient and decayed race. Roderick has the same large, luminous eye, the same slightly arched nose of delicate Hebrew model, as characterised Ligeia. He is ill with the nervous malady of his family. It is he whose nerves are so strung that they vibrate to 10 the unknown quiverings of the ether. He, too, has lost his self, his living soul, and become a sensitised instrument of the external influences; his nerves are verily like an æolian harp which must vibrate. He lives in "some struggle with the grim phantasm, Fear," for he is only the physical, post-mortem reality of a living being. 15

It is a question how much, once the rich centrality of the self is broken, the instrumental consciousness of man can register. When man becomes self-less, wafting instrumental like a harp in an open window, how much can his elemental consciousness express? It is probable that even the blood as it runs has its own sympathies and responses to the 20 material world, quite apart from seeing. And the nerves we know vibrate all the while to unseen presences, unseen forces. So Roderick Usher quivers on the edge of dissolution.

It is this mechanical consciousness which gives "the fervid facility of his impromptus." It is the same thing that gives Poe his extraordinary 25 facility in versification. The absence of real central or impulsive being in himself leaves him inordinately mechanically sensitive to sounds and effects, associations of sounds, associations of rhyme, for example—mechanical, facile, having no root in any passion. It is all a secondary, meretricious process. So we get Roderick Usher's poem, *The Haunted* 30 *Palace*, with its swift yet mechanical subtleties of rhyme and rhythm, its vulgarity of epithet. It is all a sort of dream-process, where the association between parts is mechanical, accidental as far as passional meaning goes.

Usher thought that all vegetable things had sentience. Surely all ma- 35 terial things have a form of sentience, even the inorganic: surely they all exist in some subtle and complicated tension of vibration which makes them sensitive to external influence and causes them to have an influence on other external objects, irrespective of contact. It is of this vibrational or inorganic consciousness that Poe is master: the sleep-consciousness. 40

Thus Roderick Usher was convinced that his whole surroundings, the stones of the house, the fungi, the water in the tarn, the very reflected image of the whole, was woven into a physical oneness with the family, condensed, as it were, into one atmosphere—the special atmosphere in
5   which alone the Ushers could live. And it was this atmosphere which had moulded the destinies of his family.

In the human realm, Roderick had one connection: his sister Madeline. She, too, was dying of a mysterious disorder, nervous, cataleptic. The brother and sister loved each other passionately and exclusively.
10 They were twins, almost identical in looks. It was the same absorbing love between them, where human creatures are absorbed away from themselves, into a unification in death. So Madeline was gradually absorbed into her brother; the one life absorbed the other in a long anguish of love.

15 Madeline died and was carried down by her brother into the deep vaults of the house. But she was not dead. Her brother roamed about in incipient madness—a madness of unspeakable terror and guilt. After eight days they were suddenly startled by a clash of metal, then a distinct, hollow, metallic, and clangorous, yet apparently muffled, reverberation.
20 Then Roderick Usher, gibbering, began to express himself: "*We have put her living into the tomb!* Said I not that my senses were acute? I *now* tell you that I heard her first feeble movements in the hollow coffin. I heard them—many, many days ago—yet I dared not—*I dared not speak.*"

25 It is again the old theme of "each man kills the thing he loves." He knew his love had killed her. He knew she died at last, like Ligeia, unwilling and unappeased. So, she rose again upon him. "But then without those doors there *did* stand the lofty and enshrouded figure of the Lady Madeline of Usher. There was blood upon her white robes,
30 and the evidence of some bitter struggle upon every portion of her emaciated frame. For a moment she remained trembling and reeling to and fro upon the threshold, then, with a low moaning cry, fell heavily inward upon the person of her brother, and in her violent and now final death-agonies bore him to the floor a corpse, and a victim to the terrors
35 he had anticipated."

It is lurid and melodramatic, but it really is a symbolic truth of what happens in the last stages of this inordinate love, which can recognise none of the sacred mystery of *otherness*, but must unite into unspeakable identification, oneness in death. Brother and sister go down together,
40 made one in the unspeakable mystery of death. It is the world-long

incest problem, arising inevitably when man, through insistence of his will in one passion or aspiration, breaks the polarity of himself. The best tales all have the same burden. Hate is as inordinate as love, and as slowly consuming, as secret, as underground, as subtle. All this underground vault business in Poe only symbolises that which takes place *beneath* the consciousness. On top, all is fair-spoken. Beneath, there is the awful murderous extremity of burying alive. Fortunato, in *The Cask of Amontillado*, is buried alive out of perfect hatred, as the Lady Madeline of Usher is buried alive out of love. The lust of hate is the inordinate desire to consume and unspeakably possess the soul of the hated one, just as the lust of love is the desire to possess, or to be possessed by, the beloved, utterly. But in either case the result is the dissolution of both souls, each losing itself in transgressing its own bounds.

The lust of Montresor is to devour utterly the soul of Fortunato. It would be no use killing him outright. If a man is killed outright his soul remains integral, free to return into the bosom of some beloved, where it can enact itself. In walling-up his enemy in the vault, Montresor seeks to bring about the indescribable capitulation of the man's soul, so that he, the victor, can possess himself of the very being of the vanquished. Perhaps this can actually be done. Perhaps, in the attempt, the victor breaks the bounds of his own identity, and collapses into nothingness, or into the infinite.

What holds good for inordinate hate holds good for inordinate love. The motto, *Nemo me impune lacessit*, might just as well be *Nemo me impune amat*.

In *William Wilson* we are given a rather unsubtle account of the attempt of a man to kill his own soul. William Wilson, the mechanical, lustful ego succeeds in killing William Wilson, the living self. The lustful ego lives on, gradually reducing itself towards the dust of the infinite.

In the *Murders in the Rue Morgue* and *The Gold Bug* we have those mechanical tales where the interest lies in following out a subtle chain of cause and effect. The interest is scientific rather than artistic, a study in psychologic reactions.

The fascination of murder itself is curious. Murder is not just killing. Murder is a lust utterly to possess the soul of the murdered—hence the stealth and the frequent morbid dismemberment of the corpse, the attempt to get at the very quick of the murdered being, to find the quick and to possess it. It is curious that the two men fascinated by the art of murder, though in different ways, should have been De Quincey and

Poe, men so different in ways of life, yet perhaps not so widely different in nature. In each of them is traceable that strange lust for extreme love and extreme hate, possession by mystic violence of the other soul, or violent deathly, surrender of the soul in the self.

5   Inquisition and torture are akin to murder: the same lust. It is a combat between conqueror and victim for the possession of the soul after death. A soul can be conquered only when it is forced to abdicate from its own being. A heretic may be burned at the stake, his ashes scattered on the winds as a symbol that his soul is now broken by torture and dissolved.

10   And yet, as often as not, the brave heretic dies integral in being; his soul re-enters into the bosom of the living, indestructible.

So the mystery goes on. La Bruyère says that all our human unhappiness *vient de ne pouvoir être seuls*. As long as man lives he will be subject to the incalculable influence of love or of hate, which is only inverted love.

15   The necessity to love is probably the source of all our unhappiness; but since it is the source of everything it is foolish to particularise. Probably even gravitation is only one of the lowest manifestations of the mystic force of love. But the triumph of love, which is the triumph of life and creation, does not lie in merging, mingling, in absolute identification of

20   the lover with the beloved. It lies in the communion of beings, who, in the very perfection of communion, recognise and allow the mutual otherness. There is no desire to transgress the bounds of being. Each self remains utterly itself—becomes, indeed, most burningly and transcendently itself in the uttermost embrace or communion with the other.

25   One self may yield honourable precedence to the other, may pledge itself to undying service, and in so doing become fulfilled in its own nature. For the highest achievement of some souls lies in perfect service. But the giving and the taking of service does not obliterate the mystery of otherness, the being-in-singleness, either in master or servant. On the

30   other hand, slavery is an avowed obliteration of the singleness of being.

VII.

Nathaniel Hawthorne.

Before beginning the study of Hawthorne, it is necessary again to consider the bases of the human consciousness. Man has two distinct fields of consciousness, two living minds. First there is the physical or 5 primary mind, a perfect and spontaneous consciousness centralising in the great plexuses and ganglia of the nervous system, and in the hind brain. Secondly there is the ideal consciousness which we recognise as mental, located in the brain. We are mistaken when we conceive of the nerves and the blood as mere vehicles or media of the mental conscious- 10 ness. The blood itself is self-conscious. And the great nerve-centres of the body are centres of perfect primary cognition.

What we call "instinct" in creatures such as bees, or ants, or whales, or foxes, or larks, is the sure and perfect working of the primary mind in these creatures. All the tissue of the body is all the time aware. The blood 15 is awake, the whole blood-system of the body is a great field of primal consciousness. But in the nervous system the primary consciousness is localised and specialised. Each great nerve-centre has its own peculiar consciousness, its own peculiar mind, its own primary percepts and concepts, its own spontaneous desires and ideas. The singing of a lark is 20 direct expression from the whole primary or dynamic mind. When a bee leaves its hive and circles round to sense the locality, it is attending with the primary mind to the surrounding objects, establishing a primary *rapport* between its own very tissue and the tissue of the adjacent objects. A process of rapid *physical* thought takes place, an act of the primary, 25 not the cerebral mind: the sensational, not the ideal consciousness. That is, there is a rapid sensual association within the body of the bee, equivalent to the process of reasoning; sensation develops sensation and sums up to a conclusion, a completed sum of sensations which we may call a sensual concept. 30

All thought, and mental cognition is but a sublimation of the great primary, sensual knowledge located in the tissues of the physique, and centred in the nervous ganglia. It is like the flowering of those water-weeds which live entirely below the surface, and only push their blos-soms, at one particular moment, into the light and the air above water. 35

The process of sensual reasoning, the processes of the primary mind
go on all the time, even when the upper or cerebral mind is asleep. During sleep, the first-mind thinks and makes its momentous conclusions,
sensual and sensational conclusions which are the *real* bases of all our
5   actions, no matter what our mental ideas and opinions and decisions
may be.

In the highest art, the primary mind expresses itself direct, in direct
dynamic pulsating communication. But this expression is harmonious
with the outer or cerebral consciousness.

10   At the beginning, however, of a civilisation, the upper mind cannot
adequately deal with the tremendous conclusions of the physical or primary mind. The great dynamic concepts can find no reasonable utterance. Then we have myths; after myths, legends; after legends, romance;
and after romance, pure art, where the sensual mind is harmonious with
15   the ideal mind.

Myth, legend, romance, drama, these forms of utterance merge off
into one another by imperceptible degrees. The primary or sensual
mind of man expresses itself most profoundly in myth. At the same
time myth is most repugnant to reason. Myth is the huge, concrete
20   expression wherein the dynamic psyche utters its first great passional
concepts of the genesis of the human cosmos, the inception of the
human species. Following myth comes legend, giving utterance to the
genesis of a race psyche. Beyond legend is romance, where the individual
psyche struggles into dynamic being, still impersonal. When we enter
25   the personal plane, we enter the field of art proper, dramatic, lyric,
emotional.

Myth, legend, romance, these are all utterances in defiance of reason.
They are none the less most profoundly passionally reasonable. The field
of the primary, sensual mind is so immense, that the attempt to reduce
30   myth or legend to one consistent rational interpretation is futile. It is
worse than useless to bring down every great primary myth to cosmic
terms, sun myth, thunder myth, and so on. It is still more useless to
see the phallic, procreative and parturitive meaning only. Myth is the
utterance of the primary self-knowledge of the dynamic psyche of man.
35   The dynamic or primary or sensual psyche utters, in terms more or less
monstrous, its own fundamental knowledge of its own genesis. Owing
to the great co-ordination of everything in the universe, the genesis of
the psyche of the human species is at the same time the genesis of the
sun, the moon, and the thunderbolt: indeed the genesis of everything.
40   So that, in one sense, a great primary myth means everything, and

all our interpretations are only particularisations from a colossal root-whole. For the clue or quick of the universe lies in the creative mystery. And the clue or active quick of the creative mystery lies in the human psyche. Hence, paradoxical as it may seem, if we conceive of God we must conceive of him in personal terms. But the test of wisdom lies in abstaining from the attempt to make a presentation of God. We must start from what seems to be nullity, the unknowable, the inexpressible, the creative mystery wherein we are established. We cannot become more exact than this, without introducing falsehood. But we know that the quick of the creative mystery lies, for us at least, in the human soul, the human psyche, the human anima. Hence the only form of worship is *to be*: each man to be his own self, that which has issue from the mystery, and takes form as an inscrutable self. In the soul, the self, the very man unto himself, the god-mystery is active and evident first and foremost.

The progression of man's conscious understanding is dual. The primary or sensual mind begins with the huge, profound, passional generalities of myth, and proceeds through legend and romance to pure, personal art. Parallel to this, the reasoning mind starts from the great cosmic theories of the ancient world, and proceeds, by a progress in particularisation, to establish great laws, physical and ethical, then to discover the exact and minute scientific relation between particular bodies or substances and the great laws, and finally to gain an inkling of the connection between scientific reality and creative, personal reality. The progress is a progression towards harmony between the two halves of the psyche. The approach is towards a pure unison between religion and science. The monstrosity of myth is most repugnant to reason. In the same way, the monstrosity of scientific cosmogony and cosmogenesis is most repugnant to the passional psyche. But the progress of religion is to remove all that is repugnant to reason, and the progress of science is towards a reconciliation with the personal, passional soul. The last steps remain to be taken, and then man can really begin to be free, really to live his whole self, his whole life, in fulness.

The nearest approach of the passional psyche to scientific or rational reality is in art. In art we have perfect dynamic utterance. The nearest approach of the rational psyche towards passional truth is in philosophy. Philosophy is the perfect static utterance. When the unison between art and philosophy is complete, then knowledge will be in full, not always in part, as it is now.*

Hawthorne is a philosopher as well as an artist. He attempts to understand as deeply as he feels. He does not succeed. There is a discrepancy

between his conscious understanding and his passional understanding. To cover this discrepancy he calls his work romance. Now it is evident that Hawthorne is not a romanticist in the strict sense. Romance is the utterance of the primary individual mind, in defiance of reason. The
5 two forms of romance are heroic and idyllic, Arthurian romance and *As You Like It.* In heroic romance magic is substituted to symbolise the powers of the psyche. A magic weapon such as the sword Excalibur symbolises some primal, dynamic power of the heroic psyche over the ordinary psyche. To give the sword a necessary phallic reference, as
10 some of the popular symbologists do today, is false and arbitrary.—In idyllic romance, all external conditions are made subservient to the will of the human psyche: everything occurs as you like it.

It is evident that Hawthorne belongs to neither of these categories. Yet he is not—at least in his greatest work—a realist, nor even a novelist. He
15 is not working in the *personal* plane. His great characters, Hester Prynne, Dimmesdale, Chillingworth, in *The Scarlet Letter*, are not presented spontaneously, as persons. They are abstracted beyond the personal plane. They are not even types. They represent the human soul in its passional abstraction, as it exists in its first abstract nakedness, as
20 a great, dynamic mystery, nakedly ethical, nakedly procreative. *The Scarlet Letter* is in truth a legendary myth. It contains the abstract of the fall of the white race. It is the inverse of the Eve myth, in the Book of Genesis. It contains the passional or primary account of the collapse of the human psyche in the white race. Hawthorne tries to keep up a
25 parallel rational exposition of this fall. But here he fails.

The Eve myth symbolises the birth of the upper mind, the upper consciousness which, the moment it becomes self-conscious, rebels against the physical being, and is sensible of shame because of its own helpless connection with the passional body. The serpent is the symbol of
30 division in the psyche, the knife, the dagger, the ray of burning or malevolent light, the undulating lure of the waters of the flood, the divider, which sets spiritual being against sensual being, man against woman, sex against sex, the introducer of the hostile duality into the human psyche. But the era of Christianity is the era in which the rational or upper
35 or spiritual mind has risen superior to the primary or sensual being. It is the era when, in the white race particularly, spirit has triumphed over flesh, mind over matter. The great triumph of the one half over the other half is effected.

And then comes the fall. *The Scarlet Letter* contains a precise and
40 accurate account of this Fall, dynamically logical in its exactitude. The

book scarcely belongs to the realm of art. It belongs to the realm of primary or passional ethics and ethnology,* the realm of the myth and the Morality Play.

It is the worship, upon the scaffold, of the Mother of the Maculate Conception.* It is a worship of Astarte, the Magna Mater, the great mother of physical fecundity. Only it has this strange difference; that the Great Mother is exposed on the scaffold and worshipped as an object of *sin*. This introduces the peculiar voluptuous complication.

In Christian mythology, Mary enthroned is the Mother of the Sacred Heart, pierced with seven wounds. This has many meanings. But the most obvious is, that here we have the mother of the sensual and primary body pierced in her seven sensual or physical connections, pierced, destroyed, the spiritual remainder deified. This is Mary of the Sacred Heart, with the strange symbol on her breast, of the scarlet, bleeding heart, and the sword rays. It is the sensual body pierced in its seven profound sense-activities, pierced through the seven gates of the body, in the seven great passional centres.*

Hester Prynne, on the scaffold, has a scarlet symbol on her breast. It burns and flashes with rays, sword-rays or sun-rays of golden thread. Here is Mary of the Bleeding Heart standing enthroned in the dark, Puritanical New England.

But the scarlet letter is not a bleeding heart. It is the burning symbol of the sensual mystery, the mystery of the sensual, primal psyche, angry now, in its hostility flashing like a conflagration. This is the great A, the Alpha of Adam, now the Alpha of America. It flashes with the great revenge of the serpent, as the primary or sensual psyche, which was perfectly subjected, humiliated, turns under the heel like the serpent of wrath, and bites back. Woman is wasted into abstraction as Ligeia was wasted, gone in a mental activity and a spiritual purity. Then behold, suddenly, she turns, and we have the Scarlet Woman, the Magna Mater, with her fiery insignia of the sensual self in revolt, presented for worship upon the scaffold, worship in contumely and blame. The revelation is subtle. The almost insane malice of the situation, the malicious duplicity which exalts in shame that which it worships in lust, is conveyed by Hawthorne acutely enough.

"Had there been a Papist among the crowd of Puritans, he might have seen in this beautiful woman, so picturesque in her attire and mien, and with the infant at her bosom, an object to remind him of the image of Divine Maternity, which so many illustrious painters have vied with one another to represent; something which should remind him, indeed,

but only by contrast, of that sacred image of sinless motherhood, whose
infant was to redeem the world. Here, there was a taint of deepest sin
in the most sacred quality of human life, working such effect, that the
world was only the darker for this woman's beauty, and the more lost
5   for the infant that she had borne."
     Hawthorne is a master of symbology, and further, a master of serpent
subtility. His pious blame is subtle commendation to himself. He longs,
like the serpent, for revenge, even upon himself. He is divided against
himself. Openly he stands for the upper, spiritual, reasoned being. Se-
10   cretly he lusts in the sensual imagination, in bruising the heel* of this
spiritual self and laming it for ever. All his reasoned exposition is a pious
fraud, kept up to satisfy his own upper or outward self.
     Hester Prynne is the successor of Ligeia. In Ligeia the primary or sen-
sual self was utterly submitted, and in its submission it was tortured and
15   ground to death by the triumphant husband, the spirit-worshipping or
mind-worshipping male. Ligeia herself worshipped the conscious mind.
She herself submitted the body of her own primary being to deliberate
disintegration, attempting to sublimate it altogether into mind-stuff.
Then she shrieks because she must die, leaving the destructive mental
20   being in the man triumphant. The stern vultures of passion in Ligeia are
the angry heavings of revolt, in her primary or sensual soul, against its
prostitution to the upper or spiritual or mental ego. But she suppresses
this revolt with all her will. She *keeps* the primary, sensual psyche utterly
prostitute, till it is worn away, devoured, by the spiritual psyche. Then
25   she shrieks in a frenzy of despair, and deliberately sets herself to persist
in the afterdeath, malevolently destructive still of the thing she hates
so much, the very first reality of being, the sensual or primary self in
woman. Ligeia's afterdeath malevolence destroys the body and life of
Rowena, and then spends itself. Ligeia is spent and gone. And now, as
30   from the tomb, rises the murdered body of the woman, the murdered
first-principle of being: just as the Lady Madeline of Usher rose from
the tomb and brought down her vampire brother Roderick, Roderick
who loved her to such a deathly extremity, in spiritual or mental love:
and who destroyed her.
35   Hester Prynne is the great nemesis of woman. She too is born utterly
subject. She too loves the ultra-spiritual being, Arthur Dimmesdale, the
young, saintly, almost miraculous preacher. Arthur Dimmesdale is the
very asphodel of spiritual perfection, refined till he is almost translucent
and glassy. He is far more refined than Angel Clare in *Tess*, perfect as a
40   moonstone emitting the white and sacred beam of the spirit and the holy

mind. He is so spiritual and inspired that he becomes impossible, he is a pure lambent flame sucking up and consuming the very life-stuff of mankind. But particularly he sucks up the life-stuff of the woman who loves him. Without this nourishment from her consumed, prostituted being his flame would fade out, for he belongs no more to earth. Unless the woman will be holy prostitute to him, in sacred spiritual love given to him as wax is given to the candle-flame, to be consumed into light, he is done, for his own substance is spent. Therefore the woman gives herself in sacred, virgin prostitution, and is consumed. It is what happens all the time with spiritual clergymen and their female devotees. The true being in woman is prostitute to the ghastly spiritual effulgence.

But not for ever. The hour for revenge comes. Subtly, with extreme serpent subtlety, having been held down and wasted long enough into the spiritual effulgence of Arthur Dimmesdale, the woman in Hester Prynne recoils, turns in rich, lurid revenge. She seduces the saint, and the saint is seduced. Mystically he is killed, as he must be killed. The child born of him is a little serpent, a poison blossom.

Now at last the spiritual era is at an end, but only at the beginning of the end. This is the disaster of disasters, when the woman suddenly recoils from her union with man, and strikes back at him like a serpent, secretly, from an infuriated, tormented primary soul. Through two thousand years man, the leader, has been slaying the dragon of the primary self, the sensual psyche, and the woman has been with him. But the hour of triumph is the hour of the end. In the hour of triumph the slain rises up in revenge, and the destroyer is destroyed.

When Hester Prynne seduces Arthur Dimmesdale, we have the beginning of the end: but not the end, by a long way. In the creative union between man and woman, man must take the lead,* though woman gives the first suggestion. When man, holding woman still in the bond of union, leads into prostitution and death, as man has led all humanity into the nacreous,* sanctified vampiredom of pure spiritual or intellectual being, then the bond of union breaks between the sexes. Then the deep, subconscious, primary self in woman recoils in antagonism. But it is a recoil of long, secret destructiveness, nihilism, subtle, serpent-like, outwardly submissive. Man must either lead or be destroyed. Woman cannot lead. She can only be at one with man, in the creative union, whilst he leads; or, failing this, she can destroy by undermining, by striking the heel of the male. The woman isolate or in advance of man is always mystically destructive. When man falls before woman, and she must become alone and self-responsible,* she

goes on and on in destruction, till all is death or till man can rise anew
and take his place. When the woman takes the responsible place in the
conjunction between man and woman, then the mystic creative union
is reversed, it becomes a union of negation and undoing. Whatever the
5   outward profession and action may be, when woman is the leader or
dominant in the sex relationship, and in the human progress, then the
activity of mankind is an activity of disintegration and undoing. And it
is woman who gives the first suggestion, starts the first impulse of the
undoing.
10   Man falls before woman because he has led on into a ghastly bog of
falsehood. He then clings to the woman like a child, and she becomes
the responsible party. But woe betide her, her triumph is a bitter one.
Every stride she takes is a stride of further death. With all her passion she
cherishes and nourishes her man, and yet her cherishing and nourishing
15   only destroy him more. With all her soul she tries to save life. And the
greatness of her effort only further saps the root of life, weakens the soul
of man, destroys him, and drives him into an insanity of self-destruction.
Such is the Age of Woman. Such it always has been, and always will be.
It is the age of cowardly, false, destructive men. It is the age of fatal,
20   suffocating love, love which kills like a Laocoon snake.
       Woman cannot take the creative lead, she can only give the creative
radiation. From her, as from Eve, must come the first suggestion or
impulse of new being. When however she recoils from man's leadership,
and takes matters in her own hands, she recoils in mystic destruction.
25   She cannot make a beginning, go on ahead. She can only prompt man,
not knowing herself to what she prompts him. When he will not be
prompted, woman becomes a devastating influence. She has no way
of her own. She can only follow in exaggeration the old creed. This
is evident in Hester Prynne. Hester Prynne has struck the blow that
30   will kill for ever the triumphant spiritual being in man. And yet, in
her living, she can only exaggerate the old life of self-abnegation and
spiritual purity. She becomes a sister of mercy.
       This is the puzzling anomaly of the present day. In the old day, when
woman turned in her terrible recoil, she became Astarte, the Syria Dea,
35   Aphrodite Syriaca, the Scarlet Woman. Today in her recoil, the Scarlet
Woman becomes a Sister of Mercy. She cannot help it. She must, in
her upper mind, keep true to the old faith that man has given her, the
belief in love and self-sacrifice. To this she is as it were hypnotised or
condemned. Yet, all the while, her potent self is utterly at outs with this
40   faith and this sacrifice. Darkly, she bites the heel of selfless humanity.

It is the fate of woman, that what she is, she is darkly and helplessly. What woman *knows*, she knows because man has taught it to her. What she *is*, this is another matter. She can never give expression to the profound movements of her own being. These movements can only find an expression through a man. Man is the utterer, woman is the first   5
cause. Whatever God there is,* made it so.

Hester however urges Dimmesdale to go away with her to a new country, to begin a new life. But it is doubtful if she was any more ready for this step than he. When a man responds to the prompting of a woman, towards a new life, he has not only to face the world itself,   10
but a great reaction in the very woman he takes. In her conscious self, woman is almost inhumanly conservative, reactionary. Anna Karenin,* Hester Prynne, Sue in *Jude the Obscure*, these women are never satisfied till they have shattered the man who responded to them. If Dimmesdale had fled with Hester, they would have felt themselves social outcasts.   15
And then, they would have had to live in secret hatred of mankind, like criminal accomplices; or they would have felt isolated, cut off, two lost creatures, a man meaningless except as the agent, or tool, or creature of the possessive woman; and when a man loses his meaning, the woman one way or other destroys him. She kills him by her very possessive   20
love itself. It would have been necessary for Dimmesdale in some way to conquer society with a new spirit and a new idea. And this was impossible. The time was by no means ripe. The old idea must be slowly undermined: slowly and secretly undermined. Dimmesdale, in his confession, struck his blow at the old idea. But he could not survive.   25
And it was for this reason he hated Hester at the last.

She outlived him. But she went on with the work, of secretly undermining the established form of society. Her duplicity was purely unconscious. In all her conscious passion she desired to be pure and good, a true sister of mercy. But the primal soul is inexorable. Hawthorne gives   30
the picture in all its detail, introducing the suggestion of witchcraft. The ancients were not altogether fools in their belief in witchcraft. When the profound, subconscious soul of woman recoils from its creative union with man, it can exert a tremendous invisible destructive influence. This malevolent force can invisibly press upon the sources of life in any   35
hated individual—or perhaps much more so on any loved individual— pressing, sapping, shattering life unknowably at its very sources. There is a terrible effluence from the reactionary human soul, and this effluence acts as a destructive electricity upon the centres of primary life in man, and destroys the flow, the very life itself at those centres. The   40

activity is so intensely powerful, yet so invisible, often even involuntary
on the part of the agent, that it produces ghastly and magical results.
And it is the frenzy of people harried and pressed by the destructive
power emitted from the hateful soul of an individual, woman or man,
5   who is possessed by this reaction against all creative union, that drives
communities into a sudden frenzied seeking for a victim. Then we have
the burning of witches and wizards. No passion of the human soul is
utterly misguided. And the old witch-lady, Mistress Hibbins, claims
Hester as a witch.

10   Hawthorne says of Hester: "She had in her nature a rich voluptuous
oriental characteristic—a taste for the gorgeously beautiful." This is the
aboriginal American principle working in her, the Aztec principle. She
repressed it. Even she would not allow herself the luxury of labouring
at fine, delicate stitchery. But she dressed the little Pearl vividly, and the
15   scarlet letter was gorgeously embroidered. These were her Hecate or
Astarte insignia. For the rest she was the sternest, most ascetic Puritan.

All the while, we can *see* that she is the pivot, the mystic centre of the
most implacable destruction of Dimmesdale, of his white sanctity, and
of his spiritual effulgence; nay, of more than this: she, the grey nurse, the
20   Sister of Mercy and Charity, she was a centre of mystic obstruction to the
creative activity of all life. She destroyed the Puritan being from within.
"The poor, whom she sought out to be the objects of her bounty, often
reviled the hand that was stretched forth to succour them." We know
for ourselves, that her succour was her helpless attempt to cover her
25   implacable hate, and the poor responded intuitively. "She was patient—
a martyr indeed—" Hawthorne continues, "but she forbore to pray for
her enemies, lest, in spite of her forgiving aspirations, the words of the
blessing should stubbornly twist themselves into a curse."

Yet she is not a hypocrite. Only the serpent has turned in her soul.
30   She invests herself in the sternest righteousness, to escape the doom of
her own being. But it is no good. At the very quick she is in revolt, she
is a destroyer, her heart is a source of the malevolent Hecate electricity,
flashing with serpent rays.

"She grew to have a dread of children; for they had imbibed from
35   their parents a vague idea of something horrible in this dreary woman
gliding silently through the town, with never any companion but only
one child."

The Astarte or Hecate principle has in it a necessary antagonism
to life itself, the very issue of life: it contains the elements of blood
40   sacrifice of children, in its darker, destructive mood; just as it worships

procreative child-birth, in its productive mood. The motion from the productive to the destructive activity of the Hecate principle is only a progression in intensity: intensity reached either through triumph and overweening, as in the old religions, or through opposition and repression, as in modern life. 5

"But sometimes, once in many days, or perchance in many months she felt an eye—a human eye—upon the ignominious brand, that seemed to give a momentary relief, as if half her agony were shared. The next instant, back it all rushed again, with a still deeper throb of pain; for in that brief interval, she had sinned again. Had Hester sinned alone?" 10

Hawthorne is a sorcerer, a real seer of darkness. He knows, admittedly, what it is to meet in a crowd two eyes dark with the same instant, dreadful mystery of unfathomable, indomitable destructive passion, eyes that answer in instant mystic deadly understanding, as the eye of a gipsy will sometimes answer, out of a crowd. 15

Hester's real, vital activity, however, lies in her unconscious struggle with Dimmesdale, who is polarised against her in the mystic conjunction and opposition. Once she has destroyed him, her dreadful spirit is more or less appeased. After his death, it comes to pass that the "A" on her breast is said to stand for "Abel".*—There is a devilish unconscious 20 satire—a dream irony—in this also.—She is appeased. But she lives on, a lonely, grey, dreadful woman, one of the shades of the underworld.

She is appeased, but her spirit lives on in Pearl. Pearl is the scarlet letter incarnate, as the book says. There was that in the child "which often impelled Hester to ask, in bitterness of heart, whether it were for 25 good or ill that the poor little creature had been born at all."

In her relation to Pearl, there is the same horrible division in Hester's heart. The child is the scarlet letter incarnate. Once she is compared to the demon of plague or scarlet fever—a demoniacal little creature, in her red dress. Then again she is tender and loving—but always uncertain. 30 The subtle, steely, pallid mockery is never absent from her eyes. The strange Judas principle, of betrayal, of the neutralisation of the one impulsive self against the other, this is purely expressed in Pearl. She can love with clinging tenderness—only that she may draw away and hit the mouth that kisses her, with a mocking laugh. She can hate with 35 dark passion—only to turn again with easy, indifferent friendliness, more insulting than rage. Her principle is the truly deadly principle of betrayal for betrayal's sake—the real demon principle, which just neutralises the sensual impulse with a spiritual gesture, and neutralises the spiritual impulse with a sensual gesture, creates a perfect frustration, 40

neutralisation, and laughs with recurrent mockery. This is the one single
motive of Pearl's being, this motive of neutralisation into nothingness.
And her triumph is in her jeering laugh. In the end, very fitly, she marries
an Italian nobleman. But we are not told whether she outmatched him,
5   or he her, in diabolic opposition.

Hester, inevitably, *hates* something that Pearl is. And as well she
cherishes the child as her one precious treasure. Pearl is the continuing
of her terrible revenge on all life. "The child could not be made amenable
to rules. In giving her existence a great law had been broken; and the
10 result was a being whose elements were perhaps beautiful and brilliant,
but all in disorder, or with an order peculiar to themselves, amidst which
the point of variety and arrangement was difficult or impossible to be
discovered."

This is Hawthorne's diagnosis. He did not choose to discover too
15 much, openly. But he gives us all the data. He goes on to describe
the peculiar look in her eyes—"a look so intelligent, yet inexplicable,
so perverse, sometimes so malicious, but generally accompanied by
a wild flow of spirits, that Hester could not help questioning at such
moments whether Pearl was a human child"—To answer that question,
20 Hester would have had to define what she meant by human. Pearl, by
the very openness of her perversity, was at least straightforward. She
answers downright that she has no Heavenly Father. She mocks and
tortures Dimmesdale* with a subtlety rarer even than her mother's, and
more exquisitely poisonous. But even in this she has a sort of reckless
25 gallantry, the pride of her own deadly being. We cannot help regarding
the phenomenon of Pearl with wonder, and fear, and amazement, and
respect. For surely nowhere in literature is the spirit of much of modern
childhood so profoundly, almost magically revealed.

The triangle of disruption, between Hester and Chillingworth and
30 Dimmesdale, is explicitly drawn. Chillingworth represents the sensual
male being in complete subordination, as we have him in modern life.
His principle is the sensual serpent, full of wisdom, but subjected and
dangerous. It is the subjected, even enslaved sensual male that captures
the representative female: the affinity is between these two. The acci-
35 dents of poverty and the like, which Hawthorne introduces for the sake
of probability, only make up the chain of inevitability. Hester inevitably
marries the learned old Chillingworth, who also is skilled in medicine
and the art of healing. The physician is the deadly hater. The physician
and the Sister of Mercy, these are the dark psyche in revolt, the subtle
40 destroyers. Chillingworth is skilled in the arts of the Golden Hermes,*

Nathaniel Hawthorne 253

Hermes of the Underworld, the undoer. He knows the subtle sensual reactions, such as are contained in the science of magic. He is a twisted old scholar—but potent in the sensual underworld, and diabolic there.

Still, he is humble, subjected—in symbolism, crippled and elderly; he is under the dominion of the triumphant spiritual principle; dominated, cringing, but unsubdued, malevolent in his soul. Francis Bacon is his prototype.

He marries Hester. Outwardly she believes in him as a wise, good old scholar. His taking her is a kind of theft. But inwardly she knows his principle. She enters into a tacit conspiracy—a conspiracy against the spiritual being who dominates them both. At the very beginning, Hester swears an oath of silence to Chillingworth: their oath of allegiance. For they are the two prime conspirators.

"Why dost thou smile so at me?— —Art thou like the Black Man that haunts the forest round about us? Hast thou enticed me into a bond that will prove the ruin of my soul?" Hester asks him.

"Not thy soul!" he answered, with another smile. "No, not thine."

The Black Man of the American forests is the aboriginal spirit of the primary, sensual psyche. The first settlers were all very conscious of this Black Man, their enemy.

Chillingworth, Hester, Dimmesdale, these are the triangle of destruction. Hester has thrown down the spiritual being from his pure pre-eminence. Chillingworth, the physician, the male sensual psyche subjected and turned back in recoil, must proceed with the minister's undoing. It goes on subtly and horribly. And yet Dimmesdale finally robs Chillingworth of the triumph. The spiritual being saves itself by confession upon the scaffold. The end is not yet.

As Chillingworth says: "it is all dark necessity." Yet even he dates the dark necessity from Hester's "sin." It dates from much further back— far back as Christ himself. It dates from the beginning of the triumph of the one half of the psyche, over the other half.

The ruin of Dimmesdale is horrible. He cannot conceive that his fall with Hester is not a sin. The whole world, and his whole psyche would have to be shattered before such a conception could enter. He cannot yield to the woman, commit himself to her, and flee away with her. He still holds his own.

But now there is the torture of his awakened sensual self. What is he to do with this sensual self? The old perfect flow, wherein the lower or primary self flows in gradual sublimation upwards towards a spiritual transmutation and expression is broken. The old circuit of positive spiritual being and negative sensual being is broken for ever. The two halves are in antagonism.

Dimmesdale now hates his body with morbid hate. He lusts to destroy it. He practises horrible secret tortures, wounding himself with
5   thorns, cutting himself with whips, searing himself. It is a common phenomenon, a lust of self-torture. He is the Inquisition unto himself. He has a hideous voluptuous satisfaction in the process. He is his own prostitute.

His vital belief in what he stands for is gone. All that remains is a
10 will to preservation of his appearances. Underneath the most horrible blasphemous mockery sets in.

Right to the very end, Dimmesdale must have his saintly triumphs. He must preach his great Election Sermon, and win his last saintly applause. At the same time he has an almost imbecile, epileptic impulse
15 to defile the religious reality he exists in. In Dimmesdale at this period lies the whole clue to Dostoevsky.*

This saintly minister of New England meets one of his hoary-headed deacons in the road, just before the time of the election sermon, and— "it was only by the most careful self-control that he could refrain from
20 uttering certain blasphemous suggestions that rose into his mind, concerning the communion supper." And again, as an old widow stops him for a word of comfort, he longs to whisper into her ear "a brief, pithy, and as it then appeared to him, unanswerable argument against the immortality of the soul."—Once more, as he sees a girl, "fair and
25 pure as a lily that had bloomed in Paradise", approaching him, he must cover his face in his cloak to pass by, because he knows he could not help giving her one look, full of evil suggestion, that would blight all her innocence.

It is the fatal, imbecile or epileptic state of soul, such as Dostoevsky's,
30 which makes the one half of the psyche malevolently act against the other half, in leering, malignant progress of futility.

In his very last words Dimmesdale is an actor, subtly malevolent and vicious.

"'Shall we not meet again?' whispered she, bending her face down
35 close to his. 'Shall we not spend our immortal life together? Surely, surely we have ransomed one another, with all this woe! Thou looked far into eternity with those bright dying eyes! Then tell me what thou seest!'

"Hush, Hester—hush!" said he, with tremulous solemnity. "The law we broke!—the sin here so awfully revealed!—let these alone be in thy
40 thoughts! I fear! I fear!' "

So, with a last bit of pulpit rhetoric, the perfect exemplar of the spiritual way dies, in America. The pathos, and the malignant satire, in Hawthorne's double language, his perfect, even marvellous exposition of the very deepest soul processes make this book one of the wonder-books of the world. And yet it is somewhat detestable, because of its 5 duplicity. All the way, there is the pious preaching of the conventional creed, on the ostentatious surface, whilst underneath is the lurid lust in sin, the gloating in the overthrow of that which is so praised.

After *The Scarlet Letter*, some of the *Tales* are wonderful in their two-faced reality. *The House of Seven Gables* is again a dark romance of 10 the mystic revenge, mixed with the ugliness of the coming generation, commercial and vulgar. Only the *Blithedale Romance* is really personal.

Here we have Hawthorne's waking reality, touched up with lurid dream-colours. *The Blithedale Romance* is an account, more or less, of the Brook Farm experiment. A number of the most advanced spirits 15 of America, wishing to set the perfect social example, and start the real Utopia, bought a farm, and settled themselves in, a company of advanced transcendentalists, to live in common and till the land and be perfectly at one with all things, through their common labour and their common transcendence in the Oversoul. Hawthorne stood it for a few 20 weeks. Then he shrugged his shoulders and departed.

The Brook Farm experiment is the legitimate descendant of Crèvecoeur's dreams. It is the attempt to work the sensual body from the spiritual centres. But the attempt never works.

The Brook Farmers wanted to triumph purely in the spiritual being: 25 they wanted to be transcendentally at one with all things. Their "social experiment" was a new flight into oneness and perfection. The physical or brute self must be spiritualised by labour in common, the soul must be perfected by bringing the body into line, in a brotherhood of selfless, productive toil. 30

But it was hopeless to introduce brute physical labour. Brute labour, the brute struggle with earth and herds, *must* rouse the dark sensual centres, darken the mind, isolate the being in heavy-blooded separateness. Then there is an end of spiritual oneness and transcendence.

Moreover, the clue to the movement lay in the desire to subject or dis- 35 integrate the primary sensual self. It was an attempt to perform by pleas-ant means what Dimmesdale, in his physical self-tortures, attempted by unpleasant means. The reduction of the primary spontaneous self to pure subordination, however, is never pleasant. And the process of the reduction is a process of disintegration of the primal self. And human 40 beings engaged in the toils of such disintegration must react, sooner or later, against the spiritual bond of union that is superimposed. So the Brook Farm experiment was a failure.

The individuals of the *Blithedale Romance* present a four-square
5   group, of two triangles. There are two men: Hawthorne, the I, the re-fined spiritual being, comparable to Dimmesdale; then Hollingsworth, the deep-voiced, ex-blacksmith, the patron of criminals; then Zenobia, superb, like Hester Prynne, or like Judith Hutter; and fourthly a white lily, a white weed of a sickly lily, called Priscilla, a little forlorn semp-
10 stress who turns out to be half-sister to the rich, superb Zenobia, just as Hetty Hutter was sister to Judith, or the White Lily was sister to Cora.

Now all these four are idealists, creatures of the spiritual one way. And they are all secretly seeking for the sensual satisfaction. Hawthorne is the spiritual being secretly worshipping the sensual mysteries, the
15 next generation after Dimmesdale. Hollingsworth is a descendant of Chillingworth: a dark, black-bearded monomaniac. His monomania is criminals: his one end in life is to build an asylum for criminals, of which he will be the head, the reformer. This Hephaestos of the un-derworld stubbornly adheres to his spiritual assertion. He will reform
20 all criminals. But his passion, it is obvious, is to be in communion with criminals. Potentially a criminal, the actual criminals of the state fix him like a lode-stone. He is Chillingworth without Chillingworth's intellect: Chillingworth more subject than ever, but criminally polarised.

The criminal is the man who, like Roger Chillingworth, is abject and
25 down-trodden in his sensual self, by the spiritual or social domination, and who turns round secretly on life, to bite it and poison it and mutilate it. There is a genuine *passion* at the bottom of the ultra-social individual, for criminal gratification. De Quincey in his essay on "Murder as a Fine Art", reveals this terrible reality. And this passion is Hollingsworth's
30 passion. But he maintains his spiritual dominion, and seeks to gratify his passion, and vindicate his triumphal spiritual being, in *reforming* criminals.

The connection between the two men is like that between Dimmes-dale and Chillingworth. Hawthorne falls sick at Brook Farm, and
35 Hollingsworth nurses him. There is a strong love and blood-tenderness between the two men. Hawthorne, helpless and passive between the strong, but unspeakably gentle hands of the blacksmith, is lulled in sheer sense-gratification.

But his love turns to hate. Hollingsworth wants absolute, monoma-
40 niac dominion over him, to use him. And Hawthorne will not be either dominated or used. After all, he is the finer and stronger soul of the

two. And he detests and despises the monomaniac blacksmith, who has really a lust to consume and use the other man. He is like Chillingworth, who heals in order to consume his partner.

Then there is the criss-cross of love between the men and women. Hawthorne admires, even loves the superb Zenobia, with the exotic flower in her hair, but he has no real *desire* for her. Hollingsworth also seems to love Zenobia. But he does not love her. He hates her, really. He only wants her money. Zenobia would outmatch Hollingsworth in the sensual conflict. She would beat him at his own game. The serpent in her is stronger than the serpent in him. And for this he hates her. He needs to be predominant, because, actually, he is the sensual-subjugate being, and he craves to arrogate.

Zenobia, however, loves Hollingsworth madly. She has a sister-love for Hawthorne. They understand each other. Hollingsworth almost marries her, for her money, for his criminal scheme. But poor Zenobia drowns herself.

Priscilla, the little frail sempstress, captures both men. This white, weak, ingenuous little creature has been used as a spiritualistic medium in the public shows that were then the rage in America. She has been veiled in a white veil, set on a public platform, and made to answer, as a medium, the questions of a ghastly corrupt person who turns out to be Zenobia's unconfessed husband.

Priscilla is interesting as a phenomenon. She is a real "medium". In this, she is almost like a degenerate descendant of Ligeia. Ligeia triumphs in her unspeakable submissiveness to the man, her husband. She is the passive pole of his love.

Now if we carry this process of unutterable passivity, and destructive submission, a little further, we go beyond death, and we get the little "medium", Priscilla. In Priscilla, the mystic seal of integrity, the integrity of being, is broken. She is strictly a thing, a mystic prostitute, or an imbecile. She has no being, no true waking reality, only a sleeping, automatic reality.

The covering her up with the white veil symbolises the abstracting of the upper or wakeful consciousness, leaving the under dream-consciousness free and active. It is the same as the clairvoyant gazing into the crystal. The gazing into the crystal is a process of annulling or abstracting the whole wakening consciousness, leaving the mechanical dream-consciousness in possession of the being. But in the wakeful consciousness the *being* has its presence. By destroying this consciousness—and it is a process of destruction, not of suspension, as in sleep—the core and centre and pivot of the being is gradually destroyed, and the being

becomes a thing, an incontestably marvellous *transmitter*, like a telephone apparatus, of the great *natural mechanical* vibrations in the ether,
vibrations of mechanical cause and effect. Priscilla, covered with the
veil, is abstracted from conscious being—she is a pure passive medium.
5 The director puts the questions, not to her mind, but automatically, to
her sensory-conscious *mechanical* reason. And, as a little unutterably
delicate machine, she answers automatically. There is no correspondence of telepathy or thought transmission, or even mesmerism. It is a
process of after-death, when the being is annulled, and the unimaginably
10 sensitive sensory machine remains vibrating in the flow of the great invisible forces, mechanical, psychic, animistic, the uttermost spiritualism
of material being. The whole process, however, is so inordinately delicate
and difficult, that the base tricks of mesmerism and thought transmission must form the greatest part of any public show—No medium, no
15 clairvoyant, however, can, granted the maximum of success, transmit
more than the *mechanical* possibilities of past, present, or future, those
things which depend on cause and effect, in the mechanical or causal
world. In the spontaneous or creative world, they do not exist—they
have forfeited existence. They are things,—not beings.
20   Now both men love Priscilla—Hawthorne confesses it at the very
end of his book, pops it out as if it were some wonderful secret. But
Hollingsworth gets her: she marries him: and they live in a little cottage,
and he walks, leaning on her arm, queer and aged.
    It is inevitable that both men should love Priscilla. She is the only
25 being who will so submit to them, as to give them the last horrible thrills
of sensual experience, in the direct *destruction* of the sensual body, pure
prostitution. Priscilla, passive, mediumistic, almost imbecile, is profoundly strong. Once the real living integrity of being is broken in
her, once she becomes will-less, she is stronger, less destructible than
30 any living being. Will-less, clinging, unspeakably passive, she forms,
almost like an imbecile, a pole of obscene negative passion. Towards
her the overweening sensual electricity runs in violent destructive flow,
the flow of not-being. It destroys at the very quick the correspondent.
Hollingsworth, the powerful dark blacksmith, becomes quite soon tot-
35 tering and shaky, when he has married Priscilla—and she is stronger,
alert, active. In her last mystery of not-being, the dream existence,
the somnambulist, mechanical, infernal reality such as is suggested by
the old legends of were-wolves and metamorphoses, she is established
and triumphant, and, by her very presence, almost without contact,
40 she so draws the vital electricity from the male, in a horrible sensual-
disintegrative flow, that she destroys his being as by magic. This is the

meaning of the were-wolf, and witch stories. Apuleius, with his metamorphoses, and Petronius, with his *Satyricon*,* these are not so very different, in *substance*, from Hawthorne. The obscene metamorphoses of beings into elementals and hell-principles is described more perfectly, though less explicitly, in Priscilla and Dimmesdale, and Pearl, than in these old authors.

Hollingsworth *wants* this obscene polarity with the almost imbecile Priscilla, a polarity in sheer disintegration into nought. His sensual sensations are those that he desires—the acute sensual-electric experience in the sacral ganglion. It is an experience that immediately suggests the crackling and sparkling of electricity from a battery in which it is generated. And this acute vibratory motion is set up intensely in the sacral region of the nerves of the human being, in the last processes of mystic disintegration out of being. The last lust is for this indescribable sensation—whose light we can see in the eyes of a tiger, or a wolf.

VIII.

The Two Principles.

After Hawthorne come the books of the sea. In Dana and Herman Melville the human relationship is no longer the chief interest. The sea
5 enters as the great protagonist.

The sea is a cosmic element, and the relation between the sea and the human psyche is impersonal and elemental. The sea that we dream of, the sea that fills us with hate or with bliss, is a primal* influence upon us beyond the personal range.

10 We need to find some terms to express such elemental connections as between the ocean and the human soul. We need to put off our personality, even our individuality, and enter the region of the elements.

There certainly does exist a subtle and complex sympathy, correspondence, between the plasm* of the human body, which is identical with the
15 primary human psyche, and the material elements outside. The primary human psyche is a complex plasm, which quivers, sense-conscious, in contact with the circumambient cosmos. Our plasmic psyche is radioactive,* connecting with all things, and having first-knowledge of all things.

20 The religious systems of the pagan world did what Christianity has never tried to do: they gave the true correspondence between the material cosmos and the human soul. The ancient cosmic theories were exact, and apparently perfect. In them science and religion were in accord.

When we postulate a beginning, we only do so to fix a starting-point
25 for our thought. There never was a beginning, and there never will be an end of the universe. The creative mystery, which is life itself, always was and always will be.* It unfolds itself in pure living creatures.

Following the obsolete language, we repeat that in the beginning was the creative reality, living and substantial, although apparently void
30 and dark. The living cosmos divided itself, and there was Heaven and Earth: by which we mean, not the sky and the terrestrial globe, for the Earth was still void and dark; but an inexplicable first duality, a division in the cosmos. Between the two great valves* of the primordial universe, moved "the Spirit of God," one unbroken and indivisible
35 heart of creative being. So that, as two great wings that are spread, the

260

living cosmos stretched out the first Heaven and the first Earth, terms of the inexplicable primordial duality.

Then the Spirit of God moved upon the face of the Waters.* As no "waters" are yet created, we may perhaps take the mystic "Earth" to be the same as the Waters. The mystic Earth is the cosmic Waters, and   5
the mystic Heaven the dark cosmic Fire. The Spirit of God, moving between the two great cosmic principles, the mysterious universal dark Waters and the invisible, unnameable cosmic Fire, brought forth the first created apparition, Light. From the darkness of primordial fire, and the darkness of primordial waters; light is born, through the intermediacy   10
of creative presence.

Surely this is true, scientifically, of the birth of light.*

After this, the waters are divided by the firmament.* If we conceive of the first division in Chaos, so-called, as being perpendicular, the inexplicable division into the first duality, then this next division, when   15
the line of the firmament is drawn, we can consider as horizontal: thus we have the ⊕, the elements of the Rosy Cross,* and the first enclosed appearance of that tremendous symbol, which has dominated our era, the Cross itself.

The universe at the end of the Second Day of Creation* is, therefore,   20
as the Rosy Cross, a fourfold division. The mystic Heaven, the cosmic dark Fire is not spoken of. But the firmament of light divides the waters of the unfathomable heights from the unfathomable deeps of the other half of chaos, the still unformed earth: These strange unfathomable waters breathe back and forth, as the earliest Greek philosophers say,*   25
from one realm to the other.

Central within the fourfold division is the creative reality itself, like the body of a four-winged bird. It has thrown forth from itself two great wings of opposite Waters, two great wings of opposite Fire. Then the universal motion begins, the cosmos begins to revolve, the eternal flight   30
is launched.

Changing the metaphors and attending to the material universe only, we may say that sun and space are now born. Those waters and that dark fire which are drawn together in the creative spell impinge into one centre in the sun; those waters and that fire which flee asunder in   35
the creative spell form space.

So that we have a fourfold division in the cosmos, and a fourfold travelling. We have the waters under the firmament and the waters above the firmament: we have the fire to the left hand and the fire to the right hand of the firmament; and we have each travelling back and   40

forth across the firmament. Which means, scientifically, that invisible
waters steal towards the sun, right up to feed the sun; whilst new waters
are shed away from the sun, into space; whilst invisible dark fire rolls
its waves to the sun, and new fire floods out into space. The sun is the
5   great mystery-centre where the invisible fires and the invisible waters
roll together, brought together in the magnificence of the creative spell
of opposition, to wrestle and consummate in the formation of the orb of
light. Night, on the other hand, is Space presented to our consciousness,
that space or infinite which is the travelling asunder of the primordial
10 elements, and which we recognise in the living darkness.

So the ancient cosmology, always so perfect theoretically, becomes,
by the help of our scientific knowledge, physically, actually perfect. The
great fourfold division, the establishment of the Cross, which has so
thrilled the soul of man from ages far back before Christianity, far back
15 in pagan America as well as in the Old World, becomes real to our reason
as well as to our instinct.

Cosmology, however, considers only the creation of the material universe, and according to the scientific idea life itself is but a product of
reactions in the material universe. This is palpably wrong.

20 When we repeat that on the First Day of Creation God made Heaven
and Earth we do not suggest that God disappeared between the two
great valves of the cosmos once these were created. Yet this is the modern, scientific attitude. Science supposes that once the first forces was
in existence, and the first motion set up, the universe produced itself
25 automatically, throwing off life as a by-product, at a certain stage.

It is such an idea which has brought about the materialisation and
emptiness of life. When God made Heaven and Earth, that is, in the
beginning when the unthinkable living cosmos divided itself, God did
not disappear. If we try to conceive of God, in this instance, we must
30 conceive some homogeneous rare *living* plasm, a *living* self-conscious
ether, which filled the universe. The living ether divided itself as an
egg-cell divides. There is a mysterious duality, life divides itself, and
yet life is indivisible. When life divides itself, there is no division in life.
It is a new life-state, a new being which appears. So it is when an egg
35 divides. There is no split in life. Only a new life-stage is created. This
is the eternal oneness and magnificence of life, that it moves creatively
on in progressive being, each state of being whole, integral, complete.

But as life moves on in creative singleness, its substance divides and
subdivides into multiplicity. When the egg divides itself, a new stage
40 of creation is reached, a new oneness of living being; but there appears

also a new differentiation in inanimate substance. From the new life-being a new motion takes place: the inanimate reacts in its pure polarity, and a third stage of creation is reached. Life has now achieved a third state of being, a third creative singleness appears in the universe; and at the same time, inanimate substance has re-divided and brought forth 5 from itself a new creation in the material world.

So creation goes on. At each new impulse from the creative body, All comes together with All: that is, the one half of the cosmos comes together with the other half, with a dual result. First issues the new oneness, the new singleness, the new life-state, the new being, the new 10 individual; and secondly, from the locked opposition of inanimate dual matter, another singleness is born, another creation takes place, new matter, a new chemical element appears. Dual all the time is the creative activity: first comes forth the living apparition of new being, the perfect and indescribable singleness; and this embodies the single beauty of a 15 new substance, gold or chlorine or sulphur.* So it has been since time began. The gems of being were created simultaneously with the gems of matter, the latter inherent in the former.

Every new thing is born from the consummation of the two halves of the universe, the two great halves being the cosmic waters and the 20 cosmic fire of the First Day. In procreation, the two germs of the male and female epitomise the two cosmic principles, as these are held within the life-spell. In the sun and the material waters the two principles exist as independent elements. Life-plasm mysteriously corresponds with inanimate matter. But life-plasm, in that it lives, is itself identical with 25 being, inseparable from the singleness of a living being, the indivisible oneness.

Life can never be produced or made. Life is an unbroken oneness, indivisible. The mystery of creation is that new and indivisible being appears forever within the oneness of life. 30

In the cosmic theories of the creation of the world it has been customary for science to treat of life as a product of the material universe, whilst religion treats of the material universe as having been deliberately created by some will or idea, some sheer abstraction. Surely the universe has arisen from some universal living self-conscious plasm, 35 plasm which has no origin and no end, but is life eternal and identical, bringing forth the infinite creatures of being and existence, living creatures embodying inanimate substance. There is no utterly immaterial existence, no spirit. The distinction is between living plasm and inanimate matter. Inanimate matter is released from the dead body of the 40 world's creatures. It is the static residue of the living conscious plasm, like feathers of birds.

When the living cosmos divided itself, on the First Day, then the living plasm became twofold, twofold supporting a new state of single-
5   ness, new being; at the same time, the twofold living plasm contained the finite duality of the two unliving, material cosmic elements. In the transmutation of the plasm, in the interval of death, the inanimate elements are liberated into separate existence. The inanimate material universe is born through death from the living universe, to co-exist
10 with it for ever.

We know that in its essence the living plasm is twofold. In the same way the dynamic elements of material existence are dual, the fire and the water. These two cosmic elements are pure mutual opposites, and on their opposition the material universal is established. The attraction
15 of the two, mutually opposite, sets up the revolution of the universe and forms the blazing heart of the sun. The sun is formed by the impinging of the cosmic water upon the cosmic fire, in the stress of opposition. This causes the central blaze of the universe.

In the same way, mid-way, the lesser worlds are formed, as the two
20 universal elements become entangled, swirling on their way to the great central conjunction. The core of the worlds and stars is a blaze of the two elements as they rage interlocked into consummation. And from the fiery and moist consummation of the two elements all the material substances are finally born, perfected.

25   This goes on however, mechanically now, according to fixed, physical laws. The plasm of life, the state of living potentiality exists still central, as the body of a bird between the wings, and spontaneously brings forth the living forms we know. Ultimately, or primarily, the creative plasm has no laws. But as it takes form and multiple wonderful being, it keeps
30 up a perfect law-abiding relationship with that other half of itself, the material inanimate universe. And the first and greatest law of creation is that all creation, even life itself, exists within the strange and incalculable balance of the two elements. In the living creature, fire and water must exquisitely balance, commingle, and consummate, this in continued
35 mysterious process.

So we must look for life midway between fire and water. For where fire is purest, this is a sign that life has withdrawn itself, and is withheld. And the same with water. For by pure water we do not mean that bright liquid rain or dew or fountain stream. Water in its purest is water most
40 abstracted from fire, as fire in its purest must be abstracted from water.

And so, water becomes more essential as we progress through the rare crystals of snow and ice, on to that infinitely suspended invisible element which travels between us and the sun,* inscrutable water such as life can know nothing of, for where it is, all life has long ceased to be. This is the true cosmic element. Our material water, as our fire, is still a mixture of fire and water.

It may be argued that water is proved to be a chemical compound, composed of two gases, hydrogen and oxygen. But is it not more true that hydrogen and oxygen are the first naked products of the two parent-elements, water and fire. In all our efforts to decompose water we do but introduce fire into the water, in some naked form or other, and this introduction of naked fire into naked water *produces* hydrogen and oxygen, given the proper conditions of chemical procreation. Hydrogen and oxygen are the first-fruits of fire and water. This is the alchemistic air.* But from the conjunction of fire and water within the living plasm arose the first matter, the Prima Materia* of a living body, which, in its dead state, is the alchemistic Earth.

Thus, at the end of what is called the Second Day of Creation, the alchemistic Four Elements of Earth, Air, Fire, and Water have come into existence: the Air and the Earth born from the conjunction of Fire and Water within the creative plasm. Air is a final product. Earth is the incalculable and indefinable residuum of the living plasm. All other substance is born by the mechanical consummation of fire and water within this Earth. So no doubt it is the fire and water of the swirling universe, acting upon that Earth or dead plasm which results at the end of each life-phase, that has brought the solid globes into being, invested them with rock and metal.

The birth of the chemical elements from the grain of Earth, through the consummation of fire with water, is as magical, as incalculable as the birth of men. For from the material consummation may come forth a superb and enduring element, such as gold or platinum, or such strange, unstable elements as sulphur or phosphorus, phosphorus, a sheer apparition of water, and sulphur a netted flame. In phosphorus the watery principle is so barely held that at a touch the mystic union will break, whilst sulphur only waits to depart into fire. Bring these two unstable elements together, and a slight friction will cause them to burst spontaneously asunder, fire leaping out; or the phosphorus will pass off in watery smoke. The natives of Zoruba, in West Africa, having the shattered fragments of a great pagan culture in their memory, call sulphur the dung of thunder:* the fire-dung, undigested excrement of the fierce consummation between the upper waters and the invisible fire.

The cosmic elements, however, have a twofold direction. When they move together, in the mystic attraction of mutual unknowing, then, in

5   some host, some grain of Earth, or some grain of living plasm, they embrace and unite and the fountain of creation springs up, a new substance, or a new life-form. But there is also the great centrifugal motion, when the two flee asunder into space, into infinitude.

This fourfold activity is the root-activity of the universe. We have first

10 the mystic dualism of pure otherness, that which science will not admit, and which Christianity has called "the impious doctrine of the two principles."* This dualism extends through everything, even through the *soul* or *self* or *being* of any living creature. The self or soul is single, unique, and undivided, the gem of gems, the flower of flowers, the ful-

15 filment of the universe. Yet *within* the self, which is single, the principle of dualism reigns. And then, consequent upon this principle of dual *otherness*, comes the scientific dualism of polarity.

So we have in creation the two life-elements coming together within the living plasm, coming together softly and sweetly, the kiss of angels

20 within the glimmering place. Then newly created life, new being arises. There comes a time, however, when the two life-elements go asunder, after the being has perfected itself. Then there is the seething and struggling of inscrutable life-disintegration. The individual form disappears, but the being remains implicit within the intangible life-plasm.

25 Parallel to this, in the material universe we have the productive coming-together of water and fire, to make the sun of light, the rainbow, and the perfect elements of Matter. Or we have the slow activity in disintegration, when substances resolve back towards the universal Prima Materia, primal inanimate ether.

30 Thus all creation depends upon the fourfold activity. And on this root of four is all law and understanding established. Following the perception of these supreme truths, the Pythagoreans made their philosophy, asserting that all is number, and seeking to search out the mystery of the roots of three, four, five, seven,* stable throughout all the universe,

35 in a chain of developing phenomena. But our science of mathematics still waits for its fulfilment, its union with life itself. For the truths of mathematics are only the skeleton fabric of the living universe.

Only symbolically do the numbers still live for us. In religion we still accept the four Gospel Natures, the four Evangels, with their symbols

40 of man, eagle, lion, and bull, symbols parallel to the Four Elements,

and to the Four Activities, and to the Four Natures.* And the Cross, the epitome of all this fourfold division, still stirs us to the depths with unaccountable emotions, emotions which go much deeper than personality and the Christ drama.

The ancients said that their cosmic symbols had a sevenfold or a fivefold reference.* The simplest symbol, the divided circle, ⵁ, stands not only for the first division in the living cosmos and for the two cosmic elements, but also, within the realms of created life, for the sex mystery; then for the mystery of dual psyche, sensual and spiritual, within the individual being; then for the duality of thought and sensation—and so on, or otherwise, according to varying exposition. Having such a clue, we can begin to find the meanings of the Rosy Cross, the ⊕; and for the ankh, the famous Egyptian symbol, called the symbol of life, the cross or Tau beneath the circle ⚨,* the soul undivided resting upon division; and for the so-called symbol of Aphrodite, the circle resting upon the complete cross, ♀.* These symbols too have their multiple reference, deep and far-reaching, embracing the cosmos and the indivisible soul, as well as the mysteries of function and production. How foolish it is to give these great signs a merely phallic indication!

The sex division is one of the Chinese three sacred mysteries.* Vitally, it is a division of pure otherness, pure dualism. It is one of the first mysteries of creation. It is parallel with the mystery of the first division in chaos, and with the dualism of the two cosmic elements. This is not to say that the one sex is identical with fire, the other with water. And yet there is some indefinable connection. Aphrodite born of the waters,* and Apollo the sun-god, these give some indication of the sex distinction. It is obvious, however, that some races, men and women alike, derive from the sun and have the fiery principle predominant in their constitution, whilst some, blonde, blue-eyed, northern, are evidently water-born,* born along with the ice-crystals and blue, cold deeps, and yellow, ice-refracted sunshine. Nevertheless, if we must imagine the most perfect clue to the eternal waters, we think of woman, and of man as the most perfect premiss of fire.

Be that as it may, the duality of sex, the mystery of creative *otherness*, is manifest, and given the sexual polarity, we have the fourfold motion. The coming-together of the sexes may be the soft, delicate union of pure creation, or it may be the tremendous conjunction of opposition, a vivid struggle, as fire struggles with water in the sun. From either of these consummations birth takes place. But in the first case it is the birth of a softly rising and budding soul, wherein the two principles

commune in gentle union, so that the soul is harmonious and at one with itself. In the second case it is the birth of a disintegrative soul, wherein the two principles wrestle in their eternal opposition: a soul finite, momentaneous, active in the universe as a unit of sundering. The
5   first kind of birth takes place in the youth of an era, in the mystery of accord; the second kind preponderates in the times of disintegration, the crumbling of an era. But at all times beings are born from the two ways, and life is made up of the duality.

The latter way, however, is a way of struggle into separation, isola-
10 tion, psychic disintegration. It is a continual process of sundering and reduction, each soul becoming more mechanical and apart, reducing the great fabric of co-ordinate human life. In this struggle the sexes act in the polarity of antagonism or mystic opposition, the so-called sensual polarity, bringing tragedy. But the struggle is progressive. And then at
15 last the sexual polarity breaks. The sexes have no more dynamic connection, only a habitual or deliberate connection. The spell is broken. They are not balanced any more even in opposition.

But life depends on duality and polarity. The duality, the polarity now asserts itself within the individual psyche. Here, in the individual,
20 the fourfold creative activity takes place. Man is divided, according to old-fashioned phraseology, into the upper and lower man: that is, the spiritual and sensual being. And this division is physical and actual. The upper body, breast and throat and face, this is the spiritual body; the lower is the sensual.

25 By spiritual being we mean that state of being where the self excels into the universe, and knows all things by passing into all things. It is that blissful consciousness which glows upon the flowers and trees and sky, so that I am sky and flowers, I, who am myself. It is that movement towards a state of infinitude wherein I experience my living oneness
30 with all things.

By sensual being, on the other hand, we mean that state in which the self is the magnificent centre wherein all life pivots, and lapses, as all space passes into the core of the sun. It is a magnificent central positivity, wherein the being sleeps upon the strength of its own reality, as a wheel
35 sleeps in speed on its positive hub.* It is a state portrayed in the great dark statues of the seated lords of Egypt.* The self is incontestable and unsurpassable.

Through the gates of the eyes and nose and mouth and ears, through the delicate ports of the fingers, through the great window of the
40 yearning breast, we pass into our oneness with the universe, our great

extension of being, towards infinitude. But in the lower part of the body there is darkness and pivotal pride. There in the abdomen the contiguous universe is drunk into the blood, assimilated, as a wheel's great speed is assimilated into the hub. There the great whirlpool of the dark blood revolves and assimilates all unto itself. Here is the world of living 5 dark waters, where the fire is quenched in watery creation. Here, in the navel, flowers the water-born lotus,* the soul of the water begotten by one germ of fire. And the lotus is the symbol of our perfected sensual first-being, which rises in blossom from the unfathomable waters.

In the feet we rock like the lotus, rooted in the under-mud of earth. 10 In the knees, in the thighs we sway with the dark motion of the flood, darkly water-conscious, like the thick, strong, swaying stems of the lotus that mindlessly answer the waves. It is in the lower body that we are chiefly blood-conscious.

For we assert that the blood has a perfect but untranslatable con- 15 sciousness of its own, a consciousness of weight, of rich, down-pouring motion, of powerful self-positivity. In the blood we have our strongest self-knowledge, our most powerful dark conscience. The ancients said the heart was the seat of understanding. And so it is: it is the seat of the primal sensual understanding, the seat of the passional self- 20 consciousness.

In the nerves, on the other hand, we pass out and become the universe. But even this is dual. It seems as if from the tremendous sympathetic centres of the breast there ran out a fine, silvery emanation from the self, a fine silvery seeking which finds the universe, and by means of 25 which we *become* the universe, we have our extended being. On the other hand, it seems as if in the great solar plexus of the abdomen were a dark whirlwind of pristine force, drawing, whirling all the world darkly into itself, not concerned to look out, or to consider beyond itself. It is from this perfect self-centrality that the lotus of the navel is born, 30 according to Oriental symbolism.

But beyond the great centres of breast and bowels, there is a deeper and higher duality. There are the wonderful plexuses of the face, where our being runs forth into space and finds its vastest realisation; and there is the great living plexus of the loins, there where deep calls to deep. 35 All the time, there is some great incomprehensible balance between the upper and the lower centres, as when the kiss of the mouth accompanies the passionate embrace of the loins. In the face we live our glad life of seeing, perceiving, we pass in delight to our greater being, when we are one with all things. The face and breast belong to the heavens, the 40

luminous infinite. But in the loins we have our unbreakable root, the root of the lotus. There we have our passionate self-possession, our unshakable and indomitable being. There deep calls unto deep. There in the sexual passion the very blood surges into communion, in the
5   terrible sensual oneing. There all the darkness of the deeps, the primal flood, is perfected, as the two great waves of separated blood surge to consummation, the dark infinitude.

When there is balance in first-being between the breast and belly, the loins and face, then, and only then, when this fourfold consciousness
10 is established within the body, then, and only then, do we come to full consciousness in the mind. For the mind is again the single in creation, perfecting its finite thought and idea as the chemical elements are perfected into finality from the flux. The mind brings forth its gold and its gems, finite beyond duality. So we have the sacred pentagon,*
15 with the mind as the conclusive apex.

In the body, however, as in all creative forms, there is the dual polarity as well as the mystic dualism of *otherness*. The great sympathetic activity of the human system has the opposite pole in the voluntary system. The front part of the body is open and receptive, the great valve to the
20 universe. But the back is sealed, closed. And it is from the ganglia of the spinal system that the *will* acts in direct compulsion, outwards.

The great plexuses of the breast and face act in the motion of oneing, from these the soul goes forth in the spiritual oneing. Corresponding to this, the thoracic ganglion and the cervical ganglia are the great
25 centres of spiritual compulsion or control or dominion, the great *second* or negative activity of the spiritual self. From these ganglia go forth the motions and commands which *force* the external universe into that state which accords with the spiritual will-to-unification, the will for equality. Equality, and religious agreement, and social virtue are enforced as
30 well as found. And it is from the ganglia of the upper body that this compulsion to equality and virtue is enforced.

In the same way, from the lumbar ganglion and from the sacral ganglion acts the great sensual will to dominion. From these centres the soul goes forth haughty and indomitable, seeking for mastery. These
35 are the great centres of activity in soldiers, fighters: as also in the tiger and the cat the power-centre is at the base of the spine, in the sacral ganglion. All the tremendous sense of power and mastery is located in these centres of volition, there where the back is walled and strong, set blank against life. These are the centres of negative polarity of our
40 first-being.

So the division of the psychic body is fourfold. If we are divided horizontally at the diaphragm, we are divided also perpendicularly. The upright division gives us our polarity, our for and against, our mystery of right and left.

Any man who is perfect and fulfilled lives in fourfold activity. He knows the sweet spiritual communion, and he is at the same time a sword to enforce the spiritual level; he knows the tender unspeakable sensual communion, but he is a tiger against anyone who would abate his pride and his liberty.

IX.

Dana.

Richard Henry Dana was the son of an American littérateur of the same
name, and grandson of Francis Dana, once United States Minister to
5 Russia, and Chief Justice for Massachusetts.* From this cultured and
distinguished family came the author of *Two Years Before the Mast*.
The young Dana went to Harvard, at the age of seventeen, in the
year 1832. After two years of study, an affection* of the eyes caused him
to leave the university, and turn to the sea. At the age of nineteen he
10 shipped as an ordinary sea-man on a small sailing vessel trading with the
then remote, hardly known California. He returned from this trading
voyage in 1836. And his book is an account of his experiences. On his
return, he went back to Harvard, graduated in 1837, and rose eventually
to be one of the most distinguished of American advocates. In 1879 he
15 was nominated Minister to England; but the senate refused to confirm
the appointment. He died at Rome in 1882. Such are the barest facts
concerning the author of *Two Years Before the Mast*.

The book itself is a simple, direct record of the two years spent at sea
and on the western coast. There is no apparent brilliance or profundity
20 about it. Yet it makes the deepest impression on the mind and soul.

Fenimore Cooper ran away to sea. But Cooper, like Marryatt,* became
a naval officer. Dana did not run away. He deliberately chose to go as
a labouring sea-man on a small sailing vessel. He had no thought to
distinguish himself as an officer and a gentleman. Distinction for Dana
25 lay in serving with the working men as one of themselves. This was the
first part of his achievement.

The ostensible reason for going to sea was for the sake of his eyes.
The second purpose was to achieve that oneness with labouring men,
the desire of which often afflicts gentlemen like a nostalgia. It is the
30 effort to escape from the over-conscious way of life, into the mindless
spontaneity of physical being. This passion for return to the dark blood-
consciousness is at the back of the Brook Farm experiment, and of
Tolstoi's teaching, as well as of Dana's adventure. But Dana was no
theorist, no experimentalist. Herein lies his beauty. He acts as a man
35 who follows his own intention simply, not as an apostle and example to

other men. So we have the marvellous plainness of the record, a beauty much deeper than any impassioned appeal. The perfect singleness of the man is his greatness.

But Dana does not seek only to make a return to the mindless physical spontaneity of the common sea-men. He has a last and a profounder purpose. He must achieve another conquest, a still further conquest of the self. The great impersonal deeps of the sensual self lie still unsubdued in him. The unfathomable world of waters of his deepest soul surges still beyond him, out of control. So he seeks the conquest of the sea, he pits himself against the oceans that are the cosmic body of his own sensual deeps.

Thus we have the phenomenon of the cultured young American working as a barefoot seaman before the mast, with a soul all the while profoundly, mystically active. His great goal is not the mindless return: it is the still further conquest of the lower self by the upper self, the subjection of the most profound, elemental impersonal being of his own soul, to the higher, perfected consciousness. There is no renegade in Dana. He is an ascetic priest. What the great mystics like St. John practised two thousand years ago, esoterically, Dana puts now into exoteric practice, in common life. It is a process of passional asceticism, and of supreme impersonal conflict. It is the conquest of the greatest, deepest centre of the sensual first-being.

Though Dana becomes one of the laboring seamen, the difference between him and them remains always absolute. They have lapsed into the mindless, fatal spontaneity of the deepest sensual being, a state of impersonal existence on the edge of oblivion. Dana follows too to the edge of human oblivion, to the brink of not-being, elemental, soulless. But he goes to such extreme only to master the extreme, as men climb inaccessible mountains. At the brink of passional dissolution he is conscious, deliberate, purposeful, he plants the flag of the triumphant human spirit so that it waves over the gulf of the pit, triumphant over the unfathomable deeps where the waste waters of pre-creation, or post-creation, surge elemental.

He battles with the naked waters of the Beginning and the End, the deeps of the old mystics. *There is sorrow on the sea; it cannot be quiet.** The sea is the great bitter waters of the End, the resolving asunder of the two Principles, even to the last extremity. The great waters of the Beginning are the invisible sweet waters, which mate with fire in the creative spell. The waters of the sea are the unspeakable going-asunder of the elements.

"Nothing will compare," writes Dana in the first days of the voyage, "with the *early breaking of day* upon the wide, sad ocean. There is something in the first grey streaks stretching along the eastern horizon, and throwing an indistinct light upon the face of the deep, which creates 5   a feeling of loneliness, of dread, and of melancholy foreboding, which nothing else in nature can give."—So Dana sees the dawn of the end, that dawn wherein man conquers the last wild deeps of his own being, conquers into death. He sees the naked watery universe of the *end*, where being is not; the shadow of the Last Day, or rather the penultimate day 10 of decreation, the last revelation of the sadly moving light.

Over this waste hovers the human soul, the human consciousness, the bird above the flood. This last flight of the human psyche, its mystic loneliness upon the face of the elemental deeps of being, are perfectly and unconsciously symbolised in the passage about the albatross. The 15 vessel has just rounded Cape Horn.

"This day", he writes, "we saw the last of the Albatrosses, which had been our companions for a great part of the time off the Cape. I had been interested in the bird from descriptions I had read of it, and was not at all disappointed. We caught one or two with a baited hook 20 which we floated astern upon a shingle. Their long flapping wings, long legs, and large staring eyes, give them a very peculiar appearance. They look well on the wing; but one of the finest sights that I have ever seen was an albatross asleep upon the water, during a calm, off Cape Horn, when a heavy sea was running. There being no breeze, the surface of 25 the water was unbroken, but a long, heavy swell was rolling, and we saw the fellow, all white, directly ahead of us, asleep upon the waves, with his head under his wing; now rising upon the top of a huge billow, and then falling slowly until he was lost in the hollow between. He was undisturbed for some time, until the noise of our bows, gradually 30 approaching, roused him, when, lifting his head, he stared upon us for a moment, and then spread his wide wings, and took his flight."

The mystic quality or reality of the albatross has struck mankind from the beginning. The bird is the symbol of the First Life, as it flies between the sky of Light and the naked waters. It is the living Ghost 35 or being, the embodied creative mystery which hovers between the two great valves of the primal cosmos, the upper and the lower deeps, the heavens above and the waters beneath. It is white, pristine, alone, the first and last apparition of life, upon the verge of the two great breaths; the first and last clue of perfect animate being, between the two elemental 40 surges of passional existence, sensual and spiritual duality. Dana is a mystic in spite of himself. The bird sleeps naked on the heaving gulfs of water, the man's soul sees and is accomplished in the vision.

But the real business of Dana is the fight with the sea itself. The passage round the Horn, both in the outward and homeward voyages, is a great crisis of struggle with the enveloping watery element, seas that rage against creation, in a rage of dissolution. The very dispassionate bareness of Dana's record shows the impersonal depths, the elemental consciousness from which he writes. It is a perfection of culture, far surpassing self-conscious art.

It is a fight with the sea, a fight to the death. And the man is never beaten. He cannot be overwhelmed. In all the rush of work and struggle, the soul of Dana keeps apart, watching the great seas mount round his own small body. If he is swept away, his soul will not be extinguished. It is his purpose to meet and pass through the gnashings of the waters. If he dies he dies unbeaten.* If he lives, then that which is the savage ocean of his soul will be sailed, explored, mastered. He will be master of his own deeps. The calm extremity of this great fight gives the splendid stoic hopelessness, fatality, to the style of Dana's book, as it does to the style of Thucydides.*

"Between five and six the cry of 'All starbowlines ahoy!' summoned our watch on deck, and immediately all hands were called. A great cloud of dark slate-colour was driving on us from the South-west; and we did our best to take in sail before we were in the midst of it. We had got the light sails furled, the courses hauled up, and the top-sail reef tackles hauled out, and were just mounting the fore-rigging when the storm struck us. In an instant the sea, which had been comparatively quiet, was running higher and higher; and it became almost as dark as night. The hail and sleet were harder than I had yet felt them, seeming almost to pin us down to the rigging."

In stating plain mechanical facts, Dana achieves his wonderful effect. This is the elimination of the personal element which Flaubert aimed at.* But it cannot be done deliberately. The personal element must be truly absent: it cannot be eliminated. Dana writes from his remoter centres of being—not from the personal-passional self. He writes of the great mechanical motions as they pass through the body and the soul in sleep, the movement of substance itself, which is the influence that makes our dreams. We cannot do this until we have outpassed the personal self, come to the confines of being, dispassionate and unemotional, in the ordinary sense. In the same dream mystery he watches the Isle of Juan Fernandez rise like a green cloud from the sea. He loves the island with perfect dream-recollection, he is like a ghost re-visiting the beautiful, magical places of the lost earth.

Day after day, week after week the ship sails on. The strain of the long sea-voyage is too much for these creatures of earth. The sea is too
5 strong for them. They become irritable and wasted in vitality.

Only once Dana breaks into real passion: and then he is like a man struggling in his sleep. He is writing of the flogging of one of the sailors.

"Sam was by this time seized *up*—that is, placed against the shrouds, with his wrists made fast to the shrouds, his jacket off, and his back
10 exposed. The Captain stood on the break of the deck, a few feet from him, and a little raised, so as to have a good swing at him, and held in his hand a light, thick rope. The officers stood round, and the crew grouped together in the waist. All these preparations made me feel sick and faint, angry and excited as I was. A man—a human being
15 made in God's likeness—fastened up and flogged like a beast! The first and almost uncontrollable impulse was resistance. But what could be done?—The time for it had gone by—"

Dana cannot allow this sudden violence of passion. He cannot bear to see exposed the naked back of a man, exposed to flogging. For the back
20 is the closed reality of man's integrity in isolation. In the back are the fortresses of the *will*, the back is the tower of man's volitional strength.

Now man has his perfection in fourfold activity: there is the dual sympathetic activity, sensual and spiritual, acting from the breast and the bowels; and there is the corresponding dual volitional activity, acting
25 from the upper and lower spinal ganglia, the shoulders and the loins. When any man lives fully, he lives from these four great centres of dynamic being, in four directions. Incalculable waves of vital effluence flow to and from the great sympathetic centres of breast and bowels, to and from some perfect pole in another being, or in the elemental universe.
30 Correspondingly, there is a vivid current, like an electric circuit, flowing from the volitional poles in any individual physique, to the great centres of will in another being or another anima.

It is the centres of passionate will that keep man erect. In the back, between the shoulders and in the nape of the neck are located the
35 centres of spiritual compulsion: in the lower body are the centres of sensual direction. In the young, the extreme ganglia act first, and they act before and beyond the control of the mind. Hence the whipping of schoolboys upon the buttocks, and the curious chastisement practised in some girls' schools, where the girls are beaten upon the nape of the
40 neck.

Between the captain and the sea-men of a ship a circuit of volitional control is established. But it is a circuit of productive or positive compulsion, and is polarised therefore in the shoulders. This circuit of productive compulsion, the circuit of active duty, is counterparted to some degree by a circuit of sympathy also, a sympathetic unison in   5
purpose.

Now the sea is a great disintegrative influence. The strain of months or weeks of isolation at sea disintegrates the positive connection between men, disintegrates the very unity of the soul in the individual. Also the great strain put upon a few exclusive relationships causes those relation-   10
ships to break down. So we feel the men growing slack, vague, irritable, insubordinate, whilst the Captain becomes spasmodic and domineering.

The disintegrative process has set in in the human psyche. It is like a certain electricity with which the system becomes surcharged. Men only live when the creative vital force, and when the electric vital force, which   15
is disruptive, have each their harmonious circuit around positive and negative poles. Now in these men at sea the electric disruptive force becomes surcharged. The individual loses his integrity. We feel that Sam, the negative individual *par excellence*,* is becoming soft, vague, loose, shambling, inefficient, impudent—he is losing his integrity of be-   20
ing, and becoming a loosely functioning, degenerate unit. On the other hand, the Captain, the positive or commanding nature, is becoming irritable, exacting, surcharged. The circuit round the two poles in the two men is interrupted and uncertain, the unison is breaking.

Then, just as in the heavens only a thunder-storm can release the   25
electric surcharge and set once more the true dynamic polarity between the two cosmic elements, so it is only a storm which can re-adjust these two men. It is only the flash of lightning, the flash of anger and pain striking straight into the volitional centres of the negative physique, from the positive physique, that can re-adjust the two beings, make   30
them clean and whole again. It is the electric catharsis.* The flogging therefore is a purifying process to two drossy natures. After it, there might be freshness and newness as after a storm.

It is useless to think that men can live by spiritual love and reason alone. Men have their being primarily in this circuit of passional polarity,   35
which is the basis of all creative and destructive action. The polarity may be sexual—it is always in a measure sexual—or it may be a balance of command and obedience. In either case there is a continuous vital flow or circuit of living electricty between the two beings, upon which the peace and life of each depends. If the circuit is interrupted or broken, it   40

can never be put right from the rational consciousness. Only a passional storm will readjust it. Every man must be responsible to his own soul, for his own passional acts, whether passive or active.

The Captain is perfectly exposed in his passion. When John, the
5   rather slow, benevolent, superior seaman stepped forward, and in true democratic spirit demanded of the Captain why Sam was to be flogged, the enraged Captain had John slung up too.

"As he went on, his passion increased, and he danced about on the deck, calling out as he swung the rope, 'If you want to know what I flog
10   you for, I'll tell you. It's because I like to do it!—because I like to do it!—It suits me! That's what I do it for!'

"The man writhed under the pain. My blood ran cold, I could look no longer. Disgusted, sick, and horror-struck, I turned away and leaned over the rail and looked down in the water. A few rapid thoughts of my
15   own situation, and the prospect of future revenge, crossed my mind; but the falling of the blows, and the cries of the man called me back at once. At length they ceased, and, turning round, I found that the Mate, at a signal from the Captain had cut him down.—"

It was not so very terrible after all. Sam was just as much a party to
20   it all, as the Captain. Nothing but the infliction of sharp physical pain, thrilling into the great centres of will and control, in the back, would wake him to fuller self. And nothing but sheer passion can inflict this pain: otherwise it is merely shameful and hurtful, instead of creative. The captain was implicated with Sam. There was pure polarity between
25   the two men. And the passion spent itself naturally. Each, no doubt, was purified. But the captain was ashamed.

"The flogging was seldom, if ever alluded to by us in the forecastle. If anyone was inclined to talk about it, the other, with a delicacy which I hardly expected to find among them, always stopped him, or turned
30   the subject. But the behaviour of the two men who were flogged, toward one another, showed a delicacy and a sense of honour which would have been worthy of admiration in the highest walks of life. Sam knew that the other had suffered solely on his account, and in all his complaints he said that if he alone had been flogged it would have been nothing,
35   but that he could never see that man without thinking that he had been the means of bringing that disgrace upon him; and John never, by word or deed, let anything escape him to remind the other that it was by interfering to save his ship-mate that he had suffered."

John should not have interfered in a case of impulsive passion, prop-
40   erly balanced between the Captain and Sam. Men should keep their

self-respect and the integrity of their own being. If they lose this, an electric storm becomes inevitable, a passional readjustment; or else madness sets in. The seamen know that they should not interfere in the passional readjustment, which has after all nothing abnormal in it. Only Dana is sickened, because he believes that man is a pure spiritual being, made in God's image, an item of upper consciousness. He cannot bear the passional interchange.—The captain also suffers from shame, first because he has exposed himself, secondly because he feels he has been judged and condemned by his spiritually-minded crew. This makes him morose.

The vessel arrives at the Pacific coast, and the swell of the rollers falls in our blood—the dreary coast stretches in our very tissue, Dana is so perfect at *material* creation, the realities of the water and the land substance. He gets the mystery of the principle of *substance*—which later on, Matisse or Picasso* tries to paint. It is the elemental mystery: naked substance as it is left when the waters and the fire have thrown it down.

"Not a human being but ourselves for miles; and no sound heard but the pulsations of the great Pacific!—the steep hill rising like a wall, and cutting us off from all the world—but the 'world of waters'. I separated myself from the rest, and sat down on a rock, just where the sea ran in and formed a fine spouting-horn. Compared with the plain, dull sand-beach of the rest of the coast this grandeur was as refreshing as a great rock in a weary land. It was almost the first time I had been positively alone—free from the sense that human beings were at my elbow, if not talking to me—since I had left home. My better nature returned strong upon me. Everything was in accordance with my state of feeling, and I experienced a glow of pleasure at finding that what of poetry and romance I had ever had in me had not been entirely deadened in the laborious life I had been lately leading. Nearly an hour did I sit, almost lost in the luxury of this entire new scene of the play in which I was acting, when I was aroused by the distant shouts of my companions—"

This is Dana confessing that he is a Hamlet, a self-conscious play-actor, dictated from the conscious ego. He sits and Hamletises by the Pacific. Again he has a romantic picture, a view from the ship at the entrance to San Francisco Bay—then quite wild and natural. "The tide leaving us, we came to anchor near the mouth of the bay, under a high and beautifully sloping hill, upon which herds of hundreds of red deer, and the stag, with his high-branching antlers were bounding about, looking at us for a moment, and then starting off affrighted at the noises we made for the purpose of seeing the variety of their beautiful attitudes and motions—"

It is a paradisal glimpse of America, as it is seen virgin in the eyes of Dana: a glimpse as into Eden.

5   He is not really a sea-creature—he belongs in the last resort still to the land. And if he felt one strong, but impotent passion of hate, for the Captain, he felt also one strong impulse of love or affection. This was for a Kanaka boy—Hope—a beautiful South Sea islander now sick of a white man's disease; presumably syphilis. Of him Dana writes

10   "—but the other, who was my friend, and *aikane*—Hope—was the most dreadful object I had ever seen in my life; his eyes sunken and dead, his cheeks fallen in against his teeth, his hands looking like claws; a dreadful cough, which seemed to rack his whole shattered system; a hollow, whispering voice, and an entire inability to move himself. There

15   he lay, upon a mat on the ground, which was the only floor of the oven, with no medicine, no comforts and no one to care for or help him but a few Kanakas, who were willing enough, but could do nothing. The sight of him made me sick and faint. Poor fellow! During the four months that I lived upon the beach we were continually together, both

20   in work and in our excursions in the woods and upon the water. I really felt a strong affection for him, and preferred him to any of my own countrymen there. When I came into the oven he looked at me, held out his hand, and said in a low voice, but with a delightful smile, 'Aloha, Aikane! Aloha nui!" I comforted him as well as I could, and promised

25   to ask the Captain to help him from the medicine chest."

This is the first and last time that Dana is touched *personally*—save for the case of the Captain—all through the book: and now he feels the pulse of love for a bright-eyed man of the Pacific, a real child of the ocean, full of the mystery-being of this great sea of the beyond. Hope is

30   to Dana what Chingachgook and Uncas are to Cooper—the mystic heart's-brother, the love-answerer. But in Dana's life he is a moment.

The emotion of departure from the western shore is poignantly conveyed—the sense of finality, of fatal Nevermore.* This sense of fatality, life coming to an end phase after phase, is very poignant. It

35   tears us as the ship leaves California. And yet Dana was *mad* to be off home, back to civilisation.

"When all sail had been set and the decks cleared up the *California* was a speck in the horizon, and the coast lay like a low cloud along the north-east. At sunset they were both out of sight, and we were once

40   more upon the ocean, where sky and water meet."

The voyage home is another stupendous ordeal of the waters. It is as if we passed through into another life, not belonging to this our own world. There is first the awful sense of apprehension, and the gathering mystery of passing away beyond the scope of earthly life, into the black seas.

"The days became shorter and shorter, the sun running lower in its 5 course each day, and giving less and less heat, and the nights so cold as to prevent our sleeping on deck; the Magellan Clouds in sight of a clear night; the skies looking cold and angry; and at times a long, heavy, ugly sea, setting in from the Southward, told us what we were coming to—"

They were approaching Cape Horn, in the southern winter, passing 10 into the strange dread regions of violent undoing.

"And there lay, floating in the ocean, several miles off, an immense irregular mass, its top and points covered with snow, and its centre a deep indigo. This was an iceberg, and of the largest size. As far as the eye could reach the sea in every direction was of a deep blue colour, 15 the waves running high and fresh, and sparkling in the light; and in the midst lay this immense mountain-island, its cavities and valleys thrown into deep shade, and its points and pinnacles glittering in the sun. But no description can give any idea of the strangeness, splendour, and, really, the sublimity of the sight. Its great size—for it must have been two to 20 three miles in circumference, and several hundred feet in height; its slow motion, as its base rose and sank in the water and its high points nodded against the clouds; the dashing of the waves upon it, which, breaking high with foam, lined its base with a white crust; and the thundering sound of the cracking of the mass, and the breaking and tumbling down 25 of huge pieces; together with its nearness and approach, which added a slight element of fear—all combined to give it the character of true sublimity—"

And as the ship runs further and further into danger, Dana falls sick. He had first a slight tooth-ache. Ice and exposure cause the pain to take 30 hold of all his face and head: and then the face so swelled, that he could not open his mouth to eat, and is in danger of lock-jaw. In this state he is forced to keep his bunk for three days. "At the end of the third day, the ice was very thick; a complete fog-bank covered the ship. It blew a tremendous gale from the eastward, with sleet and snow, and 35 there was every promise of a dangerous and fatiguing night. At dark, the Captain called all hands aft, and told them that not a man was to leave the deck that night; that the ship was in the greatest danger; any cake of ice might knock a hole in her, or she might run on an island and go to pieces. The look-outs were then set, and every man was put in his 40

station. When I heard what was the state of things, I began to put on my clothes, to stand it out with the rest of them, when the mate came below, and looking at my face ordered me back to my berth, saying that if we went down we should all go down together, but if I went on deck
5   I might lay myself up for life.

"In obedience to the mate's orders, I went back to my berth; but a more miserable night I never wish to spend.—"

It is the story of a man pitted in conflict against the sea, the vast, omnipotent, mystic destroyer. In contest with this Cosmic enemy, he
10 finds his own last being. He brings himself out victorious. But it is the sea itself which so tortures him, reduces his land flesh.

The almost horrific struggle round Cape Horn is the fundamental of the Dana history. It is an entry into chaos, a confusion of sleet and black ice-rain, a sea of ice and iron-like water. He fights the el-
15 ements, the elemental waters roused in all their forces of mystic violent hostility. The fight with the waters is the mystic action of Dana's life. It is not a case of overcoming obstacles that lie in the way. It is a pitting of the deliberate being against the primal waters of the polar region.

20 After the struggle, Dana is a whole man, a free consciousness. He has fought his great fight, and won. He remains integral, a triumphant consciousness, a victorious spiritual being, victorious over his deep sensual self, by his victory over the sea; and at the same time fulfilled in his deepest sensual self, fulfilled by mystic disintegration. After this, he
25 can live deliberately, according to the great social principle, free again in his own will. For in the spiritual triumph, the process of subjecting the lower self is a process of pure satisfaction in sensual distintegration.

Dana, and the ship, came through. She passed through the southern strait, skirting the polar death-mystery. And she turned north, like a
30 bird whose plumage is new and strong, flying with delight. "Every rope-yarn seemed stretched to the utmost and every thread of the canvas; and with this sail added to her the ship sprang through the water like a thing possessed. The sail being nearly all forward, it lifted her out of the water, and she seemed actually to jump from sea to sea."

35 There is great joy in the sailing ship, different from a steamer. And the reason of this is that the sailing ship subtly intervenes between the elemental forces of wind and ocean, and as a perfect resultant of the living opposing forces, she takes her chosen way. She flies in the midst of the elements as a bird does, by making herself utterly at one with

them. The wind and the rollers are her wings. She does not *overcome*, as a steamer does. She perfectly accepts.

"One night, while we were in these tropics, I went out to the end of the flying jib-boom upon some duty, and having finished it turned round and lay over the boom for a long time, admiring the beauty of the 5 sight before me. Being so far out from the deck I could look at the ship as at a separate vessel, and there rose up from the water, supported only by the small black hull, a pyramid of canvas, spreading out far beyond the hull, and towering up almost, as it seemed, in the indistinct night air, to the clouds. The sea was as still as an inland lake: the light trade 10 wind was gently and steadily breathing from astern; there was no sound but the rippling of the water under the stern; and the sails were spread out wide and high—the two lower studding sails stretching, on each side, far beyond the deck; the top-mast studding sails, like wings to the topsails; the top-gallant studding-sails spreading fearlessly out above 15 them; still higher, the two royal studding-sails, looking like two kites flying from the same string, and, highest of all, the little sky-sail, the apex of the pyramid, seeming actually to touch the stars and to be out of reach of human hand. Not a ripple upon the surface of the canvas, not even a quivering of the extreme edges of the sail, so perfectly were 20 they distended by the breeze."

It is this perfect equipoising of the self* in the midst of the great elements which gives us our joy in physical life. Machines depend upon the conquest of the external forces, so that by the intervention of machinery, we not only destroy the purest joy, but we rob ourselves of very 25 life, we become as it were deaf and numb in the elemental physical body. Every time we turn on a tap to have water, every time we turn a handle to have fire, we frustrate and annul our own life. The more appliances we have, the more applied we are, we become merely a master-appliance in ourself. 30

The machine is the perfect Neuter of all life. It exists by virtue of the pivotal vacuum, the centrality of perfect neutralisation, the potent void. Whilst we use the potent neuter machine to serve the impulses of life and creation, all is well. But when life and being are subjected to the service of the machine, productive or destructive, then all is ill, life 35 is all running into the central vacuum of the machine's pivot.

When we balance the sticks and kindle a fire, we perform the Promethean mysteries,* we poise the elements. But when we turn on an electric tap, there is as it were a wad between our sensitive, sensible body and the vivid elements. Under this wad we grow numb and atrophied. Our appliances at last exterminate us.

We have our life in the mysterious intervention between the great elements or Principles. We bring water and fire together to make our
5   seeds grow, we drive them asunder to obtain force and motion. The process is dual. And so the universe is a dual mystery of creation and decreation.

If there is a great God, the perfect Creator, there is a corresponding great god, the Undoer, the Separator. This is Zeus of the thunderbolts,
10 the earliest Ammon. The weapon of the Thunderer is the mysterious electric force. Electricity is the eternal, naked sundering force, that which liberates the perfect waters from their painful imprisonment with fire. The crash of thunder is the exploding of waters out of their conjunction with elemental fire, there in the void firmament where the
15 two are interlocked and frustrated, the creative polarity between them entangled. Then the Thunderer releases the fatal spell, there is a perfect starting asunder, in perfect creative opposition.

All our familiarity with the electric forces has not brought us any nearer to a realisation of their mystic or vitalistic action on the human
20 psyche. We have profaned the worship of the Thunderer, the terrifying Zeus. We are vulgar in our familiarity. We play with the weapons of the gods, we who are not gods, only impudent mechanics. Dana brings us to a realisation of this. He still can feel the awe and reverence before the mystery.

25 "When our watch came on deck at twelve o'clock it was as black as Erebus; not a breath was stirring; the sails hung heavy and motion-less from the yards; and the perfect stillness, and the darkness, which was almost palpable, were truly appalling. Not a word was spoken, but everyone stood as though waiting for something to happen. In a few
30 minutes the mate came forward, and in a low tone which was almost a whisper, to haul down the jib——when we got down we found all hands looking aloft, and then, directly over where we had been standing, upon the main top-gallant mast-head, was a ball of light, which the sailors name a corposant (*corpus sancti*). They were all watching it carefully,
35 for sailors have a notion that if the corposant rises in the rigging, it is a sign of fair weather, but if it comes lower down, there will be a storm. Unfortunately, as an omen, it came down and showed itself on the top-gallant yard.

"In a few minutes it disappeared and showed itself again on the fore
40 top-gallant-yard, and, after playing about for some time, disappeared

again, when the man on the forecastle pointed to it upon the flying-jib-boom end. But our attention was drawn from watching this by the falling of some drops of rain. In a few minutes low growling thunder was heard, and some random flashes of lightning came from the south-west. Every sail was taken in but the top-sail. A few puffs lifted the top-sails, 5
but they fell again to the mast, and all was as still as ever. A moment more, and a terrific flash and peal broke simultaneously upon us, and a cloud appeared to open directly over our heads, and let down the water in one body like a falling ocean. We stood motionless and almost stupified, yet nothing had been struck. Peal after peal rattled over our 10
heads with a sound which actually seemed to stop the breath in the body. The violent fall of the rain lasted but a few minutes, and was succeeded by occasional drops and showers; but the lightning continued incessant for several hours, breaking the midnight darkness with irregular and blinding flashes. 15

"During all this time hardly a word was spoken, no bells were struck, and the wheel was silently relieved. The rain fell at intervals in heavy showers, and we stood drenched through, and blinded by the flashes, which broke the Egyptian darkness with a brightness which seemed almost malignant, while the thunder rolled in peals, the concussion of 20
which appeared to shake the very ocean. A ship is not often injured by lightning, for the electricity is separated by the great number of points she presents, and the quantity of iron which she has scattered in various parts. The electric fluid ran over our anchors, topsail-sheets, and ties; yet no harm was done to us. We went below at four o'clock, leaving 25
things in the same state.—"

This is a piece of direct Shango-worship, or Thor-worship. The Thunderer is an acknowledged presence, as he sunders the water from their prison in space. Another curious instance of the process of un-creation, radical, material uncreation as it takes place with the very 30
corpuscles of the blood, is the case of scurvy reported by Dana. It is uncreation caused by the excessive salty power of the waters, over the warm-substantial body.

"The scurvy had begun to show itself on board. One man had it so badly as to be disabled and off duty; and the English lad, Ben, was in a 35
dreadful state, and was gradually growing worse. His legs swelled and pained him so that he could not walk; his flesh lost its elasticity, so that if it were pressed in, it would not return to its shape; and his gums swelled until he could not open his mouth. His breath, too, became very offensive; he lost all strength and spirit; could eat nothing; grew worse 40

every day; and, in fact, unless something was done for him, would be a dead man in a week at the rate at which he was sinking. The medicines were all gone, or nearly all gone; and if we had had a chest-full, they would have been of no use; for nothing but fresh provisions and *terra*
5   *firma* has any effect upon the scurvy."

However, they obtained half a boat-load of potatoes and onions, from a passing vessel. These they ate raw. "The freshness and crispness of the raw onion, with the earthy taste, give it a great relish to one who has been a long time on salt provisions. We were perfectly ravenous
10 after them. We ate them at every meal, by the dozen; and filled our pockets with them, to eat in the watch on deck. The chief use, however, of the fresh provisions was for the men with the scurvy. One of them was able to eat, and he soon brought himself to by gnawing upon raw potatoes; but the other, by this time, was hardly able to open his mouth;
15 and the cook took the potatoes raw, pounded them in a mortar, and gave him the juice to drink. The strong earthy taste and smell of this extract of the raw potatoes at first produced a shuddering through his whole frame, and after drinking it, an acute pain, which ran through all parts of his body; but knowing by this that it was taking strong hold,
20 he persevered, drinking a spoonful every hour or so, until, by the effect of this drink, and of his own restored hope, he became so well as to be able to move about, and open his mouth enough to eat the raw potatoes and onions pounded into a soft pulp. This course soon restored his appetite and strength; and ten days after we spoke the Solon, so rapid
25 was his recovery that, from lying helpless and almost hopeless in his berth, he was at the mast-head, furling a royal."

This is the strange account of the disintegration effect of the sea and the salt in food. Food is preserved by salt, because decomposition, which is in itself a process of living uncreation, depends on the presence of
30 living organisms, which, in a process of rudimentary creation, assume into themselves the creative presence, loose the creative bond, and release the fiery and watery principles from the organic substance, as we do in eating, and set the two streams of negative fire and negative water flowing asunder in the flux of corruption. Now the presence of salt at
35 once establishes a triumph of the watery principle within the substance, the waters triumphant or excessive or static. And all life depends on the balance of the waters with the fire. There needs a balance of sweet water and procreant fire for any organism to act. So salt which is the substance of watery preponderance, arrests, or suspends decay, in dead organic
40 substance: just as sun-drying, by abstracting the water and making a

surcharge of fire, arrests decay. In either case one Principle is held at bay, whilst the other remains static in possession.

Salt is a necessary watery stimulus in the living organic body, but if it be in excess, it causes the arrest of the fiery element and surcharge of water. Hence the dropsy-like disintegration in scurvy. The watery 5 principle in the body gradually assumes the overbalance, the excess, and starts the downthrow of the creative substance.

And there is no remedy but fresh provisions and *terra firma*, as Dana says. That is, there is no help but the positive creative principle inherent in those things which grow, the principle which unites the fiery and the 10 watery elements into a created whole: the creative presence.

And this positive principle, this Presence of the Host* is introduced into the body in the juice of the potatoes—or the limes—or the onions. Dana dwells on the relish which the *earthy* taste gives to the onion: and the very earthy smell of potato juice causes a strong shuddering through 15 the frame of the scurvy-stricken boy. This earthy smell is the scent of the Presence of the Host, and the fountain of all flower perfumes, just as earth-darkness, tar, is the fountain of all colours or dyes.* The boy is fast in the process of uncreation, under the spell of salt, and the sea, and the moon. But there is introduced the mystic latent creative principle, in 20 the juice of the potatoes, and the soft adjustment of sun-potency. He is, as it were, placed again in the womb of Geaea. Or he drinks the mystic milk of creation. It is the mystic presence of the Host itself, the creative charge within the milk, the first reality of the living substance, which will heal him and make him whole. In the living organic substance lies 25 the ever-present Host, the Ghost of organic life, the creative principle.

We must know again the God Thoth,* in his mystery of procreant substance, the underworld substance of the waters and the sun in which the active Presence is the presence of the Host, the Ghostly Creator. For the sum of Thoth knowledge is but the sum of the knowledge of what 30 happens to the scurvy-stricken boy, when he shudders with anguish smelling the earthy juice, and is filled with pain through all his fibres as the principle seeks him out. It would have been *easier* for him to lapse in the spell of uncreation. In the turning of the stream of life, he must suffer. For the Hermes is the son of the Thunderer,* he who turns, and 35 is wrathful.

X.

Herman Melville.

The greatest seer, and poet of the sea, perhaps in all the modern world, is Herman Melville. His vision is wider than that of Swinburne, and
5 more profound than that of Conrad. Melville belongs to the sea, like one of its own birds. Like a sea-bird, he seems merely to perch on the shore, he does not belong to this land. Unlike Dana, he does not go down and make a conquest of the ocean. He returns to the ocean, to become part of it. He does not pit himself against the sea. He is of it.
10 And he has that inscrutable magic and mystery of pure sea-creatures.

There is something about him that reminds one inevitably of the Vikings—those pagan Vikings who had their settlements in Greenland and Labrador, and sailed down past Nova Scotia and New England even to Florida.* The Northmen were ocean-born creatures seeking a land.
15 There were the storm-clouds of new life breaking from the sea and pouring down on the unwakened earth. Still they belonged to the sea and the waters, to the elemental water-mystery, not to the dark, earth-rich fire-mystery of the south. The blue-eyed, water-mystic people of the North cannot lose their origin. By slow absorption the blue-eyed
20 race fuses with the dark-eyed, to form new peoples, new eras. But the truest sons of the North never meet and mingle. In the end they return like Viking chiefs, to the sea whence they were born, laid in state on their ships and pushed out in flame on to the waters.* The tide has two motions, the rise and the fall. And so with the blue-eyed race. It
25 rises in flood to inundate the old, darkened, created nations, as the Nile inundates Egypt: and it retreats in the ebb, back away from creation, to the everlasting seas which stand before and after creation.

Melville makes the great return. He returns to find a home in the blue shades of the ocean, the pale, bluish underworld of the watery after-life.
30 He is like a Viking going home to the sea, encumbered with age and memories, and a sort of accomplished despair. The great Northern tide is on the ebb, the yellow, horned sea-poppy sheds its petals on the waves. Those northerners who have taken land-root fuse with the sun and ply towards a new harvest. But those who are rootless and fruitless scatter
35 into the waves.

It is to the Pacific Ocean that Melville turns. The Pacific is the first ocean, the home of all the waters. The Pacific tides brought forth the first great harvest of life, the era of the sensual mystery, the era that lies beyond the Flood, before the Glacial Period.* We do not care to believe in the vast, vanished eras of human civilisation upon which the waters of the Flood arose. Yet there must have been such eras. There must have been a vast civilisation, different from ours, a civilisation established on the perfected first-mind in man, man's primal or creative-sensual being. We cannot study even briefly the root-myths and the root-utterance of the races of the earth without having it borne upon us, that this is one utterance from one source, the stammering of a great ancient speech, that is lost. Just as the whole globe, at the present moment, is covered with one universal scientific-social body of understanding, so the whole globe, before Atlantis and the Flood, must have been fulfilled with one profound sensual-real knowledge, a knowledge embodied in deep and monstrous symbolism, symbols that had vital relationship, direct connection with life at every point. Men then *understood* in passional sensation and pulsation, in passional symbols, as we now understand universally in concepts and ideas. The All-Father, the All-Mother, the Beautifier,* the Thunderer, the Tree, these are great passional concepts, passional counterparts of our scientific ideas. This symbolistic All-Knowledge held good over the whole earth. But after its perfection came the Fall. The Eve myth only symbolises the Fall from pure sensual understanding, the birth of the upper spiritual understanding. And then came the Flood, which swept away the bulk of mankind. And after the Flood the new way of life, the spiritual-mental, struggled towards perfection. It gradually dissolved the old passional concepts into pure ideas and spiritual impulses. But even Christ is the Fruit of the Tree.* The Rood is the Tree of Sacrifice, that terrific Tree whose boughs form the Cross, the Tau, the Tree which the Druids, the Germans, the Maya worshipped,* the Tree which filled the Romans with dread and horror. And the sacred mistletoe,* fruit of the Tree, is the foreshadowing of Jesus on the Cross.—But gradually we dissolve away the monstrous Rood symbolism, we reduce Christ, the white and pearly Fruit of the Tree, to a historical fact and a pure idea or ideal. Behind the spreading, awful branches of the Rood-Screen lurks no more mystery. The vast old era of passional understanding is over, the light shines stark on altars, showing them mere furniture.

But a Day of perfect dark or sensual understanding there must have been. And we conceive that the blue sea of this Day was the Pacific Ocean, and that the lands of the Pacific knew the magnificent centuries upon centuries of primal wisdom. Egypt, and the Etruscan and Iberian
5   races, these are the last fading exemplars of the old way.* The China of our history is the utter forgetting of what was before. China and America, and the South Sea Isles, these are the sleep and the forgetting of what was before, the eternally unfinished dream.*

So the Pacific, the vastest and most profound of all the watery worlds,
10 is as the shadow of a great sleep. We cannot know how vast a reality, how mighty a civilisation the Pacific has swung down and disintegrated. Its waters are surcharged with the blue and ghostly end of immemorial centuries. It is the wide, conclusive Afterwards of manly being.

In the same way surely it is the great blue twilight of the vastest of all
15 dawns. Its waters roll latent with all the unborn beauty of the coming world of man.

It was to the great Afterwards, the heaven-under-the-wave, like the Celtic Tir-na-Og, that Melville returned. He went to the centre of the Pacific, to the South Sea Islands. And about these islands he wandered
20 and hovered like an uneasy ghost.

At the very centre of this old primeval world sleeps the living and forgetting of Samoa, Tahiti, Nukuheva, the names which trail their clouds of glory, names which no man can hear unmoved. They are the echoes from the world once splendid in the fulness of the other wisdom
25 and understanding.

But Samoa, Tahiti, Nukuheva are the sleep and the forgetting of this great life, the very living body of the sleep. And to this sleep-body Melville helplessly returned to enter again into the dream.

He enters first in Typee. Nothing is more amazing, at once actual
30 and pure dream-mystical, than his descent down the gorge to the valley of the dreadful Typee. Down this narrow, steep, horrible dark gorge he slides and struggles as we struggle in a dream, or in the act of birth, to emerge in the green Eden of the first era, the valley of the timeless savages. He had dreaded this entry, acutely, for the men of Typee had a
35 dreadful cannibal reputation.* But he finds himself at once, almost, in the purest dream-reality, the perfect sleep of a once great and wakeful civilisation.

It is absurd to speak of savages as rudimentary or undeveloped people. To look among them for the link between us and the apes is laugh-
40 ably absurd. For the savages, all savages, are the remnants of the once

civilised world-people, who had their splendour and their being in the great sensual way. No man can look at the African grotesque carvings,* for example, without seeing in them the quenched spark of a supreme understanding. The savages are not children practising. They are old, grotesque people, dreaming over their once wide-awake realities, and 5 in each dream distorting and degrading the once perfect utterance. It is indeed a sheer dream process. Any man who reads the Bushman Folk-Lore, as we have it now literally rendered,* cannot fail to be horror-struck, catching the sounds of myriad age-long distortion and age-long repetition of truths now incomprehensible, yet in their incomprehensi- 10 bility most terrifyingly resonant of a far-off past, once wise as we do not understand wisdom. These folk-stories are to the great forgotten past, what our most distorted dreams are to the wakeful reality they refer to. And the African fetishes are timelessly-repeated dream-degradations of once perfect, sensual-mystic images. 15

To return to Typee. It is inconceivable to think of Melville's delicate life among these dreaded savages of Nukuheva as a "savage" or "crude" life. It seems to have been refined beyond our conception of refinement, so delicate, so full of fine *nuances* of feeling and understanding, that it must be the "forgetting" of some most perfect and beautiful sensual 20 civilisation. True it is but the sleep-dream or living afterwards of this perfection. But even as such, it is wonderful and subtly beautiful, beyond our understanding.

The only thing Melville brings against these savages is their warfare and their cannibalism. But after all, it appears that their cannibalism is 25 in reality the dream-remembrance of an old ritual. It is, in short, the remains of the great mystic-sensual sacrament of the sensual religions, the very counterpart of our own Eucharist. Our priest says to us, in the words of Jesus: "This is my body—take, and eat." The act is one of perfect oneing. It is the mystery of unification with the Beloved, 30 through love. The Beloved yields himself to me, that I may partake of Him utterly. This is a plain statement of the process of love, as we all experience it.

But love has the opposite sense also. There is the unification through uttermost yielding to the beloved, and there is the unification through 35 the supreme *taking* of the beloved. It is this second or positive motion of love which the savage sacrament of cannibalism symbolises. "This is thy body, which I take from thee and eat." This is the unification through passional or positive love, called Pride by the Christian Church. "I take and consume thee into myself" is the statement of the original 40 sacrament. "I yield myself to thee, that thou mayest consume me into thyself," this is only the reflex or second form of the great human sacrament of love.

The savage may have forgotten the mystery implied in his sacramental observance; just as the Christian may have forgotten. He may no longer be capable of the profound, soul-shaking passion which carries him into the mystery of supreme unification. None the less, a recent African traveller asserts that—"all these tribes of Inner Africa associate quite a distinctive frame of mind with the consumption of human flesh, and, as far as this refers to the territories I myself have travelled through, I am bound to regard it as a misrepresentation of facts for any traveller to say that the Africans of the interior 'eat human flesh with the same sensation which a beef-steak gives to us.' This is not the truth, because, even if a negro has human meat upon his board several times a week, his enjoyment of it in these countries will always be connected with a definite emotion."*

Melville in Typee had found what he wanted to find, the home of the pure sensual mystery extant in living dream-reality. Having found it, he was almost satisfied. And at the same time, all he wanted was to escape again. He spent almost all his energies trying to get away from his savage hosts, who were also his captors. And he had a strange malady in his arm, which would never heal,* never whilst he was in Typee. And this because the very flesh of the white man was constituted in the spiritual form and must be gradually dissolved, like a sea pearl in land wines, before he can have the new being. The white man must remain true to his own substance and reality to the end. And therefore, later in Omoo, Melville looks almost with horror upon the white man who has the blue shark tatooed across his brow, the renegade European, sealed with the sign of the malevolent or destructive or overweening waters.

All the time Melville is tossed between these two impulses in himself: the one, the helpless desire to be given to the Pacific, to be at one with it at its very heart of age—sleep and dream; the other, the mad, irritable necessity to get back to his own cultured home, Europe, or America, the world of the white men. While he is in Typee he frets in one ceaseless fretting to get away, back to his white allegiance. And the subtle inscrutable malady in his arm will not heal. It is the sign of his own physical substantial necessity to depart: the sign of the too-active disintegration, as scurvy is a sign of the too-active disintegration of the waters.

Yet the moment he has got free, and is actually sailing away, in a voyage which will ultimately take him to America, he is overcome by the most acute and intolerable nostalgia for the island he is leaving. Almost in an agony he wants to be back again, back in the valley of Typee. He knows he has left the place he loves best on earth. Yet he is compelled to return 5 to the hell of white civilisation. And returning his arm heals almost at once.

This is the truth for him. He belongs to the white world, to the great spiritual era. Only death will perfect him in the other way. Strong as is the passion to escape the white civilisation, strong as is the nostalgic 10 longing to sleep in the sleep of the bygone sensual mystery, still stronger is the necessity to adhere, to give his allegiance to the spiritual mystery of which he is the almost finished product. He must not hurry the mystic death-process. Some part of himself has yet to finish in the white world, there is still a victory to be won in the spiritual self, over the sensual 15 self. And in the account of this contest he gives the myth of this end, in his great book *Moby Dick*.

No man that has ever written has ever created the vast and magnificent mystery of the sea, the great Pacific, as Melville has. If we cannot appreciate him it is because we have not yet come to that strange ab- 20 straction and remoteness from immediate issues, which he has reached. He is as an exoteric mystic almost on a level with St. John the Evangel, the esoteric* mystic, imprisoned on Patmos and writing the esoteric record of the Apocalypse.*

In spite of his love for the South Seas, and his passion for the islanders, 25 in spite of his sheer dislike of Christian missionaries and encroaching civilisation, Melville is still established in the spiritual mystery, he has still a further victory to win, over the sensual self. But the victory is almost the last: the cycle is almost completed.

The great sea-book, *Moby Dick*, is an account of a monomaniac hunt 30 for the great White Whale. Moby Dick himself is an old, hoary, monstrous, snow-white whale, the Leviathan of the waters. In a book of such direct and half-intentional symbols, we are forced to ask, what is Moby Dick, what does he stand for? Melville himself is floored by his own statement. He seeks in vain to know what his creation means: 35 Leviathan, that great monster.

Leviathan is closely allied to the Dragon. The Chinese have the Dragon of the Skies.* An almost predominant symbol in Africa is the crocodile: in the South Seas it is the Shark. The great Sea-Serpent used to terrify northern minds, Kraken,* the sea-monster. Besides these there 40 are the innumerable Dragons of the land, of the marshes, against which innumerable heroes like St. George* have fought.

The Dragon is malevolent in his action. The Dragon of the Sun rages: it is the great Fire principle, in its hostile motion, seeking to
5   snatch and coil man away from his central mystery of being. In the same way, the crocodile, the shark, Kraken the sea-serpent, these are the mystic hostile water-principle, that would drag men down into the waters, down from the mystic integrity of being, down from the perfection in duality, into a cosmic oneness, halfness, a malevolent identification with
10   one Principle and with all its attendant powers and forces. It symbolises that great magnetic power of the elements, attracting man or ravishing him from his superb being-in-wholeness, converting him into an elemental, a vivid force-centre, a thing of all-power, such a potency as the Devil offered to Christ at the Temptation; the power of the
15   world.*

But Moby Dick is hardly a Dragon. He is Leviathan: but he is not malevolent unless attacked. He is the oldest and supreme denizen of the seas, warm-blooded. The greatest and first warm-blooded being within the waters, he is mammal as we are, he is one with us. He is ourself, our
20   deepest water-born self. He is not a creature of watery coldness, halfness, like the shark or the huge reptiles. He is not a dragon of burning halfness, like the coiling dragon of the sun, or like the salamander.* He is whole, perfect, the deepest quick, the perfect and unquenchable spark of being, deep within the flood of the one Principle.

25   This Principle, however, is the watery principle, the salt waters which are in some unsearchable way parallel or adjunct to the deepest sensual mystery. Even the salt, spent waters of the body relate us in some way to the salt waters of the sea. Hence the White Whale is, in one of his aspects, a purely phallic symbol: for the deep sexual passion is the passion within
30   the waters, the sensual depth.

But the deep sensual reality is much more than phallic. It is a profound source of impulse and passion, and a dark way of primal, passional understanding. The hunt of Moby Dick symbolises the hunting of the primal sensual self, its final subjection to the upper consciousness. When
35   the hunt is finished, and the great white whale mastered or destroyed, then man will have conquered the most radical of his desires and passions, he will cease altogether from the old way of blind or pristine impulse, he will be perfectly controlled and self-directed.

Moby Dick is the last body of sensual being within the white race.
40   He is white, as we are, perfect in sea-reality. He is the symbol of the profound incalculable passion wherein we have our first-being. In his

wrath, he is unspeakably terrible. But when unattacked, he swims alone
and unswerving, in the pathless seas.

The captain of the ship Pequod is a monomaniac. His obsession is
the White Whale: he must kill Moby Dick. Captain Ahab is a Quaker
from Nantucket, son of the sea-going Quakers of Nantucket. He has 5
already hunted the White whale vindictively, but to his own loss, for
Moby Dick has torn off one of his legs. Still it is not so much revenge he
broods. The great sea-monster has become a symbol of sheer cunning
brute power, supreme phallic power, and the symbol works in the man's
psyche, dominating him as in a dream or a madness. He is a Quaker, a 10
sea-captain, now a monomaniac.

Ahab stumps the deck of the Pequod on an ivory leg made from
the polished bone of a sperm whale's jaw. This symbol of lameness
is very old: Hephaestos is lame in both feet.* There is a lame god in
most old religions. He is usually an underworld god of fire or of fiery 15
passion. Ahab also is branded with fire: a slender rod-like mark, lividly
whitish, runs down his tawny scorched face; it is the lightning mark.
He is branded with the terrible mark of the Thunderer.

Now Hephaestos was lamed when he was hurled by Zeus from Olym-
pus, in a quarrel between Zeus and Hera. He is one of the gods born 20
from the mystery of *sundering*, the quarrel between the two supreme
powers. So Ahab is doomed, there is a fatal limitation in his psyche. He
is the child of a quarrel between the two halves of the psyche, his reason
is unbalanced. Now the lameness refers to this lack of balance in the
psyche, a lack of reasoned control. This is true of lame gods, as well as 25
of Ahab. There is a preponderance of the passional element, thwarted
by an ineradicable self-consciousness. When Hephaestos is represented
with one leg shorter than the other, this refers to the weakness in the
upper or spiritual half of the psyche. Hence he is not a creator, only an
artificer in fire. 30

Ahab too is misbegotten. He is furiously passionate, yet ridiculously
self-conscious. There is discord and discrepancy between the two halves
of his psyche. Still he too might be a perfect artificer, a perfect sea-
captain, perfect in using the elements, a craftsman in weather and
whales. Unfortunately a mania seizes hold of him, and he cannot be 35
soothed.

Ahab has three instruments, three mates. Starbuck, the first mate,
is another Quaker Nantucketer, long, lean, earnest, steadfast, prudent,
wise. He hunts the whale from a sense of duty, respecting his quarry.
Yet even he is swept away by Ahab's monomaniac passion. Stubb, the 40
second mate, was all careless courage and jollity: "fearless as fire, and

as mechanical." He has a brief tussle with the monomaniac, but is soon
vanquished. The third mate, Flask, is all tenacity and obstinacy of will,
without imagination.

These three mates symbolise the reason, the passional impulse, and
5   the will, the three component parts of the psyche. They are the fatal
triangle of the disintegrate soul, dominated by a mania, and working
mechanically.

The fault we have to find with Melville is that he too often works his
symbols deliberately, and gives a spurious feeling, a charlatan quality to
10 his creation. He too was lame.* His conscious understanding could not
keep pace with his emotional and physical apprehension, and hence his
metaphysical symbolism staggers foolishly. He was all the time terribly
uneasy in his own soul, and he flounders wildly. For he is really beyond
the plane of personal life.

15   When he forgets himself, he is a master. The old American fault
of discrepancy between the explicit and the implicit moral, must be
allowed for in Melville as in all the rest. Beyond this, *Moby Dick* gives
the sequence of events in their subtlest, almost mechanical succession.
It would seem as if there were no real clue to it all, as if it were wild or
20 vulgar melodrama. But there is a clue, though it is almost a mechanical
one. Dana and Melville do unconsciously what the futurists aim at
doing: they are masters of the sheer movement of substance in its own
paths, free from human desire or postulation.

In the beginning, Ishmael, the *I* of the book, meets his heart's brother
25 Queequeg, the tatooed South-Sea Islander. The circumstances are curious and comic. But the powerful, tatooed harpooner, with his large, deep
eyes, fiery black and bold, opens again in Ishmael's heart the floodgates
of passional love.

"As I sat there in that now lonely room; the fire burning low, in that
30 mild stage when, after its first intensity has warmed the air, it then
only glows to be looked at; the evening shades and phantoms gathering
round the casements, and peering in upon us silent, solitary twain;
the storm booming without in solemn swells; I began to be sensible of
strange feelings. I felt a melting in me. No more my splintered hand and
35 maddened heart was turned against the wolfish world. This soothing
savage had redeemed it. There he sat, his very indifference speaking a
nature in which there lurked no civilised hypocrisies and bland deceits.
Wild he was: a very sight of sights to see; yet I began to feel myself
mysteriously drawn towards him."—So that they smoke together, and
40 are clasped in each other's arms. And the friendship is established finally

when Ishmael goes through the performance of sacrifice to Queequeg's little native idol—Yogo.*

"I was a good Christian; born and bred in the bosom of the infalliable Presbyterian Church. How then could I unite with the idolater in worshipping his piece of wood? But what is worship?—thought I. But what is worship?—to do the will of God—*that* is worship. And what is the will of God?—to do to my fellow-man what I would have my fellowman do to me—*that* is the will of God. Now Queequeg is my fellowman. And what do I wish that this Queequeg would do to me? Why, unite with me in my particular Presbyterian form of worship. Consequently, I must then unite with him; ergo, I must turn idolater. So I kindled the shavings; helped prop up the innocent little idol; offered him burnt biscuit with Queequeg; salaamed before him twice or thrice; kissed his nose; and that done, we undressed and went to bed, at peace with our own consciences and all the world. But we did not go to sleep without some little chat.

"How is it I know not: but there is no place like a bed for confidential disclosures between friends. Man and wife, they say, open the very bottom of their souls to each other: and some old couples often lie and chat over old times till nearly morning. Thus, then, lay I and Queequeg—a cosy, loving pair—"

Then Queequeg and he go over from New Bedford to Nantucket, and sign on for the voyage on the Quaker whaler, the Pequod. It is all so strangely fantastic, and yet real, actual; so fantastic, or phantasmagoric, without being actually distorted, that we wonder, and then our mind closes over in a sort of trance, we pass on into the entranced last world of the sea, with these men, and the strange, wonderful crew. It is a mythical, mystical voyage, as any cruise of the Argonauts. Yet it is all *actual*. This is the beauty—the identity of actual daily experience with profound metaphysical reality.

The voyage begins in the winter-time—strange and dark at first, as in Dana's travel.* "—in landlessness alone resides the highest truth", writes Melville rather wildly—"shoreless, indefinite as God—so, better it is to perish in that howling infinite, than be ingloriously dashed upon the lee, even if that were safety———life from the spray of thy ocean-perishing—straight up, leaps thy apotheosis!" It passes on, however, into the southern seas, and the watch for whales begins.

When he is fully at sea, moving and working with the waters, not self-consciously speculating, Melville is at his best. Then he creates the unspeakable reality of the sea-life.

"It was a cloudy, sultry afternoon; the seamen were lazily lounging about the decks, or vacantly gazing over into the lead-coloured waters. Queequeg and I were mildly employed weaving what is called a sword-mat, for an additional lashing to our boat. So still and subdued and
5 yet somehow preluding was all the scene, and such an incantation of reverie lurked in the air, that each silent sailor seemed resolved into his own silent* self—"

—And in the midst of this preluding silence, came the first cry, "There she blows! there! there! there! She blows! She blows!"—And
10 then comes the first chase, a perfect and marvellous piece of true sea-writing, the sea, and sheer sea-beings, sea-creatures on the chase. There is no stain or taint of earth—it is pure sea-motion.

' "Give way men", whispered Starbuck, drawing still further aft the sheet of his sail; "there is time to kill fish yet before the squall comes.
15 There's white water again!'—Close to!—Spring!"

'Soon after, two cries in quick succession on each side of us denoted that the other boats had got fast; but hardly were they overheard, when with a lightning-like hurtling whisper Starbuck said: "Stand up!" and Queequeg, harpoon in hand, sprang to his feet.
20 'Though not one of the oarsmen was then facing the life and death peril so close to them ahead, yet with their eyes on the intense counte-nance of the mate in the stern of the boat, they knew that the imminent instant had come; they heard, too, an enormous wallowing sound, as of fifty elephants stirring in their litter. Meanwhile the boat was still
25 booming through the mist, the waves curling and hissing around us like the erected crests of enraged serpents.

"That's his hump. *There, there*, give it to him!" whispered Starbuck.
'A short rushing sound leaped out of the boat; it was the darted iron of Queequeg. Then all in one welded motion came an invisible push
30 from astern, while forward the boat seemed striking on a ledge; the sail collapsed and exploded; a gush of scalding vapour shot up near by; something rolled and tumbled like an earthquake beneath us. The whole crew were half suffocated as they were tossed helter skelter into the white curdling cream of the squall. Squall, whale, and harpoon had all blended
35 together; and the whale merely grazed by the iron, escaped—'

So wonderful is Melville in describing violent and chaotic motion, that he can go on through a whole wild chase, utterly without waking. He is as perfect at creating stillness.

"Steering north-eastward from the Crozetts, we fell in with vast
40 meadows of brit, the minute, yellow substance, upon which the Right

whale largely feeds. For leagues and leagues it undulated round us, so that we seemed to be sailing through boundless fields of ripe and golden wheat.

"On the second day, numbers of Right Whales were seen, who, secure from the attack of a Sperm Whaler like the Pequod, with open jaws   5
sluggishly swarm through the brit, which, adhering to the fringed fibres of that wondrous Venetian blind in their mouths, was in that manner separated from the water that escaped at the lip.

"As morning mowers, who side by side slowly and seethingly advance their scythes through the long wet grass of marshy meads; even so there   10
monsters swarm, making a strange, grassy, cutting sound; and leaving behind them endless swaths of blue on the yellow sea.

"But it was only the sound they made as they parted the brit which at all reminded one of mowers. Seen from the mast-heads, especially when they paused and were stationery for a while, their vast black forms   15
looked more like masses of rock than anything else——"

This beautiful passage goes on to the apparition of the squid.

"Slowly wading through the meadows of Brit, the *Pequod* still held her way north-eastward towards the island of Java; a gentle air impelling her keel, so that in the surrounding serenity her three tall tapering masts   20
mildly waved to that languid breeze, as three mild palms on a plain. And still, at wide intervals in the silvery night, the lonely, alluring jet would be seen.

"But one transparent blue morning, when a stillness almost preter-natural spread over the sea, however unattended with any stagnant calm;   25
when the long burnished sun-glade on the waters seemed a golden finger laid across them, enjoining secrecy; when the slippered waves whispered together as they softly ran on; in this profound hush of the visible sphere a strange spectre was seen by Daggoo from the mainmast head.

"In the distance, a great white mass lazily rose, and rising higher and   30
higher, and disentangling itself from the azure, at last gleamed before our prow like a snow-slide, new slid from the hills. Thus glistening for a moment, as slowly it subsided, and sank. Then once more arose, and silently gleamed. It seemed not a whale; and yet is this Moby Dick? thought Daggoo——"   35

The boats were lowered and pulled to the scene.

"In the same spot where it sank, once more it slowly rose. Almost forgetting for the moment all thoughts of Moby Dick, we now gazed at the most wondrous phenomenon which the secret seas have hitherto revealed to mankind. A vast pulpy mass, furlongs in length and breadth,   40

of a glancing cream-colour, lay floating on the water, innumerable long
arms radiating from its centre, and curling and twisting like a nest of
anacondas, as if blindly to clutch at any hapless object within reach.
No perceptible face or front did it have; no conceivable token of either
5   sensation or instinct; but undulated there on the billows, an unearthly,
formless, chance-like apparition of life. And with a low sucking sound
it slowly disappeared again.—"

The following chapters, their account of the whale-hunts, the killing,
the cutting up, the stripping, are perfect and accurate in their rendering.
10 There are admirable accounts of the taking of the sperm oil from a
whale's head. In dilating on the brain of the sperm whale, Melville
makes the curious but significant remark—"for I believe that much of a
man's character will be found betokened in a man's backbone. I would
rather feel your spine than your skull, whoever you are— —"

15 And of the whale, he adds:—"For, viewed in this light the wonderful
comparative smallness of his brain proper is more than compensated by
the wonderful comparative magnitude of his spinal cord."

And again there are more hunts, terrible and wonderful, with touches
of profound beauty— —"As the three boats lay there on that gently
20 rolling sea, gazing down into its eternal blue moon; and as not a single
groan or cry of any sort, nay not so much as a ripple or a thought, came
up from its depths; what landsman would have thought, that beneath all
that silence and placidity, the utmost monster of the seas was writhing
and wrenching in agony!—"

25 Perhaps the most wonderful chapter is the one on the The Grand
Armada, where the Pequod chased a great herd of sperm whales, what
seems to be thousands on thousands. "Broad on both bows, at a distance
of two or three miles, and forming a great semi-circle, embracing one-
half of the level horizon, a continuous chain of whale-jets were up—
30 playing and sparkling in the noonday air."— —Chasing this great herd,
past the Straits of Sunda, and themselves chased by pirates from the
Javan coast, the whalers race on. Then the boats are lowered. The great
herd of whales, in violent motion, remained stationary.

Starbuck's boat, fast on a whale, is towed in reckless career through
35 the boiling surging chaos of monsters, even to the clear lagoon at the
centre of the herd. There, they found a sleek, a pure calm. And there
the females swam in peace, and the young whales came snuffing tamely
at the boat, like young dogs.—"But far beneath this wondrous world
upon the surface, another and still stranger world met our eyes as we
40 gazed over the side. For, suspended in these watery vaults, floated the

forms of the nursing mothers of the whales, and those that by their enormous girth seemed shortly to become mothers. The lake, as I have hinted, was to a considerable depth exceedingly transparent: and as human infants while sucking will calmly and fixedly gaze away from the breast, as if leading two different lives at a time; and while yet drawing mortal nourishment, be still spiritually feasting upon some unearthly reminiscence; even so did the young of these whales seem looking up towards us, but not at us, as if we were but a bit of gulf weed in their new-born sight. Floating on their sides, the mothers also seemed quietly eyeing us.— — — —Some of the subtlest secrets of the seas seemed divulged to us in the enchanted pond. We saw young Leviathan amours in the deep. And thus, though surrounded by circle upon circle of consternation and affrights, did these inscrutable creatures at the centre freely and fearlessly indulge in all peaceful concernments; yea, serenely revelled in dalliance and delight.—"

There is something stupendous and overwhelming in these whaling scenes, and monstrous hunts, as Melville gives them. Strange and inhuman is the chapter on ambergris. Then follows the chapter called "the Cassock"—an odd piece of phalliciam, surely unparalleled in the literature of the world. Then there is the powerful description of the "Tryworks"—the extracting oil from the blubber: the sooty, furnace-hot, oily factory of a ship at calm in the midst of the waters. And in this night of red furnaces burning on deck at sea, Melville has this strange and frightening experience of *reversion*, when he feels the ship rushing backwards from him, in the mystic reversion. 'Uppermost was the impression, that whatever swift, rushing thing I stood on was not so much bound to any haven ahead, as rushing from all havens astern. A stark, bewildered feeling, as of death, came over me. Convulsively my hands grasped the tiller, but with the crazy conceit that the tiller was, somehow, in some enchanted way, inverted.

' "My God! What is the matter with me?" thought I. Lo! in my brief sleep I had turned myself about, and was fronting the ship's stern, with my back to her prow and the compass—'

But this experience, an actual dream experience, makes a terrible impression on him. He ends with an injunction to all men, not to gaze on the red fire, when its redness makes all things look ghastly.

In some unhealthy work on the ship, Queequeg caught a fever and was like to die. "How he wasted and wasted away in those few long-lingering days, till there seemed but little left of him but his frame and tatooing. But as all else in him thinned, and his cheekbones grew sharper, his eyes, nevertheless, seemed growing fuller and fuller: they became of a strangeness of lustre; and mildly but deeply looked out at you there from his sickness, a wondrous testimony to that immortal health in him which could not die, or be weakened. And like circles on the water,

5   which, as they grow fainter, expand; so his eyes seemed rounding and rounding, like the rings of Eternity. An awe that cannot be named would steal over you as you sat by the side of this waning savage— —"

But Queequeg does not die—and the Pequod emerges from the Eastern Straits, into the full Pacific. "To my meditative Magian rover,

10 this serene Pacific once beheld, must ever after be the sea of his adoption. It rolls the midmost waters of the world— —" And in this Pacific, there are more fights.

"It was far down the afternoon; and when all the spearings of the crimson fight were done: and floating in the lovely sunset sea and sky,

15 sun and whale both died stilly together; then, such a sweetness and such a plaintiveness, such inwreathing orisons curled up in that rosy air, that it almost seemed as if far over from the deep green convent valleys of the Manilla isles, the Spanish land-breeze, wantonly turned sailor, had gone to sea, freighted with those vesper hymns.

20 "Soothed again, but only soothed to deeper gloom, Ahab, who had sterned off from the whale, sat intently watching his final wanings from the now tranquil boat. For that strange spectacle observable in all sperm whales dying—the turning of the head sunwards, and so expiring—that strange spectacls, beheld of such a placid evening, somehow to Ahab

25 conveyed a wondrousness unknown before.

"He turns and turns him to it;—how slowly, but how steadfastly his homage-rendering and invoking brow, with his last dying motions. He too worships fire';— — —"

So Ahab soliloquises: and so the warm-blooded whale turns for the

30 last time to the sun, which begot him in the waters.—But, as we see in the next chapter, it is the Thunder Fire which Ahab worships: the balls of the corposanct: the pure fire of destruction.

It is a strange storm, the electric storm on the Pequod, when the corposancts* burn in high, tapering flames of supernatural pallor, upon

35 the mast heads, and when the compass is reversed. After this all is fatality. Life itself seems electrically reversed, in these hunters of Moby Dick, they are all mad, possessed. And Ahab moves hand in hand with the poor imbecile negro boy, Pip, so dreadfully demented when they left him in the open sea, swimming alone. It is the imbecile child of the

40 sun hand in hand with the northern monomaniac, the latter dominant.

The voyage surges on and on. They meet one ship, then another. All is ordinary day-routine, and yet all is a tension of pure madness and approaching horror, the horror of the near fight. "Hither and thither, on high, glided the snow-white wings of small, unspeckled birds; these were the gentle thoughts of the feminine air; but to and fro in the deeps, far down in the bottomless blue, rushed mighty leviathans, sword-fish, and sharks; and these were the strong, troubled, murderous thinkings of the masculine sea—" It is on this day Ahab confesses his weariness, the weariness of his burden. "—But do I look very old, so very, very old, Starbuck? I feel deadly faint, bowed, and humped, as though I were Adam, staggering beneath the piled centuries since Paradise—". It is the Gethsemane of Ahab, before the last fight with the whale. The necessity to destroy—to maintain his being triumphant in one sort—it is almost too much for Ahab; the burden of the spiritual oneness.

And then they catch sight of the whale. Ahab sees him from his hoisted perch at the mast-head.—"From this height the whale was now seen some mile or so ahead, at every roll of the sea revealing his high, sparkling hump, and regularly jetting his silent spout into the air.—"

The boats are lowered, they draw near the white whale. "At length the breathless hunter came so nigh his seemingly unsuspecting prey that his entire dazzling hump was distinctly visible, sliding along the sea as if an isolated thing, and continually set in a revolving ring of finest, fleecy, greenish foam. He saw the vast involved wrinkles of the slightly projecting head, beyond. Before it, far out on the soft, Turkish-rugged waters, went the glistening white shadow from his broad, milky forehead, a musical rippling playfully accompanying the shade; and behind, the blue waters interchangeably flowed over the moving valley of his steady wake; and on either side bright bubbles arose and danced by his side. But these were broken again by the light toes of hundreds of gay fowl softly feathering the sea, alternate with their fitful flight; and like to some flagstaff rising from the pointed hull of an argosy, the tall but shattered pole of a recent lance projected from the white whale's back; and at intervals one of the cloud of soft-toed fowls hovering, and to and fro shimmering like a canopy over the fish, silently perched and rocked on this pole, the long tail feathers streaming like pennons.

"A gentle joyousness—a mighty mildness of repose in swiftness, invested the gliding whale— —"

The fight with the whale is too wonderful, and too awful, to be described apart from the book. It lasted three days. The fearful sight, on the third day, of the torn body of the Parsee harpooner, lost the

previous day, now seen lashed on to the flanks of the white whale by the
tangle of harpoon-lines, is almost too much. The awful and infuriated
whale turned upon the ship, symbol of the whole civilised world of ours.
He smote her with a fearful shock. And a few minutes later, from the last
5   of the fighting whale-boats came the cry "'The ship? Great God, where
is the ship?'—Soon they through the dim, bewildering medium saw
her sidelong fading phantom, as in the gaseous Fata Morgana; only the
uppermost masts out of water; while fixed by infatuation, or fidelity, or
fate, to their once lofty perches, the pagan harpooneers still maintained
10 their sinking look-outs on the sea. And now, concentric circles seized
the lone boat itself, and all its crew, and each floating oar, and every
lance-pole, and spinning, animate and inanimate, all round and round
in one vortex, carried the smallest chip of the Pequod out of sight.—"
    The bird of heaven, the eagle, goes down with the ship, fixed by
15 Tashtego's hammer.
    "Now small fowls flew screaming over the yet yawning gulf; a sullen
white surf beat against its steep sides; then all collapsed, and the great
shroud of the sea rolled on as it rolled five thousand years ago."
    So ends one of the strangest, and most wonderful books in the world,
20 closing up its mystery and its tormented symbolism.

INTERMEDIATE VERSION (1919)

CONTENTS

Studies in Classic American Literature

(VIII)

Nathaniel Hawthorne (II.)

The Scarlet Letter contains the inevitable triangle, the inverse trinity, the trinity of disruption. There are three people, one of whom is the ghost or go-between: in this instance maleficent. He is Roger Chillingworth. The character of Chillingworth is purely symbolistic, not personal at all. He is like a dark figure in a mystery-play, an influence rather than an individual.

Roger Chillingworth is the last incarnation of the Middle Ages, the Dark Ages. He is the last of the alchemists, first of the scientific doctors. In actual life Francis Bacon is his prototype. The difference between the alchemists and the scientists lies in their manner of knowing. The scientist "knows" mentally, and rationally. But the alchemist must trust for his profound perceptions, and for his subtlest effects, to the activities of the lower consciousness, called the Unconscious* by the psychoanalysts, vaguely known as instinct and influence in the common world. This lower or sensual consciousness apprehends by direct vibrational-contact the facts of the active material world, and it achieves its effect by something like "will," the lower, unconscious will-power which directly influences the surrounding phenomenal world.

Here we may as well admit, once and for all, that magic, Alchemy, and the Hermetic science are not such nonsense as we pretend.* They may be abhorrent. They are not nonsense.

Let us divide the world into two parts. First there is the creative world of life. The quick of creation, called the Godhead, is manifest in the living creature, first and foremost in the living human being. The creative activity is forever a mystery to us: the life-mystery. Only we know we *are* this mystery: and to what we *are*, we must submit.— The second world is the material world of death. It is from the death of the living body that Matter, inorganic Matter, and all the forces known to science, result. The great Material forces form a world of their own. This world is comprehensible. This world is subject to fixed law. This world is limited. It is the world of science.

The creative mystery is forever undefined and inexplicable, incomprehensible. It is the first term of our being. It is life itself. Life is

unlimited, and, in itself, it has no law. It even transcends the established
law of the Materio-dynamic* world.

The two worlds, living and material, creative and dynamic have a
profoundly complex relation to one another, and a scarcely comprehen-
5   sible interdependence. But let us assert, first and last, that the creative,
living world takes precedence over the material, dynamic world, and
has the ultimate control of this world.

Now science and alchemy are both seeking for the control of the
material-dynamic world. Science, however, seeks to master the dynamic
10 world by submitting to the laws of that world; and by submitting to
the laws, learning how to apply them. *Fata volentem ducunt.** The Alchemists sought the contrary. They sought to master the material world,
not by applying its own laws against itself, but by violently mastering
these laws through the force of their own material will. *Fata nolentem
15 trahunt.* The Alchemists sought for terrible will-control of the material
universe. The magicians had the same end in view. Both wanted the
master-key. Both wanted to violate the universal law, as Christ sought
to transcend the universal law. To the magicians, and to Christ alike
the motto applies: *Fata nolentem trahunt.* But it is nonsense to say that
20 the miracles of Christ, or of the magicians, are *impossible*. They are possible. But no man turns the volition of his whole creative soul towards
the mastery of the material universe without exhausting his own creative
being, and becoming, in himself, a mere term of the materio-dynamic
world, subject, fixed, limited. As long as time lasts, the greatest magi-
25 cian, and the greatest divine miracle-worker will each expend his own
creative essence in the performance of his feats, and thus destroy in
himself the very *will* by which he achieves his success. This is as true
of Christ as of Simon Magus.* Each of them expends, or as it were
explodes himself in his supreme effort of control.

30   Now Chillingworth is a mixture of Simon Magus and Jesus. He wants
to heal the world. And he wants to do it by force of his own personal *will*.
His consciousness is the dark sensual consciousness, accompanied by
that curious antique and mediaeval intellectuality, the intellectuality of
all priestcrafts, foreign for the most part to us. Jesus was *willing* utterly to
35 expend himself in order to transcend or violate the laws of the material
universe, for the sake of humanity. Chillingworth is in a quandary. He
is not willing to expend, to sacrifice himself. He is only willing to *serve*.
And he insists that, even in serving, the last word shall be left to him.
He is a servile authority.

As such he captures the woman. His principle is the serpent-wisdom. Prostrate, subjected, he is still full of dark wisdom and galvanic power. He is willing to enthrone the woman, because she, enthroned, will rest upon him. The throne of the Woman, whether Mary or Rhea,* rests upon the great serpent.

The woman enters into the compact. The power of the world is to be given to the *subject* male, the prostrate, servile, serpent-wise male. It is the accepting of Satan's offer to Jesus: the power over all the world. Hester seems to be tricked into this compact. But not so. It holds good between Chillingworth and her, to the end. She is but Judas to Dimmesdale, with Chillingworth as her Satan.

The old symbology is all brought in. The physician—Hermes of the Underworld—is distorted, crippled, like Hephaestos, to show his subjected nature. He knows all the subtle sensual reactions. His *will* works in this medium. He conquers the woman, and holds her to the end. She swears the oath with him still.

"Why dost thou smile so at me?. . . . Art thou like the Black Man that haunts the forest round us? Hast thou enticed me into a bond that will prove the ruin of my soul?"

"Not thy soul!" he answered with another smile. "No, not thine."

This is the Black Man of the American primeval forests: this demoniac *will* in the subject sensual psyche.

The game is not really between Hester and Chillingworth. As usual, she is a means between two men. The game is between Chillingworth and Dimmesdale, the two representatives of two worlds. Dimmesdale is like Jesus: he will expend himself utterly, utterly destroy himself, if he can but preserve his will, and transcend the laws of the material world: what he calls the triumph over Death. Chillingworth on the other hand seeks the same mastery for his own will, but not at the price of personal sacrifice. Though the whole world perish,* Chillingworth's will must triumph.

They are the two opposites. Neither yields to the other. The relation between them is horrible. It is a kind of satanic love. Dimmesdale will destroy himself, destroy himself utterly, pour himself out like a sacrifice on the altar, that he may vindicate the old spiritual triumph over death, the triumph of immortality in love. And Chillingworth watches, watches, goads him and tortures him with the fatal secret, the secret of man's sensual nature. Chillingworth watches, and smiles. He holds the one drop of poison that can darken the whole sun of spiritual immortality.

"It is all dark necessity," the physician says. But the necessity dates farther back than Hester's "sin." It dates as far back as Christ. Nay further, it dates further even than the triumph of the one half of the psyche over the other half. It goes right back to the beginning, to that horrible old Hebrew passion which seems radical in man, the desire of a man in his own soul to conquer the universe, to be master of life and death, by force of his own will. The old Jews discovered the Chillingworth method, the power of the sensual will. Jesus made the opposite great discovery, the power of the spiritual, self-immolating will: the great discovery that passive power is even stronger than active power. Each is but an expression of an old, horrible will-to-power-over-life-and-death. All the hideous monotheism of history is only the supreme expression of this hateful will. Why should man want power over life and death? It is a most dreary possession.

But who will win, Chillingworth or Dimmesdale? Chillingworth, it seems. In the minister the inevitable takes place. His psyche begins to disintegrate. Exert the *will* beyond a certain measure, and in its very exertion it ruptures itself. *Fata nolentem trahunt.* The horrible signs of madness set in. His lust for self-immolation becomes obscene. He tortures himself with whips and hot irons. He is the Inquisition unto himself. The horrible will which seeks power through self-immolation, power over life and death, becomes a ruptured obscenity at last.

It holds to its own purpose. Ostensibly it is whole. Right to the end Dimmesdale maintains his sanctified appearance. He must preach his great Election Sermon, and win his last saintly applause. At the same time he has an imbecile, epileptic desire to defile his own religious mysteries. In the Dimmesdale of this period lies the clue to Dostoevsky.

The saintly minister of New England meets one of his hoary-headed deacons in the road, just before the Election Sermon, and—"It was only by the most careful self-control that he could refrain from uttering certain blasphemous suggestions that rose into his mind concerning the Communion supper."—Again, as an old widow stops him for a word of comfort, he longs to whisper in her ear "a brief, pithy, and as it then appeared to him, unanswerable argument against the immortality of the soul." Once more, as he sees a young girl "fair as a lily that had bloomed in Paradise" approaching him, he must cover his face in his cloak to pass by, because he knows he could not help giving her one look, full of evil suggestion, that would blight all her innocence.

It is the fatal, imbecile or epileptic state of soul, such as Dostoevsky's, where the integrity is broken, and the one half of the psyche acts in malignant frustration of the other half, in a process of futility.

To the last Dimmesdale is an actor, subtle, malevolent. He hates the woman who is the cause of his downfall from spiritual power.   5

"Shall we not meet again?" whispered she, bending her face down close to him. "Shall we not spend our immortal life together? Surely, surely we have ransomed one another with all this woe! Thou lookest far into eternity with those bright dying eyes. Tell me what thou seest!"

"Hush, Hester—hush," said he, with tremulous solemnity. "The law   10
we broke!—the sin here so awfully revealed!—let these alone be in thy thoughts. I fear! I fear!"

With a last bit of pulpit rhetoric, the perfect exemplar of the spiritual way dies in America. He must still be superhuman and immortal. He has triumphed even now over Chillingworth. If he had died unconfessing,   15
the spiritual ascendancy in America would have received a fatal blow. But he confessed, he acknowledged the personal transgression, and the perfection of the ideal. Chillingworth was cheated of his triumph. The exponents of the spiritual way of self-abnegation still held him subject, servile.   20

It is a very great book. All the ramblings of Dostoevsky are only accumulated evidence of what is here succinctly, symbolically stated. *The Scarlet Letter* contains a marvellous and perfect exposition of the deepest soul-processes, and is one of the world's wonder-books. We can't help detesting it somewhere, for its hateful duplicity. All the way,   25
there is the hateful conventional pose, the outward pious preaching of the conventional creed, whilst underneath runs the lurid lust in sin, the gloating in the overthrow of that which is so praised.—And yet even this duplicity is necessary for a true exposition of the soul state.

The other books are not so great as *The Scarlet Letter*. *The House of the*   30
Seven Gables is a tale of the passing of the old Chillingworth order, the dark old order of the sensual will. The opposing parties are reconciled, there is a marriage. And this introduces the period of "prosperity," the barren industrial period of machine triumph.

The Blithedale Romance is less coherent, but more personal. It con-   35
tains an account, more or less, of the Brook Farm experiment. A number of the most advanced spirits of America, wishing to set the perfect so-cial example, and start the real Utopia, bought a farm and settled in, a company of spiritual transcendentalists, to live in common and to till

the land and be perfectly unified with all things. Through their pure and natural submission to the needs of man, their unison in actual *labour*, they thought to attain this spiritual triumph over life, wherein man becomes in himself infinite, he is infinity, he is identified with the
5   Oversoul, he transcends life and death.

Hawthorne stood it for a few weeks, then left. He was an artist. The artist can never have anything to do with these infinite values, this merging business, this conquest of life and death. He wants life to be life, he wants real individual values, nothing else: never, never a triumph
10 of the *will* over the spontaneous soul.

The Brook Farm experiment was in direct line from Crêvecœur. It was an attempt to work the sensual body from the spiritual centres. The attempt never works, for this reason. Once you introduce brute labour, the brute soul, the brute will, by which alone this labour is achieved,
15 starts into being full against your spiritual will. You cannot spiritualise the sensual self by *employing* the sensual self: you cannot. At the best you can but *mechanise* it. The very act of stooping and thrusting the spade into the earth calls into being the old Adam,* the dark sensual will for mastery over the inanimate earth.

20   But it was hopeless to introduce brute physical labour. Brute labour, the brute struggle with earth and herds, *must* rouse the dark sensual centres, darken the mind, isolate the being in heavy-blooded separateness. Then there is an end of spiritual oneness and transcendence.

Moreover, the clue to the movement lay in the desire to subject or dis-
25 integrate the primary sensual self. It was an attempt to perform by pleas- ant means what Dimmesdale, in his physical self-tortures, attempted by unpleasant means. The reduction of the primary spontaneous self to pure subordination, however, is never pleasant. And the process of the reduction is a process of disintegration of the primal self. And human
30 beings engaged in the toils of such disintegration must react, sooner or later, against the spiritual bond of union that is superimposed. For the whole psychic motion is frictional and separative. So the Brook Farm experiment was a failure.

The individuals of the *Blithedale Romance* present a four-square
35 group, of two triangles. There are two men: Hawthorne, the I, the re- fined spiritual being, comparable to Dimmesdale; then Hollingsworth, the deep-voiced, ex-blacksmith, the patron of criminals; then Zenobia, superb, like Hester Prynne, or like Judith Hutter; and fourthly a white lily, a white weed of a sickly lily, called Priscilla, a little forlorn semp-
40 stress who turns out to be half-sister, to the rich, superb Zenobia, just

as Hetty Hutter was sister to Judith, or the White Lily was sister to Cora.

Now all these four are nominal idealists, creatures of the spiritual one way. And they are all secretly seeking for the sensual satisfaction. Hawthorne is the spiritual being secretly worshipping the sensual mysteries, the next generation after Dimmesdale. Hollingsworth is a descendant of Chillingworth: a dark, black-bearded monomaniac. His monomania is criminals: his one end in life is to build an asylum of criminals, of which he will be the head, the reformer. This Hephaestos of the underworld stubbornly adheres to his spiritual assertion. He will reform all criminals. But his passion, it is obvious, is to be in communion with criminals. Potentially a criminal, the actual criminals of the state fix him like a lode-stone. He is Chillingworth without Chillingworth's intellect: Chillingworth more subject than ever, but criminally polarised.

The Criminal is the man who, like Roger Chillingworth, is abject and down-trodden in his sensual self, by the spiritual or social domination, and who turns round secretly on life, to bite it and poison it and mutilate it. There is a genuine *passion* at the bottom of the ultra-social individual, for criminal gratification. De Quincey in his essay on "Murder as a Fine Art," reveals this terrible reality. And this passion is Hollingsworth's passion. But he maintains his spiritual dominion, and seeks to gratify his passion, and vindicate his triumphal spiritual being, in *reforming* criminals.

The connection between the two men is like that between Dimmesdale and Chillingworth. Hawthorne falls sick at Brook Farm, and Hollingsworth nurses him. There is a strong love and blood-tenderness between the two men. Hawthorne, helpless and passive between the strong, but unspeakably gentle hands of the blacksmith, is lulled in sheer sense-gratification. It is sheer self-yielding, he yields himself up.

But his love turns to hate. Hollingsworth wants absolute, monomaniac dominion over him, to use him. And Hawthorne will not be either dominated or used. After all, the passive or spiritual soul is the finer and stronger soul of the two. And he detests and despises the monomaniac blacksmith, who has really a lust to consume and use the other man. Hollingsworth is like Chillingworth, who in healing consumes his partner.

Then there is the criss-cross of love between the men and women. Hawthorne admires, even loves the superb Zenobia, with the exotic flower in her hair, but he has no real *desire* for her. He fears her dominance, her splendid feminine arrogance and freedom. Hollingsworth also seems to love Zenobia. But he does not love her. He hates her, really. He only wants her money. Zenobia would outmatch Hollingsworth in the sensual conflict. She would beat him at his own game. The sensual being in

5 her is arrogant, and it is here that he needs submission from a woman. She would be stronger than he, for which he hates her. He would give her all the outward, spiritual pre-eminence in the world. But sensually he must arrogate, his must be the power.

Zenobia, however, loves Hollingsworth madly. She wants to possess him. She has a sister-love for Hawthorne. They understand each

10 other. Hollingsworth almost marries her, for her money, for his criminal scheme. But poor Zenobia drowns herself.

Priscilla, the little frail sempstress, captures both men. This white, weak, ingenuous little creature has been used as a spiritualistic medium

15 in the public shows that were then the rage in America. She has been veiled in a white veil, set on a public platform, and made to answer, as a medium, the questions of a ghastly corrupt person who turns out to be Zenobia's unconfessed husband.

Priscilla is interesting as a phenomenon. She is a real "medium".

20 In this, she is almost like a degenerate descendant of Ligeia. Ligeia triumphs in her unspeakable submissiveness to the man, her husband. She is the passive pole of his love.

Now if we carry this process of unutterable passivity, and destructive submission, a little further, we go beyond death, and we get the

25 little "medium", Priscilla. In Priscilla, the mystic seal of integrity, the integrity of being, is broken. She is strictly a thing, a mystic prostitute, or an imbecile. She has no being, no true waking reality, only a sleeping, automatic reality.

The covering her up with the white veil symbolises the abstract-

30 ing of the upper or wakeful consciousness, leaving the under dream-consciousness free and active. It is the same as the clairvoyant gazing into the crystal. The gazing into the crystal is a process of annulling or abstracting the whole wakening consciousness, leaving the mechanical dream-consciousness in possession of the being. But in the wakeful con-

35 sciousness the *being* has its presence. By destroying this consciousness— and it is a process of destruction, not of suspension, as in sleep—the core and centre and pivot of the being is gradually destroyed, and the being becomes a thing, an incontestably marvellous *transmitter*, like a telephone apparatus, of the great *natural mechanical* vibrations in the

40 ether, vibrations of mechanical cause and effect. Priscilla, covered with

the veil, is abstracted from creative living being—she is a pure instance of materio-dynamic existence. The director puts the questions, not to her mind, but automatically, to her sensory-conscious *mechanical* reason. And, as a little unutterably delicate machine, she answers automatically. There is no correspondence of telepathy or thought-transmission, or even mesmerism. It is a process of after-death, when the being is annulled, and the unimaginably sensitive sensory machine remains vibrating in the flow of the great invisible forces, mechanical, psychic, animistic, the uttermost spiritualism of material being. The whole process, however, is so inordinately delicate and difficult, that the base tricks of mesmerism and thought-transmission must form the greatest part of any public show—No medium, no clairvoyant, moreover, even, granted the maximum of success, can transmit more than the *material-dynamic* or *mechanical* possibilities of past, present, or future, those things which depend on cause-and-effect, in the dynamic or causal world. In the spontaneous or creative world, they do not exist—they have forfeited existence. They are things,—not beings. What is true of mediumistic revelations is true also of dreams. Dreams are expressions of the materio-dynamic world, *never* of the creative world, over which they have no power.

Now both men love Priscilla—Hawthorne confesses it at the very end of his book, pops it out as if it were some wonderful secret. But Hollingsworth gets her: she marries him: and they live in a little cottage, and he walks, leaning on her arm, queer and aged.

It is inevitable that both men should love Priscilla. She is the only being who will so submit to them, as to give them the last horrible thrills of sensual experience, in the direct *destruction* of the sensual body, pure prostitution. Priscilla, passive, mediumistic, almost imbecile, has a demon strength in her passive nullity. Once the real living integrity of being is broken in her, once she becomes will-less, she is stronger, less destructible than any living being. Will-less, clinging, unspeakably passive, she forms, almost like an imbecile, a pole of obscene negative passion. Towards her the overweening sensual electricity runs in violent destructive flow, the flow of not-being. It destroys at the very quick the correspondent. Hollingsworth, the powerful dark blacksmith, becomes quite soon tottering and shaky, when he has married Priscilla—and she is stronger, alert, active. In her last mystery of not-being, the dream existence, the somnambulist, mechanical, infernal reality such as is suggested by the old legends of were-wolves and metamorphoses, she is established and triumphant, and, by her very presence, almost

without contact, she so draws the vital electricity from the male, in a
horrible sensual-disintegrative flow, that she destroys his being as by
magic. This is the meaning of the were-wolf, and witch stories. Apuleius,
with his metamorphoses, and Petronius, with his *Satyricon*, these are
5   not so very different, in *substance*, from Hawthorne. The obscene metamorphosis of beings into elementals and hell-principles is described
more perfectly, though less explicitly, in Priscilla and Dimmesdale, and
Pearl, than in these old authors.

Hollingsworth *wants* this obscene polarity with the almost imbecile
10   Priscilla, a polarity in sheer disintegration into nought. His sensual sensations are those that he desires—the acute sensual-electric experience
in the Sacral ganglion. It is an experience that immediately suggests
the crackling and sparkling of electricity from a battery in which it is
generated. And this acute vibratory motion is set up intensely in the
15   sacral region of the nerves of the human being, in the last processes of
mystic disintegration out of being. The last lust is for this indescribable
sensation—whose light we can see in the eyes of a tiger, or a a wolf.

Studies in Classic American Literature.

(X)

Dana.

Richard Henry Dana was the son of an American littérateur of the same name, and grandson of Francis Dana, once United States minister to Russia, and Chief Justice for Massachusetts. Of this distinguished family comes the author of *Two Years Before the Mast*.

The young Dana went to Harvard in 1832, at the age of seventeen. After two years of study, trouble with his eyes caused him to leave the university. He turned to the sea. He was nineteen years of age when he shipped as an ordinary sea man on a small sailing vessel trading with the then remote, hardly-known California.—He returned from this voyage in 1836. And his book is an account of his experiences. On his return he went back to Harvard, graduated in 1837, and rose eventually to be one of the most distinguished American advocates. In 1879 he was nominated Minister to England; but the Senate refused to confirm his appointment. He died at Rome in 1882. Such are the barest facts of Dana's life.

Dana stood where the Brook Farmers had left off. They wanted the assurance of their identification with the Oversoul, union in physical labour. Like Tolstoy, through sharing common toil they wanted to be united to all men, and to the infinite. Dana was a step further on. In the first place, he sought no soul union. His desire was instinctive, a material attraction. He did not wish to return to the soil, or to be united with the Oversoul. He wanted extreme sensation. He wanted consciously to register his extreme sensations, like Edgar Allan Poe. But his reaction was not to some other individual or psyche. It was to the pure element of Water, the sea. Dana, a highly-bred, overcultured American wanted the direct physical experience of a working man, not in order to give himself over mindlessly to this experience, a unit of sensual consciousness, as the working men do; but rather to overcome this sensual reaction with his upper consciousness. He wanted consciously to *know* the sensual experience of the seas.

It was not enough for him to return to the land. Instinct told him this. The land is not a stark element. It is a mixture, it is still in a sense *life-tissue*. Men like Thoreau might watch the earth. Dana was beyond.

319

He needed the stark contact with the naked element of water. This is
actual concrete experience of the naked infinitude, as near as possible.
To know the sea, and with the consciousness to assimilate the mystery of
the sea, this is to conquer the last half of the material infinite, the infinite
5   of Matter, the death-infinite. For man, in some vast bygone epoch, has
known fire.

Single and alone Dana went to the encounter. It was to be another
great conquest of the sensual world, by the upper spiritual. Dana did not
go as the common seamen go, mindlessly, to give themselves into ulti-
10 mate communion with the sea. He did not yield to his sensual, mindless
soul. Always he was mindful, he watched. He wanted a great, elemental
extension of consciousness. The *rapport* between him and the seas was
a reaction, not a communion: combative. He approached the material
infinite in order to conquer it, not to affect a consummation. It was the
15 human will seeking a vast elemental extension of consciousness, preserving its identity in the midst of the waters. If Hawthorne, sounding
the horn at Brook Farm, saw himself as a spectre, what was Dana at sea,
a common sailor? But Dana knew his own spectral meaning. He knew
that, in face of the ultimate waters, the human soul *is* spectral: isolated,
20 facing the end. Content to be spectral, Dana faced the waters of the end.
He gave his body to be burnt by the salt waters. His consciousness he
would keep firm all the time, never yielding. It was a great achievement,
an act of investigation, whereby the human soul gains another great
circle of consciousness, extends its mysterious range further out, far
25 out over the waters.

It is this great, stark encounter which gives the extreme simplicity
and bareness, and the remarkable sense of mystic profundity to Dana's
book. Men who are not reduced, who have not reached the pitch of
elementality, will see nothing more than a pleasant account, in *Two Years
30 Before the Mast*, of by-gone sea-life. They will call it boy's reading. But
it takes a far-reaching man's soul to grasp the beauty of the statement,
the extremity of the realisation.

Dana's soul is in a sense dehumanised: better, it is elementalised.
Isolated, alone, he is not human in the ordinary sense. He is not looking
35 for things human, nor listening to human sounds. His adventure is
not an adventure of a being among beings: it is an adventure into the
material universe. He is looking at the naked element, and hearing it.
His elemental consciousness watched the primal movements of Matter,
the first Matter of all, Water, as it slides in its great inorganic motions.
40 He interposes no idea, translates into no human terms. Stark, vast,

sliding Matter he encounters in all its primordial reality. He need not anthropomorphise. His soul has its bareness and its elementality, as the sea has, Matter in its essence.

In the first pages already he gives the whole relationship. "Nothing can compare with the *early breaking of day* upon the wide, sad ocean. There is something in the first grey streaks stretching along the eastern horizon, and throwing an indistinct light upon the face of the deep, which creates a feeling of loneliness, of dread, and of melancholy foreboding, which nothing else in nature can give." So the human soul ventures wakeful and aware into the great naked watery universe of the end of life, the twilighty place where integral being ceases, where life gives out. It is life in man, facing the vast death which is the first Matter.

The same vision of life hovering tiny and isolated against the vast sliding darkness, where individuality is spent and universality supervenes, Dana conveys in his description of the albatross. The vessel has just rounded Cape Horn.—"This day we saw the last of the albatrosses, which had been our companions for a great part of the time off the Cape. I had been interested in the bird from descriptions I had read of it, and was not at all disappointed. We caught one or two with a baited hook which we floated astern upon a shingle. Their long, flapping wings, long legs, and large staring eyes give them a very peculiar appearance. They look well on the wing. But one of the finest sights that I have ever seen was an albatross asleep upon the water, during a calm, off Cape Horn, when a heavy sea was running. There being no breeze, the surface of the water was unbroken, but a long, heavy swell was rolling, and we saw the fellow, all white, directly ahead of us, asleep upon the waves, with his head under his wing; now rising upon the top of a huge billow, and then falling slowly until he was lost in the hollow between. He was undisturbed for some time, until the noise of our bows, gradually approaching, roused him, when, lifting his head, he stared upon us for a moment, and then spread his wide wings, and took his flight."

It might be Dana's vision of himself, the last, light-loving incarnation of life exposed upon the eternal waters. It is the first and last apparition of life, upon the verge of the two naked principles, aerial and watery. Between the sky of light and the ocean sleeps one single speck of life, landless, almost bodiless, incomprehensible as sea-birds are incomprehensible: almost material: ghosts of Matter, almost.

But the best of Dana is the actual conflict with the sea. In this conflict he has his consummation. It is a metaphysical, actual struggle of an integral soul with a vast, non-living, yet potent element. Dana never forgets, never ceases to watch. He must actually consciously *know*, in some way, he must master the sea in his consciousness. Which is what no sailor does. A sailor accepts, he does not master. Tiny and alone, Dana watches the great seas mount round his own small body. If he is 5 swept away, some other man will have to take up what he has begun. For the sea must be mastered by the human consciousness, in the great fight of the human soul for mastery over life and death. This is the almost scientific conquest, the *knowing of the waters*. Impartial, Dana beholds himself among the elements, calm and fatal. His style is great 10 and hopeless, the style of a perfect scientist.

"Between five and six the cry of 'All starbowlines ahoy!' summoned our watch on deck, and immediately all hands were called. A great cloud of a dark slate-colour was driving on us from the south-west; and we did our best to take in sail before we were in the midst of it. We had got 15 the light sails furled, the courses hauled up, and the top-sail reef tackles hauled out, and were just mounting the fore-rigging when the storm struck us. In an instant the sea, which had been comparatively quiet, was running higher and higher; and it became almost as dark as night. The hail and sleet were harder than I had yet felt them, seeming almost 20 to pin us down to the rigging."

It is in the dispassionate statement of plain physical facts that Dana achieves his greatness. Dana writes from the remoter, non-emotional centres of being—not from the passional-emotional self. He sees the great mechanical motions of Matter itself, he sees the soul as an isolate 25 entity, without emotional connection. He has outpassed the personal self.

So the ship battles on, round Cape Horn, then out into quieter seas. The island of Juan Fernandez, Crusoe's island, rises like a dream from the sea, like a green cloud, and like a ghost Dana watches it, feeling only 30 a faint, ghostly pang of regret for the life that was.

But the strain of the long sea-voyage begins to tell. The sea is a great disintegrative force. Its tonic quality is its disintegrative quality. It burns down the tissue, liberates energy. And after a long time, this burning-down is destructive. The psyche becomes destroyed, irritable, 35 frayed, almost dehumanised.

So there is trouble on board the ship, irritating discontent, friction unbearable, and at last a flogging. This flogging rouses Dana for the first and last time to passion.

"Sam was by this time seized up—that is, placed against the shrouds, 40 with his wrists made fast to the shrouds, his jacket off, and his back exposed. The captain stood on the break of the deck, a few feet from him, and a little raised, so as to have a good swing at him, and held in his hand a light, thick rope. The officers stood round, and the crew grouped together in the waist. All these preparations made me feel sick and faint, angry and excited as I was. A man—a human being made in God's likeness—fastened up and flogged like a beast! The first and almost uncontrollable impulse was resistance. But what could be done?—The time for it had gone by—"

Dana cannot resist: he is sick and faint. His whole being is contravened. A man is a being made in God's likeness, a spiritual being, a *knowing* thing. And here is a violent demonstration of his ungodlike, unspiritual nature, a sheer contradiction of the Logos in him. The naked back of the seaman is uncovered and exposed. First violation. For the back is blind, sealed, utterly private in its nakedness, not to be known. The back is the field of man's individual volition, from the back he *wills.*—Then the naked back is flogged with a rope. Second violation. For man is made in God's image, he is already perfected, a Logos.—And finally, another man does the flogging. Third violation. For are not all men equal, all sons of God, all spiritual beings, each one a Logos?

Dana is violated in his deepest being. But he cannot act. He can effect nothing. Because he too is wrong. He is too much a scientist, a theorist, a logician.—As a matter of fact, a man is a unique, single being, "made in God's image," so long as he keeps the pure integrity of his being. Once he loses or forfeits the integrity of his single being, he becomes subject to the laws of Force and Matter. Again, even though a man be ultimately, or primarily an "image of God," yet, in the actual business of living he is part, not only of a great human system, but even of a vital system. However we may argue against it, the vital force itself flows from man to woman, and from man to man, in a physical, dynamic circuit. Whatever we may be, in our own vital being we are dynamically polarised one by another. However man and woman may assert their individual independence, yet a life-circuit encompasses them, and makes one the positive, commanding pole, one the negative, receptive pole. Any disruption of this polarised vital circuit causes disruption in all life. In the same way, the vital circuit flows through men. One man is the positive, commanding pole, others are negative and receptive. Men are so born, and so constituted, and will ever be so born and so constituted. *Fata nolentem trahunt.* True, the first, the primal reality is the reality of the unique, individual soul in each man. But the integrity of this very soul depends on the acceptance of the great sub-condition, the condition of polarity, the condition of command or obedience.

By circumstance, and probably by nature, the seaman Sam and the captain of the ship are polarised in the vital circuit, the former as negative
5   pole of obedience, the latter as positive pole of command. So long as each maintains himself in the circuit, each maintains the purity and dignity of his own inviolate, integral being. But during the long voyage, the integrity of the soul tends to weaken. Sam becomes slack, loose, slobbery, disobedient. And the captain becomes inflamed and overbearing. The
10   poles of the vital flow are shaken, the circuit becomes interrupted. At each end there is a sort of storm. It is like electricity. There is an over-balance, a surcharge, a lack of connection. And then violent friction of escaping current sets up a storm. The storm is an explosion and a readjustment.
15   It is as ridiculous to quarrel with anger and with passionate violence, as it is to quarrel with thunder. No doubt, in a perfect peaceable world there would never be a thunderstorm. But such talk is nonsense. There comes a mal-adjustment of the aerial electricity. This is readjusted by a violent storm. Would we rather the horrid sultriness lasted for ever,
20   rather than experience the violence of thunder? The same with Sam and the Captain. Would we rather each continued loose, unformed, inflamed, not himself, would we rather each lost his vital integrity, rather than suffer the storm of readjustment? It is nonsense. There are other ways of punishment? True. But your moral punishments, your poisons
25   and confinements do not purify the soul. They sodden it. Thunder may not break out. It may slowly swale away, slowly dissipate. But is there the sharp glad newness that follows a thunder-storm? There is not. No punishment could be so pure and purifying, so liberating, as this self-same flogging upon the back. It is a direct stimulus-by-pain upon the
30   very centres of the human will, which are situated in the back. It is a veritable stormy transfer of the loose electricity to its true poles again. It is a refreshing and renewing of the degraded individual.

We must guard forever against positive tyranny. But our danger today is negative tyranny, the tyranny of millions of loose, formless Sams es-
35   caping from the true circuit of their polarity, and vitiating not only their own being, but the being of all the others, those who should constitute the positive pole.

The captain suffered most. Afterwards, he could not bear the expo-sure of himself, his own passion. Sometimes man is not himself. He is
40   a mere centre of violent passional disturbance. Men are always terrified

of exposing themselves in this state. For this reason healthy sensual love seeks darkness and retreat. But the captain was naked in passion.

"As he went on, his passion increased, and he danced about on the deck, calling out as he swung the rope, 'If you want to know what I flog you for, I'll tell you. It's because I like to do it!—because I like to do it!—It suits me. That's what I do it for!'

"The man writhed under the pain. My blood ran cold, I could look no longer. Disgusted, sick, and horror-struck, I turned away and leaned over the rail and looked down in the water. A few rapid thoughts of my own situation, and the prospect of future revenge, crossed my mind; but the falling of the blows, and the cries of the man called me back at once. At length they ceased, and, turning round, I found that the Mate, at a signal from the Captain, had cut him down—"

After all, it was not so terrible. The captain evidently did not exceed the true passional measure. There was no vindictiveness, even no violation. All would have been well, save for the *moral* verdict. And this came from theorists like Dana and the seaman John, rather than from the sailors themselves. The sailors understand the passional morality, not the ethical. They respect the violent readjustments of the naked force.

"The flogging was seldom, if ever alluded to by us in the forecastle. If anyone was inclined to talk about it, the other, with a delicacy which I hardly expected to find among them, always stopped him, or turned the subject—"

Two men had been flogged: the second and elder, John, for interfering and asking the captain why he flogged Sam. It is whilst flogging John that the Captain shouts "If you want to know what I flog you for, I'll tell you—"

"But the behaviour of the two men who were flogged," Dana continues, "toward one another, showed a delicacy and a sense of honour which would have been worthy of admiration in the highest walks of life. Sam knew that the other had suffered solely on his account, and in all his complaints he said that if he alone had been flogged it would have been nothing, but that he could never see that man without thinking that he had been the means of bringing that disgrace upon him; and John never, by word or deed, let anything escape him to remind the other that it was by interfering to save his ship-mate that he had suffered.—"

As a matter of fact, it was John who ought to have been ashamed for bringing confusion and false feeling into a clear issue. Conventional morality apart, John is the reprehensible party, not Sam or the captain. It is the Johns of this world who stultify life, swathe it and strangle it with false emotions, dictated from a theory. And it is the Danas who, fixing the theory and the moral deduction, are ten times damnable. In this case, however, owing to conventional ethics, it was upon the Captain that the stigma remained. He should have remembered the awful powers 5 of public opinion: particularly Dana.

The vessel arrives at the Pacific coast, and the swell of the rollers falls in our blood—the dreary coast stretches wonderful, on the brink of the unknown.

"Not a human being but ourselves for miles—the steep hill rising 10 like a wall, and cutting us off from all the world—but the 'world of waters.' I separated myself from the rest, and sat down on a rock, just where the sea ran in and formed a fine spouting-horn. Compared with the dull, plain sand-beach of the rest of the coast this grandeur was as refreshing as a great rock in a weary land. It was almost the first time I had 15 been positively alone— — —My better nature returned strong upon me.—I experienced a glow of pleasure at finding that what of poetry and romance I had ever had in me had not been entirely deadened in the laborious life I had been lately leading. Nearly an hour did I sit, almost lost in the luxury of this entire new scene of the play in which I was 20 acting, when I was aroused by the distant shouts of my companions."

So Dana sits and Hamletises by the Pacific—chief actor in the play of his own existence. But in him, self-consciousness is again nearing the mark of scientific indifference to self.—He gives us a pretty picture of the then wild, unknown bay of San Francisco.—"The tide leaving 25 us, we came to anchor near the mouth of the bay, under a high and beautifully sloping hill, upon which herds of hundreds of red deer, and the stag, with his high-branching antlers were bounding about, looking at us for a moment, and then starting off affrighted at the noises we made for the purpose of seeing the variety of their beautiful attitudes 30 and motions—"

Two moments of real passion Dana experiences: one moment of strong but impotent hate for the Captain, one strong impulse of pitying love for the Kanaka boy, Hope—a beautiful South Sea Islander sick of a white man's disease, phthisis or syphilis. Of him Dana writes "—but the 35 other, who was my friend, and aikane—Hope—was the most dreadful object I had ever seen in my life; his eyes sunken and dead, his cheeks fallen in against his teeth, his hands looking like claws; a dreadful cough, which seemed to rack his whole shattered system; a hollow, whispering voice, and an entire inability to move himself. There he lay, upon a mat 40 on the ground, which was the only floor of the oven, with no medicine, no comforts, and no-one to care for or help him but a few kanakas, who were willing enough, but could do nothing. The sight of him made me sick and faint. Poor fellow! During the four months that I lived upon the beach we were continually together, both in work and in our excursions in the woods and upon the water. I really felt a strong affection for him, and preferred him to any of my own countrymen there. When I came into the oven he looked at me, held out his hand and said in a low voice, but with a delightful smile, 'Aloha, Aikane! Aloha nui!' I comforted him as well as I could, and promised to ask the Captain to help him from the medicine chest.—"

We have felt the pulse of hate for the Captain—now the pulse of love for the bright-eyed man of the Pacific, a real child of the ocean, full of the mystery-being of that great sea. Hope is to Dana what Chingachgook is to Cooper—the hearts-brother, the answerer. But in life he is barely more than a moment to Dana: a living being, and therefore far more ephemeral than a moral judgment.

Dana was mad to leave the Californian coast, to be back in the civilised east. Yet he feels the poignancy of departure when at last the ship draws off. The Pacific is his glamour-world: the eastern States his world of actuality, scientific, materially real.

"When all sail had been set and the decks cleared up the *California* was a speck in the horison, and the coast lay like a low cloud along the north-east. At sunset they were both out of sight, and we were once more upon the ocean, where sky and water meet."

The description of the voyage home is wonderful. It is as if the seas rose up to prevent the escape of this subtle explorer. Dana seems to pass into another world, another life, not of this earth. There is first the sense of apprehension, then the passing right into the black deeps. Then the waters almost swallow him up, with his triumphant consciousness.

"The days became shorter and shorter, the sun running lower in its course each day, and giving less and less heat, and the nights so cold as to prevent our sleeping on deck; the Magellan Clouds in sight of a clear night; the skies looking cold and angry; and at times a long, heavy, ugly sea, setting in from the Southward, told us what we were coming to—"

They were approaching Cape Horn, in the southern winter, passing into the strange, dread regions of the violent waters.

"And there lay, floating in the ocean, several miles off, an immense irregular mass, its top and points covered with snow, its centre a deep indigo. This was an iceberg, and of the largest size. As far as the eye

could reach the sea in every direction was of a deep blue colour, the
waves running high and fresh, and sparkling in the light, and in the
midst lay this immense mountain-island, its cavities and valleys thrown
into deep shade, and its points and pinnacles glittering in the sun. But no
5   description can give any idea of the strangeness, splendour, and, really,
the sublimity of the sight. Its great size—for it must have been two to
three miles in circumference, and several hundred feet in height; its
slow motion, as its base rose and sank in the water and its points nodded
against the clouds; the dashing of the waves upon it, which, breaking
10 high with foam, lined its base with a white crust; and the thundering
sound of the cracking of the mass, and the breaking and the tumbling
down of huge pieces; together with its nearness and approach, which
added a slight element of fear—all combined to give it the character of
true sublimity—"
15   But as the ship ran further and further into trouble, Dana became
ill. First it is a slight toothache. Ice and exposure cause the pain to take
hold of all his head and face. And then the face so swelled, that he could
not open his mouth to eat, and was in danger of lock-jaw. In this state he
was forced to keep his bunk for three or four days.—"At the end of the
20 third day, the ice was very thick; a complete fog-bank covered the ship.
It blew a tremendous gale from the eastward, with sleet and snow, and
there was every promise of a dangerous and fatiguing night. At dark,
the Captain called all hands aft, and told them that not a man was to
leave the deck that night; that the ship was in the greatest danger; any
25 cake of ice might knock a hole in her, or she might run on an island and
go to pieces. The look-outs were then set, and every man was put in his
station. When I heard what was the state of things, I began to put on
my things, to stand it out with the rest of them, when the mate came
below, and looking at my face ordered me back to my berth, saying if
30 we went down we should all go down together, but if I went on deck I
might lay myself up for life.—In obedience to the mate's orders, I went
back to my berth; but a more miserable night I never wish to spend—."
        It is the story of a man pitted in conflict against the sea, the vast,
almost omnipotent material element. In contest with this cosmic enemy,
35 man finds his further ratification, his further vindication. He comes out
victorious, but not till the sea has tortured his living, integral body, and
made him pay something for his triumph in consciousness.
        The horrific struggle round Cape Horn, homewards, is the crisis of
the Dana history. It is an entry into chaos, a heaven of sleet and black
40 ice-rain, a sea of ice and iron-like water. Man fights the element in all

its roused, mystic hostility to life. This fight is the inward crisis and triumph of Dana's soul. He goes through it all consciously, enduring, *knowing*. It is not a mere overcoming of obstacles. It is a pitting of the deliberate consciousness against all the roused, hostile, anti-life waters of the Pole.

After this fight, Dana has achieved his success. He has entered into a new state of mind, a new field of consciousness is awake in him, he has won to a fuller self. He is victorious over the vast primordial element, the one-half of the world of death. Now he can continue in a further, progressive social life: a higher materialist.

So the ship passes through the strait, skirts the polar death-mystery, and turns northward, home. She seems to fly with new strong plumage, free. "Every rope-yarn seemed stretched to the utmost, and every thread of the canvas; and with this sail added to her the ship sprang through the water like a thing possessed. The sail being nearly all forward, it lifted her out of the water, and she seemed actually to jump from sea to sea."

Beautifully the sailing-ship nodalises the forces of sea and wind, converting them to her purpose. There is no violation, as in a steam-ship, only a winged centrality. It is this perfect adjusting of ourselves to the great elements, the perfect equipoise between them and us, which gives us a great part of our life-joy. The more we intervene machinery between us and the naked forces, the more we numb and atrophy our own senses. Every time we turn on a tap to have water, every time we turn a handle to have fire or light, we deny ourselves and annul our being. The great elements, the earth, air, fire, water, are there like some great mistresses whom we woo and struggle with, whom we heave and wrestle with. And all our appliances do but deny us these fine embraces, take the miracle of life away from us. The machine is the great Neuter. It is the eunuch of eunuchs. In the end it emasculates us all. When we balance the sticks and kindle a fire, we partake of the mysteries. But when we turn on an electric tap there is as it were a wad between us and the dynamic universe. We do not know what we lose by all our labour-saving appliances. Of the two evils it would be much the lesser to lose all machinery, every bit, rather than to have, as we have, hopelessly too much.

When we study the pagan Gods, we find they have now one meaning, now another. Now they belong to the creative essence, and now to the material-dynamic world. First they have one aspect, then another. The greatest god has both aspects. First he is an originator of *life*. Then he is mystic dynamic lord of the essential physical forces. So Zeus is Father, and Thunderer.

Nations that worship the material-dynamic world, as all nations do in their decadence, seem to come inevitably to worship the Thunderer.

5 He is Ammon, Zeus, Wotan and Thor, Shango of the West Africans. As the creator of man himself, the Father, is greatest in the creative world, the Thunderer is greatest in the material world. He is the god of destruction and of earthly blessing, the god of the bolt and of sweet rain.

10 So that electricity seems to be the first, intrinsic principle among the Forces. It has a mystic power of readjustment. It seems to be the overlord of the two naked elements, fire and water, capable of mysteriously enchaining them, and of mysteriously sundering them from their connections. When the two great elements become hopelessly mixed,

15 entangled, the sword of the lightning can separate them. The crash of thunder is really not the clapping together of waves of air: the explanation is nonsense. Thunder is the noise of the explosion which takes place when the waters are loosed from the elemental fire, when old vapours are suddenly decomposed in the upper air by the electric force. Then

20 fire flies fluid, and the waters roll off in purity. It is the liberation of the elements from hopeless conjunction. Thunder, the electric force, is the counterpart in the material-dynamic world of the life-force, the creative mystery itself, in the creative world.

Dana gives a wonderful description of a tropical thunderstorm.

25 "When our watch came on deck at twelve o'clock it was as black as Erebus; not a breath was stirring; the sails hung heavy and motionless from the yards; and the perfect stillness, and the darkness, which was almost palpable, were truly appalling. Not a word was spoken, but everyone stood as though waiting for something to happen. In a few

30 minutes the mate came forward, and in a low tone which was almost a whisper, gave the command to haul down the jib— —When we got down we found all hands looking aloft, and then, directly over where we had been standing, upon the main top-gallant mast-head, was a ball of light, which the sailors name a corposant (*corpus sancti*). They were

35 all watching it carefully, for sailors have a notion that if the corposant rises in the rigging, it is a sign of fair weather, but if it comes lower down, there will be a storm. Unfortunately, as an omen, it came down and showed itself on the top-gallant yard.

"In a few minutes it disappeared and showed itself again on the fore

40 top-gallant-yard, and, after playing about for some time, disappeared

again, when the man on the forecastle pointed to it upon the flying-jib-boom end. But our attention was drawn from watching this by the falling of some drops of rain. In a few minutes low growling thunder was heard, and some random flashes of lightning came from the southwest. Every sail was taken in but the top-sail. A few puffs lifted the topsails, but they fell again to the mast, and all was as still as ever. A minute more, and a terrific flash and peal broke simultaneously upon us, and a cloud appeared to open directly over our heads and let down the water in one body like a falling ocean. We stood motionless and almost stupified, yet nothing had been struck. Peal after peal rattled over our heads with a sound which actually seemed to stop the breath in the body. The violent fall of the rain lasted but a few minutes, and was succeeded by occasional drops and showers; but the lightning continued incessant for several hours, breaking the midnight darkness with irregular and blinding flashes.

"During all this time hardly a word was spoken, no bell was struck, and the wheel was silently relieved. The rain fell at intervals in heavy showers, and we stood drenched through, and blinded by the flashes, which broke the Egyptian darkness with a brightness which seemed almost malignant, while the thunder rolled in peals, the concussion of which appeared to shake the very ocean. A ship is not often injured by lightning, for the electricity is separated by the great number of points she presents, and the quantity of iron which she has scattered in various parts. The electric fluid ran over our anchors, topsail-sheets and ties; yet no harm was done to us. We went below at four o'clock, leaving things in the same state."

Dana is wonderful at relating these mechanical, or dynamic-physical events. He could not tell about the being of men: only about the *forces*. He gives another curious instance of the process of de-creation, as it takes place within the very corpuscles of the blood. It is *salt* this time which arrests the life-activity, causing a static arrest in Matter, after a certain sundering of water from the fire of the warm-substantial body.

"The scurvy had begun to show itself on board. One man had it so badly as to be disabled and off duty; and the English lad, Ben, was in a dreadful state, and was gradually growing worse. His legs swelled and pained him so that he could not walk; his flesh lost its elasticity, so that if it were pressed in, it would not return to its shape; and his gums swelled until he could not open his mouth. His breath, too, became very offensive; he lost all strength and spirit; could eat nothing; grew worse every day; and, in fact, unless something was done for him, would be a

dead man in a week at the rate at which he was sinking. The medicines
were all gone, or nearly all gone; and if we had had a chest full, they
would have been of no use; for nothing but fresh provisions and terra
firma has any effect upon the scurvy."

5   However, a boat-load of potatoes and onions was obtained from a
passing ship. These the men ate raw. "The freshness and crispness of
the raw onion, with the earthy taste, gave it a great relish to one who
has been a long time on salt provisions. We were perfectly ravenous
after them. We ate them at every meal, by the dozen; and filled our
10   pockets with them, to eat in the watch on deck. The chief use, however,
of the fresh provisions was for the men with the scurvy. One was able
to eat, and he soon brought himself to by gnawing upon raw potatoes;
but the other, by this time, was hardly able to open his mouth; and the
cook took the potatoes raw, pounded them in a mortar, and gave him
15   the juice to drink. The strong earthy taste and smell of this extract
of the raw potatoes at first produced a shuddering through his whole
frame, and after drinking it, an acute pain, which ran through all parts
of his body; but knowing by this time that it was taking strong hold, he
persevered, drinking a spoonful every hour or so, until, by the effect of
20   this drink, and of his own restored hope, he became so well as to be able
to move about, and open his mouth enough to eat the raw potatoes and
onions pounded into a soft pulp. This course soon restored his appetite
and strength; and ten days after we spoke the Solon, so rapid was his
recovery that, from lying helpless and almost hopeless in his berth, he
25   was at the mast-head, furling a royal."

This is the strange effect of the disintegrating effect of the sea, and
of salt in food. Certain substances seem active against the life-principle
itself, thus providing, in small quantities, a stimulus. Salt, sulphur, the
acids, are instances. They all seem to have a mysterious power for driv-
30   ing asunder the fire and water which are in vital combination in a living
organism, preventing any further conjunction of fire and water, so that
growth and decay—which after all depends on life—are alike arrested.
Salt is one of the elements in which water seems predominant and
vindictive. It has a curious power to penetrate into all living tissue,
35   liberating the water from its conjunction. Hence the dropsy-like symptoms of scurvy.* Any substance which is in the grip of salt seems to be
in the grip of the overweening watery principle, and procreant fire is
excluded. It is strange to try to think what effect the salt seas must have
upon the atmosphere of the world.

Acids seem the opposite of salt. They seize upon the latent, vital fire. They burn. And acids, vegetable acids, are the antidote to scurvy. Acid alone would not do. It needs the pure vegetable juice, in which the vital principle is still alive. Acid counteracts the salt-activity, but it is the positive creative principle, present in the juice of potatoes, or onions, or limes, which restores the creative activity to its living ascendance in the body. The vital world triumphs over the material. Dana mentions the relish which the *earthy* taste gives the onion. It is the taste of created substance, the juice is the living milk of Geaea.

We have to know the two worlds, the creative and the material. We have to try to discover their mutual relationship. Certainly all life depends on a perfect conjunction of fire and water. Certainly the life-spell, the creative mystery, effects this pure conjunction, or consummation. Certainly in the *dynamic* world, the great force of pure sundering is thunder. And certainly in the *material* world, there are various substances which, given their preponderance, can effectively bar out one element from conjunction with the other, besides causing a sundering in the first place. After a certain sundering, they cause a static arrest. If it be salt, then fire is shut out, the spell of water becomes fixed. No organism can then live. If it be acid, the advent of water is shut out, the spell of fire is triumphant. So acids easily explode when fire is added: for then the complete preponderance of one element occurs, and there is disunion. And so salt melts down. And so sulphur burns. Sulphur and the acids are irritable, overcharged with fire. Salt and phosphorus are irritable, overcharged with water, Each of these acts upon the body, in small quantities, as a stimulus. In large quantities, they cause death. The reason is obvious.

Science, to whom the material dynamic world is given over, knows none of the great secrets of Matter or of *dunamis*.*

Studies in Classic American Literature

(XI)

Herman Melville (1)

The greatest seer and poet of the sea, perhaps in all the world, is
Herman Melville. His vision is far more real than that of Swinburne,
for he does not personify or humanise, and far more profound than that
of Conrad, for he does not emotionalise. Melville belongs to the sea,
like one of its own birds. Like a sea-bird, he seems to have nothing of
the land in him. He does not pit himself against the sea, he is of it.
And so he has that strange inscrutable magic and mystery of the pure
sea-creatures, the same untranslateable speech, and, oddly, the same
curious repulsiveness, or inferiority of order. One cannot help feeling
that he is lapsing from the creative order of life, into the material order
of existence, where eternity is a concrete substance, as water is eternal.
It is one of the last flights of the consciousness, away into the boundless,
where it loses itself.

There is also something about Melville which reminds us of the
Vikings: those Vikings, inhuman, like sea-birds, creatures of the watery mystery, who sailed from their settlements in Greenland down
past Labrador to Nova Scotia, and even to Florida. They were Northmen, ocean-born, seeking the sun. Some met and mingled with the
dark, earth-rich fiery creation of the south. Some lapsed in extreme ice.
Some persisted unchanged. The blue-eyed, water-mystic people of the
North have not yet lost their allegiance and origin. They are not yet
fused into being. Creatures of the one preponderant mystery, they are
almost elementals, not beings, wonderful, primordial to us. The dead
Viking chiefs are pushed out in flames into the ocean, given in death to
the fire-consummation. And the living either seek a living consummation, or they too return at last to the seas, carrying the death-fires with
them.

Melville is like one pushed out in flame again to the sea. The sea
claims him, as its own. The sea never quite loses its spell over the blue-
eyed people. They love it, as the dark-eyed hate it. For the dark-eyed
people are people of an old creation, created under the sun from the
waters, sun-children. Their brown eyes are brown like the earth, which
is tissue of bygone life, complicated, compound. The sun-spell is the

stronger. They belong more to the fire-mystery, the earth-mystery quick with fire. The water is inherent in them too. But the fire preponderates. They are children of the old, old world.

Melville makes the great return. He would really melt himself, an elemental, back into his vast beloved element, material though it is. All his fire he would carry down, quench in the sea. It is time for the sea to receive back her own, into the pale, bluish underworld of the watery after-life. He is like a Viking going home to the sea, encumbered with age and memories, and a sort of accomplished despair, almost madness. The great Northern cycle of which he is the returning unit has completed its round, accomplished itself, flowered from the waters like forget-me-nots and sea-poppies, and now returns into the sea, giving back its consciousness and its being to the vast material element, burying its flames in the deeps, self-conscious and deliberate. So blue flax and yellow, horned sea-poppies fall into the waters and give back their created sun stuff to the watery end, the watery infinite.

It is to the Pacific ocean Melville returns: the great, original ocean, fire-impregnated. This is the first of all the waters, immemorial. Its mysteries are grander, profounder, *older* than those of the Atlantic. Without doubt the great era of the previous world perfected itself about the Pacific. Without doubt the Pacific has known a vast previous civilisation, before the geological cataclysms.* Without doubt its sleep is vastly impregnated with dreams unfathomable to us, it holds a great quenched epoch within itself. The China, the Japan, those lands historically known to us, they are only an aftermath. Of what went before, the vast Pacific civilisation, we can never know anything. The geological cataclysms intervene.

For many thousands of years the Pacific lands must have been passing through the process of disturbing dreams, some good, mostly bad, dreams of the great sensual-mystic civilisations which once were theirs, and which are now ten times forgotten and re-forgotten by the very peoples themselves. Egypt and India no doubt are young civilisations,* forerunners of Europe. But China, Japan, the Aztecs, Maya, Incas, Polynesians—surely these are all only echoes and re-echoings of what is immemorially bygone, re-echoed a million times, each time fainter.

There must have been some universal body of knowledge over the world in the unknown past, just as there is now. There must have been inter-communication over all the globe, as there is now, and a universal understanding, as, potentially, there is now. The Pacific Ocean must have been the vast cradle of the civilisation of that geologically-incomprehensible world, and what is now Europe must have been the hinterland.

But all exact knowledge is gone for ever. We have some fragments, almost barren remains, curious forms of an almost mathematical cosmology, found in Korea, native Argentine, the Soudan, similar abstract forms;* also degraded mythologies. How much is survival, how much is legend, who knows? The surviving mythologies tell us almost less than nothing of the great sensual understanding these people had. And we lack the proper intelligence to understand.

Something similar happens much closer to us. We do not know how completely we have lost all comprehension of even Mediaeval Christianity. We shall soon have lost the *mystery* of Christianity altogether, even while we keep dogmas and ethical creeds and ritual services intact. Already we *cannot understand* what happended to St. Francis when he fell at the feet of the peasant. We have lost the faculty for experiencing the terrible shock of the revelation of present *otherness*, the crash of submission, and the subsequent gush of relaxation into the divine love, which sweeps the individual away in a divine unconsciousness or superconsciousness, bears him like a piece of flotsam on the flood of infinitude, in that motion of infinite uniting which is infinitude itself. This is the very crisis of Christian experience, and already we have lost all conception, or *even remembrance* of it. It has passed from our range of passional experience, and become a verbal term.—The same with the mystery of the Eucharist. Since the transubstantiation disputes, and the rationalising of the sacrament,* the Holy Communion has become really a barren performance. The profound, passional *experience* it was to the Mediaeval christian is beyond our comprehension. We do not even choose to know. Because we do not choose to admit the sensual apprehension. We do not choose that the blood shall act in its own massive, inscrutable consciousness. We are artificial little products, really.

The Pacific Ocean holds the dream of immemorial centuries: in the same way it is nascent with a new world. It is the great blue twilight of the vastest of all evenings, the most wonderful of all dawns. This great ocean, with its peoples, is still latent with the coming unknown. The Atlantic is again superseded. Never was so vast a reality as the Pacific has swung down into disintegration. Its waters are surcharged with the blue, ghostly end of immemorial peoples. But it rolls also latent with all the unborn issues of the coming world of man.

It was to this Pacific Ocean, then, that Melville returned, the great bourne, the heaven under the wave, like the Celtic Tir-na-Og. And he went to the centre of the Pacific, to the South Sea Islands. Among these islands he wanders like an uneasy ghost seeking its rest, and never finding it. For he cannot yet identify himself with the great sea, he cannot yet escape his European self, ideal and ethical as it is, chain-bound.

At the very centre of the old primeval world sleeps the living and forgetting of the South Sea Isles, Samoa, Tahiti, Nukuheva, places with the magic names. Wordsworth hints at the sleep-forgotten past magnificence of human history in his "trailing clouds of glory do we come." Tahiti, Samoa, Nukuheva, the very names are clouds of glory. They are echoes from the world once splendid in the fulness of the other way of knowledge.

But Samoa, Tahiti, Nukuheva are the sleep and the forgetting of this great life, the very body of dreams. And to this dream Melville helplessly returns. He enters first in *Typee*. Nothing is more startling, at once actual and dream-mystical, than his descent down the gorges to the valley of the dreadful Typee. Down this narrow, steep, horrible dark gorge he slides and struggles as we struggle in a dream, or in the act of birth, or in some cloacal apprehension, to emerge in the green Eden of the first, or last era, the valley of the timeless savages. He had dreaded this entry acutely, for the men of Typee had a dreadful cannibal reputation. But they are good and gentle with him, he finds himself at once in a pure, mysterious world, pristine.

It is absurd to speak of savages as "children," young, rudimentary people. To look among them for the link between us and the ape is laughably absurd. Of all childish things, science is one of the most childish and amusing. The savages, we may say *all* savages, are remnants of the once civilised world-people, who had their splendour and their being for countless centuries in the way of sensual knowledge, that conservative way which Egypt shows us most plainly, mysterious and long-enduring. It is we from the north, starting new centres of life in ourselves, who have become young. The savages have grown older and older. No man can look at the African grotesque carvings, for example, or the decoration patterns of the Oceanic islanders, without seeing in them the infinitely sophisticated soul which produces distortion from its own distorted psyche, a psyche distorted through myriad generations of degeneration. No one can fail to see the quenched spark of a once superb understanding. The savages are not children practising. They are old, grotesque people, dreaming over their once wide-awake realities, and

in each dream producing a new distortion. It is a real dream-process, a process of continuing almost mechanically in life long after creative living has ceased: a sort of slow, infinitely slow degeneration, back towards Matter and Force. It is something like the long, thousand-year sleep of
5 toads.* Any man reading the Bushman Folk-Lore, as we have it now literally rendered, must feel horror-struck, catching the sounds of myriad age-long distortions and age-long repetitions in human communication, communication become now unintelligible, yet in its incomprehensibility most terrifyingly resonant of so far-off a past, that the soul faintly
10 re-echoes in horror. The ideographs* are so complicated, the sound-groups must convey so many unspeakable, unfeelable meanings, all at once, in one stroke, that it needs myriads of ages to achieve such unbearable concentration. The savages are not simple. It is we who are simple. They are unutterably complicated, every feeling, every term of theirs
15 is untranslateably agglomerate. So with the African fetishes. They are timelessly-repeated dream-degradations of some once perfect, sensual-mystic image, and each distortion contains centuries of strange, slow experience, for which we have no reference.

    So Melville's life among the Typee. It is inconceivable to think of
20 that life in Nukuheva as "savage." It is refined, and concentrated, and self-understood to a degree which makes our life look laughably crude. True, it is unscientific. But subjectively it is beyond us.

    Melville brings against them nothing, save their lack of European morals, the wildness of their warfare, and their cannibalism. Their lack
25 of morals he does not mind. The cannibalism fills him with a fear and horror to me unaccountable. For surely he must have assisted at the Christian Communion-Supper, he must have heard the words "This is my body, take, and eat." After all, cannibalism seems everywhere to have primarily a ritualistic, sacramental meaning. It is no doubt the remains
30 of the mystic Eucharist of the sensual religions, the very counterpart of our Eucharist. "This is thy body which I take from thee and eat," says the sensual communicant, in his ecstasy of consummation in pride. The savage may have forgotten the mystery implied in his observance: but, to judge from the traveller's reports, not nearly so much as we have forgot-
35 ten *our* mystery. The savage seems to know the sacred, passional reality of the act. In Typee they observed the strictest secrecy.* There was evidently a real passional comprehension of the sacrament, the mystery of *Oneing* which takes place when the communicant partakes of the body of his vanquished enemy. It is the mystery of final unification, ultimate
40 oneing, as in our sacrament. The act is only reversed. Frobenius, after

travelling in Africa, says "all the tribes of Inner Africa associate quite a distinctive frame of mind with the consumption of human flesh and, as far as this refers to the territories I myself have travelled through, I am bound to regard it as a misrepresentation of facts for any traveller to say that the Africans of the interior 'eat human flesh with the same sensation which a beefsteak gives to us.' This is not the truth, because, even if a negro has human meat upon his board several times a week, his enjoyment of it in these countries will always be connected with a definite emotion." 5

Melville found in Typee almost what he wanted to find, what every man dreams of finding: a perfect home among timeless, unspoiled savages. There, in Nukuheva, the European psyche, with its ideals and its limitations, had no place. Our artificial ethical laws had never existed. There was naked simplicity of life, with subtle, but non-mental understanding, *rapport* between human beings. And it was too much for the American Melville, idealist of all idealists still. For him, life must be an *idea*, essentially an idea. It must be a progression towards an ideal: a life dedicated to some process or goal of consciousness. He could never let be. He could never really let go. His will was always clinched, forcing life in some direction or other, the direction of ideal transcendence. Man must be an ideal consciousness: this was a fixed principle in him. 10 15 20

And therefore, beautiful, free as it was, the life in the island became a torture to him. The very freedom was a torture. If he had been *constrained*, he could have borne it. But he was free and cherished: only he might not depart. And so he spent all his energies contriving to escape. 25

One would have thought that now his gnawing restlessness would have ceased: that now his fretful spirit would be appeased. But no—on the contrary, he was mad to escape, mad to run back to that detestable America which he always had been driven to run away from: America of the increasing insane, hateful industrialism, competition, fight for existence, survival of the fittest. He had to go back to it. It enshrined his ideal, hideous as it was, and he was an idealist. He needed the struggle, struggle, struggle into further ideal consciousness. The true sensual existence, though he longed for it achingly, was yet a torture and a *nullification* to him. This is the quandary of the idealist, the man who stakes all his being on his upper consciousness. He cannot be free and full, and he cannot be made free. He cannot even enjoy his own being. He can only delight in cutting himself in two. 30 35

So Melville. He loved his savage hosts. But he never knew the sacred reality of their lives, lived in mindless, naked spontaneity. Such a life 40 of spontaneity was null to him, just nothing. He could only understand *forcing* in some direction.

He had not fulfilled his own destiny. And so, escape he must, or die. Whilst in Typee he had a strange malady in his arm, which would never
5   heal. Such maladies are due to an interruption in the vital circuit. The poles of his vital flow were broken. The escaping current destroyed him in his wound. The moment the poles were restored, the wound began to heal: that is, the moment he was on board a white ship again.

The white man must remain true to his own destiny. And there-
10 fore, later on in Omoo, Melville looked with horror on the renegade Englishman who had the blue shark tattooed across his brow, the mystic sign that he had joined the savages utterly, accepted their life finally. Melville was horrified at the renegade. Us he would interest, as a kind of forerunner.

15 But Melville must remain true to his white destiny, the destiny of the Christian white races, of conquering life and death by submission. This mad desire, this ideal, this conquest of life and death still possessed Melville. Man had submitted to man, in martyrdom and death, till at last the ideal of submission was established. Kings had fallen,
20 men were equal, a oneness in submission and humility and meek love was established, or at least accepted as the highest reality. Life was conquered. Now death must be conquered: the kingdom of death: Matter itself. The scientists conquered the forces, by applying them. Remained only to know the sheer stuff of death, the eternal elements, eternal as
25 indestructible Matter. What Dana began, Melville must utterly finish. It was his destiny. He would have died in Typee, though he loved it. Destiny did not permit him to stay, any more than it will allow a leaf from one tree to be stuck livingly on to another tree. The malady in his arm proved to Melville the malady, or malaise of his psy-
30 che. It was a sign of his physical, substantial, and spiritual necessity to depart.

Yet the moment he is free, and is actually sailing away, in a voyage that will ultimately take him to America, oh, the acute and intolerable nostalgia he feels for the island he is leaving. His whole *desire* is that way:
35 his aspiration is another way. Typee is his paradise, that he longs for. But he is not ready for paradise. The simple spontaneity of life itself, spontaneous being, this is the goal of his desire but the prison of his aspiration. He must strive, strive, strive in a given direction, towards a goal of triumphant consciousness and self-extinction. Striving, his arm
40 heals at once.

It is a great necessary sacrifice, his giving himself up to the conscious conquest of the sea. From such sacrifices we inherit our possibility of grand freedom in the future. Having triumphed over death, there is no further need to triumph: no need for more of the insatiable striving. We can be confident and at home in ourselves.

In *Omoo*, the book which succeeds *Typee*, Melville continues his wanderings among the South Sea Islands. No man gives us the Pacific quite as Melville does: and we feel that his is the *real* Pacific. It is not really emotional or even stupendous. It is just *there*, immediate. If we cannot appreciate it, it is because we are not far enough on, not abstracted, not sufficiently resolved. We are still too much in our own practical, rather trivial world of machines and arbitrary ideals. The Pacific has no ideals. It has no fixed goal to strive after. There, each thing is itself, *arrivé*.* And this is what the European can't bear. He must have a sense of *getting on*.

So Melville roams, sails, wanders, a vagabond, a hired land-worker, a ship's hand. *Omoo* is a curious book. It has no unity, no purpose, no anything, and yet it is one of the most real, actual books ever written about the South Seas. It seems like reality itself. Melville, at his best, is the perfect life-accepter. At his worst, he is a professional mystic and transcendentalist. At his best, he is just a man, accepting life. But when we say, just a man, we don't mean a common anybody. Rarest of all things to find is a man who can really accept life, without imposing some theory or some arbitrary goal. Melville is no amateur at living. He is the perfect epicurean, eating the world like a snipe, dirt and all baked in one *bonne bouche*. He takes the crude, dirty realities along with the rest. Essentially, Melville is one of the most cultured men that have ever written. All the finicking niceties of "delicate" or "moral" individuals seem so cheap, so boorish in the end. That man is perfectly educated who knows how to meet life sensitively and responsively in every one of its moods and aspects. Your picker and chooser, your elegant and your Tolstoy are alike half-educated, ill-bred, clownish.

Melville knows how to live, and living he *knows* life. This is the highest pitch of culture. He has really no purpose in mind, no scheme of life for himself. In his actual living he is quite spontaneous, non-moral. All the time, he is the living quick of the moment.

This is the free Melville, who has escaped from Typee. But he is not ultimately free. A long, thin, fine chain is round his ankle, the chain of the old christian purpose, the purpose of the conquest of life and death, by meekness and "love." He is curious: in his immediate living

quite non-moral; and yet he keeps the whole block of the Christian tenets intact at the back of his mind, in a sort of cupboard. His brain, some part of it, is a tablet of stone, on which the old ethic is engraved. No matter what his first-consciousness may be; the spontaneous consciousness of
5 the blood which surges and returns, the first-consciousness of the great nerve-centres which are our physical, and basic first-minds, this, the living reality of our waking being, can be annulled again in a minute. The ethic fixed in his brain is like some fatal millstone.

The old will, the old purpose is fixed in him. He, who seems so
10 truly spontaneous, is in reality a monomaniac, possessed by a fixed idea of further spiritual triumph, further idealisation. The end is not yet reached. Suddenly he starts from his peace and his happy-go-lucky wandering, starts off on the old maniacal quest, the quest of the infinite, the triumph over life and death. It seems as if man will never be able to
15 accept life and death, perfectly and splendidly, till he has effected this triumph over life and death, and proved his infinitude. Not till he has in real experience accomplished his triumph and known his infinitude, will he realise that infinitude is nothing, and mastery over life is less than nothing. To be able to live in sheer full spontaneity, because of the perfect
20 harmony between the conscious intelligence and the unconscious, pre-conscious prompting, urging of the very life itself, the living soul-centre itself, this is the whole goal of our ambition, our education, our perfect culture. But this, being the state of flowering in us, is hardest to come to. We have first to go through all the processes of mastering life and
25 mastering death, achieving the hollow triumph of our own nothingness, before we can cease from such "triumphs," and be ourselves from the centre.

Studies in Classic American Literature

(XII)

Herman Melville (2)

Herman Melville's biggest book* is *Moby Dick, or The White Whale.* It is a story of the last hunt. The last hunt, the last conquest—what 5 is it?

Before we turn to *Moby Dick* itself, let us return once more to the old theory of human consciousness. We know that the ancients were not concerned with the study of mental consciousness, not psychology as we know it. For them the seat of consciousness, in the first place, was the 10 heart: then the stomach and liver. These are the great fountains of blood-consciousness. But the initiated went further. They knew of the great dynamic nerve-centres, the great ganglia, which form the first-minds of the human psyche. The ganglia form a dual system, sympathetic and volitional. The sympathetic occupy the fore part of the body, and 15 act as recipient or negative poles; the latter occupy the back part of the body, they are the spinal ganglia, and they act as the compelling or positive poles of the dynamic vital force. The body is further divided by the diaphragm. The ganglia above the diaphragm we have called the spiritual ganglia, the centres of physical perception; the ganglia below 20 the diaphragm we call the sensual ganglia, centres of physical absorption and psychic assimilation. The ancient study of man concerned itself with this study: the ancient psychology referred to this primary psyche. But all knowledge was conserved by a special initiated class. It was not made public. It was esoteric, to be attained only in stages of initiation. 25 The fragments of Anaximander, Anaximenes, Pythagoras, Heraklitos* give broken hints. The Manicheans and the Gnostics give further hints. But to these the Christian world deliberately and necessarily stopped its ears. Yet while straining the gnat it swallowed the camel.* It admitted— after much hesitation, certainly—the Apocalypse. 30

Now John the Evangel was evidently one of the initiated—like Plato. And while welcoming Jesus, he saw that Jesus was only a term in the old system, a direction given to the old order. He would have preserved an *esoteric* Christianity alongside the exoteric. The early Christians set their face dead against any of the old learning, and therefore the Apocalypse 35 was admitted only after every clue to its meaning was apparently destroyed. Esoteric Christianity died with the Gnostics and Manicheans:

or was destroyed with them. The corpse remained in the Book of
Revelations.

John the Evangel accepted supreme consciousness as the supreme
goal of a human being. There is a degree of consciousness to which man
5 can attain, after centuries of *perception*—and pure perception means
self-abnegation—wherein a man realises Allness, or infinitude. It is as
if man looked and looked and saw and perceived and perceived and
comprehended until he reached that mystic crisis where he perceived
the All and comprehended Allness. This is a true psychic state, to be
10 verified by every individual of sufficient comprehensive intelligence, and
to be examined by science. William James began to study the state of
consciousness wherein man knows All, or Allness.* This All or Allness
is the Infinite which everybody babbles about:* a true *subjective*, as well
as objective reality.

15 This subjective reality of the Infinite was the goal of great mystics like
St. John. It is the goal of every common individual who aspires today,
or has aspired for the last two thousand years. It is nothing special and
fantastic. It is the desire for the experience of the great peace, which
passes all understanding*—a desire inherent in every human heart.

20 Now the esoteric mystics scientifically examined the way to this
supreme experience, this supreme state of consciousness or being, called
peace, or perfection, or infinitude. "Be ye also perfect," says Paul.*
Empirically, the esoterics determined the process. The early fathers ab-
horred this empiricism. To them it was anathema. They insisted on the
25 way of blind faith. The same process took place, through blind faith, in
two thousand years, as had taken place in the psyche of St. John, through
initiation and empiric knowledge, in a certain number of years—twenty,
thirty, or forty.

The progress towards the goal of supreme consciousness, mental
30 consciousness, is a progression in the conquest of the lower ganglia by
the upper. The diaphragm divides the body horizontally. St. John counts
the "cities," the centres of consciousness, as seven in all.* He is counting
only the voluntary centres of the spinal system, since it is these alone
that must be "conquered." There are three below the diaphragm, three
35 above—and then the last, the supreme, the New Jerusalem, the brain,
where full comprehension takes place. These seven cities are sometimes
seven gateways: though the gateways are usually the seven orifices of the
human body. The mouth corresponds to the first of the lower ganglia: the
solar plexus with its voluntary pole, the lumbar ganglion;* the nostrils to
40 the lower hypogastric plexus, with the sacral ganglion:* also balancing

the sexual and watery orifice; whilst the ears, in which, say the magicians, all the senses can be summed up, correspond to the last ganglion, the cocygeal,* and the faecal orifice.

In the process of conquest, the thoracic ganglion* conquers the lumbar ganglion: that is, the circuit of polarity is established, with the thoracic ganglion as the positive and the lumbar ganglion the negative. Then the human being has voluntary control over the first appetites. And then also he has his first great field of consciousness: the mediaeval consciousness, in history. Secondly the cervical ganglia* conquer the sacral ganglion. This is a great conquest. A vast new circuit of life is set up. The individual now conquers the deeper appetites, like the sexual, and makes these subject to the consciousness, and to conscious control. He has also a great new "vision," he *sees* what has never been seen before. And there is also a vast new field of intelligence, of mental understanding.—The period of this circuit of human consciousness has been from the Renaissance till now. Now the last and lowest of the centres of our being remains to be conquered, and man will be made "whole," he will "know in full."* Then he will have peace. He will at last be free to be his own very self. Up till now, it has all been *process*. Up till now, human beings, like trees in a forest, have each one been struggling up to full height. After this comes the flowering, each from its own individual self and source. Up till now, all has been what some sects call "becoming"*— the process of becoming full grown. The season of blossom, when each individual blossoms with his own single self, this lies still ahead.

American art symbolises the destruction, decomposition, mechanising of the fallen degrees of consciousness. Franklin and Crêvcœur show the mechanising of the shallowest instincts and passions, appetites; Cooper and Melville the deeper worship-through-contumely of the fallen sexual or sacral consciousness; Poe the direct decomposition of this consciousness; and Dana and Melville the final hunting of the same consciousness into the very Matter, the very watery material last home of its existence, and its extinction there. Remains the entry into the last state, and into fulness, freedom.

St. John said "there shall be no more sea."* That was esoteric. Exoterically, Dana and Melville say the same. The Sea, the great Waters, is the Material home of the deep sacral–sexual consciousness. To the very depths of this home Melville pursues the native consciousness in himself, and destroys it there. When he has really destroyed his sacral–sexual consciousness, destroyed or overthrown it, then John's prophecy will be fulfilled. There will be no more sea.

Moby Dick is the story of this last symbolic hunt. Moby Dick is
a great white whale, the Leviathan of the waters. He is old, hoary,
monstrous, and snow-white; unspeakably terrible in his wrath; having
been repeatedly attacked, he swims now alone in the great, pathless seas.
5   He is the last warm-blooded tenant of the waters, the greatest and last.
He is the deep, free sacral consciousness in man. He must be subdued.
In himself he is warm-blooded, even lovable. But he must go. Curious
are his counterparts in the world. The whole of the South Pacific seems
to worship, in hate, the Shark or the Crocodile, the great cold-blooded
10 tenants, lords of the water, fiendish and destructive lords. Curious how
shark and crocodile patterns, with grinning teeth, dominate aboriginal
decoration-designs in those regions.* The same crocodile worship is
found in Africa, very wide-spread.—In China, however, the dragon,
the Leviathan is the dragon of the sun: as the mantis, surely another
15 dragon of the sun, dominates the Bushmen.* Is not this the inordinately
ancient relic of the pre-Flood worship, a relic from that era when the
upper consciousness was the anathema, and the glory and the triumph
was all in the sensual understanding, incomprehensible to us now.

Melville writes in the peculiar lurid, glamorous style which is natural
20 to the great Americans. It gives us at first a sense of spuriousness. To
some it merely seems wordy and meaningless, unreal. It comes, I think,
from the deliberate attempt in America not only to dethrone, but to
murder the lower consciousness. It is the same inverted worship-in-
contumely, t[he[?]] self-frustrating worship of the very thing hated, so
25 that the reaction goes beyond reason, into lustful destructiveness, like
criminality.

This very murder of the lower consciousness means, of course, the
kill[ing] of the creative reality in man altogether and the triumph of
the materi[al] dynamic will. Matter and dynamics take the place of
30 creative impulse and exfoliation, in such American souls. And it is
this which gives a repellant quality to American art, repellant even to
the Americans themselves. Sometimes the evidence of this murder-
process, this criminal triumph of dynamic Matter over life-being, is so
repulsive that we cannot read the books: or, on the other hand, to the
35 life-destroyers it is so attractive that they find such evidence the mark
of the very highest quality in a book. But, surely, shall we not admit that
the Americans only go to the extreme, where we do not venture: and
from the extreme one may learn the last word.

So, in beginning *Moby Dick*, we must be prepared for the curious
40 lurid style, almost spurious, almost journalism, and yet *not* spurious:

on the verge of material unreality, still real. The book starts off with a semi-metaphysical effusion about *water*, and about the author's attraction to this element;* it goes on with some clumsy humorisms, till it arrives in the sea-town of New Bedford.* Then actual experience begins. It is curiously like bald material record, touched-up into journalese: neither veritable nor created. One cannot help feeling that the author is spurious, pretentious, and an amateur, wordy and shoddy. Yet something glimmers through all this: a glimmer of genuine reality. But it is not a reality of real, open-air experience. It is a reality of what takes place in the musty cellars of a man's soul, what the psychoanalysts call the unconscious. There is the old double set of values; the ostensible Melville, a sort of Emersonian transcendentalist, and the underneath Melville, a sort of strange underworld, under-sea creature looking with curious, lurid vision on the upper world. It is the incongruous mixture of ideal heaven and rotten rubbish heaps. The reality comes out of the rotten rubbish heaps, drowned, under-sea stuff.

It is no use pretending that Melville writes like a straight-forward, whole human being. He is hardly a human being at all. He gives events in the light of their last reality: mechanical, material, a semi-incoherent dream-rendering. What the futurists have tried hard to do, Dana and Melville have pretty well succeeded in doing for them. These two are masters of the sheer movement of *substance* in its own paths, free from all human postulation or control. The result is nearly like artifice, a sort of rank journalism. But we must restrain our too hasty judgment. A good deal of the awkward stupid quality comes from the sense of the vulgar, mental world at the author's elbow, to which he must kow-tow.

Melville tries to square himself with the intellectual world by dragging in deliberate transcendentalism, deliberate symbols and "deeper meanings."* All this is insufferably clumsy and in clownish bad taste: self-conscious and amateurish to a degree, the worst side of American behaviour. When however he forgets all audience, and renders us his sheer apprehension of the world, he is wonderful, his book commands a stillness in the soul, almost awe.

Let us repeat that it is in rendering the sheer naked slidings of the elements, and the curious mechanical cause-and-effect of material events, that he is a master. For near as he is to sheer materialism, the central creative spark is still unquenched, the integral soul is present, if alone. His mind lags far, far behind his physical comprehension. His mind is cumbered up with a hopeless aggregation of fixed ideas, which spin on together like little wheels. But his bodily knowledge moves naked,

a living quick among the stark elements. In sheer physical, vibrational
sensitiveness, like a mai vellous wireless-station, he registers the effects
of the outer world. And he records also, almost beyond pain or pleasure,
the extreme transitions of the isolated, far-driven soul, the soul which
5   is now alone, without human connection.

The first days in New Bedford introduce the only human being who at
all enters into the soul of Ishmael, the "I" of the book. This is Queequeg,
the tattooed, powerful South Sea harpooneer, whom Melville loves
almost as Dana loves "Hope." The advent of Ishmael's bed-mate is
10 amusing and unforgettable. But later the two swear "marriage," in the
language of the savages. For Queequeg has opened again the flood-gates
of love and human connection in Ishmael.

"As I sat there in that now lonely room; the fire burning low, in that
mild stage when, after its first intensity has warmed the air, it then
15 only glows to be looked at; the evening shades and phantoms gathering
round the casements, and peering in upon us silent, solitary twain; I
began to be sensible of strange feelings. I felt a melting in me. No
more my splintered hand and maddened heart was turned against the
wolfish world. This soothing savage had redeemed it. There he sat, his
20 very indifference speaking a nature in which there lurked no civilised
hypocrisies and bland deceits. Wild he was; a very sight of sights to see;
yet I began to feel myself mysteriously drawn towards him."—So they
smoke together, and are clasped in each other's arms. The friendship
is finally sealed when Ishmael offers sacrifice to Queequeg's little idol,
25 Gogo.

"I was a good Christian, born and bred in the bosom of the infallible
Presbyterian Church. How then could I unite with the idolater in worshipping his piece of wood? But what is worship?—thought I. But what
is worship?—to do the will of God—*that* is worship. And what is the
30 will of God?—to do to my fellow-man what I would have my fellow-man
do to me—*that* is the will of God. Now Queequeg is my fellow-man.
And what do I wish that this Queequeg would do to me? Why, unite
with me in my particular Presbyterian form of worship. Consequently,
I must then unite with him; ergo, I must turn idolater. So I kindled
35 the shavings; helped prop up the innocent little idol; offered him burnt
biscuit with Queequeg; salaamed before him twice or thrice; kissed his
nose; and that done, we undressed and went to bed, at peace with our
own consciences and all the world. But we did not go to sleep without
some little chat. How it is I know not; but there is no place like bed for
40 confidential disclosures between friends. Man and wife, they say, open

the very bottom of their souls to each other; and some old couples often lie and chat over old times till nearly morning. Thus, then, lay I and Queequeg—a cosy, loving pair—"

Elsewhere Ishmael says of Queequeg that he loved him for his "large, deep eyes, fiery black and bold." 5

The two men go over from New Bedford to Nantucket, and there sign on for the Quaker whaling-ship, the *Pequod.* It is all strangely fantastic, phantasmagoric. Yet is it unreal? We pass on into the midst of the sea with this strange ship and its incredible crew. It is a mythical, mystical voyage as any Argonaut voyage ever was. Yet it is curiously *actual.* This 10 is the beauty—the identity of daily experience with profound mystic experience.

The voyage begins, like Dana's, in the winter-time, strange and dark at first. There is a mystery about the captain—he keeps hidden. The secret gradually emerges. The Quaker Ahab, the captain, a man in the 15 prime of life, is a prey to a monomania. He walks with an ivory stump, made from the sea-ivory. For Moby Dick, the great white whale, tore off his leg at the knee. So Ahab is now a monomaniac, and the ship is out on a maniacal cruise, the hunt of the almost mythical white whale.

It would be too long to unravel the amazing symbolism of the book.— 20 Starbuck, the first mate, is another Quaker Nantucketer, long, earnest, steadfast, prudent. He is a man of reason and forethought, intrepid, yet wise enough to say— "I will have no man in my boat who is not afraid of a whale."—But he inclines to superstition. At the bottom of him is a sense of fatality, rooted in a great fear. This makes him succumb at last, 25 in spite of himself, to Ahab's criminal madness.

Stubb, the second mate, is a man of spontaneous courage and jollity— "fearless as fire, and as mechanical," Ahab says of him. He is a mindless sailor delighting in sensation for sensation's sake. After a brief tussle, he too becomes a mere instrument of Ahab's hunt; a perfect instrument 30 moreover.

Flask, the third mate, is stubborn, obstinate, distinguished for his tenacity. He has no imagination, no vision at all. To him "the wondrous whale was but a species of magnified mouse, or water-rat— — —This ignorant, unconscious fearlessness of his made him a little waggish in 35 the matter of it—." None the less, he is an admirable whalesman.

These three mates symbolise the three parts of the psyche, reason, impulsive passion, and blind will. But all these three elements are subject to the monomania in Ahab. Ahab is the force which drives them on the fearful, fatal chase. 40

Melville cannot have known what his own symbols meant. Yet he used them half-deliberately: never *quite* sure. Then again, he forgets them and moves into pure actuality. It is curious how actuality of itself, in deep issues, becomes symbolic.

5   The three harpooneers, Queequeg, the Polynesian, Tashtego, the North-American Indian, and Daggoo, the great, black negro, are of three races.—Then, strangely and secretly, far more strangely than in Conrad,* is introduced a boat's-crew of fire-worshipping, sunwor-shipping Parsees, men for Ahab's own boats. All races, all creeds, the
10   fire-worship and the sea-worship, are all united to engage in the great disastrous hunt.

When at last the ship is fully in the South Seas, then the pure beauty comes out. Melville is at his best when moving and working with the waters, and not self-consciously speculating. Yet it is the author's very
15   attempt to get at some mystery behind the show of things which leads him to his highest beauty. The effort is made in a struggle of mystic speculation: then comes the lovely result, in a piece of sheer revelation.

Like Dana, Melville is impressed by the albatross. But he must rather clumsily philosophise, he is in somewhat bad taste.—"I remember the
20   first albatross I ever saw. It was during a prolonged gale, in waters hard upon the Antarctic seas. From my forenoon watch below I ascended to the overclouded deck; and there, dashed upon the main hatches, I saw a regal, feathery thing of unspotted whiteness, and with a hooked, Roman bill sublime. At intervals it arched forth its vast, archangel
25   wings— —. Wondrous throbbings and flutterings shook it. Though bodily unharmed, it uttered cries, as some king's ghost in supernatural distress. Through its inexpressible, strange eyes methought I peeped to secrets not below the heavens— —the white thing was so white, its wings so wide, and in those for ever exiled waters, I had lost the miser-
30   able warping memories of traditions and of towns.—I assert then, that in the wondrous bodily whiteness of the bird chiefly lurks the secret of the spell—"

—We must remember that Melville's albatross is a prisoner, caught by a bait on a hook. The whole description occurs in a note to the
35   Chapter on *Whiteness*. The author dilates upon the whiteness of the whale, Moby Dick, and on the strange, supernatural spell which is cast by pure whiteness. We attribute whiteness to refraction.* The sheer mechanical fusion of water and light, or Matter and light, or Matter and fire, causes white incandescence, whether of foam or of burning. In
40   the same way, the utter absorption or drowning of the one element in

the other causes blackness, like black flame or black water. The other colours reveal the mysterious degrees of interpenetration between the two.

How lovely it is to be at sea with the *Pequod*: all the seas are there, so wonderful, so utterly sea-like, with barely a grain of earth interposed: the perfect reality of sea-life.

"It was a cloudy, sultry afternoon; the seamen were lazily lounging about the decks, or vacantly gazing over into the lead-coloured waters. Queequeg and I were mildly employed weaving what is called a sword-mat, for an additional lashing to our boat. So still and subdued and yet somehow preluding was all the scene, and such an incantation of reverie lurked in the air, that each silent sailor seemed resolved into his own invisible self—"

In the midst of this preluding silence came the first cry: "There she blows! there! there! there! She blows! She blows!"—And then comes the first chase, a marvellous piece of true sea-writing, the sea, and sheer sea-beings on the chase, sea-creatures chased. There is scarcely a taint of earth—pure sea-motion.

"Give way men," whispered Starbuck, drawing still further aft the sheet of this sail; "there is time to kill fish yet before the squall comes. There's white water again!—Close to!—Spring!" Soon after, two cries in quick succession on each side of us denoted that the other boats had got fast; but hardly were they overheard, when with a lightning-like hurtling whisper Starbuck said: "Stand up!" and Queequeg, harpoon in hand, sprang to his feet.—Though not one of the oarsmen was then facing the life and death peril so close to them ahead, yet with their eyes on the intense countenance of the mate in the stern of the boat, they knew that the imminent instant had come; they heard, too, an enormous wallowing sound, as of fifty elephants stirring in their litter. Meanwhile the boat was still booming through the mist, the waves curling and hissing around us like the erected crests of enraged serpents.

' "That's his hump. There! there, give it to him!" whispered Starbuck. —A short rushing sound leapt out of the boat; it was the darted iron of Queequeg. Then all in one welded motion came a push from astern, while forward the boat seemed striking on a ledge; the sail collapsed and exploded; a gush of scalding vapour shot up near by; something rolled and tumbled like an earthquake beneath us. The whole crew were half suffocated as they were tossed helter-skelter into the white curdling cream of the squall. Squall, whale, and harpoon had all blended together; and the whale, merely grazed by the iron, escaped—'

Melville is a master of violent, chaotic physical motion, he can keep up
a whole wild chase without a flaw. He is as perfect at creating stillness.
The ship is cruising on the Carrol Ground, south of St Helena.*—
"It was while gliding through these latter waters that one serene and
5 moonlight night, when all the waves rolled by like scrolls of silver; and
by their soft, suffusing seethings, made what seemed a silvery silence,
not a solitude; on such a silent night a silvery jet was seen far in advance
of the white bubbles at the bow.—"

Then there is the description of Brit. "Steering north-eastward from
10 the Crozetts, we fell in with vast meadows of brit, the minute, yellow
substance upon which the Right whale largely feeds. For leagues and
leagues it undulated round us, so that we seemed to be sailing through
boundless fields of ripe and golden wheat. On the second day, numbers
of Right whales were seen, secure from the attack of a Sperm whaler like
15 the *Pequod*, with open jaws sluggishly swam through the brit, which,
adhering to the fringed fibres of that wondrous Venetian blind in their
mouths, was in that manner separated from the water that escaped at the
lip. As morning mowers who side by side slowly and seethingly advance
their scythes through the long wet grass of the marshy meads; even
20 so these monsters swam, making a strange, grassy, cutting sound; and
leaving behind them endless swaths of blue on the yellow sea. But it was
only the sound they made as they parted the brit which at all reminded
one of mowers. Seen from the mast-heads, especially when they paused
and were stationary for a while, their vast black forms looked more like
25 masses of rock than anything else—"

This beautiful passage brings us to the apparition of the squid.

"Slowly wading through the meadows of brit, the *Pequod* still held her
way north-eastward towards the island of Java; a gentle air impelling her
keel, so that in the surrounding serenity her three tall, tapering masts
30 mildly waved to that languid breeze, as three mild palms on a plain.
And still, at wide intervals in the silvery night, that lonely, alluring jet
would be seen.

"But one transparent blue morning, when a stillness almost preter-
natural spread over the sea, however unattended with any stagnant calm;
35 when the long burnished sunglade on the waters seemed a golden finger
laid across them, enjoining secrecy; when all the slippered waves whispered together as they softly ran on; in this profound hush of the visible
sphere a strange spectre was seen by Daggoo from the mainmast head.

"In the distance, a great white mass lazily rose, and rising higher and
40 higher, and disentangling itself from the azure, at last gleamed before

our prow like a snow-slide, new slid from the hills. Thus glistening for
a moment, as slowly it subsided, and sank. Then once more arose, and
silently gleamed. It seemed not a whale; and yet, is this Moby Dick?
thought Daggoo——"

The boats were lowered and pulled to the scene.

"In the same spot where it sank, once more it slowly rose. Almost
forgetting for the moment all thoughts of Moby Dick, we now gazed
at the most wondrous phenomenon which the secret seas have hitherto
revealed to mankind. A vast pulpy mass, furlongs in length and breadth,
of a glancing cream-colour, lay floating on the water, innumerable long
arms radiating from its centre, and curling and twisting like a nest of
anacondas, as if blindly to clutch at any hapless object within reach.
No perceptible face or front did it have; no conceivable token of either
sensation or instinct; but undulated there on the billows, an unearthly,
formless, chance-like apparition of life. And with a low sucking sound
it slowly disappeared again.—"

The following chapters, with their account of whale-hunts, the killing,
the stripping, the cutting up, are magnificent records of actual happening. Then comes the queer tale of the meeting of the *Jeroboam*, a whaler
met at sea, all of whose men were under the domination of a religious
maniac, one of the ship's hands. There are detailed descriptions of the
actual taking of the sperm oil from a whale's head. Dilating on the smallness of the brain of a sperm whale, Melville significantly remarks—"for
I believe that much of a man's character will be found betokened in
his back-bone. I would rather feel your spine than your skull, whoever you are—." And of the whale, he adds—"For, viewed in this light,
the wonderful comparative smallness of his brain proper is more than
compensated by the wonderful comparative magnitude of his spinal
cord."

In among the rush of terrible, awful hunts come touches of pure
beauty.

"As the three boats lay there on that gently rolling sea, gazing down
into its eternal blue noon; and as not a single groan or cry of any sort,
nay not so much as a ripple or a thought, came up from its depths;
what landsman would have thought, that beneath all that silence and
placidity the utmost monster of the seas was writhing and wrenching
in agony!—"

Perhaps the most stupendous chapter is the one called "The Grand
Armada," at the beginning of Volume III. The *Pequod* was drawing
through the Sunda Straits towards Java when she came upon a vast host

of sperm whales. "Broad on both bows, at a distance of two or three miles, and forming a great semi-circle embracing one-half of the level horizon, a continuous chain of whale-jets were up-playing and sparkling in the noon-day air—"—Chasing this great herd, past the Straits of
5   Sunda, themselves chased by Javan pirates, the whalers race on. Then the boats are lowered. At last that curious state of inert irresolution came over the whales, when they were, as the seamen say, gallied. Instead of forging ahead in huge martial array, they swam violently hither and thither, a surging sea of whales, no longer moving on. Starbuck's boat,
10 made fast to a whale, is towed in amongst this howling Leviathan chaos. In mad career it cockles through the boiling surge of monsters, till it is brought into a clear lagoon in the very centre of the vast, mad, terrified herd. There, a sleek, pure calm reigns. There the females swam in peace, and the young whales came snuffing tamely at the boat, like dogs. And
15 there the astonished sea-men watched the love-making of these amazing monsters, mammals, now in rut far down in the sea.— "But far beneath this wondrous world upon the surface, another and still stranger world met our eyes as we gazed over the side. For, suspended in these watery vaults, floated the forms of the nursing-mothers of the whales, and
20 those that by their enormous girth seemed shortly to become mothers. The lake, as I have hinted, was to a considerable depth exceedingly transparent; and as human infants while sucking will calmly and fixedly gaze away from the breast, as if leading two different lives at a time; and while yet drawing mortal nourishment, be still spiritually feasting upon
25 some unearthly reminiscence, even so did the young of these whales seem looking up towards us, but not at us, as if we were but a bit of gulf-weed in their newborn sight. Floating on their sides, the mothers also seemed quietly eyeing us.———Some of the subtlest secrets of the seas seemed divulged to us in this enchanted pond. We saw young Leviathan
30 amours in the deep. And thus, though surrounded by circle upon circle of consternation and affrights, did these inscrutable creatures at the centre freely and fearlessly indulge in all peaceful concernments; yea, serenely revelled in dalliance and delight.—"
    There is something really overwhelming in these whale-hunts, almost
35 superhuman or inhuman, bigger than life, more terrific than human activity. The same with the chapter on ambergris: it is so curious, so real, yet so unearthly. And again in the chapter called The Cassock— surely the oddest piece of phallicism in all the world's literature.
    After this comes the amazing account of the Try-works, when the
40 ship is turned into a sooty, oily factory in mid-ocean, and the oil is

extracted from the blubber. In the night of the red furnace burning on deck, at sea, Melville has his startling experience of reversion. He is at the helm, but has turned to watch the fire: when suddenly he feels the ship rushing backward from him, in mystic reversion.—"Uppermost was the impression, that whatever swift, rushing thing I stood on was not so much bound to any haven ahead, as rushing from all havens astern. A stark, bewildered feeling, as of death, came over me. Convulsively my hands grasped the tiller, but with the crazy conceit that the tiller was, somehow, in some enchanted way, inverted. 'My God! What is the matter with me!' thought I!—"

This dream-experience makes a great impression on him. He ends with an injunction to all men, not to gaze on the red fire when its redness makes all things look ghastly.

After some unhealthy work on the ship, Queequeg caught a fever and was like to die.— "How he wasted and wasted in those few, long-lingering days, till there seemed but little left of him but his frame and tattooing. But as all else in him thinned, and his cheek-bones grew sharper, his eyes, nevertheless, seemed growing fuller and fuller; they took on a strangeness of lustre; and mildly but deeply looked out at you there from his sickness, a wondrous testimony to that immortal health in him which could not die, or be weakened. And like circles on the water, which, as they grow fainter, expand; so his eyes seemed rounding and rounding, like the circles of Eternity. An awe that cannot be named would steal over you as you sat by the side of this waning savage—"

But Queequeg did not die—and the *Pequod* emerges from the Eastern Straits, into the full Pacific. "To my meditative Magian rover, this serene Pacific once beheld, must ever after be the sea of his adoption. It rolls the midmost waters of the world—"

In this Pacific the fights go on.—"It was far down the afternoon; and when all the spearings of the crimson fight were done; and floating in the lovely sunset sea and sky, sun and whale both died stilly together; then, such a sweetness and such a plaintiveness, such inwreathing orisons curled up in that rosy air, that it almost seemed as if far over from the deep green convent valleys of the Manilla isles, the Spanish land-breeze had gone to sea, freighted with these vesper hymns.—Soothed again, but only soothed to deeper gloom, Ahab, who had sterned off from the whale, sat intently watching his final wanings from the now tranquil boat. For that strange spectacle observable in all sperm whales dying—the turning of the head sunwards, and so expiring—that strange spectacle, beheld of such a placid evening, somehow to Ahab conveyed a wondrousness unknown before. 'He turns and turns him to it;—how slowly, but how steadfastly, his homage-rendering and invoking brow, with his last dying motions. He too worships fire';— — —"

So Ahab soliloquises: and so the warm-blooded whale turns for the
5   last time to the sun, which begot him in the waters.

But as we see in the next chapter, it is the Thunder-fire which Ahab really worships: that livid fire of which he bears the brand, from head to foot.—It is storm, the electric storm on the *Pequod*, when the corposants burn in high, tapering flames of supernatural pallor upon the mast-
10   heads, and when the compass is reversed. After this all is fatality. Life itself seems mystically reversed. In these hunters of Moby Dick there is nothing but madness and possession. The captain Ahab moves hand in hand with the poor imbecile negro boy, Pip, who has been so cruelly demented, left swimming alone in the vast sea. It is the imbecile child of the
15   sun hand in hand with the northern monomaniac, captain and master.

The voyage surges on. They meet one ship, then another. It is all ordinary day-routine, and yet all is a tension of pure madness and horror, the approaching horror of the last fight. "Hither and thither, on high, glided the snow-white wings of small, unspeckled birds; these were
20   the gentle thoughts of the feminine air; but to and fro in the deeps, far down in the bottomless blue, rushed mighty leviathans, sword-fish and sharks; and these were the strong, troubled, murderous thinkings of the masculine sea—"—On this day Ahab confesses his weariness, the weariness of his burden. "—But do I look very old, so very, very
25   old, Starbuck? I feel deadly faint, and bowed, and humped, as though I were Adam staggering beneath the piled centuries since Paradise—"
It is the Gethsemane of Ahab, before the last fight: the Gethsemane of the human soul seeking the last self-conquest, the last attainment of extended consciousness—infinite consciousness.
30   At last they sight the whale. Ahab sees him from his hoisted perch at the mast-head.—"From this height the whale was now seen some mile or so ahead, at every roll of the sea revealing his high, sparkling hump, and regularly jetting his silent spout into the air.—"

The boats are lowered, to draw near the white whale. "At length
35   the breathless hunter came so high his seemingly unsuspecting prey that his entire dazzling hump was distinctly visible, sliding along the sea as if an isolated thing, and continually set in a revolving ring of finest, fleecy, greenish foam. He saw the vast involved wrinkles of the slightly projecting head, beyond. Before it, far out on the soft, Turkish-
40   rugged waters, went the glistening white shadow from his broad, milky

forehead, a musical rippling playfully accompanying the shade; and
behind, the blue waters interchangeably flowed over the moving valley
of his steady wake; and on either side bright bubbles arose and danced
by his side. But these were broken again by the light toes of hundreds of
gay fowl softly feathering the sea, alternate with their fitful flight; and   5
like to some flagstaff rising from the pointed hull of an argosy, the tall
but shattered pole of a recent lance projected from the white whale's
back; and at intervals one of the clouds of soft-toed fowls hovering, and
to and fro shimmering like a canopy over the fish, silently perched and
rocked on this pole, the long tail-feathers streaming like pennons.   10

"A gentle joyousness—a mighty mildness of repose in swiftness, invested the gliding whale— —"

The fight with the whale is too wonderful, and too awful, to be described apart from the book. It lasted three days. The fearful sight on the
third day, of the torn body of the Parsee harpooneer, lost on the previous   15
day, now seen lashed on to the flanks of the white whale by the tangle
of harpoon-lines, has a mystic dream-horror. The awful and infuriated
whale turns upon the ship, symbol of this civilised world of ours. He
smites her with a fearful shock. And a few minutes later, from the last of
the fighting whale-boats comes the cry " 'The Ship! Great God, where   20
is the ship?'—Soon they through the dim, bewildering mediums saw
her sidelong fading phantom, as in the gaseous Fata Morgana; only the
uppermost masts out of the water; while fixed by infatuation, or fidelity,
or fate, to their once lofty perches, the pagan harpooneers still maintained their sinking look-outs on the sea. And now, concentric circles   25
seized the lone boat itself, and all its crew, and each floating oar, and
every lance-pole, and spinning, animate and inanimate, all round in one
vortex, carried the smallest chip of the *Pequod* out of sight—"

The bird of heaven, the eagle, St. John's bird, goes down with the
ship, nailed by Tashtego's hammer, the hammer of the Indian.   30

"Now small fowls flew screaming over the yet yawning gulf; a sullen
white surf beat against its steep sides; then all collapsed; and then the
great shroud of the sea rolled on as it rolled five thousand years ago."

So ends one of the strangst and most wonderful books in the world,
closing up its mystery and its tortured symbolism. It is an epic of the   35
sea such as no man has equalled; and it is a book of esoteric symbolism
of profound significance.

Studies in Classic American Literature

(XIII)

Whitman.

Whitman is the last and greatest of the Americans. He is the fulfilmen[t]
5 of the great old truth. But any truth, immediately it is fulfilled, accom-
plishe[d,] become *ipso facto** a lie, a deadly limitation to truth. Never is
this more fully exemplified than here. In Whitman lies the greatest of
all modern truths. And yet many really thoughtful men, in Europe at
least, insist even today that he is the greatest of modern humbugs,* the
10 arch-humbug. A great truth—or a great lie—which? A great prophet,
or a great swindle—which?

    Both! The answer becomes tiresome nowadays. This is the age of
paradoxes*—till paradoxes are a real nuisance to us. But let us sit down
to them. St. John talks of the glory of the heavens opening at the tri-
15 umph of the rider on the white horse.* The white horse symbolises the
spiritual vital energy: like Jung's *libido*.* The rider is the human self,
or soul: or the archetype, the Paraclete; Jesus, archetype of the human
soul. The triumph is when the last of the chakras, the centres of primary consciousness, is finally vanquished. When the lowest centre of
20 consciousness, the cocygeal ganglion, is at last subdued and brought
into subject polarity by the corresponding upper conscious centre, the
cerebellum,* or some particular quick in the cerebellum, then the whole
circuit of perfect consciousness is established in the human being. There
is a magnificent accession into wholeness, full knowledge, symbolically,
25 into *light*. The esoterics say that some latent body, the pineal body
presumably,* bursts into activity, and the human being suddenly finds
himself with a terrible new vision, a new eye having opened:* there is
the awful vision now of Allness, infinitude, Wholeness, the Whole is
revealed. The mystics say that a tremendous great light crashes into
30 the human psyche,* like a great thunder, and that this is the supreme
moment of consummation and of peril for the new seer. For many seers
died in the stress of this supreme moment.

    That may well be. What it has taken us two thousand years to accom-
plish, they brought to pass in a life-time, through scientific stages of
35 initiation. With us, the thunder of the light and the peril of the stress is
spread over several generations. There are other accompanying effects

also, unnoticed by the great seers, who could swoon into their Nirvana,*
their Infinite, Boundless, or whatever they might call it, without thought
of anything further. They thought a final goal was reached, a consummation and an end. We find that this end is only a phase, a stage in a
process. They thought they might rest forever in their Nirvana, like a
larvum in a cocoon. We find we must struggle, gnaw our way even out
of the cocoon, the quiescent chrysalis state, and burst into new being,
take a new mode of life and locomotion.

Whitman, however, is the best modern example of the great triumph into infinitude, Allness, the glory of the infinite Light. If we
read his paeans, his chants of praise and deliverance and accession,
what do we find? Chaoti[c] surges of vehemence, catalogues, lists, enumerations, and all-embracing acceptance. "Whoever you are, to you
endless announcements."—"And of these one and all I weave the song
of myself."—"Lovers, endless lovers."

It is all one cry: I am everything and everything is me. I accept
everything—nothing is rejected.

"I am he that aches with amorous love;
  Does the earth gravitate? does not all matter, aching, attract all
    matter?
  So the body of me to all I meet or know."

This is Whitman. It is his accession into wholeness, his knowledge in
full. Now he is unified with everything, *consciously*. Now, consciously, he
embraces all things into a oneness with himself. Now he sees all things
as one with himself. Drunk with this new vision, really drunk with the
strangest wine of infinitude, he pours forth his paeans, his chants of
praise. It is a man's maximum state of consciousness. It is a state of
living infinitude, when man really knows in full, when really he sees,
not as through a glass, darkly, but distinctly and in totality. Supreme
consciousness, and the divine drunkenness of supreme consciousness,
this is Whitman's revelation. The clue, the connecting mystery, is love,
sympathy, St Paul's "charity"*—"And whoever walks a furlong without
sympathy walks to this own funeral drest in his own shroud," shouts
Whitman. A man who is not so keen on supreme consciousness is inclined to answer "Humbug." Both are right. By vivid, imaginative sympathy, or love, Whitman is identified with whatever and whoever he sees,
or even thinks of. This is the clue to his cryptic "One Identity." It is the
same Allness. But a man who does not find his reality in Allness or infinitude is tempted to find Whitman a humbug. Some men find the highest

reality in the single, separate distinctness of the soul, an even starry aloofness: a supreme isolation: an isolation reached by infinite rejection, a rejection of All, leaving the one soul alone. This is another form of infinitude, the infinite of pride or rejection, symbolised by Saint Teresa
5   as a point:* the infinite of the *point*: the negative infinite. This is, in the end, the Russian infinite, the Russian "supreme state." Each supreme state is paradoxical to the other, and yet, in the very last issue, identical with the other, like the positive and negative infinity in mathematics. Each supreme state, in the end, becomes the highest form of egoism.
10   Whitman however goes his own way. By virtue of vivid imaginative sympathy, or love, he can enter into all things and all beings, he can become in his own person the whole world, the whole universe, and the whole of eternity. It is the actual attaining to a Godhead. Item by item he identifies himself with the universe, and this accumulative identity
15 he calls democracy, *en masse*, and so on. List after list of additions to himself he gives us: we read till we are stupefied, or carried away. For each item is indeed an extension of the being, it is a vivid addition to the soul, imaginative. There is no good and no evil. Nothing is repudiated or rejected. Every being, every creature, every substance, every experience,
20 every phenomenon enters in. Whitman must experience *everything*, in his own person. It is the progress towards democracy, en masse, infinity—what you like.

But this process of extreme physical sympathy, universal sympathy, *merging*, as Whitman rapturously calls it, must obviously be made at
25 some expense somewhere. The *consciousness*, the mental consciousness is the great gainer, gainer to infinity. But a man cannot endlessly merge into all things without endlessly departing from his own integral, single self. And at the very moment when he really surpasses into the infinite he passes away from himself, from his own integral, single being. So
30 that the very moment of his accession into infinitude is the moment of his soul-death. Obviously, there can be no *final* accession into infinitude until physical death and dissemination takes place. The body is finite. But the process is a process of straining at the bonds of the integral self, it is a process of actual death to the self.
35   The goal of the *spirit*, or the consciousness, may be Infinity. But once the spirit, or the consciousness, surpasses into the Infinite, the single soul is dead. The self is dead. The Infinite is therefore Death.

No one knows this better than Whitman. The burden of some of his loveliest and greatest songs is Death, always Death, Death. Even the
40 supreme happiness at last is in Death.

It is impossible to persist in universal passional sympathy without a great violation to the real, single self. Whitman conceives happiness, in his first poems, as a state of rapturous merging away from himself into the surrounding world, human, animal, vegetable, intellectual, whatever it be. But such a state is only *poignantly* or destructively happy, half happy. It is a continual strain in one direction. It has its ghastly collapses into nothingness.

The great danger is the *breaking* of the integral self, the breaking of the integral oneness of the being, when a state of imbecility, or epilepsy, or madness supervenes. It is common, not only as religious mania. And Whitman, knowing the weariness of the strain, and probably knowing the danger of decomposition setting in in the soul, knows also the saving beauty of death, where all things are solved.

Man must seek his great goal of consciousness infinitude, his ecstasy of oneing with all things. It is his fulfilment. But he must remember, that beyond such fulfilment, the human soul then must assume its own integral singleness, and spontaneity, and creative reality. *After* the great fulfilment, the human soul becomes free to be itself, to blossom spontaneously from itself. Before this, all is a process of "becoming."

Every soul, before it can be free, and whole in itself, spontaneously blossom[ing] from itself, must know this accession into Allness, infinitude. Thus far Whitman is a great prophet. And he shows us the process of oneing: he is a true prophet. The falsehood creeps in when we accept this "oneing" as a goal, and not as a process, a means to a different end altogether.

But Whitman shows us the process of the oneing. It is a process of unificatio[n.] It is a process, in the individual psyche, of unifying the consciousness, bringing all under one control, into a unified knowledge. That is, it is a process of establishing a pure polarity between the lower sensual body and the upper spiritual body, with the lower body as the negative, subject pole. The lower centres of consciousness must be reduced to subject polarity. The circui[t] of dynamic consciousness is thus established, full consciousness floods the mind, there is complete control and unification.

With great courage and beauty Whitman describes this process: almost as the esoteric priest-hoods of the past must have known it. He seeks to merge, not only in the spirit, but bodily even, with all things. It is his own physical body which he seeks to fuse and merge in one unspeakable coalescence with the body of the universe. If he go too far, he will cause the disintegration even of his own *physical* psyche.

But he must go far enough, or he is never fulfilled. It is man's eternal dilemna.

Whitman's method of fusing, or transfusing, was to constitute himself the negative pole in the sensual flow. He sought one form of grati-
5   fication, one continuous ecstasy—the ecstasy of giving himself utterly, passing like a spent breath into the body of the other, in an ecstasy of acute, physical passing away, away from himself, in a self-loss keen and delirious as death or sheer delight—the terrible blade-cut of the sensual death, in the negative polarity.

10   There is, of course, another method—a seeking of the ecstasy of positive possession, cumulating in almightyness. Then the sensual polarity in a man is positive, and he utterly envelops the other being, catching up and consuming, as it were, the other being, into an ecstatic sensual unification with his self. Then he envelops his recipient in the flame of
15   himself, till the recipient is rapt away into himself. This is the culminative sensual physical ecstasy of infinitude: the *sensual-positive* infinite, which is at the same time the spiritual *negative* infinite, the *consciousness* reduced to a point.

But Whitman's way is the way of sensual negation, and spiritual
20   positivity, when sensually he lapses like spilt blood, to a point almost of nothingness, whilst spiritually and consciously he becomes boundless, he knows everything.

The process of establishing the sensual centres as the negative centres was once known as a scientific process. Now it takes place hap-hazard.
25   But it is always the same process. The upper or spiritual self gathers the passion[ ] experience of the lower, sensual self, violates, as it were, the lower self, and assumes command.

First there is the conquest of the first appetites, hunger, thirst, and so on, and of the first emotions, human and parental affection, fear of
30   pain, and such-like: all those impulses and desires which bubble up into our psyche at the great abdominal centre, the solar plexus, and which maintain themselves volitionally in the lumbar ganglion. The solar plexus and the lumbar ganglion are conquered from the thoracic ganglion, and the first circuit of control is set up, and the first field of
35   consciousness opens in the mind.

Secondly the great appetites of the hypogastric plexus, the great corresponding will of the sacral ganglion must be conquered. This means sexual desire, the love of man for woman, and some deep appetites such as love of wine. Now Whitman, singing of the mystery of touch,
40   tells us of the process. He tells of the mystery of the touch of the

hands and fingers, those living tendrils of the upper spiritual centres, upon the lower body: the hands and fingers gathering and controlling the sheer sex motions. It is one of the first steps in the transfer of the control from the lower spontaneous centres to the upper: and it has its accompanying increase of mental consciousness[.] The upper self reacts 5 upon the lower, seizes control, and establishes a circuit.

But the touch of the hands is only the beginning of a great involved process. Not only the fingers reap the deep forces, but the mouth and tongue in kissing and so on, the nostrils in scent of secret sweat and hair, the eyes in seeing, the ears in gathering the sounds of sensual blood- 10 resonance, from the voice in speech, from music, from the beat of the pulse. All this Whitman minutely and continually describes. It is the transferring to the upper centres, the thoracic and cervical ganglia, of the control of the deep lumbar and sacral ganglia; it is the transferring to the upper sympathetic centres, breast, hands, mouth, face, of the dark, 15 vital secrets of the lower self. The lower sensual centres are explored and subjected and *known* by the upper self.

This is what makes Whitman again so monstrous, a shattering half-truth, a devastating, thrilling half-lie. Everything is transferred into the upper self, and the mental consciousness. It is a process of sheer self- 20 consciousness. Whitman is almost a monomaniac, obsessed by the *idée fixe** of his own person.

It is this extreme self-consciousness which makes athletes. The athlete is one whose whole upper consciousness is occupied with his own physique, his own sensual realities. He is a creature of complete control, 25 complete transfer, an almost automatic physical self-consciousness. In him the dark spontaneity of the rich sensual centres is gone entirely. He has no spontaneity. He is a self-obsessed physical automaton.

The same is true of Whitman's women, his "athletic mothers." Whitman goes to a woman simply and solely for merging, and for 30 the state of consciousness, and self-consciousness, liberated during this merging. He has no idea that each woman is, in truth, a *being*, a single, instant being, no[t] in any way to be generalised. To Whitman each woman is a Female, a Womb, the Magna Mater. All he sought was the experience of the sensual merging into the woman, the sinking himself again into her 35 womb: and, at the same time, the birth of a still greater, dominant *consciousness* in himself. The two experiences concur: the sensual merging, utter self-loss, and the spiritual self-realisation, triumphant. So he sings the woman, the great womb of space: the Female— "with bent head and arms folded over the breast"—She is the self-absorbed, mindless womb. 40

"As I see my soul reflected in Nature
As I see through a mist, One with inexpressible completeness,
sanity, beauty
See the bent head, and arms folded over the breast, the Female
5   I see."

It is no wonder men complain of the humbug. It is a wonder more
wome[n] do not complain. For surely it is humbug to translate the
individual into a function—an integral woman into a Female, a Womb.
And yet, there is the terrific truth of it too.

10   "This the nucleus—after the child is born of woman, man is born
of woman
This is the bath of birth, this merge of small and large, and the
outlet again[."]

Quite true, it is the bath of birth. Quite true, man is born again of
15   woman, in sheer merging. But not born without a concurrent death. He
is born again in the spiritual upper being, born in the upper *consciousness*.
But in the powerful, rich, dark sensual self, he is destroyed, reduced,
annulled. And this reduction or annulling of any part of the psyche, if
carried too far, results in the disintegration of the very being of man or
20   woman, real death, damnation. Which Whitman knows. And hence the
violent reaction between man and woman, the inevitable hate in love.
For as man loves that which is his bath of birth, so he hates mystically
that which is his death. "The womb, the tomb," as somebody sings:*
for it is both a bath of birth and a lake of death to a man's being.—The
25   same is true for a woman. While exalted, she is destroyed: till she must
hate the very exaltation.
Whitman keeps a great deal of this dark: hence the humbug. Hence
also the Whitmanesque vehemence. "Methinks the gentleman doth insist too much."* Men must always insist heavily on a half-truth.
30   But Whitman, for all that, did not merge himself altogether into
woman. He found he could not. For in the first place, he was too proud
to render up his free independence of being, too much a male to submit
his very being to a woman's *will*. And in the second place, short of utter
self-abnegation, he found that the last stages of merging were impossible
35   between beings so categorically different as man and woman. Man must
either yield himself to complete absorption and inglutination* by the
woman—a debâcle far too ignominious for a great man like Whitman.—
or he must reconsider, and seek elsewhere his last mystic unification.

There is a final polarisation, a final circuit of vital being impossibl[e] between man and woman. Whitman found this empirically. Empirically he found that the last circuit of vital polarisation goes between man and man. This was known to the esoterics and the priest-hoods thousands of years before Plato. Whitman is the first in modern life, truly, from   5 sheer empiric necessity, to re-assert this truth. And here he does not shout nor insist. His vehemence is gone. Hesitatingly, reluctantly, cryptically, he begins to speak of the love of comrades, the new love, upon which the new world, the new democracy will be established. Wistfully, sadly, without making himself too plain, he writes *Calamus*, giving the   10 great hint. It is his most wistful theme—the love of comrades—manly love.

We know that the deep, passional human relations are a vital circuit between two beings. A vital circuit has its poles of establishment, like an electric circuit. The great passional emotions of family love, for   15 example, are polarised in the solar plexus and the lumbar ganglion[.] So a woman feels her "bowels drawn" to a child. And so a man feel[s] that the loss of a child "breaks his reins."*—Deeper, we find that sexual love of a man for a woman is polarised in the hypogastric plexus and the sacral ganglion. The sexual consummation between man and woman   20 is the fiery, electric establishing of the perfect life-current, the vital circuit between the two. The two poles are brought together and the great life-circuit is established, upon which the very life and being and equilibrium of man and woman depend. Hence the vast mysterious power of sexual love, and of marriage. Hence also the vast importance   25 of the sexual act itself. It is the forever-refreshing establishment and re-adjustment of the circuit of life, upon which both beings depend for their real, spontaneous living. The whole of mankind is made up of units of man and woman. And therefore all human life rests upon this circuit of vital polarity.   30

But this is not the end. Deeper than the hypogastric and sacral centres lie the cocygeal. The vagina, as we know, is the orifice to the hypogastric plexus, which, in the old words "is situated amid the waters." It is the advent to the great source of being, and it is the egress of the bitter, spent waters of the end.* But beyond all this is the cocygeal centre.   35 There the deepest and most unknowable sensual reality breathes and sparkles darkly, in unspeakable power. Here, at the root of the spine, is the last clue to the lower body and being, as in the cerebellum is the last upper clue. Here is the dark node which relates us to the centre of the earth, the plumb-centre of substantial being. Here is our last and   40 extremest reality. And the port, of egress and ingress,* is the fundament, as the vagina is port to the other centre.

So that, in the last mystery of established polarity, the establishment is between the poles of the cocygeal centres. The last perfect balance is between two men, in whom the deepest sensual centres, and also the extreme upper centres, vibrate in one circuit, and know their electric establishment and readjustment as does the circuit between man and woman. There is the same immediate connection, the same life-balance, the same perfection in fulfilled consciousness and being.

As the hypogastric plexus is as well the clue to the bitter, departing waters of the end, so is the cocygeal the clue to the fiery corruption which is also one stream of our being. As the circuit between man and woman embraces the stream of the watery corruption,* so does the other circuit embrace the stream of fiery corruption, which we have been so afraid to know: and with which Rabelais,* and many other humorists, have mocked us.—Indeed this nodality of the cocygeal centre of consciousness explains many disregarded facts: for instance, the innumerable jokes connected with the seat,* and also the time-old whipping of boys upon that region.

But Whitman's "manly love," like all other love, has its laws. It is not truly a *merging*. Merging means the breaking-down of the soul's integrity, and a flowing into formlessness, decomposition, death. The true relation rests on an established polarity, where one being indeed is negative in his polarity, the other positive, but where both maintain their sheer single, separate integrity, their inviolable singleness of being. It is a relation of two stark individuals, equal in their pure oppositeness or duality. They are balanced stark and extreme one against the other, beyond emotion, beyond all merging, existing in the last extreme of mutual knowledge, almost beyond feeling, so deeply abstracted or concentrated. They are balanced on the edge of death: and their relationship is the root of greatest life and being. Hence *Calamus*.

About this reality, as usual, Whitman spoke a half-truth. He knew the extremity and the strange, ultimate reality. He knew the death and the life. Yet he mixed all up with emotion and merging, that merging which is the breaking-down of being. He believed in fusion—which is pure loss. Not fusion, but delicately-adjusted polarity, is life. Fusion is death. The Greek paiderasty* was a form of fusion, or merging. There the one being possessed utterly the other, possessed, absorbed, consumed, superimposing his will and his intention. The lover caught his beloved at the nascent point of adolescence, and as it were *stole* the sex-flow, tapped the very source of being in the boy. There was no equality, no equilibrised duality, no delicately-suspended true polarity. It was a prostitution like any other prostitution: or else a merging. A prostitution means a using one being for the gratification and increase of the other being, without any true duality, true polarised circuit. It is a destructive 5 process, like merging. They are both processes of disintegration at the life-centres.

So that, in the last passion of merging, or possession, Whitman was drawn to the deepest life-centres. He discovered manly love, love of comrades. He knew a new world would depend on this newly-discovered 10 love. And yet in the next breath it is death, death, all death. So he confesses himself, quiveringly, in *Calamus*. This manly love is the strange calamus, which has its pink-tinged root by the pond, and sends up its leaves of comradeship.* This same love is found again in *Drum-Taps*: for it is the cohering passion of all fearless soldiery; and again, it is 15 the cohering principle, the final fusing-passion of great Democracy, Whitman's en-masse. And then—

> "Yet you are beautiful to me, you faint-tinged roots, you make
> me think of death,
> Death is beautiful from you (what indeed is finally beautiful 20
> except death and love?)
> I think it is not for life I am chanting here my chant of lovers,
> I think it must be for death,
> For how calm, how solemn it grows to ascend to the
> atmosphere of lovers, 25
> Death or life, I am then indifferent, my soul declines to prefer,
> (I am not sure but the high soul of lovers welcomes death
> most)
> Indeed, O death, I think now these leaves mean precisely the
> same as you mean " 30

So from *Calamus*. What a very great poet Whitman is, at his best! At last he will stand with Shakspeare or Dante, then.

Again, from *Sea-Drift*, a lovely and great poem:*

> "Whereto answering, the sea
> Delaying not, hurrying not, 35
> Whisper'd me through the night, and very plainly before
> day-break,
> Lisp'd to me the low and delicious word death,

And again death, death, death, death,
Hissing melodious, neither like the bird nor like my arous'd
child's heart,
But edging near as privately for me rustling at my feet,
5   Creeping thence steadily up to my ears and laving me softly all
over,
Death, death, death, death, death.—"

Again, in *Memories of President Wilson.**

"Come lovely and soothing death
10   Undulate round the world, serenely arriving, arriving,
In the day, in the night, to all, to each
Sooner or later delicate death.

Praised be the fathomless universe
15   For life and joy, for objects and knowledge curious,
And for love, sweet love—but praise! praise! praise!
For the sure-enwinding arms of cool-enfolding death."*

It takes the greatest soul of all to be quite straightforward and direct. In the long run rhetoric and circuitous elaboration and gorgeous
20   language must take second place. Perhaps no man has led us as far as
Whitman. He is the leader. And a humbug. But not only a humbug,
not by any means. In his most blatant poems, rather a humbug. But
elsewhere, very great and single and fearless, one of the splendidest
souls. They talk in America now about Paul Fort and such-like Gallic
25   ephemera:* even they stunt about Sappho, when there is no Sappho.*
Truly modern Americans are not worthy of the great Americans that
have been. No race or people is yet worthy of the best Whitman.
   If we look at Whitman's verse form, again we see a dual intention.
At its best it springs purely spontaneous from the well-heads of con-
30   sciousness. The primal soul utters itself in strange pulsations, gushes
and strokes of sound. At his best Whitman gives these throbs naked and
vibrating as they emerge from the quick. They follow, pulse after pulse,
line after line, each one new and unforeseeable. They are lambent, they
are life itself. Such are the lines. But in the whole, moreover, the whole
35   soul speaks at once: sensual impulse instant with spiritual impulse,
and the mind serving, giving pure attention. The lovely blood-lapping
sounds of consonants slipping with fruit of vowels is unsurpassed and

unsurpassable, in a thousand lines. Take any opening line, almost.—
"Out of the cradle endlessly rocking—" or again—"By the bivouac's
fitful flame—" or "When lilacs last in the dooryard bloom'd"—it goes
straight to the soul, nothing intervenes. There is the sheer creative gesture, moving the material world in wonderful swirls. The whole soul   5
follows its own free, spontaneous, inexplicable course, its contractions
and pulsations dictated from nowhere save from the creative quick itself. And each separate line is a pulsation and a contraction. There is
nothing measured or mechanical. This is the greatest poetry.

But sometimes, again, Whitman dumps us down cartloads of mate-   10
rial, cartload after cartload. All is shovelled out uninspired. How weary
one grows of *A Song for Occupations*, for example!

Yet there we are! I, being what I am, salute you, Whitman, before any
other man, because I owe the last strides into freedom to you. And in
saluting you, I salute your great America.   15

APPENDIX I

Reading Notes for *The Scarlet Letter* (1917)

NOTE ON THE TEXT

The text follows DHL's autograph manuscript, 9 pages (Roberts E382e, BucU) here reproduced in quasi-facsimile. The original is inscribed on unnumbered pages in a lined notebook which also contains farm accounts dating from 1926 to 1929, almost certainly entered by one of the Hocking family; the inside front cover of the notebook has printed calendars for 1907 and 1908. The text here has been transcribed line for line, with underlining as in the original, and the original's spacing reproduced as far as possible. A 1973 transcription (see Introduction, footnote 108) has not been recorded. Deletions are recorded between angle brackets ⟨⟩; additions are recorded as half brackets ⌈⌉.

READING NOTES FOR
THE SCARLET LETTER

Study of Sin.
Hester is the lady again – she is Ligeia
no longer in revolt against herself, her   5
   own passion
p. 70   Sacred Image of Madonna – but
   here "deepest sin in most sacred quality
   of human life."
Roger Chillingworth – symbol of   10
old Europe in America – all mind and
malice, a devil (misshapen from the hour of my birth)
Dimmesdale is the last, young
Christianity – the William Wilson of
Goodness   but hypocrite, coward   15
now.
Hester "My child ⟨shall⟩ ⌐must⌐ seek a heavenly
⌐85⌐ father: she shall never know an
   earthly one. "
p. 92   Chillingworth's speech   20
   95   Magic, or devil worship "Art thou the black
   man etc"
      "Not thy soul, ⟨not⟩ ⌐No⌐ not thine "
99.   She did not flee.
101.   Her work became the fashion   25
⟨Pearl⟩ – Hester had in her character a rich,
voluptuous, Oriental Characteristic – a taste
for the gorgeously beautiful – Cf. Aztecs*
103.   She will not allow herself even the luxury
of fine handicraft – She does coarse work   30
This betoken[s] "something that might be deeply wrong beneath"
She was a christian in act "but she forbore to
pray for her enemies, lest prayer should turn to
curse." For the first time, the woman is in spite of
herself in revolt.   35

But "the spot never grew callous."
The scarlet letter gave her a new sense – the
Sin-detecting sense. – The letter was "red-hot (108)
Pearl: "her nature lacked reference and adaptation
5   (111)   to the world into which she was born "
     "in giving her existence a great law had been
     broken – "
     112   Her mother, while Pearl was yet an infant, grew
     acquainted with a certain peculiar look – – – – So intelligent
10   yet inexplicable, so perverse, sometimes so malicious –"
     p. 113–114.
     p. 115. Pearl hated the other children
     116   All this enmity & passion Pearl had inherited,
     by inalienable right, out of Hester's heart – ,
15   117.   She never created a friend, but seemed always
     to be sowing broadcast the dragon's teeth.
     119.   Hester sees her own face mirrored in Pearl's eyes
     but "fiend-like, full of smiling malice."
     120.   "He did not send me – I have no heavenly
20   Father " – This is the whole crux – Pearl is
     a child without a precedent God, she
     exists isolated, per se.
     She was accounted a demon-child
     The demon is Mephistophelian, a negative agent
25   124   "She was the unpremeditated offspring of the passionate
     moment." This momentaneity is hard for us to
     understand or sympathise with, it's none the less the
     clue to a lost life.
     p. 198 –
30   p. 125.   "Behold, verily, there is the woman of the
     Scarlet letter, & of a truth, moreover, there is of the
     likeness of the Scarlet Letter running along by her side. Come,
     let us fling mud at them.
     "She resembled, in her pursuit of them, an infant
35   pestilence – the Scarlet fever, or some such half fledged angel
     of judgment – whose mission i⟨s⟩⌈t⌉ was to punish the sins
     of a rising generation."
     130.   Her quick & mobil⟨l⟩e interest – her momentaneity
     p. 142. The Black Man in the Woods. – the
40   native spirits

p. 162. "Hath she any discoverable principle of being?"
"None, save the freedom from a broken law."
Roger Chillingworth is Dimmesdale's other
self, the sceptical Reason, the tormentor,
the mocker.   5
174 – Dimmesdale – hypocrite "Above all
things else, he loathed his own miserable soul."
Scourge ! – and vigils, looking at his own
face !
176. The only truth that continued to give Mr D. a   10
real existence on this earth was the anguish in his
inmost soul.
184 The dread of public exposure!
186. Sky – signs – occultism – the A in
the sky   15
190. "The next day – – he preached a discourse which
was held to be the richest & most powerful etc –"
197. Marble coldness of Hester "her life had turned
from passion to thought."
198. "It is remarkable that persons who speculate   20
the most boldly often conform with the most perfect
quietude to the external regulations of Society
She might have been a prophetess
199. "Was existence worth accepting to Whole race
of women – For herself, no "   25
"A woman never overcomes these problems
by exercise of thought."
200 – Roger Chillingworth is become a devil –
yet he had been "kind, just, true, & of constant
207   if not warm affection "*   30
209 "It is our fate. Let the black flower blossom
as it will."
210 "Be it sin or no – – I hate the man."
212 And it seemed a fouler offence committed by Roger
Chillingworth – that – – he had persuaded her to   35
fancy herself happy by his side."
221 – this gaiety of Pearl's – "Perhaps this too, was
a disease, and but the reflex of the wild energy with
which Hester had fought against her sorrows before Pearls
birth ' – "She wanted – a grief – "   40

223   "Once in my life I met the Black Man –
and this letter is his mark."

230   They meet in the forest.

231   "of penance I have had enough. Of
penitence there has been none"

233.   " – disorganise & corrupt his ⟨whole⟩ ⌈spiritual⌉ ⟨being⟩.
Its result, on earth – – – insanity and hereafter,
that alienation from the Good & True, of which
madness is perhaps the earthly type."

234   Blacker or fiercer frown –
                235
"What we did had a Consecration of its own."

237   "Think for me, Hester. Thou art Strong. Resolve
        for me."

2   "Wilt thou die for very weakness."
"The judgment of God is on me."

238   "I am powerless to go. (")⌈I⌉ dare not
quit my post."

2⟨3 . . .⟩⌈40⌉   "The tendency of her fate & fortunes had set
his face."

241   "But this had been a sin of passion, not of
principle, nor even purpose."X

242   "that the breach which guilt has once made
into the human soul is never, in this mortal state,
repaired."
        "Wherefore should I not snatch the solace
allowed to the condemned culprit before his execution

243   " – of breathing the wild, free, atmosphere of
an unredeemed, unchristianised, lawless region."

        " – there was inevitably a tinge of the
devotional in his mood."
"This is already the better life "

244.   She throws away the Scarlet Letter

24⟨5⟩⌈6⌉. – Pearl is a ⟨n⟩⌈N⌉ atur⟨-⟩Kind – "the small
denizens of the w⟨oo⟩ilderness hardly took pains
to move out of her path " – infant dryad*

254 – She resumes the Scarlet Letter.

255   Pearl kisses the Scarlet Letter

256   Pearl washes off the minister's kiss

260   He wanted to preach the election Sermon

263   "it was only by the most careful self-
control that the former could refrain from
uttering certain blasphemous Suggestions
that rose in his mind, respecting the Communion
Supper."   5
264   "deep, pithy unanswerable argument
against immortality of human soul " – to
drop in widow's ear
265 – "teach wicked words to knot
of little Puritan Children."   10
266.   Old Mistress Hibbins
271 "His inspiration in writing
the Election Sermon
305 – Roger Chilingworth – "Madman – I can
yet save you."   15
306.   "Better? – Yea; so we may both die, &
little Pearl ⟨n⟩die with us."
314   "It is a curious subject of observation and
enquiry, whether hatred & love be not the
same thing at bottom."   20
315   Pearl marries foreign aristocracy

[in ink in another hand:]
    Thomas Stanley Hocking
       Tregarthen Farm
          Zinnor*   25
             St. Ives.
                Cornwall.
    July 7th 1921.
       Thursday.
          Stanley Hocking   30
             Stanley Hocking

APPENDIX II

Foreword to Studies in Classic American Literature (1920)

NOTE ON THE TEXT

The text follows a photocopy of DHL's autograph manuscript, 6 pages (Roberts E382.5a, Smith). The Textual apparatus records the readings of the typescript (Roberts E382.5c, Smith), *New Republic* (Per) and *Phoenix* (A1).

Foreword to Studies in Classic American Literature.

"America has no *tradition*. She has no culture-history."
Therefore, she is damned.

Europe invariably arrives at this self-congratulatory conclusion,— usually from the same stock starting–point, the same phrase about tra- 5 dition and culture. Moreover it usually gets Americans in the eye, for they really haven't anything more venerable than the White House, or more primitive than Whistler.* Which they ought to be thankful for, boldly proclaiming their thankfulness.

Americans in Italy, however, are very humble and deprecating. They 10 know their nakedness, and beg to be forgiven. They prostrate themselves with admiration, they knock their foreheads in front of our elegant fetishes. Poor, void America, crude, barbaric America, the Cinquecento knew her not.* *How* thankful she ought to be! She doesn't know when she is well off. 15

Italy consists of just one big arrangement of things to be admired. Every step you take, you get a church or a coliseum between your eyes, and down you have to go, on your knees in admiration. Down go the Americans, till Italy fairly trembles with the shock of their dropping knees. 20

It is a pity. It is a pity that Americans are always so wonderstruck by our—note the possessive adjective—cultural monuments. Why they are any more mine than yours, I don't know—except that I have a British passport to validify my existence, and you have an American. However.. 25

After all, a heap of stone is only a heap of stone—even if it is Milan cathedral. And who knows that it isn't a horrid bristly* burden on the face of the earth? So why should the *Corriere della Sera* remark with such sniffy amusement: "Of course they were duly impressed, and showed themselves overcome with admiration—"—*they* being The Knights of 30 Columbus, *i Cavalieri di Colombo*.*

The Knights of Columbus were confessedly funny in Milan. But once more, why not? The dear, delicate-nosed, supercilious Anna Comnena found Bohemund and Tancred and Godfrey of Bouillon funny enough,

381

in Constantinople long ago.* And well-nurtured Romans never ceased
to be amused by the gaping admiration of Goths and Scythians* inside
some forum or outside some temple. Until the hairy barbarians stopped
gaping and started to pull the wonder to pieces.

5   Of course, Goths and Scythians and Tancred and Bohemund had
no tradition behind them. Luckily for them, for they would never have
got so far with such impedimenta. As a matter of fact, once they *had*
a tradition they were fairly harnessed. And if Rome could only have
harnessed them in time, she might have made them pull her ponderous
10   uncouth Empire across a few more centuries. However, men with such
good names as Alaric and Attila* were not going to open their mouths
so easily to take the bit of Roman tradition.

You might as well sneer at a lad for not having a grey beard as jibe at
a young people for not having a tradition. A tradition, like a bald head,
15   comes with years, fast enough. And culture, more often than not, is a
weary saddle for a jaded race.

A thing of beauty is a joy for ever.* Let us live in hopes. But it isn't
the end of all joys. There are as good fish in the sea as ever came out
of it: quite as good as that prickly sea-urchin of Milan cathedral, Oh
20   Knights of Columbus. As for the sea—la mer, c'est moi. La mer, c'est
aussi vous,* ô Chevaliers de Colombe. Which is to say, there are quite as
many wonders enfathomed in the human spirit as ever have come out
of it: be they Milan Cathedral or the Coliseum or the Bridge of Sighs.*
And in the strange and undrawn waters of the Knights of Columbus,
25   what wonders of beauty etc. do not swim unrevealed? A fig for the spiny
cathedral of Milan. Whence all this prostration before it?

A thing of beauty is a joy for ever. But there's more than one old joy.
It isn't the limit. Do you expect me to gasp in front of a Ghirlandaio,*
that life has reached its limit, and there's no more to be done? You can't
30   fix a high-water mark to human activity: not till you start to die. Here is
Europe swimming in the stagnation of the ebb, and congratulating itself
on the long line of cathedrals, coliseums, Ghirlandaios which mark the
horizon of the old high water: people swarming like the little crabs in
the lagoons of Venice, in seas gone dead, and scuttling and gaping and
35   pluming themselves conceitedly on the vision of St. Marks and San
Giorgio,* looming up magic on the sky-and-water line beyond.

Alas for a people when its tradition is established, and its limits of
beauty defined. Alas for a race which has an exhibition of modern paintings such as the one in the Gardens at Venice, in this Year of Grace 1920.*
40   What else is left but to look back to Tintoret.* Let it look back then.

Let the beauty of Venice be a sort of zenith to us, beyond which there is no seeing. Let Lincoln cathedral* fan her wings in our highest heaven, like an eagle soaring at our pitch of flight. We can do no more. We have reached our limits of beauty. But these are not the limits of all beauty. They are not the limit of all things: only of *us*.

Therefore St. Marks need be no reproach to an American. It isn't *his* St. Marks. It is ours. And we like crabs ramble in the slack waters and gape at the excess of our own glory. Behold our golden Venice, our Lincoln cathedral like a dark bird in the sky at twilight. And think of our yesterdays! What would you not give, O America, for our yesterdays! Far more than they are worth, I assure you. What would not *I* give for your tomorrows.

One begins to understand the barbarian rage against the great monuments of civilisation. "Go beyond *that*, if you can," we say to the American, pointing to Venice among the waters. And the American humbly admits that it can't be done. Rome said the same thing to Attila, years gone by. "Get beyond Aquileia, get beyond Padua,* you barbarian." Attila promptly kicked Aquileia and Padua to smithereens, and walked past. Hence Venice. If Attila or some other barbaric villain hadn't squashed the cities of the Adriatic head, we should have had no Venice. Shall we bewail Aquileia, or praise our Venice? Is Attila a reprehensible savage, or a creator in wrath?

Of course it is simpler for America. Venice isn't really in her way, as Aquileia was in the way of Attila, or Rome in the way of the Goths. Attila and the Goths *had* to do some kicking. The Americans can merely leave us to our monuments.

There are limits. But there are no limits to the human race. The human race has no limits. The Milanese fished that prickly sea-bear of a cathedral out of the deeps of their own soul, and have never been able to get away from it. But the Knights of Columbus depart by the next train.

Happy is the nation which hasn't got a tradition, and which lacks cultural monuments. How gay Greece must have been, while Egypt was sneering at her for an uneducated young nobody, and what a good time Rome was having, whilst Hellas was looking down a cultured and supercilious nose at her. There's as fine fish in the sea as ever came out of it.

America, therefore, should leave off being *quite* so prostrate with admiration. Beauty is beauty, and must have its wistful, time-hallowed dues. But the human soul is father and mother of all man-created beauty.

An old race, like an old parent, sits watching the golden past. But the golden glories of the old are only fallen leaves about the feet of the young. It is an insult to life itself to be *too* abject, too prostrate before Milan cathedral or a Ghirlandaio. What is Milan cathedral but a prickly,
5 empty burr dropped off the tree of life! The nut was eaten even in Sforza days.*

What a young race wants is not a tradition nor a bunch of culture monuments. It wants an inspiration. And you can't acquire an inspiration as you can a culture or a tradition, by going to school and by
10 growing old.

You must first have faith. Not rowdy and the tub-thumping, but steady and deathless, faith in your own unrevealed, unknown destiny. The future is not a finished product, like the past. The future is a strange, urgent, poignant responsibility, something which urges inside
15 a young race like sap, or like pregnancy, urging towards fulfilment. This urge you must never betray and never deny. It is more than all tradition, more than all law, more than all standards or monuments. Let the old world and the old way have been what they may, this is something other. Abide by that which is coming, not by that which has come.

20 And turn for the support and the confirmation not to the perfected past, that which is set in perfection as monuments of human passage. But turn to the unresolved, the rejected.

Let Americans turn to America, and to that very America which has been rejected and almost annihilated. Do they want to draw sustenance
25 for the future? They will never draw it from the lovely monuments of our European past. These have an almost fatal narcotic, dream-luxurious effect upon the soul. America must turn again to catch the spirit of her own dark, aboriginal continent.

That which was abhorrent to the Pilgrim Fathers and to the Spaniards,
30 that which was called the Devil, the black Demon of savage America, this great aboriginal spirit the Americans must recognise again, recognise, and embrace. The devil and anathema of our forefathers hides the Godhead which we seek.

Americans must take up life where the Red Indian, the Aztec, the
35 Maya, the Incas left it off. They must pick up the life-thread where the mysterious Red race let it fall.* They must catch the pulse of the life which Cortes and Columbus murdered. There lies the real continuity— not between Europe and the new States, but between the murdered Red America and the seething White America. The President should
40 not look back towards Gladstone or Cromwell or Hildebrand,* but

towards Montezuma. A great and lovely life-form, unperfected, fell with Montezuma. The responsibility for the producing and the perfecting of this life-form devolves upon the new American. It is time he accepted the full responsibility.

It means a surpassing of the old European life-form. It means a departure from the old European morality, ethic. It means even a departure from the old range of emotions and sensibilities. The old emotions are crystallised forever among the European monuments of beauty. There we can leave them, along with the old creeds and the old ethical laws, outside of life. Montezuma had other emotions, such as we have not known or admitted. We must start from Montezuma, not from St. Francis or St. Bernard.

As Venice wedded the Adriatic,* let Americans embrace the great, dusky continent of the Red Man. It is a mysterious, delicate process, no theme for tub-thumping and shouts of Expositions. And yet it is a theme upon which American writers have touched and touched again, uncannily, unconsciously, blindfold as it were. Whitman was almost conscious: only the political democracy issue confused him. Now is the day when Americans must become fully, self-reliantly conscious of their own inner responsibility. They must be ready for a new act, a new extension of life. They must pass the bounds.

To your tents, O Israel.* Listen to your own, don't listen to Europe.

Florence. 1920.*

APPENDIX III

Foreword (1922)

NOTE ON THE TEXT

The text follows the carbon-copy typescript, 2 pages (TCC7, Roberts E382p, Smith).

STUDIES IN CLASSIC AMERICAN
LITERATURE
BY
D. H. LAWRENCE

Foreword.

It is high time Americans became American, and ceased to hang on to   5
the skirts of Europe. It is time now they grew up, artistically, and left
off behaving like schoolboys let loose from European school-masters.
Tub-thumping and yawping won't do it. If you are going to act from
one centre, you must find that centre in yourself. It is no use chasing it
over all the old continents. It is no use stirring a foot outside America.   10
It is no use yawping* in the ear of your old schoolmasters. Down into
your own self you must go, and find the centre, the clue there. To your
tents, O Americans.*

Never was such a barren absence of creative criticism as in the
U. S. A. Never did any body of people approach its own produc-   15
tions so cautiously and sniffishly* as the Americans; unless indeed these
products be Edison inventions or patent foods.*—The real American
literature—"Oh," say the current Americans, "it is so *unreal*. What, all
that mass of words!" Yes, all that mass of words, and pearls before swine
too.   20

Heaven knows what Americans mean by *reality*. Heaven knows what
anybody means. Telephones, tinned meat, Charlie Chaplin, and World-
Salvation, presumably. All of which seems to be broken bits of nightmare, especially World-Salvation, which apparently is the American
speciality. Save yourselves, O Americans!   25

Two bodies of literature seem to contain a quick, from which the
future may develop: the Russian and the American. Why how? The
American! Yes, dear sirs: but nothing up to date. The *classic* Americans,
if you please. The *classic* Americans. And on a par too, with those voluminous Russians. Poor thin volumes of Hawthorne, Melville, Whitman,   30
Poe, against the piles of Dostoevsky and Tolstoy and Turgenev! Oh
don't trouble. The one lot is as weighty as the other, if the scales be true.

Certainly the Americans are less explicit: all implicit, only implicit.
Which is just the contrary with the Russians: they are too explicit. The
Russian hates the *implied*—as we all do, at last. But better a deep reality   35

implied, than triviality explicit. Not that the Russians are trivial: indeed
no. But up-to-date Americans are.

Nothing is so agonisedly shy as sheer truth. The Americans had, and
have, a new body of truth to bring into the world. So they swaddled
5   it in an ark of indiscernible green, and stuffed it among the bulrushes.
No[t] so much as a Miriam* to keep an eye on it! And yet, you can't
put a new baby in the street, to let it look after itself. You must protect
it. What must you do then, with an enemy baby? The Americans did
the Moses-in-the-bulrushes trick. It was a howling, heathen, dangerous
10   Egypt, for a baby Moses—that U. S. A. Whereas every Russian is at
least a born Miriam. But Uncle Sam—a Pharaoh implacable.

Now we have to lift Moses out of the bulrushes. So now, look out
for the Egyptians. Hi there, what baby is that?—Now am I the roused
Princess, tooth and nail will I fight for my Moses, and my own skin.
15   *A moi, le vrai Israel.**

APPENDIX IV

Nathaniel Hawthorne's *Blithedale Romance* (1920–1)

NOTE ON THE TEXT

The text follows the corrected ribbon-copy typescript, 12 pages (TS3, Roberts E382h, UT). The Textual apparatus also records the readings of *Symbolic Meaning* (E2).

Nathaniel Hawthorne's *Blithedale Romance*

The character in the allegory of *The Scarlet Letter* we have not mentioned. Roger Chillingworth is the actual husband of Hester; he appears as the evil figure in the trinity. A physician, he belongs to the old mediaeval school of medicine and alchemy rather than to modern science. Mysterious herbs, and black magic seem to be his instruments of healing.

He is an old man, older than Hester, with a grey beard and a twisted body—the magician of old. But he is the magician on the verge of modern science, like Francis Bacon, his great prototype.

We are apt to assume that there is only one mode of science—our own. We have decided that, because the old Hermetic science and alchemy and astrology are all displaced today, they were therefore quite fallacious. But if we choose to see only the failure and the fraud in the alchemistic sciences, and only the success of our own, it is our own affair.

Is there indeed no way of examining the phenomena of the world except our own way? A true act of scientific study or discovery is today an act of submission. The true scientist divests himself of his own assurance and devotes himself indefatigably to the phenomenon he wishes to analyse and comprehend, until such time as he receives the desired enlightenment. Our true scientific process is the same as our religious process, a pure self-abnegation on the part of the postulant. This reverential humility, this extreme devotion to the phenomenon under investigation is the pure act of the upper or spiritual consciousness. The lower or sensual centres are abnegated. And when the scientist, through pure *inward* submission to the unresolved phenomenon, has at last apprehended its actual nature, he can then, by another act of self-abnegation proceed to convert his new knowledge into power, power for the common good.

In ancient science, of which Alchemy and Astrology and the Hermetic science are only mutilated remains, the process was just the opposite. Instead of the act of supreme self-denial and devotion before his object, the Alchemist sought to perform the supreme act of authority and command. He would not humbly, religiously *seek*; he would *compel* the material world to yield up its secret to him. There is a world of difference between the two processes, and between the results obtained.

The alchemistic knowledge was *de facto* esoteric. It *could not* be common knowledge. It *must* be secret, private, by its very nature.

We imagine that, because our humility has brought us such great gain, we have exhausted the field of science and knowledge. We imagine
5 that our exoteric knowledge, held by us all in common, having given us such immense power over the natural forces, is the one and the true knowledge. But as a matter of fact we are driven at last to conclude that all our knowledge is only half-knowledge, all our power is only a half of power, and an inferior half at that.

10 If we think a moment we realise that our whole science assumes the subordination of life to the great mechanistic forces. The great forces, the great planets, these are abiding and unchanging. Life is a flux, a sort of atmosphere depending on the planets, a mere product of the forces. Life is the subordinate reality: Force, Matter, the eternal planets, these
15 are primordial. That is the true scientific opinion today. Our science tends all the time to the assertion that life is a mere outcome of certain conjunction of specific forces: a made thing, manufactured in the great and fascinating factory of the cosmos, at a certain point in time.

Now the ancient science held just the opposite. Let us repeat that
20 the alchemy and astrology which dribbled on into our era was but a distorted remains. And still at its core we can discern a central truth different from the truth that sustains all our knowledge. To the ancient scientist, *life* was the first mover. It was life which produced the universe, not the universe which produced life. Life certainly must precede death:
25 there could be no death if there were no life. And to the far-off pagan scientists the universe as we have it is only the great permanent death-result from the great preceding life-phases. Dead life is Matter and Force. All matter was once, in some way, alive, just as the dust of a dead man's bones was once alive. All dust was once bones and flesh. All
30 Matter was once tissue. But in the great post-mortem reaction between the shed dust and the shed, naked elements of fire and water the material universe has been set up.

Though this material universe is set up in apparent independence of the living, it is not even now independent of life. The life-mystery
35 still has the final sway over the mechanistic forces and the material universe. The independence of the material universe is an illusion. The illusion comes owing to the fact that the life-power in *one individual* cannot easily affect the motion of the natural phenomena. But, though the phenomenal universe has its own fixed laws, these laws themselves
40 are subject ultimately to direct life-control.

Our science has reached the point of declaring that all laws are immutable, and can be brought to the service of man through their very immutability. Man submits, and in submission triumphs.

The ancient scientist held the opposite. He held that even the sun is but a cast-off burning breath of life, cast away like a breath emitted, but still not exempt from life. All is part of life, and therefore subject to change.* For in life, nothing is immutable. And, therefore, since the great sun is still within the bounds of life, he may be arrested in his course and made to stand still in mid-heaven, if such be the life-will: that is, if it be the supreme will of the *living*. If it be the supreme will of the living that the sun should stand still in heaven, then the sun will stand still. For life means the living: nothing else. How then exert this supreme will?

This was the basis and the problem of the enormous pre-historic science of the world: how to use, to exert the supreme will. To us it seems nonsense. The sun will not stand still, even if we *will* our heads off. But that, the ancients would tell us, is because we are fools who know nothing about the sacred powers of the life-will which is in us. In the ancient sense, we have no will: none of that tremendous Old-Testament power which moved worlds.* We have only the will which to them was unholy, the will to submission, and triumph through submission.

Now Roger Chillingworth was of the old order: what we call the order of sensual knowledge and power, which has become for us mere abracadabra.* He was mediaeval, a descendant from the pagan world through Simon Magus and Roger Bacon, to the point where old Francis Bacon left off. He believed in the powers of the sensual will. Modern science also has come to the point where it must grant a supreme and terrifying power to *will*. But with us, as with Nietzsche, will is something conscious,* or at least selfless, spiritual: a form of triumph through supreme transcending of self through abnegation, as in Christ. Even the hypnotist, though he hypnotises his patient, makes a sacrifice also of himself. The Germans went to war in a spirit of self-immolation which they intended should raise them to the highest power. The supreme will of today is like the will in Ligeia. The supreme will of the Pharaohs was just the opposite: an all-extension of the centripetal* self, all-powerful, magical, in our sense mindless. It was not *actually* mindless: it had a great science of its own, embodied in the priesthood. But according to our conception of mind and of science, it was mindless and futile.

The old way of sensual understanding and power fell into disrepute with the Greeks, and with the Christians the one supreme sin was the sin of pride. Naturally. Therefore those remnants of the sensual understanding which lived on in the Christian era lived on stigmatised. And this is Roger Chillingworth: he persists, but he is stigmatised. His slight physical deformity* is the symbol. He is the serpent of the

5   Creation myth. Woman bruises his head, but he bruises her heel: for he is the indestructible reality of our sensual being, which always strikes at us through woman.

In this myth of the second Fall, it is the serpent who marries Eve, it is the spiritual Adam who is brought down to prostitution. Hester

10 marries Chillingworth: the woman gives herself to the stigmatised one, the dark alchemist who must needs masquerade as a healer. It is the reversal of the great order of our era. The mother is now enthroned upon the Serpent again, not upon the dove or the cloud of light.

Hester swears her oath with him to the end. She is his great accom-
15 plice in the pulling-down of the spiritual man.

"Why dost thou smile so at me— — —Art thou not like the Black Man that haunts the forest round us? Hast thou not enticed me into a bond which will prove the ruin of my soul?"

"Not thy soul!" he answered with another smile. "No, not thine."

20 The close fight goes on between the two men, Dimmesdale the pure preacher, and the old Roger. Each of them is fixed in his own way, the one ancient, stigmatised, sensual, the other exalted and spiritual. Each of them represents the fatal old doctrine "Pereat mundus—"*

It is a satanic hatred, closely akin to love. The men, through their
25 sheer oppositeness of mode and being, gravitate together in a helpless attraction of mutual hate and mutual love. Dimmesdale will suffer all tortures rather than admit he has fallen. He will suffer all destruction if he may still vindicate the old triumph of spirit over death, the triumph of immortality in selfless love. But it is already too late. Chillingworth holds
30 the one drop of poison that can darken the sun of spiritual immortality: man's irremediable being in sensuality.

Christ made the great revelation that passive power is greater than active power.* Passive power has been accumulating through a long era; is still accumulating. But mystically, essentially, it is already broken. The
35 world is like Dimmesdale, it has its Chillingworth in the dark races. It has had its Hester in Germany.

But like Dimmesdale, it persists even after it has fallen. Nothing is more horrible than the disintegration that sets in in the minister's soul. He becomes obscene and dreadful, all the while preserving his sancti-
40 fied mode. The fatal self-division takes place in his psyche, incipient

epilepsy or imbecility, the desire to defile most horribly the thing he holds most holy. Dostoevsky's whole essence is in these last days of Arthur Dimmesdale.

At the last the saintly minister cheats the satanic physician. By *confessing* his fall he expiates, he throws himself at the feet of mercy, he 5 leaves the great *ideal* intact. He refutes the woman, the sensual union with her.

"Shall we not meet again?" whispered she, bending her face down close to him. "Shall we not spend our immortal life together? Surely, surely we have ransomed one another with all this woe! Thou look- 10 est far into eternity with those bright dying eyes. Tell me what thou seest!"

"Hush, Hester—hush," said he, with tremulous solemnity. "The law we broke!—the sin here so awfully revealed! let these alone be in thy thoughts. I fear! I fear!" 15

So he dies, and both Chillingworth and Hester are cheated of their triumph. Woman still has no place save as the Mater Dolorosa, and the sensual being no acceptance save as the hated serpent.

The Scarlet Letter is a profound and wonderful book, one of the eternal revelations. Those who look for realism and personal thrills may jeer at 20 it. It is not thrilling in the vulgar way. But for those who talk about the profundities of Dostoevsky, it is far more profound than the epileptic Russian, and for those who talk about the perfection of the French novel, it is more perfect than any work of fiction in French. True, Hawthorne classes it as a romance, and thus puts it almost in line with the *Morte* 25 *D'Arthur.* But as a matter of fact it is greater than any romance, and its concentrated *perfection* is a matter of wonder to any artist. It is a romance as much as the Book of Job or the Book of Ruth is a romance, and as little as *Don Quixote.** It is the lasting representative book of American literature. If it displeases us in any particular, it is in the way the ethical 30 Hawthorne embroiders over the artist Hawthorne. The deepest joy is the pride of sin: and all the preaching is so lugubrious and moral. This touch of cant or falseness, duplicity, is however absolutely essential to the fallen Puritan psyche, and therefore artistically true. The lust of sin goes simultaneous with the solemn condemnation of sin. Which is 35 peculiarly American. And this book is the myth of the fallen Puritan psyche, in the New World.

No other work of Hawthorne's is supreme. *The House of the Seven Gables* is a tale of the passing of the dark old Chillingworth order, which was mediaeval, touched with the supernatural. The magic spends 40 itself, the black old proud blood perishes. The young generations are reconciled in a glow of commercial prosperity, modern America.

There are wonderful stories in *Twice Told Tales*. But *The Blithedale Romance* has another element. Here Hawthorne approaches actuality,
5   his own actual doings. The story opens with a more or less true picture of Brook Farm, where the American transcendentalists made their famous experiment. A number of the great idealists, wishing to initiate the social Utopia, bought a farm and united to live in common, to till the ground and eat the bread their own hands had raised, at the same time lifting
10   their souls to that perfect harmony with the Oversoul which was for them the goal of life.

The experiment was in direct line from Crêvecoeur: nature sweet and pure, and brotherhood in toil. It was the old attempt to idealise that which you cannot idealise, heavy physical work and physical, sensual
15   reaction. You cannot dig the ground with the spirit. In the long run, you realise you are fighting the natural elements. The very act of stooping and thrusting the heavy earth calls into play the dark sensual centres in a man, at last, that old Adam which is the eternal opposite of the spiritual or ideal being. Brute labor, the brute struggle with the beast and herd
20   must rouse into activity the primary centres, darken the mind, induce a state of animal mindlessness, and pivot a man in his own heavy-blooded isolation. This is what the transcendentalists wanted, but in an ideal manner. Which is as good as saying they wanted fire which did not burn.

The real clue to the movement lay in this desire of the self-conscious
25   idealists for the sensual unconsciousness of the peasant. They thought they could get it ideally, or idyllically—like Marie Antoinette playing dairymaid. They went for it in earnest. And some enjoyed it. But the experiment was a failure, like all the others of the same sort. The temper of an idealist is too frictional. He is too-much engaged in sublimating the
30   natural brute in himself—which is a frictional, reducing process—to be able to live in physical contact with others. Hawthorne at once knew the falseness of the attempt. Never, he says, did he feel himself more spectral than when he was winding the horn to summon the laborers to their tasks. A more self-conscious scarecrow never stood in a field than
35   the author of the *Scarlet Letter*. No doubt he would have quite liked to be a brute, in the healthy sense of the word, if he could have been it without forfeiting his whole established ideal nature.

The characters in the tale present a four-square group—of two triangles. There is the superb Zenobia, with her tropic flower in her hair,
40   her proud voluptuousness; there is a forlorn little sempstress called

Priscilla, another festering White Lily; there is the I, the teller of the story, the sensitive idealist young man; and there is Hollingsworth, the ex-blacksmith, deep-voiced, black-bearded, patron of criminals.

We have something of the same four-square group as in *Deerslayer*. Zenobia is lurid with a suggestion of sin, Priscilla is touched with im- 5 becility. But in Hollingsworth is a new element. He is a monomaniac, fascinated by criminals. His one aim in life is to build an asylum for crim- inals, which he shall superintend. It is strictly the criminal in himself, the dark luster,* taking on a beneficent form.

Hollingsworth is the sensual type, stigmatised, but rising now to self- 10 arrogance and revenge. He is dark, passionate, obscure—a blacksmith. The sensitive young man is nursed by him, tenderly. Hollingsworth has the strong blood-gentleness, the frail newcomer is lapped in warmth and restoration. So that the two men love each other warmly, at first. The young, frail, thoughtful man, the I of the story, feels a deep love 15 for his sombre nurse. Which love turns to hate, when he realises that Hollingsworth wants to dominate him absolutely, with monomaniac overbearing. He will not be dominated. He turns at last in anger and contempt from the Hephaestos of the underworld, finds him unintelli- gent and stupidly overbearing, criminal really. 20

Both men pretend to love Zenobia, the lurid woman who has become a sort of tropic idealist. And Zenobia has a passion for the criminal- saving blacksmith, who only cares for her because her money will build his asylum.

Both men, we are told, actually love Priscilla. The story is worthy 25 of Poe, should really, after the beautiful opening, have been carried out in Poe's manner. Priscilla is a degenerate descendant of Ligeia. In her the will-to-submission is carried to obscenity. She has been used as a spiritualistic medium by a corrupt person who turns out to be Zenobia's husband. Priscilla is the famous Veiled Lady of the public spiritualist 30 shows at that time so popular in America. Poe should have dealt with all this part of the story.

Priscilla is the psychic prostitute. In her the integral being is gone, leaving her a sort of thing or instrument, repulsive really. When she is covered with the white veil, in the public shows, her trivial up- 35 per consciousness is obliterated, she remains an automatic instrument. Apart from her subjectivity to the suggestion which comes from the "professor," she is actually a medium.

Which means, that she exists under the cloth as a sort of wireless instrument. The apparatus of the human consciousness is much more 40 delicate than any telegraphic apparatus. It can register vibrations which no wireless can register. It can report from the unseen. It does so all the time, in our deep pre-conscious soul. But it can register direct in isolate *mental* messages. On one condition only, however.

5   That the central being is obliterated in the medium herself, leaving her only an instrument. And when she is reduced to this mere telegraphic apparatus, what is it she can report? Nothing but *things*: items of consciousness which exist, as wireless messages exist, in vibrations and impression upon the so-called ether. Should we expect souls to
10   communicate to each other through a medium? Should we expect the dead to need a telephone to speak to us? It is absurd. The dead, if they die and rest, enter into a oneness with life, they are made so *at one* with us, that the thought of a medium is a mere vulgar profanity. And those dead who die and are not at rest, are they going to ring us up on the
15   faulty and silly telephone of a medium like Priscilla? They too can speak *direct*, within us, as they do.

A medium can tell us *nothing* from the dead or the living. What she can do, and all she can do, is to report the scattered pieces of *detached* consciousness which are littered, like torn bits of paper, upon the im-
20   pressible ether—or electricity, call it what you will.* She communicates nothing. She only picks up random bits of thought-impression from her atmosphere.

Another thing a medium *might* do—what the oracles tried to do. Supposing that the whole universe of time and phenomena were a re-
25   morseless chain of cause and effect, then a medium might, by the subtlest transmission and interpretation of the vibrations in the vital ether, forecast an event in the future. But the universe of time and phenomena is *not* a chain of cause-and-effect. It depends, as we know, upon the life-mystery. And the life-mystery knows no absolute cause and effect. It
30   can vary any law at any minute, it does actually create *new fate* every moment. So that mediumistic foretelling of event, though not absolutely nonsensical, must forever be a chancy business. Life itself sets the limit to all enquiry beyond life. The living soul, in its own fulness, contains all it needs to know. Impertinent enquiry is forever made useless by
35   the perfect immediacy of all things which are in life, and by the eternal incalculability of life, and hence of phenomenon.

APPENDIX V

XIII. Whitman (1921–2)

NOTE ON THE TEXT

The text follows the carbon-copy typescript, 2 pages (TCC7, Roberts E382p, Smith). A corrected copy of the previous textual stage (TCC6) presumably served as the setting-copy for the *Nation and Athenaeum* (Per 1), while the text in the *New York Call* (Per 2) was set from Per 1. The Textual apparatus records all the variants of TCC6, Per 1, Per 2 and *Symbolic Meaning* (E2).

XIII.

Whitman.

Whitman* is the last and the greatest of the Americans. One of the greatest poets of the world, in him an element of falsity troubles us still. Something is wrong: we cannot be *quite* at ease in his greatness. 5

This may be our own fault. But we sincerely feel that something is overdone in Whitman: there is something that is too much. Let us get over our quarrel with him first.

All the Americans, when they have trodden new ground, seem to have been conscious of making a breach in the established order. They have 10 been self-conscious about it. They have felt that they were trespassing, transgressing, or going very far, and this has given a certain stridency, or portentousness, or luridness to their manner. Perhaps that is because the steps were taken so rapidly. From Franklin to Whitman is a hundred years. It might be a thousand. 15

The Americans have finished in haste, with a certain violence and violation, that which Europe began two thousand years ago or more. Rapidly they have returned to lay open the secrets which the Christian epoch has taken two thousand years to close up.

With the Greeks started the great passion for the ideal, the passion 20 for translating all consciousness into terms of spirit and ideal or idea. They did this in reaction from the vast old world which was dying in Egypt. But the Greeks, though they set out to conquer the animal or sensual being in man, did not set out to annihilate it. This was left for the Christians. 25

The Christians, phase by phase, set out actually to *annihilate* the sensual being in man. They insisted that man was in his reality *pure spirit*, and that he was perfectible as such. And this was their business, to achieve such a perfection.

They worked from a profound inward impulse, the Christian religious 30 impulse. But their proceeding was the same, in living extension, as that of the Greek esoterics such as John the Evangel or Socrates.* They proceeded, by will and by exaltation, to overcome *all* the passions and all the appetites and prides.

The appetites, passions and prides are on certain planes, in the human psyche. In the first plane we have the appetite of meat and drink, luxury, self-ostentation and vanity and selfishness—to give them all their bad names. This field we find to be active in the abdomen, the stomach and
5 liver of the ancients. The centres of consciousness for these appetites are the great solar plexus and the lumbar ganglion. These centres therefore must be conquered. That is, the cardiac plexus and the thoracic ganglion of the upper body must establish a circuit of polarity with the solar plexus and lumbar ganglion of the lower body, in which circuit the lower centres
10 shall be the submissive or negative, the upper the positive. This entails a *conquest* of the two lower centres by the two upper. Which conquest once established, man is in full control of his lower appetites, and is able, if so need be, to deny them altogether, even to death. And this is the first great step in the progress towards pure spiritual being, and liberty.
15 It took Europe until the Renaissance to accomplish it.

The next and deeper field of the passions is the field of sex and of love for power or regnant glory. The great dynamic centres of these passions are the hypogastric plexus and the sacral ganglion of the lower body. These also must be conquered, the profound appetites subjected. Our
20 history since the Renaissance has been the history of the conquest of kings and sex. In the individual, the conquest is made by the cervical plexus and the cervical ganglia, which seize control of the hypogastric plexus and the lumbar ganglion, and establish the circuit which hold the two great centres of the lower body subjected or negative.
25 But as we know, the fields of consciousness, the *cities*, are seven. We have explored or opened out the four great ones. Still remains the lowest plane and the highest plane, and the final city, the "New Jerusalem."

Now so far, in Europe, the conquest of the lower self has been objective. That is, man has moved from a great impulse within himself,
30 unconscious. But once the conquest has been effected, there is a temptation for the conscious mind to return and finger and explore, just as tourists now explore battlefields.* This self-conscious *mental* provoking of sensation and reaction in the great affective centres is what we call sentimentalism or sensationalism. The mind *returns upon* the affective
35 centres, and sets up in them a deliberate reaction.

And this is what all the Americans do, beginning with Crèvecoeur, Hawthorne, Poe, all the transcendentalists, Melville, Prescott, Wendell Holmes,* Whitman, they are all guilty of this provoking of mental reactions in the physical self, passions exploited by the mind. In Europe,
40 men like Balzac* and Dickens, Tolstoi and Hardy, still act direct from

the passional motive and not inversely, from mental provocation. But the aesthetes and symbolists, from Baudelaire and Maeterlinck* and Oscar Wilde onwards, and nearly all later Russian, French, and English novelists set up their reactions in the mind and reflect them by a secondary process down into the body. This makes a vicious living and a spurious art. It is one of the last and most fatal effects of idealism. Everything becomes self-conscious and spurious, to the pitch of madness. It is the madness of the world of today. Europe and America are all alike: all the nations self-consciously provoking their own passional reactions from the mind, and *nothing* spontaneous.

And this is our accusation against Whitman, as against the others. Too often he deliberately, self-consciously *affects* himself. It puts us off, it makes us dislike him. But since such self-conscious secondariness is a concomitant of all American art, and yet not sufficiently so to prevent that art from being of rare quality, we must get over it. The excuse is that the Americans have had to perform in a century a curve which it will take Europe much longer to finish, if ever she finishes it.

Whitman has gone further, in actual living expression, than any man, it seems to me. Dostoevsky has burrowed underground, into the decomposing psyche. But Whitman has gone forward in life-knowledge. It is he who surmounts the grand climacteric* of our civilisation.

Whitman enters on the last phase of spiritual triumph. He really arrives at that stage of infinity which the seers sought. By subjecting the *deepest centres* of the lower self, he attains the maximum consciousness in the higher self: a degree of extensive consciousness greater, perhaps, than any man in the modern world.

We have seen Dana and Melville, the two adventurers, setting out to conquer the last vast *element*, with the spirit. We have seen Melville touching at last the far end of the immemorial prehistoric Pacific civilisation, in *Typee*. We have seen his terrific cruise into universality.

Now we must remember that the way, even towards a state of infinite comprehension, is through the externals towards the quick. And the vast elements, the cosmos, the big things, the universals, these are always the externals. These are met first and conquered first. That is why science is so much easier than art. The quick is the living being, the quick of quicks is the individual soul. And it is here, at the quick, that Whitman proceeds to find his experience of infinitude, his vast extension or concentrated intensification into Allness. He carries the conquest to its end.

If we read his paeans, his chants of praise and deliverance and accession, what do we find? All embracing, indiscriminate passional acceptance: surges of chaotic vehemence of invitation and embrace, catalogues, lists, enumerations.—"Whoever you are, to you endless announcements—"—"And of these one and all I weave the song of myself"—"Lovers, endless lovers."

5   Continually the one cry: I am everything and everything is me. I accept everything in my consciousness: nothing is rejected.*

"I am he that aches with amorous love;
Does the earth gravitate? does not all matter, aching, attract all
matter?
10   So the body of me to all I meet or know."

At last everything is conquered. At last the lower centres are conquered. At last the lowest plane is submitted to the highest. At last there is nothing more to conquer. At last all is one, all is love, even hate is love, even flesh is spirit. The great oneness, the experience of infinity, 15 the triumph of the living spirit, which at last includes *everything*, is here accomplished.

It is man's accession into wholeness, his knowledge in full. Now he is united with everything. Now he embraces everything into himself, in a oneness. Whitman is drunk with the new wine of this new great experi- 20 ence, really drunk with the strange wine of infinitude. So he pours forth his words, his chants of praise and acclamation. It is man's maximum state of consciousness, his highest state of spiritual being. Supreme spiritual consciousness, and the divine drunkenness of supreme consciousness. It is reached through embracing love. "And whoever walks 25 a furlong without sympathy walks to his own funeral dressed in his own shroud." And this supreme state, once reached, shows us the One Identity in everything, Whitman's cryptic *One Identity*.

Thus Whitman becomes in his own person the whole world, the whole universe, the whole eternity of time. Nothing is rejected. Because 30 nothing opposes him. All adds up to one in him. Item by item he identifies himself with the universe, and this accumulative identity he calls Democracy, En Masse, One Identity, and so on. With his lists of additions to himself at last he either stupefies us or carries us away. But for *him*, each item is a vivid passional imaginative act, an addition to the 35 soul. And so he reaches his consummation in Allness.

But this state, even when reached, is only one state of soul or being, one state, among others. Even at its maximum, it is only a halfness, to tell the truth. Even infinity is dual. Those seated Egyptian kings, they knew another infinity: dark, subtle, the infinity of pride and all-triumphant might, the grand Almighty of the Old Testament. They too covered the universe: but not by extension, but by intensification. They intensified All into their own imperial souls, grandly. They were pivotal, not all-extended.

So that even at its maximum, Whitman's state of Allness is only a half 5 of Allness. And when man is at his maximum of extended being and intensified being also, he is even then only at the two extremes of himself. True, he must reach those extremes. At his very greatest, he should reach *both* extremes. And then he will know the reality of his own being, pivotal in the single and unique self, extensive through imaginative 10 sympathy over the whole universe, intensive through passional pride of being until he is quick of the external All. But even at his greatest, though he embrace the universe and though by intensity he form the potent clue to the universe, a man is no more than himself. Even in his greatest states, he is only himself: just his own single self. Though he 15 be all, he is only *himself* in all.

And this is the last and final truth. Always the last truth is at the quick. And the quick is the single individual soul, which is never more than itself, though it embrace eternity and infinity, and never *other* than itself, though it include all men. Each vivid soul is unique, and though 20 one soul embrace another, and include it, still it cannot *become* that other soul, or livingly dispossess that other soul. In extending himself, Whitman still remains himself, he does not become the other man, or the other woman, or the tree, or the universe: in spite of Plato.*

Which is the maximum truth, though it appears so small in contrast to 25 all these infinites and En Masses and Democracies and Almightinesses. The essential truth is that a man is himself, and only himself, throughout all his greatnesses and extensions and intensifications.

The second truth which we must bring as a charge against Whitman is the one we brought before, namely, that his Allness, his One Identity, 30 his En Masse, his Democracy, is only a half-truth, an enormous half-truth. The other half is Jehovah, and Egypt, and Sennacherib: the other form of Allness, terrible and grand, even as in the Psalms.*

Now Whitman's way to his Allness, he tells us, is through endless sympathy, *merging*. But in merging you must merge *away* from some- 35 thing, as well as towards something, and in sympathy you must depart from one point to arrive at another. Whitman lays down this law of sympathy as the one law, the direction of merging as the one direction. Which is obviously wrong. Why not a *right-about-turn*? Why not turn slap back to the point from which you started to merge? Why not *that* 40 direction, the reverse of merging, back to the single and overweening self? Why not, instead of endless dilation of sympathy, the retraction into isolation and pride?

Why not? The heart has its systole diastole, the shuttle* comes and
5 goes, even the sun rises and sets. We know, as a matter of fact, that all life lies between two poles, and is a motion back and forth between these poles. The direction is twofold. Whitman's *one direction* becomes a hideous tyranny, once he has attained his goal of Allness. His One Identity is a prison of horror, once realised. For identities are manifold
10 and each jewel-like, different as a sapphire from an opal. And the motion of merging becomes at last a vice, a nasty degeneration, as when tissue breaks down into a mucous slime. Even Whitman personally tended to this vice of disintegration and merging soppiness,* in his later days. There must be the sharp retraction into isolation, following the expan-
15 sion into unification, otherwise the integral being is overstrained and will break, break down like disintegrating tissue into slime, imbecility, epilepsy, vice, like Dostoevsky.

And one word more. Even if you reach the state of infinity, you can't sit down there. You just physically can't. You either have to strain still
20 further into universality, and become vaporish or slimy: or you have to hold your toes and sit tight* and practise Nirvana; or you have to come back to common dimensions, eat your pudding and blow your nose and be just yourself; or die and have done with it. A grand experience is a grand experience. It brings a man to his maximum. But even at his
25 maximum a man is not more than himself. When he is infinite he is still himself. He still has a nose to wipe. The state of infinity is *only* a state, even if it be the supreme one.

But in achieving this state Whitman opened a new field of living. He drives on to the very centre of life, and sublimates even this into
30 consciousness. Melville hunts the remote white whale of the deep-est passional body, tracks it down. But it is Whitman who captures the whale. The pure sensual body of man, at its deepest remoteness and intensity, this is the White Whale. And this is what Whitman captures.
35 He seeks his consummation through one continual ecstasy: the ec-stasy of *giving himself*, and of being taken. The ecstasy of his own reaping and merging with another, with others; the sword-cut of sensual death. Whitman's motion is always the motion of *giving himself*. This is my body, take, and eat. It is the great sacrament. He knows nothing of
40 the other sacrament, the sacrament in pride, where the communicant

envelops the victim and host in a flame of ecstatic consuming, sensual gratification and triumph.

Whitman's is the method of giving himself. But first he gives himself to himself. It is the reaping of the lower body, by the upper. First he reaps his own body. When he tells us of the mystery of touch, he tells 5 how the hands and fingers, those gateways, those seekers of the upper consciousness, travel upon the lower body and gather their knowledge of it. His hands and fingers *know* him. They provoke and gather the sheer sex reactions. They transfer the control of the lower spontaneous centres to the upper, the great motions of the hypogastric plexus are 10 provoked and reaped from the cervical or upper plexuses. The upper body seizes control and establishes a circuit. The result is an increase in a certain sort of mental consciousness. The result, if the practice be continuous, is also vice, the vice of masturbation, the vice of the mouth, all the strange vices the modern human being is capable of have their 15 explanation here: the transferring of the action of the lower centres to the upper: the *inversion* of primal reactions.

Whitman tells us the actual physical process of the transfer of the lower sensual self into the upper self: hands, mouth in touch and licking and in taste, nostrils in scent of sweat and flesh, ears in hearing: all 20 perform the great transfer of the lower reactions of the upper. The thoracic and cervical ganglia gain control of the lumbar and the sacral ganglia. This gives Whitman also some of the painful *idée fixe* of his own person, his own special form of self-consciousness, his most objectionable *trait*. 25

But he is concerned with others beside himself: with Woman, for example. But what is Woman to Whitman? Not much. She is a great function—no more. Whitman's "athletic mothers of these States" are depressing. Muscles and wombs: functional creatures: no more.

"As I see my soul reflected in Nature 30
As I see through a mist, One with inexpressible
completeness, sanity, beauty,
See the bent head, and arms folded over the breast, the
Female I see."

That is all. The woman is reduced, really, to a submissive function. 35 She is no longer an individual being, with a living soul. She must fold her arms and bend her head and submit to her functioning capacity. Function of sex, function of birth.

"This the nucleus—after the child is born of woman, man is
   born of woman,
   This is the bath of birth, this merge of small and large, and
   the outlet again—"

5   So, man enters into the womb of woman, whence the child issued,
to be born again there. True enough, in sex man finds a passional
consummation which fulfils him. For Whitman, love between him and
a woman did not mean a balanced relationship between two human
beings, each individual and single, polarised in perfect equilibrium, but
10   never merged. Love with a woman meant for him the merging of himself
completely into the woman, sexually. He entered deep into the bath of
birth, the bath of sex.

And this is again the supreme merging, for the sexual beings which
we are. It is a complete at-onement, becoming at one with the opposite
15   half of human nature. It is a reaching of a state of infinitude. Man
merges into woman, at the supreme moment they become one. They are
consummated, they are one flesh, one being. The two separate halves
suddenly fuse, there is wholeness, completeness, perfection. It is the
maximum experience for man and woman.

20   The maximum experience. But what then? You can't stay there. An
experience is an experience. It is a fulfilment, perhaps. But you cannot
persist in a state of crisis of fulfilment. You have to come sober again.
You are changed after the great bath of birth. You are re-born. But you
are still yourself, and only yourself, though this self is wonderful and
25   new.

To insist on the continuance of this crisis of passional oneing with
the woman is as bad as to persist in a state of exalted drunkenness. It is
merely vicious and destructive. You have to return to your own limits,
she to hers. The best of it is, that in this return each can instinctively take
30   a new attitude. Each becomes a separate human being. But there is still
a beautiful correspondence of affection, understanding, an equilibrium
which maintains the man and the woman true to herself and himself,
each distinct, yet balanced one with the other. And this is the state of
marriage.

35   But then, beyond the state of marriage, beyond the equilibrium between man and woman, there is another plane of life. After marriage
is consummated, after the beautiful equilibrium is established, there is
still, for greater individuals, another field of being to open. The marriage
remains permanent, eternal. But there is something else.

The woman has her children. Essentially, man does not have children, only heirs. Woman has children. And what has man?—his work? True, but if work only means provision for the wife and children, mankind has fallen into the fatal meaningless return upon itself. Work means something beyond labour for provisions. It means, in some way, a new field of creative living.

This is what we have forgotten. We have tried to make of work a mere heaping up of provision for human life. With the result that we find human life an intolerable prison, we turn blindly to destruction. Blind destruction is no way out of the hopeless automatic utilitarianism of modern life. After bouts of destruction, the hopeless automatic utilitarian activity starts afresh, more vigorously: only to meet, in a short time, a new earthquake in the human psyche.

Humanity is in a state of violent oscillation between the poles of production and destruction. We have lost our centrality. We have fallen out of our orbit. We have lost our *raison d'être.**

Remains to recover it. Let us go back to Whitman. Woman is the bath of birth to man. And after the bath, what then? We can't remain forever in the bath.

What does the bath of birth mean? It means an experience of pure conjunction, consummation with another being, and then a more perfect recovery of the living self. In conjunction and consummation there must be a pure polarising of the beings consummated. And this is what actually does happen. The great vital centres of the lower body, like tremendous centres of electric force, are brought at last into pure conjunction. There is a tremendous blazing adjustment into a new unison. And a whole new field of life is opened, a new circuit of being is established. Man and woman are actually born of each other. They are two new beings, with new feelings and new understanding, perfectly polarised with each other in a living vital circuit which has never been established before. Each is now in a greater measure himself, more fully, more perfectly, almost finally himself. But not quite. The woman has still to be a mother. And the man has to go forward into another field of life, beyond the woman. It is so.

In marriage, the polarisation is actually established between the hypogastric plexus in man and in woman, and between the terrific sacral ganglia. This is the clue to real marriage: this tremendous vital circuit which exists *all the time* between the powerful life-poles in the two beings, once it is established. Rupture this vital circuit, and you rupture the life-flow in each of the two beings. It is torment and disaster, a

horrible mutilation to both parties, once the great dynamic circuit has been established. But do not let us imagine that mere accidental social and technical marriage will establish the terrific and dynamic circuit of connubial life. It won't. This is one of the mysteries of love: that the
5   great balance in living polarity can only be consummated between certain specific individuals. The higher the being, the more terribly difficult to establish a pure circuit with another being.—But once established, this pure circuit is life itself, being itself, to the man and the woman. Hence the sacredness of marriage, true, consummate marriage. It will
10 always be so. True marriage is a tremendous life-state, a state of being, a state of creative existence.

But even so, it is not finally conclusive. For woman there is the new polarity of motherhood, when a new little being is actually polarised with her. And for man?—There is the new polarisation from the deepest and
15 last of the life-centres.

Below the powerful hypogastric plerus and the lumbar ganglion, which two centres open their flashing dynamos fully at adolescence, there are other final centres. And when the great centres which control sex and manhood and womanhood are established in their grand and
20 living polarity, the terrific vital circuit established like the orbits of the spheres, then it becomes incumbent on man to open up the last, the deepest centres.

And these are the cocygeal centres, situate at the very base of the spine. The cocygeal plexus and ganglion, these are the last, most secret,
25 most *extreme* dynamic centres of our being. And these also must be conquered: these must not only be conquered, they must be established in a new external polarity as well.

In moving forward to this great, last conquest, man is alone. He departs alone, as Dana and Melville departed. Man is now womanless.
30 He is at the extreme of being. And at the extreme of being, man is alone, womanless. At the extreme of being, where life is at its highest, and where it is at its nearest to death, the male is alone, projected beyond the female. At this extreme stage, the female has her young, man has his final activity apart. From the deepest centres streams the blue fire of a
35 peacock's tail, issues the moon-throbbing of a nightingale's song, from the males alone.

Acting from the last and profoundest centres, man acts womanless. It is no longer a question of race continuance. It is a question of sheer, ultimate being, the perfection of life, nearest to death. Acting from these centres, man is an extreme being, the unthinkable warrior, creator, mover and maker.

And the polarity is between man and man. Whitman alone of all moderns has known this, positively. Others have known it negatively, *pour épater les bourgeois.** But Whitman knew it positively, in its tremendous knowledge, knew the extremity, the perfectness, and the fatality.

Even Whitman becomes grave, tremulous, before the last dynamic truth of life. In *Calamus* he does not shout. He hesitates; he is reluctant, wistful. But none the less he goes on. And he tells the mystery of manly love, the love of comrades. Continually he tells us the same truth: the new world will be built upon the love of comrades, the new great dynamic of life will be manly love. Out of this inspiration the creation of the future.

The strange Calamus has its pink-tinged root by the pond, and it sends up its leaves of comradeship, comrades at one root, without the intervention of woman, the female. This comradeship is to be the final cohering principle of the new world, the new Democracy. It is the cohering principle of perfect soldiery, as he tells in *Drum-Taps.* It is the cohering principle of final *unison* in creative activity. And it is extreme and alone, touching the confines of death. It is something terrible to bear, terrible to be responsible for. It is the soul's last and most vivid responsibility, the responsibility for the circuit of final friendship, comradeship, manly love.

> "Yet you are beautiful to me you faint-tinged roots, you make me
>   think of death,
> Death is beautiful from you (what indeed is finally beautiful
>   except death and love?)
> I think it is not for life I am chanting here my chant of lovers, I
>   think it must be for death,
> For how calm, how solemn it grows to ascend to the atmosphere
>   of lovers,
> Death or life, I am then indifferent, my soul declines to prefer,
> (I am not sure but the high soul of lovers welcomes death most)
> Indeed, O death, I think now these leaves mean precisely the
>   same as you mean—"

Here we have the deepest, finest Whitman, the Whitman who knows the extremity of life, and of the soul's responsibility. He has come near now to death, in his creative life. But creative life must come near to death, to link up the mystic circuit. The pure warriors must stand on

the brink of death. So must the men of a pure creative nation. We shall
have no beauty, no dignity, no essential freedom otherwise. And so it is
from *Sea-Drift*, where the male bird sings the lost female: not that she
is lost, but lost to him, who has had to go beyond her, to sing on the
5   edge of the Great Sea, in the night. It is the lost voice on the shore.

"Whereto answering, the sea
Delaying not, hurrying not,
Whisper'd me through the night, and very plainly before
day-break,
10   Lisp'd to me the low and delicious word death,
And again death, death, death, death,
Hissing melodious, neither like the bird nor like my arous'd
child's heart,
But edging near as privately for me rustling at my feet,
15   Creeping thence steadily up to my ears and laving me softly all
over,
Death, death, death, death, death—"

What a great poet Whitman is: great like a great Greek. For him the
last enclosures have fallen, he finds himself on the shore of the last sea.
20   The extreme of life: so near to death. It is a hushed, deep responsibility.
And what is the responsibility? It is for the new great era of mankind.
And upon what is this new era established? On the perfect circuits of
vital flow between human beings. First, the great sexless normal relation
between individuals, simple sexless friendships, unison of family and
25   clan and nation and group. Next the powerful sex relation between man
and woman, culminating in the eternal orbit of marriage. And finally
the sheer friendship, the love between comrades, the manly love which
alone can create a new era of life.

The one state however does not annual the other: it fulfils the other.
30   Marriage is the great step beyond friendship and family and national-
ity, but it does not supersede these. Marriage should only give repose
and perfection to the great previous bonds and relationships. A wife
or husband who sets about to annul the old, pre-marriage affections
and connections ruins the foundations of marriage. And so with the
35   last, extremest love, the love of comrades. The ultimate comradeship
which sets about to destroy marriage destroys its own *raison d'être*.
The ultimate comradeship is the final progression from marriage, it is
the last seedless flower of pure beauty, beyond purpose. But if it destroys marriage it makes itself purely deathly. In its beauty, the ultimate

comradeship flowers on the brink of death. But it flowers from the root of all life, upon the blossoming of the tree of life, when marriage opens its fruitful flowers a little lower down.

The life-circuit now depends entirely upon the sex-unison of marriage. This circuit must never be broken. But it must be still surpassed. We cannot help the laws of life. We have kept it excluded. Only savage humour has corrected us.

Obviously, the last, final relationship is even a more dangerous responsibility than marriage. If the relation between man and woman should not be prostituted, how much more should this passional relation between man and man not be prostituted!

If marriage is sacred, the ultimate comradeship is utterly sacred, since it has no ulterior motive whatever, like procreation. If marriage is eternal, the great bond of life, how much more should this bond be eternal, being the great life-circuit which borders on death in all its round. The new, extreme, sacred relationship of comrades awaits us, and the future of mankind depends upon the way this relation is entered upon by us. It is a relation between fearless, honorable, self-responsible men, a balance in perfect polarity. In fearlessness and honor men go forward, from the last, deepest impetus of manly belief and unison, on towards the breaking of the old system and the making of a new world. We can never have a new world without a new belief. And we shall never again believe in remote or abstract gods. The next belief is to be a hot belief of men in each other, a culminating belief, culminating in a final leader and hero.

Whitman shows us the last step of the old great way. But he does not show us the first step of the new. His great Democracy is to be established upon the love of comrades. Well and good. But in what direction shall this love flow? Into more *en masse*?

As a matter of fact the love between comrades is always and inevitably a love between a leader and a follower. The one comrade is leader, the other the passionate believer and answerer. And neither can live without the other. This is always true; true of David and Jonathan, Orestes and Pylades,* of every great manly friendship since time began. It is a relationship in perfect leadership and perfect liege love. This is the very flower and perfection of love. And upon this the next great epoch will be established. Upon the mystery of passionate leadership and passionate answer: the supreme *active* love relationship between men, when men act in a miracle of unison, making a new world out of the passion of their belief, and in the great inspiration of a culminating leader.

What makes the great classic friendships tragic, deathly, is that all the passion is present, but no belief. So it was, really, in Whitman's case. His comradeship was an emotional end in itself, and therefore deathly. Any love as an emotional end in itself is always deathly to *men*. Men

5 must have *purpose* before everything.

Whitman went to the brink of death in his Calamus and love of comrades. One more step in *en masse* was simple death. What then?

Let us take our stand on the extreme tip of life, where he has led us. But let us turn round. There is no stride onwards possible, in democracy,

10 in En Masse, in merging. The next stride is the gulf of the bottomless pit. Stride one step further in democracy and merging, and down you go, down the bottomless pit.

Let us accept this love of comrades, but not on the downward slope. Not in the Whitman sense of abandon and self-merging. Never. Let us

15 turn round and look each other square in the face. Manly love means action, or it means nothing. It means building the world afresh, and smashing the obsolete form, or else it means only vice.

It means profound, passional *constructive* belief, or it means degeneration. It means that one man out of two shall accept the sacred re-

20 sponsibility of leadership, while the other man accepts the joy of liege adherence. That is manly love. The glad proposition, and the heroic answer, and men tackling the world like heroes.

And the love culminates. Each leading soul knows a leader still beyond him. Each leading soul not only leads, but has his own leader whom he

25 follows through a thousand deaths. And this leader again has a greater soul ahead of him; and so on till we reach the last, the final leader of men, the sacred tyrannus.

This is true democracy. No hopeless mechanism of hereditary kings. No disaster of mass-rule. But a marvellous progression in passional

30 belief, up to the supreme man. It does not matter where the supreme man was born, nor how. In the great culminating wave of manly love, which is manly belief, he is lifted up upon the faith of myriads. The true democracy! It is not a looking downwards, to the humblest man. It is not a sinking and merging downwards towards the mass. The love of

35 comrades is no matter of mere sympathy and emotion. On the contrary. Let us turn our backs on all this emotion and merging and en masse. Let us search out belief in our soul, and let belief be the first term of manly love. Belief in our own power to build the world afresh, and then, still greater, the passionate belief in the man who stands next ahead of

40 us, striving forward. Who turns round with his face fierce with love,

and in his eyes, greater even than the light of love, the undying light of manly purpose. Then onward in manly purpose, onward, let love give fuel to the flame of purpose. Onward, always following the leader, who when he looks back has a flame of love in his face, but a still brighter flame of purpose.

That is the true democracy. That is what America is waiting for. Not any more of this en-masse business, slipping down the bottomless pit of a false emotionalism. Not any more mob-humility. But leaping up each soul like a flame, leaping flame by flame, towards the heroic soul that burns the very zenith. The grand culmination of soul-chosen leaders up till we reach the perfect leader, the tyrannus* who when he looks round has love in his face, and a wonderful light of purpose that is beyond even love, beyond all love, beyond all men's understanding. The light in the soul of the greatest hero: that the beacon of all our faith.

Whitman was a wonderful poet. He brought us to the world's edge, beyond where any other man has gone. This American, this Columbus of the soul. The world's edge! But it is no use crowding over the edge into chaos. Now let us take our stand, turn round, and see the world we have to tackle, to break and re-create, lying stretched out there. And let us catch the flame of belief from eye to eye, leaders seeking for leaders, for a leader. Let us cry out to our leaders whom we love, our leading comrades whom we more than love, whom we fiercely believe in. Let us cry out to our leaders whom we passionately love and believe in, to take our love and give us leadership.

Whitman! The last of the very great poets. And the ultimate. How lovely a poet he is. His verse at its best springs sheer out of his soul, spontaneous, like the song of a bird. For a bird doesn't rhyme and scan.—The miracle of pure spontaneity. The whole soul speaks at once, in a naked spontaneity so unutterably lovely, so far beyond rhymes and scansion; just as the full loveliness of a loved woman is in her perfect nakedness, not her dressed-up splendour.

"Out of the cradle endlessly rocking—"

APPENDIX VI

XII. Whitman (1922)

NOTE ON THE TEXT

The text follows DHL's autograph manuscript, 10 pages (MS8, Roberts E382q, Smith). Deletions are recorded between angle-brackets⟨ ⟩; additions are recorded as half brackets ⌈ ⌉.

XII.

Whitman.

Post mortem effects?
But what of Walt Whitman?
The "good gray poet." 5
Was he a ghost, with all his physicality?
The good gray poet.
Post mortem effects. Ghosts.
A certain ghoulish insistency. A certain horrible pottage of human
parts. A certain stridency and portentousness. A luridness about his 10
beatitudes.
DEMOCRACY! THESE STATES! EIDOLONS!
LOVERS, ENDLESS LOVERS!
ONE IDENTITY!
ONE IDENTITY! 15
I AM HE THAT ACHES WITH AMOROUS LOVE.
You bet!
Do you believe me, when I say post mortem effects?
When the Pequod went down, she left many a rank and dirty steam-
boat still fussing in the seas. The Pequod sinks with all her souls, but 20
their bodies rise again to man innumerable tramp steamers, and ocean-
crossing line(s)rs. Corpses.
What we mean is that people may go on, keep on, and rush on,
without souls. They have their ego and their will, that is enough to keep
them going. 25
So that you see, the sinking of the Pequod was only a metaphysical
tragedy after all. The world goes on just the same. The ship of the soul is
sunk. But the machine-manipulating body works just the same: digests,
chews gum, admires Botticelli and aches with amorous love.
I AM HE THAT ACHES WITH AMOROUS LOVE. 30
What do you make of that? I AM HE THAT ACHES. First
generalisation. First uncomfortable universalisation. WITH
AMOROUS LOVE! Oh god! Better a belly-ache. A belly-ache is
at least specific. But the ACHE of AMOROUS LOVE!
Think of having that under your skin. All that! 35
I AM HE THAT ACHES WITH AMOROUS LOVE.
Walter, leave off. You are not HE. You are just (an isolated) ⌈a limited⌉
Walter. And your ache doesn't include all Amorous Love, by any means.
If you ache you only ache with a small bit of amorous love, and there's

so much more ⟨amorous love that⟩ stays outside the cover of your ache,
that you might be a bit ⟨modester⟩ ⌈milder⌉ about it.
I AM HE THAT ACHES WITH AMOROUS LOVE.
CHUFF! CHUFF! CHUFF!
5   CHU-CHU-CHU-CHU-CHUFFFF!
Reminds one of a steam-engine. A locomotive. They're the only
things that seem to me to ache with amorous love. All that steam inside
them. Forty million foot-pounds pressure. The ache of ⟨amorous love.⟩
⌈AMOROUS LOVE.⌉ Steam-pressure. CHUFF!
10   An ordinary man aches with love for Belinda, or his Native Land, or
the Ocean, or the Stars, or the Oversoul: if he feels that an ache is in
the fashion.
It takes a steam-engine to ache with ⟨amorous love⟩ ⌈AMOROUS
LOVE⌉. All of it.
15   Walt was really too superhuman. The danger of the superman is that
he is mechanical.
⌈They talk of his "splendid animality." Well, he'd got it on the brain,
if that's the place for animality.⌉
"I am he that aches with amorous love;
20   Does the earth gravitate, does not all matter, aching, attract all matter?
So the body of me to all I meet or know."
What can be more mechanical? The difference between life and matter is that life, living things, living creatures, have the instinct of turning right away from some matter, and of blissfully ignoring the bulk of
25   ⟨all⟩ ⌈most⌉ matter, and of turning towards only some certain bits of
specially selected matter. As for living creatures all helplessly hurtling
together into one great snowball, why, most very living creatures spend
the greater part of their time getting out of the sight, smell⟨,⟩ or sound of
the rest of living creatures. ⌈Even bees only cluster on their own queen.
30   And that is sickening enough. Fancy all white humanity clustering on
one another like a lump of bees.⌉
No Walt, you give your self away. Matter <u>does</u> gravitate, helplessly.
But men are tricky-tricksy, and they shy all sorts of ways.
Matter gravitates because it <u>is</u> helpless and mechanical.
35   And if you gravitate the same, if the body of you gravitates to all you
meet or know, why, something must have gone seriously wrong with
you. You must have broken your main-spring.
You must have fallen also into mechanisation.
I only know that my body does⌈n't⌉ ⟨anything but⟩ ⌈by any means⌉
40   gravitate to all I meet or know. I find I can shake hands with a few people.
But most I ⟨dont want⟩ ⌈wouldn't⌉ touch with a long prop.

Your mainspring is broken, Walter, my dear. The mainspring of your own individuality. And so you run down with a great whirr, merging with everything.

I am everything and everything is me and so we're all One in One Identity, like the Mundane Egg, which has been addled quite a while.   5
"Whoever you are, to endless announcements— — — —"
"And of these one and all I weave the song of myself."

Do you, my boy? Well then it just shows you haven't got any self. ⌐It's a mush, not a woven thing. A hotch-potch, not a tissue. Your Self.⌐

Oh Walter Walter, what have you done with it? What have you done   10
with yourself? With your own individual self? For it sounds as if it had all leaked out of you when you made water, leaked into the universe when you peed. Oh Walter, you're a leaky vessel.

Post-mortem effects. The individuality had leaked out of him at his seams, like out of a leaky barrel.   15

I remember an American girl* whose parents had lived in the town where Whitman ⟨had lived⟩ ⌐resided⌐ when he was old, told me that the neighbours fairly hated Walter because he used to walk in his little back yard — he lived in a row — stark naked and fat and excited with his own nudity and his grey beard. "His nasty little back yard," ⟨a⟩⌐A⌐rabella   20
⟨S⟩⌐s⌐aid. And that he used to stop the little girls coming home from school, with senile amorousness.

No no, don't lay this down to poetry. These are post mortem effects. And Walt's great poems are really huge fat tomb-plants, great rank graveyard growths.   25

All that false exuberance. All those lists of things boiled in one pudding-cloth, the skin of Walt! No no!

I don't want all those things inside me, thank you.

"I reject nothing," says Walt. ⟨If⟩

If that is so, Walter, you must be a pipe open at both ends, so everything   30
runs through.

Post mortem effects.

"I embrace ALL," says Walter. "I weave all things into myself."

Do you really! There can't be much left of you when you've done.

"And whoever walks a furlong without sympathy walks to his own   35
funeral dressed in his own shroud."

Take off your hat then, Walter, my funeral procession of one is passing.

This ⟨al⟩ awful Whitman. This post mortem poet. This poet with the private soul leaking out of him all the time. All his privacy leaking   40
out in a sort of dribble, oozing into the universe.

Walt becomes in his own person the whole world, the whole universe, the whole eternity of time. As far as his rather sketchy knowledge of history ⟨would⟩ ⌜will⌝ carry him, that is. Because to <u>be</u> a thing he ha⟨s⟩⌜d⌝ to know it. In order to assume the identity of a thing, he
5   ha⟨s⟩⌜d⌝ to know that thing. He ⟨could never have assumed⟩ ⌜was not able to assume⌝ one identity with Charlie Chaplin, for example, because Walt didn't know Charlie. What a pity! He'd have done poems, paeans and what not, Chant⟨,⟩⌜s,⌝ Songs of Cinematernity.
    "Oh Charlie my Charlie, another film is done – "
10   ⟨But a⟩⌜A⌝s soon as Walt <u>knew</u> a thing, he assumed a One Identity with it. If he knew that an Esquimo sat in a kyak, immediately there was Walt being little and yellow and greasy, sitting in a kyak.
    Now my dear Walter, will you tell me exactly what a kyak is?
    Who is he that demands petty definition? Let him behold me <u>sitting</u>
15   <u>in a kyak.</u>
    I behold no such thing, Walter. I behold a rather fat old man full of a rather senile, self-conscious sensuality. Animality on the brain.
    DEMOCRACY. EN MASSE. ONE IDENTITY
    The universe, in short, adds up to ONE.
20   ONE.
    1.
    Which is Walt.
    His poems, Democracy, En Masse, One Identity, they are long sums in addition and multiplication, of which the answer is invariably
25   MYSELF.
    He reaches the state of ALLNESS.
    In a nasty little back-yard, with the neighbours pulling down their back blinds to shut the view out.
    Of course I am being personal, I intend to be.
30   Whitman was never really an esquimo. Never even saw one. It was all just prize conceit.
    Whitman being everything! Just think of it! The cheek! Had never even been out of America. Impudent provincial.
    Another proof that a little learning is a dangerous thing.
35   My, wouldn't Walt have been startled if he'd been forced to realise what an actual esquimo is! Because of course Walter blandly assumed that all esquimos are minor little Walts.
    Post mortem effects.
    As a matter of fact, all these Infinites and Alls and En Masses and
40   Democracies and One Identities are just the frog puffing himself up till he bursts.

I remember, when I was a little boy with other boys, watching them push a fine straw up the back passage of a frog and blow up this straw till the frog was like a balloon.

Some malign fiend must have been doing a parallel thing to Whitman.

MERGE! says Walter.

MERDE!* say I.

Merge, merge, merge! Merging, merging, merging, sings Walter.

So we've all got to slither down the slimy chute of sympathy into the—infinite cess-pool, it seems to me. Nasty naked old men in back yards.

ONE DIRECTION! insists Whitman.

Never, you slimy democratic ⟨bully⟩ animal.

ONE DIRECTION! re-iterates America, more loudly.

Sh — — t!

ALLNESS! sings Walter.

B — — — S! sing I.

ONE IDENTITY! chants the democratic En Masse.

F — — K it! comes my antiphony.

All right then, you grand Idealist, be infinite. Sit on your infinity, then, as on the privy seat. And don't come off it.

The Infinite!

Post mortem effects!

Poor Walter, dominated by the idée fixe of his own person and his own private parts. Tainted with the "exposure" dementia.

Post mortem effects.

Masturbation, Song of Myself.

Post mortem effects.

Woman!

"A woman waits for me —"

He might as well have said: "The female end waits for my maleness." Oh beautiful generalisation and abstraction! Oh biological function.

"Athletic mothers of these ⟨s⟩⌈S⌉tates — " Muscles and wombs. They needn't have had faces at all.

"As I see myself reflected in Nature,
As I see through a mist, One with inexpressible completeness, sanity,
   beauty,
See the bent head, and arms folded over the breast, the Female I see."

Everything was female to him: even himself. Nature just one great function.

"This is the nucleus — after the child is born of woman, man is born
   of woman,
This is the bath of birth, the merge of small and large, and the outlet
   again —"

5   Can't you just see Walt ⟨just⟩ oozing himself into the womb of a
woman, then getting out by the back door. Trying to ⟨dive⟩ ⌜creep⌝
head and shoulders into the womb of woman, and crawl out again.
Bath of birth, indeed! Bath of imbecility, to men who go to it in that
way.

10   "The Female I see —"
If I'd been one of his women, I'd have given him Female. With a flea
in his ear. He'd have got his bath in hot water.
Always wanting to merge himself into the womb of a woman.
"The Female I see —"

15   And when he found he couldn't, then wanting to merge into some-
thing else. But always going back to the old want, the womb.
Anything, so long as he could merge himself.
Just a vice. A chronic disease. A sort of white flux.
Post mortem effects.

20   He found, like all men find, that you can't really merge in a woman,
though you may go a long way. You can't manage the last bit. So you
have to give it up, and try elsewhere. If you insist on merging.
In Calamus he changes his tune. He doesn't shout and thump and
exult any more. He begins to hesitate, reluctant, wistful.

25   The strange calamus has its pink-tinged root by the pond, and it
sends up its leaves of comradeship, comrades from one root, without
the intervention of woman, the female.
So he sings of the mystery of manly love, the love of comrades. Over
and over he says the same thing: the new world will be built on the love

30   of comrades, the new great dynamic of life will be manly love. Out of
this manly love will come the inspiration for the future.
Will it though? Will it?
Comradeship! Comrades! This is to be the new Democracy: of Comrades. This is the new cohering principle in the world: comradeship.

35   Is it? Are you sure, Walt?
It is the cohering principle of true soldiery, we are told in "Drum
Taps." It is the cohering principle in the new unison for creative activity.
And it is extreme and alone, touching the confines of death. Something
terrible to bear, terrible to be responsible for. Even Walter felt it. The

soul's last and most poignant responsibility, the responsibility ⟨for⟩ ⌜of⌝ comradeship, of manly love.

"Yet you are beautiful to me, you faint-tinged roots, you make me think of death.
Death is beautiful from you (what indeed is finally beautiful except   5
death and love?)
I think it is not for life I am chanting here my chant of lovers, I think it must be for death,
For how calm, how solemn it grows to ascend to the atmosphere of lovers,   10
Death or life, I am then indifferent, my soul declines to prefer
(I am not sure but the high soul of lovers welcomes death most)
Indeed, O death, I think now these leaves mean precisely the same as you mean — "

This is strange, from the exultant Walt.   15
Death!
Death is now his chant! Death!
Merging! And Death! Which is the final merge.
The great merge into the womb. Woman.
And after that, the merge of comrades: man-for-man love.   20
And almost immediately with this, death, the final merge of death.

There you have the progression of merging. For the great mergers, woman at last becomes ⟨ined⟩ inadequate. For those who love to extremes. Woman is inadequate for the last merging. So the next step, is the merging of man-for-man love. And this is on the brink of death. It   25
slides over into death.

David and Jonathan. And the death of Jonathan.
It always slides into death.
The love of comrades.
Merging.   30
So that if the new Democracy is to be based on the love of Comrades, it will be based on death too. It will slip so soon into death.

The last merging. The last Democracy. The last love. The love of Comrades.
Fatality. And fatality.   35
Whitman would not have been ⟨a⟩ ⌜the⌝ great poet ⌜he is⌝ if he had not taken the last steps and looked over into death. Death, the last merging, that was the goal of his manhood.

To the mergers, there remains the brief love of comrades, and then Death.

But why merge? Why merge any more? Why love any more?

5 Any man whose soul didn't go down in the Pequod: Whitman's soul went down: will know that he doesn't want to merge any more. That he doesn't want to love any more.

Man doesn't want to love any more. The desire is gone.

What then?

The Pequod went down with the White soul. The ship of the soul 10 went down. But we were not all on board. Or we were not entirely on board.

The mergers. The conscious mergers. The conscious lovers. Conscious love. ⌈Love on the brain.⌉

Make an end of it all.

15 Have no merging. Have no ⟨s⟩love. Have no sex. Cut it out.

Cut it out, till we get into a new mode.

Cut love out. Cut sex out. Cut out all merging, all uniting. Cut yourself off isolate. Keep only your silent loyalties. And wait.

Wait.

20 Wait for what?

Wait till we get clear.

"Whereto answering, the sea
Delaying not, hurrying not
Whispered me through the night, very plainly before day-break,
25 Lisp'd to me the low and delicious word death,
And again death, death, death, death
Hissing melodious, neither like the bird nor like my arous'd child's
        heart,
But edging near as privately for me rustling at my feet,
30 Creeping thence steadily up to my ears and laving me softly all over,
Death, death, death, death, death —"

Whitman is a very great poet, of death, not of life. A very great post mortem poet, of the transitions of the soul after it has died in its integrity. The poet of the soul's post mortem disintegration, on the confines of 35 death. Après moi le déluge.

But we have all got to die, and disintegrate.

We have got to die in life, too, and disintegrate while we live.

But even then the goal is not death.

Something else will come.

"Out of the cradle endlessly rocking —"
Though I'm not sure about a <u>cradle.</u> Damn cradles.
We've got to die first, anyhow. And disintegrate while we still live.
Only we know this much. Death is not the <u>goal.</u> And Love, and
merging, are now only part of the death-process. Comradeship — part   5
of the death-process. Democracy — part of the death-process. The new
Democracy — the brink of death. One Identity — death itself.
We have died, and we are still disintegrating.
But IT is finished.
<u>Consummatum est.</u>   10
Jesus was only an intermediary god, any way. Not a primary god.
And love is only an intermediary thing. Not a primary thing.
Love is not a fundamental thing. As life drives us deeper and deeper,
we pass certain borders, and love ceases to be of first-rate importance.
It comes to an end. Something else takes its place.   15
Love is an intermediary thing. As Jesus is intermediary between the
Father and the Holy Ghost: to use the weary old symbol of our Trinity.
When life is at its deepest, there is no love. And that is why Whitman's
love of Comrades won't work. ⟨It is a misapplication.⟩ ⌈Something there
is, but it is not love. To function as love, in the deepest self, is just a   20
fatality.⌉
When we are living from our very deepest selves, there is no com-
radeship, there is no friendship, there is no equality. For comradeship,
⟨equality,⟩ ⌈friendship,⌉ and love all presume equality between lovers
and comrades. And in the deepest self, there is no sense of equality   25
⌈left⌉, there is no possibility of equal Communion.
⟨There is something else, quite different, much more profound.⟩
⟨The power of the Holy Ghost.⟩
⌈But marriage is still possible. So long as you do <u>not</u> base it on love.
Stark marriage. This holds the first clue to vital inequality, non-equality. 30
Equality is superseded, when you get deep enough. And love is su-
perseded. You find something else.
You find your own stark isolation. And the presence of the Holy
Ghost(s).⌉
Each man to himself is isolate. And ⟨to⟩ ⌈in⌉ each isolate man ⟨comes⟩   35
⌈lives⌉ the Holy Ghost. Only to him in his isolation.
You can't ⟨know⟩ ⌈have⌉ the Holy Ghost in company. The Pentecostal
flame*⟨is something different.⟩ ⌈belongs to love: a common inspiration.⌉
You can only ⟨know⟩⟨⌈be with⌉⟩ ⌈⌈have⌉⌉ the Holy Ghost when you are
alone.   40

When you are alone, you ⟨know⟩ ⌜⌜may⌝⌝ ⌜have⌝ the Holy Ghost. And the ⟨active⟩ ⌜strange⌝ power ⟨of⟩ ⌜that⌝ the ⟨h⟩⌜H⌝oly Ghost ⌜is⌝. Because the Holy Ghost is a ⟨great unseen⟩ ⌜⟨personal⟩⌝ power ⟨coming to you.⟩ ⌜in your land.⌝

5   ⟨⟨Th⟨e⟩⌜is⌝ ⟨Ghostly⟩ ⟨⟨Power⟩⟩ is what⟩ ⌜⌜The innermost power that⌝⌝ supersedes the spell of love: the ⟨Power of⟩ the Holy Ghost ⟨within you.⟩ ⌜in your ⟨hinterland.⌝ ⟩ ⌜⌜lone country.⌝⌝

Once you accept the ⟨Power of the⟩ Holy Ghost, the world of love and loving fades into rubbish. And Jesus is relegated to a second place.

10 The Holy Ghost, and the Father, ⟨are⟩ the ⟨superior⟩ ⌜major⌝ gods of our ⟨t⟩⌜T⌝rinity. Jesus ⟨is⟩ the intermediary.

The world of love fades into rubbish: like a dead empire. Then you ⟨see⟩ ⌜recognise⌝ the new-comers, those who ⟨know⟩ ⌜get⌝ the⌜ir⌝ power ⟨of⟩ ⌜from⌝ the Holy Ghost.

15 You see the ⟨new comers.⟩ ⌜new foreigners.⌝ And the ⟨new-comers⟩ ⌜foreigners⌝ see one another, and recognise one another. As far as the world of love goes, it is the brand of Cain. ⟨It is t⟩⌜T⌝he curse of Ishmael. But to the men who ⟨know⟩ ⌜have ⟨⟨found⟩⟩⌝ ⌜⌜got⌝⌝ the power of the ⟨h⟩⌜H⌝oly Ghost, it is a new ⟨splendour.⟩ ⌜title.⌝ They ⟨walk in

20 splendour,⟩ ⌜go with another strength,⌝ like a dark night with stars.

The ⟨new comers⟩ ⌜foreigners⌝ see one another, ⟨invested in⟩ ⌜and ⟨⟨recognise⌝⟩⟩ ⌜⌜feel⌝⌝ the new ⟨mystery of⟩ ⌜communion in⌝ power. The power of the Holy Ghost ⟨.⟩ ⌜of each other.⌝

The hierarchies of the power of the Holy Ghost ⟨that is within us.⟩

25 ⌜of us.⌝

Once it was the hierarchies of the power of the Father. Now it ⟨t⟩ is another thing. Nothing to do with begetting: with Fatherhood. Having to do only with isolate manhood. Men in their isolation taking rank according to the Holy Ghost which is within them. Placed by the Holy

30 Ghost in new hierarchies of power. Not crowned, but imbued. An aura, not a sceptre. But powers in the land. And ranged in hierarchies.

EXPLANATORY NOTES

EXPLANATORY NOTES

Note. Explanatory notes to the essays are asterisked in the text when they contain something other than simple reference or corrections to DHL's quotations. Notes providing the sources of direct quotations from the authors about whom DHL is writing (or notes simply showing the state of the text from which he quoted) are not provided with asterisks in the text; the errors and variants in DHL's quotations are, however, recorded, in square brackets, text taken from the edition from which he was working. Annotations are only provided at the point of the first appearance of the detail being annotated; so, for example, a quotation or an author's dates are annotated only in the notes to the essay in which such details first appear. References to the Bible are, unless otherwise noted, to *KJB*. The abbreviation *P* signifies a paragraph break; the mark / signifies a line break.

Foreword (Final Version 1923)

11:7 **let the precious cat out of the bag.** I.e. disclose a secret, often by mistake; see DHL's 1920–1 novel *Mr Noon*, ed. Lindeth Vasey (Cambridge, 1984), 185:24–6.

11:11 *Et interrogatum ... est inventus!"* Nonsense verse (Latin and English) of unknown origin, but perhaps dating from DHL's time at Nottingham High School, 1898–1901: 'And it was asked by everyone: / "Where is that Toad-in-the-Hole?" / And it was repeated by everyone: / "He hasn't been found!" '

11:18 **this missing link** Hypothetical extinct animal or animal group, formerly thought to be intermediate between anthropoid apes and man. The term was invented by the Scottish geologist Sir Charles Lyell (1795–1875) in 1851. In 1929, DHL quoted a correspondent – 'evidently a woman of education and means' – who wrote to him 'out of the blue ... "You, who are a mixture of the missing-link and the chimpanzee" ' ('The State of Funk', *Phoenix II*, ed. Warren Roberts and Harry T. Moore, 1968, p. 569).

11:25 **Telephones, tinned meat, Charlie Chaplin, water-taps, and World-Salvation,** Telephones using the electromagnetic principle were the 1876 invention of the US scientist Alexander Graham Bell (1847–1922) ... tinned meat (or more commonly tinned beef) had been known since the middle of the eighteenth century, but (like most tinned products) was in mass production from the 1870s ... Chaplin was an enormously successful British film-maker, actor and comedian (1889–1977) who worked in Hollywood and had (most recently) directed *The Kid* (1920) ... water-taps

433

434 *Explanatory notes*

(faucets in USA) were in common use by the 1890s: DHL referred in 1924 to the 'bright brass taps' installed by a woman attempting to improve a New Mexican ranch before the First World War as an indication of the advance of civilisation (*St. Mawr*, ed. Brian Finney, Cambridge, 1983, 147:6–10) – though see too 117:29–30 . . . DHL may be referring ironically to the League of Nations (founded in 1920 with the aim of preserving world peace: see his 1920 essay 'Education of the People', *Reflections* 161:18) or to Andrew Carnegie's $10 million donation in 1910 as an Endowment for International Peace (see note on 21:14).

11:33 **French . . . Marinetti . . . Irish** France was the home of much modern European art (see note on 12:6) . . . Filippo Tommaso Marinetti (1876–1944), Italian poet, who in 1909 founded the Futurist movement (see note on 12:6) and whose manifestos DHL read in 1914 (see *Letters*, ii. 180–3) . . . DHL almost certainly refers to James Joyce, Irish novelist (1882–1941), whose *Ulysses* (1922) he had read in November 1922 (*Letters*, iii. 335, 345) while revising *Studies*.

12:2 **Sherwood Anderson,** American writer (1876–1941) whose reputation was made by his novel *Winesburg, Ohio* (1919), which DHL read in December 1919: 'gruesome it is . . . good, I think, but somehow hard to take in: like a nightmare one can hardly recall distinctly' (*Letters*, iii. 426).

12:5 **Tolstoi, Dostoevsky, Tchekov, Artzibashev** Count Leo Tolstoy (1828–1910), novelist and philosopher (see note on 105:18); Fyodor Dostoevsky (1821–81), novelist (see note on 14:16); Anton Chekhov (1860–1904), short-story writer and dramatist: all of whom DHL had read between 1905 and 1912. Less well known now is Mikhail Petrovich Artzybashev (1878–1927), novelist, whose novel *Sanine* (1907) DHL read in 1913 (*Letters*, ii. 33, 70).

12:6 **French modernism or futurism** 'Modernism' meaning early twentieth-century literature, poetry, drama and art characterised by formal experiment was not a term used in DHL's time, and the fact that the Futurist movements were most extensively developed in Italy and Russia suggests that DHL's phrase refers simply to contemporary French art and literature. He knew something of the work of Marcel Proust (1871–1922), Anatole France (1844–1924) – 'a very graceful piffler, and so *easy* that to me he becomes impossibly difficult' (*Letters*, iii. 350) – and Henri Barbusse (1873–1935); and he knew the art of Paul Cézanne (1839–1906) and Pierre Puvis de Chavannes (1824–98). His new (September 1922) friendship with Mabel Dodge Sterne (see note on 41:8) would also have given him insights into artistic movements in Paris – e.g. around Gertrude Stein (1874–1946) and her salon – before the First World War. Futurism was an artistic movement that arose in Italy early in 1909; painters especially associated with it were Umberto Boccioni (1882–1916), Carlo Carrà (1881–1966) and Gino Severini (1883–1966). For DHL's comments, see *Letters*, ii. 182–4. See too 134:24.

12:17 **swaddled in ... the babe.** See Exodus ii. 3–10; the word 'swaddled' here and at 12:18 means 'tightly wrapped in long strips of linen' – 'swaddling clothes' – and almost certainly derives from the story of the Christ-child (see Luke ii. 7).

The Spirit of Place (Final Version 1923)

13:4 **children's books.** Books by James Fenimore Cooper, Richard Henry Dana and Herman Melville in particular suffered this fate (for dates and biographies, see notes on 42:2, 105:2 and 122:3). DHL himself records how he 'read Fenimore Cooper, as a boy' (32:31), and in March 1916 he recommended Melville to his Russian friend S. S. Koteliansky (1880–1955) as one of a list of authors of children's books (*Letters*, ii. 589). Three months later, in June 1916, he recommended to Koteliansky the 'beautiful literature for boys, adventurous and romantic' which existed in English: he cited Cooper's *The Last of the Mohicans* and *The Deerslayer*, Melville's *Moby-Dick* and Dana's *Two Years Before the Mast* (*Letters*, ii. 615). *The Last of the Mohicans* – see note on 55:7 – was, e.g., published 'Arranged for Youth' in an illustrated Routledge edition of 1890 (shortened by cuts normally of whole paragraphs, amounting to about 25,000 words: e.g. the last eleven pages were omitted), and 'Adapted for use in Schools' in a George Bell & Sons edition of 1909; Dana's *Two Years Before the Mast* had appeared in Routledge's Every Boy's Library in 1877 and in Blackie's School and Home Library in 1894.

13:10 **Lucretius ... Apuleius ... Tertullian ... Augustine ... Athanasius.** DHL's grasp of the classical world may in part be explained by his possession of a 'classical dictionary' in 1917 which he had sent on to him in 1918 (iii. 236). Titus Lucretius Carus (?96–55 BC), Roman poet and philosopher, expounded the Epicurean atomist theory of the universe; in 1899 the German classicist F. Marx suggested that he came from southern France or Spain: cf. 'Iberian Spain' (13:11). The idea was not, however, accepted; and it is possible that DHL is confusing Lucretius with the poet Lucan (Marcus Annaeus Lucanus, AD 39–65), born in Cordoba in Spain ... Apuleius (AD ?125–?180), Latin writer, born in Madaura in what is today Libya, studied in 'old Carthage' (13:11) near Tunis, celebrated for his serio-comic novel *The Golden Ass* (see too note on 259:2) ... Quintus Septimius Florens Tertullianus (AD ?160–?220), Christian theologian born (and dying) in Carthage, writing in Latin rather than Greek, originator of much Christian terminology ... St Augustine (AD 354–430), one of the Fathers of the Christian Church, born in Tagaste in what is today Libya (13:11), became Bishop of Hippo in what is today Algeria (13:12) ... St Athanasius (AD ?296–373), patriarch of Alexandria in Egypt, championed Christian orthodoxy against Arianism and other heresies (see notes on 180:24, 206:14 and 266:12), but wrote in Greek, so that DHL's 'high-brow Romans' (13:8) were unlikely to have read him; see note on 167:14.

13:14 **Poe or Hawthorne** See notes on 66:2 and 81:3.

14:4 **Plato**   Greek philosopher (427–?347 BC).

14:8 **the *Scarlet Letter*,**   See note on 81:3.

14:16 **Dostoevsky . . . a little horror.**   DHL first commented on the Christianity of
Dostoevsky in February 1916, when he argued that '1. He has a fixed will, a mania to be
absolute, to be God. 2. Within this will, his activity is two-fold: a. To be self-less, a pure
Christian, to live in the outer whole, the social whole, the self-less whole, the universal
consciousness. b. To be a pure, absolute self, all-devouring and all-consuming.' DHL
saw the first type (the spiritual) exemplified in *The Idiot* (1868: see note on 64:39), and
the second (the sensual) in Dmitri Karamazov in *The Brothers Karamazov* (1879–80:
see notes on 103:29 and 254:16). Even at this stage, DHL was insisting that 'They
are great parables, the novels, but false art . . . People are not fallen angels, they are
merely people. But Dostoevsky uses them all as theological units, they are all terms of
divinity . . . They are bad art, false truth' (*Letters*, ii. 543–4).

14:25 **to point a moral and adorn a tale.**   'The Vanity of Human Wishes' (1749)
by Samuel Johnson (1709–84), l. 219 ['To . . . moral, or . . .'].

14:36 **freedom of worship.**   The Pilgrim Fathers (see 15:9): Separatists who sailed
on the ship the *Mayflower*, expecting to land in Virginia, but who came ashore further
north and founded Plymouth Colony in Massachusetts in 1620.

14:39 **stopped at home and fought for it.**   I.e. in the English Civil War (1642–9),
in the rebellion against James II (1688) and in the various attempts to achieve religious
tolerance. The First Version essay adds 'with Cromwell' (174:3), i.e. in the time of
Oliver Cromwell (1599–1658) during the English Civil War, but thereby points up
a serious problem: one of the consequences of the Civil War was the dominance in
Parliament of the Presbyterian party, who were totally opposed to religious toleration
(in 1646, for example, a bill was passed which punished with death those who denied
doctrines relating to the Trinity and the Incarnation).

15:1 **The land of the free!**   From 'The Star-Spangled Banner' (1814) by Francis
Scott Key (1779–1843): 'O say, does that star-spangled banner yet wave / O'er the
land of the free and the home of the brave?'

15:7 **the truth about Queen Victoria,**   DHL is probably thinking of poems by
Walt Whitman (see note on 148:2) in which the European ruler is presented as
the unelected and potentially tyrannical ruler (from ruling families stained with the
blood of their subjects), as in the poem 'Song of the Broad-Axe' (*LG* 155–65: see
note on 148:2 for details of the text used here); of the contrast between American
democracy and European monarchy found in the same poem; and of the sense of
European monarchy being now mythic rather than actual found in 'Song of the
Exposition':

> Pass'd! pass'd! for us, forever pass'd, that once so mighty world,
>   now void, inanimate, phantom world,

Embroider'd, dazzling, foreign world, with all its gorgeous
   legends, myths,
Its kings and castles proud, its priests and warlike lords
   and courtly dames,
Pass'd to its charnel vault, coffin'd with crown and armour on . . .
                            (*LG* 167–8)

15:20 **"Henceforth be masterless."** Stuart P. Sherman used the phrase (not apparently a quotation from verse or drama) in his essay on Emerson (see note on 33:12) in *Americans* (New York, 1922), p. 78, to summarise the attitude of a 'true liberator' who 'strikes off the old shackles but immediately . . . suggests new service, a fuller use of our powers'. DHL was sent Sherman's book for review sometime after 12 December 1922 (*Letters*, iii. 355, 359), by which time all twelve of the essays of *Studies* had either gone to New York for typing or had been parcelled up to go; he would have been able to incorporate the phrase during his revision of the typescript of *Studies* in January 1923. DHL's review of Sherman (which also quotes the remark) had gone to the *Dial* by 16 January 1923 (viii. 59) and appeared in the *Dial*, lxxiv (May 1923), 503–10 (reprinted in *Phoenix* 314–21); the revised typescripts of all the essays in *Studies* were sent to Seltzer on or shortly after 19 January 1923 (iv. 369). See Introduction p. 49 and n. 95; see too notes on 81:18, 85:40, 100:8 and 149:21.

16:18 **"Ca Ca Caliban / Get a new master, be a new man.."** 'Ban, Ban, Ca-Caliban, / Has a new master – get a new man': Caliban's song of rebellion in Shakespeare's *The Tempest* (*c.* 1611), II. ii. 196–7. The semi-human creature has been the servant of Prospero, but – made drunk by Stephano and Trinculo – decides to serve them instead.

16:19 **Liberia or Haiti.** Liberia was founded as an independent state in 1847, for slaves returning to Africa; the island of Haiti (French from 1697) freed itself 1804–6 under the black leader Jean Jacques Dessalines, and declared itself a republic.

17:7 **the American Eagle** On the dollar coin and later on the dollar bill: the Bald Eagle is the national bird of the USA. By 15 October 1922, DHL had written his poem 'Eagle in New Mexico' (*Letters*, iv. 322).

17:10 **the Spaniards filled most of America.** The Spaniards began the conquest of the North and South American continents and until the start of the nineteenth century were still a significant power in North America (as well as dominant elsewhere); Louisiana was acquired by Spain from the French in 1763 (though recovered by France in 1800) and only became part of the United States through the 'Louisiana Purchase' of 1803. As late as 1821 the Spanish still controlled the Vice-Royalty of New Spain (which would become the central and western United States) as well as large areas of Central and South America.

17:23 **the terrific religions of Egypt.** The development of religion in Ancient Egypt showed a society with many gods giving way to one dominated by a small number of single deities. The god Horus (often pictured as a falcon) was identified with the living Pharaoh; the sun-god Ra, the crocodile-god Sebek and the god Osiris (linked with the Nile and with vegetation) were also extremely important.

18:22 **invisible magnetism...migrating birds...unforeknown goal.** DHL's confidence (probably derived from some knowledge of the work of Dr E. von Middendorff, who had studied migration paths in Eastern Siberia coinciding with the direction of the magnetic pole) was not shared by his contemporaries: 'The only plausible attempts to give definite shape to the idea of a special sense are based on an assumed sensitivity to the phenomenon of terrestrial magnetism. No evidence of any magnetic sense has ever been obtained, however, despite a good deal of experiment' (Arthur Landsborough Thomson, *Bird Migration*, 1936, p. 206). The ninth edition of the *Encyclopaedia Britannica* (1909) agreed: the magnetic theory was 'not at all borne out by the observed facts of Migration in North America' (iii. 769).

18:28 **Orestes pursued by the Eumenides.** In *The Eumenides* (458 BC) by Aeschylus (?525–?456 BC), Orestes (who has killed his mother Clytemnestra, the murderer of his father Agamemnon) is pursued by the avenging Furies.

Benjamin Franklin (Final Version 1923)

20:2 **Benjamin Franklin.** Printer, journalist, scientist, diplomat and writer, with honorary doctorates from St Andrews (1758) and Oxford (1762): born Boston 1706, died Philadelphia 1790 (see notes on 23:30, 24:2, etc.) He was best known for his yearly publication *Poor Richard's Almanack* (1733–58) under the pseudonym of Richard Saunders, and *The Way to Wealth* (1758). He published *Experiments and Observations on Electricity* (1751–4) and his *Autobiography* was published posthumously; the Everyman edition which DHL used, *Benjamin Franklin's Autobiography* (1908), contained not only the *Autobiography* (*BFA* 1–204) but also W. Macdonald's account of the rest of Franklin's life (*BFA* 207–314). In other cheap reprints (e.g. Cassell's National Library edition, Introduction by Henry Morley, 1905), 'Chastity' was omitted from the list of virtues (p. 94) and other changes also made.

20:4 **The Perfectibility Of Man!...the Ford car!** Phrase often linked with William Godwin (1756–1836), leading political philosopher and theorist of the Romantic period. His book *An Enquiry concerning the Principles of Political Justice* (1793) spoke out against all forms of tyranny (in government, marriage and property) and claimed justice and freedom for all, on the basis of the supremacy of reason: it argued that 'man is perfectible' and that 'every perfection or excellence that human beings are competent to conceive, human beings...are competent to attain' (Book I, chap. 5)...Henry Ford (1863–1947) was President of the Ford Motor Co. until 1919; its most successful car, the Model T (of which more than 15 million were sold), was in production 1908–27. DHL may have been making a particular point, writing in the late autumn of 1922: the Ford car ('Lizzie') belonging to Knud Merrild and Kai Götzsche, with whom DHL and FL moved to the Del Monte ranch in December 1922 (see note on 32:29), was always breaking down; see *Letters*, iii. 347.

20:10 **dummy standards.** Either dummy in the sense of the baby's dummy or pacifier (see *Mr Noon*, ed. Vasey, 141:3–8), or 'pretended, unreal'.

20:12 **Abraham Lincoln...Roosevelt or Porfirio Diaz?** Abraham Lincoln (1809–65), sixteenth President of the United States (1861–5)... Theodore Roosevelt (1858–1919), twenty-sixth President (1901–9)... Porfirio Díaz (1830–1915), President of Mexico (1877–80, 1884–1911), effectively a dictator.

20:19 **Yale College...Harvard College?** Yale University (in New Haven, Connecticut, founded in 1701) and Harvard University (in Cambridge, Massachusetts, founded in 1636) were originally founded as Colleges, and only acquired the status of University in the late nineteenth century. Cf. the reference to 'Yale College' in the Introduction to the Everyman edition of Cooper's *The Deerslayer* which DHL probably used (*DS* vii), and in his copy of *Moby Dick* to the whale ship as 'my Yale College and my Harvard' (*MD* 100).

20:32 **"satisfy the professors of every religion, but shock none."** See *BFA* 112. Franklin added to his autobiography some notes made early in life (around 1731): 'I find one purporting to be the substance of an intended creed, containing, as I thought, the essentials of every known religion, and being free of every thing that might shock the professors of any religion.'

21:7 **But me no buts,** Phrase dating from the eighteenth century but popularised by the novelist Sir Walter Scott (1771–1832) in *The Antiquary* (1816): ' "I heartily wish I could, but" – "Nay, but me no buts..." ' (chap. xi).

21:13 **"That there is [20:34]...here or hereafter."** *BFA* 112 ['...one God...he governs...his providence...he ought...by adoration...'].

21:14 **Andrew Carnegie,** American philanthropist and millionaire (1835–1919); see note on 11:25.

21:20 **Wanamaker...Aloft on a pillar of dollars.** A department store (and city institution) in Philadelphia: DHL only included the reference during revision in 1922–3...cf. St Simeon Stylites, Syrian monk (AD ?390–459), first of the ascetics who lived on pillars.

21:32 **Hail Columbia!** Song by Joseph Hopkinson (1770–1842) in praise of the USA: 'Hail, Columbia! happy land! / Hail, ye heroes! heaven-born band!'; Columbia both because of the discovery of America by Christopher Columbus (?1451–1506) in 1492, and because the capital of the country has since 1791 been in Washington, in the District of Columbia (DC).

21:34 **The soul of man is a dark forest...Hercynian Wood that scared the Romans so,** Cf. the remark by Proust (see note on 12:6) 'Votre âme est bien, comme parle Tolstoï, une forêt obscure' (*Les Plaisirs et les jours*, Paris, 1896, 'Fragments de comédie italienne', no. vii, sect. 4 ['Your soul is certainly, as Tolstoy said, a dark forest']. However, cf. 'The heart of man is a dark forest – that is one of the sayings they have in Brazil' (J. M. Coetzee, *Foe*, 1986, p. 11)...Hercynia silva, the wooded region of central Germany (now Mittelgebirge); in the time of Julius Caesar (100–44 BC), the border between the Celts and the Germans. A regular theme in DHL post-1918; see e.g. *Movements* 45:12–46:24; *Mr Noon*, ed. Vasey, 249:14–16; 'A Letter from Germany' (1924) (*Phoenix* 107–8).

22:1 **in bounds** The reading of MS8 (p. 13); A1's 'in pound' (p. 16) has been judged an error, although a typescript or proof correction by DHL (punning on the meanings 'enclosure' and 'money') is a possibility.

22:3 **barbed wire fence.** Originally 'barb-wire' (see 29:14): dating from the 1860s and 1870s, to fence sheep in (and cattle out).

23:18 1 **TEMPERANCE [22:6]...and Socrates.** *BFA* 99–100 ['...to dullness; drink...or yourself; *i.e.*, waste...time; be always employ'd...unnecessary actions... extreams; forbear...injuries so much...cloaths, or...health or offspring...']... Socrates (470–399 BC), teacher and philosopher, best known through the dialogues written by his pupil Plato.

23:21 **A Quaker friend...an afterthought.** *BFA* 109: 'My list of virtues contain'd at first but twelve; but a Quaker friend having kindly informed me that I was generally thought proud...I added *Humility* to my list.'

23:23 **Alcibiades** Athenian general and statesman (450–404 BC); appears in Plato's *Symposium*, disputing with Socrates over love.

23:25 **wise in your own conceit,** Cf. Proverbs xxvi. 12: 'Seest thou a man wise in his own conceit? there is more hope of a fool than of him.'

23:28 **put his spoke in."** I.e. have his say, interfere (*OED2* 3a).

23:30 **the first of Americans** As one of the original signatories for the thirteen rebellious British colonies of the Declaration of Independence in July 1776 (*BFA* 273–4), Franklin was always regarded as one of the founding fathers of his country.

23:34 **conduct charts are lost to us...Order was his stumbling block.** See note on 187:23...*BFA* 106: 'In truth, I found myself incorrigible with respect to Order'.

24:2 Snuff-coloured little man! DHL may well have been thinking of the much-reproduced painting by the American artist John Trumbull (1756–1843) of Franklin, Thomas Jefferson and others at the signing of the Declaration of Independence in 1776: Franklin appears not very tall, rotund ('Middle-sized, sturdy' – 24:19), with a quantity of white hair; he is dressed in black with a white cravat, but the black is curiously pale on the chest and shoulders, as if stained by snuff (easily spilled and scattered by snuff-takers).

24:6 swept and lighted the streets of young Philadelphia. See *BFA* 149–50; Franklin was responsible for 'the bill . . . for lighting as well as paving the streets' (150), and made proposals for cleaning the streets of Philadelphia (149–53).

24:7 invented electrical appliances. See *BFA* 143, 183–7; Franklin was actually conducting experiments with electricity (see note on 24:17) rather than inventing appliances. DHL is probably recalling his invention of a new kind of stove (139–40).

24:8 a moralising club in Philadelphia, In 1727 Franklin created the 'Junto', a society for free discussion, and in 1744 a Philosophical Society (*BFA* 71–3, 131).

24:11 member of all the important councils of Philadelphia, and then of the American Colonies. He became Deputy Postmaster for Philadelphia (*BFA* 122) and a member of the Philadelphia Assembly (137); he became President of the executive council of Pennsylvania and by 1770 was 'invested with the Agentship for four of the colonies' (245).

24:13 the cause of American Independence at the French Court . . . economic father of the United States. Following the Declaration of Independence, Franklin was sent as the first envoy to the Court of Louis XVI, and was largely responsible for persuading the French government to support the newly broken-away thirteen states of the USA against its old enemy Great Britain; in 1778 an agreement with Spain and France was signed, an army supplied in 1780 and a fleet in 1781, and considerable financial aid obtained. Franklin also played a crucial part in the adoption of the US Constitution proposed in Philadelphia in 1787 and ratified in 1789.

24:14 infra dig, 'Beneath one's dignity' (from the Latin phrase *infra dignitatem*).

24:17 thunders of electricity, Franklin was famous for flying a kite in a thunderstorm, with a key attached to it, to attract a lightning strike; see *BFA* 187 and 213–14.

24:23 books of Venery were about hunting deer. The primary meaning of the word is indeed the practice or sport of hunting game, or the game to be hunted. But the second meaning (dating from the fifteenth century) is 'the practice or pursuit of sexual pleasure, the indulgence of sexual desire' (*OED2*).

24:25 as a little child, Cf. Matthew xviii. 3.

24:29 impeccable husband *BFA* 82–3 and 95–6 describe Franklin's marriage.

24:30 **Pioneer, Oh Pioneers!** Cf. Whitman's poem 'Pioneers! O Pioneers!' (*LG* 194–7): see note on 148:2 for details of the text used here.

24:34 **my father... yearly almanack** Arthur John Lawrence (1846–1924), coalminer; see John Worthen, *D. H. Lawrence: The Early Years 1885–1912* (Cambridge, 1991), pp. 10–12... annual book of tables giving statistical information about the phases of the moon, tides, etc., often decorated with pictures and mottos, and with predictions about the year to come.

25:4 **thorns in young flesh.** Proverbial, from 2 Corinthians xii. 7 ('There was given to me a thorn in the flesh'); cf. DHL's 1913 story 'The Thorn in the Flesh' in *The Prussion Officer and Other Stories* (1914).

25:19 **to settle some disturbance among the Indians.** See *BFA* 144; 'a treaty being to be held with the Indians at Carlisle', in Pennsylvania.

25:34 **made** The reading of Per ('made') was typed in TCC7 as 'had made'. TCC7 (p. 33) survived into MS8 as p. 17 for 25:18–26:2, so this correction – and that at 25:40 – have been taken from Per.

25:40 **"We found [25:20]... all the sea coast——"** *BFA* 145 ['... women, quarreling... dark-colour'd... half naked... firebrands... form'd... imagin'd; there... misbehav'd... their old counselors... acknowledg'd... upon the rum; and... saying, "*The... whatever use he design'd any thing... said: 'Let... with,' and... so.*" And,... for cultivators... inhabited the sea-coast.'].

26:8 **Chicago... Pittsburgh, Pa.?** Founded in 1803, made a city in 1837... in the early twentieth century, the largest (and ugliest) steel-producing town in North America; founded near a British fort in 1764, made a city in 1816.

26:10 **Kultur** Culture (German), with – at that date – a pejorative implication.

26:24 **an automatic piano** Either a 'player piano' or more likely a 'pianola', using punched piano rolls and operated either with a handle or electrically: the cabinet stood beside a normal piano and operated its keys. Very popular in the 1920s: see, e.g., DHL's story 'Glad Ghosts', *The Woman Who Rode Away and Other Stories*, ed. Dieter Mehl and Christa Jansohn (Cambridge, 1995), 194:6–16. The 'victrola' of 28:36 was invented *c.* 1905 by the Victor Talking Machine Co. as its own version of the gramophone (or phonograph) patented by the Gramophone Co. (see too note on 213:23).

26:37 **He who runs may read.** Constant (and now proverbial) misquotation from Habakkuk ii. 2 ('that he may run that readeth it'). See, e.g., Alfred Lord Tennyson (1809–92), 'The Flower' (1864), ll. 17–18 ('Read my little fable: / He that runs may read').

27:3 **Bacchus,** Roman god of wine and fruitfulness (counterpart of the Greek god Dionysus: see note on 178:38).

28:36 **cat-o-nine-tails.** Rope whips, supposedly with nine knotted thongs, traditionally used for the punishment of flogging in the army and navy.

29:5 **Mr Pierpont Morgan...Mr Nosey Hebrew** Both John Pierpont Morgan (1837–1913) and his son John Pierpont Morgan Jr (1867–1943) were famous bankers and millionaires (the latter helping the financing of the American contribution to the First World War)...gibe about rich Jews with large noses.

29:21 **at Paris judiciously milking money out of the French monarchy** See note on 24:13, and *BFA* 295–300.

30:1 **Benjamin Franklin to Woodrow Wilson** Franklin died in 1790: Thomas Woodrow Wilson (1856–1924) was twenty-eighth President (1913–21) (see note on 33:1).

30:29 **any Russian nihilist.** Ivan Turgenev (1818–83), Russian novelist and dramatist, called the Russian anarchists 'nihilists': e.g. his character Bazarov in *Fathers and Sons* (1862), tr. 1895 (see *WL* note on 86:36; see too note on 225:6). The name was popularised, so that by the early twentieth century 'anarchist' and 'nihilist' tended to be linked; e.g. in Conrad's *The Secret Agent* of 1907, with its central figure of Vladimir Verloc. The tendency was increased in the popular imagination following the overthrow and murder of Tsar Nicholas I in the revolutions of 1917–18.

31:3 **squirrels running in...cages.** A squirrel-cage was a small cylindrical framework made to rotate by a small animal (in scientific experiments usually a rat or mouse) moving inside it; hence, a repetitive and purposeless task.

Henry St. John de Crèvecoeur (Final Version 1923)

32:3 **Crèvecoeur...at Caen...1735.** DHL acquired his information from Warren Barton Blake's Introduction to the Everyman edition of *Letters From an American Farmer* (hereafter *LAF*), pp. viii–x. Michel-Guillaume Jean de Crèvecoeur (1735–1813) went to England at the age of nineteen; shortly afterwards he joined the French general Louis Joseph Montcalm, Marquis de Saint-Véran (1712–59), in Canada (where the latter commanded the French troops, only to die during the defence of Quebec against the English). In 1759 Crèvecoeur went to the colony of New York and travelled extensively; he took the names 'Hector Saint John' when he became a naturalised American in 1765 (DHL's forms 'Henry', 'Henri' and 'Crèvecoeur' in all the versions of the essay he himself wrote are unaccountable). He married Mehitabel Tippet (DHL's 'New England girl'), daughter of a merchant from Yonkers, New York, in 1769 (p. x) and purchased the farm 'Pine Hill' in Orange County, New York. He left the farm during the War of Independence and ironically, given his Tory sympathies, was (in 1779) imprisoned by the British on suspicion of being a spy. In 1780 he returned to Europe and published – first in London (1782), then in Paris (1784) – his *Letters* (revised for the French edition). He was sent as French consul to New York in 1783, after the War of Independence, but by then his wife was dead, his farm burned and his children scattered; he remained as consul until 1790, returning only once (for two years) to France. In 1790 he finally returned to France and died at Sarcelles, on the outskirts of Paris. His *Sketches of Eighteenth-Century America* were published only in 1925; they give a far more sceptical picture of his age than his *Letters*.

32:11 Tom Payne. Thomas Paine (1737–1809), political pamphleteer, born in England, arrived in Philadelphia in 1774 with letters of introduction from Franklin; his enormously influential pamphlets *Common Sense* (1776) and *Crisis* (1776–83) supported the colonists' fight for independence.

32:13 stunt, Originally US student slang, which DHL here uses clumsily but deliberately: something done to attract attention.

32:23 Rousseau's ... Madame d'Houdetot, Jean Jacques Rousseau (1712–78), French-Swiss writer and philosopher, author of the autobiographical *Confessions* (1782) ... Élisabeth de La Live de Bellegarde, Comtesse d'Houdetot (1730–1813); Rousseau saw in her many of the 'natural' qualities he celebrated in his *Julie ou la Nouvelle Héloïse* (1761). She is discussed in the Everyman Introduction (*LAF* xviii–xix).

32:28 Hazlitt ... Shelley ... Coleridge ... Bristol. William Hazlitt (1778–830), critic and essayist, close friend when young of Coleridge; the Everyman Introduction mentioned that he wrote about Crèvecoeur (*LAF* vii) ... Percy Bysshe Shelley (1792–1822), poet and social reformer ... the poet Samuel Taylor Coleridge (1772–1834) was one of the three leading figures in the Pantisocratic movement centred in Bristol (the second largest city after London, and the largest port in Great Britain in the 1790s); he lived there for several months in 1795. It was proposed that a group – 'the friends of liberty' – should set out for the USA to settle on the Susquehanna river, 150 miles w. of Philadelphia. Various groups and individuals did go, but Coleridge had become disillusioned by August 1795: see Richard Holmes, *Coleridge, Early Visions* (1989), pp. 87–102; see too note on 76:38. A note in *LAF* explicitly linked Crèvecoeur's book with Pantisocracy and Coleridge (pp. 237–8). DHL had done some reading in the Romantic period in July 1916, borrowing *Trelawny's Recollections of the Last Days of Shelley and Byron* (*Letters*, ii. 625) and acquiring (ii. 633) a copy of *Reminiscences of the English Lake Poets* by Thomas De Quincey (1785–1859), the latter probably as part of the 'tattered but complete set of De Quincey's Works' (iii. 407 n. 4) which he acquired in Cornwall: his Zennor address (April 1916–October 1917) is inscribed in it (UN). See too note on 79:35.

32:29 Some of us ... all the way. DHL arrived in the USA (at San Francisco) on 4 September 1922; lived in Taos, New Mexico, until the end of November; and then lived on the Del Monte Ranch (18 miles n. of Taos) on Lobo Mountain from December 1922 to March 1923. In December he finished writing the final version of *Studies* and in January completed the revision of the typescript (see note on 15:20). His experiences on Lobo presumably led to his comments on how he 'tiptoed into the Wilds and saw the shacks of the Homesteaders' (34:7).

33:1 Woodrow Wilson's wrung heart and wet hanky. Possibly a reference to the attempted policy of 'Peace without Conflict' which Wilson carried on before the USA joined the First World War in April 1917, or to his 'Fourteen Articles' of January 1918, when he outlined the principles on which any peace after the war should be based; or to his successful attempts (beginning in 1916) to create the League of Nations (for which he was awarded the Nobel Peace Prize for 1919). Given the comment at 137:20–1, however, it is most likely to refer to Wilson's attempts 1918–19 to achieve a just peace at the Treaty of Versailles (signed on 28 June 1919); see DHL's comments on Wilson in January 1919 (*Letters*, iii. 318).

33:12 Thoreau and Emerson worked it up. The writer Henry David Thoreau (1817–62) and the idealist and thinker Ralph Waldo Emerson (1803–82) were both Transcendentalists and close friends. Between 1845 and 1847 Thoreau lived by Walden Pond near Concord (on land owned by Emerson) on what he could grow and catch; he published *Walden; or Life in the Woods* in 1854, while Emerson's first published pamphlet was entitled *Nature* (1836); he followed it with *Essays* (1841) and *Essays Second Series* (1844).

33:15 Chateaubriand. Francois René Vicomte de Chateaubriand (1768–1848), French writer and politician, noted for his melancholy, dreamy lyricism as a writer in, e.g., his *Mémoires d'outre-tombe* (1849–50).

33:25 Amiable Spouse ... I have no name. / I am the Infant Son—"...shafts of the plough...potato patch. Crèvecoeur addresses himself to 'a beloved wife, my faithful helpmate' (*LAF* 210) but not to an 'Amiable Spouse'...parody of 'Infant Joy' (1794), ll. 1–2, by William Blake (1757–1827): 'I have no name: / I am but two days old'; see 33:29; cf. too 'the infant' (*LAF* 24)...'Often, when I plough my low ground, I place my little boy on a chair which screws to the beam of the plough' (*LAF* 25)...the 'potato patch' is DHL's invention.

33:27 Neighbours, whom no doubt he loved as himself, to build a barn, There is no such episode in *LAF*; in Letter III, however, his neighbours help 'Andrew, the Hebridean' to build a house (*LAF* 84–6). See Matthew v. 43.

33:28 Innocent Simplicity of one of Nature's Communities. DHL's ironical version of the narrator's attitude, not a quotation from *LAF*.

33:31 a deep-breasted daughter of America, Classical heroic cliché, often 'deep-bosomed' (from the Greek vathykolpos).

33:34 Ahoolibah, See note on 32:3.

33:39 Healthy Offspring...Children of Nature...Wilds...Simple Toil... Honest Sweat Although Crèvecoeur refers to 'my blooming offspring' (*LAF* 218), none of the other words or phrases is used in *LAF*.

34:4 *Im Bild*, In the picture (German).

34:14 Bernadin de St. Pierre...François Le Vaillant, Jacques Henri Bernardin de Saint-Pierre (1737–1814), author of the idyllic novel *Paul et Virginie* (1787), which DHL knew by December 1910 (see *Letters*, i. 205, *WL* 124:22 and *FWL* 110:38), and one of the forerunners of Romanticism ... François le Vaillant (1753–1824), traveller and ornithologist, author of *Voyage dans l'intérieur de l'Afrique* (1790), *Histoire naturelle*

446 Explanatory notes

des Oiseaux d'Afrique (1799) and *Histoire naturelle d'une partie d'Oiseaux nouveaux et rares de l'Amérique et des Indes* (1801).

34:15 Marie Antoinette Born 1755; wife from 1770 (and queen from 1774) of the French King Louis XVI (1754–93); guillotined in Paris in October 1793. At her palace of the Petit Trianon, the queen developed (from 1782) the so-called 'Hameau', a farm with thatched cottages, stables, barn, etc.; she took a great interest in its development and at times fed the hens there and carried in the milk.

34:32 Garden Suburb or a Brook Farm The Garden City (or Suburb), designed to bring together the advantages of urban life with pleasantly green surroundings, was an invention of the English Parliamentary Secretary Sir Ebenezer Howard (1850–1928) who published *Garden-Cities of Tomorrow* in 1902. Brook Farm was the location of an attempt at communal living (1841–7) in which Nathaniel Hawthorne and others engaged; see note on 99:20.

34:33 Robinson Crusoe . . . high-brow of high-brows. Hero of the novel *The Life and Strange Surprizing Adventures of Robinson Crusoe of York, Mariner* (1719) by the English writer Daniel Defoe (1660–1731) . . . Crusoe is actually the son of a Yorkshire merchant.

35:9 "I am astonished [35:4] . . . astonishing dexterity." *LAF* 27 ['. . . crows which . . .']. Kingbirds are large, insect-catching birds of the genus *Tyrannus*; the Eastern Kingbird is also known as the Bee Martin. See also 35:18.

35:11 the ideal turtle. I.e. the voice of the turtle dove (cf. Song of Solomon ii. 10), sweetly and peacefully cooing.

35:17 "One being Who made all things, and governs the world by His providence." Cf. *BFA* 112 ['That there is one God, who made all things. That he governs the world by his providence'].

35:23 The horse . . . is the friend of man, and man is the friend of the horse . . . my sly old Indian pony, Not a direct quotation: Crèvecoeur, however, refers to ploughing as a task when 'my labour flows from instinct, as well as that of my horses; there is no kind of difference between us in our different shares of that operation' (*LAF* 17). He also describes the 'docility of my horses' (22), 'the sagacity of those animals which have long been the tenants of my farm' (26) and thinks of horses as – compared with cattle – 'more generous animals' (28). He also observes the 'kindness and affection' which people show their horses (161) . . . DHL's horse in the winter of 1922–3, 'Laddie', was a 'high sorrel thoroughbred that nearly splits me as I split my logs with wedges' (*Letters*, iv. 370, 360).

35:25 Man . . . is the friend of man. Not a direct statement; in Letters II and III, in particular, Crèvecoeur presents his fellow Americans as extraordinarily kind and generous to each other: 'a general decency of manners prevails throughout' (*LAF* 47): strangers meet 'with hospitality, kindness, and plenty everywhere' (57). In Letter IX, however, he sees 'avarice, rapine and murder, equally prevailing in all parts' (167) and states that 'Everywhere one part of the human species are taught the art of shedding the blood of the other' (170).

35:33 **Some great hornets ... free of flies.** *LAF* 35–6.

35:38 **pugnaciously ... so American** An English seventeenth-century word, from the Latin *pugnax*; the adverbial form, however, first appeared in C. A. Goodrich's revision of Noah Webster's *American Dictionary of the English Language* (New York, 1847).

36:4 **Swallows built their nest [35:36] ... little rascals of wrens.** *LAF* 34–5; Crèvecœur refers to his 'piazza' (34), not his veranda; there was only one swallow's nest and one wren's nest; there is no mention of 'adobe'; there was no return of the swallows again to be driven out; the wren simply removed the nesting material from the swallow's nest to its own box, and Crèvecoeur moved the box to ensure the action was not repeated. Nor does Crèvecoeur entirely approve; he refers to the wren's 'selfishness' (34), 'injustice' (35) and 'plunder' (35).

36:10 **shot a kingbird [36:6] ... like Jonah up the seashore;** *LAF* 26–7; see Jonah i. 17, ii. 10.

36:30 **The humming-bird. "Its bill is [36:15] ... the winged species.—"** *LAF* 179 ['... calix ... blossoms, ... that serve ... feeds, it ... immovable though ... pieces: for ... side: most ... parts it ... parent; who ... it the smallest ... beautiful of ...'].

36:32 **read about humming birds elsewhere, in Bates and W. H. Hudson,** Henry W. Bates's book *The Naturalist on the River Amazon* (1910), which DHL read in 1919 (*Letters*, iii. 315, 317, 340), and W. H. Hudson's *South American Sketches* (1909), which DHL apparently read in 1910 (*Letters*, i. 151). DHL asked Amy Lowell in August 1916 whether there were still humming-birds in the USA, 'as in Crèvecoeur?' (*Letters*, ii. 645). Keith Sagar has pointed out that DHL's poem 'Humming-Bird', though in *Birds, Beasts and Flowers* (1923) giving as its place of writing 'Española' (on the Rio Grande, suggesting that it was written in 1922–3), was actually written in Sicily in 1921, probably also drawing upon Bates and Hudson (*D. H. Lawrence: Life into Art*, 1985, pp. 215–16).

37:2 **"Often, in [36:39] ... them to do."** *LAF* 27–8 ['Often in ... fences where ... earth as ...'].

37:7 **St. Francis,** St Francis of Assisi (?1181–1226), founder of the Franciscan order, and traditionally remembered for his love for brother animals and sister birds – see *The Little Flowers of St. Francis*, tr. W. Heywood (1906), p. 26: 'and he went into the field and began to preach to the birds ... on this wise: "My sisters the birds"'. Cf. DHL: 'I have never been to Assisi – but that I feel I must consult the birds before I claim sistership with them – they might object to my lack of feathers' (*Letters*, iii. 712).

37:10 The *Letter* about snakes and humming-birds   Letter X ('On Snakes; and on the Humming Bird'). Starting here, DHL used pp. 46–51 of his copy of TCC7 when assembling his final manuscript (crossing out the first seven lines of p. 46).

37:26 "Strange was [37:13] ... contracted its own."   *LAF* 180–1 ['... ground mutually ... entwined, seemed ... water snake ... outstretched; the ... superiority, it ...'].

37:28 "uncommon and beautiful."   *LAF* 180.

37:30 a sheer ophiolater ... ophiolatry,   Ophiology is the branch of zoology concerned with snakes (*ophis* is Greek for 'snake'): while 'ophiologist' and 'ophiological' are standard terms, 'ophiolater' and 'ophiolatry' ('one who worships snakes', and 'the worship of snakes': Greek -*latria*, from *latreia* 'worship' cf. 'Mariolater' and – 'Mariolatry') are DHL's coinage.

37:31 that coiled Aztec rattlesnake carved in stone.   Almost certainly the superb Aztec carving (in granite) in the British Museum (no. 1849. 6–29.1). DHL wrote this long before going to Mexico in April 1923 but was well acquainted with the exhibits of the British Museum: see notes on 214:8, 268:36, and 346:12. He was still recalling 'an Aztec rattlesnake' in 'Him with his Tail in his Mouth' in 1925 (see *Reflections* 316:33).

37:39 a line of shipping ... under the wigwams.   DHL draws upon the Everyman Introduction, which describes Crèvecoeur's 'packet-line – the first established between New York and a French port ... Lorient in Brittany' (*LAF* xx–xxi) ... *LAF* 221 ['You may therefore, by means of anticipation, behold me under the Wigwam ...'].

38:3 the last letter ... to man.   Letter XII.

38:7 inclined to be vile,   Cf. the hymn 'From Greenland's Icy Mountains' by Bishop Reginald Heber (1783–1826): 'What though the spicy breezes / Blow soft o'er Ceylon's Isle; / Where every prospect pleases, / And only man is vile' (ll. 9–12).

38:16 Touchingly and vividly ... within the wigwam.   Cf. *LAF* 221–3; but Crèvecoeur writes that while he 'can plough, sow and hunt, as occasion may require ... my wife, deprived of wool and flax, will have no room for industry' (*LAF* 222); he makes no reference to maize or to weaving.

38:17 his tender offspring   Cf. 'Their tender minds' (*LAF* 227), 'my blooming offspring' (218).

38:19 under the greenwood tree,   Play on the title of the novel (1872) by Thomas Hardy (1840–1928); see also 'Study of Thomas Hardy', *Hardy* 22:14–21.

38:29 crazy ... for this.   'Extremely fond'; never simply an Americanism, being first used in 1779 in England, but DHL considered it characteristically American.

40:2 "I must tell you [39:28] ... alter their temper...."   *LAF* 51–2 ['... woods, which ... that grow and live ... thoughts but ... wolves to destroy ... bears to kill ... foxes to catch ... property, they ... gloomy, and unsociable ... no neighbours ...'].

40:16 "the apprehension...their tender years" *LAF* 214 ['...dangerous at...'].

40:28 "By what power [40:16]...of credit. *LAF* 214 ['...pass, that...people, can...war, who at...captivity; when...sorrow, they...Indianised, that...parents for protection against...'].

40:32 "There must be [40:29]...become Europeans...." *LAF* 215 ['there must ...Europeans!'].

40:33 **Our cat and another,** In Nottinghamshire, 'our cat' would commonly be said to someone – often a child – talking too much: their 'tale' (i.e. 'tail') being too long.

41:8 **Especially white women Americans...inside the machine;** DHL is thinking of women such as Mary Austin (1868–1934) and Mabel Dodge Sterne (1879–1962) – the latter shortly to marry the Native American Tony Luhan – both of whom worked in defence of the Pueblo: see Esther Lanigan Stineman, *Mary Austin: Song of a Maverick* (New Haven, 1989), pp. 152–8, 171–9. Mary Austin was a regular visitor to Taos (see *The Plays*, ed. Hans-Wilhelm Schwarze and John Worthen, Cambridge, 1999, pp. 687–8); Mabel Sterne had invited DHL to Taos but he and Frieda moved up to the Del Monte Ranch (see note on 20:4). As soon as he had arrived in Taos in September she had 'immediately sent me motoring off to an Apache gathering 120 miles away across desert' (*Letters*, iv. 296). On 27 September DHL noted that 'We are kept busy – being driven out in the car over the desert to wild places' (*Letters*, iv. 312); he ended with a considerable dislike for 'these women in breeches and riding-boots and sombreros, and money and motor-cars and wild west' (*Letters*, iv. 314).

Fenimore Cooper's White Novels (Final Version 1923)

42:2 **Fenimore Cooper's** James Fenimore Cooper (1789–1851) – 'of good family' (44:28) – grew up on his prosperous father's estate near Lake Otsego; his father founded Cooperstown near the Susquehanna river in upper New York state, not (DHL's error) 'by Lake Champlain' (44:29, 58:36), near the Canadian border, which was the setting of a number of Cooper's novels (e.g. *The Last of the Mohicans*). In 1802, Cooper studied at Yale but was expelled; he served briefly in the merchant navy, but in 1811 married Susan De Lancey and subsequently lived as a gentleman farmer and writer at Scarsdale, New York, and in New York City. He paid a long visit to England and France (1826–33), some of the time as American consul, and was a thoroughgoing 'gentleman of culture' (44:29–30). He returned to Cooperstown in 1835 and lived there until his death.

42:10 **The Aztec...the Incas...The Red Indian, the Esquimo, the Patagonian** The Aztec civilisation of central Mexico reached its peak 80–100 years before the first Europeans arrived on the continent; the civilisation was destroyed by the Spanish under Hernando Cortés (1485–1546) in the first half of the sixteenth century: see note on 197:10...the Inca empire (the name belonged to the ruler) centred on Peru and lasted from around 1100 until it was destroyed by the Spanish under Francisco Pizarro (1478–1541) also in the first half of the sixteenth century . . . the American population grew from 3.9 million in 1790 to 31.3 million in 1860; and especially in expansion west of the Mississippi the indigenous Native American population was displaced; Andrew Jackson (1767–1845), seventh President (1829–37), pursued a particularly aggressive policy towards the Native Americans, who more than once were defeated in battle and massacred, with the survivors confined to reservations . . . the Eskimo peoples (Inuit) had their traditional ways of life radically changed by the movement of Americans and Canadians into their traditional fishing and hunting grounds . . . Patagonia (now part of Argentina) was fought over by the Argentineans and Chileans in the late nineteenth century and possessed by Argentina in 1902 but the (always small) population was not displaced. Cf. DHL's comment in the 1920 'Foreword': 'America must take up life where the Red Indian, the Aztec, the Maya, the Incas left it off' (384:34–5).

42:11 *Où sont les neiges d'antan?*   From *Le Grand Testament, Ballade des Dames du Temps Jadis*, by François Villon (1431–63), French poet; 'Where are the snows of yesteryear?' (tr. Dante Gabriel Rossetti). Cf. *Letters*, i. 157.

42:25 **Happy Hunting Ground.**   Supposed Native American name for the after-life to which hunters go; see, e.g., *DS* 111, 113.

44:6 **Malice!**   Cf. DHL's feeling (in his October 1922 essay 'Indians and an Englishman') of what he experienced on first encountering Native Americans: 'a jeering, malevolent vibration . . . ridicule. Comic sort of bullying. No jolly, free laughter. Yet a great deal of laughter. But with a sort of gibe in it' (*Phoenix* 96).

44:9 **Supposing an Indian loves a white woman, and lives with her.**   It would have been hard for DHL in 1922 not to have been thinking of Tony Luhan and Mabel Sterne (see note on 41:8), currently living together in Mabel's house in Taos.

44:21 **oneing.**   *OED2* records no use of the word in this sense since 1480; the word has, since the 1920s, come to mean 'joining in one, uniting' in a religious sense which has nothing to do with DHL's usage. See 60:1, 184:39, 270:5.

44:25 **Cooper his success.**   With the essayist and short-story writer Washington Irving (1783–1859), Cooper was the most popular American literary author in the United States and Europe through the mid-nineteenth century. To take just one novel during its first fifty years: *The Last of the Mohicans* was published in London, New York and Paris in 1826; there had been twelve new editions in London by 1875 and numerous editions published in Philadelphia and New York.

44:33 **Austin Dobson . . . Andrew Lang**   Both poets and men of letters of the 1890s and known for their learning, range of reference, wit and preciosity: Henry Austin Dobson (1840–1921) famous for his poem 'Ars Victrix', tr. of poem by Théophile Gautier (1811–72) . . . Lang (1844–1912): see his poem 'Brahma' in imitation of Emerson (see note on 33:12).

44:36 *raffiné* ... hoydenish, Refined (French) ... wild, boisterous and female.

45:2 a Frenchman, who says, *"L'Amérique est pourrie avant d'être mûre."* 'America is rotten before being ripe.' In Cooper's *Homeward Bound* (see note on 45:7), Paul Powis says of America:

> 'I do not go quite so far in describing her demerits as some of the countrymen of Mademoiselle Viefville have gone.'
> 'And what may that have been?' asked the governess eagerly, in English.
> '*Pourrie avant d'être mûre. Mûre*, America is certainly far from being; but I am not disposed to accuse her yet of being quite *pourrie*.' (*HB* 415)

DHL misquoted 'mûre' as 'muri' and ascribed the phrase to 'some Frenchman seventy years ago' when writing to Waldo Frank on 15 September 1917 (*Letters*, iii. 160), showing that he knew the Cooper novel by then, but also suggesting that his knowledge may have originated some time earlier.

45:4 **Baudelaire learned his lesson from America.** Charles Baudelaire (1821– 67), French poet, art critic and essayist; his poems *Les Fleurs du Mal* (1855, 2nd edn 1861) demonstrate a radical stress on the darker sides of individuality and sexuality; he also translated (from 1854) the work of Edgar Allan Poe and was much influenced by his critical writing.

45:7 *Homeward Bound, Eve Effingham, The Spy, The Pilot* ... **the Leatherstocking Series.** Published in 1838, 1839 (originally as *Home as Found*), 1821 and 1823 respectively ... the five books which became known as the 'Leatherstocking Novels' are *The Pioneers* (1823), *The Last of the Mohicans* (1826), *The Prairie* (1827), *The Pathfinder, or the Inland Sea* (1840), *The Deerslayer, or the First Warpath* (1841); the chronological order of events within the novels does not, however, follow their order of publication (see 55:3–21).

45:10 **father ... uncle,** Edward, Eve and John Effingham.

45:19 **parvenu ... demagogue,** Economic or social upstart ... political agitator who appeals through crude oratory: Steadfast Dodge, misremembered by DHL as Septimus (45:21).

45:26 **the Venus de Milo.** Broad-hipped and armless Greek sculpture discovered in 1820 in ruins on the island of Melos and today in the Louvre (45:29). Loerke in *WL* 434:2 thinks her 'a bourgeoise', but cf. DHL's comment of January 1914 (*Letters*, ii. 137). DHL imagines Dodge's response (45:26–7).

45:30 **The original Vandals** Members of a Germanic people which raided Roman provinces in the third and fourth centuries before devastating Gaul (406–9), conquering Spain (409–18) and North Africa (429–42), and sacking Rome (455). See *Movements* 61:40–62:8, 85:8–13.

45:36 **the Bargello ... the Piazza di San Marco** Palazzo del Bargello – really the Palazzo del Podestà – built 1254–1346 and now the National Museum for Italian sculpture: it contains, e.g., the Donatello *David* and *St George* ... the piazza in front of the eleventh-century basilica of San Marco.

46:6 a few German bombs fell upon Rheims cathedral   The Germans bombarded Reims (in n.w. France), and set fire to and severely damaged the Cathedral (built between 1211 and 1300) on 19 September 1914; it was restored after the First World War with aid provided by the USA.

46:10 peace hath her victories.   Sonnet 'To the Lord General Cromwell, May 1652', ll. 10–11, by John Milton (1608–74): 'peace hath her victories / No less renowned than war' (see too note on 14:39).

46:11 Dodge-town   Where Dodge lives (with a population of eighteen): once Dodgetown – 'but this did not last long, being thought vulgar and commonplace' (*HB* 228) – subsequently changed to Dodgeborough, then to Dodgeville; Dodgeople and Dodgeopolis are also suggested (229). DHL may also be playing on Cooperstown (44:29) and thinking of Dodge City, Kansas, on the Arkansas river. See too note on 47:18.

46:14 the Rhine, or the Coliseum: The river Rhine, 1,320 km long, running from the Swiss Alps to the coast of Holland, for the greater part through Germany: boat trips on the Rhine are a popular tourist attraction ... properly the Colosseum: the Flavian Amphitheatre, one of the most impressive surviving ruins of ancient Rome and a necessity for tourists, 186 m long, built AD 70–80.

46:23 "Mr Effingham? Pleased to meet you, Mr Effingham"... "Pleased to meet you, Mr Dodge."   Not a quotation: DHL paraphrases and interprets ('Pleased to meet you' being thought vulgar in middle-class England). Dodge invites himself into the Effinghams' cabin: 'Mr. Effingham gave their visitor a polite reception ... marked with a little more than usual formality, by way of letting it be understood that the apartment was private; a precaution that he knew was very necessary in associating with tempers like those of Steadfast. All this was thrown away on Mr. Dodge ...' Eventually Dodge addresses Eve:

'We have had a considerable pleasant time, Miss Effingham, since we sailed from Portsmouth,' he observed familiarly.

Eve bowed her assent, determined not to take to herself a visit that did violence to all her habits and notions of propriety. But Mr. Dodge was too obtuse to feel the hint conveyed in mere reserve of manner. (*HB* 92)

46:41 As a true democrat...right is might.   Cf. 'Ultra as a democrat and an American' (*HB* 230). Dodge also expresses his belief in 'Equal laws, equal rights, equality in all respects, and pure, abstract, unqualified liberty, beyond all question, sir' (*HB* 95) ... cf. the closing exhortation of Abraham Lincoln's address of 27 February 1860: 'Let us have faith that right makes might' (*Lincoln's Speeches and Letters*, introduction by James Bryce, J. M. Dent & Co., 1907, p. 156).

47:8 **has the Effinghams on the hip.** Cf. Shakespeare's play *The Merchant of Venice*, I. i. 42: 'If I can catch him once upon the hip'. From wrestling: to catch someone at a disadvantage.

47:18 **the Dodge dilemma.** John F. and Horace E. Dodge founded their car company in 1912; both died in the influenza outbreak of 1920, and the company was sold to the Chrysler Corporation in 1928; for Ford see note on 20:4.

48:8 **Eve! And birds of paradise. And apples!** As 48:10 makes clear, a reference to Eve in the Garden of Eden (or 'Paradise'): see Genesis ii. 9, 17; iii. 1–6.

48:17 **that apple of Sodom** Or 'Dead Sea Fruit'; traditionally of external beauty but disappointing and hollow: when touched, turning to dust and ashes.

48:24 **Mr Dodge [48:19]...knickerbockers...below the belt...a bit nearer.** The conversation (48:19–24) is wholly invented by DHL...from 1859, the name given to baggy breeches fastened with a band at the knee or above the ankle; the garment – and the pattern – confirming the impression of inelegance...'below the belt' is 'not allowed', from boxing: the mixed metaphor here is suggestive...there is no evidence in the novel that Dodge is attracted to Eve.

49:4 **Septimus at the Court of King Arthur.** Cf. the novel *A Connecticut Yankee at King Arthur's Court* (1889) by Mark Twain (1835–1910).

49:8 **Excalibur...knighthood...kingship.** Arthur became king because he alone could draw the sword Excalibur from the stone in which it was fastened; he used it to ennoble the knights of his Round Table.

49:17 **your fifth rib?** Proverbial from at least the seventeenth century as the place where someone may effectively be killed: from the killing of Ashael by Abner in 2 Samuel ii. 23 ('smote him under the fifth rib, that the spear came out behind him').

49:21 **the *Contrat Social*,** As developed by Rousseau and others, the theory that a voluntary agreement is entered into by individuals (who desire the protection which society affords them) to give up some of their liberty, and that this results in the formation of the state or of organised society.

49:25 **flaps** There may be a memory of the image of the insect in Pope's 'Epistle to Dr Arbuthnot' (1735), ll. 308–9: 'Yet let me flap this bug with gilded wings – / This painted child of dirt, that stinks and stings.'

49:37 **These States.** Strongly reminiscent of Whitman (see note on 148:2): cf. the titles 'France, The 18th Year of these States' (*LG* 200) and 'Europe, The 72nd and 73rd Years of These States' (*LG* 226); cf. too 'By Blue Ontario's Shore', l. 60: 'These States are the amplest poem' (*LG* 286).

50:4 **"Naked to the waist...truncheon of a spear—"** 'The Chapel in Lyoness', ll. 5–8, in *The Defence of Guenevere and Other Poems* (1858) by William Morris (1834–96)

['... was I, ... spear.']. DHL referred to the poem in 'The Shades of Spring' (1911); see *The Prussian Officer and Other Stories*, ed. John Worthen (Cambridge, 1983), 110:30–3.

50:7 Rights of Man. Although the phrase had been used twice in poems by William Cowper (1731–1800) in the early 1780s (see 'The Task', iv. 680, and 'Charity', l. 28), the phrase became current, and by the second decade of the nineteenth century was proverbial, from its use as the title of a pamphlet (1791) justifying the French Revolution by Tom Paine ('The natural and imprescriptible rights of man ... are liberty, property, security, and resistance of oppression').

50:11 the first smartly-tailored "suit," that ever woman wore. Not a reference to women in trousers, but to 'a costume', the combination of a matching coat (or jacket) and skirt. *OED2* – recording 'recent use' – offers a 1913 reference to 'linen suits and frocks in exclusive styles'.

50:18 I never had a great-grandfather. DHL told the story of how his mysterious (paternal) great-grandfather was supposed to have been a French refugee from the Revolution of 1789–93 who had fought against Napoleon at Waterloo (1815), and how his grandfather was subsequently brought up in a military establishment in England (see, e.g., *Letters*, iii. 282); cf., however, Worthen, *The Early Years*, p. 7.

50:19 in education ... I'm merely scrappy. DHL attended Nottingham High School September 1898–July 1901, leaving at the age of sixteen. He was a pupil teacher in Eastwood 1902–5, sitting the King's Scholarship Examination in December 1904 and the University of London matriculation examination in June 1905. He then studied for his teacher's certificate at Nottingham University College 1906–8.

Fenimore Cooper's Leatherstocking Novels (Final Version 1923)

52:25 flitted round Europe so uneasily. Cf. the Everyman edition of Cooper's *The Prairie*, Introduction anonymous, which DHL was probably using: 'in July, 1826, Cooper landed in England ... crossed to France ... and then settled for a time in Paris' (*PR* vii).

52:29 "In short ... humble self." The quotation does not appear in the first edition of Cooper's letters, published the year DHL arrived in the USA (*Correspondence of James Fenimore-Cooper*, ed. James Fenimore Cooper, 2 vols., New Haven, 1922), nor in any other of the sources DHL had used (e.g. the Introductions to the Everyman editions of the novels). In the *Correspondence*, however, a letter from Cooper of 12 October 1826 to William Jay, from Paris, offers some significant parallels: Cooper supplies a list of twenty-six titled or distinguished people with whom he had been dining (including Count de Villèle, Count Appolini, the Papal Nuncio, Viscount Granville and the Russian and Spanish Ambassadors) and ends 'next – your humble servant' (p. 102): later in the letter he comments on how 'The Duke of Villahermosa led Mrs Canning, your humble servant led the – rear' (p. 104). DHL had either read that letter in the *Correspondence* and was recreating it, or was creating a pastiche from what someone had quoted to him.

53:11 the flesh goes tired on my bones. FL noted that 'My flesh grows weary on my bones' was 'one of Lawrence's expressions when somebody held forth to him' (*"Not I, But the Wind..."*, Santa Fe, The Rydal Press, 1934, p. 304). Cf. 'my flesh wearies upon my bones' in *David* (*The Plays*, ed. Schwarze and Worthen, 92:27); see Job xix. 20 ('My bone cleaveth to my skin and to my flesh') and Ecclesiastes xii. 12 ('much study *is* a weariness of the flesh').

53:14 Mr Snippy Knowall 'Snippy' usually means 'fault-finding, snappish, sharp'; DHL links it with 'know-all', one who pretends to know everything.

53:30 Louis Quatorze hôtel in Paris, See the Everyman Introduction: 'The hotel itself... had been the home of a French ducal family in the time of Louis XIV' (*PR* viii).

54:15 "It was...Apollo...young Mohawk." Quoted in the Everyman Introduction (*PR* vii) ['... that in drawing Indian character he...picture, rather...revolting though...see the Apollo...']. Benjamin West (1738–1820), American painter, exclaimed 'My God, how like it is to a young Mohawk warrior!' when shown the Apollo Belvedere in Rome (John Galt, *The Life and Studies of Benjamin West*, 1816, p. 105); Apollo was the Greek god of light, poetry and music, the son of Zeus and Leda.

54:38 American Odyssey...Circes and swine...Ithacus Circe was an enchantress in Greek mythology, daughter of Helios and Aia; she appears in Homer's *Odyssey* as one who detains travellers on the island of Aeaea and turns them into pigs: see too 97:33–4 and note... there is no such character as Ithacus in the *Odyssey*. Ithaca is Odysseus' homeland; this must be DHL's error or shorthand for Odysseus.

55:7 *The Last of the Mohicans*: It seems probable that DHL did not have a copy to hand when writing the essay. He assumes that the character actually called 'Hawk-eye' – 'the white man whom we shall call Hawk-eye, after the manner of his companions' (*LOM* 26, 30: the name should be added to the list DHL gives at 55:22–3) – is called 'Natty' or 'Leatherstocking'; the 'last of the Delawares' is Uncas, and DHL's plot summary also ignores the name – Alice – of Cora's sister; he replaces it with 'Lily' at 61:33.

55:14 in a chair on DHL revised MS8 (p. 50) to read 'seated a chair on on'; he almost certainly meant 'seated in a chair on' – cf. 61:23 and 220:31 – rather than the reading created by the typist or typesetter of A1, 'seated on a chair on' (p. 72).

55:35 girning, Showing their teeth in rage and disappointment.

56:8 Chingachgook, the Great Serpent. E.g. Natty's comment: 'Chingachgook, which signifies big sarpent, is really a snake, big or little' (*LOM* 58).

58:2 Abraham Lincoln...self-murdering note Lincoln (see note on 20:12) was assassinated by John Wilkes Booth on 15 April 1865.

58:5 a *pis aller*. A last resort (French).

59:7 **a young ... Effingham for a husband.** In *The Pioneers*, Elizabeth Temple marries Oliver Effingham.

59:9 **prunes and prisms** Mrs General, in *Little Dorrit* (1857) by Charles Dickens (1812–70), supplies her young female charge with exercises in genteel elocution and 'very good words for the lips ... especially prunes and prism' (Book II chap. v): plosives were not to be made too explosive.

59:40 **a sort of evasion.** DHL originally wrote 'a lie' in MS8 (p. 55) and revised to the above reading. The typist or typesetter of A1 read the last word as 'vision'; cf. 61:3.

60:23 **The letter killeth.** 2 Corinthians iii. 6 ('the letter killeth, but the spirit giveth life'): used as motto on the title page of *Jude the Obscure* (1895) by Thomas Hardy.

60:31 **Cooper ... travelled west and saw the prairies,** DHL misremembers; although (as the Everyman Introduction points out) Cooper 'chose entirely new scenes' for *The Prairie* and 'resolved to cross the Mississippi and wander over the desolate wastes of the remote Western prairies', he never did so: the closest he ever came was when chiefs of the Native American western tribes visited Washington (*PR* vii).

60:34 **Kentuckian men ... their wolf-women,** A good deal of *The Prairie* is set in Kentucky ... see note on 61:8.

60:40 **Frank Norris' novel, *The Octopus*.** *The Octopus: a Story of California* (London, 1901), by Benjamin Franklin (Frank) Norris (1870–1902). First novel of an unfinished trilogy entitled *The Epic of the Wheat*; it describes the war between the wheat grower and the railroad trust. DHL knew it by 1909: see *Love Among the Haystacks and Other Stories*, ed. John Worthen (Cambridge, 1987), 42:32, and *Letters*, i. 172.

61:1 **the West of Bret Harte** Francis Brett Harte (1836–1902), American short-story writer, who joined in the California gold rush in 1854 and became a journalist in San Francisco; he used his experiences of the west in stories such as 'The Luck of Roaring Camp' (1868) and specialised in stories of 'local colour' employing eccentrics and outsiders as characters.

61:8 **Ishmael ... his huge sons and his were-wolf wife.** The squatter Ishmael Bush – 'pariah-like' because he has passed his 'life ... on the skirts of society' (*PR* 66) – plays a large part in the novel, as do his sons and his wife Esther.

61:9 **like Cyclops** A race of giants in Homer's *Odyssey* with a single eye in the middle of the forehead; one Cyclops, Polyphemus, detains Odysseus and his sailors.

61:39 *borné.* Narrow, limited (French).

62:4 **Adonis rather than Apollo** See 54:15 and note; David Gamut is briefly seen as the 'disciple of Apollo' (*LOM* 20), but only for musical reasons. Alice, however, also sees Uncas 'as she would have looked upon some precious relic of the Grecian chisel' (*LOM* 53).

62:13 **"lilies that fester,"** Shakespeare's sonnet 94, line 14 ('Lilies that fester, smell far worse than weeds'); see too 101:23.

62:30 **Magua—shot from a height [62:28] ... the bird that flies in the high, high sky,** See *LOM* 382: 'his dark person was seen cutting the air with its head downwards, for a fleeting instant ... in its rapid flight to destruction' ... as a proof of his skill, Deerslayer shoots a high-flying eagle (*DS* 437–8) though it is not – in spite of 62:31 – 'invisible'.

62:41 **a more comfortable Jasper.** I.e. Jasper Western (*PF* 117).

63:11 **a bit of perfect paste.** I.e. an artificial (not a real) gem.

64:3 **"castle ... ark,"** See *DS* 25, 27–9, 39, 51–2.

64:11 **just as war has been declared.** I.e. the war between England and France for Canada; the war had actually begun in 1756 and is supposed to be in its 'third year' (*LOM* 7), but on its title page the book is 'a narrative of 1757'.

64:14 **Thomas Hardy's ... sensual and pure,** See DHL's 1914 'Study of Thomas Hardy', *Hardy* 46:5–8: 'There is the dark, passionate, arrogant lady ... There is the fair, passionate, submissive lady'; in chap. IX DHL stresses the opposition in *Jude the Obscure* of the fair, innocent and pure Sue with the dark, sinful and sensual Arabella. See too notes on 60:23 and 88:15.

64:37 **"who governs all things by his providence,"** See *BEA* 112 ['That he governs the world by ...'].

64:39 **Dostoevsky's Idiot,** DHL read *The Idiot* in March 1915; its central figure is the saintly Prince Mishkin. See 131:35; and also see *Letters*, ii. 311, 537 and 543.

65:10 **a tale told by an idiot,** *Macbeth* V. i. 26–7.

65:14 **He says: "Hurt nothing unless you're forced to."** Nothing in *Deerslayer* exactly corresponds to this, but Deerslayer regularly makes similar remarks: e.g. 'I know it's war between your people and mine, but that's no reason why human mortals should slay each other, like savage creatures that meet in the woods' (*DS* 106); ''twould have been wrong to kill a human mortal without an object' (*DS* 117). He also refuses to shoot a buck (see next note) and regrets killing the eagle (see note on 62:30).

65:16 **he puts a bullet through the heart of a beautiful buck,** DHL misremembers; it is Hurry Harry who shoots the 'noble' buck as it drinks from the lake (*DS* 44); Deerslayer refuses to shoot it.

Edgar Allan Poe (Final Version 1923)

66:2 **Edgar Allan Poe.** Poe (1809–49), poet and short-story writer, was born in Boston, but orphaned and brought up in Richmond, Virginia, by John Allan; he worked as a journalist all his life. DHL was using the 1906 Everyman edition of

Tales of Mystery and Imagination, which contained 'Ligeia' (1838), 'Eleonora' (1839), 'Berenice' (1845), 'The Fall of the House of Usher' (1839), 'William Wilson' (1839), 'The Murders in the Rue Morgue' (1840), 'The Gold-Bug' (1843), 'The Pit and the Pendulum' (1843) and 'The Cask of Amontillado' (1846).

66:34 *Ligeia* and *The Fall of the House of Usher*   DHL had linked the stories in *The Crown* (1915): 'He is immersing himself within a keen, fierce, terrible reducing agent. This is true of the hero of Edgar Allan Poe's tales, *Ligeia*, or the *Fall of the House of Usher*... In the name of love, what horrors men perpetrate, and are applauded!' (*Reflections* 284:11–16).

67:34 **master of his own fate,**   Versions of lines from 'Invictus' by W. E. Henley (1849–1903) regularly appear in *Studies*; see 158:22–3 and notes on 87:29, 249:6. Here, cf. 'I am the master of my fate' (l. 15).

68:14 **Joseph Glanville** [68:10]... **feeble will."**   Joseph Glanvill, philosopher (1636–80)... *TMI* 155. The epigraph is, however, apparently Poe's invention.

68:39 **Poe tried alcohol, and any drug he could lay his hand on.**   DHL would have learned about Poe's drinking from the Everyman Introduction (*TMI* x–xi); Bedloe in 'A Tale of the Ragged Mountains' takes morphine (23), Roderick Usher in 'The Fall of the House of Usher' has a 'guttural utterance, which may be observed in the lost drunkard, or the irreclaimable eater of opium' (132), and the narrator of 'Ligeia' (to DHL indistinguishable from Poe: it is 'his own story' – 69:18–19) is 'wild with the excitement of an immoderate dose of opium' (165).

68:41 **his wife: his cousin: a girl with a singing voice.**   The Everyman Introduction recounts how, when he was twenty-six, Poe married his cousin Virginia Clemm (1823–47), and describes her singing (p. x). At 69:16, DHL apparently refers to Poe's wife as 'Lucy', but may simply be continuing the train of thought started in the Cooper essay and its heroine 'Lily' (see note on 55:7).

69:9 **the sympathetic ganglia**   DHL developed his theories of plexuses, ganglia and the affective and volitional centres between 1917 and 1919. A plexus is a complex network of nerves, blood vessels or lymphatic vessels: a ganglion is a complex knot or encapsulated collection of nerve-cell bodies. In part DHL also adopted the language of the chakras ('the centres of primary consciousness' – 358:19–20) which theosophy took over from Hindu mythology: to a writer in the magazine *Theosophy* in March 1888, for example, the chakras were the 'vital and important sympathetic plexuses and preside over all the functions of organic life' (p. 373). DHL's most important source was Janes Pryse's *The Apocalypse Unsealed* (New York, 1910), which he probably read in 1917 (*Letters*, iii. 150 and n. 3), and which provided not only a diagram of 'The Gnostic Chart Concealed in the Apocalypse' (p. [25]), showing the seven chakras in the four main areas of the body, but also an anatomical torso showing 'The Seven Principal Ganglia' (p. 17). Pryse thus grafted on to the idea of the chakras his own version of twentieth-century anatomical fact, so that it encompassed more organs and was mostly expressed in scientific terminology; and in this DHL followed him. See

Reflections xxxi–xxxii. The first appearance of the new language would be in the 1918–19 published versions of the Crèvecoeur essay, 'Fenimore Cooper's Anglo-American Novels' and 'Nathaniel Hawthorne', and in the Melville essay written for the Intermediate Version (1919); it was crucial to the Intermediate Version (1919) Whitman essay. The first appearance of his new language in book form was in *Psychoanalysis and the Unconscious* (written January 1920 and published May 1921). The American artist Earl Brewster (1878–1957), preoccupied with Buddhist philosophy, heard DHL talk about the 'solar plexus' in May 1921 but apparently without the language of ganglia; and by the time the Whitman essay was revised in 1920–2 (see Appendix V), the language had (as here) to some extent been simplified. In 'Education of the People' (written June–July 1920), the theory appears in DHL's writing about the spanking of babies and children: 'Rouse the powerful volitional centres at the base of the spine, and those between the shoulders. Even with stinging rods, rouse them' (*Reflections* 142:11–12).

69:15 **Ligeia! A mental-derived name.** I.e. one which Poe invented; not a name from the classical period.

69:33 **"In stature [69:28]...my shoulder."** *TMI* 156 ['...study save...']

69:39 **His *machine à plaisir*, as somebody says.** A reference to the description of women in chap. ix of *Mademoiselle de Maupin* (1835) by Théophile Gautier (see note on 44:33): 'Ce sont des machines à plaisir' ['They are pleasure-machines']. DHL referred to the novel in *St. Mawr*, ed. Finney, 113:35, and repeated this phrase from it in February 1929 (*Letters*, vii. 179).

70:1 **in terms of matter—jewels, marble, etc.** In 'The Fall of the House of Usher', 'pearl and ruby glowing' (*TMI* 16); 'black granite', 'pearly teeth' and 'ruby-drops' in 'Ligeia' (163, 166, 167).

70:8 **È *finita la commedia*!** Cf. 'La commedia è finita' ['the comedy is over']: the last words of the opera *I Pagliacci* (1892), music and libretto by Ruggiero Leoncavallo (1858–1919), which DHL saw on 31 March 1911 (*Letters*, i. 247).

70:11 **"They were...our race"** *TMI* 157.

70:13 **"They were even fuller...tribe of Nourjahad** *TMI* 157 ['...tribe of the valley of...'].

70:15 **"The hue of the orbs...great length"** *TMI* 157.

70:19 **"The brows...the *expression*."** *TMI* 157–8 ['..."strangeness,"...eyes, was...'].

70:26 **"Ah, word [70:20]...passion to discover...."** *TMI* 158 ['...discover.'].
Democritus (?460–?370 BC), the Greek philosopher, of Abdera, on the coast of Thrace, developed the atomist theory of matter; it is unclear why Poe assigns a well to him, unless he were thinking of the Democritus fragment B172: 'Deep water is useful for many purposes – and then again it is bad: for there is danger of drowning.'

70:27 **each man kills the thing he loves.** From 'The Ballad of Reading Gaol' (1898) by Oscar Wilde (1854–1900), pt 1: 'Yet each man kills the thing he loves'. See too 78:13.

71:10 **at being vamped** Two senses of the word are appropriate: 'being invented or fabricated' (*OED2* 1.c.) and 'being attracted and exploited' (*OED2* v³.2.) – the latter a fashionable sense belonging to the second decade of the twentieth century, and an abbreviation of 'vampire'.

71:22 **an index" (he really meant indication)** DHL is being pedantic; 'index' has meant 'indication' since the seventeenth century (*OED2* 4.b.).

71:24 **"An intensity [71:20] . . . its existence."** *TMI* 159 ['. . . *intensity* . . . speech, . . . index,'].

71:34 **"Of all the women [71:27] . . . habitually uttered."** *TMI* 159.

71:37 **Condors!** Probably the great vulture of California (*Cathartes californianus*), resembling the South American condor in size and other characteristics.

72:11 **are "had."** 'Cheated', slang from the early nineteenth century ('have' *OED2* 15.c.).

72:18 **"That she [72:13] . . . to idolatry."** *TMI* 160 ['. . . only, was . . .'].

72:20 **"How had I . . . such confessions?"** *TMI* 160.

72:28 **"How had I [72:20] . . . capable of expressing."** *TMI* 160–1 ['how had . . . only, that . . . alas! all . . .'].

72:33 **"And from them . . . which he hath."** Cf. Matthew xxv. 29 ('For unto every one that hath shall be given, and he shall have abundance: but from him that hath not shall be taken away even that which he hath').

73:16 **"Out, out [73:9] . . . Conqueror Worm."** *TMI* 161 ['Out—out are the . . . form, . . . tragedy, . . .'].

73:17 **William Blake poem.** DHL is perhaps thinking of 'The Sick Rose', with its 'invisible worm / That flies in the night, / In the howling storm' (ll. 2–4).

73:25 **" 'Oh God!' [73:19] . . . feeble will.' "** *TMI* 161–2 ['O God!'. . . . will with its . . .'].

73:26 **Anche troppo.** Also too much (Italian).

73:28 **has not God said . . . not be forgiven?** Christ says at Matthew xii. 31: 'All manner of sin and blasphemy shall be forgiven unto men: but the blasphemy against the Holy Ghost shall not be forgiven unto men'; see also note on 98:7.

74:7 **Ligeia dies. The husband goes to England,** See *TMI* 162.

74:12 **Rowena Trevanion, of Tremaine.** 'Tre-' is a common Cornish and Welsh prefix to the names of people and places: 'Saxon-Cornish' is, however (as DHL suggests), a strange mixture.

74:22 **"In halls [74:14]...her purity..—"** *TMI* 164 ['...perceiving;...more to demon than to...oh...august, the beautiful, the...'].

74:26 **It is the ghostly Ligeia who pours poison into Rowena's cup.** See *TMI* 166.

74:39 **William James and Conan Doyle and the rest** William James (1842–1910), American philosopher and psychologist, stated that 'Facts, I think, are yet lacking to prove "spirit return"', but he was nevertheless 'somewhat impressed' by the 'favourable conclusions' of spiritualists ('Postscript', *The Varieties of Religious Experience*, New York, 1902)...Sir Arthur Conan Doyle (1859–1930), English author (best known as the creator of Sherlock Holmes), joined the Psychical Research Society in 1891 and was a firm believer in communications from the spirit-world after death; he published *The New Revelation* early in 1918...the 'rest' might have included Sir Oliver Lodge (1851–1940), president of the Society for Psychical Research (1901–4): cf. *Letters*, ii. 440.

75:2 **Lemures,** In Roman mythology, the spirits of the dead.

75:10 **Valley of Many-coloured Grass,** *TMI* 170 ['...of the...Many-Coloured...'].

75:12 **River of Silence,** *TMI* 170.

75:12 **the god Eros** In Greek mythology, the god of love, son of Aphrodite (see note on 267:25).

75:29 **"Toutes ses dents étaient des idées,"** *TMI* 180 ['toutes...'].

75:37 **In psychoanalysis almost every trouble in the psyche is traced to an incest-desire.** DHL alludes to Freud: see, e.g., *The Interpretation of Dreams* (1913), chap. V, section D (β). 'The Fall of the House of Usher' is very discreet: 'sympathies of a scarcely intelligible nature had always existed between them' (*TMI* 139).

76:3 **The root of all evil** Cf. 1 Timothy vi. 10 ('The love of money is the root of all evil').

76:6 **prismatically decomposed, giving ecstasy.** I.e. white light, for an ultimate ecstatic experience.

76:13 **Béranger...le touche il résonne."** Pierre-Jean de Béranger, French poet (1780–1857), whom DHL knew by July 1917 (iii. 136)...*TMI* 128: 'His heart is a suspended lute; the moment one touches it, it sounds' (from 'Le Refus', 1831: the original reads 'Mon coeur...').

76:19 **"I reined [76:15]...eye-like windows."** *TMI* 129.

76:21 **Minute fungi... the eaves.** Poe almost word for word: 'Minute *fungi* over-spread the whole exterior, hanging in a fine tangled web-work from the eaves' (*TMI* 130).

76:23 **Gothic archways... encrimsoned light** Poe almost word for word (*TMI* 131).

76:24 **"an air of stern, deep, irredeemable gloom"** *TMI* 131 ['An air... deep, and...'].

76:29 **large, luminous eye... delicate Hebrew model,** Poe almost word for word (*TMI* 132).

76:34 **some struggle... phantasm, Fear,"** *TMI* 133 ['... FEAR'].

76:38 **a harp in an open window,** I.e. an 'Aeolian harp' – a rectangular sounding box with 8–10 strings across its open side – which interested a number of the Romantics: cf. Coleridge and his poem 'Effusion XXXV' (1795), later re-titled 'The Aeolian Harp'.

77:6 **fervid facility of his impromptus."** *TMI* 135 ['... *facility... impromptus*']. Roderick plays the guitar (134) and sometimes sings to his own playing (135).

77:12 *The Haunted Palace,* *TMI* 136–7.

77:16 **all vegetable things had sentience.** *TMI* 137: 'an opinion of Usher's... was that of the sentience of all vegetable things'.

77:33 **a mysterious disorder, nervous, cataleptic.** Cf. *TMI* 134: 'The disease of the Lady Madeline had long baffled the skill of her physicians. A settled apathy, a gradual wasting away of the person, and frequent although transient affections of a partially cataleptical character, were the unusual diagnosis.' 'Cataleptic' means a disturbance of consciousness, occurring, e.g., in schizophrenia, which leads to the prolonged maintenance of rigid postures.

77:35 **They were twins,** Usher explains this only after Madeline has died (*TMI* 139).

77:39 **Roger,** DHL's error for 'Roderick', in a passage he added while revising the final typescript or the proofs.

78:5 **Her brother... incipient madness... unspeakable terror and guilt.** Cf. *TMI* 139: 'He roamed from chamber to chamber with hurried, unequal, and objectless step'; the narrator is aware of 'the mere inexplicable vagaries of madness, for I beheld him gazing upon vacancy for long hours, in an attitude of the profoundest attention, as if listening to some imaginary sound.' The narrator also observes 'a species of mad hilarity in his eyes' (*TMI* 140), how 'a tremulous quaver, as if of extreme terror, habitually characterised his utterance' (*TMI* 139), and is not surprised that 'his condition terrified – that it infected me' (*TMI* 139). The word 'guilt', however, appears nowhere in Poe's text.

78:7 **a distinct, hollow, metallic, and clangorous, yet apparently muffled, reverberation.** *TMI* 143 ['. . . muffled reverberation'].

78:8 **gibbering,** Cf. *TMI* 143: 'in a low, hurried, and gibbering murmur'.

78:12 **"We have [78:8] . . . not speak."** *TMI* 143–4 ['. . . in the . . . speak!'].

78:23 **"But then [78:15] . . . had anticipated."** *TMI* 144 ['but then . . . there DID . . . death-agonies, bore . . .'].

78:34 **merge,** See note on 153:11.

79:3 **perfect hatred,** Fortunato is walled up alive by Montresor (*TMI* 117:8).

79:21 ***Nemo me . . . impune amat.*** Montresor's Latin motto (*TMI* 209), also the motto of the Crown of Scotland and of all Scottish regiments: 'No-one provokes me with impunity' . . . 'No-one loves me with impunity.'

79:35 **De Quincey** DHL is thinking of the essay 'On Murder considered as One of the Fine Arts' (1827).

80:14 **La Bruyère . . . être seuls.** Jean de la Bruyère (1645–96), French writer and aphorist; aphorism no. 99 in 'De l'homme', *Les Caractères* (1688–99), reads (in part) 'Tout notre mal vient de ne pouvoir être seuls' ['All our unhappiness comes from not being able to be alone'], and states that dissipation, ignorance, jealousy, forgetfulness of self and of God all derive from that failure. The aphorism was derived from Blaise Pascal (1623–62), *Pensées* (1669), ii. 139: 'tout le malheur des hommes vient d'une seule chose, qui est de ne savoir pas demeurer en repos, dans une chambre' ['all the unhappiness of man derives from a single thing, which is not knowing how to stay quiet, in one room'].

80:18 **do not live to eat,** Now traditional apothegm – 'We must eat to live, not live to eat' – originally from *L'Avare* (1668), III. v ('Il faut manger pour vivre et non pas vivre pour manger'), by Molière (1622–73).

80:32 **love killed him.** Not literally, though the circumstances of Poe's death in 1849 were kept mysterious in the Everyman Introduction, which stated that – having been made drunk by 'a gang of ruffians' – he was found 'dying in some sordid place' (*TMI* xi). DHL, perhaps thinking of Ibsen's *Hedda Gabler* (1890) and the death of Løvborg, may have believed this meant a brothel. In fact Poe was found on Election Day in an alcohol-related stupor inside a Baltimore tavern which also served that day as a polling-place, was taken to hospital, and died several days later either of alcohol-related causes or of exposure to the elements.

Nathaniel Hawthorne and *The Scarlet Letter*
(Final Version 1923)

81:3 *The Scarlet Letter.* The first novel of his maturity (1850) by Nathaniel Hawthorne (1804–64), New England writer of novels and short stories. Hawthorne's first American ancestor had arrived in Massachusetts as early as 1630; he himself studied with Longfellow (see note on 81:15), and worked as a journalist, tax inspector and surveyor for the port of Salem (described in the novel's opening chapter). See too note on 99:20. In 1837 he published the first series of *Twice-Told Tales* (the second in 1841) and in 1846 *Mosses from an Old Manse.* *The Scarlet Letter* is set in the Boston area; it alludes to a number of real-life people and events – e.g. Anne Hutchinson (*TSL* 198), the Rev. John Wilson (*TSL* 81–5, 131–5, 139–40, 180–2, 303, 314) and Governor John Winthrop, whose death-bed in 1649 is attended in the novel by Wilson, Hester Prynne and Chillingworth (*TSL* 181, 183–4, 189).

81:8 *As You Like It...Forest Lovers...Morte D'Arthur.* Shakespeare's play (*c.* 1598), with a celebrated (and at times idyllic) woodland setting (see too note on 92:40); at 244:10–12, DHL notes that 'In idyllic romance, all external conditions are made subservient to the will of the human psyche: everything occurs as you like it'... novel (1898) by the novelist, poet and essayist Maurice Hewlett (1861–1923); DHL knew it by March 1909 (*Letters,* i. 120) and it influenced his own story 'A Fragment of Stained Glass' (1907–11) (see *The Prussian Officer,* ed. Worthen, note on 92:13)... prose romance (1485) by Sir Thomas Malory (d. 1471) of ideal and heroic knighthood, set in a landscape of castles, dragons, maidens needing rescue, love and honour.

81:12 **earthly story with a hellish meaning.** A parable is proverbially defined as 'an earthly story with a heavenly meaning'.

81:15 **Longfellow** Henry Wadsworth Longfellow (1807–82), American poet and prose writer, a college friend of Hawthorne at Bowdoin (see *TSL* vii).

81:18 **"never saw him in time."... "frail effulgence of eternity."** DHL's source for the first quotation (given accurately at 82:7) was certainly the essay on Hawthorne in Sherman's *Americans* (see note on 15:20 for DHL's knowledge of the book and his opportunity for using material from it in his revision of *Studies*). Sophia Hawthorne wrote of her husband in her journal: 'I have never thought of him as in time' (quotation taken from Julian Hawthorne's *Nathaniel Hawthorne and His Wife,* New York, 1889, i. 373); Sherman quotes first the whole passage, then the phrase 'never thought of him as in time' (*Americans,* pp. 136, 138).

The second quotation (in *OED2,* 'effulgence' is 'splendid radiance, *lit.* and *fig.*') is apparently DHL's invention, linking a reminiscence of Shelley's phrase 'the white radiance of eternity' (*Adonais,* 1821, LII, 463) to two remarks of Hawthorne ('I was basking quietly in the sunshine of eternity' and 'we are... inheritors of eternity', *Americans,* pp. 130 and 129, both quoted from Hawthorne's *American Note-Books,* 7 April and 4 October 1840). DHL himself would use the word 'effulgence' twice in his

1923 collection *Birds, Beasts and Flowers* (*The Complete Poems of D. H. Lawrence*, ed. Vivian de Sola Pinto and Warren Roberts, 1964, i. 288, 328).

82:15 the meaning of the Cross symbol. Cf. DHL's poem 'Tortoise Shell': 'The Cross, the Cross / Goes deeper in than we know' (*Complete Poems*, ed. Pinto and Roberts, i. 354).

83:29 a beautiful, cultured woman... outrages me." DHL may have had in mind Lady Ottoline Morrell (1873–1938), whom he met in 1915; it is probably not a coincidence that, in *Women in Love*, Hermione Roddice (a character with strong links with Ottoline Morrell) should hit Rupert Birkin (a character with strong links with DHL himself) over the head; or that Birkin should remark to her 'If one cracked your skull perhaps one might get a spontaneous, passionate woman out of you, with real sensuality' (*WL* 42:35).

83:34 condemned to manual labour... died first. The eldest son George (1876–1967) of Arthur Lawrence and Lydia Lawrence (1851–1910) worked briefly as a miner before going into business in Nottingham; the second son, William Ernest (1878–1901), became a clerk and worked in London; the third son, DHL, trained and worked as a school-teacher. Arthur survived Lydia by fourteen years.

84:11 *Co-ordinate!* To bring into proper combined order as parts of a whole. There may possibly be a reminiscence of Emerson on Shakespeare: 'An omnipresent humanity co-ordinates all his faculties' (*Representative Men: Shakespeare*, 1844, *Works*, i. 362).

84:25 The blood must be *shed*, says Jesus. Cf. Matthew xxvi. 28 ('For this is my blood of the new testament, which is shed for many for the remission of sins').

85:3 aeroplane *sensation* There is no precedent in *OED2* for the use of 'aeroplane' as an adjective, but the dictionary gives many examples of its use in the first thirty years of the twentieth century as an adjectival noun: 'aeroplane ambulance' (1914), 'aeroplane duty' (1923), etc. In 'Education of the People' (1920), DHL referred to 'aeroplane thrills' (*Reflections* 132:7–8).

85:10 Dimmesdale... Hester... seduce him. Hawthorne gives no details of the seduction: DHL's 'gloatingly' (85:17) is unwarranted.

85:26 "Seduce me, Mrs Hercules." I.e. as opposed to the clichéd romantic demand made to the heroic male: 'Save me, Mr Hercules!' Cf. 'The Wilful Woman': 'Mr Hercules had better think twice' (*St. Mawr*, ed. Finney, 199:33–4).

85:35 Alpha... Adama! The first letter of the Greek alphabet ... DHL's coinage.

85:38 gold thread... upon the scaffold See *TSL* 66: 'fantastic flourishes of gold thread' ... Hester Prynne stands on the platform of the pillory, 'displayed to the surrounding multitude, at about the height of a man's shoulders above the street' (*TSL* 70).

85:39 the Magna Mater... Abel! The Great Mother, the great female principle, worshipped by the Romans from 204 BC (see Sir James George Frazer, *The Golden*

Bough, 1890–1915, Part IV, i, 263) and identified with Astarte at 91:13; a Semitic goddess, sometimes called the Syrian goddess, 'latterly of lunar nature' (Sir Edward B. Tylor, *Primitive Culture*, 1903, ii. 301, which DHL read in April 1916 – *Letters*, ii. 593). Pryse's *The Apocalypse Unsealed* described 'the Goddess Rhea, who was also called Cybêle, Astartê . . . Her numerous temples abounded in "consecrated women", and as the *Magna Mater*, "the Great Mother" of these prostitutes, she was worshipped with shameless orgiastic rites' (p. 184). Cf. DHL's August 1917 letter to the writer, socialist, Jungian psychoanalyst and Zionist Dr David Eder (1865–1936): 'I should like to talk to you also about the lunar myth – the lunar trinity – father – mother – son, with the son as consort of the mother, the *magna Mater*. It seems to me your whole psycho-analysis rests on this myth . . .' (*Letters*, iii. 150). See too 106:20 and *WL* 200:12–21, 246:30 . . . Abel was the son of Adam and Eve, killed by his brother Cain (Genesis iv. 8).

85:40 **Admirable!** As David Ellis pointed out (*Dying Game*, p. 629), probably derived from Sherman's quotation in *Americans* of Hawthorne's own description in 'Endicott and the Red Cross' (1842) of a woman wearing an 'A', and his suggestion that it might lead people to believe it meant 'Admirable or anything rather than Adulteress' (pp. 141–2). DHL must have added it to the typescript of the *Studies* in January 1923.

86:1 **Mary of the Bleeding Heart . . . Mater Adolorata!** I.e. of the Sacred Heart: a common representation of the Virgin Mary in Roman Catholic iconography . . . 'Adolorata' (unlike Mater, 'mother') is not Latin; DHL is playing on words like 'adultery', 'adorata' and 'adulate' and creating an appropriate combination to stand against the conventional term 'Mater Dolorosa', 'sorrowful mother' (Latin): the Virgin Mary, sorrowing for the dead Christ.

86:18 **"Had there [86:12] . . . the world."** *TSL* 70 ['. . . sinless motherhood . . .'].

86:23 **"Here was [86:21] . . . had borne."** *TSL* 70–1 ['Here, there was the . . . and the more . . . infant that she . . .'].

86:31 **wipe off the mud with your hair, another Magdalen.** See John xii. 3 and Luke vii. 36–50 for Mary Magdalen wiping Jesus' feet with her hair; another version appears at Mark xiv. 3–9. Cf. too *Letters*, iii. 179–80.

86:33 **duchesses used to stitch themselves coronets.** DHL presumably refers to needlework or embroidery, and to the stitching of coronets on (e.g.) handkerchiefs.

87:9 **To the pure all things etc.** See Titus i. 15.

87:19 **whipping it, piercing it with thorns, macerating himself.** The single reference in the novel is: 'In Mr. Dimmesdale's secret closet, under lock and key, there was a bloody scourge. Oftentimes, this Protestant and Puritan divine had plied it on his own shoulders, laughing bitterly at himself the while, and smiting so much the more pitilessly because of that bitter laugh' (*TSL* 174–5). There is no mention of piercing with thorns, nor of 'searing' (254:5), though Hester does feel her breast seared by 'the burning letter' when about to remove it (*TSL* 298); and though it is suggested that the letter 'A' on Dimmesdale's flesh may be a result of his 'inflicting a hideous torture on himself', this is 'conjectural' (*TSL* 311) and other explanations are provided. To macerate is to wear away the body by fasting: it is Dimmesdale's 'custom, too, as it has been that of many other pious Puritans, to fast . . . as an act of penance' (*TSL* 175).

87:21 **give it what for,** I.e. punish it, hurt it (slang).

87:29 **I am the master . . . the Captain of my soul . . . clutch of circumstance,"** etc., etc. Further versions of 'Invictus' by Henley, ll. 5–6, 13–16 (see note on 67:34).

> In the fell clutch of circumstance
> I have not winced nor cried aloud . . .
>
> It matters not how strait the gate,
> How charged with punishments the scroll,
> I am the master of my fate;
> I am the captain of my soul.

See too 158:22–3.

87:32 **Achilles Heel** As a baby, Achilles was dipped in the river Styx to make his body invulnerable: the heel by which his mother held him, however, remained a small (but eventually fatal) weakness.

87:35 **"For the will therein lieth, which dieth not— —"** From the epigraph to Poe's *Ligeia* by 'Glanvill': see note on 68:14 ['And the . . .'].

87:37 **The Scarlet Woman . . . Sister of Mercy . . . in the late war.** Cf. Revelation xvii. 1–5 . . . strictly speaking, member of a Roman Catholic sisterhood founded in Dublin 1827; but the name is popularly applied to any nursing sisterhood, and Hester is 'self-ordained a Sister of Mercy, or, we may rather say, the world's heavy hand had so ordained her . . . The letter was the symbol of her calling' (*TSL* 194) . . . the First World War.

87:39 **Hester urges . . . having any.** See *TSL* chaps. xix and xx. Dimmesdale refuses to go away by himself, but at their forest meeting accepts a journey away with Hester: it is not correct that 'He didn't see the point' (88:8). His reactions when he returns from the forest further reveal his emotional attachment to Hester. Roger Chillingworth, however, discovers their plan, and arranges to travel with them; Dimmesdale gives his final sermon, is impelled to mount the scaffold and tell the truth. He says to Hester 'Is not this better than what we dreamed of in the forest?' (*TSL* 306); then dies.

88:3 *Plus ça change . . . même chose.* 'The more things change, the more they are the same': now proverbial, originally coined by Alphonse Karr (1808–90) in *Les Guêpes* (1849) ['. . . *change et plus . . .*'].

88:13 dree out his weird. Correctly 'dree his weird', endure his suffering; archaism first revived by Scott in *The Antiquary*, chap. xxxii. DHL is perhaps also thinking of the other meaning of 'dree', to draw.

88:15 As Angel Clare...hated Tess...Jude...hated Sue: DHL had first discussed these characters from Hardy's novels *Tess of the D'Urbervilles* (1891) and *Jude the Obscure* (1895) in chap. IX of 'Study of Thomas Hardy'; see *Hardy* 97:3–100:36, 101:5–122:29. Angel Clare leaves Tess because of her rape by another man before their marriage; Jude Fawley, however (as DHL tacitly admits), continues to love Sue Bridehead.

88:31 '"Shall we not [88:24]...I fear!"' *TSL* 309 ['...close to his...Surely, we...eyes! Tell...hush!' said...thoughts! I...'].

89:8 Hester...a public nurse. Here, and at 90:30–1, DHL follows the Introductory chapter's account of Hester's later years: 'It had been her habit, from an almost immemorial date, to go about the country as a kind of voluntary nurse, and doing whatever miscellaneous good she might' (*TSL* 43). Although Hester watches by the death-bed of Governor Winthrop (*TSL* 183), it is to measure him for his grave-clothes: she lives by her needle-work (see *TSL* 100–2). DHL's statement that she 'becomes at last an acknowledged saint' (89:8–9) refers to her time in New England after Pearl's marriage, when she 'gained from many people the reverence due to an angel' (*TSL* 43).

90:38 sugar-plum...scorpion A small sweet, made of boiled sugar...cf. Luke xi. 12 ('if he shall ask an egg, will he offer him a scorpion?').

91:9 "She had...gorgeously beautiful." *TSL* 103 ['...Oriental...beautiful,'].

91:13 Hecate Goddess of the underworld in Greek myth, used by Shakespeare *c*. 1604 in *Macbeth* IV. i.

91:15 the Mormons Popular name for members of the Church of Jesus Christ of the Latter-Day Saints, religious group founded in the USA in 1830. Their original, much-publicised belief in polygamy was, after 1890, rarely put into practice.

91:19 grey nurse, The colour grey is regularly associated with Hester: see *TSL* 254, 258, 273, 275, 276, 315; and see below, 95:26.

91:24 ithyphallic images With an erect penis: such sculptures were carried in the ancient festivals of Bacchus. Seltzer replaced the phrase with 'images of sex-worship', although 'ithyphallic' was allowed to appear a page later (p. 141).

91:29 "The poor...succour them." *TSL* 104 ['...stretched forth to...'].

91:34 "She was...a curse." *TSL* 104 ['...martyr, indeed...for enemies...'].

91:40 "She grew...one child." *TSL* 105 ['...one only...'].

92:8 **"But sometimes [92:3] . . . sinned alone?"** *TSL* 106 ['. . . still a . . . for, in that brief interval, . . . had sinned anew . . .'].

92:26 **my first lover,** Presumably Jessie Chambers (1887–1944): see Worthen, *The Early Years*, pp. 152–63.

92:37 **an Italian Count** DHL's assumption; Pearl's husband is titled and not English, and her letters bear 'armorial seals . . . unknown to English heraldry' (*TSL* 316). Hester has mentioned to Dimmesdale the possibility of escaping to 'pleasant Italy' (*TSL* 238), and that may have determined DHL.

92:40 **And so . . . rot and rot.** Shakespeare's *As You Like It*, II. vii. 26–7; DHL taught the play to his pupils in Croydon in 1911 (*Letters*, i. 245).

93:3 **"which often . . . born at all."** *TSL* 198 ['and which . . . ask, in . . . for ill or good that . . .'].

93:10 **Her own mother . . . demon of plague, or scarlet fever,** It is not Hester Prynne who makes the comparison but the narrator, describing Pearl's response to children who mock her: 'She resembled, in her fierce pursuit of them, an infant pestilence – the scarlet fever, or some such half-fledged angel of judgement' (*TSL* 125). It is not, either, Hester but 'neighbouring townspeople' who use the word 'demon' about Pearl (*TSL* 121, 122, 295, 315). The inaccuracies do not appear in the First Version (1918–19) of the essay.

93:13 *understanding,* Cf. 'Pearl's wonderful intelligence' (*TSL* 120): Hawthorne does not, however, use the word 'understanding' about her.

93:14 **a hit across the mouth,** Pearl never does this, though she pelts her mother's breast with flowers (*TSL* 119); but cf. Gudrun Brangwen in *FWL* 157:22–9.

93:22 **smarm.** Fulsome flattery, derived from the grease or oil applied to hair: DHL's use here predates the first *OED2* (1937) usage of the noun in this sense, though the verb 'smarm' and adjective 'smarmy' had been common from the late nineteenth century.

93:28 **"sadness."** Cf. Hester looking 'sadly' (*TSL* 119) into Pearl's eyes when the child is throwing flowers at her, and feeling 'inexpressibly sad' (*TSL* 117).

93:33 **"The child . . . to discover."** *TSL* 111 ['. . . to be discovered." '].

94:4 **"a look . . . human child."** *TSL* 113 ['. . . intelligent, so . . .'].

94:8 **flatly refuses any Heavenly Father,** *TSL* 120, 136.

94:22 **Francis Bacon . . . Roger Bacon.** Philosopher, essayist and statesman (1561–1626), often thought of as a scientist (his statue was alongside that of Sir Isaac Newton on the University College of Nottingham building which DHL attended) because of his classification of the sciences in *The Advancement of Learning* (1605), where he referred to 'degenerate natural magic, alchemy, astrology' as subjects dependent

upon 'imagination and belief' (II. viii. 3)... Franciscan monk, scholar and scientist
(1214–92), whose *Opus Majus* is a compendium of all the sciences of his age.

94:25 **the Hermetic philosophies.** I.e. the occult philosophical and theosophical
writings ascribed to Hermes Trismegistus (the Greek name for the Egyptian god
Thoth) by the neo-Platonists (in particular relating to alchemy); the subject of much
discussion by Helena Petrovna Blavatsky in *Isis Unveiled* (1877), e.g. i. 406–7, 507.
Theosophy in modern times is a system claiming 'a knowledge of nature profounder
than is obtained from empirical science, and contained in an esoteric [intended only
for a selected or initiated minority] tradition of which the doctrines of the various
historical religions are held to be only the exoteric [intended for more than a selected
or initiated minority] expression' (*OED2*).

94:29 **Shakspere's whole tragic wail** Cf. DHL's poem 'When I read Shakespeare—'
(1928): 'When I read Shakespeare I am struck with wonder / that such trivial people
should muse and thunder / in such lovely language' (ll. 1–3).

94:37 **her last oath,** Misleading: DHL is referring to the 'oath' she swears to
Chillingworth at the start of the novel to keep his secret (*TSL* 95); the First
Version (1918–19) explicitly places the oath 'At the very beginning' (253:11).

95:3 ' "Why dost [94:39]...thy soul!"' *TSL* ['...thou like...round about
us...thou enticed...bond that...soul," he answered,...not thine!"].

Hawthorne's *Blithedale Romance* (Final Version 1923)

96:3 *Blithedale Romance.* Hawthorne's third novel (1852); see note on 99:20.

96:24 **like so many other Crowned Heads, has abdicated his authority.** Four
European monarchs vanished 1917–22: in Russia, with the execution of Nicholas II
(1868–1918, ruled 1894–1917) on 16 July 1918; in Germany, with the abdication of
Kaiser Wilhelm II (1859–1941, ruled 1888–1918) on 10 November 1918: in Austria
and in Hungary, with the abdication of Karl I & IV (1887–1922, ruled 1916–18) on 11
and 13 November 1918; and in Turkey, with the sultanate ended by Kemal Atatürk
(1881–1938) in 1922, the last ruler having been Abd ül-Hamid II (1876–1909), who
had lost his throne to the 'Young Turks'.

97:6 **in a pickle.** In an awkward situation.

97:29 **like Cleopatra...drowns a lover a night...Nilus Flux...Candida!**
DHL's knowledge of Cleopatra would have derived from legend, from Plutarch's *Lives*,
from Shakespeare's play *Antony and Cleopatra* (*c.* 1608) and from the play *Caesar and
Cleopatra* (1901) by the Anglo-Irish dramatist George Bernard Shaw (1856–1950);
he would only have found in legend the idea that Cleopatra had her lovers drowned
(though immersing a lover in her river Nile has a sexual meaning too), but he would
have found in Shakespeare the identification of Cleopatra with the river Nile
(I. v. 25) as well as the form 'Nilus' (V. ii. 52). 'Flux' means a flow or discharge

and also a kind of instability (cf. 'white flux' 153:7) – things which DHL associated with a certain kind of dominant female sexuality ... by a movement of thought which may well include *Antony and Cleopatra*'s use of the word 'discandy' (IV. x. 33) and the memory of Shaw's *Caesar and Cleopatra*, almost certainly a reference to Shaw's earlier play *Candida* (1895): the dominant female Candida chooses her husband Jacob Morell, rather than go off with the man who loves her, the poet Eugene Marchbanks, because her husband is the weaker man and so needs her more.

97:31 **Pearl ... before swine.** See Matthew vii. 6 ('Give not that which is holy unto the dogs, neither cast ye your pearls before swine, lest they trample them under their feet, and turn again and rend you').

97:33 **when Circe lies with a man, *he's* a swine after it,** Homer gives no warrant for DHL's assumption that Circe seduced men before transforming them.

97:37 **Doom! What a beautiful northern word.** The word derives from the Old English *dōm* and the Old Norse *dómr*, meaning 'judgement'; a 'doom ring' was, e.g., a circle of stones forming the boundary of an Old Norse place of judgement.

97:39 **Who will write that Allegory?** Cf. the Middle English allegory *Pearl* (*c*. 1380).

98:5 **Now Pearl ... let's drop you in the vinegar.** Meaning 'make life nastier – and sourer – for you', but also a continuation of the Cleopatra theme. If a vinegar (or wine) were sufficiently (i.e. undrinkably) acid, it would dissolve many things, including pearls; but Cleopatra's legendary method of demonstrating extravagance (recorded by Pliny) has little scientific basis.

98:7 **the Holy Ghost. "*It shall not be forgiven him.*"** I.e. 'the blasphemy against the Holy Ghost shall not be forgiven unto men' (Matthew xii. 31); see too note on 73:28.

98:10 **The Father forgives: the Son forgives:** See, e.g., Ecclesiasticus ii. 11 ('For the Lord is full of compassion and mercy, longsuffering, and very pitiful, and forgiveth sins') and Ephesians i. 3–7 ('Jesus Christ ... In whom we have redemption through his blood, the forgiveness of sins, according to the riches of his grace').

98:13 **the Holy Ghost is within you ...*is* you:** Cf. 1 Corinthians vi. 19 ('your body is the temple of the Holy Ghost which is in you').

98:29 *Quos vult perdere Deus, dementat prius.* Common Latin translation (usually *Quos Deus vult perdere ...*) of an unknown and anonymous Greek tragedian's line appended in a scholium to the *Antigone* of Sophocles (498–406 BC): 'Those whom God wishes to destroy, he first drives mad'; cf. the variant 'Jupiter' for 'Deus' at 206:30.

98:31 **Battening on** Feeding gluttonously on.

98:38 *The House of the Seven Gables* Hawthorne's third novel (1851); the 'Father' (98:39) is presumably Judge Jaffrey Pynchon, 'dark-browed, grisly-bearded' (chap. viii), who dies towards the end of the novel; his only son, however, dies before he does.

99:2 these new vacuum cleaners. *OED2* gives 1903 as the first recorded date of usage of 'vacuum cleaner'; by the mid-1920s they were fairly common in the USA and Britain.

99:9 the black cloth of a camera I.e. when the photographer puts his head under a black cloth covering the shutter (and plate) of a plate camera, to check the exposure.

99:10 Vivat industria! Long live industry! (Latin).

99:14 America ... nothing but a Main Street. A reference to *Main Street* (New York, 1920), the novel which first established the reputation of Sinclair Lewis (1885–1951): a devastating account of American small-town provincialism. DHL read it in February 1922 'and it gave me horrors' (*Letters*, iv. 201).

99:20 Brook Farm experiment. Hawthorne was one of the participants in the group which took over Brook Farm (near West Roxbury, Massachusetts), to experiment with the idea of a better life than any which could be found in conventional society (a similar experiment to Thoreau's life beside Walden Pond). The project lasted 1841–7, although the sceptical Hawthorne himself left after a few months, in 1841; others involved included the writer George Ripley (1802–80), who directed the experiment, and Dana; ideas for it also came from John Sullivan Dwight (1813–93), who joined in November 1841, William Ellery Channing the Younger (1818–1901) and Theodore Parker (1810–60). DHL's reference to 'bookfarming' (99:31–2) refers to Hawthorne's use of Brook Farm in *The Blithedale Romance*: cf. the 'Preface' (*BR* 1–3). In Taos in October 1922, DHL discussed the failure of the experiment when out riding with Maurice Lesemann (Nehls, ii. 195).

99:24 the Oversoul, Ralph Waldo Emerson's name for the deity regarded philosophically as the supreme spirit which animates the universe; his essay 'The Over-Soul' defines it as the 'eternal ONE ... within which every man's particular being is contained' (*Essays 1st and 2nd Series*, Everyman's Library, 1906, p. 150).

100:5 winding the horn Archaism and/or poeticism (originally sixteenth-century) for 'blowing a note or signal on'. E.g. 'Ode to Evening' (1746) by William Collins (1721–59): 'Or where the beetle winds / His small but sullen horn' (ll. 11–12). Hawthorne's horn is literal: 'I shall sound the horn at daybreak' says Silas Foster (*BR* 37), and it sounds 'harsh, uproarious, inexorably drawn out, and as sleep-dispelling as if this hard-hearted old yeoman had got hold of the trump of doom' (*BR* 39). See also next note.

100:8 "Never did I feel more spectral," Not a quotation from the novel, although the word 'spectral' – a favourite with idealist American writers – appears three times in it (*BR* 97, 109, 209). The 1920–1 version of the essay (see Appendix IV) confirms that DHL was rephrasing a passage from Hawthorne's journal quoted in the Everyman

Introduction: ' "The real Me... was never an associate of the community: there has been a spectral Appearance there sounding the horn at daybreak, and milking the cows, and hoeing potatoes and raking hay, toiling in the sun and doing me the honour to assume my name. But this spectre was not myself." / That this spectral self had fully done its other work *The Blithedale Romance* is the original and unseen witness' (*BR* vii–viii). Most of the journal passage was also quoted by Stuart Sherman in *Americans*, p. 131.

100:22 **amiable spouse... sanctum sanctorum** Hawthorne married Sophia Peabody in 1842: his wife had borne two children by 1849... holy of holies (Latin).

100:28 **The narrator: whom we will call Nathaniel.** In the novel, he is Miles Coverdale. This may be an indication of DHL's fading memory of the book (see notes on 100:8, 101:3, 101:28, 101:30). In the First Version (1918–19) he is 'Hawthorne, the I' (256:5).

100:31 **Margaret Fuller,** Sarah Margaret Fuller (1810–50), American writer, journalist and pioneering feminist; acquaintance of Hawthorne, Emerson and Thoreau, she edited (1840–2) the journal of the Transcendentalists the *Dial* (in which Hawthorne published essays) and wrote the influential *Woman in the Nineteenth Century* (1845).

101:3 **Zenobia's Husband... by the back door.** Professor Westervelt actually makes his first appearance in the novel in the wood, where he addresses the narrator (*BR* 92–8).

101:8 **The two men... surpassing the love of women,** Cf. David's lament for Jonathan, 2 Samuel i. 26 ('thy love to me was wonderful, passing the love of women'). See note on 154:16.

101:11 **Hephaestos of the underworld.** The (lame) Greek god of fire and metal-working (Roman equivalent Vulcan).

101:28 **Zenobia... goes off without her flower.** The most obvious sign that DHL's memory of the novel had faded by 1922: Zenobia dramatically drowns herself at the end of the book, murdered in effect by Hollingsworth, who has spurned her in favour of Priscilla; the body is recovered and buried at Blithedale. She does, however, take the 'jewelled flower' out of her hair just before her suicide (*BR* 229). In the First Version (1918–19), DHL had simply noted 'But poor Zenobia drowns herself' (257:15–16).

101:30 **loved Prissy all the while.** This confession does not, however, appear in the *Débacle*, as DHL suggests, but at the very end of the *Conclusion*: the confession forms the last sentence of the last chapter of the book, 'Miles Coverdale's Confession' (*BR* 250).

101:34 **leaning totteringly on the arm... Gone are all dreams of asylums,** An exaggeration; even in the First Version (1918–19) of the essay, Hollingsworth simply 'walks, leaning on her arm' (258:23), but in the novel he walks without leaning on Priscilla at all, simply with 'a childlike or childish tendency to press close, and closer still, to the side of the slender woman whose arm was within his'; and though Priscilla is 'protective and watchful' she is also marked by 'a deep, submissive, unquestioning reverence' towards her companion (*BR* 245) . . . Hollingsworth also accuses himself of being 'busy with a single murderer' (*BR* 246): i.e. himself.

102:20 **A wireless apparatus . . . taking down messages.** As is explicit in the 1920–1 version, DHL describes wireless telegraphy apparatus receiving and trans- mitting messages (400:7–9). Marconi's development could send messages 14 km in 1897 and intercontinental wireless-telegraphy was being used experimentally by 1906. 'Broadcasting' was only developed in the early 1920s: the first experimental radio broadcast took place in December 1920 but regular broadcasts did not start in Europe until 1923–4.

102:25 **unknown magnetos,** A magneto is normally either a small electric gen- erator (often for providing the spark in an internal combustion engine) in which a magnetic field is produced by a permanent magnet, or the *combining form* indicating magnetism or magnetic properties, as in 'magnetosphere'.

103:12 **Rien de certain.** Nothing certain (French).

103:29 **by this time he stinketh.** Said to Christ about Lazarus – dead for four days – by his sister Martha, before Christ brought Lazarus back to life (John xi. 39); there may also be a reminiscence of the story of Father Zossima in Dostoevsky's *The Brothers Karamazov*, whose saintly corpse unforgettably stinks (Book 7, chap. 1). See too 122:30 and note on 147:13.

Dana's *Two Years Before the Mast* (Final Version 1923)

105:2 *Two Years Before the Mast.* Richard Henry Dana (1815–82) published the book in 1840; it was re-issued with an additional 'Concluding Chapter' in 1869. It can be established that DHL used the Nelson's Classics edition (n.d. [1912]), with an anonymous Introduction; he had a copy of the book in May 1916 (*Letters*, ii. 614) and on 12 June 1916 recommended it to Koteliansky: 'Dana's *Two Years* you can get for 6d – (Nelsons)' (*Letters*, ii. 615). He was not to know that the Nelsons Classics edition omitted two chapters completely, incorporated chapter titles which Dana had not supplied, did not print the 'Concluding Chapter' included in most texts (e.g. in the 1912 Everyman edition, Introduction by J. E. Patterson), and introduced extensive cuts throughout, in words, phrases and paragraphs. The mutilated text and Introduction were also used in the edition issued by Blackie and Son Limited (n.d. [*c.* 1904]), the Introduction in both editions providing information DHL could probably not have obtained from anywhere else (see notes on 272:5, 8), but textual differences confirm that it was the Nelson's Classics text which he used. Few of his quotations suffered much, as it happened, but it was obviously unfortunate that his reading text should have mutilated Dana's novel so badly.

105:7 **Novels like Thomas Hardy's and pictures like the Frenchman Millet's.** E.g. *The Return of the Native* (1878) and *Tess of the D'Urbervilles* by Thomas Hardy;

Jean François Millet (1814–75) was famous for his pictures of peasants at work in the fields: e.g. *The Gleaners* (1857).

105:13 **Thomas Hardy's pessimism**   Taken for granted here, as in the 'Study of Thomas Hardy' (*Hardy* 49:36 and note); pessimism had been a commonplace of Hardy criticism during the late nineteenth century (see, e.g., Michael Millgate, *Thomas Hardy*, 1987, p. 321).

105:16 **slow Laocoön snake.**   In Greek mythology, a great snake killed the Trojan priest of Apollo and his two sons by strangling them. See *Letters*, i. 136.

105:18 **Tolstoi had it,**   See, e.g., *Anna Karenina* (1877), Part Two, chaps. 12–13, with their celebration of the spring; Tolstoy also founded a school for peasant children in 1860.

106:5 **Transcendentalism.**   The religio-philosophical teaching of the New England school of thought: 'What is popularly called Transcendentalism among us, is Idealism' (Emerson, *Lectures*, 'The Transcendentalist', 1842).

106:17 **Giovanni Verga;**   Italian writer (1840–1922), much concerned with the lives of peasants in Sicily; in 1922 DHL translated his novel *Mastro-Don Gesualdo* (1889: tr. 1923), and would follow that with Verga's short stories *Vita dei Campi* (1880: tr. as *Little Novels of Sicily*, 1925) and the short stories in *Cavalleria Rusticana* (1880: tr. 1928).

106:22 **Swinburne tried, in England.**   DHL is probably thinking of 'The Triumph of Time' (1866), stanzas 33–8, by the English poet Algernon Charles Swinburne (1837–1909): e.g. 'I will go back to the great sweet mother, / Mother and lover of men, the sea' (ll. 257–8).

106:27 **Dana's eyes failed ... at Harvard.**   'Young Dana, while at Harvard University, which he entered in 1832, became troubled with an affection of the eyes that prevented him from continuing his studies' (*TYB* i); the reason for his eye problem had been an attack of measles in 1831. He himself comments that he went to sea in 1834 'to cure ... by a long absence from books and study, a weakness of the eyes which had obliged me to give up my pursuits' (*TYB* [7]).

106:34 **KNOW THYSELF.**   Written up in Greek (gnothi safton) in the temple at Delphi: 'From the gods comes the saying "Know thyself"' (Juvenal, *Satires*, xi. 27).

107:14 **"Nothing can [107:10] ... nature can give."**   *TYB* 11 ['Nothing will ... *with the* ... wide sad ...'].

107:28 **"—But one of [107:19] ... took his flight."**   *TYB* 34 ['but one ... rising on the ... wings and ...'].

108:7 **KNOWLEDGE ... the Tree. The Cross.**   DHL makes the common link between the Tree of the Knowledge of Good and Evil in the Garden of Eden (see Genesis ii. 17) and the tree – or cross – on which Christ was crucified.

108:19 "Between five [108:10] . . . the rigging." *TYB* 29 ['. . . starbowlines* . . . reef-tackles . . . *pin us down* . . .']. Dana provides asterisked footnotes for some of his terms: 'Starbowlines' are 'the starboard watch' (*TYB* 29).

108:24 **Juan Fernandez, Crusoe's island,** The supposed original of the uninhabited island occupied by Robinson Crusoe: see note on 34:33.

109:4 "Sam was [108:35] . . . gone by—" *TYB* 83 ['Sam by this time was seized *up* . . . hand the bight of a thick, strong rope . . . and almost faint . . . what was to be . . . gone by.'].

109:9 "made in God's image?" Cf. Genesis i. 26 ('And God said, Let us make man in our image').

109:20 **Man doth not live by bread alone,** Matthew iv. 4 ['Man shall not . . .'].

109:30 **gorgon** Terrible, ugly, literally petrifying; an adjective last previously used in 1827, according to *OED2*.

109:33 **played the very old Harry with** Damaged, ruined ('old Harry' is the devil).

110:29 **take away jam for tea?** DHL parodies the alternative punishment mentioned in Herman Melville's *White-Jacket, or The World in a Man-of-War* (1850; New York, 1892), p. 132: 'to "stop" a seaman's *grog* for a day or a week'.

110:31 **swale away** To waste away, like a guttering candle or like a tumour which can be dissipated (see 'sweal away' in *Sons and Lovers*, ed. Helen Baron and Carl Baron, Cambridge, 1992, 419:14).

111:31 **Spare the rod . . . the *ideal* child.** Proverbial (without DHL's '*ideal*'), from 'Hudibras', Part II (1664), i. 844, by Samuel Butler (1612–80); cf. 'Education of the People': 'A parent *owes* the child all the natural passional reactions provoked. If a child provokes anger, then to deny it this anger, the open, passional anger, is as bad as to deny it food or love' *(Reflections* 148:12–15).

112:2 **John . . . Jack-tar . . . Logos . . . Mediator, Interceder . . . Paraclete.** The name John reverberates in this text, as writer of the Apocalypse and as gospel-writer (see notes on 145:34, 293:24 and 403:32); the name dwindles into Jack, as here, and is translated into Johannus (112:6) . . . familiar name for common sailor . . . God as the Word (John i. 1) . . . 'Mediator' is applied regularly to Christ as one who mediates between God and man; so is 'interceder' (cf. 'intercession' at Romans viii. 26–7) . . . the Holy Ghost, the Advocate, though in Pryse's *Apocalypse Unsealed* also the '*speirêma*' or kundalini (pp. 10–11, 16), the energy of the serpent-coil at the base of the spine.

112:3 "Why are you . . . man, Sir?" *TYB* 83 ['What are you going to flog that man for, sir?']

112:4 **had got his dander up.** Originally US colloquial for getting angry.

112:6 **Johannuses.** I.e. 'Johns': the character in Dana is the Swede Johannes.

112:13 **Herman Melville's ships** See note on 122:3.

112:15 **Melville... to be flogged. In** *White Jacket.* See *White-Jacket*, chap. lxvii ('White-Jacket arraigned at the Mast'), pp. 263–5: the narrator is determined not to be flogged ('would have taken it as the last insult' – 112:15) and intends to rush the captain overboard, killing them both.

112:22 **Saviourism** Not in *OED2*: DHL's coinage. See too 157:9.

113:9 **"As he went [112:39]...cut him down—"** *TYB* 85 ['...on his...about the...suits me!...cold. I...look on no...down into the...and of the...revenge crossed...blows and...mate...captain...down.'].

113:20 **"The flogging...the subject—"** *TYB* 89 ['...seldom if...others ...him or...subject.'].

113:24 **"If you want...tell you—"** *TYB* 85 ['...you.'].

113:33 **"But the behaviour [113:25]...had suffered.—"** *TYB* 89–90 ['...flogged toward...another showed...never could...shipmate...suffered.'].

114:19 **"Not a human [114:8]...my companions."** *TYB* 113 ['...miles; and no sound heard but the pulsations of the great Pacific! the...world but..."world of waters!"...plain, dull...alone–' '...upon me. Everything was in accordance with my state of feeling, and I...I ever had...deadened by...which I had been so long acting...companions,'].

114:20 **Hamletises** To be self-consciously thoughtful: according to *OED2*, 'very rare'. This is one of only four recorded instances from the twentieth century, all from DHL (see *WL* 187:4, and *The First and Second Lady Chatterley Novels*, ed. Dieter Mehl and Christa Jansohn, Cambridge, 1999, 400:12,16). DHL also knew what it was to be 'Hamletty' (see *Letters*, i. 269).

114:29 **"The tide [114:23]...and motions—"** *TYB* 183 ['...antlers, were...off, affrighted...noises which we...motions.'].

114:30 **now, and the Presidio!** A military post, from the Spanish for 'garrison' (the city at one time being under Spanish rule); DHL and Frieda landed at San Francisco on 4 September 1922 and would have seen it overlooking the harbour. It was, however, there in Dana's time too (*TYB* 176), being referred to again in chap. xxi of the uncut version of the novel (see note on 105:2).

114:34 **the Kanaka boy...phthisis or syphilis.** Strictly, a native Hawaiian; but see Melville, *Typee*: 'The word "Kannaka" is at the present day universally used in the South Seas by Europeans to designate the islanders' (*TYP* 73 n. 1)...disease that causes wasting away of the body, especially tuberculosis; syphilis was introduced into the islands of the central Pacific in the course of the eighteenth century.

115:11 **"—but the other [114:35]...the medicine chest.—"** *TYB* 195 ['... *aikane*...life: his...system, a...no one...Kanakas...hand, and..."*Aloha, Aikane!*

Aloha nui!" . . . medicine-chest.']. Dana gives no explanation of 'aloha', 'aikane' or 'nui' (perhaps 'hullo', 'brother', 'now').

115:28 **"When all sail . . . water meet."** *TYB* 220. The *California* was another (and larger) ship working for the firm which employed Dana on the brig *Pilgrim*.

115:38 **"The days . . . coming to—"** *TYB* 229 ['. . . southward . . .']. The Magellan clouds – usually Magellanic clouds – 'consist of three small nebulae in the southern part of the heavens – two bright, like the Milky Way, and one dark. When off Cape Horn they are nearly overhead' (*TYB* 26).

116:17 **"And there lay [116:1] . . . true sublimity—"** *TYB* 238–9 ['. . . snow, and its centre of a deep indigo colour . . . water, and its high points . . . sublimity.'].

116:21 **in danger of lock-jaw.** *TYB* 242: having the jaws immovable from tonic spasm of the muscles of mastication. Tetanus is not implied.

116:35 **"At the end [116:22] . . . to spend—."** *TYB* 242–3 ['. . . the captain called . . . my clothes to . . . life. / In . . . spend.'].

117:1 **The horrific struggle round Cape Horn, homewards,** *TYB* chap. xxx is called 'Doubling Cape Horn', but *TYB* chap. xxix ('Bad Prospects') is even more 'horrific'.

117:12 **He has carried his consciousness open-eyed through it all.** Cf. DHL's tribute to Maurice Magnus at the end of his 'Memoir' (written between November 1921 and January 1922: *Memoir of Maurice Magnus*, ed. Keith Cushman, Santa Rosa, California, 1987): 'He carried the human consciousness unbroken through circumstances I could not have borne . . . He fought it open-eyed. He went through it and *realised* it all' (pp. 100–1).

117:22 **"Every rope-yarn . . . sea to sea."** *TYB* 259 ['. . . utmost and . . . of canvas . . .'].

117:23 **nodalises** I.e. concentrates in a node (in physics the point at which one of two displacements is at zero, the other at maximum). DHL's invention as a verb; the only citation in *OED2* is from *The Rainbow* (ed. Kinkead-Weekes, 408:36)

117:37 **an electric tap . . . a wad** DHL is re-christening the electric switch (named well before the First World War): he is unlikely to be referring to the 'tap' of an electric transformer (for which *OED2* cites a use in 1900) . . . some kind of a pad, or wadding, to prevent direct contact: DHL's usage does not exactly correspond with any in *OED2*, and is apparently uninfluenced by dialect use.

118:6 **Zeus is Father, and Thunderer.** In Greek mythology the Father of the gods (see next note). DHL was interested in the way in which classical and pre-classical mythology, Jewish mythology and the American Native American animist religion which he was starting to encounter in North America could be brought together. In his play *David* (1926), for example, he would refer to the Old Testament God as 'the

Thunder' (7:26), drawing on 1 Samuel vii. 10, Psalms xviii. 13, xxix. 3, lxxvii. 18 and lxxxi. 7, while in revision he frequently replaced the words 'God' and 'Lord' by words with animist connections, including 'Bolt' and 'Thunderer'. In such ways he could replace the concept of a personal God with something more primitive. For DHL on animism, see 'The Hopi Snake Dance' (1924) in *Mornings in Mexico* (1927) and 'New Mexico' (1928), *Phoenix* 146–7.

118:9 **Ammon ... Wotan ... Thor, Shango** The classical name of the Egyptian god Amen, identified by the Greeks with Zeus ... supreme god in Germanic mythology ... the Norse god of thunder, depicted as holding a hammer (emblematic of the thunderbolt) ... the Yoruba god of thunder (the cult also surviving in the West Indies). DHL would have learned about the last from *VOA* 204–27, chap. xi ('The Kingly Thunder-God'), which he read in April 1918 (*Letters*, iii. 233); in April 1919 he had drawn 'a little man: a thunder-evoker, from an African symbol' (*Letters*, iii. 349, 363) to be engraved on a present for Kot: he presumably took it from Frobenius. See too notes on 289:4, 292:16 and 293:40.

119:28 **"When our [118:28]... same state."** *TYB* 267–70 ['... every one ... tone, which ... jib. The {13 lines omitted} and there ... rigging it ... down there ... down, and ... yard-arm. / In ... flying-jibboom-/end ... low grumbling ... topsail ... moment more and ... heads, and ... stupefied ... no bells were ... malignant; while ...']. Erebus is a place of darkness between earth and Hades: the image 'dark as Erebus' being extant from 1839 ... a corposant – *corpus sancti* (saint's body) or *corpus sanctum* (holy body) (Latin), *corpo santo* (Old Spanish) – is the ball of fire sometimes seen on a ship's rigging during a storm ... Egyptian darkness is intense darkness (cf. Exodus x. 22).

120:5 **"The scurvy [119:35]... the scurvy."** Disease caused by lack of vitamin C and exposure. *TYB* 272–3 ['... was daily growing ... all, or ... *terra firma* ...'].

120:26 **"The freshness [120:7]... furling a royal."** *TYB* 274–5 ['... earthy taste, give ... in our watch ... One of them was ... raw potato ... by this that ...']. To 'speak' in this context is to hold communication with, signal, etc. (*OED2* 33b, nautical use). A royal is 'a light sail, next above the top-gallant sail' (*TYB* 27).

120:29 **phosphorus,** One of the non-metallic elements, highly inflammable, undergoing steady combustion at ordinary temperatures, hence glowing in the dark; widely distributed in nature in combination with other elements. In 'The Two Principles' (originally designed as an introduction to the Dana and Melville essays) it is a 'strange, unstable' element: 'In phosphorus the watery principle is so barely held that at a touch the mystic union will break ... the phosphorus will pass off in watery smoke': see 265:31–8. See too *Sons and Lovers*, ed. Baron and Baron, 464:35 and n.

120:32 **the living milk of Gea.** Properly Gaea or Gaia: the goddess of the earth in Greek mythology, who bore Uranus and by him Oceanus, Cronos and the Titans.

120:37 **The way up, and the way down.** In John Burnet's *Early Greek Philosophy* (1908 edn), which DHL first read in July 1915 and wished to refer to again in September

1916 (*Letters*, ii. 364–5, 652), he found Herakleitos' saying that 'The way up and the way down is one and the same' (p. 138): see *FWL* 477, Explanatory note on 159:6.

120:39 a lawyer... once almost an ambassador. Dana was admitted 'to the Massachusetts Bar in 1840, and ... rose to be one of the most distinguished advocates of the American law courts' (*TYB* ii); US Attorney for Massachusetts 1861–6. 'In 1879 [actually 1876], Mr. Dana was nominated to the position of minister to England; but, after a long contest, the Senate failed to confirm the appointment' (*TYB* iii).

121:10 Dana's small book In the Nelson's Classics edition, a small octavo (11 cm × 16 cm) of 282 pages.

Herman Melville's *Typee* and *Omoo* (Final Version 1923)

122:3 *Typee... Omoo*. Published 1846 and 1847. The Everyman editions which DHL originally used both had anonymous Introductions. *TYP* was unfortunately based on the New York revised edition of 1846, which cut many of the references to religion and missionaries (see notes on 125:39 and 126:2). Herman Melville (1819–91) was a 'northerner', born 'at New York on August 1st, 1819' (*TYP* vii), of an upper-middle-class family which (following his father's death in 1832) was in poor circumstances; he was not 'sea-born' (123:22) although he went 'to sea as a cabin-boy' (*TYP* vii), nor originally from New England (134:2), though that is where he settled after his travels (he had Hawthorne, to whom he would dedicate *Moby-Dick*, as a nearby Berkshires neighbour 1850–1). He first went to sea in June 1839 on a trans-Atlantic packet plying between New York and Liverpool – see *Redburn* (1849). He sailed in the whaler *Acushnet* out of Fairhaven on 3 January 1841 but in June 1842 deserted in the Marquesa islands – see *Typee*. After a month ashore, he joined a second whaler, the *Lucy Ann*, but deserted again in Tahiti – see *Omoo*. In November 1842 he joined the whaler *Charles and Henry* for six months, being discharged in the Hawaiian islands in August 1843; he signed on the frigate *United States* for the return voyage to the USA, where he arrived in October 1844 – see *White-Jacket* (1850). All his voyages contributed to *Moby-Dick* (1851). He had been farming on a part-time basis ever since 1850; after the crushing failures of *Pierre* (1852) (see note on 131:23) and *The Confidence-Man* (1857), he took a job as a customs inspector in New York; he subsequently published only occasional poetry volumes, and in 1891 (the year he died) wrote his final short novel *Billy Budd* (1924).

122:8 Joseph Conrad's... Lord Jim. In *Lord Jim* (1903) by Joseph Conrad (1857–1924), Jim feels profoundly guilty for his act of cowardice in deserting the *Patna* (which he believes to be sinking), and spends the rest of his short life either escaping the notoriety or trying to make amends for his failure; cf. DHL's 1912 comment 'I cannot forgive Conrad for being so sad and for giving in' (*Letters*, ii. 465).

122:11 half-seas-over. Normally 'drunk', but here with its original meaning of 'half way between one state and another', like a ship half-overwhelmed by the sea (see *Letters*, iii. 683).

122:14 **yellow-bearded Vikings...beaked ships.** The legend of Vikings with yellow beards is probably the result of their portrayal in nineteenth-century paintings...Norse ships equipped with a *barð* (Old Norse) – a beak on the prow, often carved – were called *barði*, beaked ships.

122:20 **brown** See Textual apparatus: DHL must have tried to patch up his text after the typist or typesetter omitted several lines (see next entry in apparatus).

122:23 *allzu menschlich* 'All too human': cf. the book *Menschliches, Allzumenschliches* (1878–9) by Friedrich Nietzsche (1844–1900).

122:25 **Blue-eyed people...keen and abstract...like a Viking** DHL drew Jessie Chambers's attention, *c.* 1906, to the sentence 'fair hair and blue eyes are a deviation from the type and almost constitute an abnormity' in his copy of the 'Metaphysics of Love' (*Essays by Schopenhauer*, ed. Mrs Rudolf Dircks, Walter Scott Ltd, n.d., p. 189; E. T., *A Personal Record*, p. 111); DHL's own eyes were – according to Richard Aldington – 'the most brilliant blue' (Nehls, i. 236). DHL created a series of strikingly fair-haired, blue-eyed and 'northern' characters: e.g. William in *Sons and Lovers*, fair-haired, with blue eyes and 'a touch of the Dane or Norwegian about him' (ed. Baron and Baron, 11:10–11, 16, 69:40) and Gerald Crich (*WL* 14:28–36, 58:40).

122:30 **Balder the beautiful...dead,** Cf. the poem 'Balder Dead' (1853–4) by the English poet and essayist Matthew Arnold (1822–88). In Norse mythology, Baldr – a beautiful young god, son of Odin and Frigg – was killed by the blind god Hod, misled by the malicious Loki. DHL himself had constructed a version of the myth in *Women in Love*, with the death of its fair-haired central character Gerald being influenced by the activity of the malicious Loerke.

122:31 **sea-poppies** I.e. the common horned poppy, *Glaucium luteum*; see 288:32.

123:7 **Let water conceive no more with fire.** Reminiscent of the fragments of Herakleitos, as explained in Burnet, *Early Greek Philosophy*, pp. 130–68: 'The fire in us is perpetually becoming water' – ideally, fire and water should be 'evenly balanced' in the soul (pp. 151, 153).

123:10 **merman turn away from his human wife and children,** Cf. Arnold's poem 'The Forsaken Merman' (1847–9), in which the merman pleads with his human partner (not wife) to come back to him and to their children. DHL suggests exactly the opposite.

123:10 **seal-woman forget the world of men,** In September 1917 DHL got to know (via the musician Cecil Gray, 1895–1951: see his *Musical Chairs*, 1948, pp. 28–9) the *Songs of the Hebrides*, ed. Marjorie Kennedy-Fraser (1917); see *Letters*, iii. 164 n. 6, and *Kangaroo*, ed. Bruce Steele (Cambridge, 1992), 245:12, for a transcription of the seal-woman's song. In so far as she sings in no human language, the seal-woman may be 'remembering only the waters'.

123:16 **Woman, what...It is finished.** *Consummatum est.* John ii. 4, a common biblical reference in DHL (cf. *FWL* 96:9, 396:11–12, 428:32, and 'Tortoise Family

Connections', *Complete Poems*, ed. Pinto and Roberts, i. 357)... Christ's last words: John xix. 30 (and Vulgate version).

123:18 Basta! Enough! (Italian).

123:25 *Der Grosse oder Stille Ozean*. 'The Great or Still Ocean', as Frieda called the Pacific while she and DHL were living in Australia in May 1922 (*Letters*, iii. 249): today slightly old-fashioned German for the 'Pazifische Ozean'.

123:30 To sleep is to dream: Cf. *Hamlet* III. i. 64–5: 'To die, to sleep, / To sleep: perchance to dream.'

123:35 Maoris, the Tongans, the Marquesans, the Fijians, the Polynesians: The Polynesian peoples spread to the island groups of the central Pacific Ocean; they include the Tongans and the inhabitants of the Marquesa Islands, and the Maoris who migrated to New Zealand. The Fijians, however, are today classed as belonging to the Melanesian group.

123:40 South Sea Islanders belong to the Stone Age. I.e. to the period before metal was used in tools, also known as the Neolithic period; the ethnographer Lt-General A. Lane-Fox Pitt-Rivers described in 1874 how the Fijians, 'at the time of their discovery were still in the stone age' (*The Evolution of Culture and Other Essays*, ed. J. L. Myres, Oxford, 1906, p. 14), and his remarks were frequently repeated; cf. 'Until influenced by European civilisation, they ['Negroes in Polynesia'] were in the stone age' (E. D. Laborde, *Australia, New Zealand and the Pacific Islands*, 1932, p. 249).

124:12 the lotus was always in flower... bygone world, before Egypt. Cf. DHL's description of his feelings in Ceylon in April 1922: 'One could quite easily sink into a kind of apathy, like a lotus on a muddy pond' (*Letters*, iv. 228)... DHL is wrong to name China and Japan (124:7, 12) as examples of pre-Egyptian civilisations – something he only did in the Final Version of the essay. Previously he had been careful to stress that he meant Chinese and Japanese civilisations in so far as they echoed previous civilisations. Chinese civilisation only started to flourish between 2200 and 1500 BC, while Japan dates its origins back only to 660 BC. The first Egyptian dynasties, however, ruled 2850–2660 BC, and the great age of pyramid building was under the 4th dynasty, 2590–2470 BC. DHL wrote in April 1922 how Ceylon 'made an enormous impression on me – a glimpse into the world before the Flood. I can't get back into history – The soft, moist elephantine pre-historic has sort of swamped in over my known world' (*Letters*, iv. 234). Cf. the 'soft, uncreate past' at 127:1.

124:38 Samoa, Tahiti, Raratonga, Nukuheva: DHL, on his journey across the Pacific in August 1922, stopped at Raratonga (in the Cook Islands) for one day and Tahiti for two, finding the former 'Such a lovely island... it's really almost as lovely as one expects these South Sea Islands to be' (*Letters*, iv. 284); Tahiti was 'lovely – but Papeete [the port] disappointing' (*Letters*, iv. 286). Samoa lay to the west, the Marquesa Islands (of which Nukuheva is one) to the east of his journey. He added Raratonga to his list (which otherwise comes from Melville's experiences) after his own Pacific journey.

124:40 **a sleep and a forgetting... "Trailing clouds of glory."** From 'Ode. Intimations of Immortality from Recollections of Early Childhood' (1807) by William Wordsworth (1770–1850): 'Our birth is but a sleep and a forgetting' (l. 58), 'But trailing clouds of glory do we come' (l. 64).

125:5 **Delenda est Chicago.** Play on the saying of Marcus Porcius Cato (the Elder, 234–148 BC), Roman statesman and writer: 'Delenda est Carthago' – 'Carthage must be destroyed' (from Plutarch's *Life of Marcus Cato*, xxvii). Cf. *Letters*, ii. 650.

125:7 **paradise "regained."** Cf. Milton's *Paradise Regained* (1674).

125:12 **in *Typee*... cannibals of Nukuheva.** Chaps. 7–10 describe the journey.

125:22 **Child of Nature... Noble Savage** Phrase first used in English in the early seventeenth century but popularised by the philosophical novel *The Child of Nature improved by Chance* (tr. 1774) by the French philosopher Claude Adrien Helvétius (1715–71); it was, e.g., used by Cowper in *The Task* (1784), iv. 623, and by Wordsworth in 'To a Young Lady' (1802) l. 1 ('Dear Child of Nature...'). Cf. too DHL in 'On Human Destiny' (1924): 'Let us dismiss the innocent child of nature. He does not exist, never did, never will, and never could' (*Phoenix II*, ed. Roberts and Moore, p. 624)... the phrase 'noble savage' originates in *The Conquest of Granada* (1672), I. i. 3, by John Dryden (1631–1700).

125:28 **"immoral,"** E.g. the narrator's account of the arrival of the *Dolly* in Nukuheva harbour, when she is boarded by Marquesan girls whose 'abandoned voluptuousness... I dare not attempt to describe' (*TYP* 13); and the examination to which he and Toby are subjected by the Typee girls, when 'my feelings of propriety were exceedingly shocked' and Toby is 'immeasurably outraged' (*TYP* 76). The narrator finds, however, the local practice of polygamy surprising but intelligent (*TYP* 202–4); he constantly stresses that it is the whites who are actually immoral: 'Alas for the poor savages when exposed to the influence of these polluting examples!' (*TYP* 13).

125:34 **"This is... remembrance of me."** From the Communion service of the Church of England: 'Take, eat, this is my body which is given for you... Drink ye all of this, for this is my blood of the New Testament... Do this, as oft as ye shall drink it, in remembrance of me' (*Book of Common Prayer*).

125:39 **Herman chose to be horrified.** In chap. 4 the narrator explains that 'the word "Typee" in the Marquesan dialect signifies a lover of human flesh', and on arriving among the Typees, the narrator and Toby fear they may be eaten (*TYP* 75, 97–9): cannibalism is 'horrible and fearful' (212), and the sound of drums during an 'inhuman feast' gives the narrator 'a sensation of horror which I am unable to describe' (246). However, even in the Everyman edition, which omitted some of the narrator's enlightened ideas (see note on 122:3), cannibalism is only practised 'upon the bodies of slain enemies', while 'those who indulge in it are in other respects humane and virtuous' (212). In the full text the narrator asks whether cannibalism is any worse than the European's practice of hanging, drawing and quartering traitors, or the white man's 'remorseless cruelty', and suggests that 'so far as the relative wickedness of the parties is concerned, four or five Marquesan Islanders sent to the United States as Missionaries might be quite as useful as an equal number of Americans despatched to the Islands in a similar capacity' (*Typee*, ed. G. Thomas Tanselle, Library of America, 1982, pp. 150–1).

126:2 **wild methods of warfare.** The white man's methods of warfare in particular were censored in the Everyman edition; a sentence was cut which declared that such methods 'are enough of themselves to distinguish the white civilised man as the most ferocious animal on the face of the earth' (*Typee*, ed. Tanselle, p. 150). Nevertheless, the narrator of *Typee* does note of the Islanders how 'the heads of enemies killed in battle are invariably preserved, and hung up as trophies in the house of the conqueror' (*TYP* 206).

126:6 **fly even in Paradisal ointment ... the first was a ladybird.** Originally from Ecclesiastes x. 1: some small or trifling circumstance which spoils the enjoyment of a thing; cf. DHL's 1909 story 'The Fly in the Ointment', *Love Among the Haystacks*, ed. Worthen, 49–53 ... presumably Eve.

126:15 **Home and Mother,** Evidence that – by the time the essay in its Final Version was complete – DHL had consulted Raymond Weaver's book on Melville (see Introduction note 62). Melville's full text at this point describes how the 'only two English words' the narrator teaches Marheyo are ' "Home" and "Mother" ' (*Typee*, ed. Tanselle, p. 280), but the Everyman text DHL had used had reduced the sentence to 'emphatically pronounced one expressive word I had taught him – "Home" ' (*TYP* 258). The quotation of the two words does not appear in any version of the essay before 1923, but appears in Weaver: 'Under these circumstances he taught old Marheyo two English words: *Home* and *Mother*' (*Herman Melville*, p. 212).

126:21 **hibiscus flowers ... frangipani** DHL commented on the 'great red hibiscus' he saw on Raratonga (*Letters*, iv. 284) ... probably the tropical shrub *Plumeria rubra* (Red Jasmine), with its waxy and heavily scented red flowers, first brought from the West Indies but also to be found in the Pacific Ocean.

126:26 **under a vacuum, in the South Seas.** DHL described his feeling, in Ceylon, of being under 'a bell-jar of heat ... the feeling that there is a lid down over everything' (*Letters*, iv. 227).

126:29 **Gauguin couldn't really go back:** The French painter Paul Gauguin (1848–1903) decided to live and work in Tahiti in 1891, but came back to Paris in 1893; he returned to Tahiti in 1895 and, after a suicide attempt, in 1897 went to live and work in the Marquesa Islands, where he died.

127:20 **like warm mud.** Cf. DHL's comments on Ceylon: 'the heads of elephants and buffaloes poking out of primeval mud ... the tropics have something of the world before the flood – hot dark mud and the life inherent in it' (*Letters*, iv. 233–4).

127:21 **the Saurian...*Noli me tangere.*** Strictly, reptiles belonging to the order *Sauria*, but from the early nineteenth century popularly applied to extinct lizard-like creatures; see, e.g., *WL* 101:11–13 ... 'Touch me not': Christ's words to Mary Magdalene after his resurrection, in the Vulgate version (John xx. 17).

127:29 **"reformers" and "idealists" who glorify the savages in America.** DHL would probably have included Mabel Luhan and Mary Austin (see note on 41:8) in this category, and perhaps the campaigner for Native American rights John Collier (1884–1968) too (see Ellis, *Dying Game*, pp. 64–5).

127:35 **his leg...would not heal.** The leg is swollen (*TYP* 79) and no treatment helps (80–1). It then gets better, but (suddenly) far worse again (240, 252); and it is for this reason, above all others – to answer DHL's question 'O God, why wasn't he happy?' (126:21–2) – that the narrator wishes to leave.

128:16 **a boat-hook full in the throat...dearest savage friends...sank him,** Mow-Mow, who only enters the narrative at *TYP* 244, is not a friend of the narrator but 'the only chief present, whom I had been much in the habit of seeing' (257); when the narrator 'dashed the boat-hook at him', it 'struck him just below the throat', but he comes to the surface again immediately afterwards: 'never shall I forget the ferocious expression of his countenance' (263). Weaver, however (see note on 126:15), presents the episode very much as DHL does and is almost certainly responsible for his reading: 'One profoundly silent noon, as Melville lay lame and miserable under Kory-Kory's roof, Mow-Mow, the one-eyed chief, appeared at the door, and leaning forward towards Melville, whispered: *Toby pemi ena* – "Toby has arrived." That evening Mow-Mow's dead body floated on the Pacific, a boat-hook having been mortally hurled at his throat. And it was Melville who hurled the boat-hook' (*Herman Melville*, p. 212).

128:24 **When he really...it Purgatory.** Not in the texts of *Typee, Omoo* or *White-Jacket*, in none of which is the narrator's return to his own home described (*White-Jacket* ends with his saying goodbye to his shipmates, p. 370).

129:2 **The mills of God were grinding inside him,** Cf. l. 1 of 'Retribution', tr. Longfellow, *Sinngedichte* (1653), III. ii. 24, by Friedrich von Logau (1604–55): 'Though the mills of God grind slowly, yet they grind exceeding small.' Cf. *Letters*, ii. 35.

129:5 **injustice and folly of missionaries...of brutal sea-captains...of governments,** Evidence of DHL's awareness of the full text of *Typee*, as Weaver described it in *Herman Melville* (e.g. p. 207); almost all the descriptions of missionaries (e.g. *Typee*, ed. Tanselle, pp. 14–15, 229–34, 248) had been omitted from the Everyman edition...see, e.g., *TYP* 14 ('arbitrary and violent in the extreme')...mostly omitted from the Everyman edition (e.g. *Typee*, ed. Tanselle, p. 238).

129:15 **the craziest, most impossible of whaling ships.** The *Julia* is mentioned in *Typee* (*TYP* 263–4) but described (with 'crazy old hull') in *Omoo* (*OMO* 39).

129:18 **his leg ... began quickly to get well.** 'I soon began to recover' (*OMO* 35).

129:22 **intolerable nostalgia ... for the island he has left.** 'I ... felt weighed down by a melancholy that could not be shaken off. It was the thought of never more seeing those, who ... had ... treated me kindly. I was leaving them for ever' (*OMO* 4).

129:29 **Fata Morgana.** A deception, a mirage, originally that in the Strait of Messina attributed to the sorcery of the enchantress Morgan le Fay in the King Arthur legends; see too 145:25.

130:3 **a beach comber.** In DHL's period, a settler on the islands of the Pacific Ocean, living by fishing 'or often by less reputable means' (*OED2*). The description in the Intermediate Version (1919) (see 341:16–17) is more accurate.

130:9 **epicurean ... eating the world like a snipe ... *bonne bouche*.** Devoted to sensual pleasures, especially food and drink ... 'snipe' has been 'an opprobrious or abusive term' (*OED2*) since the sixteenth century, but although the bird, long-beaked and inhabiting marshy places, was regularly eaten, it was not notoriously gluttonous: 130:20 ('ate his snipe') confirms that DHL is thinking of the snipe as food ... tasty titbit (French).

130:11 **Doctor Long Ghost.** The original doctor of the *Julia*, 'he went by the name of the long Doctor, or ... Doctor Long Ghost' (*OMO* 8).

130:32 **a white man ... his brow,** Lem Hardy, 'a renegado from Christendom and humanity' (*OMO* 26). It is, however, untrue that Melville 'couldn't bear it': Hardy 'fled the parish workhouse when a boy ... it is just this sort of men ... uncared for by a single soul, without ties, reckless, and impatient of the restraints of civilization, who are occasionally found quite at home upon the savage islands of the Pacific. And, glancing at their hard lot in their own country, what marvel at their choice?' (*OMO* 27).

130:36 **American man-of-war ... *White Jacket*.** The *United States*, recreated as the *Neversink*: see notes on 110:29, 122:3 and 132:7.

131:3 **twenty-five his wild oats were sown ... back to Home and Mother,** Melville returned to the USA from the South Seas in the autumn of 1844, when he was twenty-five; Weaver describes how 'Melville's disillusionment began at home' with 'The romantic idealisation of his mother ...' (*Herman Melville*, p. 338).

131:8 **He married ... an ecstasy of a courtship ... fifty years of disillusion.** Melville married Elizabeth Shaw in 1847; they were married for forty-four years, until his death in 1891 at seventy-two. Weaver commented: 'By the very ardour of his idealisation, Melville was foredoomed to disappointment in marriage ... their marriage was for each a crucifixion' (*Herman Melville*, p. 340).

131:18 **lovey-doveyness** Maudlin affection: DHL's noun from 'lovey-dovey' (late nineteenth-century slang) is the first citation in *OED2*.

131:23 *Pierre* *Pierre; or, the Ambiguities*, Melville's first non-seagoing novel, was 'received with a hostility beyond that of any other of his books'; reviews commented that it was 'utterly unworthy of Mr. Melville's genius', 'a dead failure' and the 'craziest fiction extant' (Watson G. Branch, 'Introduction', *Melville: The Critical Heritage*, 1974, pp. 30–1). See too Weaver, pp. 342–3.

131:36 **The meek...Sermon on the Mount...a litany of white vice.** See Matthew v. 5, 8 ... Matthew v–vii ... i.e. a long recital of spiritual demands and commands.

132:7 **Jack Chase, in *White Jacket*.** See *White-Jacket*, pp. 16–19.

Herman Melville's *Moby Dick* (Final Version 1923)

133:3 *Moby Dick, or the White Whale.* The erroneous title of the Everyman edition which DHL was using; the title of the American edition was *Moby-Dick; or, The Whale* and of the English edition *The Whale* (1851). The Everyman edition also omitted the brief 'Epilogue' which explains how Ishmael survives the wreck and can thus narrate it: DHL's comment at 145:39, 'So ends one of the strangest and most wonderful books in the world', suggests that he did not know of the missing 'Epilogue'. See JoEllyn Clarey, 'D. H. Lawrence's *Moby-Dick*: A Textual Note', *Modern Philology*, lxxxiv (November 1986), 191–5. See too notes on 133:13 and 141:37.

133:13 **Leviathan, not a Hobbes sort.** Thomas Hobbes (1588–1679), English political philosopher, published his justification of absolute sovereignty, *Leviathan*, in 1651; Melville quoted its opening sentence (including the phrase 'that great Leviathan, called a Commonwealth or State') in the 'Extracts' which should appear at the start of the novel but which in the Everyman edition were printed at the end (*MD* 497).

133:16 **frigate-bird distortions,** Any bird of the genus *Fregata* and family *Fregatidae*, of tropical and sub-tropical seas, with a wide wingspan; it was popularly believed hardly ever to alight, and to fly with incredible swiftness.

133:21 **He never coils like the Chinese dragon of the sun.** DHL was probably thinking (as in *Apocalypse and the Writings on Revelation*, ed. Mara Kalnins, Cambridge, 1980) of 'The long green dragon with which we are so familiar on Chinese things...There he coils, on the breasts of the mandarins' coats, looking very horrific, coiling round the centre of the breast and lashing behind with his tail': 'His coils within the sun make the sun glad, till the sun dances in radiance...It is the same dragon which, according to the Hindus, coils quiescent at the base of the spine of a man' (124:34–5, 37–8; 124:39–125:1, 3–5). In 1917–18, too, DHL would have read in Blavatsky, *Isis Unveiled*, i. 550: 'The tradition of the Dragon and the Sun...has awakened echoes in the remotest parts of the world. It may be accounted for with perfect readiness by the once universal heliolatrous religion.' See too 293:37–294:5, 20–21.

133:34 **Nobody can be...so amateurishly.** The First (1918–19) and Intermediate (1919) Versions of the essay show what DHL is objecting to; see e.g. 346:19–26, 39—347:7.

134:4 *au grand sérieux.* With great seriousness (French).

134:10 **wormwood and gall.** See Lamentations iii. 19: 'Remembering mine affliction and my misery, the wormwood and the gall'; wormwood is a plant yielding a bitter extract, gall is the type of an intensely bitter substance.

134:24 **a futurist long before futurism found paint.** See note on 12:6.

134:26 **over the border: psychiatry.** DHL regards analysis of the soul's needs not only as something 'Almost spurious' (134:26) but as the job of psychiatric analysis, not of the creative imagination. 'Psychiatry' was used from the mid-nineteenth century to mean 'medical treatment of diseases of the mind'.

134:31 **hugged in bed by a huge tatooed South Sea Islander,** See *MD* 24, 27.

134:32 **offering burnt offering to the savage's little idol,** See *MD* 50. See note on 297:2 for evidence of DHL's distance from the text when he corrected Roberts E382i in 1918–19.

135:3 **New Bedford** Ishmael (see next note) spends the weekend in New Bedford (on the coast of Massachusetts) on his way out to Nantucket Island, where he seeks a place on a whaling ship (*MD* 12).

135:4 **Ishmael, the "I" of the book.** Abraham's son by Hagar, the maid of Abraham's wife Sarah (Genesis xvi. 11–16, xxi. 9–21, xxv. 12–18) – 'And he will be a wild man; his hand will be against every man, and every man's hand against him' (xvi. 12); displaced by Abraham's lawful son Isaac and cast out by Sarah, he grows up in the wilderness and becomes an archer (xxi. 20); hence the reference to him at 136:4–5 as 'the hunted . . . the hunter'.

135:6 **harpooneer,** 'Now *rare*' (*OED2*), last recorded use 1874.

135:8 **The advent . . . swear "marriage,"** *MD* 23–7, 50.

135:20 **"As I sat there [135:11] . . . drawn towards him."—** *MD* 49 ['. . . twain; the storm booming without in solemn swells; I . . . splintered heart . . . maddened hand were . . .'].

135:28 **"I was a . . . to do to my fellow-man . . . of God.—"** *MD* 50 ['. . . Christian; . . . with this wild . . . worship? thought . . . fellowman . . . fellowman to do . . . God.']. Cf. Christ's commandment: 'Thou shalt love thy neighbour as thyself' (Mark xii. 31).

135:41 **"Now Queequeg [135:30] . . . loving pair—"** *MD* 50–1 ['Now, . . . fellowman . . . him in his . . . chat. *P* How . . . like a . . . there open . . . pair.'].

136:10 **"large, deep eyes, fiery black and bold."** *MD* 48 ['. . . bold,'].

136:13 **Quaker whaling-ship, the *Pequod*.** See note on 136:27.

136:18 **The Argonauts . . . Ulysses . . . the Circes . . . the wicked hussies of the isles.** The heroes who sailed with Jason in quest of the Golden Fleece . . . see notes on 54:38 and 97:33 . . . e.g. the Nymph Calypso (who imprisons Odysseus in her cave) and (perhaps) the beautiful but virtuous Nausicaa, the daughter of King Alcinous.

136:27 **You are some time . . . Ahab: the mysterious Quaker.** Ahab is frequently mentioned in chaps. XVI–XX, but seen for the first time (cf. 136:33–4) only in chap. XXVII (*MD* 107). The owners of the *Pequod*, Captains Bildad and Peleg, are both Quakers, 'named with Scripture names' (*MD* 68). It is never stated that Ahab is a Quaker, though his name is Biblical, from 1 Kings xvi–xxii: 'Ahab of old, thou knowest, was a crowned king!' (*MD* 74).

136:32 **Oh captain, my captain, our fearful trip is done.**" Whitman's 1865 poem on the death of Lincoln ['O Captain! my Captain! . . . done,']; see 150:22 and 151:14.

136:37 **Moby Dick . . . tore off Ahab's leg** See *MD* 67, 108–9.

137:8 **Starbuck:** See *MD* 100–2; DHL's method of listing mates and harpooners is modelled on Melville's own.

137:11 **Stubb: "Fearless as fire, and as mechanical."** For Stubb, see *MD* 103. The remark is a version of Ahab's comment 'did I not know thee brave as fearless fire (and as mechanical) I could swear thou wert a poltroon' (*MD* 474). Stubb himself remarks 'I am a coward; and I sing to keep up my spirits' (*MD* 433).

137:16 **Flask . . . water-rat— —"** See *MD* 104 ['. . . or at least water-rat,']

137:22 **Mr Wilson . . . at the Peace Conference . . . wives along.** President Woodrow Wilson's wife Edith Bolling Galt Wilson (b. 1872) attended the celebration dinner at the Élysée Palace with him on 27 June 1919, the evening before the signing of the Treaty of Versailles; see *The Times*, 28 June, p. 14, and *Memoirs of Mrs. Woodrow Wilson* (1939), pp. 319–23.

137:28 **Queequeg,** See *MD* 23–31, 52–4, 104.

137:29 **Tashtego,** See *MD* 104–5.

137:31 **Daggoo,** See *MD* 105.

137:37 **only after . . . Parsees.** They appear only at the end of chap. XLVI, *MD* 189.

138:2 **Stars and Stripes. Beaten with many stripes.** The stars on a blue field on the US national flag correspond to the current number of states; the red and white stripes represent the thirteen original states . . . Luke xii. 47: 'And that servant, which knew his lord's will, and prepared not himself, neither did according to his will, shall be beaten with many stripes.'

138:16 **compare Melville with Dana, about the albatross.** For Dana, see 107:19–28.

138:29 **"I remember [138:17] . . . of the spell—"** *MD* 165 n. 1 ['. . . below, . . . dashed upon . . . intervals, . . . vast archangel wings, as if to embrace some holy ark. Wondrous flutterings and throbbings . . . eyes, . . . heavens. As Abraham before the angels, I bowed myself; the white . . . towns. [11 lines omitted] I assert, then, . . . spell;'].

138:30 **a bait on a hook.** 'But how had the mystic thing been caught? . . . with a treacherous hook and line, as the fowl floated on the sea' (*MD* 165 n. 1).

138:33 **P. and O. boat, nearly empty . . . lascar crew** Between 18 and 27 May 1922, DHL and Frieda travelled from Perth to Sydney on board the P. and O. boat *Malwa*, getting 'glimpses of the Australian coast' (138:36): there were 'less than thirty passengers second class' (*Letters*, iii. 244) . . . DHL noted that they had 'all Indian servants on board here' (*Letters*, iii. 243), but may have meant by that Lascars (i.e. from the East Indies), normal on a P. and O. boat travelling around Australia: a Lascar crew was involved in a shipwreck shortly afterwards (*Letters*, iii. 249).

139:1 **about "whiteness."** E.g. *MD* chap. XLI 'The Whiteness of the Whale', containing the footnote on the albatross (see note on 138:29).

139:12 **"It was a [139:6] . . . invisible self—"** *MD* 187 ['. . . self.'].

139:14 **"There she . . . She blows!"** *MD* 188 ['. . . she . . . she . . .'].

139:39 **' "Give way [139:18] . . . iron, escaped—'** *MD* 196–7 ['. . . way, men . . . close to! Spring!' *P* Soon . . . feet. *P* Though . . . *There, there* . . . Starbuck. *P* A . . . leaped out . . . welded commotion . . . an invisible push . . . escaped.'].

140:8 **"It was [140:3] . . . the bow.—"** *MD* 202–3.

140:25 **"Steering north-eastward [140:9] . . . anything else—"** *MD* 239 ['. . . substance, upon . . . Right Whale . . . wheat. *P* On . . . Right Whales . . . seen who, secure . . . Sperm Whaler . . . fringing fibres . . . lip. *P* As . . . mowers, who . . . of marshy . . . blue upon . . . sea. *P* But . . . mastheads especially . . . like lifeless masses . . . else.']

141:4 **"Slowly wading [140:27] . . . thought Daggoo— —"** *MD* 241–2 ['. . . held on her . . . northeastward . . . sun glade . . . enjoining some secrecy; when the . . . and yet is . . . Daggoo.'].

141:16 **"In the [141:6] . . . disappeared again.—"** *MD* 242 ['in the . . . life. *P* As with . . . again,'].

141:19 **The following . . . actual happening.** See chaps. LIX, LX, LXVI–LXIX, LXXI.

141:21 **the *Jereboam* . . . ship's hands.** See chap. LXX; the man believes himself to be the archangel Gabriel and 'had gained a wonderful ascendancy over almost every body in the *Jeroboam*' (*MD* 272).

141:22 **taking of the sperm oil** See chaps. LXXVI–LXXVII.

141:26 **"for I . . . you are—."** *MD* 303.

141:29 **"For, viewed . . . spinal cord."** *MD* 303.

141:37 "As the [141:32]...in agony!—" *MD* 309 ['...nay, not...or a bubble came...placidity, the...agony!']. DHL's 'not so much as a ripple or a thought, came' (rather than 'not so much as a ripple or a bubble came') demonstrates his use of the Everyman edition; his eye skipped line 7 (which starts 'bubble came') to line 8 (which starts 'thought,') before returning to line 7.

141:39 "The Grand Armada," Chap. LXXXVI.

141:40 drawing through the Sunda Straits towards Java The odd construction is perhaps influenced by *MD* 331: 'the *Pequod* was now drawing nigh to these straits; Ahab proposing to pass through them into the Javan sea...'

142:4 "Broad on...noonday air,—"— *MD* 331 ['...at the distance...semi-circle,...one half...'].

142:5 Javan pirates, *MD* 332.

142:7 that curious...gallied. Mixture of DHL and Melville: 'that strange perplexity of inert irresolution'; 'they were, as the seamen say, gallied' (*MD* 333); Melville gave a scholarly footnote (*MD* 333 n. 1) commenting on 'gallied' – frightened.

142:13 sleek, *MD* 336 comments on 'that smooth satin-like surface, called a sleek, produced by the subtle moisture thrown off by the whale in his more quiet moods' and *OED2* confirms that 'Broad oily tracks, or "sleeks"' may be 'produced by the recent passage of a party of cetaceans' (1840); but the word is also related to 'slick', 'A smooth place or streak on the surface of water, usually caused by the presence of some oily or greasy substance' (*OED2* 3.a.).

142:14 the young whales...like dogs. 'Like household dogs they came snuffling round us, right up to our gunwales, and touching them' (*MD* 336).

142:28 "But far beneath [142:16]...eyeing us.— — — *MD* 336–7 ['...while suckling...at the time...reminiscence;—even...Gulfweed...new-born...us.'].

142:33 Some of [142:28]...and delight.—" *MD* 337–8 ['...deep. *P* And...consternations...delight.'].

142:36 chapter on ambergris: Chap. XCI (*MD* 355–7).

142:37 chapter..."The Cassock" Chap. XCIV (*MD* 364–5).

142:39 the Try-works, Chap. XCV (*MD* 365–9).

143:10 "Uppermost was [143:5]...thought I!—" *MD* 368 ['...ahead as...what is...me? thought I.'] Ishmael, rather than Melville, is at the helm of the *Pequod*.

143:13 an injunction...look ghastly. See *MD* 368: 'Look not too long in the face of the fire, O man!...believe not the artificial fire, when its redness makes all things look ghastly.'

143:17 like to die. Old-fashioned usage: 'likely to die'.

143:26 "How he wasted [143:17] . . . waning savage—" MD 412 ['. . . wasted away in . . . few long-lingering . . . cheekbones . . . they became of a strange softness of . . . the rings of . . . savage.'].

143:30 "To my . . . the world—" MD 416 ['To any meditative . . . world.'].

144:4 homage-rendering The typesetter or typist of Roberts E382q (p. 152) apparently misunderstood DHL's indications to close up the space round a spaced dash ('homage – rendering') to make it a hyphen and deleted 'ag' as well, to produce 'home-rendering' (see Textual apparatus).

144:5 "It was far [143:31] . . . fire';— — —" MD 427 ['. . . done: and . . . stilly died . . . such plaintiveness . . . Manilla . . . land-breeze, wantonly turned sailor, had . . . hymns. P Soothed . . . turning sunwards of the head, and . . . conveyed before. P "He . . . it,—how . . . fire;'].

144:8 the next chapter, Actually chap. CXVIII ('The Dying Whale' had been chap. CXV).

144:9 livid sundering A1 (p. 234) divided at 'liv-', so its reading 'liv-ing' may well have been a misreading by the typesetter duplicating the ending of the next word, rather than a change DHL made in proof.

144:10 the brand, from head to foot. Ahab has been 'branded' by a 'slender, rod-like mark, lividly whitish . . . Threading its way out from among his grey hairs . . . till it disappeared in his clothing'; we are told that he may have been born with it, or that it may have 'come upon him . . . in an elemental strife at sea' (MD 107–8); he himself says that, as a fire-worshipper, he was 'in the sacramental act so burned by thee, that to this hour I bear the scar' (MD 435).

144:12 the corposants . . . upon the mast-heads . . . the compass is reversed. MD 434–7, 443; see note on 119:28.

144:16 hand in hand . . . negro boy, Pip . . . demented, left swimming alone See MD 457, 447–8, 357–9.

144:19 The voyage . . . then another. Cf. 'The intense Pequod sailed on . . .' (MD 462) . . . meetings are described with the Jeroboam (271–6), the Virgin (303–13), the Rosebud (349–55), the Samuel Enderby (377–83), the Bachelor (424–6), the Rachel (453–6) and finally the Delight (462–3).

144:26 "Hither and [144:21] . . . masculine sea—" MD 463 ['Hither, and . . . sword-fish, and . . . sea.'].

144:26 his weariness, MD 464 ['oh, weariness! heaviness!'].

144:29 "—But do . . . since Paradise—" MD 465 ['But . . . faint, bowed . . . Adam, staggering . . .'].

144:30 the Gethsemane   The garden near Jerusalem where Jesus spent his last night before being crucified (Matthew xxvi. 36–56).

144:36 hoisted perch... "From this... the air.—" *MD* 467: Ahab is being hoisted by rope to the main royal masthead when he sees the whale ['... high sparkling... air.'].

145:15 "At length [144:37]... gliding whale——" *MD* 268–9 ['... prey, that... head beyond... soft Turkish-rugged... over into the... the painted hull... the cloud of... fro skimming like... tail feathers... whale.'].

145:17 The fight... lasted three days.   Chaps. CXXXII–CXXXIV, one chapter for each day.

145:20 the torn body... now seen lashed... harpoon-lines,   See *MD* 488: 'Lashed round and round to the fish's back... the whale had reeled the involutions of the lines around him... the half torn body of the Parsee was seen'.

145:32 "The Ship [145:23]... out of sight—"   *MD* 492 ['The ship... out of water... lookouts... sight.']. See too note on 129:29.

145:34 the eagle, St John's bird, the Red Indian... American,   The Evangelistic Beast for St John... the eagle (and its feathers) played an essential part in the religious life and decorative art of the Native Americans of the Southwest.

145:38 "Now small... years ago."   *MD* 493 ['... collapsed, and the...'].

146:39 the war... all flotsam.   The First World War... floating wreckage from a ship.

147:1 Quien sabe... señor?   Who knows, sir? (Spanish)

147:7 *Boom!* as Vachel Lindsay would say.   See, e.g., ll. 5–9 of 'The Congo' (1914) by the American poet Vachel Lindsay (1879–1931):

> Beat an empty barrel with the handle of a broom,
> And as they were able
> Boom, boom, BOOM,
> With a silk umbrella and the handle of a broom,
> Boomlay, boomlay, boomlay, BOOM.

147:13 Post mortem effects,   Changes which occur after death, as a result of death. The phrase is apparently unknown outside DHL's own writing, but the Poe essay in its First Version (1918–19) refers to 'The process of the decomposition of the body' as 'a life process of post-mortem activity' (229:13–14). Cf. *MD* 364, where the cutting up of the whale and the removal of the valuable products are 'this post-mortemising of the whale' (post-mortem examination involves surgery). At 148:8, however, the word 'Ghosts' stands in apposition to the phrase, so that it clearly relates not only to decomposition, but also to a 'process' of change; Pryse, in *The Apocalypse Unsealed*, had referred to a phantasm which 'comes into existence only after the death of the physical body' (pp. 12–13)

147:14 **Cetus, the Whale.** Latin. Christ was linked not with the whale but with the fish from the second century AD: *ICHTHYS* (Greek for fish) being drawn from the formula *I*esous *CH*ristos *TH*eou *Y*ios *S*oter (Jesus Christ, Son of God, Saviour). See too Blavatsky, *Isis Unveiled*, ii. 256–7.

Whitman (Final Version 1923)

148:2 **Whitman.** Walt Whitman (1819–92) grew up in Brooklyn, New York, and was originally a printer and teacher. He became a journalist and newspaper editor; in 1855 he published the first of seven editions of *Leaves of Grass* (12 untitled poems and a preface) which for the rest of his life he enormously extended and revised, to a final total of 389 poems. He worked as a volunteer nurse in army hospitals during the Civil War (1863–4) and in the Department of the Interior until fired in 1866 by the Secretary, who had found an annotated copy of *Leaves of Grass* on Whitman's desk. He then found employment in the Attorney General's office until partially incapacitated by a stroke in 1873 which compelled him to move to his brother's home in Camden, New Jersey, the unlovely city in which he spent his last two decades. DHL was apparently using the slightly bowdlerised 1912 Everyman edition *Leaves of Grass (1) & Democratic Vistas*, which included no poems after Whitman's 1867 edition and contained errors such as the title 'I Sing of the Body Electric' for 'I Sing the Body Electric' (*LG* 80); plans for a second Everyman volume to include the rest of *Leaves of Grass* and thus '*complete the work*' (*LG* xiv) came to nothing.

148:5 **"good gray poet."** The first book about Whitman, *The Good Gray Poet*, by his friend and public advocate William D. O'Connor, was published in New York in 1866.

148:11 **beatitudes.** Matthew v. 3–11.

148:13 **DEMOCRACY!** ... **EIDOLONS** ... **ENDLESS LOVERS!** Whitman wrote constantly of Democracy: he referred to 'The greatness of Love and Democracy', invoked 'Democracy!' and 'Democracy's lands' ('Starting from Paumanok', l. 132, 156, 193, *LG* 17, 18, 19), while the first poem in *LG* ('One's-Self I Sing') stressed the word 'Democratic' (l. 2, *LG* 1) . . . 'Eidólons' are 'images, spectres, phantoms', the accent marking Whitman's unconventional pronunciation of the word: see his poem 'Eidólons' (4) . . . first cited in the Intermediate Version (1919) of the essay (Roberts E382b) as 'Lovers, endless lovers', but not a quotation from Whitman; however, a synthesis of his poetic language. 'Endless' and 'lovers' are very common words in *LG*; see, e.g., note on 150:18 and 'Song of Myself', l. 477: 'Endless unfolding of words of ages!' (43); see too 'And that all the men ever born are also my brothers, and the women my sisters and lovers' ('Song of Myself', l. 86, *LG* 28): 'Every room of the house do I fill with an arm'd force, / Lovers of me, bafflers of graves' (ll. 1012–13, *LG* 64): 'My lovers suffocate me! / Crowding my lips, thick in the pores of my skin' (ll. 1169–70, *LG* 70).

148:14 **ONE IDENTITY!** 'Our Old Feuillage', l. 77: 'Singing the song of These, my ever-united lands – my body no more inevitably united, part to part, and made out of a thousand diverse contributions one identity, any more than my lands are inevitably united and made ONE IDENTITY' (*LG* 147). Cf. too Whitman's phrase 'Always a knit of identity' ('Song of Myself', l. 47, *LG* 26).

148:16 **I AM HE...AMOROUS LOVE.** Title and first line of a poem in the *LG* section *Children of Adam* (*LG* 93), quoted in full at 149:23–6.

148:28 **chews gum, admires Botticelli** Gum chewing was quintessentially American, its practice ('A piece of gum to chaw') first recorded in Philadelphia in 1842 (*OED2* 1 d.). Americans regularly made the pilgrimage to Europe (see the 1920 'Foreword' in Appendix II), in particular to Florence, where in the Uffizi they could see the most famous paintings by Sandro Botticelli (1444–1510): DHL refers to 'those poor English and Americans in front of the Botticelli Venus' in 'Introduction to these Paintings', *Phoenix* 557.

149:13 **Forty million foot-pounds pressure.** A mixture of two different kinds of measurement: foot-pounds are units of energy or work required to raise one pound weight one foot, but steam-locomotives had their boiler pressure denoted in pounds per square inch (a locomotive boiler of the period ran at between 130 and 175 pounds per square inch). Locomotive power can also, however, be measured in horse-power, and a locomotive might be rated at 1,000 horse-power: as 40 million foot-pounds per second are equivalent to over 72,000 horse-power, DHL is exaggerating.

149:15 **Belinda...his Native Land,** DHL may perhaps be thinking of literary heroines; e.g. 'The Rape of the Lock' (1712–14) by Alexander Pope (1688–1744), *Belinda* (1801) by Maria Edgeworth (1767–1849) and *Belinda* (1883) by Rhoda Broughton (1840–1920)...cf. Scott's 'The Lay of the Last Minstrel' (1805), vi. 3: 'This is my own, my native land!'; DHL discusses the line in his 1923 essay 'On Coming Home', *Reflections* 177–83.

149:19 **superhuman...superman** Although the adjective 'superhuman' dates from the seventeenth century, from the mid-1890s it was sometimes used as a noun to translate Nietzsche's German *Übermensch* ('a superhuman'), an ideal superior being evolved from the normal human type... 'superman' was (following G. B. Shaw's *Man and Superman* of 1903) the more common translation.

149:21 **his "splendid animality."** Not apparently a quotation, but in 1856 Thoreau had commented on Whitman's writing: 'It is as if the beasts spoke', and John Cowper Powys had referred in 1915 to Whitman's 'boisterous animal-spirits' (*A Century of Whitman Criticism*, ed. E. H. Miller, Bloomington, 1969, pp. 5, 147). As DHL inserted this sentence into MS8 after the previous and subsequent sentences had been written, it is possible that he was responding to a sentence he could very recently have read in Sherman's *Americans*: 'Mr. George Santayana represents him as a kind of placid animal wallowing unreflectively in the stream of his own sensations' (p. 170); in 1900,

Santayana had referred to Whitman's 'hairiness and animality' (*Whitman: The Critical Heritage*, ed. Milton Hindus, 1971, p. 270).

149:26 **"I am he ... meet or know."** *LG* 93.

149:34 **Even bees ... their own queen.** Some bees swarm with the old queen-bee; others remain behind with the new queen. Bees, however, do not transfer loyalty from one hive to another.

149:38 **tricky-tricksy,** DHL's coinage; 'tricksy' probably in the sense both of 'tricky, cunning, cheating' (*OED2* 3) and of 'needing careful handling' (*OED2* 4).

150:10 **touch with a long prop.** I.e. the more usual idiom 'touch with a barge-pole' – keep at a considerable distance. A 'prop' (or 'clothes-prop') would be used for raising a washing line well clear of the ground.

150:17 **the Mundane Egg,** Many ancient nations believed the world to be egg-shaped (or hatched from an egg laid by the creator), an idea taken up by Theosophy; see Helena Blavatsky, *The Secret Doctrine* (1888), i. 65, 359–68, and Blavatsky, *Isis Unveiled*, ii. 214: 'the *mother-principle*, the mundane egg, or universal womb'.

150:19 **"Whoever you ... endless announcements— — — —"** 'Starting from Paumanok', l. 189 ['... to you endless announcements!'] (*LG* 19).

150:20 **"And of these ... the song of myself."** 'Song of Myself', l. 329 (*LG* 37).

150:23 **Oh Walter Walter** See note on 136:32.

150:31 **lists of things boiled in one pudding-cloth!** Some kinds of pudding – made, e.g., with bread-crumbs rather than suet – would be boiled in a cloth to keep the various ingredients together until they amalgamated during cooking. Many of Whitman's poems contain such 'catalogs': e.g. 'Song of Myself', where much of section 15 describes the characteristic behaviour of different figures such as The youth / The Wolverine / The squaw / The connoisseur / The deck-hands / The young sister / The one-year wife (ll. 288–94, *LG* 35–6).

150:33 **"I reject nothing,"** Not quite a quotation: but cf. 'By Blue Ontario's Shore', l. 11: 'I reject none, accept all, then reproduce all in my own forms' (*LG* 284). Cf. too 'Song of the Open Road', ll. 23–4: 'They pass, I also pass, anything passes, none can be interdicted, / None but are accepted, none but shall be dear to me' (*LG* 124); and 'City of Ships', ll. 13–14: 'I have rejected nothing you offer'd me – whom you adopted I have adopted, / Good or bad I never question you – I love all – I do not condemn anything' (*LG* 247).

150:37 **"I embrace ALL ... I weave all things into myself."** Not a quotation: but cf. 'Song of Myself', l. 329: 'And of these one and all I weave the song of myself' (*LG* 37).

151:2 **"And whoever walks ... his own shroud."** 'Song of Myself', l. 1272 ['... drest in his shroud'] (*LG* 74). See too DHL's own 'Retort to Whitman' (1929):

'And whoever walks a mile full of false sympathy / walks to the funeral of the whole human race' (*Complete Poems*, ed. Pinto and Roberts, ii. 653).

151:15 **paeans... Chants, Songs of Cinematernity... is done—"** Paeans are songs of praise... chants is a word frequently used in *LG*: e.g. '*chanting the chant of battles*' ('As I ponder'd in Silence', l. 17, *LG* 2) and 'For you a programme of chants' ('Starting from Paumanok', l. 39, *LG* 13). Whitman also referred to 'the following chants' at l. 2 of the last poem of the section 'Inscriptions', 'Thou Reader' (*LG* 11)... 'Songs of Eternity' is neither a poem nor a group of poems by Whitman, but 'Song' is extremely common: e.g. 'Song of Myself' (*LG* 24–77), 'Song of the Open Road' (*LG* 123–32)... see note on 136:32.

151:17 **an Esquimo sat in a kyak,** There seem to be no direct references either to Eskimos or to kyaks (or kayaks) in Whitman, but cf. 'Song of the Broad-Axe', l. 206: 'Seal-fishers, whalers, arctic seamen breaking passages through the ice' (*LG* 163); and 'Salut Au Monde!', ll. 124–6: 'I see the regions of snow and ice, / I see the sharp-eyed Samoiede and the Finn, / I see the seal-seeker in his boat poising his lance' (*LG* 119). Closest of all, perhaps, is 'Song of Myself', ll. 339–40, when Whitman offers himself as 'At home on Kanadian snow-shoes or up in the bush, or with fishermen off Newfoundland, / At home in the fleet of ice-boats, sailing with the rest and tacking' (*LG* 38).

151:24 **DEMOCRACY. EN MASSE.** Cf. 'One's-Self I Sing', ll. 1–2, in 'Inscriptions': 'One's-Self I sing, a simple separate person, / Yet utter the word Democratic, the word En-Masse' (*LG* 1); see too 'Song of Myself', l. 478: 'And mine a word of the modern, the word En-Masse' (*LG* 43).

151:29 **His poems, Democracy, En Masse, One Identity,** Not titles but leading ideas in Whitman's poems (at 152:8, 'ONE DIRECTION!' is not a quotation from Whitman either).

152:22 **"A woman waits for me—"** Title and first line of a poem in the *LG* section 'Children of Adam' (*LG* 87).

152:25 **"Athletic mothers of these States—"** Not a quotation from Whitman, but cf. 'To Foreign Lands', l. 2: 'America, her athletic Democracy' (*LG* 3); 'Our Old Feuillage', ll. 61–2: 'The athletic American matron speaking in public to... the individuality of the States' (*LG* 146); and 'By Blue Ontario's Shore', l. 191: 'Have you vivified yourself from the maternity of these States?' (*LG* 292).

152:31 **"As I see... Female I see."** 'I Sing the Body Electric', ll. 72–4 ['... head and...'] (*LG* 83); see note on 148:2.

152:37 **"This is the nucleus... the outlet again—"** 'I Sing the Body Electric', ll. 64–5 ['This the... This the... birth, this the... again.'] (*LG* 83).

153:11 **merge in a woman... *insist* on merging.** Cf. 'Song of Myself', l. 381: 'This the thoughtful merge of myself, and the outlet again' (*LG* 39).

153:12 *Calamus* A section of *LG* added to the collection in 1860, the poems composed mostly the previous year, and organised around the theme of manly love. Calamus is a large, aromatic rush with spear-shaped leaves.

153:17 **manly love, the love of comrades.** Frequent throughout *LG* but see 'For You O Democracy', ll. 8–9: 'By the love of comrades, / By the manly love of comrades' (*LG* 99). See too 'Starting from Paumanok', ll. 88, 92, 94: 'these are to found their own ideal of manly love, indicating it in me': 'I will write the evangel-poem of comrades and of love': 'And who but I should be the poet of comrades?' (*LG* 15).

153:26 **cohering principle... *Drum-Taps*.** None of the words DHL makes crucial – 'cohering', 'principle' or 'soldiery' – actually appears in the *Drum-Taps* section of *LG* (first published separately in 1865), but cf. 'Over the Carnage Rose Prophetic a Voice' l. 22, describing how the Union will be re-made by love and affection: '(Were you looking to be held together by lawyers? / Or by an agreement on a paper? or by arms? / Nay, nor the world, nor any living thing, will so cohere.)' (*LG* 265). The word 'cohering' appears a number of times elsewhere in *LG*.

154:3 **"Yet you are [153:31]... as you mean—"** 'Scented Herbage of My Breast', in *Calamus*, ll. 10–16 ['... me you... faint tinged... you, (what... O I think... most,) / Indeed O... you mean,'] (*LG* 97).

154:16 **David and Jonathan... the death of Jonathan.** See 1 Samuel xix–xx and 2 Samuel i. 17–27; cf. note on 101:8.

154:39 **"Whereto answering [154:30]... death, death—"** 'Out of the Cradle Endlessly Rocking', ll. 165–73 ['... sea, ... death.'] (*LG* 215).

155:4 *Après moi le déluge.* 'After me [or us] – the flood': words supposedly spoken by Madame de Pompadour (1721–64) ['... nous le...'].

155:9 **"Out of the cradle endlessly rocking—"** First poem in the section 'Sea-Drift' (*LG* 210–15).

155:31 **Pisgah. Pisgah sights... Moses.** The mountain from which Moses (just before he died) saw the Promised Land (Deuteronomy xxxiv. 1–4). A favourite DHL image: cf. *The Rainbow*, ed. Mark Kinkead-Weekes (Cambridge, 1989), 181:13, and his 1924 essay 'Climbing down Pisgah' (*Phoenix* 740–4). He would also have found a reference to 'Pisgah top' in Melville's *White-Jacket*, p. 372.

156:13 **Emerson... tiresome "superiority" of the soul.** Emerson insisted that the soul 'is not the intellect or the will, but the master of the intellect and the will; is the vast background of our being, in which they lie...' (*Essays 1st and 2nd Series*, p. 151).

156:15 **down among the potsherds.** Like Job, infected with boils by Satan: 'And he took him a potsherd to scrape himself withal' (Job ii. 8); a potsherd is a fragment of pot.

156:23 **The Open Road.** Cf. 'Song of the Open Road' (*LG* 123–32).

157:2 **sympathy,** I.e. 'feeling with' (157:3). Cf. 'A Song of Joys', l. 23: 'O the joy of that vast elemental sympathy which only the human soul is capable of generating and emitting in steady and limitless floods' (*LG* 149); see too note on 151:2.

157:13 **As leave** DHL's frequent form of 'as lief' – as well, as readily. See too *Reflections* 77:32–3 and n.

157:18 **"In my Father's house are many mansions."** John xiv. 2.

157:36 **Jesus' LOVE ... Paul's CHARITY.** E.g. Matthew xix. 19 and John xv. 13 ... 1 Corinthians xiii. 1–13.

157:40 **beyond Calvary.** Where Christ was crucified (Luke xxiii. 33).

158:7 **Like Flaubert and the leper.** 'La Légende de Saint Julien l'Hospitalier' (1877) by Gustave Flaubert (1821–80), in which Julien is asked by a leper: ' "Take off your clothes, because I need the warmth of your body! ... Come close, warm me! Not with your hands! no! your whole body." Julien spread himself out completely on him, mouth to mouth, stomach to stomach.' See too 160:1 and *Memoir of Maurice Magnus*, ed. Cushman, p. 100.

158:34 **the negro slave ... the prostitute ... the syphilitic.** E.g. 'Song of My-self', ll. 189–98 (*LG* 32). Whitman regularly linked the people DHL listed; e.g. 'Song of the Open Road', l. 19: 'The black with his woolly head, the felon, the diseas'd, the illiterate person, are not denied' (*LG* 123); 'A Song for Occupations', ll. 24–7: 'Because you are diseas'd, or rheumatic, or a prostitute ... Do you give in that you are any less immortal?' (*LG* 180); and 'Song of Myself', l. 376: 'The heavy-lipp'd slave is invited, the venerealee is invited' (*LG* 39).

159:13 **"Bear ye ... Love thy ... do unto me."** Paul in Galatians vi. 2 ... Leviticus xix. 18 and Christ in Matthew xix. 19 ... Christ in Matthew xxv. 40 ['Inasmuch as ye have done it unto one of the least of these my brethren, ye have done it unto me'].

159:29 **the Priapic mysteries.** The secrets of the phallic cult devoted to Priapus, the Greek god of gardens and vineyards, normally represented with an erect penis.

160:2 **Bubi de Montparnasse** Central character ('Bubu') in *Bubu of Montparnasse* (1901) by Charles-Louis Philippe (1874–1909). The prostitute (Berthe Méténier) living with Bubu finds that she has syphilis; he is at first horrified – 'the pox, Berthe had the Pox' (tr. Laurence Vail, Paris, 1932, p. 89) – but after getting drunk one afternoon, he reasons that not having syphilis 'would detract in some way from his glory': 'If he didn't have the pox then it was high time he had it' (p. 107). He goes home, makes love to Berthe in the kitchen and is infected.

161:32 **Chapala. 1923** DHL read proof and made his final revisions in Mexico during May–June 1923 (see Introduction). His previous revision (done in the winter of 1922–3 at the Del Monte Ranch) had been commemorated by 'LOBO, NEW MEXICO.' as printed in A1 (p 264).

I. The Spirit of Place (First Version 1918–19)

167:14 **Athanasius,** DHL's insistence on Athanasius' religious passion 'voicing itself in Latin' (167:13–14) is wrong: see note on 13:10.

167:33 **Virgil and Cicero and Tacitus,** Publius Vergilius Maro (70–19 BC), Roman poet; Marcus Tullius Cicero (106–43 BC), Roman consul and writer, often regarded as writing the purest form of Latin prose; Publius Cornelius Tacitus (AD ?55–?120), Roman historian. DHL drew upon Tacitus when writing his own history book in 1918–19: see *Movements* xix–xx, xl, 33–4.

169:3 **a universal mystic language,** Blavatsky takes the existence of such a 'once universal mystery language' for granted; see, e.g., *The Secret Doctrine*, i. 308–9: 'Mr Ralston Skinner, of Cincinnati', suggests that it was 'the language of the world and of universal use, possessed, however, as it became more and more moulded into its arcane forms, by a select class or caste' (i. 309). For Blavatsky, the tenets of the esoteric philosophy were taught 'in every religion, *ante* as well as *post* diluvian, in India and Chaldea, by the Chinese as by the Grecian sages' (i. 278).

169:18 **symbology . . . psychometry . . . psycho-analysis** The science or study of symbols . . . the scientific measurement of the duration and intensity of mental states . . . David Eder would be one of those DHL was thinking of as a scientist of the 'subtler psychic activities' (169:16).

170:19 **Spanish and Venetian sailors** E.g. the Spanish voyages of discovery to America 1492–1502, led by Columbus. Venice, however, although renowned for its effectiveness as a sea-power, was always more concerned with European politics and trade with the East (e.g. India and the East Indies) than with America, and the Italians most concerned with the discovery of America were not Venetian: Amerigo Vespucci (?1454–1512) was from Florence and John Cabot (1450–98) probably from Genoa, as was Columbus himself.

170:40 **Roman history [170:35] . . . Gaul . . . Constantinople** DHL had described exactly this change in *Movements* 16–24; the shift of the Roman empire capital to Constantinople (20:34) took place in AD 334.

171:4 **Athens . . . Sardis . . . Ecbatana . . . Treves,** Imperial capitals: ancient and modern capital of Greece . . . ancient city and capital of Lydia in West Asia Minor . . . ancient city in Iran (on the site of the modern Hamadān), capital of Media and royal residence of the Persians and Parthians . . . French name (properly Trèves) for Trier, ancient Roman capital and one of the oldest towns in central Europe.

171:11 **the time of Diocletian** Gaius Aurelius Valerius Diocletianus (AD 245–313), Roman Emperor (AD 284–305) who divided the empire into four units; see *Movements* 17:8–18:1.

171:33 **Celtic Christianity ... quite apart from the whole Italian-Germanic Christianity** For roughly 150 years, at the end of the Roman empire – the period *c.* 400–550 – Celtic Christianity was effectively cut off from Rome, and a number of early practices were therefore preserved. At the end of the sixth century, the Celtic Bishops who met St Augustine of Canterbury (d. 604) were still refusing to conform with Rome by changing the date of Easter, as well as their tonsure and baptismal practices (it was Augustine's mission to establish the authority of the Roman see over the Celtic church). DHL is also thinking of the massive emigration to the USA in the mid-nineteenth century from Ireland and Scotland (see 172:8, 177:27, 30).

172:18 **the Celtic Tir na Og.** Normally 'tír na nóg', the fabled land of perpetual youth, an Irish version of Elysium; sometimes conceived as three phantom islands.

172:24 **Vikings should sail to Greenland and Labrador.** The Vikings had discovered Greenland *c.* 900 and settled it by 984; Leif Eiriksson had discovered Labrador ('Helluland') by *c.* 1000. The Vikings went still further south, to Nova Scotia ('Markland') for certain, though the exact location of the 'Vinland' colonies visited by Bishop Eirik in 1121 is still disputed. See note on 288:14.

173:2 **Cortes [172:36] ... Montezuma, the priest-emperor ... embraced the Spanish** DHL draws his information from the *History of the Conquest of Mexico* (1843) by William Hickling Prescott (1796–1859). Hernán Cortés (1485–1547), Spanish soldier, landed in Mexico in February 1519 and by November had fought his way to Tenochtitlán, the Aztec capital, where he imprisoned the last Aztec emperor Montezuma (or Moctezuma) II (1466–1520); the latter swore allegiance to Spain in 1520 (Prescott, p. 324) but was killed during an uprising. See too note on 197:10.

174:13 **the Spaniards of the Inquisition** The Holy Office, the judicial institution of the Roman Catholic Church, for the suppression of heresy and the punishment of heretics, started in the thirteenth century; the Spanish Inquisition (with the Inquisitor General at its head) was renowned in the sixteenth century for the ferocity of its investigations, and was only abolished in 1834.

174:20 **a gloomy passion ... to destroy or mutilate life at its very quick,** E.g. the early Christian theologian and pioneer in Biblical analysis Origen (185–254), born in Alexandria, who deliberately underwent castration.

174:29 **Bernard of Clairvaux ... Martin Luther,** Cistercian monk (1090–1153) who founded the Abbey of Clairvaux ... German monk (1483–1546), principal founder of Protestantism; see *Movements* 130:32–3, 146:19–21, 175:3–181:18.

174:32 **Calvinism** Theological system of John Calvin (1509–64, theologian and ecclesiastical reformer) and his followers, characterised by emphasis on predestination and justification by faith.

175:33 **fakir-like ... St. Anthony frenzied in celibacy,** Like the Hindu devotee and naked ascetic ... Anthony the Egyptian hermit (AD ?251–?356), commonly regarded as the founder of European monasticism.

175:21 **the first Yankees** The origin of the name is much disputed; 'the most plausible' (*OED2*) explanation is that a version of the Dutch *Janke*, 'John', became an (originally derogatory) designation of English colonists in New England and was in use by the 1683, so indeed used 'After only two generations in New England'.

176:37 **the Jews.** 1917–18 marked DHL's development of a number of theories about the Jews: e.g. Jews knowing the truth but betraying it (*Letters*, iii. 144); their hatred of mankind (*Letters*, iii. 242–3); and (appropriately here) in letters to his Jewish friend Koteliansky about 'the conscious ego' and the 'ultra-conscious Jew' (*Letters*, iii. 137, 284). Cf. too *WL* 428:13-21.

177:37 **salt-licks.** Places to which animals go to lick exposed natural deposits of salt.

178:9 **transubstantiation.** A complete transmutation: an example of the word being used outside the Christian context (see note on 336:26).

178:22 **blue gentian flower ... edelweiss flower ... shaped like snow-crystals.** Any of the blue-flowered varieties of the genus *Gentiana*; cf. DHL's poem 'Bavarian Gentians' (*Complete Poems*, ed. Pinto and Roberts, ii. 697, 963) ... the Edelweiss (*Leontopodium alpinum*), growing in often barely accessible rocky places in the Swiss mountains, is remarkable for its star-shaped white flower.

178:38 **put forth ... grapes, like the ship of Dionysos** Greek god of wine and fruitfulness; in 1916 DHL had described as 'very lovely and delightful' a picture of 'Dionysos in a ship with ... the mast a tree with grapes, sailing over a yellow sea' which he had found in the Loeb *Hesiod, The Homeric Hymns*: an illustration from a Greek vase. See *Letters*, ii. 517 and no. 2.

II. Benjamin Franklin (First Version 1918–19)

180:14 **the Millennium of the world.** Here, the time of peace and happiness, in the distant future.

180:18 **The magicians knew ... what it was to create a being out of the intense *will* of the soul.** Blavatsky quotes an account of the creation of a spirit flower (*Isis Unveiled*, ii. 610) and cites an authority declaring that 'The magician ... can compel the presence and assistance of spirits of lower grades of being than himself' (i. 367), but no authority for DHL's assertion has been found.

180:20 **Mary Shelley ... Frankenstein's monster.** Mary Wollstonecraft (Godwin) Shelley, wife of Percy Bysshe Shelley (see note on 32:28), published her novel *Frankenstein* in 1818.

180:24 **According to the early creed, the only power that the Almighty Creator could *not* confer ... was this same power of creation.** Not precisely true of any of the early Christian creeds, but they were indeed part of a process of defining, as integral to orthodoxy, the dogma of creation from nothing, which then reserved creation – in this specific sense of necessity – to God alone. DHL is probably thinking of the Athanasian creed and the Nicene creed (see note on 206:19), both insisting that although the three persons of the Trinity are one person, yet their capacities are different. In the Athanasian creed, 'The Father is made of none: neither created, nor begotten. The Son is of the Father alone: not made, nor created, but begotten.' The Nicene creed stressed some of the same points ('God the Father Almighty, Maker of heaven and earth . . . Jesus Christ . . . being of one substance with the Father, By whom all things were made'). Cf. incidentally Cooper: ' "Is the power to give life to inanimate matter the gift of man?" "I would it were!" ' (*PR* 71).

182:20 **the universe is a bush which burns for ever . . . consuming itself and yet never consumed;** Cf. Exodus iii. 2. Burnet, *Early Greek Philosophy*, quotes Herakleitos: 'This world . . . was ever, and ever shall be an ever-living Fire, with measures of it kindling, and measures going out' (p. 134).

182:34 **always Now.** Cf. DHL's poem 'Manifesto' (1917): 'We shall not look before and after. / We shall *be, now.* / We shall know in full. We, the mystic NOW' (*Complete Poems*, ed. Pinto and Roberts, i. 268).

183:8 **The reality . . . the rose in flower . . . the snake in brindled colour, the tiger in his stripes.** Language strongly reminiscent of DHL's 'The Reality of Peace' (1917) (e.g. *Reflections* 47:3–4, 52:9, 37:21, 38:30, 43:21).

183:20 *adsum* I am present (Latin): traditionally the answer to a roll-call.

184:7 **Congreves . . . Addisons . . . Smolletts . . . Robert Burns.** Cf. William Congreve (1670–1729), famous for the wit and suggestiveness of plays such as *The Way of the World* (1700) . . . Joseph Addison (1672–1719), English essayist and poet, founder of the *Spectator*, correct and pious, thus misplaced in this list of the exuberant and self-indulgent . . . Tobias George Smollett (1721–71), Scottish novelist, whose robust picaresque novels include *Roderick Random* (1748) . . . Robert Burns (1759–96), Scottish poet whose dialect, rebellious and often bawdy poems DHL admired, and whom he recreated as 'Jack Haseldine' in his 'Burns Novel' (see *Love Among the Haystacks*, ed. Worthen, 201–11).

184:20 **Shelley . . . Verlaine . . . Swinburne . . . Tolstoi,** See note on 32:28: Shelley was notorious for his belief in (and practice of) free love, as well as for poems such as 'Prometheus Unbound' (1819) and 'When the lamp is shattered' (1822) . . . Paul Verlaine (1844–96), French poet, famous for the sensuality of poetry such as in *Romances sans Paroles* (1874) . . . Swinburne (see note on 106:22) was notorious in the 1860s and 1870s for the passion and encoded sexuality of his writing in, e.g., *Poems and Ballads* (1860) . . . see note on 12:5; cf. DHL's description of Tolstoy's contradictions over love in 'The Novel' (1925): 'where would any of Leo's books be, without the phallic splendour? . . . Leo worshipped the human male, man as a column of rapacious and living blood'. However, 'Tolstoi had that last weakness of a great man: he wanted

Explanatory notes

the absolute: the absolute of love, if you like to call it that' (*Hardy* 180:16–17, 187:1–2, 26–7).

185:39 **the old** *virtus* DHL's reworking of the Latin 'manliness, courage' with at least two of the archaic meanings of 'virtue' as (e.g. in *KJB*): 'The power or operative influence inherent in a supernatural or divine being' and 'Physical strength, force, or energy' (cf. Mark v. 30, Luke vi. 19).

187:23 **He drew up a table** [187:19] ... **he does not give us his marked chart ... "Order."** In fact the Everyman edition from which DHL was working not only supplied the table DHL describes (*BFA* 102) – though with the days of the week along the top and not 'down the side' – but also marked it.

TEMPERANCE						
Eat not to dullness						
Drink not to elevation						
S.	M.	T.	W.	T.	F.	S.
T						
S *	*		*		*	
O **	*	*		*	*	*
R		*		*		
F	*			*		
I		*				
S						
J						
M						
C						
T						
C						
H						

The Everyman table reproduced above also erroneously placed the two 'Sunday' marks against 'Order' rather than 'Silence' (see, e.g., *Benjamin Franklin's Autobiography*, ed. J. A. Leo Lemay and P. M. Zall, New York, 1986, p. 133), thus making Franklin's failure still worse.

189:10 **a printer's workman, in London, for a short time.** Franklin was in London from November 1724 to July 1726, working most of the time as a printer's apprentice.

190:18 **the great Greek-Christian will-to-knowledge** DHL is probably thinking of the Socratic obligation to 'Know thyself' and the corresponding Christian demand for complete moral consciousness of, and responsibility for, one's behaviour.

III. Henry St. John de Crèvecoeur (First Version 1918–19)

193:19 **I am I,** Cf. 'Foreword to "Sons and Lovers"' (1913) (*Sons and Lovers*, ed. Baron and Baron, 472:9–12), 'Study of Thomas Hardy' (*Hardy* 13:7), 'The Crown' (*Reflections* 254:39), etc.

194:13 **Shelley sought... spiritual consummation,** See note on 214:6.

195:12 **"Now [195:8]... sweet and pure... That is my spouse... fountain of life."** DHL, not Crèvecoeur.

195:22 **Châteaubriand** The circumflex on Chateaubriand is incorrect: see note on 33:15.

195:25 **Arcadians,** I.e. inhabitants of Arcadia (the idealised rural site of pastoral poetry), themselves rustic or bucolic, or leading the simple life.

196:9 **Dmitri Karamazov... exposed naked, is virtually killed.** In *The Brothers Karamazov*, Dmitri is tried for the murder of his father and found guilty (Book 12, chap. 14).

196:27 **the God-King.** 'The kings of Egypt were deified in their lifetime... "It has never been doubted that the king claimed actual divinity; he was the 'great god,' the 'golden Horus,' and son of Ra"' (Frazer, *The Golden Bough*, chap. VIII). But cf. also 'Democracy' (September–October 1919) on the 'king-god', who 'extends the dominion of his own consciousness and will over all things' (*Reflections* 72:10–11).

196:30 **Napoleon... his brief ascendancy.** Napoleon Bonaparte (1769–1821) came to power in 1799 but was Emperor of France for only eleven years (1804–15).

197:10 **the dark-lustrous mantle of the feathers of birds,** DHL's reference strongly suggests his debt to Prescott's *History of the Conquest of Mexico*, which described human sacrifice (pp. 38–41) and also 'mantles of feather-work exquisitely made' and 'the gorgeous feather-work in which they excelled' (pp. 19, 22) (examples of Aztec feather-work, including a head-dress presented to Cortés by Montezuma, survive). DHL noted the 'Aztec' quality of 'the gorgeously beautiful' as early as his 1917 notes on *The Scarlet Letter*; see note on 373:28.

198:23 **It is like Herodotus... invent or repeat fables.** Greek historian (490–?425 BC), famous for his *History* dealing with the causes and events of the wars between the Greeks and the Persians. DHL refers to such anecdotes as Arion being carried to Taenarum on the back of a dolphin.

IV. Fenimore Cooper's Anglo-American Novels
(First Version 1918–19)

204:9 **Science ... asserted ... law of polarity**   Nineteenth-century biologists, in particular, had described how laws of polarity were observed by nature – Herbert Spencer, e.g., discussed this in *Principles of Biology* (1864–7), I. ii. iv. 181 – and discoveries about the polarities of eggs were being made 1895–1924; but Jungian psychology (see notes on 217:10, 236:26 and 358:16) also insisted that the psyche was essentially polarised between opposite, dual poles, and DHL's awareness of scientific assertions 'of late' would probably have included this in his sense of 'knowledge, which is the very beginning of psychology' (204:28).

204:33 **the Eleusinian mysteries,**   Religious festival, held in September at the town of Eleusis in Attica (about 23 km w. of Athens) in classical times, in which initiates celebrated Persephone, Demeter and Dionysos; at 205:24–6 DHL describes one of the rituals.

205:8 **St. John gives us ... upper or spiritual dynamic consciousness,**   See, e.g., Pryse, *The Apocalypse Unsealed*, pp. 64, 70, though DHL is here moving away from his source into his own re-working of Pryse's ideas.

206:7 **Gnostics, the Manicheans ... Greek esotericism ... Persian,**   Gnostics – to the Christians various heretical sects, some Greek – claimed to have superior knowledge ('gnosis') on various spiritual matters; some, e.g., believed that the spiritual element in man could be released from its bondage in matter; others that there were more gods than one; see, e.g., Blavatsky, *Isis Unveiled*, ii. 155–7. The word can, however, be used for esoteric groups more generally. The Manicheans believed (also heretically) that a primordial conflict between dark and light was central to the universe and its structures (the group was named after the supposed Persian prophet Mani, *c.* third century AD); see note on 266:12. Blavatsky's *The Secret Doctrine*, ii. 389, brings them together with the Gnostics ... by 'Greek esoterics', DHL would have meant writers like Pythagoras (see Burnet, *Early Greek Philosophy*, pp. 84–112) ... by 'Persian' he would have meant teachers like Mani and also the Zoroastrians, Zoroaster being the 'teacher and instructor of Pythagoras' (Blavatsky, *Isis Unveiled*, ii. 141).

206:14 **the intricacies ... of the Homoousion.**   A Homoousian was a Christian who believed that the Son was of the same substance with the Father, as opposed to a Homoiousian, who believed that the Son was of like (but not identical) substance with the Father: a refinement of the Arian heresy (see next note).

206:19 **the Council of Nice, and the General Councils,**   The council of Nicaea, the first General Council of the Church, was held in AD 325 to settle the Arian controversy, provoked by the teaching of Arius of Alexandria that Christ was not of one substance with the Father, but a created being raised to the status of the Son of God by the Father. The Nicene Council condemned Arianism as a heresy and promulgated the Nicene Creed (authorised at the next General Council of the Church, at Constantinople in AD 381); its teaching was taken further by the so-called Athanasian Creed, dating from the fourth century. See too note on 180:24.

206:21 unreadable riddle of the Apocalypse. Cf. DHL's review in 1924 of Dr John Oman's book on *Revelation*: 'old symbols have many meanings, and we only define one meaning in order to leave another undefined. So with the meaning of the Book of Revelation. Hence the inexhaustibility of its attraction' (*Apocalypse*, ed. Kalnins, 42:1–4).

211:21 pursuits at sea, fleeing scoundrels, lords in disguise, shipwrecks, ferocious savages of the Sahara Plot events of *Homeward Bound*: the *Montauk* is pursued (the novel's subtitle was *The Chase: A Tale of the Sea*), and Henry Sandon is a criminal on the run; as well as one real baronet (Sir George Templemore) there is a false baronet on board, while the *Montauk* is at one point boarded and captured by Arabs.

212:30 disquality I.e. difference: *OED2* dismisses it as a 'nonce-word' meaning 'defect', first used in 1863.

213:23 wound up ⌊213:19⌋ ... let me not be wound up." With its clockwork – the motive power of many gramophones (phonographs) until the 1930s – wound up: see 213:29 ... the phrase 'let me not be' is frequent in *KJB*: e.g. Psalm xxv. 2 ('O my God, I trust in thee, let me not be ashamed'.

213:33 St. Francis ... astonished peasant, See note on 37:7. DHL uses the same reference in 'Education of the People': 'Saint Francis was ready to fall in rapture at the feet of the peasant' (*Reflections* 102:10–11). Admonished by a peasant 'fall not short of that which men hope to find thee', St Francis 'cast himself to earth ... and kneeled him down before that villain and kissed his feet' (*The Little Flowers of St. Francis*, p. 92).

213:35 Father Zosimus ... Dmitri Karamazov. In *The Brothers Karamazov*, Father Zossima prostrates himself to Dmitri in Book 2, chap. 6.

214:6 The tiger ... Shelley ... the lamb. There is no evidence in the writing of Shelley to support this, but cf. DHL's analysis of Shelley in 'Study of Thomas Hardy': 'In the ordinary sense, Shelley never lived. He transcended life ... Why should he insist on the bodylessness of beauty, when we cannot know of any save embodied beauty' (*Hardy* 71:8–9, 13–14).

214:8 to Sennacherib ... the winged and burning lion. Sennacherib (murdered 681 BC) was the most famous King of Assyria 705–681 BC: having invaded Judah twice, he lost and then re-took Babylon in 689 BC, when he totally destroyed it. No particular link between him and lions can be established; DHL may be thinking of his predecessor Assurnasirpal II (883–859 BC) who appears in a famous alabaster relief at the British Museum hunting lions from his chariot. In 1914 DHL had gone to the Museum (see note on 268:36) and was deeply impressed by the 'Assyrian sculpture' (*Letters*, ii. 218); he was still recalling an Assyrian carving of 'a she-lion' in 'Him with his Tail in his Mouth' in 1925 (see *Reflections* 316:23–4).

V. Fenimore Cooper's Leatherstocking Novels
(First Version 1918–19)

216:5 Orpheus into hell, Orpheus, poet and lyre-player, managed (through the expressive power of his music) to penetrate Hades (hell) in search of his dead wife Eurydice, but was obliged to return without her.

216:28 Doppelgänger Ghostly counterpart of a living person (German); see *The Trespasser*, ed. Elizabeth Mansfield (Cambridge, 1981), 115:2.

217:10 Longfellow and Prescott, See note on 81:15; Longfellow's best-known writing for English readers of DHL's generation would have been *The Song of Hiawatha* (1855), a poem in fifteen parts about Native American life; the Swiss psychoanalyst Carl Gustav Jung (1875–1961) examined it for its revelation of the pre-sexual stage of development and the 'terrible mother' (*Psychology of the Unconscious*, pp. 191–3) ... DHL knew both *The History of the Conquest of Peru* (1847) by Prescott – he sent a copy to Katherine Mansfield in 1918 (*Letters*, iii. 327) – and *The History of the Conquest of Mexico* (see note on 173:2); both were in Everyman's Library. See too *The Plumed Serpent*, ed. L. D. Clark (Cambridge, 1987), note on 79:33.

217:39 Hurry Harry and Hetty Hutter In *Deerslayer*; see above, pp. 63–4.

220:9 the Sons of Anak. See Numbers xiii. 1–33; Anak is Hebrew for 'giant'. Moses sent thirteen observers to 'spy out the land of Canaan' (17) who reported its fruitfulness, but also warned that 'the people be strong that dwell in the land' (28) and that in Hebron are 'Ahiman, Sheshai, and Talmai, the children of Anak' (22); there follows an 'evil report of the land ... there we saw the giants, the sons of Anak, which come of the giants' (32–3). In Milton's *Samson Agonistes* (1671), l. 528, a type of the gigantic; since then proverbial.

220:20 some sensuous, soft, Asiatic or Polynesian quality, DHL may be thinking of the first appearance of the young Pawnee Native American Hard-Heart: 'the secondary features of his face were slightly marked with the well-known traces of his Asiatic origin'; he wears 'a light robe of the finest dressed deer-skin ... His leggings were of bright scarlet cloth' (*PR* 202–3).

221:36 twice ... into death, At least five hostile Native Americans fall to spectacular deaths in *The Last of the Mohicans*: one is knifed and falls 'sullenly and disappointed down the irrecoverable precipice' (74); another goes over a waterfall, 'with a sullen plunge, into that deep and yawning abyss' (72). But in each of the three episodes which describe a fall after a shooting, Hawk-eye shoots his opponent from below, not 'from overhead': he shoots a man who falls 'headlong among the clefts of the island' (73); he shoots a Huron in a tree: 'the limbs of the victim trembled and contracted, the head fell to the bosom, and the body parted the foaming waters, like lead' (79); and he shoots Magua (382: see note on 62:30).

223:1 **wing-covered seraph** Cf. the description of the seraphim in Isaiah vi. 2 ('each one had six wings: with twain he covered his face, and with twain he covered his feet, and with twain he did fly').

223:9 **anima,** Although the word has become strongly associated with Jung, he was not using the word (taken from Plato) in 1918 to describe the innermost "soul" of the individual, mediated between consciousness and the collective unconscious, and – in men – always female in nature. Jung's first use in this sense would come only in 1920 with *Psychological Types*, first translated in 1923 by Godwin Baynes (see *Letters*, i. 475 n. 3 and iii. 377 n. 4); but even the 1920 reference 'was so cryptic that one could not have guessed the importance he already attached to the idea' (John Kerr, *A Most Dangerous Method*, 1994, pp. 502–3).

223:14 **the flower that generates the seed in the first instance,** Cf. 'Study of Thomas Hardy', *Hardy* 12:38–9.

224:2 *amour propre,* Self respect (French).

224:31 **Ellen ... the admirable young female of *Oak Openings*.** Ellen Wade (*PR* 14) ... Margery Waring in Cooper's late novel *The Oak Openings; or, The Bee-Hunter* (1848): 'almost uniformly called Blossom by her acquaintances', she has 'that happy admixture of delicacy and physical energy which is, perhaps, oftener to be met in the American girl of her class than in the girl of almost any other nation' (chap. V).

225:6 **Hardy ... Turgenev ... Irish verse.** For Thomas Hardy, see notes on 38:19, 60:23, 64:14 and 88:15: DHL may be thinking of what in 1914 he called 'the background of dark, passionate Egdon, of the leafy, sappy passion and sentiment of the woodlands' (*Hardy* 28:36–7) ... see note on 30:29: DHL read Turgenev's *A Sportsman's Sketches* (1895) in November 1916, just after *Deerslayer*, and described it as 'so very *obvious* and coarse, beside the lovely mature and sensitive art of Fennimore Cooper or Hardy' (*Letters*, iii. 41: an error probably induced by the misspelling of the name in the Everyman catalogue) ... DHL is probably thinking of the verse of the 'Celtic Twilight', for example by W. B. Yeats, whom he also described as 'sickly' (*Letters*, ii. 248).

227:11 **candid ... candescent:** White, pure ... glowing white hot ('rare' in *OED2*).

227:14 **scotched snake,** *Macbeth* III. ii. 13 was in the past generally printed and spoken as 'We have scotch'd the snake, not killed it': i.e. the snake rendered only temporarily harmless. Now proverbial (*OED2* 2.a.), 'scotched' is actually a conjectural emendation of the Folio text's 'scorch'd' – i.e. slashed with a knife (*OED2* v³) – made by the Shakespearean editor Lewis Theobald (1688–1744) in 1733, but now generally discredited.

228:6 **the hand ... laid on him ... far out on the water.** *DS* 73:3.

VI. Edgar Allan Poe (First Version 1918–19)

229:8 **seething down** Although 'seething' suggests agitation, as in boiling liquid, DHL uses the word in a sense akin to *OED2* 3 to mean 'reducing' (cf. 'seething back' at 229:10 and 'reduced back' at 229:16); at 229:23 it clearly has the underlying meaning of reduction rather than expansion. 'Reduction' is an important concept in DHL's philosophical thinking: e.g. 'The Crown', *Reflections* 293:10–12; *Twilight in Italy*, ed. Paul Eggert (Cambridge, 1994), 131:35.

230:1 **phosphorescence of decay.** Cf. *Sons and Lovers*, ed. Baron and Baron, 464:35 and n.; *The Rainbow*, ed. Kinkead-Weekes, 294:21; *Twilight in Italy*, ed. Eggert, 176:37.

230:6 **how the dead bury their dead.** Referring to one of DHL's favourite biblical quotations, 'Let the dead bury their dead' (Matthew viii. 22); see *FWL* 186:31, 301:12; *Letters*, ii. 627, 638; *Reflections* 41:35; Nehls, i. 440.

230:9 **fall into the ground and perish before it can bring forth new life.** Cf. John xii. 24: 'Except a corn of wheat fall into the ground and die, it abideth alone: but if it die, it bringeth forth much fruit.'

230:23 **a living dead.** The use of 'a dead' as a singular noun for 'one who is dead' is now obsolete (*OED2* B.1.a., last used 1691). Some African tribes speak of 'a living dead', an Ogbanje – e.g. a child only on loan to this world, who will shortly be called back to the other world – but DHL's phrase does not appear to have that meaning.

230:15 **a lodestone ... the soft metal.** Cf. *The Rainbow*, ed. Kinkead-Weekes, 296:28–36.

233:1 **The learning ... known in woman.** 'I have spoken of the learning of Ligeia: it was immense – such as I have never known in woman' (*TMI* 159).

233:4 **one of ... the world.** Matthew iv. 8–9.

236:26 **Jung ... all life is a matter of lapsing towards, or struggling away from, mother-incest.** DHL's access at this date to the work of Jung was via his conversations with David Eder and from Jung's book *Psychology of the Unconscious* (1918), which he had borrowed from Koteliansky and read by 5 December 1918 (see *Letters*, iii. 301); cf. Jung's description of 'the longing to go back to the mother, which is opposed to the adaptation to reality' (p. 184), 'the paralysing longing for the mother' (p. 204), and DHL's description of the book's concentration on the 'Mother-incest idea' (*Letters*, iii. 301).

VII. Nathaniel Hawthorne (First Version 1918–19)

243:38 knowledge will be in full, not always in part, as it is now. Cf. 1 Corinthians xiii. 12: 'For now we see through a glass, darkly; but then face to face: now I know in part; but then shall I know even as also I am known.'

245:2 ethnology, The branch of anthropology that deals with races and peoples, their origins and relations with one another.

245:5 the Mother of the Maculate Conception. The opposite of the Virgin Mary (whose conception was 'immaculate', without stain of original sin): stained, spotted.

245:17 seven profound sense-activities . . . seven gates . . . seven great passional centres. Sight, hearing, touch, taste and smell are traditionally the five senses; it is not clear which two 'activities' DHL is adding to them . . . 'gates' is traditional for entrances to the body: two eyes, two nostrils, mouth, anus and urethra; cf. DHL's 1919 poem 'Seven Seals', *Complete Poems*, ed. Pinto and Roberts, i. 153–4. Pryse in *The Apocalypse Unsealed* points out that 'gateway' is derived from 'orifice', though to him there are 'twelve orifices of the body' (p. 33) . . . see notes on 267:6 and 344:32.

246:10 bruising the heel Cf. Genesis iii. 15.

247:28 In the creative union between man and woman, man must take the lead, Cf. DHL's comments on 5 December 1918: 'I do think men must go ahead absolutely in front of their women, without turning round to ask for permission or approval from their women. Consequently the women must follow as it were unquestioning. I can't help it, I believe this' (*Letters*, iii. 302).

247:31 nacreous, Pearly, hard, brilliantly white.

247:40 alone and self-responsible, A considerable change from 1914, when DHL had explained his hope that his 1913 novel 'The Sisters' (later to become *The Rainbow* and *Women in Love*) would show 'woman becoming individual, self-responsible, taking her own initiative' (*Letters*, ii. 165).

249:6 Whatever God there is, Cf. Henley's 'Invictus', l. 3 ('I thank whatever gods may be'), and 'The Garden of Proserpine' by Swinburne, ll. 83–4, to which Henley was indebted ('We thank with brief thanksgiving / Whatever gods may be').

249:12 Anna Karenin Heroine of *Anna Karenina*: see note on 105:18.

251:20 After his death . . . stand for "Abel". The 'A' is interpreted as 'Abel' long before Dimmesdale's death (which occurs at *TSL* 310); see, e.g., *TSL* 194.

252:23 mocks and tortures Dimmesdale See, e.g., *TSL* 162, where Pearl throws a prickly burr at Dimmesdale and – seeing his 'nervous dread' – 'clapped her little hands in the most extravagant ecstacy'.

252:40 the Golden Hermes, 'Golden' probably because of the long association between Hermes Trismegistus and alchemists' attempts to turn base metal into gold.

253:28 **As Chillingworth . . . dark necessity."** *TSL* 209.

254:13 **his great Election Sermon,** *TSL* 271–2.

254:16 **whole clue to Dostoevsky.** Smerdyakov, the murderer in *The Brothers Karamazov*, is epileptic, as Dostoevsky himself was; the latter suffered his first epileptic attack in 1850, following his arrest, imprisonment and sentence to forced labour the previous year.

254:21 **meets one . . . communion supper."** *TSL* 263: the Deacon is actually 'hoary-bearded' ['. . . mind, respecting . . .'].

254:24 **an old widow . . . the soul."** *TSL* 264.

254:28 **a girl . . . all her innocence.** *TSL* 264–5: DHL paraphrases 'to blight all the field of her innocence with one wicked look' (265).

254:40 **" 'Shall we not [254:34] . . . I fear!' "** *TSL* 309 ['. . . to his. 'Shall . . . seest!" . . . Hester–hush . . .'].

259:2 **Apuleius, with his metamorphoses . . . Petronius, with his** *Satyricon*, *The Golden Ass* of Apuleius was subtitled *Transformations* or *Metamorphoses* . . . Gaius Petronius (d. AD 66), supposed author of the *Satyricon*, a picaresque account of the licentiousness of society.

VIII. The Two Principles (First Version 1918–19)

260:8 **primal** DHL appears to be using this in the particular sense – relating to the needs, fears, behaviour which form the origins of emotional life – employed by Freudian psychology, and first recorded in 1918 (*OED2* 1.b.), rather than in the older sense of 'primitive' or 'original'. The dominant 'primal' male is the object of the child's Oedipal desires to murder him.

260:14 **plasm** The living matter, protoplasm.

260:18 **radio-active,** First used in 1898 to define a substance undergoing spontaneous nuclear decay with a consequent emission of radiation; employed figuratively from 1905 to mean 'intensely active'. DHL may however (like others) be influenced in his use of the word by 'radio' (*OED2* 3) as is suggested by his gloss 'connecting with all things, and having first-knowledge of all things' (260:18–19). See *WL* 332:24 and Explanatory note.

260:27 **The creative mystery . . . always will be.** Cf. Birkin's consoling certainty, in the revision of *Women in Love* done between 1917 and 1919, that 'If humanity ran into a cul de sac, and expended itself, the timeless creative mystery would bring forth some other being . . . The game was never up' (*WL* 479:3–7).

260:33 **in the beginning [260:28] . . . Heaven and Earth . . . two great valves** DHL reworks Genesis i. 1–4 and John i. 1, amalgamating Genesis i. 4 ('And God divided the light from the darkness') with his favourite theory of systole / diastole, the two movements of the heart valve (see 408:4).

261:3 the Spirit of God ... the waters. Genesis i. 2.

261:12 Surely this is true, scientifically, of the birth of light. Blavatsky, *The Secret Doctrine*, i. 40–1, says that 'Light is inconceivable except as coming from some source which is the cause of it; and as, in the instance of primordial light, that source is unknown ... therefore it is called "Darkness" by us ... Darkness, then, is the eternal matrix in which the sources of light appear and disappear.' Moving between The Waters and the cosmic fire, between darkness and darkness, light is born.

261:13 waters ... divided by the firmament. Genesis i. 6–7.

261:17 the ⊕ ... the Rosy Cross, One of the symbols recovered by the recreation of Rosicrucianism in the nineteenth century (the movement, originally an offshoot of masonry, led by R. W. Little); associated with the development of the Theosophical society, and its name appropriated by that society. Blavatsky calls this the astronomical cross of Egypt (*The Secret Doctrine*, ii. 557).

261:20 the end of the Second Day of Creation Genesis i. 8 (see too 'the First Day' at 262:20, 263:21: Genesis i. 5).

261:25 as the earliest Greek philosophers say, Cf. Burnet, *Early Greek Philosophy*: 'The statements of Aristotle [recording the philosophy of Thales] may be reduced to three: (1) The earth floats on water. (2) Water is the material cause of all things. (3) All things are full of gods' (pp. 47–8).

263:16 gold or chlorine or sulphur. See later in the essay for DHL's explanation of two elements of this strange conjunction: gold because it is a 'superb and enduring element', sulphur because it is a 'strange, unstable' element: it was also (along with mercury and salt) one of the three alchemical properties (see Blavatsky, *The Key to Theosophy*, 1900, p. 301). Chlorine is one of the non-metallic elements, a heavy gas.

265:3 invisible element ... between us and the sun, 'With the ancients, the divine luminiferous substance which pervades the whole universe' (Blavatsky, *The Key to Theosophy*, p. 299). See too note on 400:20.

265:15 the alchemistic air. Cf. also 'alchemistic Earth' (265:17): 'the alchemistic Four Elements of Earth, Air, Fire and Water' (265:18–19). Alchemy compared the four elements to the spiritual, mental, psychic and physical planes of human existence (see Blavatsky, *The Key to Theosophy*, p. 301).

265:16 Prima Materia Original matter (Latin).

265:40 Zoruba ... sulphur the dung of thunder: The Yoruba people of the w. region of Nigeria ... a misremembering of Frobenius: 'Sulphur, called Emi-Orun, or sun-dung' (*VOA* i. 250). An Ara-dung is a meteorite or thunderbolt (i. 209, 219).

266:12 **"the impious doctrine of the two principles."** St Augustine referred scathingly to 'your doctrine of two principles' in his attack on the Manichean heresy, 'Reply to Faustus the Manichean' (*The Works of Aurelius Augustine*, ed. Marcus Dodds, Edinburgh, 1872, v. 398). The Gnostics in the second century and the Manicheans in the fourth and fifth both questioned whether there were one or two first principles at work in the universe; orthodox Christianity came to be defined by the answer 'one'. See too Blavatsky, *Isis Unveiled*, ii. 489: 'the Two Brothers, the Good and Evil Principles, appear in the Myths of the Bible'.

266:34 **the Pythagoreans... asserting that all is number... the mystery of the roots of three, four, five, seven,** Cf. Burnet, *Early Greek Philosophy*: 'It was this... that led Pythagoras to say all things were numbers'; 'many of Hellenes think Pythagoras said things were made *of* number' (pp. 307–8). But although Pythagoras was responsible for discovering the numerical basis of harmonic intervals (pp. 106–7), and the Pythagoreans apparently explained some things by means of numbers – 'the "right time"... was seven, justice was four, and marriage three' (pp. 107–8) – they were not responsible for the study of square roots, as this suggests.

267:1 **the four Gospel Natures, the four Evangels... the Four Elements... the Four Activities... the Four Natures.** Presumably the different characters of the four gospel-writers; see note on 293:24... see, e.g., Blavatsky, *Isis Unveiled*, pp. 146–7... i.e. the four alchemical substances water, air, fire and earth... unclear, unless it refers to the 'four principal winds coming from the four cardinal points' (ibid. p. 147)... the Four Natures is certainly theosophical, and refers either to 'the physical quaternary, composed of four' (*The Key to Theosophy*, p. 89) – 'the physical body, Life or the vital principle, the astral body, the seat of animal passions and desires' (90) – or to 'the four kingdoms of nature... 4. *Animal kingdom*. 3. Vegetable Kingdom. 2. Mineral Kingdom. 1. Elements' (Blavatsky, *Isis Unveiled*, i. 329).

267:6 **a sevenfold or a fivefold reference.** Sevens in particular can be found everywhere: 'There must have been some reason why this figure [seven] was universally accepted as a mystic calculation... the Pythagoreans called the number seven the vehicle of life, as it contained body and soul' (Blavatsky, *Isis Unveiled*, ii. 417–18). However, 'Lao-Tze, in his *Tao-te-King*, mentions only five principles, because he, like the Vedântins, omits to include two principles, namely, the Spirit... and the physical body...' (Blavatsky, *The Key to Theosophy*, p. 116).

267:6 **the divided circle,** ⊕, Blavatsky discusses versions of this in *The Secret Doctrine*, i. 360–1, 433, and ii. 581.

267:14 **the ankh... the cross or Tau beneath the circle** ⚵, A tao cross with a loop on the top, symbolising eternal life, 'Isis with the... rope' (Jung, *Psychology of the Unconscious*, p. 153)... the 'handled cross' (see Blavatsky, *Isis Unveiled*, ii. 254), shaped like the Greek letter tau (τ). Blavatsky, *The Secret Doctrine*, says that 'the ansated Egyptian cross, or *tau*, the... Swastica, and the Christian cross have all the same meaning' (i. 657).

267:15 **the so-called symbol of Aphrodite...♀.** Also known as the mirror of Venus (speculum veneris): the symbol of the female, included by Jung in *Psychology of the Unconscious*, p. 153, and discussed by Blavatsky in *The Secret Doctrine*, ii. 546–7, 583, 600 . . . see note on 267:25.

267:20 **the sex division is one of the Chinese three sacred mysteries.** DHL's knowledge of Chinese thought would have been filtered through the understanding of western writers such as Annie Besant (1847–1933); her book *The Ancient Wisdom; an Outline of Theosophical Teachings* (1897) had suggested that Taoism saw man as a trinity of spirit, mind and body (pp. 11–12), and some such summary is likely to lie behind DHL's remark. The Taoist philosopher Chu-hsi had stated that 'From the Way of Heaven, male is born. Following the Way of Earth, female is born', and that 'The Tao produced One; One produced Two; Two produced Three; Three produced all things', while the philosopher Lü suggested something parallel to DHL's 'sex division' in his comment that, within 'The Mystery of Earth', 'Without spirit there is no substance, without substance there is no spirit. Spirit is active, substance receptive.' It is also, however, possible that DHL has in mind the so-called 'Three Treasures' of traditional oriental thought, though the 'sex division' is not one of those.

267:25 **Aphrodite born of the waters,** Greek goddess of love and beauty; the sperm of Zeus fell into the sea and Aphrodite was born of the resultant 'foam'. Blavatsky in *The Secret Doctrine* sums up the underlying mythology when she states that 'Water is . . . the feminine principle. Venus Aphrodite is the personified Sea' (i. 458).

267:29 **blonde, blue-eyed, northern...water-born,** Cf. Gerald Crich (*WL* 14: 28 36) . . . *OED2* cites this passage as the only known use of the adjective (reworking the common 'water-borne'); see note on 269:7.

268:35 **as a wheel sleeps in speed on its positive hub.** Cf. *The Rainbow*, ed. Kinkead-Weekes, 135:11–16; see too 'The Reality of Peace', *Reflections* 51:3–6.

268:36 **the great dark statues...seated lords of Egypt.** DHL's interest in ancient Egypt is first recorded in 1914 when he discovered, from the Egyptian sculpture in the British Museum, how 'We want to realise the tremendous *non-human* quality of life . . . coming unseen and unperceived as out of the desert to the Egyptians' (*Letters*, ii. 218); he could have seen the two black-granite seated figures of Amenophis III (18th Dynasty) from his Mortuary Temple in Thebes (cf. 'Those seated Egyptian kings' – 00:00). See also *Letters*, ii. 293, 521 n. 3, 556, and *WL* 98:37, 318:10–16.

269:7 **the water-born lotus,** The water-lily of Egypt and Asia, treated symbolically in Hindu and Buddhist thought.

270:14 **sacred pentagon,** Polygon with five sides; DHL probably means the word in a use the *OED2* defines as 'rare': i.e. 'pentacle', 'pentagram' or 'pentangle', one of the oldest sacred symbols, used by the Pythagoreans and other magicians; often seen (as in the Pentangle of Solomon, or the Endless Knot) as a magical defence against evil.

IX. Dana (First Version 1918–19)

272:5 an American littérateur ... Chief Justice for Massachusetts. DHL acquired this information from the Introduction (p. [i]) to the Nelson's Classics edition he was using (see note on 105:2), as he did all the biographical details down to 272:16 (pp. ii–iii).

272:8 an affection The word 'affection' – meaning 'disease' – was used in the Nelson's Classics Introduction, p. [i].

272:21 Marryatt, Frederick Marryat (1792–1848), English writer, served in the Navy from 1806 (as a captain from 1825); he wrote numerous books about the sea after his retirement in 1830, many of them – e.g. *Mr. Midshipman Easy* (1836) – popular as boys' literature (cf. *Letters*, ii. 588).

273:35 the deeps of the old mystics ... *There is sorrow on the sea; it cannot be quiet.* Blavatsky lists water and waters as the 'mystic, primordial substance' in Judaism, Scandinavian and other northern mythologies, Chaldean legend, Mexican mythology and alchemy (Blavatsky, *Isis Unveiled*, i. 133) ... Jeremiah xlix. 23.

275:15 If he dies he dies unbeaten. Reminiscent of DHL's remarks about tragedy in his 'Preface' to *Touch and Go*, written in July 1919: 'He may be killed, but the resistant, integral soul in him is not destroyed. He goes through, though he dies' (*The Plays*, ed. Schwarze and Worthen, 365:33–4).

275:19 Thucydides. DHL acquired a copy of *The History of the Peloponnesian War* by the Greek historian (471 – *c*. 401 BC) in the spring of 1916: 'He is a very splendid and noble writer, with the simplicity and the directness of the most complete culture and the widest consciousness. I salute him. More and more I admire this true classic dignity and self responsibility' (*Letters*, ii. 592). He was still reading Thucydides in June and July 1916, at the same time as he was reading Dana and Melville (*Letters*, ii. 614, 634), and in the novel he wrote April–November 1916 he showed Birkin reading Thucydides (*FWL* 93:5–6, 94:13–14).

275:32 which Flaubert aimed at. See note on 158:7; DHL is here characterising Flaubert as the type of the impersonal writer, as he did elsewhere: see, e.g., *Letters*, ii. 101; 'German Books: Thomas Mann', *Phoenix* 308.

277:19 *par excellence*, Beyond comparison (French: by way of excellence).

277:31 the electric catharsis. DHL may have been influenced by the use of the term (originally Aristotle's for the effect of tragedy on its spectators) in Freudian psychoanalysis from 1909 ('emotional catharsis') to mean relieving an abnormal excitement by re-associating the emotion with the memory of the event which was its cause; see *OED2*.

279:15 **Matisse or Picasso** Henri Matisse (1869–1954), French painter and sculptor; Pablo Picasso (1881–1973), Spanish painter. Deleted in Roberts E382r: 'Picaesa' (p. 12). In a 1916 revision of *Women in Love*, Picasso is a painter with an 'almost wizard, sensuous apprehension of the earth': see *FWL* 233:37.

280:33 **Nevermore.** From 'The Raven' (1845) by Edgar Allan Poe; see *Sons and Lovers*, ed. Baron and Baron, 271:23 and n. (Jung quoted and commented on the poem in *Psychology of the Unconscious*, p. 35; see note on 236:26.)

283:21 **"One night [283:3]...by the breeze."** *TYB* 262–3; not in other versions of the essay ['... it seemed in ... trade-wind ... under the stem ... studding-sails ... studding-sails ... string; and ... sky-sail ...']. A flying jib-boom is an additional spar forming an extension of the bowsprit. Studding-sails are light sails set outside the square sails on booms, only carried in a fair wind; skysails are light sails, again only employed in fair weather.

283:22 **equipoising of the self** The last previous citation in *OED2* of the word 'equipoising' – 'holding in balance' – was *c.* 1790.

283:38 **the Promethean mysteries,** 'Prometheus is also the *Logos* of the ancient Greeks' (Blavatsky, *Isis Unveiled*, p. 298).

287:12 **this Presence of the Host** DHL's reworking of the language of the Roman Catholic Mass describing the 'real presence' or 'corporal presence' of Christ in the 'Host', the wafer or bread of the Mass. He also describes the Host (traditionally the body of Christ, originally meaning a victim for sacrifice) as the 'Ghostly Creator' (287:29) – thus referring to the other two persons of the Trinity, the Holy Ghost and God the Father.

287:18 **earth-darkness, tar, is the fountain of all colours or dyes.** There seems no conventional or scientific authority for this statement: tar is the black or dark-coloured solid or liquid obtained by the destructive distillation of wood, coal or other organic substance.

287:27 **the God Thoth,** In Egyptian mythology, a moon deity, scribe of the gods and protector of learning and the arts; hence, perhaps, DHL's reference to 'Thoth knowledge' (287:30); associated by the Greeks with Hermes Trismegistus (see next note).

287:35 **the Hermes is the son of the Thunderer,** Hermes was son of Zeus by the nymph Maia.

X. Herman Melville (First Version 1918–19)

288:14 **Vikings ... even to Florida.** No archaeological evidence exists of the Vikings further s. than Newfoundland, and scholarship in the early twentieth century located them in the n.e. part of America. Blavatsky, however, had asserted that 'The

Northmen who visited the continent in the tenth century' had come ashore in central America (*Isis Unveiled*, i. 592); and the 1847 revision by I A Blackwell of the influential *Northern Antiquities* (originally written by Paul Henri Mallet as the *Introduction à l'Histoire de Dannemarc* and translated by Thomas Percy: reprinted 1859, 1882 and 1902) identified Florida as a possible landfall for Leif and the Vikings: 'vessels may have been driven across the Atlantic as far south as Florida' (1902 reprint, p. 266).

288:23 **pushed out in flame on to the waters.** Again (see note on 122:14) nineteenth-century paintings of mythological subjects may be responsible for the idea: see, e.g., *Funeral of a Viking* (1893) by Sir Frank Dicksee (1853–1928), in Manchester City Art Galleries, which shows a ship literally being 'pushed out' into the waves. Evidence for ship cremation is actually hard to come by, although ship burial was regularly practised in Viking Age Scandinavia; but the young god Baldr (see note on 122:30) was said to have been cremated in a ship sent drifting out to sea, as were two early Norwegian kings. In the Shetlands, in January, the Up Helly Aa festival culminates in the ritual burning of a replica Viking ship.

289:4 **the era that lies beyond the Flood, before the Glacial Period.** DHL had some knowledge of the pre-Flood and Atlantis writings of his time, and is probably drawing on more than one source here. By 1917 (*Letters*, iii. 150) he had been attracted to the ideas of Atlantis and pre-history he had found in Blavatsky's *The Secret Doctrine*, which linked the biblical story of Noah to the Atlantis myth, while Frobenius's *Voice of Africa*, which DHL knew by April 1918 (see note on 118:9), claimed that a West African civilisation, before Egypt and Carthage, 'gave rise to the Atlantis myth' (*Letters*, iii. 233); see, e.g., *VOA* i. 319–49 (chap. XV, 'Atlantis'). In March 1919 (*Letters*, iii. 340 and n.) DHL acquired a copy of Thomas Belt's *The Naturalist in Nicaragua* (1873; Everyman edn 1911), with its own version of the origins of Atlantis (see note on 335:22).

289:20 **All-Father ... All-Mother ... Beautifier** Versions of an omnipotent power: one of the names of the Norse God Odin, *Al-fa∂ ir* ... DHL's creation of a female equivalent ... *OED2* gives 1612 as first use of the word, describing God as 'Beautifier of the Sacrifice'.

289:29 **Christ is the Fruit of the Tree.** Cf. 'The tree-worship, the worship of the Tree of Life seems always to have entailed human sacrifice. Life is the fruit of that Tree. But the Tree is dark and terrible, it demands life back again. With its branches spread it becomes a Cross. And in our hymns even today we speak of Jesus "hung on the Tree" ' (*Movements* 51:21–5). Cf. too Genesis iii. 3: 'of the fruit of the tree which *is* in the midst of the garden, God hath said, Ye shall not eat of it'. St Paul also referred to the resurrected Christ as 'the firstfruits of them that slept ... Christ the firstfruits' (1 Corinthians xv. 20, 23). DHL would also have seen an illustration in Jung, *Psychology of the Unconscious*, facing p. 153, of 'Christ on the Tree of Life', showing the cross as a tree with leaves. See too Virginia Hyde, *The Risen Adam* (Pennsylvania, 1992), pp. 153–7.

289:31 The Rood... the Cross... which the Druids, the Germans, the Maya worshipped, The Rood is the Cross on which Jesus was crucified: also a crucifix, especially one set on a beam or screen ... cf. DHL on Celtic and Druid tree-worship in *Movements* 51:11–20; it is possible that he knew about the four Mayan gods (the *Bacabs*) who held up the world on their shoulders and were not only each associated with a particular tree but were thought to take on the form of trees. He had read about Malayan beliefs in tree-spirits and tree-worship, in Tylor, *Primitive Culture*, ii. 215, where he would also have found many other examples of tree-worship: e.g. i. 476, ii. 223. He could also have read about tree-worship in Frazer's *Golden Bough*, *The Magic Art*, vol. ii, chap. IX, 'The Worship of Trees', pp. 7–58, which discusses 'Aryan' tree-worship (see, e.g., *Fantasia of the Unconscious*, chap. iv), and may have confused the races and countries.

289:32 the sacred mistletoe, Supposedly held in veneration by the Druids; see Éliphas Lévi [Alphonse Louis Constant], *The History of Magic*, tr. A. E. Waite (1913), pp. 229–31.

290:5 Egypt, and the Etruscan and Iberian races, the last fading exemplars of the old way. See note on 124:12; in 1927 DHL linked the Egyptians and the Spanish with the Etruscans as 'peoples ... from the pre-historic Mediterranean world' (*Sketches of Etruscan Places and Other Essays*, ed. Simonetta de Filippis, Cambridge, 1992, 27:5–8).

290:8 unfinished dream. The Wordsworthian context of 'the sleep and the forgetting' (see note on 124:40) suggests another reminiscence of the 'Ode': 'Where is it now, the glory and the dream?' (l. 57).

290:35 cannibal reputation. The very first mention of the Marquesa Islands in *Typee* provokes a reference to 'cannibal banquets' (chap. I).

291:2 African grotesque carvings, See, e.g., the carving described in *WL* 74:9–19, 78:36–79:24, in part in chap. vii, 'Fetish' (see 291:14).

291:8 Bushman Folk-Lore, as we have it now literally rendered, A reference to *Specimens of Bushman Folk Lore, collected by the late W. H. I. Bleek and Lucy C. Lloyd*, ed. Lucy C. Lloyd (1911); no other collection fits DHL's description. See note on 346:15.

292:16 a recent African traveller [292:8]... definite emotion." Named in the Intermediate Version of the essay as Leo Frobenius; see note on 118:9. The quotation is from *VOA*, i. 13 ['all the cannibal tribes ... a quite ... flesh and, ... of the facts ... 'eat human meat ... has a human joint upon ...']; the previous four pages of *VOA* are mostly about cannibalism.

292:22 a strange malady in his arm, which would never heal, DHL misremembers *Typee* (the error is repeated at 292:37 and 293:6): the narrator has a leg problem. See note on 127:35.

293:23 **an exoteric ... the esoteric** Replacing in Roberts E382s (p. [13] 9): 'a practical ... the abstract'. Pryse had commented: 'the infelicitous word esoteric being used in this work merely because the English language appears to afford no happier one' (*Apocalypse Unsealed*, p. 9).

293:24 **St. John the Evangel ... Patmos ... the Apocalypse.** The gospel-writer St John (usually 'the evangelist': this usage is very uncommon but occurs a number of times in DHL's work, so is unlikely to be a result of the typist abbreviating the word) was perhaps exiled to the island of Patmos in the Aegean *c.* AD 95 and at one time was supposed to have written *The Revelation of St. John the Divine* (otherwise called *Apocalypse*) there; see D. H. Lawrence, *Apocalypse*, ed. Mara Kalnins, Cambridge, 1979, 66:18–20). Roberts E382s p. [13] 9 originally ended with the words 'writing the esoteric': DHL added 'record of the Apocalypse' in ink when replacing the next twelve pages with five handwritten pages.

293:38 **The Chinese ... Dragon of the Skies.** See note on 133:21.

293:40 **the crocodile ... the Shark ... Kraken,** DHL may have noted Frobenius's discovery of a 'fine carved crocodile' (*VOA*, i. 91) and his illustrations of 'The Crocodile Temple in Idena' and of two quartz crocodiles (301), and also have read how crocodile images were 'still worshipped' (300); he would also have found sacred alligators in Tylor's *Primitive Culture*, ii. 379, as well as a chapter on crocodile worship in Blavatsky's *Secret Doctrine* ... see Tylor, *Primitive Culture*, ii. 379 ... the Kraken was a mythical sea-monster of enormous size, supposedly seen off the Norwegian coast: first named and identified in the mid-eighteenth century.

294:2 **St. George** Patron saint of England, d. AD ?303, hero of a legend in which he killed a dragon.

294:15 **as the Devil offered to Christ ... the power of the world.** See Luke iv. 5–6: 'And the devil ... showed unto him all the kingdoms of the world in a moment of time. / And the devil said unto him, All this power will I give thee, and the glory of them.'

294:22 **the salamander.** Amphibian mythically reputed to live in fire without being harmed.

295:14 **Hephaestos is lame in both feet.** I.e. Hephaistos: in Greek mythology, the lame god of fire and metal-working (Vulcan in Roman mythology); his lameness is explained at 295:19–20. DHL originally wrote 'lame in one foot' (p. 12).

296:10 **He too was lame.** Not literally.

297:2 **Queequeg's little native idol—Yogo.** See note on 134:32; the idol is called 'Yojo' (*MD* 63). In Roberts E382s, the word had been typed as 'Gogo' and DHL himself adjusted it to 'Yogo' (p. [25] [19] 15).

297:32 **in the winter-time ... as in Dana's travel.** See *MD* 12: 'a Saturday night in December'. Dana's voyage actually starts on 14 August (*TYB* [7]), but the return voyage is explicitly 'in the very dead of winter' (221).

297:36 "—in landlessness ... leaps thy apotheosis!" *MD* 95 ['... safety! ... Up from the ...']. The quotation did not appear in subsequent versions of the essay.

298:7 **silent** The error of 'silent' for 'invisible' *(MD* 187), unique to this version of the essay, indicates either that someone subsequently did some checking of quotations, or (more likely) that the next version of the essay (Roberts E382i) derived not from Roberts E382s but from the now lost manuscript original which preceded it.

302:34 **the corposancts** DHL's spelling (not used by Melville) may represent an attempt to recover the Latin original 'corpus sanctum'.

(VIII) Nathaniel Hawthorne II. (Intermediate Version 1919)

309:16 **the Unconscious** According to *OED2*, the word was previously 'used in the purely descriptive sense'; its first dated reference to the psychoanalytic meaning is to Freud in 1912: 'now comes to imply ... ideas keeping apart from consciousness'.

309:23 **magic, Alchemy, and the Hermetic science are not such nonsense as we pretend.** Cf. DHL to Mark Gertler, 28 April 1918: 'I have been reading another book on Occultism. Do you know anybody who cares for this – magic, astrology, anything of that sort. It is very interesting, and important – though antipathetic to me. Certainly magic is a reality – not by any means the nonsense Bertie Russell says it is' *(Letters,* iii. 239). See too Blavatsky, *Isis Unveiled,* i. 502–3.

310:2 **Materio-dynamic** DHL's coinage, after the original eighteenth-century model 'serio-comic': 'materio' perhaps from the Italian. The meaning does not seem distinct from 'material-dynamic' at, e.g., 310:9.

310:11 *Fata volentem ducunt.* From the 107th letter of Seneca (AD 4–65), 'Ducunt volentem fata, nolentem trahunt' ('The fates lead the willing, they drag the unwilling'): see 310:14–15.

310:28 **Simon Magus.** A Samaritan sorcerer of the first century AD; after being converted to Christianity, he tried to buy miraculous powers from the Apostles (Acts viii. 9–24). He is also identified as the founder of a Gnostic sect, and is said to have met his death in attempts to fly. DHL could have found a great deal about him in Lévi's *History of Magic,* pp. 180–6.

311:4 **Mary or Rhea,** Mothers of the gods: the Christian Virgin Mary, mother of Christ; the Greek mythological wife of Cronos and mother of several gods, including Zeus.

311:30 **Though the whole world perish,** Cf. George Herbert (1593–1633), 'Vertue', ll. 14–16: 'Only a sweet and virtuous soul ... / ... though the whole world turn to coal, / Then chiefly lives.'

314:18 **the spade into the earth ... the old Adam,** Cf. the (now proverbial) slogan of the 1381 English peasants' revolt led by Wat Tyler: 'When Adam delved and Eve span / Who was then the gentleman?' The unregenerate condition or character; cf.

the 'old man' of Romans vi. 6. A favourite reference of DHL: cf. his stories 'The Old Adam' (1911) and 'New Eve and Old Adam' (1913).

(X) Dana (Intermediate Version 1919)

332:36 **dropsy-like symptoms of scurvy.** The two illnesses actually have very different symptoms: dropsy being characterised by puffiness and swellings from the accumulation of watery fluid in various parts of the body, scurvy by general debility, foul-smelling breath, tenderness of gums, subcutaneous eruptions and pains in the limbs.

333:29 *dunamis.* DHL recreates an English version of the Greek noun (meaning 'power') lying behind 'dynamic': dynamis.

(XI) Herman Melville (1) (Intermediate Version 1919)

335:22 **the previous world perfected itself about the Pacific ... a vast previous civilisation, before the geological cataclysms.** Blavatsky quotes Louis Jacolliot's version of a vast continent occupying the space of the Pacific Ocean, now sunk, the home of 'a civilization more ancient than that of Rome, of Greece, of Egypt, and of India', with the Sandwich Islands, New Zealand and Easter Island being the 'three summits of this continent' (*Isis Unveiled*, i. 594–5); while Belt, in *The Naturalist in Nicaragua*, had also argued for a lost central Pacific civilisation: 'On numerous islands in Polynesia are cyclopean ruins utterly out of keeping with their present size and population' (p. 207). Civilisations in Mexico, South America and China were among the very earliest locations of developed cultures, as important as the civilisations which developed in the Nile, Euphrates, Indus and Ganges deltas.

335:32 **Egypt and India ... young civilisations,** See note on 124:12; Indian civilisation started to flourish very early, around 4000 BC, though the first ruler of a large part of the continent did not rule before 250 BC.

336:7 **an almost mathematical cosmology, found in Korea ... Argentine, the Soudan, similar abstract forms;** DHL's primary source or sources for such remarks remain unidentified, but he summarised them in the 'Foreword' to *Fantasia of the Unconscious* (1922): 'in the great world previous to ours a great science and cosmology were taught esoterically in all countries of the globe, Asia, Polynesia, America, Atlantis and Europe'; some of his justification for the comments lay in his reading of Belt's *The Naturalist in Nicaragua*.

336:26 **the transubstantiation disputes ... rationalising of the sacrament,** Disagreement over whether the whole substance of the bread and wine changes into the substance of the body and blood of Christ, when consecrated in the Eucharist, was crucial in dividing the Protestant churches from the Roman Catholic Church in the sixteenth century; the Church of England in 1562, for example, offered the 'rational' explanation that 'the Bread which we break is a partaking of the Body of

Christ ... the Cup of Blessing is a partaking of the Blood of Christ', while transubstantiation 'is repugnant to the plain words of Scripture ... and hath given occasion to many superstitions' (*Book of Common Prayer: Articles of Religion*, XXVIII).

338:5 **thousand-year sleep of toads.** Although toads are the subjects of many myths – that they are poisonous, or have a precious jewel in their heads, or are the familiars of witches – no-one beside DHL appears to have believed that they sleep for 1,000 years. He, however, used them as a type of the enduring; cf. his 1926 short novel *The Virgin and the Gipsy*, 1930, pp. 154–5: 'The will, the ancient, toad-like, obscene *will* in the old woman, was fearful ... It belonged to the old, enduring race of toads, or tortoises'; and 'Mother and Daughter' (1928), *The Lovely Lady* (1933), p. 115: 'he sat, with short thighs, like a toad, as if seated for a toad's eternity'.

338:10 **The ideographs** Signs or symbols used in writing systems such as those of China or Japan, which directly represent concepts or things rather than employing words or sets of words for them.

338:36 **the strictest secrecy.** See, e.g., the events of chap. XXXII.

341:14 *arrivé.* In its place (French).

(XII) Herman Melville (2) (Intermediate Version 1919)

343:4 **Melville's biggest book** Perhaps a value judgement, but also literally true: in Everyman, *Moby Dick* was 504 pages, *Typee* 279 pages and *Omoo* 328 pages.

343:26 **fragments of Anaximander, Anaximenes, Pythagoras, Heraklitos** DHL first read these in 1915; see *Letters*, ii. 364–5, 652, and Burnet, *Early Greek Philosophy*, pp. 50–71, 72–9, 84–112, 130–68.

343:29 **straining the gnat it swallowed the camel.** Proverbial, from Matthew xxiii. 24 ('blind guides, which strain at a gnat, and swallow a camel').

344:12 **William James began to study ... All, or Allness.** DHL may be thinking of the chapter on 'Mysticism' in *The Varieties of Religious Experience* (1902); Jessie Chambers says that he liked the book (E. T., *A Personal Record*, p. 113) but in May 1919 he denied having read it (*Letters*, iii. 355) ... i.e. universality: a concept which (like 'Oneness') James would have regarded as a mystical pronouncement (see *Pragmatism*, 1907, pp. 148–55).

344:13 **the Infinite which everybody babbles about:** E.g. E. F. Jourdain, *On the Theory of the Infinite in Modern Thought* (1911), Sydney Turner Klein, *Science and the Infinite* (1912), Theophilus Parsons, *The Infinite and the Finite* (1918) and – perhaps the actual source DHL had in mind – Ralph Waldo Trine's extremely popular book *In Tune with the Infinite*, first published 1897, reprinted 1900, 1915, 1921, etc.; it had sold 26,000 copies by 1899, and was quoted in William James's *The Varieties of Religious Experience* (pp. 99–100, 385).

344:19 **peace which passes all understanding** Philippians iv. 7 ('the peace of God, which passeth all understanding').

344:22 **"Be ye also perfect," says Paul.** Christ commanded: 'Be ye therefore perfect, even as your Father which is in heaven is perfect' (Matthew v. 48); Paul wrote 'Make you perfect in every good work to do his will' (Hebrews xiii. 21).

344:32 **St. John ... "cities," ... seven in all.** *KJB* declares that it is to be sent to 'the seven churches which are in Asia' (Revelation i. 11), and names them (Ephesus, Smyrna, Pergamos, Thyatira, Sardis, Philadelphia and Laodicea): but also refers to seven golden candlesticks, stars, spirits of God, lamps of fire, seals, horns, eyes, angels, trumpets, etc., etc. (Revelation i. 12, ii. 1, iii. 1, iv. 5, v. 1, v. 6, viii. 6). In DHL's account, however, the New Jerusalem (Revelation xxii. 2) is the seventh and last city (344:35): it is (as he remarked in 1923) 'the mind enthroned' (*Letters*, iv. 460). Pryse provided a map of the seven cities in Asia and commentary (pp. 93–4).

344:39 **the lumbar ganglion;** The knot of nerve-cells centred on the region between the lowest ribs and the hip-bone.

344:40 **lower hypogastric plexus ... the sacral ganglion:** The bundle of nerves most closely linked with the sexual organs ... the ganglion below the base of the spine.

345:3 **the last ganglion, the cocygeal,** Properly spelled 'coccygeal': of or belonging to the coccyx, the very bottom of the spine.

345:4 **the thoracic ganglion** Centred on the area between the ribs.

345:9 **the cervical ganglia** The ganglia associated with the womb and neck of the vagina; it is hard to see how DHL can oppose them to the 'sacral ganglion' (see above), but it is probable that by 'cervical' he meant 'belonging to the neck' (at 363:13 he specifically referred to the cervical ganglion as one of the 'upper centres').

345:18 **"know in full."** Not a *KJB* phrase; but cf. 1 Corinthians xiii. 12 ('now I know in part, but then shall I know even as also I am known').

345:22 **what some sects call "becoming"** E.g. an 1860 comment by the high Anglican theologian Edward Pusey (1800–82): 'Our life is a "becoming" rather than a simple "being".' Cf. too *OED2*'s citation of a sermon by Frederick William Robertson (1816–53): 'Everything else is in a state of becoming, God is a state of Being.'

345:34 **"there shall be no more sea."** Revelation xxi. 1 ['and there was no...']; DHL's phrasing was probably influenced by the construction of xxi. 4 ('And God shall wipe away all tears from their eyes').

346:12 **shark and crocodile patterns, with grinning teeth, dominate aboriginal decoration-designs in those regions.** DHL is probably referring to the British Museum's collection of artefacts from the 'South Pacific' (346:8).

346:15 **as the mantis... dominates the Bushmen.** Section I (pp. 1–37) of 'Mythologies, Fables, Legends and Poetry' in *Specimens of Bushman Folk Lore*, ed. Lloyd (see note on 291:8), is entirely about 'The Mantis', not simply an insect but a wise and magic-performing elder; e.g. 'The Mantis formerly, when inconvenienced by darkness, took off one of his shoes and threw it into the sky, ordering it to become the Moon' (p. 53). As late as January 1929 DHL would recall the translations, 'in which the qualities of things seemed to be in continual change' (Nehls, iii. 296).

347:3 **a semi-metaphysical effusion about *water*, and about the author's attraction to this element;** Chap. I (*MD* 7–11).

347:4 **some clumsy humorisms... the sea-town of New Bedford.** Chaps. I–II (*MD* 12–14).

347:29 **deliberate transcendentalism... "deeper meanings."** See, e.g., chap. XLI, 'The Whiteness of the Whale' (*MD* 163–70).

350:8 **far more strangely than in Conrad,** There is no apparent direct comparison with Conrad to be made, but in *Lord Jim* (see note on 122:8), the crew of the *Patna* is Malaysian, apart from the five white officers.

350:37 **refraction.** A word unused in Melville's chapter.

352:3 **Carrol Ground, south of St Helena.** An 'unstaked, watery locality' (*MD* 202).

(XIII) Whitman (Intermediate Version 1919)

358:6 ***ipso facto*** By that very fact (Latin).

358:9 **many really thoughtful men... insist even today that he is the greatest of modern humbugs,** E. g. the Scottish journalist Peter Bayne, who referred to Whitman in 1875 as 'a demonstrated quack', while the English poet Swinburne (see note on 106:22) had written that Whitman was 'usually regarded by others than Whitmaniacs as simply a blatant quack – a vehement and emphatic dunce' (*Whitman: The Critical Heritage*, ed. Hindus, pp. 165, 199).

358:13 **This is the age of paradoxes** The idea of the logical paradox had infiltrated philosophical discussion from the turn of the twentieth century; paradoxes such as the 'Liar Paradox' and 'Russell's paradox' remained important in philosophical discussion down to the 1960s.

358:15 **St. John talks... the white horse.** Revelation xix. 11–21.

358:16 **Jung's *libido*.** Although today Freud is especially associated with the concept of the libido – psychic drive and energy, especially that linked with the sexual instinct – Jung was equally committed to the idea: *Psychology of the Unconscious* (see note on 236:26) includes chapters entitled 'Aspects of the Libido', 'The Conception and the Genetic Theory of Libido' and 'The Transformation of the Libido'. In his 'Introduction' to *Fantasia of the Unconscious* (written in June 1921) DHL again referred to 'Jung's *Libido*'.

358:22 **the cerebellum,** One of the main divisions of the vertebrate brain, situated in man above the medulla oblongata and beneath the cerebrum; its function is the co-ordination of voluntary movements and the maintenance of bodily equilibrium.

358:26 **some latent body, the pineal body presumably,** The pineal gland, behind the third ventricle of the brain, is the only organ of the brain which is single; it had been suggested from the early eighteenth century that it might be the seat of the soul, and in the late nineteenth century it was compared to an unpaired eye. The 'pineal or parietal eye' has actually some function in lizards, for example, comparable to those of an actual eye; but there was a long tradition of Hindu mysticism which declared that the god Shiva had a third eye, of insight and destruction, looking both up and down, and which identified the pineal gland with the 'third eye', the eye of clairvoyance and second sight (see next note). See too Blavatsky, *The Key to Theosophy*: 'the pineal body is in truth the very seat of the highest and divinest consciousness in man – his omniscient, spiritual and all-embracing mind' (p. 119).

358:27 **a new eye having opened:** The opening of the third eye was known as 'Satori', (enlightenment). The idea was well known to DHL; he would have read in Pryse about the 'pineal body, the "third eye" ' (*Apocalypse Unsealed*, p. 38), and DHL's friend Dorothy Brett (1883–1977) recalled him, in Oaxaca in the autumn of 1924, saying to her 'Good gracious . . . Have you never heard of the third eye?' (*Lawrence and Brett*, Philadelphia, 1933, p. 176).

358:30 **The mystics say that a tremendous great light crashes into the human psyche,** Jung, e.g., describes how 'stars come from the disc of the sun to the mystic, "five-pointed, in quantities, filling the whole air. If the sun's disc has expanded, you will see an immeasurable circle, and fiery gates which are shut off " ' . . . In Mysticism the inwardly perceived, divine vision is often merely sun or light' (Jung, *Psychology of the Unconscious*, p. 54).

359:1 **their Nirvana,** Final release from the cycle of reincarnation, attained by the extinction of individual desires, culminating (in Buddhism) in absolute blessedness, and in Hinduism in absorption into Brahman, the ultimate impersonal and divine reality of the universe. See Blavatsky, *Isis Unveiled*, i. 291–2. Freudian psychology also used the word to describe the death-instinct; DHL's friend Barbara Low actually christened this instinct the 'Nirvana principle', as acknowledged by Freud in *Beyond the Pleasure Principle* (1920), *Standard Edition of the Complete Psychological Works*, vol. XVIII, 56.

359:32 **St Paul's "charity."** 1 Corinthians xiii. 2–8, 13.

360:5 **symbolised by Saint Teresa as a point:** In her autobiography, St Teresa (1515–77) explains her experience of 'rapture', of 'the extreme loneliness in which the soul finds itself': 'it rises far above itself and above all creation. God then so strips it of everything that, strive though it may, it can find no companion on earth. Nor, indeed, does it wish for one; it would rather die in its solitude' (tr. J. M. Cohen, chap. XX).

363:22 *idée fixe* A fixed idea, an obsession (French).

364:23 **"The womb, the tomb," as somebody sings:** Cf. Shakespeare's sonnet 86, ll. 3–4 ('That did my ripe thoughts in my brain inhearse, / Making their tomb the womb wherein they grew?').

364:29 **"Methinks the gentleman doth insist too much."** Cf. *Hamlet*, III. ii. 242 ('The lady doth protest too much, methinks').

364:36 **inglutination** Not in *OED2*; but also used is DHL's *Psychoanalysis and the Unconscious* (1922), chap. I. To 'conglutinate' is to cause the edges of a wound or fracture to join or stick together during the process of healing; 'inglutition' is 'rare' (last recorded 1803) for 'the action of swallowing'. DHL's coinage suggests that ingestion may mean an absorption *in* the other.

365:18 **"bowels drawn" to a child . . . the loss of a child "breaks his reins."** I.e. deeply and sympathetically attracted to ('bowels' in archaic and dialect usage meaning 'sympathies') . . . reins are, archaically and in dialect, the seat of the feelings: so 'breaks his heart'.

365:35 **amid the waters."** . . . the bitter, spent waters of the end. Cf. the Latin saying 'nascimur inter faeces et urinam' ('we are born amidst excrement and urine'), 'water' being common for 'urine'. Fluid contained in the amniotic cavity (the 'bag of waters') is, too, exuded from the womb down the birth canal ('the breaking of the waters') shortly before a baby is born. The phrase 'amid the waters' also appears in Milton's *Paradise Lost* (1667), VII. 262 . . . death is sometimes accompanied by the spontaneous evacuation of urine.

366:1 **the port, of egress and ingress,** Cf. 'each mystic port / Of egress from you' in DHL's 1919 poem 'Seven Seals', *Complete Poems*, ed. Pinto and Roberts, i. 154.

366:13 **the fiery corruption . . . the stream of the watery corruption,** The evacuation respectively of faeces and urine.

366:15 **Rabelais,** François Rabelais (?1494–1553), French writer famous for *The Heroic Deeds of Gargantua and Pantagruel* (1534) which includes numerous episodes in which people shit and fart. The child Gargantua, e.g., in the translation by Sir Thomas Urquhart (1611–60), 'beshit himself every hour' while 'barytonising with his tail' (chap. VII).

366:18 **the seat,** I.e. the buttocks.

366:37 **Greek paiderasty** Homosexual relations between boys and men: accepted spellings are 'pederasty' or 'paederasty'.

367:14 **its pink-tinged... leaves of comradeship.** See, e.g., the poems 'Scented Herbage of My Breast' and 'For You, O Democracy' in the section 'Calamus' (*LG* 96, 99).

367:33 *Sea-Drift*, **a lovely and great poem:** A section, not a poem (*LG* 210–23).

368:8 *Memories of President Wilson.* Error for 'Memories of President Lincoln', the penultimate section of poems in the book DHL was using (*LG* 274–83). Woodrow Wilson was President when DHL was writing: see note on 30:1.

368:17 **"Come lovely** [368:9]... **cool-enfolding death."** 'When Lilacs Last in the Dooryard Bloom'd', ll. 135–42 (*LG* 279) ['... death, ... each, ... Prais'd ... universe, ... joy, and ...'].

368:25 **Paul Fort... Gallic ephemera:** French poet (1872–1960), best known for the *Ballades Françaises* which he started to publish in 1896. DHL originally spelled Fort with an 'e' at the end, but deleted it; and also originally wrote 'little' and then deleted it.

368:25 **there is no Sappho.** Very little is known factually about the Greek poet Sappho; she was writing in the sixth century BC and she journeyed to Sicily before returning to the island of Lesbos, where she is supposed to have gathered around her a circle of young women; in one account she killed herself by jumping into the sea (see *Hardy* 53:4–5, *WL* 191:13). DHL's scepticism belongs to his period, when (as also happened with Homer) it was suggested that no historical individual of that name had ever lived, and that the poetry she was supposed to have written had simply been assigned to her. New fragments of her poems were, however, discovered in the twentieth century.

Reading notes for *The Scarlet Letter* (1917)

Note: where the page reference DHL supplies and the allusion to the text (including quotation of the Everyman text) are both accurate, in most cases no quotation has been given.

373:4 **Hester is the lady again** Cf. 'She was ladylike, too, after the manner of the feminine gentility of those days' (*TSL* 68).

373:7 **Sacred Image of Madonna** Cf. 'Had there been a Papist among the crowd of Puritans, he might have seen in this beautiful woman, so picturesque in her attire and mien, and with the infant at her bosom, an object to remind him of the image of Divine Maternity, which so many illustrious painters have vied with one another to represent' (*TSL* 70).

373:9 **here "deepest sin in most sacred quality of human life."** 'Here, there was the taint of deepest sin in the most sacred quality of human life' (*TSL* 70).

373:12 **all mind and malice, a devil (misshapen from the hour of my birth)** A number of passages contribute to this summary: cf. 'The intellect of Roger Chillingworth had now a sufficiently plain path before it. It was not, indeed, precisely that which he had laid out for himself to tread. Calm, gentle, passionless, as he appeared, there was yet, we fear, a quiet depth of malice, hitherto latent, but active now, in this unfortunate old man' (*TSL* 167); 'In a word, old Roger Chillingworth was a striking evidence of man's faculty of transforming himself into a devil, if he will only, for a reasonable space of time, undertake a devil's office' (*TSL* 204); 'Misshapen from my birth-hour' (*TSL* 91).

373:19 **"My child ... earthly one."** ' "And my child must seek a heavenly father; she shall never know an earthly one!" ' (*TSL* 85).

373:22 **"Art thou ... black man etc "** 'Art thou like the Black Man that haunts the forest round about us?' (*TSL* 95).

373:23 **"Not thy soul ... not thine "** ' "Not thy soul," he answered, with another smile. "No, not thine!" ' (*TSL* 95).

373:24 **She did not flee.** 'Hester Prynne, therefore, did not flee' (*TSL* 99).

373:25 **Her work became the fashion** Cf. 'By degrees, not very slowly, her handiwork became what would now be termed the fashion' (*TSL* 101).

373:28 **Hester had ... gorgeously beautiful – Cf. Aztecs** 'She had in her nature a rich, voluptuous, Oriental characteristic – a taste for the gorgeously beautiful' (*TSL* 103); see note on 197:10.

373:31 **She will not ... wrong beneath"** Cf. 'Much of the time, which she might readily have applied to the better efforts of her art, she employed in making coarse garments for the poor. It is probable that there was an idea of penance in this mode of occupation, and / that she offered up a real sacrifice of enjoyment in devoting so many hours to such rude handiwork' (*TSL* 102–3); 'something doubtful, something that might be deeply wrong beneath' (*TSL* 103).

373:34 **"but she forbore ... turn to curse."** Cf. 'She was patient—a martyr, indeed but she forebore to pray for enemies, lest, in spite of her forgiving aspirations, the words of the blessing should stubbornly twist themselves into a curse' (*TSL* 104).

374:1 **"the spot never grew callous."** 'From first to last, in short, Hester Prynne had always this dreadful agony in feeling a human eye upon the token; the spot never grew callous' (*TSL* 105).

374:3 **a new sense ... Sin-detecting sense.** 'she felt or fancied, then, that the scarlet letter had endowed her with a new sense' (*TSL* 106).

374:3 **"red-hot** 'red-hot with infernal fire' (*TSL* 108).

374:7 **"her nature ... been broken –"** 'Her nature appeared to possess depth, too, as well as variety; but—or else Hester's fears deceived her—it lacked reference and adaptation to the world into which she was born. The child could not be made amenable to rules. In giving her existence a great law had been broken' (*TSL* 111).

374:10 **Her mother ... so malicious –"** 'Her mother, while Pearl was yet an infant, grew acquainted with a certain peculiar look, that warned her when it would be labour thrown away to insist, persuade or plead. / It was a look so intelligent, yet inexplicable, perverse, sometimes so malicious' (*TSL* 112–13).

374:11 **p. 113–114.** The pages are concerned with Hester's daughter Pearl, and her violent mood-swings.

374:12 **Pearl hated the other children** Cf. 'Pearl was a born outcast of the infantile world' (*TSL* 114); 'Pearl saw, and gazed intently, but never sought to make acquaintance. If spoken to, she would not speak again. If the children gathered about her, as they sometimes did, Pearl would grow positively terrible in her puny wrath, snatching up stones to fling at them, with shrill, incoherent exclamations, that made her mother tremble, because they had so much the sound of a witch's anathemas in some unknown tongue' (*TSL* 115).

374:14 **All this ... Hester's heart** 'All this enmity and passion had Pearl inherited, by inalienable right, out of Hester's heart' (*TSL* 116).

374:16 **She never ... dragon's teeth.** *TSL* 117.

374:18 **Hester sees ... smiling malice."** Cf. 'Once this freakish, elvish cast came into the child's eyes while Hester was looking at her own image in them, as mothers are fond of doing; and / suddenly for women in solitude, and with troubled hearts, are pestered with unaccountable delusions she fancied that she beheld, not her own miniature portrait, but another face in the small black mirror of Pearl's eye. It was a face, fiend-like, full of smiling malice' (*TSL* 118–19).

374:23 **"He did not ... demon-child** Cf. ' "He did not send me!" cried she, positively. "I have no Heavenly Father!" ' (*TSL* 120); 'the neighbouring townspeople ... had given out that poor little Pearl was a demon offspring' (*TSL* 121).

374:26 **"She was the ... passionate moment."** Cf. 'she seemed the unpremeditated offshoot of a passionate moment.' (*TSL* 124).

374:29 **p. 198** DHL may be thinking of the following sentence: 'The child's own nature had something wrong in it which continually betokened that she had been born amiss—the effluence of her mother's lawless passion—and often impelled Hester to ask, in bitterness of heart, whether it were for ill or good that the poor little creature had been born at all' (*TSL* 198).

374:37 **"Behold, verily [374:30] ... rising generation."** ' "Behold, verily, there is the woman of the scarlet letter: and of a truth, moreover, there is the likeness of the scarlet letter running along by her side! Come, therefore, and let us fling mud at them!" ... She resembled, in her fierce pursuit of them, an infant pestilence—the scarlet fever, or some such half-fledged angel of judgment—whose mission was to punish the sins of the rising generation' (*TSL* 125).

374:38 **Her quick & mobile interest – her momentaneity** Cf. 'the quick and mobile curiosity of her disposition was excited by the appearance of those new personages' (*TSL* 130).

374:40 **The Black Man in the Woods. – the native spirits** Cf. 'Had they taken her from me, I would willingly have gone with thee into the forest, and signed my name in the Black Man's book too, and that with mine own blood!' (*TSL* 142).

375:5 **"Hath ... mocker.** Chillingworth asks, of Pearl, 'Hath she any discoverable principle of being?' and Dimmesdale replies: 'None, save the freedom of a broken law' (*TSL* 162).

375:9 **Dimmesdale ... own face!** Dimmesdale feels that he is a 'subtle, but remorseful hypocrite ... above all things else, he loathed his miserable self!' (*TSL* 174). Followed by: 'He kept vigils, likewise, night after night, sometimes in utter darkness, sometimes with a glimmering lamp, and sometimes, viewing his own face in a looking-glass, by the most powerful light which he could throw upon it' (*TSL* 175).

375:12 **The only ... inmost soul.** *TSL* 176.

375:13 **The dread of public exposure!** 'with the new energy of the moment, all the dread of public exposure, that had so long been the anguish of his life, had returned upon him' (*TSL* 184).

375:15 **Sky – signs ... the sky** Dimmesdale looks at the sky: 'Nothing was more common, in those days, than to interpret all meteoric appearances, and other natural phenomena that occurred with less regularity than the rise and set of sun and moon, as so many revelations from a supernatural source' (*TSL* 186). 'We impute it, therefore, solely to the disease in his own eye and heart that the minister, looking upward to the zenith, beheld there the appearance of an immense letter—the letter A—marked out in lines of dull red light' (*TSL* 187).

375:17 **"The next ... powerful etc –"** 'The next day, however, being the Sabbath, he preached a discourse which was held to be the richest and most powerful, and the most replete with heavenly influences, that had ever proceeded from his lips' (*TSL* 190).

375:19 **Marble ... to thought."** 'Much of the marble coldness of Hester's impression was to be attributed to the circumstance that her life had turned, in a great measure, from passion and feeling to thought' (*TSL* 197).

375:23 **"It is ... a prophetess** 'It is remarkable that persons who speculate the most boldly often conform with the most perfect quietude to the external regulations of society. The thought suffices them, without investing itself in the flesh and blood of action. So it seemed to be with Hester. Yet, had little Pearl never come to her from the spiritual world, it might have been far otherwise. Then she might have come down to us in history, hand in hand with Ann Hutchinson, as the foundress of a religious sect. She might, in one of her phases, have been a prophetess' (*TSL* 198).

375:27 **"Was ... of thought."** 'Indeed, the same dark question often rose into her mind with reference to the whole race of womanhood. Was existence worth accepting even to the / happiest among them? As concerned her own individual existence, she had long ago decided in the negative, and dismissed the point as settled ... A woman never overcomes these problems by any exercise of thought' (*TSL* 198–9).

375:30 **200 – Roger Chillingworth ... warm affection"** There is nothing on p. 200 exactly fitting the first part of this note, except the remark that – for Dimmesdale – 'A secret enemy had been continually by his side, under the semblance of a friend and helper' (*TSL* 200): i.e. Chillingworth. Three pages later, however: 'In a word, old Roger Chillingworth was a striking evidence of man's faculty of transforming himself into a devil, if he will only, for a reasonable space of time, undertake a devil's office' (*TSL* 204). Chillingworth then asks Hester: 'Was I not, though you might deem me cold, nevertheless a man thoughtful for others, craving little for himself—kind, true, just and of constant, if not warm affections? Was I not all this?' (*TSL* 207).

375:33 **"It is ... the man."** 'It is our fate. Let the black flower blossom as it may!' (*TSL* 209). ' "Be it sin or no," said Hester Prynne, bitterly, as still she gazed after him, "I hate the man!" ' (*TSL* 211).

375:36 **And it ... his side."** 'And it seemed a fouler offence committed by Roger Chillingworth than any which had since been done him, that, in / the time when her heart knew no better, he had persuaded her to fancy herself happy by his side' (*TSL* 211–12).

375:40 **this gaiety ... a grief –"** 'Gaiety' is a word only used about Pearl later (*TSL* 275); here, she is characterised by 'never failing vivacity of spirits'; she does not have 'the disease of sadness'. 'Perhaps this, too, was a disease, and but the reflex of the wild energy with which Hester had fought against her sorrows before Pearl's birth' (*TSL* 221). 'She wanted—what some people want throughout life—a grief that should deeply touch her, and thus humanise and make her capable of sympathy. But there was time enough yet for little Pearl' (*TSL* 222).

376:2 **"Once ... his mark."** ' "Once in my life I met the Black Man!" said her mother. This scarlet letter is his mark!" ' (*TSL* 223).

376:5 **"of penance ... been none "** Dimmesdale says to Hester: 'Of penance, I have had enough! Of penitence, there has been none!' (*TSL* 231).

376:9 **" – disorganise ... earthly type."** 'the sufferer's conscience had been kept in an irritated state, the tendency of which was, not to cure by wholesome pain, but to disorganize and corrupt his spiritual being. Its result, on earth, could hardly fail to be insanity, and hereafter, that eternal alienation from the Good and True, of which madness is perhaps the earthly type' (*TSL* 233).

376:10 **Blacker ... frown –** 'Never was there a blacker or a fiercer frown than Hester now encountered' (*TSL* 234).

376:12 "What . . . own." *TSL* 235.

376:16 "Think . . . on me." Dimmesdale says: ' "Think for me, Hester! Thou art strong. Resolve for me!" ' She asks: ' "Wilt thou die for very weakness?" "The judgment of God is on me," answered the conscience-stricken priest' (*TSL* 237).

376:18 "I am . . . my post." Hester suggests that Dimmesdale escape; he answers 'I am powerless to go. Wretched and sinful as I am, I have had no other thought than to drag on my earthly existence in the sphere where Providence hath placed me. Lost as my own soul is, I would still do what I may for other human souls! I dare not quit my post . . .' (*TSL* 238).

376:20 "The tendency . . . his face." 'The tendency of her fate and fortunes had been to set her free' (*TSL* 240).

376:22 "But . . . even purpose." *TSL* 241. The note is followed by a large 'x' in ink.

376:25 "that . . . repaired." *TSL* 242.

376:27 "Wherefore should . . . execution 'wherefore should I not snatch the solace allowed to the condemned culprit before his execution?' (*TSL* 242).

376:29 " – of . . . region." 'It was the exhilarating effect—upon a prisoner just es- caped from the dungeon of his own heart—of breathing the wild, free atmosphere of an unredeemed, unchristianised, lawless region' (*TSL* 243).

376:31 " – there . . . mood." *TSL* 243.

376:32 "This is . . . better life " 'This is already the better life!' (*TSL* 243).

376:33 She throws . . . Letter 'So speaking, she undid the clasp that fastened the scarlet letter, and, taking it from her bosom, threw it to a distance among the withered leaves' (*TSL* 243).

376:36 –Pearl . . . infant dryad 'Naturkind' (German): 'child of nature'. 'The small denizens of the wilderness hardly took pains to move out of her path' (*TSL* 246). Pearl 'became a nymph child, or an infant dryad' (*TSL* 247).

376:37 She resumes . . . Scarlet Letter. 'With these words she advanced to the margin of the brook, took up the scarlet letter, and fastened it again into her bosom' (*TSL* 245).

376:38 Pearl . . . Scarlet Letter 'In a mood of tenderness that was not usual with her, she drew down her mother's head, and kissed her brow and both her cheeks. But then—by a kind of necessity that always impelled this child to alloy whatever comfort she might chance to give with a throb of anguish—Pearl put up her mouth and kissed the scarlet letter, too' (*TSL* 255).

376:39 Pearl . . . minister's kiss 'The minister—painfully embarrassed, but hoping that a kiss might prove a talisman to admit him into the child's kindlier regards—bent forward, and impressed one on her brow. Hereupon, Pearl broke away from her mother, and, running to the brook, stooped over it, and bathed her forehead, until the unwelcome kiss was quite washed off and diffused through a long lapse of the gliding water' (*TSL* 256).

376:40 **He wanted . . . election Sermon**   'on the third day from the present, he was to preach the Election Sermon' (*TSL* 259).

377:5 **"it was [377:1] . . . Supper."**   'it was only by the most careful self-control that the former could refrain from uttering certain blasphemous suggestions that rose into his mind, respecting the communion-supper' (*TSL* 263).

377:8 **"deep . . . widow's ear**   The widow enjoys being 'refreshed with a word of warm, fragrant, heaven- / breathing Gospel truth, from his beloved lips, into her dulled, but rapturously attentive ear. But, on this occasion, up to the moment of putting his lips to the old woman's ear, Mr. Dimmesdale, as the great enemy of souls would have it, could recall no text of Scripture, nor aught else, except a brief, pithy, and, as it then appeared to him, unanswerable argument against the immortality of the human soul' (*TSL* 263–4).

377:10 **"teach . . . Children."**   Dimmesdale feels a great urge to 'teach some very wicked words to a knot of little Puritan children who were playing there, and had but just begun to talk' (*TSL* 265).

377:11 **Old Mistress Hibbins**   A 'reputed witch-lady' (*TSL* 266).

377:13 **His inspiration . . . Sermon**   'Then flinging the already written pages of the Election Sermon into the fire, he forthwith began another, which he wrote with such an impulsive flow of thought and emotion, that he fancied himself inspired' (*TSL* 271).

377:15 **Roger . . . save you."**   'the old man rushed forward, and caught the minister by the arm. / "Madman, hold! what is your purpose?" whispered he. "Wave back that woman! Cast off this child! All shall be well! Do not blacken your fame, and perish in dishonour! I can yet save you! . . ." ' (*TSL* 304–5).

377:17 **"Better . . . with us."**   'Better? Yea; so we may both die, and little Pearl die with us!' (*TSL* 306).

377:20 **"It is . . . at bottom."**   *TSL* 314.

377:21 **Pearl . . . aristocracy**   Pearl apparently marries: 'Letters came, with armorial seals upon them, though of bearings unknown to English heraldry' (*TSL* 316).

377:25 **Thomas Stanley Hocking . . . Tregarthen . . . Zinnor**   Youngest son (b. 1900) of the Hocking family, who lived at Lower Tregerthen Farm, Zennor: the spellings suggest the local pronunciation.

Foreword to Studies in Classic American Literature

381:8 **haven't anything more venerable than the White House, or more primitive than Whistler.** DHL is (provocatively) wrong. The official Washington residence of the US President was originally built in 1792 and refashioned in 1824, but the Palace of the Governors in Santa Fe was, e.g., built in 1610, and there are many extant mid-eighteenth-century buildings; parts of the Pueblo buildings in Taos probably date from the twelfth century. James Abbott McNeill Whistler (1834–1903) was a US painter and etcher especially well known in Europe, but there were many earlier successful and well-known US painters, e.g. Washington Allston (1779–1843) and John James Audubon (1785–1851); and in the realm of naive (or primitive) painting, Edward Hicks (1780–1849).

381:14 **the Cinquecento knew her not.** I.e. the sixteenth century. The phrasing is appropriately archaic, cf. *KJB*: 'the world knew him not' (John i. 10) and Matthew i. 24–5: 'Joseph . . . knew her not'.

381:27 **Milan cathedral . . . horribly bristly** DHL had no fondness for the exceptionally ornate and pinnacled cathedral of Mariae Nascenti in Milan, as he showed in a letter of 23 October 1913: 'Milano, with its imitation hedge-hog of a cathedral' (*Letters*, ii. 88).

381:31 *Corriere della Sera . . . i Cavalieri di Colombo.* The foremost Milan newspaper printed on 27 August 1920, p. 3, in a section called "Corriere Milanese", an (unsigned) article entitled 'UN TRENO SPECIALE DI AMERICANI I "CAVALIERI DI COLOMBO"'. The 'Knights' were described as a 'Freemasonry association' and details were given of their origin, their social function and the dates of their arrival in and departure from Milan – they wore the colourful badge of the Knights of Columbus. DHL offers a version of the *Corriere*'s phrase 'i viaggiatori si mostrarono assai ammirati, specialmente del Duomo' ('the travellers showed themselves sufficiently admiring, particularly of the Cathedral'). He had been in Milan around 15–17 August 1920, but was in Venice 26 August–1 September, where he must have seen a copy of the newspaper. The Knights were a Fraternal Roman Catholic men's organisation in the USA and Canada, founded 1882.

382:1 **Anna Comnena. . . Bohemund. . . Tancred. . . Godfrey of Bouillon. . . Constantinople long ago.** See *Movements* 124:21–3: 'Anna Comnena, daughter of the emperor [Alexius I (1048–1118)], a young, clever princess, wrote her memoirs in which we may still read her account of the visit of these Crusaders to her father's capital [Constantinople]'. Bohemond and Tancred were both Norman lords of southern Italy. Godfrey of Bouillon (d. 1100), descendant of Charlemagne, led the successful attack on Jerusalem and was later idolised in legend as the perfect Christian knight; they were all involved in the first Crusade, 1096–9. DHL's information came from Gibbon's *Decline and Fall of the Roman Empire*, chap. lviii, footnote 76: 'Her fastidious delicacy complains of their strange and inarticulate names, and indeed there is scarcely one that she has not contrived to disfigure with the proud ignorance, so dear and familiar to a polished people.'

382:2 **Goths and Scythians** Enemies of Rome (see next note); the Huns originally came from Scythia.

382:11 **Alaric and Attila** Alaric, king of the Visigoths, invaded Italy in 401; Attila invaded Gaul with the Huns in 451.

382:17 **A thing of beauty is a joy for ever.** *Endymion*, Book I, l. 1, by John Keats (1795–1821).

382:21 **la mer, c'est moi ... c'est aussi vous,** DHL parodies the remark attributed to Louis XIV (1638–1715) 'L'État c'est moi' ('I am the state') ... 'it's you too'.

382:23 **the Coliseum or the Bridge of Sighs.** In Rome (see note on 46:14) and Venice respectively, the Ponte dei Sospiri being a sixteenth-century covered bridge between the Doge's palace and the prisons.

382:28 **Ghirlandaio,** Domenico Ghirlandaio (1449–94), Italian painter, who worked in Florence (his masterpiece is often thought to be the set of frescos in the Sanctuary of the church of Santa Maria Novella).

382:36 **St. Marks and San Giorgio,** The Basilica of San Marco (ninth–fourteenth centuries) looks across the lagoon to the church of San Giorgio Maggiore (built 1566–1610).

382:39 **exhibition of modern paintings ... in the Gardens at Venice, in this Year of Grace 1920.** The 'Biennale' has (since 1895) been held every two years in the pavilions of the International Exhibition of Modern Art, in the Giardini Publici.

382:40 **Tintoret.** I.e. Jacopo Tintoretto (1519–94), Venetian painter, whose work DHL could have seen in Venice's Galleria dell'Accademia and in many Venetian churches.

383:2 **Lincoln cathedral** Described in DHL's *Sons and Lovers*, ed. Baron and Baron, 280:35–281:7, and *The Rainbow*, ed. Kinkead-Weekes, pp. 183–95.

383:17 **Aquileia.... Padua,** Attila utterly destroyed the city of Aquileia (at the head of the Adriatic) in 452, and it was not rebuilt; Padua was also severely damaged.

383:6 **Sforza days.** I.e. in the time of the Duke of Milan, Francesco Sforza, in the mid-fifteenth century (the Castello Sforzesco was built 1451–66), and the next two generations of Sforzas.

384:36 **They must pick up the life-thread where the mysterious Red race let it fall.** In 1925, DHL commented sarcastically on a remark by the critic Edwin Muir – 'Mr. Lawrence has picked up a thread of life left behind by mankind'

('D. H. Lawrence', *Nation*, New York, 11 February 1925, cxx, 150) – 'Darn your socks with it, Mr Muir?' (*Reflections* 243:5–6). It would seem likely that Muir was referring to this 1920 essay.

384:40 **Gladstone...Hildebrand,** William Ewart Gladstone (1809–98), English politician and four times prime minister... the monastic name of Pope Gregory VII (1020–85).

385:13 **Venice wedded the Adriatic,** The Doge of Venice performed the annual ceremony of the marriage with the sea when he threw his ring into the sea from the Bucintoro, near the Porto di Lido, and it was retrieved by a young fisherman.

385:22 **To your tents, O Israel.** 2 Kings xii. 16: a favourite quotation of DHL's (see, e.g., his June 1921 'Introduction' to *Fantasia of the Unconscious*). Per printed 'America' for 'Israel'.

385:23 **1920.** The textual variants of the reprint of Per in *The NEW REPUBLIC Anthology 1915–1935*, ed. Geoff Conklin (New York, 1936), pp. 129–34, have not been recorded. DHL's piece was followed by Walter Lippmann's response 'The Crude Barbarian and the Noble Savage' in 1920 (and in the reprint).

Foreword (1922)

389:12 **yawping** Cf. Whitman's 'Song of Myself', section 52: 'I too am not a bit tamed, I too am untranslatable, / I sound my barbaric yawp over the roofs of the world' (*LG* 77)

389:14 **To your tents, O Americans.** See note on 385:22.

389:17 **sniffishly** Probably DHL's coinage. *OED2* recognises only 'sniffingly', 'sniffily' (the latter first used 1900) and 'sniffish' (from 1933).

389:18 **Edison inventions...patent foods.** Thomas Alva Edison (1847–1931) patented more than 1,000 inventions, including the phonograph, the incandescent electric lamp and the microphone... artificial 'proprietary food preparation', protected by a patent (first *OED2* reference 1871).

390:6 **ark...bulrushes...Miriam** Exodus ii. 1–10...Miriam was the sister of Moses and Aaron.

390:15 *A moi, le vrai Israel.* To me, the real Israel (French).

Nathaniel Hawthorne's *Blithedale Romance* (1920–1)

395:7 **subject to change.** DHL may be thinking of Herakleitos' fragments such as 'The sun is new every day', 'You cannot step twice into the same rivers', 'All things come into being and pass away through strife' and 'It rests by changing' (Burnet, *Early Greek Philosophy*, pp. 135, 136, 137, 139).

395:20 **Old-Testament power which moved worlds.** E.g. Joshua x. 12–13 ('Then spake Joshua to the Lord . . . and he said in the sight of Israel, Sun stand thou still upon Gibeon; and thou, Moon, in the valley of Ajalon. And the sun stood still, and the moon stayed . . . So the sun stood still in the midst of heaven, and hasted not to go down about a whole day').

395:24 **abracadabra.** A cabalistic word traditionally used by conjurors, and used in certain Gnostic writings, 'now often used in the general sense of a spell, or pretended conjuring word' (*OED2*): perhaps related to Greek *Abrasax*, a Gnostic deity.

395:29 **with us, as with Nietzsche, will is something conscious,** DHL was influenced by the stereotype of Nietzsche embodied in the title *Der Wille zur Macht* (1887, tr. as *The Will to Power* in 1906); cf. his 1914 comment 'The Wille zur Macht is a spurious feeling' ('Study of Thomas Hardy', *Hardy* 104:15).

395:35 **centripetal** Acting, moving, or tending to move towards a centre; the opposite of centrifugal.

396:4 **His slight physical deformity** One of Chillingworth's shoulders 'rose higher than the other', a 'slight deformity of the figure' (*TSL* 75–6).

396:23 **the fatal old doctrine "Pereat mundus—"** From the saying attributed to Emperor Ferdinand I of Germany (1503–64): 'Fiat justitia, et pereat mundus' ('Let justice be done, though the world perish').

396:33 **Christ . . . passive power is greater than active power.** E.g. 'Blessed are the meek: for they shall inherit the earth . . . I say unto you, That ye resist not evil: but whosoever shall smite thee on the right cheek, turn to him the other also . . . Love your enemies, bless them that curse you, do good to them that hate you, and pray for them which despitefully use you and persecute you' (Matthew v. 5, 39, 44).

397:29 **Book of Job or the Book of Ruth . . . *Don Quixote*.** Books of the Bible noted for their portrayal of suffering, and their symbolic quality . . . novel (1605) by Miguel de Cervantes (1547–1616) which satirises chivalric romance.

399:9 **the dark luster,** Both 'one who lusts' – 'Rare' in *OED2*, but used, e.g., in Charlotte Brontë's *Jane Eyre* (1847), III. v. – and the obsolete or US form of 'lustre'. Cf. too note on 197:10.

400:20 **ether—or electricity, call it what you will.** 'Ether' was – until *c.* 1900–20 – scientifically believed to be the substance permeating the whole of planetary and stellar space, and the medium through which waves of light (and radio waves) passed. In colloquial usage, 'ether' was the source of radio signals, which came 'over' it. DHL suggests that the 'medium' may receive messages as a radio set does, or directly, in the form of electrical impulses.

XIII. Whitman (1921–2)

403:3 Whitman. Per2 quotes two sentences (3:17–18, 20–1) here and notes that DHL is the author of *The Rainbow, Sons and Lovers, The Lost Girl, Women in Love,* 'etc.'; the article is illustrated with drawings of Whitman and DHL.

403:32 John the Evangel or Socrates. See note on 145:34; St John was later described by DHL as 'surely a cultured "Greek" Jew, and one of the great inspirers of mystic, "loving" Christianity' (*Apocalypse*, ed. Kalnins, 66:18–20): hence the link with the Greek philosopher (see note on 23:18).

404:32 just as tourists now explore battlefields. DHL was probably thinking of tourists visiting Belgium and France following the end of the First World War in November 1918, but battlefield tourism dated back at least as far as the Franco-Prussian War: cf. 'Numerous English tourists, bound for a gape at the battle-field of Sedan' (*Daily News,* 4 October 1870).

404:38 Wendell Holmes, Oliver Wendell Holmes (1809–94), American poet and essayist, author of *The Autocrat of the Breakfast-Table* (1858); see Introduction, p. xxxii.

404:40 Balzac Honoré de Balzac, French novelist (1799–1850), author of *Eugénie Grandet* (1833) and other novels which DHL admired (see *Letters,* i. 91–2).

405:2 Maeterlinck Maurice Maeterlinck (1862–1949), Belgian poet and dramatist (see *Letters,* i. 237 and n. 1).

405:21 Dostoevsky has burrowed underground ... the grand climacteric The phrase suggests in particular *Notes from the Underground* (1864) ... crucial or critical moment.

406:6 I am everything ... is rejected. Not a quotation: see note on 150:32.

407:24 in spite of Plato. Plato never suggested that human beings might become each other; this is presumably an allusion to the Platonic idea that nothing except the universal forms or ideas were real, and that the everyday objects of sense perception had no actual substance, being merely shadows.

407:33 Jehovah ... Egypt ... in the Psalms. Types of absolute authority; Jehovah the Old Testament God, celebrated by Moses (e.g.) as 'a man of war ... Thy right hand, O Lord, is become glorious in power: thy right hand, O Lord, hath dashed in pieces the enemy' (Exodus xv. 3, 6) ... the Pharaohs of Egypt were absolute rulers ... see note on 118:6 and, e.g., 'Clouds and darkness are round about him: righteousness and judgment are the habitation of his throne. / A fire goeth before him, and burneth up his enemies round about' (Psalms xcvii. 2–3).

408:4 shuttle I.e. the shuttle of a weaver's loom, which passes back and forwards at speed.

408:13 soppiness, I.e. mawkish sentiment, facile emotion, DHL's usage long predating the earliest (1974) *OED2* citation.

408:21 hold your toes and sit tight DHL is thinking of the seated Buddha; Earl Brewster remembered how 'In later years he used often to say ... "Oh I wish he would *stand up!*" ' (Nehls, ii. 119).

411:16 *raison d'être.* Reason for existing (French).

413:5 *pour épater les bourgeois.* I.e. to shock the bourgeois (French).

415:34 Orestes and Pylades, For Orestes see note on 18:28; Pylades, his close friend and helper, was the son of Strophius. They enter together, e.g., at the start of Aeschylus' play *The Libation Bearers.*

417:11 tyrannus Latin for absolute (sometimes illegitimate) ruler, lord: from the Greek.

Whitman (1922)

423:16 an American girl Named as 'Arabella' at 424:24–5. From *c.* 20 October to 29 November 1917, DHL and FL had shared a flat with Dorothy ('Arabella') Yorke (b. 1892), 'elegant but poor' (*Letters*, iii. 183), whose family came from Camden, New Jersey. See Kinkead-Weekes, *Triumph to Exile*, pp. 410, 416–17. Her memories may have influenced DHL's essay in its 1918 and 1919 forms, as well as the 1922 manuscript in which they actually appeared.

425:6 MERDE! '*SHIT*!' (French)

429:38 The Pentecostal flame Pentecost, deriving from the Jewish holiday of Shavuoth observed fifty days after the first day of Passover, is now also a festival of the Christian church observed on the seventh Sunday after Easter (Whit-Sunday), commemorating the descent of the Holy Spirit (or Holy Ghost) on to the heads of the assembled disciples in the form of 'cloven tongues like as of fire' (Acts ii. 1–4).

TEXTUAL APPARATUS

VARIORUM APPARATUS
(MANUSCRIPT AND TYPESCRIPT VARIANTS)

TEXTUAL APPARATUS

In the apparatus, whenever the reading of the base-text is adopted (see Introduction and 'Note on the Texts'), it appears within the square bracket with no symbol. When a reading from a source later than the base-text has been preferred, it appears with its source-symbol within the square bracket; this is always followed by the reading of the base-text. Other rejected readings follow the square bracket, in the sequence indicated for each essay, with their first source given. Further variants from other states follow in the sequence indicated. In the absence of information to the contrary, the reader should assume that a variant recurs in all subsequent states. The following symbols are used editorially:

Ed.   = Editor
~   = Substitution for a word in recording a punctuation or capitalisation
           variant
Om.   = Omitted
/   = Line or page break
P   = New paragraph
= Internal division
R   = Autograph corrections by DHL to a state of the text (e.g. authorial
           corrections to the typescript for Franklin, *TSR*)
C   = Correction made by someone other than DHL (e.g. TCC7C, MS8C)
[ ]   = Editorial emendation or addition
{ }   = Partial variant reading
⟨ ⟩   = Deleted text
⌈ ⌉   = Added text
[type]   = Typed correction (in Variorum apparatus)

When the symbol ~ (swung dash) is used in the Textual apparatus to record the repetition of a word including an apostrophe, it indicates that the word **including the apostrophe** has been correctly transmitted. Where an apostrophe has not been correctly transmitted, or where one has been inserted in a subsequent state of text, the swung dash is not employed.

The following symbols (see Introduction, 'Texts') are used to distinguish states of the text for pp. 544–631 of this apparatus.

TS1 = Typed ribbon copy E382g, E382r, E382s
Per = *English Review*

543

MS2 = Autograph manuscripts E382b, E382f, E382i, E382l, E382n
TS3 = Typed ribbon copy E382h
TS4 = Typed ribbon copy E382m
TS5 = Typed ribbon copy E382k
TCC5 = Typed carbon copy E382j
TCC6 = Typed carbon copy E382d
TCC7 = Typed carbon copy E382p
MS8 = Autograph manuscript E382q
MS9 = Autograph manuscript E382a
TS10 = Typed ribbon copy E382c
A1   = First American edition (Seltzer)
E1   = First English edition (Secker)
E2   = Second English edition (*Symbolic Meaning*)

Final Version

The order of texts is *MS8*, *A1*, *E1*, except for 'Foreword'. (Earlier texts – *TS1*, *Per*, *MS2* – are used to correct *MS8*.)

Foreword

The order of texts is *MS8*, *A1* (*E1* omitted it).

11:1 Foreword. *Ed.*] STUDIES IN CLASSIC AMERICAN LITERATURE/BY/ D.H.LAWRENCE/ Foreword. *MS8* FOREWORD *A1*
11:3 up,] ~ *A1*
11:12 inventus? *A1*] inventus? I merely ask. *MS8*
11:18 recreant *A1*] truant *MS8*
11:22 Co?] ~.? *A1*

11:23 American. *A1*] American. Yes sir, all those pearls before swine. *MS8*
11:24 Telephones] Telephone *A1*
12:5 Tchekov] Chekhov *A1*
12:12 Americans] American *A1*
12:15 meaning. They revel in subterfuge. *A1*] meaning, as a screen even for themselves. *MS8*

The Spirit of Place

13:4 childishness *A1*] subterfuge *MS8*
13:4 part. *P* The] ~. The *E1*
13:6 But] ~, *A1*
13:8 Third and Fourth] third ~ fourth *A1*
13:12 Africa:] ~; *A1*
13:17 blabbed] babbled *E1*
13:19 the] a *A1*
13:29 "different" *A1*] new *MS8*

13:32 round *MS8*. *E1*] around *A1*
13:33 cut,] ~ *E1*
13:33 Cutting away...is left. *A1*] Like a woman who feels as if her baby were being cut out of her. *MS8*
14:3 Away *A1*] To hell *MS8*
14:8 the] *The A1*
14:10 false *A1*] liar *MS8*

14:11 art speech] art-speech *A1*
14:12 art speech] art-speech *A1*
14:12 prevaricates so terribly, *A1*] lies so terribly on the surface. *MS8*
14:14 Like *A1*] Like that *MS8*
14:25 tail] tale *A1*
14:27 function *MS8, E1*] functions *A1*
14:37 more *A1*] far more *MS8*
15:4 fellow countrymen] fellow-countrymen *E1*
15:7 No] ~, *A1*
15:10 Freedom] ~, *A1*
15:20 "Henceforth be masterless." *A1*] *Om. MS8*
15:23 *positively want to A1*] positively want to *MS8*
15:23 always been ... are *not A1*] never found that *MS8*
15:24 Unless] ~, *E1*
15:24 of course they are *A1*] they positively want to be *MS8* of course, they are *E1*
15:25 made or in the making *A1*] which is a sign of failure to live *MS8*
15:32 control *A1*] master *MS8*
16:2 new *A1*] *Om. MS8*
16:11 rebellion against *A1*] hatred of *MS8*
16:16 Whatever else ... masterless. *A1*] *Om. MS8*
16:18 man..] ~. *A1*
16:27 The masterless. *A1*] *Om. MS8*
16:29 man..] ~. *A1*
16:35 Even no God Almighty. *A1*] *Om. MS8*
16:36 "humanity" *A1*] free-and-easiness *MS8*
17:7 "We are ... Hen-Eagle. *A1*] *Om. MS8*
17:10 Yankees too] ~, ~, *A1*
17:10 refuted] refused *A1*
17:11 humanism *A1*] easiness *MS8*

17:15 old *A1*] real *MS8*
17:15 spontaneity *A1*] easiness *MS8*
17:25 melting pot] melting-pot *E1*
17:30 died] dies *A1*
17:34 obeying some ... unrealised ... [17:39] shout of freedom. *Ed.*] in a homeland, and their spirit, their blood is flowing in unison with the vast vibration of their homeland. Men are free when they are in a homeland, at one with that homeland, and united in carrying out the great unknown of that homeland. *MS8* obeying some ... unrealized ... shout of freedom. *A1*
17:40 shout *A1*] shout of freedom *MS8*
18:1 just *A1*] *Om. MS8*
18:1 The moment ... doing. Men *A1*] They *MS8*
18:3 the deepest self *A1*] IT *MS8*
18:4 And there ... [18:6] be sure. *A1*] IT? What is IT? *P* IT is many things, more than I know. But for one thing, IT is the spirit of place. The spirit of the continent of America. Americans will be free when they are doing what IT likes, and not that they themselves like. *MS8*
18:11 Perhaps at ... [18:14] than Europe. *A1*] And this is where Americans have a hard job. They have to break the old spell in themselves and in the world. And then they have to submit themselves to IT, the great unrevealed spirit of the American continent. *MS8*
18:15 all *A1*] the old *MS8*
18:17 IT being ... idealistic halfness. *A1*] But see how difficult it

is, when nobody knows what
IT is. Can't know, until out
of themselves they begin to
make a revelation of IT. *MS8*
IT . . . halfness. *E1*
18:19 then:] ~; *A1*
18:20 Driven *A1*] Drawn *MS8*
18:21 magnetism brings *A1*] mag-
netisms bring *MS8*
18:22 it brings the *A1*] they bring
MS8
18:24 Unless of course] ~, ~ ~, *E1*
18:25 vulgarly cocksure of our ready-
made *A1*] without any *MS8*
18:27 obey *A1*] obey IT *MS8*
18:27 counter *A1*] counter to IT *MS8*
18:28 round] around *A1*
18:30 their own wholeness *A1*] IT *MS8*

18:31 cocksure, ready-made destinies
A1] destiny *MS8*
18:33 Which will . . . whole men? *A1*]
Om. MS8
18:36 progressive *A1*] open *MS8*
18:38 the old thing *A1*] masters *MS8*
18:39 a figment . . . for much *A1*] an
instrument, it can never be a
master *MS8*
19:1   phrase *A1*] instrument *MS8*
19:2   people. Then . . . own wholeness. *A1*] people, and you throw
the tool down. Basta! *MS8*
19:5   mastery] master *E1*
19:8   negative *A1*] open *MS8*
19:10 whole soul *A1*] Daimon *MS8*
19:13 "Henceforth be . . . mastered.
A1] *Om. MS8*

Benjamin Franklin

20:3   Of] of *A1*
20:5   theme! The perfectibility . . .
car! *A1*] theme. *MS8*
20:5   I am not . . . contrivance. *A1*]
Om. MS8
20:10 me, according . . . standards. *A1*]
me. *MS8*
20:12 Roosevelt or Porfirio Diaz? *A1*]
Om. MS8
20:13 patient ass *A1*] object *MS8*
20:14 doing, playing . . . in a *A1*] doing
in this *MS8*
20:14 jacket? *A1*] ~ ! *MS8*
20:15 patience *A1*] utterance *MS8*
20:19 College *A1*] college *MS8*
20:20 fugitive *A1*] bitter *MS8*
20:27 Franklin *A1*] Daddy Franklin
MS8
20:28 man. He . . . dummy American.
A1] cuss. *MS8*
21:5   Which cost nothing. *A1*]
Benjamin worshipping
Benjamin *MS8*

21:6   *But—— P* (But *Ed.*] ~—, *P*
(But *MS8* ~—" But *A1*
~——" But *E1*
21:7   Lord.)] ~. *A1*
21:8   *man*] *men A1*
21:13 *hereafter." Ed.*] ~.) *MS8* ~." *A1*
21:14 millionaire *Ed.*] magnate *MS8*
millionaire, *A1*
21:18 The everlasting Wanamaker.
A1] *Om. MS8*
21:20 Aloft . . . of dollars *A1*] Winged
with the dollar *MS8*
21:27 thing,] ~ *E1*
21:30 all Benjamin . . . back garden
A1] Benjamin was a bit of a sage
bush *MS8*
21:31 in to] into *E1*
21:32 Hail Columbia! *A1*] Well, we
just shan't. *MS8*
21:36 man!] ~? *A1*
21:37 fencing *A1*] ticketting *MS8*
22:1   bounds] pound *A1*
22:1   forever] for ever *E1*

22:2 them] they *E1*

22:4 trotted *A1*] trotted round *MS8*

22:22 i.e.] i. e., *A1* i.e., *E1*

22:25 INDUSTRY *A1*] ~. *MS8*
INDUSTRY *E1*

23:18 Socrates./————] ~. *A1*

23:23 two *A1*] two worthies *MS8*

23:25 "Aren't you *E1*] Be not *MS8*
Aren't you *A1*

23:26 Ben? *A1*] ~. *MS8*

23:27 "Henceforth be... his spoke
... of masterlessness. *A1*] *Om.*
MS8 "Henceforth... His spoke
... masterlessness. *E1*

23:34 *not*] not *A1*

24:3 The immortal ... insurance policy.
A1] *Om. MS8*

24:4 Benjamin *A1*] But Benjamin
MS8

24:11 Colonies] colonies *A1*

24:14 *infra dig A1*] as good as forgot
ten *MS8 infra dig. E1*

24:22 And, by ... hunting deer. *A1*]
Om. MS8

24:24 naiveté] naïveté *A1*

24:25 become again] again become
A1

24:34 almanack] almanac *E1*

24:37 woman] women *E1*

24:38 hatched,] ~ *E1*

25:4 are thorns in young flesh *A1*]
did me harm *MS8*

25:5 Because] ~, *E1*

25:5 I dislike policy altogether;
though *A1*] and that *MS8*

25:7 it's still... hatched. It *A1*] yet it
MS8

25:13 outside, *MS8, E1*] ~ *A1*

25:16 corral *A1*] corrall *MS8*

25:17 Benjamin! Sound, satisfied Ben!
Ed.] Benjamin! *MS8* Benjamin.
Sound, satisfied Ben! *A1*

25:18 State,] ~ *A1*

25:19 writes:— *P* "We] ~: # *P* "We
A1

25:22 half naked] half-naked *E1*

25:25 be well] well be *A1*

25:34 made *Ed.*] had made *MS8 see
notes*

25:35 rum] the rum *E1*

25:40 sea coast————" *P* This *Ed.*] sea
coast—" *P* This *MS8* seacoast
..." # *P* This *A1* seacoast. ..."
P This *E1*

26:1 complacency, *MS8, E1*] ~ *A1*

26:4 Oh] ~, *A1*

26:5 Benjamin!] Franklin! *A1*

26:7 cultivated *A1*] cultivate *MS8*

26:8 Pittsburgh *A1*] Pittsburg *MS8*

26:8 Pa.?] ~? *E1*

26:10 it *A1*] *Om. MS8*

26:13 paragon? *A1*] paragon? *P* Damn
Benjamin and his Providence
and his lists of virtue and his cultivators of the earth. Damn him
and his barbed wire! *MS8*

26:17 Benjamin] ~, *E1*

26:19 tap." *A1*] tap." *P* Damn you,
Benjamin. *MS8*

26:26 believe.] ~: *A1*

26:27 "That I ... [26:31] gods come
... recognise... [26:36]
and women."] # *"That
I ... gods, come ... recognize
... and women." # A1* [*A1* and
E1 have in italics and regular
paragraphs]

26:39 Benjamin. *A1*] ~ *MS8*

27:11 to the gods... Recognise... all
order. *Ed.*] for your own soul,
and don't let anybody be it
for you. *MS8* to... Recognize
... order. *A1*

27:18 you, or... recognise... Ghost.
Ed.] you. *MS8* you, or...
recognize... Ghost. *A1*

27:22 Don't waste ... your emotion. *A1*] *Om. MS8*

27:26 serve *A1*] busily serve *MS8*

27:26 Holy Ghost *A1*] gods *MS8*

27:27 mankind *A1*] man *MS8*

27:30 other man is not me *A1*] gods come and go, and the soul is patient *MS8*

28:5 CLEANLINESS *A1*] Cleanliness *MS8*

28:10 Obey the ... recognise ... to command. *Ed.*] *Om. MS8* Obey ... recognize ... command. *A1*

28:17 offspring *MS8*, *E1*] off-spring *A1*

28:22 See all ... the barren. / ——— *Ed.*] Recognise the changes in yourself, and in other men or women. / ——— *MS8* See ... barren. *A1*

28:28 wholeness *A1*] gods *MS8*

28:33 useful *A1*] *Om. MS8*

28:36 cat-o-nine-tails] cat-o-nine tails *A1*

29:7 bit] ∼, *E1*

29:10 And why] ∼ ∼, *E1*

29:10 trap *A1*] mouse-trap *MS8*

29:13 barb-wire] barbed-wire *A1*

29:13 corral *A1*] corrall *MS8*

29:14 barb-wire] barbed-wire *A1*

29:15 *Work*] "∼ *A1*

29:15 WORK!] ∼ !" *A1 WORK!" E1*

29:17 Holy Ghost *A1*] odd gods *MS8*

29:26 "Henceforth be masterless." *A1*] *Om. MS8*

29:29 government] Government *A1*

29:40 recreant *A1*] truant *MS8*

30:3 Theoretic and materialistic. *A1*] *Om. MS8*

30:5 course] ∼, *E1*

30:7 Either we ... Benjamin or ... usually unconscious *A1*] IT does things inside us *MS8* Either ... Benjamin, or ... unconscious *E1*

30:11 or outside us *A1*] *Om. MS8*

30:12 the deeps ... inside us *A1*] IT *MS8*

30:20 the inner gods, should *A1*] IT, will *MS8*

30:29 a slow] slow *A1*

30:34 was] ∼, *E1*

30:34 still is] ∼ ∼, *E1*

30:39 the past *A1*] all masters *MS8*

31:5 lies *A1*] stinks *MS8*

31:6 barb-wire] barbed-wire *A1* barbed wire *E1*

Henry St. John de Crèvecoeur

For *TCC7* pages (37:10-end) surviving into *MS8*, *Per* is the ultimate source, e.g. 38:9 (second entry).

32:2 Henry Ed.] HENRY *MS8* HECTOR *A1*

32:9 *from E1*] from *MS8* From *A1*

32:15 him then] ∼, ∼, *E1*

32:22 favourite *A1*] favorite *MS8*

32:24 were of course] ∼, ∼ ∼, *E1*

32:25 *from an E1*] From An *MS8 From an A1*

32:32 prototype *MS8, E1*] protoype *A1*

32:34 Joan] John *A1*

33:12 it,] ∼ *A1*

33:13 over,] ∼ *A1*

33:14 *Letters A1*] Letters *MS8*

33:19 Amiable *A1*] Aimable *MS8*

33:23 Son—] ∼——— *A1*

33:24 I.S.] I. S. *A1*

33:26 A.F.] A. F. *A1*

33:28 Amiable *A1*] Aimable *MS8*

33:32 methodist] Methodist *A1*

33:32 Amiable *A1*] Aimiable *MS8*

34:3 the Healthy . . . occasion, and] *Om. A1*

34:4 Amiable *A1*] Aimiable *MS8*

34:7 Amiable *A1*] Aimiable *MS8*

34:11 Jean] John, *A1*

34:13 Jean] John *A1*

34:13 Bernadin] Bernardin *A1*

34:14 François *A1*] Francois *MS8*

34:14 Nature Sweet and Pure] Nature-Sweet-and-Pure *E1*

34:20 human being] Human Being *A1*

34:24 So *MS8, E1*] ~. *A1*

34:25 Nature-Sweet-and-Pure *A1*] Nature Sweet and Pure *MS8*

34:25 Nature] nature *A1*

34:40 toil etc.] ~, etc., *A1*

35:4 *Letters A1*] Letters *MS8*

35:17 providence] Providence *A1*

35:25 Man] ~, *A1*

35:25 Whereupon *A1*] Then *MS8*

35:26 farm; so *A1*] farm, and *MS8*

35:26 refrains from mentioning *A1*] never mentions *MS8*

35:26 *Letters,* for fear . . . premises. *E1*] Letters. *MS8 Letters,* for fear . . . premises. *A1*

35:30 Amiable *A1*] Aimiable *MS8*

35:34 Amiable *A1*] Aimiable *MS8*

35:34 S.] S., *A1*

35:34 told. And] ~, and *A1*

35:36 verandah] veranda *E1*

36:2 triumph,] ~ *E1*

36:6 kingbird] king-bird *E1*

36:10 kingbird] king-bird *E1*

36:15 sewing needle] sewing-needle *E1*

36:15 bee] Bee *A1*

36:19 When] Where *A1*

36:25 favourable *A1*] favorable *MS8*

36:30 species.—] ~. *A1*

36:31 tartar] Tartar *A1*

36:31 ink spots] ink-spots *E1*

36:32 humming birds] humming-birds *A1*

36:32 W.H.Hudson] W. H. Hudson *A1* W.H. Hudson *E1*

36:34 lion. P Birds *Ed.*] ~. / Birds *MS8* ~. Birds *A1*

37:7 air," *A1*] ~", *MS8*

38:6 sophisticated] ~, *E1*

38:9 Indian,] Indians *E1*

38:9 *à la Per*] a la *TCC7* à la *TCC7C, MS8*

38:11 pre-determined] predetermined *E1*

38:36 *Letters A1*] Letters *MS8*

38:36 wish-fulfilment *MS8, E1*] wish-fulfillment *A1*

38:37 isolate] ~, *A1*

39:13 *know*] know *A1*

39:18 Oh] ~, *A1*

39:24 take] takes *A1*

39:24 fancy] ~, *E1*

40:5 husbandman,] ~ *E1*

40:10 ideal] idea *A1*

40:19 readopt *E1*] re-/ adopt *Per* re-adopt *TCC7*

40:22 sorrow *Per, A1*] sorry *TCC7*

Fenimore Cooper's White Novels

For the part of the *TCC7* page surviving into *MS8, Per* is the ultimate source: 45:1–20 ('Cooper quotes . . . a month.')

42:5 Savage =] ~ = = *A1*

42:12 again] *Om. A1*

42:29 new-comer *MS8, E1*] newcomer *A1*

42:31 numbers] ~, *E1*

42:32 demon] ~, *E1*

43:17 the glorification of the savages *A1*] a reconciliation between the souls of the two races *MS8*

43:19 desire to glorify him *A1*] desire,
        for a reconciliation *MS8*
43:25 intellectualise *Ed.*] love *MS8*
        intellectualize *A1*
43:25 man] Man *A1*
43:30 consideration] ~, *E1*
43:34 woman.—] ~. *A1*
44:6   on.—] ~. *A1*
44:23 Red man] ~ Man *A1*
44:24 success,] ~ *E1*
44:29 Coopers-Town] Cooperstown *A1*
44:33 fleabites] flea-bites *A1*
44:34 finely-drawn] finely drawn *E1*
45:1   are. Cooper] ~. *P* Cooper *A1*
45:2   *"L'Amérique . . . mûre." Per, A1*]
        "L'Amerique est pourrie avant
        d' etre mure." *TCC7* "L'Amérique
        . . . mûre." *MS8R* "L'Amérique
        . . . mûre." *E1*
45:6   Leatherstocking Series] *Lea-*
        therstocking Series A1
45:9   *Homeward Bound Ed.*] home-
        ward bound *Per* "Homeward
        Bound" *MS8R*
45:13 is a] is *A1*
45:17 female— *TCC7C*] ~,— *Per*
        ~. *A1*
45:20 *done Per*] done *TCC7* "done"
        TCC7C
45:20 Oh] ~, *A1*
45:33 Come] come *A1*
45:37 exclaiming] ~, *A1*
45:37 else] ~, *E1*
45:39 know—"] ~"— *A1*
46:2   Marks] Mark's *A1*
46:3   upside down *MS8, E1*]
        upside-down *A1*

46:6   cathedral] Cathedral *A1*
46:7   one,] ~⸴ *E1*
46:7   five-minute] five-minutes' *A1*
46:13 had] has *A1*
46:23 meet *A1*] Meet *MS8*
46:33 does] ~, *E1*
46:37 Dodgetown] Dodge-town *E1*
47:6   No] ~, *A1*
47:13 Dodges.] ~? *A1*
47:18 dilemma. Since] ~. *P* Since *A1*
47:34 Sight] sight *A1*
47:35 superiority?] ~. *A1*
47:36 Somehow,] ~ *E1*
47:39 i. e.] i.e. *E1*
48:3   er—] ~—— *E1*
48:7   Eve! *P* Think] ~! Think *A1*
48:8   apples!] ~. *A1*
48:19 Mr *Ed.*] ~. *MS8*
48:25 away!"—] ~!" *A1*
48:26 Hence,] ~ *E1*
48:26 her *A1*] her / her *MS8*
49:4   Court *MS8, E1*] court *A1*
49:5   Hello] ~, *A1*
49:15 Excalibur).] ~.) *A1*
49:29 propellers *A1*] propellors *MS8*
49:37 propellers *A1*] propellors *MS8*
49:37 propelling] ~. *A1*
49:38 amazing, ludicrous, *MS8, E1*]
        ~ ~ *A1*
49:40 forever] for ever *A1*
50:1   I] ~, *E1*
50:4   spear—] ~—— *E1*
50:11 suit,"] ~" *A1*
50:21 Well] ~, *A1*
50:37 man, so *Ed.*] ~, So *MS8* ~. So
        A1

Fenimore Cooper's Leatherstocking Novels

52:9   No] ~, *A1*
52:14 ego] ~, *E1*
52:16 pin] ~, *E1*

52:21 National] national *E1*
52:24 as] that *E1*
52:25 course] ~, *E1*

52:34 Grouch] grouch *A1*
53:1 Cooper's *A1*] Coopers *MS8*
53:2 MRS *Ed.*] ~. *MS8* MRS. *E1*
53:2 COOPER |] ~ *A1* COOPER *E1*
53:2 WORK.] ~ *A1* WORK *E1*
53:3 WORK |] ~ *A1* WORK *E1*
53:4 WIFE |] ~ *A1* WIFE *E1*
53:5 THE DEAR CHILDREN] THE DEAR CHILDREN *A1* THE DEAR CHILDREN *E1*
53:12 Oh] ~, *A1*
53:20 Cardinals *A1*] cardinals *MS8*
53:24 self.] ~ *E1*
53:26 to his WIFE *A1*] *Om. MS8* to his WIFE *E1*
53:27 versus] *vs. A1*
53:27 HÔTEL *Ed.*] HÔTEL *MS8* HOTEL *A1* HOTEL *E1*
53:28 wish-fulfilment] Wish Fulfilment *A1*
53:28 ACTUALITY *Ed.*] ACTUALITY *MS8* Actuality *A1*
53:28 versus] *vs. A1*
53:29 versus] *vs. A1*
53:30 Fenimore] ~, *E1*
53:30 hôtel] hotel *E1*
53:32 butterflies] Butterflies *A1*
53:34 déjeûner] déjeuner *A1*
53:36 actuality,] ~ *E1*
54:3 Monsieur Fénimore … américain] *Monsieur Fenimore Cooper, le grand écrivain américain A1*
54:6 Fenimore arm-in-arm] ~, ~, *E1*
54:6 odd] old *E1*
54:11 Wish] wish *E1*
55:3 *Pioneers*: *Ed.*] ~— *MS8* ~: *A1*
55:7 *Mohicans*:] ~: *A1*
55:10 Scout] scout *A1*
55:12 *Prairie*:] ~: *A1*
55:14 in a chair on *Ed.*] on *MS8* a chair on on *MS8R* on a chair on *A1* *see notes*
55:16 *Pathfinder*:] *The Pathfinder*: *A1*

55:18 sergeant] Sergeant *A1*
55:19 *Deerslayer*:] ~: *A1*
55:22 There] These *A1*
55:35 girning] grinning *A1*
55:37 men like] ~, ~ *E1*
55:38 resistance *A1*] terror *MS8*
55:39 common-sense] common-/ sense *A1* commonsense *E1*
56:3 soil] Soil *A1*
56:6 When the … down again. *A1*] *Om. MS8*
56:11 the white man *A1*] white men *MS8*
56:12 loves *A1*] love *MS8*
57:4 this.] ~: *A1*
57:41 life-throb] life throb *E1*
58:11 *pis-aller*] *pis aller A1*
58:12 that. Chiefly] ~, chiefly *A1*
58:23 The] the *A1*
58:38 frontier-village,] ~ *E1*
59:2 Natty] Matty *E1*
59:6 fact] ~, *E1*
59:8 tiresomely,] ~ *A1*
59:17 wood-fires] woodfires *A1*
59:19 woodsmen] woodsman *E1*
59:21 turkey-shooting] turkey shooting *E1*
59:28 could] would *A1*
59:38 Cooper however] ~, ~, *A1*
59:40 evasion] vision *A1 see notes*
60:1 And nevertheless] ~, ~, *A1*
60:19 season. *P* The] ~. The *A1*
60:25 severed] ~, *A1*
60:27 Letter] letter *E1*
60:33 a sense] sense *A1*
60:37 crime,] ~; *A1*
61:15 west] West *A1*
61:30 myth-meaning] myth-/ meaning *A1* myth meaning *E1*
61:32 time,] ~ *E1*
61:37 Major *A1*] young Major *MS8*
62:4 the Last] The last *E1*
62:12 white lily] White Lily *A1*

62:18   childless, *MS8, E1*] ~ *A1*
62:18   men] ~, *E1*
62:26   hurling] hurtling *E1*
62:29   *Deerslayer Ed.*] Deerslayer *MS8*
        Deerslayer, A1 Deerslayer, *E1*
62:34   glamour *A1*] glamor *MS8*
62:38   blond] blonde *A1*
63:2   camp-fire] campfire *A1*
63:6   What ever] Whatever *A1*
63:11   gem *A1*] lovely, lovely gem
        MS8
63:12   setting, so ... pretense of reality
        A1] setting better than any real
        stone in platinum *MS8* setting,
        so ... pretence of reality *E1*
63:13   *Deerslayer Ed.*] Deerslayer *MS8*

63:16   ever has] has *E1*
63:27   blond-bearded] blonde bearded
        A1
63:28   hemlock-tree,] hemlock tree *A1*
64:3   ark," *A1*] ~", *MS8*
64:8   blond] blonde *E1*
64:23   philosophic,] ~ *A1*
64:26   forever] for ever *A1*
64:37   God] ~, *A1*
65:1   direction.—] ~. *A1*
65:7   life": *Ed.*] ~:" *MS8* ~," *A1*
65:21   American] America *A1*
65:25   course] ~, *E1*
65:27   these] there *A1*
65:33   stoic] ~, *A1*

Edgar Allan Poe

For *TCC7* pages surviving into *MS8*, *Per* is the ultimate source: 75:6–80:16.

66:7   dual:] ~. *A1*
66:20   great,] ~ *A1*
67:4   flaming, frictional] *Om. A1*
67:4   That is coition.] *Om. A1*
67:12   life,] ~ *A1*
68:12   great will] great Will *A1*
68:21   god] God *A1*
68:21   he] He *A1*
68:36   *women*] women *A1*
68:40   wife:] ~; *A1*
68:40   cousin:] ~, *A1*
69:3   blood-vessels *MS8, E1*] blood/
        vessels *A1*
69:25   woman *A1*] woman-lover *MS8*
69:26   Even *A1*] Even unto *MS8*
69:32   voice] ~, *E1*
69:36   chair-springs and mantel-pieces
        A1] a mechanism *MS8* chair-
        springs and mantelpieces *E1*
69:37   instrument,] ~ *E1*
70:1   matter—] ~, *A1*
70:1   etc.— *A1*] ~— *MS8* ~.,— *E1*

70:7   brain, and *A1*] brain and blood.
        And *MS8*
70:7   È] E *A1*
70:12   folks'—] ~. *A1*
70:13   Nourjahad— — —" Which]
        ~—" Which *A1* ~"—which *E1*
70:14   black,] ~ *A1*
70:15   length"—suggests *MS8, E1*]
        ~."—Suggests *A1*
70:16   —"The] "~ *A1*
70:17   however,] *Om. A1*
70:17   eyes] ~, *E1*
70:19   to] to as *A1*
70:20   cat.—] ~— *E1*
70:23   midsummer] mid-/ summer *A1*
        mid-summer *E1*
70:26   discover ....] ~.... *A1*
70:37   blood, through ... of coition.]
        blood. *A1*
70:39   And] ~, *A1*
70:40   to *get*] or *get A1*
71:1   Knowledge] knowledge *A1*

71:37 Condors!] ∼. *A1*

72:3 Vultures *A1*] vultures *MS8*

72:5 then] ∼, *A1*

72:18 Oh] ∼, *A1*

72:20 cursed).] ∼.) *A1*

72:25 now] *Om. A1*

72:32 have] hath *A1*

72:35 birds] ∼, *E1*

72:35 Ligeia] ∼, *E1*

72:36 them,] ∼; *E1*

73:4 Fooled] Foiled *A1*

73:18 Blake too] ∼, ∼, *A1*

73:18 knowers] Knowers *A1*

73:19 Oh] O *A1*

73:22 Conqueror] conqueror *A1*

73:23 the will . . . to the] the/ the *A1* the *E1*

73:26 Anche troppo] *Anche troppo A1*

73:31 high falutin] high-falutin *E1*

73:31 all] ∼, *E1*

73:32 leave off . . . leave off *A1*] yield . . . yield *MS8*

74:2 forget, bids . . . limits. *A1*] forget. *MS8*

74:17 me] *Om. A1*

74:22 purity. —" etc. *Ed.*] ∼.." " etc *MS8* ∼ . . ." etc. *A1*

74:31 she too] ∼, ∼, *A1*

74:35 Rowena] ∼, *A1*

74:35 her *A1*] *Om. MS8*

74:36 re-appears] re-/ appears *A1* reappears *E1*

75:12 out *A1*] *Om. MS8*

75:16 mental *A1*] destructive *MS8*

75:18 Coition] The embrace of love *A1*

75:20 sex-intercourse] love-making *A1*

75:21 daytime] all *A1*

75:28 "Toutes . . . idées,"] *"Toutes ses dents étaient des idées," A1*

75:35 longing *Per, A1*] loving *TCC7*

76:6 We want it continually. *A1*] *Om. MS8*

76:8 be resisted] ∼ ∼, *E1*

76:8 We ought to decide . . . with craving. *A1*] *Om. MS8*

76:12 Son cœur . . . Sitôt . . . il *Per*] Son coeur . . . Sitot . . . il *TCC7* Son coeur . . . Sitôt . . . il *MS8R* *Son coeur est un luth suspendu; / Sitôt qu'on le touche il A1*

76:13 résonne *Per*] resonne *TCC7* résonne *A1*

76:21 eaves *Per, E1*] eves *TCC7*

76:33 æolian *Per, A1*] aeolian *TCC7*

76:38 self-less] selfless *E1*

77:8 inordinately] ∼, *E1*

78:1 this] his *A1*

78:7 hollow,] ∼ *A1*

78:29 forever] for ever *A1*

78:29 Ghost] ghost *A1*

78:33 love, love, love, *A1*] ∼, ∼, ∼/ ∼, *MS8*

78:36 Each must . . . certain limits. *A1*] *Om. MS8*

78:39 this underground . . . symbolises . . . consciousness.] this/ that which takes place *beneath* the consciousness. / underground vault business in Poe only symbolizes *A1* this underground . . . symbolizes . . . consciousness. *E1*

79:2 the *Per*] *Om. TCC7*

79:9 bounds] bonds *A1*

79:23 Wilson, . . . Wilson,] ∼ . . . ∼ *E1*

79:27 following out *Per*] the following out of *TCC7*

79:39 self: an . . . accepts limits. *A1*] self. *MS8*

80:11 evil. And Love] ∼, and love *A1*

80:13 unhappinesses *viennent A1*] unhappiness *vient MS8* unhappiness *viennent E1*

80:35 art in *MS8, E1*] Art ∼ *A1*

Nathaniel Hawthorne and
The Scarlet Letter

81:7   it's *MS8, E1*] its *A1*

81:7   *D'Arthur A1*] D' Arthur *MS8*

81:10 the] *The E1*

81:16 sucking doves] sucking-doves *E1*

81:16 Hawthorne's ... time." Which
       ... eternity." *Ed.*] *Om. MS8*
       Hawthorne's ... time," which
       ... eternity." *A1* Hawthorne's
       ... time," which ... eternity." *E1*

81:23 disagreeable *A1*] terrible *MS8*

82:1   case;] ~: *A1*

82:3   the *Scarlet Ed.*] the Scarlet *MS8*
       The Scarlet A1

82:5   warbles *A1*] cackles *MS8*

82:7   So convincingly ... in time."
       A1] That is the darling blue-
       eyed Natty waving his parson's
       sleeves. *MS8*

82:9   Knowledge] knowledge *A1*

82:10 had intercourse] lived *A1*

82:11 Many a time] Yes, he had *A1*

82:12 Knowledge-poison] knowledge-
       poison *A1*

82:15 Cross] cross *A1*

82:17 momentaneously *A1*] monta-
       neously *MS8*

82:17 blood knowledge] blood-
       knowledge *A1*

82:18 mind knowledge] mind-
       knowledge *A1*

82:18 Blood knowledge] Blood-
       knowledge *A1*

82:19 Blood knowledge] Blood-
       knowledge *A1*

82:24 appendage] *Om. A1*

82:24 Lord, just look at it behaving!]
       Lord! *A1*

82:24 l] And Eve! l *A1*

82:25 what Eve has got to match]
       about Eve *A1*

82:34 pryed] pried *A1*

82:35 in the act] *Om. A1*

82:36 said] ~, *A1*

82:36 hide, we've] ~. We've *A1*

82:39 self-watching] ~, *A1*

82:40 UNDERSTANDING] un-
       derstanding *A1*

83:2   Cross] cross *E1*

83:27 I] ~, *A1*

83:37 blood: as the act of coition.]
       blood. *A1*

83:41 does *A1*] ever does *MS8*

84:3   laborer] labourer *A1*

84:4   acts,] ~ *A1*

84:10 heads. *A1*] heads, the devils.
       MS8

84:11 *Co-ordinate!*] ~. *A1*

84:12 the blood] blood *A1*

84:19 Fall!] ~. *A1*

84:23 UNDERSTAND. That is to
       intellectualise the blood. *Ed.*]
       UNDERSTAND, damn it.
       MS8 UNDERSTAND. That
       is to intellectualize the blood.
       A1 UNDERSTAND. That is to in-
       tellectualize the blood. *E1*

84:28 extremely extremely] extre-
       mely *A1*

85:2   fluttery] fluttering *A1*

85:11 *first*] first *A1*

85:16 Sin] sin *A1*

85:17 Oh] ~, *A1*

85:21 course] ~, *E1*

85:34 A.] *A. A1*

85:34 Alpha. Alpha! *A1*] Alpha of
       America. Alpha! America! *MS8*

85:35 American! *A1*] *Om. MS8*

85:36 A.] *A. A1*

85:37 insignia *A1*] insignia of Ame-
       rican woman *MS8*

85:39 A.] *A. A1*
85:40 Able! Admirable! *Ed.*] Able!
    MS8 Abel! Admirable! *A1*
86:1 A.] *A. A1*
86:1 Adolorata] Adolerata *A1*
86:2 A. ... A.] *A. ... A. A1*
86:2 Abel! Adultery. Admirable! *A1*]
    Abel. America. Adultery. *MS8*
86:4 is perhaps] ~, ~, *A1*
86:4 penned,] ~. *A1*
86:9 A.] *A. A1*
86:10 Alpha *A1*] America. Alpha *MS8*
86:10 Abel.] ~, *A1*
86:10 A.] *A. A1*
86:10 America. *A1*] *Om. MS8*
86:11 The Scarlet Letter] *The Scarlet
    Letter A1*
86:17 Sinless] sinless *A1*
86:22 effect, *TS1*] ~ *MS8*
86:25 symbols] ~, *A1*
86:27 Oh] ~, *A1*
86:29 sacred saint] Sacred Saint *A1*
86:31 witches] witch's *A1*
87:9 things] ~, *A1*
87:21 mind,—] ~, *A1*
87:25 set] get *A1*
87:28 Captain] captain *A1*
87:28 Hurray! "In...etc., etc. *A1*]
    Hurray! *P* The Penitentes in
    New Mexico are still at it. *MS8*
87:30 Goodbye] Good-bye *A1*
87:31 So] ~, *A1*
87:31 touched *A1*] tickled *MS8*
87:31 weak spot *A1*] tit-bit *MS8*
87:35 not——] ~—— *A1*
87:37 Oh prophet] ~, Prophet *A1*
88:9 woman,] ~ *E1*
88:11 her:] ~; *E1*
88:19 females] ~, *A1*
88:24 ' "Shall] " '~ *A1*
88:24 again?"] ~?' *A1*
88:25 "Shall] '~ *A1*
88:26 another, *TS1*] ~ *MS8*

88:26 looked *TS1*] lookest *MS8*
88:27 Then tell *TS1*] Tell *MS8*
88:28 seest!" '] ~!' " *A1*
88:29 ' "Hush] " '~ *A1*
88:29 hush,"] ~,' *A1*
88:29 "The] '~ *A1*
88:30 — let *TS1*] let *TCC7* Let *MS8*
88:31 fear!" '] ~!' " *A1*
88:36 belief. Or] ~, or *E1*
89:11 lie] life *A1*
89:14 Sister of Mercy saint] Sister-of-
    Mercy Saint *A1*
89:16 witch. Which] ~, which *A1*
89:23 Woman,] ~. *A1*
89:24 American woman] ~ ~, *A1*
89:28 *genuinely*;] ~: *A1*
89:38 willy nilly] willy-nilly *A1*
89:40 appearance, like Ligeia. *A1*]
    appearance. *MS8*
90:1 faltering *A1*] living *MS8*
90:20 meekly. *A1*] meekly, the bitch.
    MS8
90:27 willy nilly] willy-nilly *A1*
90:39 oh] ~, *A1*
90:39 destroys him *A1*] tears out his
    entrails *MS8*
91:8 rich voluptuous *TS1*] ~, ~,
    MS8
91:11 laboring] labouring *A1*
91:11 stitchery] stitching *A1*
91:14 characteristic—] ~—— *E1*
91:24 ithyphallic images] images of
    sex-worship *A1*
91:27 phallic] *Om. A1*
92:1 —Can't] ~ *A1*
92:1 silently"? *E1*] ~?" *MS8*
92:2 but of] but *A1*
92:13 crowd:] ~, *A1*
92:15 gipsy *MS8, E1*] gypsy *A1*
92:26 lover,] ~ *A1*
92:27 vols.] volumes *A1*
92:28 gipsy *MS8, E1*] gypsy *A1*
92:30 oh] ~, *A1*

92:35 produce *A1*] spawn *MS8*
92:36 produced *A1*] spawned *MS8*
92:37 produce *A1*] spawn *MS8*
92:39 ripe,] ~. *A1*
92:40 then] ~, *E1*
93:14 diabolical] diabolic *A1*
93:17 not *A1*] never *MS8*
93:19 oh] ~, *A1*
93:19 serve] serves *A1*
93:28 sadness." Which] ~," which *A1*
93:34 course] ~, *E1*
93:37 Hester of course ~, ~ ~, *A1*
94:6 borne *A1*] spawned *MS8*
94:13 The chickens... trussed. *A1*]
    Om. MS8
94:18 scarlet letter *Ed.*] Scarlet letter
    MS8 Scarlet Letter *A1*

94:20 physician] ~, *E1*
94:24 mediaeval] mediæval *A1*
94:25 christian] Christian *A1*
94:29 Shakspere's] Shakespeare's *E1*
94:39 ' "Why] "~ *A1*
94:39 me— —] ~ — *A1*
94:40 round] around *A1*
95:2 soul?" '] ~?" *A1*
95:3 ' "Not] "~ *A1*
95:3 soul!" '] ~!" *A1*
95:5 this other *A1*] another *MS8*
95:7 Saint] saint *A1*
95:14 the game *A1*] it *MS8*
95:16 up *A1*] up pure *MS8*
95:22 were] ~, *A1*
95:24 like] as *A1*

Hawthorne's *Blithedale Romance*

96:5 Sin] sin *A1*
96:6 Commandments] command-
    ments *A1*
96:11 sin:] ~, *E1*
96:19 Man] man *A1*
96:21 bring on *A1*] come to the
    scratch with *MS8*
96:29 it's *A1*] it *MS8*
96:29 thing:] ~— *E1*
96:32 in,] ~ *E1*
96:32 wrong. Because] ~, because *E1*
97:2 do wrong] *do wrong A1*
97:6 *half*-genuine] half-genuine *A1*
97:12 him. *A1*] him. Tra-la-la. *MS8*
97:20 Pearls,] ~ *A1*
97:21 may. Because] ~, because *E1*
97:22 Men with... name. *A1*] *Om.*
    MS8
97:24 Oh... Oh] ~, ...~, *A1*
97:24 Oh] ~, *A1*
97:25 blemish.] ~! *A1*
97:33 *he's A1*] he's *MS8*
97:34 Not *she. A1*] And *MS8*
97:34 impeccable *A1*] *Om. MS8*

97:35 oh] ~, *A1*
97:38 Doom] doom *E1*
98:1 against:] ~; *E1*
98:2 Son *A1*] Beloved Son *MS8*
98:5 Now] ~, *A1*
98:13 YOU] You *A1*
98:14 breach] break *A1*
98:17 you:] ~, *E1*
98:21 Oh] ~, *A1*
98:24 smell *A1*] stink *MS8*
98:31 bat-like] batlike *A1*
98:33 god] God *A1*
98:34 you. P Hawthorne's] ~. # P
    Hawthorne's *A1*
98:35 *Scarlet Ed.*] Scarlet *MS8 The*
    Scarlet A1
99:9 Vivat industria] *Vivat Industria*
    A1
99:11 Oh] ~, *A1*
99:11 ironist.] ~! *A1*
99:19 *The Ed.*] "The *MS8* the *A1*
99:27 quarreling] quarrelling *A1*
99:28 Which is... physical work. *A1*]
    Om. MS8

99:31 And that's *A1*] That's *MS8*
99:31 bookfarming. *A1*] bookfarming. Those that didn't turn to the inventing of machines that should settle hard work, break its back for ever. *MS8*
99:34 blood knowledge] blood-knowledge *A1*
99:35 This] That *A1*
99:39 another. And] ~—and *E1*
100:6 laborers] labourers *A1*
100:7 turnips.] ~, *A1*
100:16 Oh] ~, *A1*
100:22 amiable *A1*] aimiable *MS8*
100:25 —It] ~ *A1*
100:26 opening. *P Dramatis Personae. P* I.]~. # ~ *Personæ: P* I. *A1*
100:28 The] —~ *A1*
100:30 *Zenobia.* A] ~: a *A1*
100:37 séances] seances *A1*
101:4 Plot I.] *Plot I.—A1*
101:10 on] to *A1*
101:11 Hephaestos] Hephæstos *A1*
101:11 a] *Om. A1*
101:13 Plot II.] *Plot II.—A1*
101:17 contemptuously,] ~ *A1*
101:19 Plot III.] *Plot III.—A1*
101:20 which of course] ~, ~ ~, *E1*
101:21 Plot IV.] *Plot IV.—A1*
101:23 Plot V.] *Plot V.—A1*
101:23 vapourously] vaporously *A1*
101:26 Also she . . . half-sister. *A1*]*Om. MS8*

101:27 Débâcle. *P* Nobody] # *Débâcle* # *P* Nobody *A1*
101:30 he too] ~, ~, *A1*
101:31 Conclusion. *P* A] # *Conclusion* # *P* A *A1*
101:36 Lady. *P* There] ~ # *P* There *A1*
102:13 table cloth] tablecloth *A1*
102:14 sleep",] ~," *A1*
102:15 *individual,*] ~ *E1*
102:18 do,] ~ *E1*
102:22 underconscious] under-conscious *A1*
102:26 all,] ~ *E1*
102:27 underconscious] under-conscious *A1* under-/conscious *E1*
102:37 of the] of a *A1*
103:1 messages." Because] ~," because *E1*
103:2 consciousnesses] consciousness *A1*
103:3 has] ~, *E1*
103:3 have] ~, *E1*
103:9 mustering] maturing *A1*
103:12 Rien de certain] *Rien de certain A1*
103:15 deal is] ~ ~, *E1*
103:16 be] ~, *E1*
103:21 practices *A1*] practice *MS8*
103:22 of material vibrations *A1*] *Om. MS8*
103:29 by this time he stinketh] fell *A1*
103:39 so] ~, *A1*
104:7 materialistic *A1*] egoistic *MS8*

Dana's *Two Years Before the Mast*

For *TCC7* pages surviving into *MS8*, *MS2* is the ultimate source (107:10–109:4, 112:39–120:28), and the order of texts is *MS2, TCC7, TCC7C, MS8, MS8C, MS8R, A1, E1.*

105:1 The *Ed.*] The *MS8* THE *A1*
105:3 You *MS8, E1*] YOU can't idealize brute labour. That is to say, you can't idealize brute labour, without coming undone as an idealist. *P* You *A1*

105:17 mother earth] mother-earth *E1*
105:21 mother earth] mother-earth *E1*
105:23 mother earth] mother-earth *E1*
105:26 soil *A1*] Soil *MS8*
105:27 And of the pocket. *A1*] *Om. MS8*
106:4 spirit home-land]
     spirit-home-land *E1*
106:10 No] ~, *A1*
106:22 tried,] ~ *A1*
106:37 KNOW,] know, *A1*
106:38 KNOW] know *A1*
107:3 not to know] not-to-know *A1*
107:12 eastern *MS2*] Eastern *TCC7*
107:14 give." So *MS2*] ~." P So
     TCC7
107:16 twilighty *MS2*] twilight *TCC7*
107:19 "—But] "~ *A1*
107:20 during a calm, *MS2*] *Om.*
     TCC7
107:27 him, when, *MS2*] ~; ~ *TCC7*
107:29 best *A1*] *Om. MS8*
108:2 alone,] ~ *A1*
108:14 light sails *MS2*] lightsails
     TCC7 light-/ sails *E1*
108:15 fore-rigging] fore-/ rigging *A1*
     forerigging *E1*
108:22 passional-emotional *MS2*]
     passional emotional *TCC7*
108:22 self. *A1*] self. He sees the great
     mechanical motions of Matter
     itself, he sees the soul as an iso-
     late entity, without emotional
     connection. He has outpassed
     the personal self. *MS8*
108:23 out *MS2*] *Om. TCC7*
108:28 great disintegrative *MS2, A1*]
     great disintegration *TCC7*
109:4 by—] ~—— *A1*
109:8 whipped? Because ... [109:16]
     blasphemy. *P* And as]
     whipped? *P* As *A1*
109:28 life interchange]
     life-interchange *A1*

109:31 Gods-of-the-machine] gods-
     of-the-machine *A1*
109:34 is,] is, with *A1*
109:37 an abstract *A1*] a bloody *MS8*
110:6 life: or anti-life. *A1*] life. *MS8*
110:11 unstable,] ~ *A1*
110:26 re-finding] refinding *A1*
110:39 makes *A1*] make *MS8*
111:5 beside *A1*] by *MS8*
111:11 whack! down] Whack! ~ *A1*
111:14 captain's] Captain's *A1*
111:21 smarting] smarty *A1*
111:21 captain] Captain *A1*
111:35 To him ... a Sam! *A1*] *Om.*
     MS8
112:1 Interceder *E1*] Intercedor
     MS8
112:2 The popular Paraclete. *A1*]
     Om. MS8
112:3 Sir] sir *A1*
112:5 interfered-with] interfered
     with *A1*
112:9 captain] Captain *A1*
112:15 he too] ~, ~, *A1*
112:18 Interceder *E1*] Intercedor
     MS8
112:19 Saviour] saviour *A1*
113:1 —because *MS2*] —Because
     TCC7
113:2 what *MS2, A1*] why *TCC7*
113:3 ran *MS2*] run *TCC7*
113:4 sick, *MS2*] ~ *TCC7*
113:4 horror-struck *MS2*]
     horror-stricken *TCC7*
113:9 Captain *MS2*] captain *TCC7*
113:9 down— *MS2*] ~. *TCC7*
113:17 ever *MS2*] ~, *TCC7*
113:20 subject— *MS2*] ~. *TCC7*
113:21 elder *MS2*] the elder *TCC7*
113:22 whilst *MS2*] while *TCC7*
113:23 Captain *MS2*] captain *TCC7*
113:23 shouts *MS2*] ~, *TCC7C*
113:24 you—] ~—— *A1*

113:33 ship-mate] ship-/ mate *A1*
    shipmate *E1*
113:33 suffered.—] ∼. *A1*
113:37 re-adjustment] readjustment
    A1
114:2 your Danas] you Danas *E1*
114:4 Oh] O, *A1* O *E1*
114:6 dreary *MS2*] weary *TCC7*
114:12 coast *MS2*] ∼, *TCC7*
114:14 alone— — —] ∼. . . .*A1*
114:14 —I *MS2*] ∼ *TCC7*
114:22 self.—He *MS2*] ∼. *P* He
    TCC7
114:25 deer,] ∼ *E1*
114:26 stag,] ∼ *E1*
114:29 motions—] ∼—— *A1*
114:32 Captain *MS2*] captain *TCC7*
114:35 "—but *MS2*] —"∼ *TCC7*
114:36 his eyes . . . his teeth,] *Om. A1*
115:1 no-one *MS2*] no one *TCC7*
115:2 kanakas *MS2*] Kanakas
    TCC7
115:10 Captain *MS2*] captain *TCC7*
115:11 chest.—] ∼. *A1*
115:12 Captain *MS2*] captain *TCC7*
115:13 saviour-like] Saviour-like *A1*
115:19 mad *MS2*, *MS8R*] made
    TCC7
115:19 Californian] California *A1*
115:23 masters] master *A1*
115:25 had *MS2*, *A1*] has *TCC7*
115:29 seas *MS2*] sea *TCC7*
115:38 to— *MS2*] ∼. *TCC7*
116:10 to *MS2*] or *TCC7*
116:11 sank *MS2*] sunk *TCC7*
116:12 dashing *MS2*] lashing
    TCC7
116:17 sublimity—] ∼—— *A1*
116:19 pain *MS2*] pains *TCC7*
116:22 days.—] ∼. *A1*
116:26 Captain *MS2*] captain *TCC7*
116:26 all *MS2*] the *TCC7*
116:34 —In *MS2*] ∼ *TCC7*

116:35 spend—. *MS2*] ∼. *TCC7*
117:9 KNOWS] knows *A1*
117:14 And from . . . us, we . . . him
    homage. *A1*] So he can go
    home and— — *MS8* And . . .
    us; we . . . homage. *E1*
117:16 skirts *MS2*] strikes *TCC7*
117:23 nodalises *MS2*, *MS8R*]
    moralises *TCC7* nodalizes *A1*
117:28 forces, *MS2*] ∼ *TCC7*
117:29 water, *MS2*, *E1*] ∼ *TCC7*
117:31 mistresses *MS2*] mistress
    TCC7
117:34 Neuter] neuter *A1*
117:37 is as it were] ∼, ∼ ∼ ∼,
    E1
118:1 Gods *MS2*] gods *TCC7*
118:9 Shango *MS2*, *MS8R*] Shanys
    TCC7
118:10 Father, *MS2*] ∼ *TCC7*
118:17 connections] connexions *E1*
118:23 mystery *MS2*] ·, *TCC7*
118:34 jib— — *MS2*] ∼. — *TCC7* ∼.
    E1
118:39 weather,] ∼; *E1*
119:2 top-gallant-yard] top-gallant
    yard *E1*
119:3 flying-jib-boom end] flying-
    jib-boom-end *A1*
119:6 south-west *MS8*, *E1*]
    southwest *A1*
119:12 stupified *MS2*] stupefied
    TCC7
119:25 quantity *MS2*] quality *TCC7*
119:30 *forces MS2*] forces *TCC7*
119:31 de-creation *MS2*] re-creation
    TCC7 recreation *A1*
120:3 chest-full] chest-/ full *A1*
    chestfull *E1*
120:7 raw. "The] ∼. *P* "The *A1*
120:8 gave] give *A1*
120:11 in *MS2*] on *TCC7*
120:16 drink *MS2*] suck *TCC7*

120:19 time] *Om. A1*
120:24 Solon *MS2*] *Solon TCC7*
120:26 mast-head *MS2*] mast-/ head
        TCC7 masthead *A1*
120:28 in] *Om. A1*
120:29 connection] connexion *E1*

121:1   It is . . . achievement. *A1*] *Om.*
        MS8
121:7   much. *A1*] much. Knowledge
        is nothing. *MS8*
121:16 forever] for-/ ever *A1* for ever
        E1

Herman Melville's *Typee* and *Omoo*

122:15 viking] Viking *A1*
122:17 human of the living humus *A1*]
        homo sum business *MS8*
122:20 brown] blue *A1 see notes*
122:21 earth and . . . principally the]
        rain and *A1*
122:23 *allzu*] *Allzu A1*
122:32 church-bell] church bell *E1*
122:34 element] elements *A1*
123:3   Like] As *E1*
123:17 fire] Fire *A1*
123:20 humanity: our *MS8*] humanity
        and *A1*
123:26 aeons] æons *A1*
123:31 And oh] ~, ~, *A1* ~, ~ *E1*
123:33 again. Dreams:] again: *A1*
123:36 dreams.] ~? *E1*
124:2   Age:] ~; *A1*
124:17 knows.] ~? *E1*
124:26 the] *Om. A1*
124:28 out,] away, *A1*
125:5   Delenda est] *Delenda est A1*
125:5   Chicago *Ed.*] Cartago *MS8*
        Chicago *A1*
125:11 *Typee A1*] Typee *MS8*
125:11 dreaded] dread *A1*
125:15 savages *A1* Savages *MS8 see notes*
125:20 *truly*] truly *A1*
125:21 Châteaubriand's *A1*] Chat-
        eaubriand's *MS8, E1*
125:33 time:] ~. *A1*
125:37 sip *A1*] drink *MS8*
125:40 horrified. Though] ~; though,
        E1

125:40 course] ~, *E1*
126:2   —Thirdly] ~, *E1*
126:7   it,] ~. *A1*
126:8   like] as *E1*
126:16 fast] far *A1*
126:21 on] in *A1*
126:21 Oh] O *A1*
126:32 time and *A1*] *Om. MS8*
127:8   now are] are now *A1*
127:10 life development]
        life-development *A1*
127:11 on in life-development . . .
        inside us that] on in us that *A1*
        on, and *E1*
127:13 And our . . . retrogression. *A1*]
        It is part of the onward Even
        blindly smash. *MS8*
127:20 She has . . . *tangere. A1*] *Om.*
        MS8
127:23 take a . . . direction, onwards
        A1] realise their lives *MS8*
127:31 back. And] ~, and *E1*
127:31 the civilised *Ed.*] *Om. MS8* the
        civilized *A1*
127:32 he knew *A1* as he knew it *MS8*
127:32 savages. He] ~; he *E1*
127:33 to. He . . . to. And] ~, he . . . ~,
        and *E1*
127:34 sick. It] ~; it *E1*
127:37 condition. Sick] ~—sick *E1*
127:37 miserable. Ill] ~, ill *E1*
128:4   Yet, as . . . [128:6] on ourselves.
        A1] *Om. MS8*
128:7   Savages] savages *A1*

128:10 prostitute *A1*] bend *MS8*
128:10 by returning *A1*] back *MS8*
128:15 escaped. And] ~, and *E1*
128:21 had] has *A1*
128:21 begins *A1*] begin *MS8*
128:22 Paradise."] ~"— *E1*
128:25 even worse than *A1*] an even worse *MS8*
128:25 a soft hell, *A1*] *Om. MS8*
128:26 him,] ~ *E1*
128:40 forever] for ever *E1*
129:9 knows.] ~? *E1*
129:12 ground] grind *A1*
129:17 *Julia*] ~, *E1*
129:20 Yet] ~, *A1*
129:21 oh] ~, *A1*
129:23 past. What] ~—what *E1*
129:24 don't *MS8, E1*] won't *A1*
130:2 Melville] ~, *E1*
130:3 beach comber] beachcomber *A1*
130:15 neer-do-well] ne'er-do well *A1*
130:20 snipe] ~, *A1*
130:21 afterwards. Which] ~, which *E1*
130:24 the] this *A1*

130:32 tatooed] tattooed *E1*
130:41 chain:] ~, *E1*
131:6 doorstep. Like] ~,—like *E1*
131:9 just] had just *A1*
131:17 will,] ~ *E1*
131:17 love. He... understanding. *A1*] love. *MS2* love; he... understanding. *E1*
131:19 lovey-dovey *A1*] *Om. MS8*
131:20 love. No] ~: no *E1*
131:20 mountain-lion] mountain lion *E1*
131:21 cat. And] ~; and *E1*
131:22 after. Not] ~—not *E1*
131:29 idealists:] ~, *E1*
131:30 woman *A1*] women *MS8*
131:30 feels herself *A1*] feel themselves *MS8*
131:31 good. *P* It] ~. It *A1*
132:8 relationship:] ~; *E1*
132:8 mating:] ~; *E1*
132:14 *viennent A1*] *vient MS8*
132:16 Melville however] ~, ~, *A1*
132:16 this] his *A1*
132:17 Life] life *A1*
132:25 bushes. Which] ~—which *E1*

Herman Melville's *Moby Dick*

For *TCC7* pages surviving into *MS8* (134:38–136:16, 138:21–146:2), *MS2* is the ultimate source, and the order of texts is *MS2, TS5, TS5C, TCC7, TCC7C, MS8, MS8C, MS8R, A1, E1. MS2* is *not* cited when substantive revisions in *TS5* are accepted as authorial; *TS5* and *TS5C* are only recorded when they affected the typing of *TCC7*.

133:3 *Moby ... Whale. Ed.*] "Moby Dick, or the White Whale." *MS8 MOBY DICK ... Whale. A1*
133:12 lovable] loveable *E1*
133:14 warm-blooded,] ~ *E1*
133:14 lovable] loveable *E1*
133:24 journalese] journalism *A1*

134:2 ethical-mythical-transcendentalist] ethical mythical-transcendentalist *A1*
134:3 Hawthorne] ~, *A1*
134:4 *sérieux*. You] *serieux*, you *A1*
134:6 do I care *A1*] the hell does it matter *MS8*
134:6 Life] life *A1*

134:7   drink *A1*] cup of tea *MS8*
134:11 *sérieux] serieux A1*
134:12 Oh] ~, *A1*
134:12 brays! brays! brays! *A1*] brays!
        MS8
134:19 more:] ~; *E1*
134:31 tatooed] tattooed *A1*
134:32 the] this *A1*
134:32 frock coat] frock-coat *A1*
134:39 In *MS2*] For *TCC7* For with
        MS8R
134:39 physical,] ~ *E1*
135:4   namely] ~, *A1*
135:5   tatooed *Ed.*] tattooed *MS8*
135:6   harpooneer *TS5C*] harpooner
        MS2, TCC7
135:7   bed-mate] bedmate *A1*
135:9   connection] connexion *E1*
135:11 room; *MS2*] ~, *TS5*
135:12 mild *MS2, A1*] wild *TCC7*
135:14 twain; *MS2*] ~: *TCC7*
135:20 smoke] smoked *E1*
135:25 thought I . . . is worship?—]
        Om. A1
135:27 fellow-man . . . fellow-man
        MS8, E1] fellowman . . .
        fellowman *A1*
135:28 —"Which] "— ~ *A1*
135:29 logic.—] ~. *A1*
135:30 fellow-man *MS8, E1*] fellow-/
        man *A1*
135:31 me? *MS8, E1*] ~. *A1*
135:32 then] *Om. A1*
135:41 cosy *MS8, E1*] cozy *A1*
135:41 pair—" *P* You would . . .
        [136:11] was all. *MS8R*]
        pair—" The sophistry with
        which he justifies his act of
        idolatry is amusing, and very
        characteristic of Melville. He
        continually spins an ideal
        logic to fit his new acts.
        The ideal logic is apt to be

boring. Plainly, he cared nothing about worship, and he
loved Queequeg. Elsewhere
he says he loved the savage's
"large, deep eyes, fiery black
and bold." *TS5* pair—"*P* The
sophistry . . . and bold." *TCC7*
pair——" *P* You would . . . was
all. *A1 see also entries to* 136:10
136:4   more,] ~ *E1*
136:6   KNOWN," *A1*] ~", *TCC7*
        KNOWN," *E1*
136:10 doubt,] ~ *E1*
136:13 whaling-ship] whaling ship *A1*
136:14 whaling-voyage] whaling voy-
        age, *A1*
136:17 Circes *A1*] Circe's *MS8R*
136:18 isles *A1*] shore *MS8R*
136:19 *Pequod*'s *Ed.*] Pequod's *MS8R*
        Pequod's A1
136:20 soul-history] soul history *A1*
136:20 sea-yarn] sea yarn *A1*
136:21 sea-yarns] sea yarns *A1*
136:22 sea-man's] seaman's *A1*
136:25 feeling *A1*] words *MS8*
136:27 god-fearing] God-fearing *A1*
136:29 fate.] ~, *E1*
136:32 "Oh captain . . . done."] "Oh,
        captain . . . done." [set as reg-
        ular paragraph] *A1*
136:34 him?] ~! *E1*
136:35 Oh] ~, *A1*
136:36 whale,] ~ *E1*
137:1   right] ~, *A1*
137:12 Must be afraid too, really. *A1*]
        Om. MS8
137:16 mouse,] ~ *E1*
137:16 water-rat— —] ~—— *A1*
137:18 sea-men] seamen *A1*
137:18 whale-men] whalemen *A1*
137:18 first class] first-class *E1*
137:20 crew, at . . . wives along. *A1*]
        crew. *MS8*

137:27 harpooneers] harpooners *A1*
137:28 tatooed] tattooed *A1*
137:33 harpoons] ~, *A1*
137:34 *white*] *White A1* white *E1*
137:36 fireworshipping]
       fire-worshipping *A1*
137:40 American.] ~? *A1*
138:6 White Whale] white whale *A1*
138:14 book. With] ~, with *E1*
138:15 meaning. And] ~, and *E1*
138:16 albatross.] ~— *E1*
138:17 sententious.—] ~. *E1*
138:18 gale,] ~ *A1*
138:19 overclouded *MS2*]
       overcrowded *TS5*, *E1*
       over-crowded *A1*
138:19 deck;] ~, *A1*
138:20 regal,] ~ *A1*
138:20 feathery *MS2*] feathered *TS5*
138:21 hooked, *MS2*] ~ *TS5*
138:22 wings——. Wondrous *Ed.*]
       ~— . Wonderous *MS2* ~—
       . wonderous ~ *TS5* ~—.
       Wondrous *TS5C* ~—. Won-
       derous *TCC7* ~.—Wondrous
       A1 ~—wondrous *E1*
138:24 king's *MS2*] King's *TS5*
138:24 inexpressible, *MS2*] ~ *TS5*
138:26 heavens—— *MS2*] ~— *TS5*
138:28 —I] ~ *E1*
138:29 spell—] ~ — *A1*
138:31 albatross] ~, *A1*
138:32 southern] Southern *A1*
138:35 tried] ~, *A1*
138:35 southern] Southern *A1*
138:39 One] Who *A1*
139:9 subdued] ~, *E1*
139:11 air, *MS2*] ~ *TS5*
139:11 resolved *MS2*, *E1*] reselved *A1*
139:12 self— *MS2*] ~.— *TS5* ~——
       E1
139:14 She blows! She *MS2*] she *TS5*
       She *TCC7*

139:17 earth— *MS2*, *E1*] ~,— *TS5*
139:18 ' "Give *MS2*] "~ *TS5* " '~ *A1*
139:18 men," *MS2*] ~,' *A1*
139:19 "there *MS2*] '~ *A1*
139:20 Spring!"*MS2*] ~!' *A1*
139:23 "Stand up!" *MS2*] "~ ~!
       TCC7 '~ ~!' *MS8R*
139:25 with] *Om. A1*
139:29 curling *MS2*] curbing *TS5*
139:31 ' "That's *Ed.*] "~ *MS2* '~
       MS8R " '~ *A1*
139:31 there *MS2*] There *TS5*
139:31 him!" *MS8*, *A1*] ~!' *MS8R*
139:37 half suffocated *MS2*]
       half-suffocated *TS5*
139:38 curdling] curling *TCC7*
139:39 escaped—'] ~—" *TS5*, *TCC7*
       ~.—" *TS5C* ~——" *A1*
140:1 motion,] ~; *E1*
140:3 St *MS2*] ~. *TS5*
140:8 bow.—] ~—— *A1*
140:9 north-eastward *MS2*] north /
       eastward *TCC7*, *E1*
       northeastward *A1*
140:10 Crozetts, *MS2*] Crozells *TS5*
       Crozello *TCC7*
140:11 Right *MS2*, *TCC7C*, *MS8C*]
       light *TCC7* right *A1*
140:12 undulated *MS2*, *MS8R*] mod-
       ulated *TCC7*
140:14 Right *MS2*, *TCC7C*, *MS8C*]
       light *TCC7* right *A1*
140:14 Sperm *MS2*] sperm *TS5*
140:15 *Pequod*, with *MS2*] Pequod.
       With *TS5 Pequod*. With
       TCC7C
140:15 jaws *MS2*] jaws they *TS5*
140:18 morning *MS2*] moving *TCC7*
140:18 who] ~, *A1*
140:18 by side] ~ ~, *A1*
140:23 mast-heads *MS2*, *MS8R*] mast
       heads *TS5* mast-/ heads *E1*
140:25 else—] ~—— *A1*

140:26 apparition *MS8, E1*] apparia-
        tion *A1*
140:27 brit; *MS2*] ~, *TS5*
140:28 north-eastward]
        northeastward *A1*
140:29 tall, *MS2, A1*] ~ *TS5*
140:31 intervals *MS2*] ~, *TS5*
140:33 "But *TS5C, TCC7C, MS8C*]
        ~ *MS2, TCC7*
140:33 transparent blue] transparent-
        blue *A1*
140:39 "In *TS5C, TCC7C, MS8C*] ~
        MS2, TCC7
141:4 Daggoo——*MS2*] ~— *TS5*
        ~——*A1*
141:15 sound *MS2*] *Om. TS5*
141:16 again.—] ~. *A1*
141:17 whale-hunts] whale hunts *E1*
141:25 back-bone] backbone *A1*
141:26 are—. *MS2*] ~— *TS5, TCC7*
        ~.— *TS5C* ~—— *E1*
141:26 adds— "For] ~: *P* "For *TCC7*
141:30 hunts] ~, *E1*
141:34 thought, *MS2*] ~ *TS5*
141:37 agony!—"*MS2*] ~!"— *TS5*
        ~!" *TCC7*
141:38 "The Grand Armada," *MS2,
        TS5C*] "~ ~ ~", *TS5, TCC7
        The Grand Armada, A1*
141:39 Volume *MS2, TCC7, MS8,
        A1*] volume *TS5, TCC7C,
        MS8C*
141:39 *Pequod A1*] Pequod *MS8*
142:2 semi-circle] semicircle *E1*
142:4 air—"— *MS2*] ~." *TS5*
142:7 whales *MS2, TCC7C, MS8C*]
        whalers *TS5, A1*
142:8 array, *MS2*] ~ *TS5*
142:10 Leviathan *TS5*] leviathan *MS2*
142:13 There, *MS2*] ~ *TS5*
142:15 sea-men *MS2*] seamen *TS5*
142:16 sea.—] ~— *E1*
142:18 eyes *MS2*] ~, *TS5*

142:19 nursing-mothers *MS2*] nur-
        sing mothers *TS5*
142:24 mortal] moral *A1*
142:28 us.— — — *MS2*] ~.— *TS5,
        A1* ~.— —/ *TCC7*
142:33 delight.—] ~—— *A1*
142:37 "The Cassock" *TCC7C,
        MS8C*] The ~ *MS2, TCC7*
        the ~ *TS5 The Cassock A1*
142:38 oddest] oldest *A1*
142:40 a *MS2*] the *TS5*
143:4 reversion.—] ~— *E1*
143:7 stark, bewildered] stark bewil-
        dering *E1*
143:10 'My *MS2*] ~ *TS5*
143:10 me!' thought I!—] ~? thought
        I!— *TS5* ~. I thought! *TCC7*
        ~, I thought! *A1*
143:13 had] has *A1*
143:13 evoked *TS5C, TCC7C,
        MS8R*] cooked *TS5, TCC7*
143:17 die.—] ~. *E1*
143:19 tatooing *Ed.*] tattooing *MS8*
143:26 savage—] ~—— *A1*
143:30 midmost *MS2*] utmost *TS5*
143:30 world—] ~—— *A1*
143:31 on.—] ~: *E1*
143:31 afternoon;] ~, *E1*
143:32 done;] ~, *E1*
143:33 then, *MS2*] ~ *TS5*
143:37 hymns.—] ~. *E1*
143:38 had sterned] has steered *A1*
143:40 spectacle] ~, *A1*
144:2 conveyed a *MS2*] conveyed/
        TCC7 conveyed *A1*
144:3 'He *MS2, A1*] "~ *TS5* ~
        TCC7
144:3 it;— *MS2*] ~; *TS5*
144:4 homage-rendering]
        home-rendering *A1 see notes*
144:5 fire';— — — *Ed.*] ~;— — —
        MS2, TCC7 ~;—— *TS5* ~;
        ...' *A1* ~ ...' *E1*

144:9   worships: *MS2*, *A1*] ~; *TCC7*
144:9   livid] living *A1*
144:10 foot.—It] ~; it *E1*
144:10 on *MS2*] of *TS5*
144:12 mast-heads *MS2*] mast-head *TCC7* masthead *A1*
144:14 captain Ahab] ~, ~, *A1*
144:22 small, *MS2*] ~ *TS5*
144:22 unspeckled *MS2*] unspecked *TCC7*
144:26 sea—] ~—— *E1*
144:26 —On *MS2*] ~ *TS5*
144:27 "—But *MS2*] "~ *TS5*
144:29 Paradise—] ~—— *E1*
144:34 mast-head.—] masthead.— *A1* masthead— *E1*
144:36 air.—] ~. *A1*
144:38 unsuspecting *MS2*] unsuspectful *TS5*
145:2   Turkish-rugged *MS2*] Turkish rugged *TCC7*
145:14 "A *TS5C*, *TCC7C*, *MS8C*, *A1*] ~ *MS2*, *TCC7*
145:15 whale——— *MS2*, *TCC7*] ~—— *TS5* ~—— *A1*
145:18 harpooneer *MS2*, *TS5C*] harpooner *TS5*, *TCC7*
145:20 harpoon-lines] harpoon lines *A1*
145:23 whale-boats *MS2*, *E1*] whale boats *A1*
145:23 cry *MS2*] ~. *TCC7* ~: *A1*
145:23 Ship *MS2*] ship *TS5*
145:24 —Soon] ~ *E1*

145:24 they] ~, *A1*
145:24 mediums] ~, *A1*
145:27 harpooneers *MS2*, *TS5C*] harpooners *TS5*, *TCC7*
145:28 look-outs] lookouts *A1*
145:28 now,] ~ *A1*
145:32 sight—] ~—— *A1*
145:33 St *Ed.*] ~. *MS8*
145:33 the Red . . . the American, *A1*] *Om. MS8*
145:34 Tashtego's] Tastego's *A1*
145:35 Spirit] spirit *A1*
146:1   esoteric *MS2*] exoteric *TS5*
146:13 Ah] ~, *A1*
146:18 Spirit] spirit *A1*
146:24 —He] ~ *E1*
146:25 race. He] ~; he *E1*
146:27 mental *A1*] *Om. MS8*
146:33 our own] our/our *A1* our *E1*
146:34 Our . . . ideal consciousness. *A1*] Which is slow but fatal suicide. *MS8*
146:38 god . . . god] God . . . God *A1*
146:38 *Pequod A1*] Pequod *MS8*
147:1   Quien sabe? . . . señor?] *Quien sabe? Quien sabe, señor? A1*
147:2   Neither Spanish . . . any answer. *A1*] *Om. MS8*
147:5   business-like] businesslike *A1* business-/ like *E1*
147:14 Because, in . . . little fishes. *A1*] *Om. MS8*

Whitman

For 155:18 to end the order is *MS9*, *TS10*, *TS10C*, *A1*, *E1*. *MS2* is the original source for poetry quotations and is used to correct mistakes in *MS8* which were carried over from *TCC7* (e.g. 149:24), and the order is *MS2*, *TCC7*, *TCC7C*, *MS8*, *A1*, *E1*. The reader may also consult the diplomatic transcription of MS8 in Appendix VI.

148:5   gray] grey *A1*
148:7   gray] grey *A1*
148:16 LOVE. *A1*] LOVE. *P* You bet! *MS8* Love. *E1*

148:23 will,] ~; *E1*
148:33 Oh god] ~, God *A1*
148:33 belly-ache . . . belly-ache] bellyache . . . bellyache *A1*

148:34 of] OF *A1* OF *E1*

149:10 CHU—CHU—CHU—
CHU—CHUFFFF] CHU-
CHU-CHU-CHU-CHUFF
A1 CHU-CHU-CHU-CHU-
CHUFF *E1*

149:23 love;] ~: *A1*

149:24 gravitate? *MS2*] ~, *TCC7*

149:37 No] ~, *A1*

149:37 your self] yourself *A1*

150:4 main-spring] mainspring *E1*

150:6 Your Moby... Dead mentalised. *Ed.*] *Om. MS8* Your
Moby... Dead mentalized. *A1*

150:11 Walt Whitman *A1*] Walter, my
dear *MS8*

150:14 You have... mentalised... of
it. *Ed.*] *Om. MS8* You have
... mentalized... of it. *A1*

150:17 Identity] Indentity *A1*

150:18 while. *P* "Whoever] ~./ #
"Whoever *A1*

150:19 announcements————"]
~——*A1*

150:21 you? *A1*] you, my boy? *MS8*

150:21 Well then] ~, ~, *A1* ~ ~, *E1*

150:22 Self] self *A1*

150:23 Oh Walter] ~, ~, *A1*

150:25 you, *A1*] you when you made
water, *MS8*

150:25 universe. *A1*] universe when
you peed. Oh Walter, you're a
leaky vessel. *MS8*

150:26 Post-mortem *MS8, E1*] Post
mortem *A1*

150:26 him. *A1*] him at his seams,
like out of a leaky vessel.
P I remember an American
girl whose parents had lived
in the town where Whitman
⟨had lived⟩ ⌜resided⌝ when
he was old, told me that
the neighbours fairly hated

Walter because he used to walk
in his little back yard—he lived
in a row—stark naked and fat
and excited with his own nudity and his grey beard. "His
nasty little back yard," ⟨a⟩⌜A⌝
rabella ⟨S⟩⌜s⌝ aid. And that he
used to stop the little girls coming home from school, with senile amorousness. *MS8*

150:27 No] ~, *A1*

150:27 post mortem] post-mortem *E1*

150:31 pudding-cloth!*A1*]pudding-
cloth, the skin of Walt! *MS8*

150:31 No] ~, *A1*

150:34 one *A1*] Walter, you *MS8*

150:37 Whitman *A1*] Walter *MS8*

150:39 When you've... One Identity.
A1] *Om. MS8*

151:3 my *A1*] Walter, my *MS8*

151:4 post mortem] post-mortem *E1*

151:10 thing,] ~ *E1*

151:13 paeans] pæans *A1*

151:13 Cinematernity. *P* "Oh *Ed.*] ~/
P "Oh *MS8* ~./ # "Oh, *A1*

151:14 Charlie] ~, *A1*

151:14 done—] ~——*A1*

151:16 Esquimo] Eskimo *E1*

151:19 Now *A1*] Now my dear
Walter, *MS8*

151:22 thing. *A1*] thing, Walter. *MS8*

151:23 sensuosity. *A1*] sensuality. Animality on the brain. *MS8*

151:29 Democracy... Identity]
*Democracy, En Masse, One
Identity A1*

151:33 And what...[152:21] ALL-
NESS. *P* "A *Ed.*] In a nasty little back-yard, with the neighbours pulling down their back
blinds to shut the view out.
P Of course I am being
personal, I intend to be. *P*

Whitman was never really an esquimo. Never even saw one. It was all just prize conceit. *P* Whitman being everything! Just think of it! The cheek! Had never even been out of America. Impudent provincial. *P* Another proof that a little learning is a dangerous thing. *P* My, would n't Walt have been startled if he'd been forced to realise what an actual esquimo is! Because of course Walter blandly assumed that all esquimos are minor little Walts. *P* Post mortem effects. *P* As a matter of fact, all these Infinites and Alls and En Masses and Democrac/[ies] and One Identities are just the frog puffing himself up till he bursts. *P* I remember, when I was a little boy with other boys, watching them push a fine straw up the back passage of a frog and blow up this straw till the frog was like a balloon. *P* Some malign fiend must have been doing a parallel thing to Whitman. *P* MERGE! says Walter. *P MERDE!* say I. *P* Merge, merge, merge! Merging, merging, merging, sings Walter. *P* So we've all got to slither down the slimy chute of sympathy into the infinite cesspool, it seems to me. Nasty naked old men in back yards. *P* ONE DIRECTION! insists Whitman. *P* Never, you slimy democratic ⟨bully⟩ animal. *P* ONE DIRECTION! reiterates America, more loudly.

P Sh - - t! *P* ALLNESS! sings Walter. *P* B - - - S! sing I. *P* ONE IDENTITY! chants democratic En Masse. *P* F - - k it! comes my antiphony. *P* All right then, you grand Idealist, *be* infinite. Sit on your infinity, then, as on the privy seat. And don't come off it. *P* The Infinite! *P* Post mortem effects! *P* Poor Walter, dominated by the *idée fixe* of his own person and his own private parts. Tainted with the "exposure" dementia. *P* Post mortem effects. *P* Masturbation, Song of Myself. *P* Post mortem effects. *P* Woman! *P* "A *MS8* And what... ALLNESS./ # "A *A1* And what ... ALLNESS./ # "A *E1 see also entries to* 152.17

151:34   Esquimo... Esquimo *A1*] Eskimo... Eskimo *E1*
151:35   Esquimoness *A1*] Eskimoness *E1*
151:37   Esquimos *A1*] Eskimos *E1*
151:39   Esquimo *A1*] Eskimo *E1*
152:4   Everything *A1*] everything *E1*
152:11   wildernesses. As *A1*] ~, as *E1*
152:11   road, *A1*] ~— *E1*
152:18   motorcars *A1*] motor-cars *E1*
152:22   me—] ~——— *A1*
152:23   femaleness *A1*] female end *MS8*
152:24   Oh... Oh] ~, ...~, *A1*
152:25   States—] ~——— *A1*
152:27   my soul *MS2*] myself *TCC7*
152:27   Nature *MS2*] ~, *TCC7*
152:37   again—] ~——— *A1*
152:38   "The *A1*] Can't you just see Walt ⟨just⟩ oozing himself into the womb of a woman, then

getting out by the back door.
Trying to ⟨dive⟩ ⌐creep⌐ head
and shoulders into the womb
of woman, and crawl out again.
Bath of birth, indeed! Bath of
imbecility, to men who go to it
in that way. *P* "The *MS8*
152:38 see—] ~——— *A1*
153:1 Female. With] ~, with *E1*
153:2 ear. *A1*] ear. He'd have got his
      bath in hot water. *MS8*
153:3 something or other *A1*] a
      woman *MS8*
153:5 see—" *Ed.*] see—" *P* And
      when he found he couldn't,
      then wanting to merge into
      something else. But always go-
      ing back to the old want, the
      womb. *MS8* see——" *A1*
153:7 horror. *A1*] vice. A chronic dis-
      ease. *MS8*
153:9 like] as *E1*
153:11 elsewhere. If] ~ if *E1*
153:22 Democracy:] ~ *E1*
153:23 comradeship] Comradeship *A1*
153:24 sure? *A1*] sure, Walt? *MS8*
153:25 *Drum-Taps. Ed.*] Drum-Taps
      MS2 Drum Taps. *TCC7*
      "Drum Taps." *TCC7C Drum
      Taps. A1*
153:28 Walt Whitman *A1*] Walter
      MS8
153:32 death, *MS2*] ~ *TCC7* ~.
      TCC7C
153:39 prefer, *MS2*] ~ *TCC7*
154:3 mean—] ~ ——— *A1*
154:13 step,] ~ *A1*
154:20 Comrades] comrades *A1*
154:29 Death. *A1*] Death. *P But why
      merge?* Why merge any more?
      Why love any more? *P* Any
      man whose soul didn't go down
      in the *Pequod*: Whitman's soul

went down: will know that
he doesn't want to merge any
more. That he doesn't want to
love any more. *P* Man doesn't
want to love any more. The desire is gone. *P* What then? *P*
The *Pequod* went down with
the white soul. The ship of
the soul went down. But we
were not all on board. Or we
were not *entirely* on board. *P*
The mergers. The conscious
mergers. The conscious lovers.
Conscious love. ⌐Love on the
brain.⌐ *P* Make an end of it all.
P Have no merging. Have no
⟨s⟩ love. Have no sex. Cut it
out. *P* Cut it out, till we get into
a new mode. *P* Cut love out.
Cut sex out. Cut out all merging, all uniting. Cut yourself off
isolate. Keep only your *silent*
loyalties. And wait. *P* Wait. *P*
Wait for what? *P* Wait till we
get clear. *MS8*
154:31 hurrying not, *MS2*] ~ ~
      TCC7
154:32 Whisper'd *MS2*] Whispered
      TCC7
154:32 and *MS2*] *Om. TCC7*
154:32 day-break] daybreak *A1*
154:34 death,/ *MS2*] ~/ *TCC7* ~./
      A1
154:35 melodious] melodions *A1*
154:38 Creeping *A1*] /"~ *MS8*
154:39 death—] ~——— *A1*
155:1 the end *A1*] death, not *MS8*
155:1 post mortem] post-mortem *E1*
155:2 as it loses *A1*] after it has died
      in *MS8*
155:3 last shout and shriek *A1*] post
      mortem disintegration *MS8*
155:4 le] *de A1*

155:8   come. *P* "Out] ∼./ # "Out
        A1
155:9   rocking—] ∼. *A1*
155:10 We've *A1*] Though I'm not
        sure about a *cradle.* Damn cra-
        dles. *P* We've *MS8*
155:13 death process] death-process
        A1
155:16 is finished] IS FINISHED *A1*
        IS FINISHED *E1*
155:17 *est.* # Whitman . . . [161:32]
        Chapala. 1923 *Ed.*] *est. P* Jesus
        was only an intermediary god,
        any way. Not a primary god.
        P And love is only an inter-
        mediary thing. Not a primary
        thing. *P* Love is not a fun-
        damental thing. As life drives
        us deeper and deeper, we pass
        certain borders, and love ceases
        to be of first-rate importance.
        It comes to an end. Some-
        thing else takes its place. *P*
        Love is an intermediary thing.
        As Jesus is intermediary be-
        tween the Father and the Holy
        Ghost: to use the weary old
        symbol of our Trinity. *P* When
        life is at its deepest, there is no
        love. And that is why Whit-
        man's love of comrades won't
        work. ⟨It is a misapplication.⟩
        ⌐Something there is, but it is
        not love. To function as love,
        in the deepest self, is just a
        fatality.⌐ *P* When we are living
        from our very deepest selves,
        there is no comradeship, there
        is no friendship, there is no
        equality. For comradeship,
        ⟨equality,⟩ ⌐friendship,⌐ and
        love all presume equality be-
        tween lovers and comrades.

And in the deepest self, there is no sense of equality ⌐left⌐, there is no possibility of equal communion. *P* ⟨There is something else, quite different, much more profound. *P* The power of the Holy Ghost.⟩ *P* ⌐But marriage is still possible. So long as you do *not* base it on love. Stark marriage. This holds the first clue to vital inequality, non-equality. *P* Equality is superseded, when you get deep enough. And love is superseded. You find something else. *P* You find your own stark isolation. And the presence of the Holy Ghost⟨s⟩.⌐ *P* Each man to himself is isolate. And ⟨to⟩ ⌐in⌐ each isolate man ⟨comes⟩ ⌐lives⌐ the Holy Ghost. Only to him in his isolation. *P* You can't ⟨know⟩ ⌐have⌐ the Holy Ghost in company. The Pentecostal flame ⟨is something different.⟩ ⌐belongs to love: a common inspiration.⌐ You can only ⟨know⟩ ⟨⟨⌐be with⌐⟩⟩ ⌐⌐have⌐⌐ the Holy Ghost when you are alone. *P* When you are alone, you ⟨know⟩ ⌐⌐may⌐⌐ ⌐have⌐ the Holy Ghost. And the ⟨active⟩ ⌐strange⌐ power ⟨of⟩ ⌐that⌐ the ⟨h⟩⌐H⌐oly Ghost⟨.⟩ {is.} Because the Holy Ghost is a ⟨great⟩ ⟨unseen⟩ ⟨⟨⌐personal⌐⟩⟩ power ⟨coming to you.⟩ ⌐in your land.⌐ *P* ⟨⟨Th⟨e⟩⌐is⌐⟩⟩ ⟨Ghostly⟩ ⟨⟨Power is what⟩⟩ ⌐⌐The innermost power that⌐⌐ supersedes the spell of love: The ⟨Power of⟩ the Holy Ghost ⟨within you.⟩ ⌜in your ⟨⟨hinterland.⌝⟩⟩ ⌜⌜lone country.⌝⌝ *P* Once you accept the ⟨Power of the⟩ Holy Ghost, the world of love and loving fades into rubbish. And Jesus is relegated to a second place. *P* The Holy Ghost, and the Father, ⟨are⟩ the ⟨supreme⟩ ⌜major⌝ gods of our ⟨t⟩⌜T⌝rinity. Jesus ⟨is⟩ the intermediary. *P* The world of love fades into rubbish: like a dead empire. Then you ⟨see⟩ ⌜recognise⌝ the new-comers, those who ⟨know⟩ ⌜get⌝ the⌜ir⌝ power ⟨of⟩ ⌜from⌝ the Holy Ghost. *P* You see the ⟨newcomers.⟩ ⌜new foreigners.⌝ And the ⟨newcomers⟩ ⌜foreigners⌝ see one another, and recognise one another. As far as the world of love goes, it is the brand of Cain. ⟨It is t⟩⌜T⌝he curse of Ishmael. But to the men who ⟨know⟩ ⌜have ⟨⟨found⌝⟩⟩ ⌜⌜got⌝⌝ the power of the ⟨h⟩⌜H⌝oly Ghost, it is a new ⟨splendour.⟩ ⌜title.⌝ They ⟨walk in splendour,⟩ ⌜go with another strength,⌝ like a dark night with stars. *P* The ⟨newcomers⟩ ⌜foreigners⌝ see one another, ⟨inverted in⟩ ⌜and ⟨⟨recognise⌝⟩⟩ ⌜⌜feel⌝⌝ the new ⟨mystery of⟩ ⌜communion in⌝ power. The power of the Holy Ghost⟨.⟩ ⌜of each other.⌝ *P* The hierarchies of the power of the Holy Ghost ⟨that is within us.⟩ ⌜of us.⌝ *P* Once it was the hierarchies of the power

of the Father. Now it ⟨t⟩ is another thing. Nothing to do with begetting: with Fatherhood. Having to do only with isolate manhood. Men in their isolation taking rank according to the Holy Ghost which is within them. Placed by the Holy Ghost in new hierarchies of power. Not crowned, but imbued. An aura, not a sceptre. But powers in the land. And arranged in hierarchies. *MS8 see also entries to* 161:31

155:18   # Whitman *Ed.*] (Contd from proof) *P* Whitman *MS9* (continued from proof) *P* Whitman *TS10* # *P* Whitman *A1*

155:32   aesthetic] æsthetic *A1*

156:11   conception,] ~ *E1*

156:18   and the phallus] *Om. A1*

156:18   oh soul] Oh Soul *TS10*

156:20   vagina] body *A1*

156:22   Calamus] calamus *TS10*

156:22   soul] Soul *TS10*

156:31   Charity] charity *A1*

156:31   Love] love *TS10*

156:32   Nor] Not *A1*

156:32   Good Works] good works *A1*

156:36   feet *MS9, A1*] fleet *TS10*

156:39   direction,] ~ *E1*

157:3   Love] love *A1*

157:3   says sympathy *MS9, A1*] ~ Sympathy *TS10*

157:7   Salvation] salvation *A1*

157:8   salvation *MS9, A1*] Salvation *TS10*

157:10   saviour] Saviour *TS10*

157:11   salvation *MS9, A1*] Salvation *TS10*

157:24   salvation *MS9, TS10C*] Salvation *TS10*

157:25   opens] ~, *TS10*

157:31 today . . . today *MS9, A1*]
      to-day . . . to-day *TS10C, E1*
157:36 Jesus' *TS10*] Jesus *MS9*
158:1 attempt,] ~ *E1*
158:5 en masse] *en masse E1*
158:6 of love] ~ Love *TS10*
158:9 itself,] ~; *E1*
158:11 soul] Soul *TS10*
158:12 soul] Soul *TS10*
158:16 salvation] Salvation *TS10*
158:17 soul] Soul *TS10*
158:17 then *MS9, TS10C*] *Om. TS10*
      there *A1*
158:22 fate.] ~, *E1*
158:29 love-compulsion,] ~; *E1*
158:30 habit. For] ~—for *E1*
158:34 syphilitic. Which] ~—which *E1*
159:11 merging,] ~ *TS10*
159:12 burdens."—] ~": *E1*
159:12 thyself."—] ~": *E1*
159:20 help. Since] ~, since *E1*

160:1 body:] ~; *A1*
160:3 syphilis:] ~; *A1*
160:4 love,] ~; *TS10*
160:13 Charity!,] ~! *A1*
160:15 your soul's . . . and phallus] the
      body *A1*
160:19 lips or phallus] body *A1*
160:38 proximity:] ~; *E1*
160:39 from] from the *TS10*
161:2 Therefore] ~, *A1*
161:5 phallus] body *A1*
161:8 road. And] ~, and *E1*
161:12 charity] Charity *TS10*
161:13 anything] ~, *E1*
161:24 edge] Edge *TS10*
161:31 souls. # Chapala. 1923] *Om.*
      TS10 souls./ # LOBO, NEW
      MEXICO. / # THE END *A1*
      souls./ # LOBO, NEW
      MEXICO. / # THE END *E1 see*
      notes

First Version

The Spirit of Place

The order of the texts is *Per, E2.*

167:13 Libya] Lybia *E2*
167:29 and Poe] or Poe *E2*
168:16 simulacra *E2*] simulcra *Per*
170:18 space-wards] space-/ wards *E2*
170:20 of] on *E2*
171:5 been] ~, *E2*

171:23 borne] born *E2*
176:24 womenfolk *Ed.*] women-/ folk
      Per women-folk *E2*
177:8 ocean] Ocean *E2*
177:30 in] on *E2*

Benjamin Franklin

186:1 follows:—] ~: *E2*
186:3 none *E2*] done *Per*

189:1 impulsive,] ~ *E2*
189:35 coast——] ~— *E2*

Henry St. John de Crèvecœur

The order of texts is *Per, E2, TCC7, TCC7C.*

191:3 France in . . . century] France,
      at Caen, in the year 1735
      TCC7

191:5 there with the French in their]
      with Montcalm in the *TCC7*
191:14 *littérateur]* litterateur *TCC7*

191:16   the] *Om. TCC7*
191:16   Romanticists,] ~ *TCC7*
191:17   Coleridge,] Coleridge, Hazlitt,
         TCC7
191:21   stern] hard *TCC7*
192:15   wildly *Per, TCC7*] widely *E2*
192:21   wholeness] the wholeness
         TCC7
192:29   third] —~ *TCC7C*
193:32   mysteriously] mysterious *TCC7*
195:1   naïve] naive *TCC7*
195:4   seating] seeing *TCC7*
195:11   sweet,] ~ *TCC7*
195:11   deep-breasted] deep, breasted
         TCC7
195:22   Châteaubriand] Chateaubriand
         TCC7
195:22   Bernadin *Per, TCC7*] Bernardin
         E2
195:25   suburb *Per, TCC7*] suburbs *E2*
195:30   mechanical,] ~ *TCC7*
195:38   almost *Per, TCC7*] *Om. E2*
196:8   fright *E2, TCC7C*] fight *Per,*
         TCC7
196:25   culminating, *Per, TCC7*] ~ *E2*

196:39   America] American *TCC7*
196:40   savage] savages *TCC7C*
197:19   king-birds *TCC7*] king-/
         birds *Per* kingbirds *E2*
198:33   for, *Per, TCC7*] ~ *E2*
199:5   curiously] ~, *TCC7*
199:27   cold, *Per, TCC7*] ~ *E2*
199:39   passionate, *Per, TCC7*] ~ *E2*
200:22   Nature *Per, TCC7*] nature *E2*
200:24   ophiolatory *Per, TCC7*] ophi-
         olatry *E2*
200:26   Nature *Per, TCC7*] nature *E2*
200:41   Men *Per, TCC7*] Man *E2*
201:1   *à la*] à la *TCC7*
201:38   *will*] will *TCC7*
201:40   life] ~, *TCC7*
201:41   is *Per, TCC7*] is *E2*
202:8   take *Per, TCC7*] takes *E2*
202:23   neighbours, *Per, TCC7*] ~; *E2*
202:27   Nature *Per, TCC7*] nature *E2*
203:3   readopt *E2*] re-/ adopt *Per*
         re-adopt *TCC7*
203:6   sorrow] sorry *TCC7*
203:31   sensual] *Om. TCC7* essential
         TCC7C

Fenimore Cooper's Anglo-American Novels

206:25   ourself] ourselves *E2*
206:40   we believe we] we *E2*
211:39   real] ~, *E2*

213:15   supermachine *E2*] super-/
         machine *Per*
213:30   secondarily] ~, *E2*

Fenimore Cooper's Leatherstocking Novels

216:9   lifetime] life-time *E2*
217:5   external,] ~ *E2*
218:6   Continent] continent *E2*
219:7   kind,] ~; *E2*
219:15   Men] Man *E2*

220:23   ferocity,] ~ *E2*
220:24   Great] great *E2*
224:5   abode.] ~ *Per*
224:16   perhaps] ~, *E2*

Edgar Allan Poe

229:4   progressive] ~, *E2*
231:23   lieth,] ~ *E2*
232:16   Nourjahad....] ~.... *E2*
232:28   discover....] ~.... *E2*

233:15   not....] ~.... *E2*
234:33   Conqueror] conqueror *E2*
235:38   god] God *E2*
238:21   I *now*] I ~ *E2*

Nathaniel Hawthorne

The order of texts is *TS1*, *Per*, *E2*. (*Per* ends at 252:28 see Introduction.)

241:3 Hawthorne,] ~ *Per*
241:5 First] ~, *Per*
241:6 centralising *Per*] located *TS1*
241:7 system,] ~ *Per*
241:8 Secondly] ~, *Per*
241:8 ideal *Per*] ordinary *TS1*
241:8 consciousness] ~, *Per*
241:16 awake,] ~; *Per* ~: *E2*
241:31 thought,] ~ *Per*
241:32 physique,] ~ *Per*
241:34 blossoms,] ~ *Per*
241:35 moment,] ~ *Per*
242:1 mind go] ~, ~ *Per*
242:3 sleep,] ~ *Per*
242:3 conclusions,] ~— *Per*
242:4 conclusions] ~, *Per*
242:8 pulsating *Per*] *Om. TS1*
242:14 sensual *Per*] primary *TS1*
242:17 sensual *Per*] dynamic *TS1*
242:19 time] ~, *Per*
242:25 planc,] ~ *Per*
242:25 proper,] ~— *Per*
242:28 profoundly] ~, *Per*
242:29 primary,] ~ *Per*
242:29 immense,] ~ *Per*
242:33 procreative] ~, *Per*
242:37 co-ordination] co-/ ordination
       Per coordination *E2*
242:39 indeed] ~, *Per*
243:1 root-whole. For] ~. *P* For
       Per
243:5 him] Him *Per*
243:9 this,] ~ *Per*
243:12 mystery,] ~ *Per*
244:2 Now] ~, *Per*
244:10 —In] ~ *Per*
244:11 will of the human *Per*] individual *TS1*
244:14 not—] ~, *Per*
244:14 work—] ~, *Per*

244:17 spontaneously,] ~ *Per*
244:20 great,] ~ *E2*
244:21 is in truth] ~, ~ ~, *Per*
244:31 lure] line *Per*
244:32 spiritual . . . sensual being, *Per*]
       Om. TS1
244:35 sensual *Per*] physical *TS1*
244:36 era] ~, *E2*
244:40 this Fall *Per*] the fall *TS1*
245:3 Morality Play] morality play
       Per
245:6 difference;] ~: *Per*
245:7 Great Mother] grcat mother
       Per
245:9 Christian *Per*] christian *TS1*
245:11 is,] ~ *Per*
245:14 breast,] ~ *Per*
245:15 heart,] ~ *Per*
245:21 Puritanical] puritanical *Per*
245:23 sensual, *Per*] passional, *TS1*
245:28 abstraction] ~, *Per*
245:29 purity *Per*] abnegation *TS1*
246:3 effect,] ~ *Per*
246:6 and] ~, *Per*
246:16 male.] ~; *Per*
246:24 prostitute,] ~ *Per*
246:26 afterdeath] after death *E2*
246:32 Roderick, Roderick] ~—~,
       Per
246:35 She too . . . She too] ~, ~, . . .
       ~, ~, *Per*
247:1 impossible,] ~; *Per*
247:2 pure *TS1*, *E2*] ~, *Per*
247:6 him,] ~ *Per*
247:6 love] ~, *Per*
247:8 Therefore] ~, *Per*
247:9 prostitution *Per*] love *TS1*
247:11 ghastly *Per*] nasty *TS1*
247:21 secretly, from *Per*] like
       TS1

247:25 slain rises *Per*] dead rise *TS1*
247:25 revenge,] ~ *Per*
247:26 Dimmesdale,] ~ *Per*
247:27 end,] ~ *E2*
247:34 nihilism, *Per*] Om. *TS1*
247:36 man,] ~ *Per*
248:3 conjunction *Per*] union *TS1*
248:4 reversed,] ~; *Per*
248:6 progress *Per*] relationship *TS1*
248:7 And *Per*] And yet *TS1*
248:9 undoing. *Per*] new life. But with her it can never be more than a suggestion, a vague, blind gesture. Man must make it sure and definite. *TS1*
248:12 her,] ~; *Per*
248:19 It is the age of fatal ... snake. *Per*] Om. *TS1*
248:21 lead,] ~; *Per*
248:22 radiation *Per*] suggestion *TS1*
248:23 When however] ~, ~, *Per*
248:23 leadership,] ~ *Per*
248:33 day,] days, *Per*
248:35 Today] To-day, *Per*
248:35 recoil,] ~ *Per*
248:38 is] ~, *Per*
248:38 were] ~, *Per*
248:38 hypnotised] hypnotized *E2*
249:1 is,] ~ *Per*
249:6 is,] ~ *Per*
249:7 Hester however] ~, ~, *Per*
249:10 woman,] ~ *Per*
249:11 self,] ~ *Per*
249:15 Hester,] ~ *Per*
249:16 then,] ~ *Per*
249:20 She kills ... love itself. *Per*] Om. *TS1*
249:24 Dimmesdale,] ~ *Per*
249:25 confession,] ~ *Per*
249:27 work,] ~ *Per*

249:28 society] Society *E2*
249:31 detail] details *Per*
249:34 man,] ~ *Per*
249:34 exert] exact *Per*
249:40 itself] ~, *Per*
250:10 rich voluptuous] ~, ~, *Per*
250:15 her *Per*] here *TS1*
250:17 while,] ~ *E2*
250:18 sanctity,] ~ *Per*
250:19 effulgence; nay] ~. Nay *Per*
250:20 Sister of Mercy and Charity] sister ~ mercy ~ charity *Per*
250:24 ourselves, *Ed.*] outselves, *TS1* ourselves *Per*
250:26 indeed—] ~, *Per*
250:30 righteousness,] ~ *Per*
250:31 revolt,] ~; *Per*
250:40 mood *Per*] aspect *TS1*
251:1 procreative *Per*] Om. *TS1*
251:1 mood *Per*] aspect *TS1*
251:6 months] ~, *Per*
251:10 interval,] ~ *Per*
251:13 indomitable] ~, *Per*
251:13 passion,] ~— *Per*
251:14 instant mystic] ~, ~, *Per*
251:19 death,] ~ *Per*
251:19 to pass *Per*] Om. *TS1*
251:20 devilish] ~, *Per*
251:31 steely,] ~ *E2*
252:19 child"—To *Ed.*] child"—But to *TS1* child." To *Per*
252:19 question,] ~ *Per*
252:20 Pearl,] ~ *E2*
252:28 revealed. P The] ~. # II. P The *E2* [*Per* ends]
252:39 Mercy *E2*] mercy *TS1*
253:14 "Why] " '~ *E2*
253:14 me?— —Art] me?' inquired Hester. ... 'Art *E2*
253:16 soul?" Hester asks him.] soul?' *E2*
253:17 "Not] " '~ *E2*
253:17 soul!"] ~,' *E2*

253:17 "No... thine."]   '~ ... ~.' "
E2
253:19 psyche] psche E2
253:28 "it] "... ~ E2
253:28 is all] has all been a E2
253:33 psyche] ~, E2
253:40 expression] ~, E2
254:10 Underneath] ~, E2
254:13 great] Om. E2
254:18 election sermon] Election Sermon E2
254:18 and—] ~ E2
254:19 he] the former E2
254:20 mind,] ~ E2
254:20 concerning] respecting E2
254:21 communion supper]
        communion-supper E2
254:23 and] ~, E2
254:24 soul Ed.] Soul TS1 human soul
        E2
254:30 the other] its other E2
254:34 Shall we... life together?] Om.
        E2
254:36 surely] ~, E2
254:36 looked] lookest E2
254:37 eternity] ~, E2
254:37 eyes!] ~. E2
254:37 Then] ~, E2
254:37 seest!] ~? E2
254:38 "Hush] " '~ E2
254:38 Hester—] ~, E2
254:38 hush!"] ~!' E2
254:38 "The] '~ E2
254:40 thoughts!] ~. E2
255:3   even] Om. E2
255:4   processes] ~, E2
255:9   Tales E2] Tales TS1
255:10 of Ed.] of TS1 of the E2
255:12 the] The E2
255:17 Utopia] utopia E2
255:30 toil. P But Ed.] ~./ But TS1
        ~. But E2

255:32 dark] ~, E2
255:38 primary] ~, E2
256:4   the] The E2
256:6   deep-voiced,] ~ E2
256:8   and fourthly] ~, ~, E2
256:22 lode-stone] lodestone E2
256:24 criminal E2] Criminal TS1
256:28 "Murder E2] ~ TS1
256:29 Art", Ed.] ~, TS1 ~" E2
256:29 Hollingsworth's E2] Hollingworth's TS1
256:31 reforming] reforming E2
256:35 Hollingsworth E2] Hollingworth TS1
256:35 nurses E2] nursed TS1
256:38 sense-gratification]
        self-gratification E2
257:6   Hollingsworth E2] Hollingworth TS1
257:8   her] the E2
257:20 platform,] ~ E2
257:23 medium". Ed.] ~" TS1 ~." E2
257:34 under dream-consciousness]
        under-dream consciousness
        E2
257:37 wakening] waking E2
258:2   natural mechanical]
        natural-mechanical E2
258:8   thought transmission]
        thought-transmission E2
258:14 show—] ~. E2
258:17 causal] casual E2
258:19 things,—] ~, E2
258:20 Priscilla—] ~. E2
258:37 somnambulist] somnabulist
        E2
259:1   were-wolf,] ~ E2
259:1   Apulieus E2] Apuleius TS1
259:5   explicitly] explicity E2
259:5   Dimmesdale,] ~ E2
259:10 sacral E2] Sacral TS1
259:15 a wolf] a/a wolf E2

The Two Principles

260:13 correspondence,] ~ *E2*
260:34 "the] "The *E2*
262:15 America] ~, *E2*
262:23 was] were *E2*
262:32 egg-cell] egg-shell *E2*
263:28 is an] as an *E2*
264:11 twofold] two fold *E2*

266:3 twofold *Ed.*] two-fold *Per*
269:10 under-mud *Ed.*] under-/ mud *Per* undermud *E2*
269:31 Oriental] oriental *E2*
269:35 great] deep *E2*
269:37 the lower] lower *E2*

The editorial emendations for the **First Version** essays 'Dana' and 'Herman Melville' have been included in the Variorum apparatus (see below, pp. 613–19).

Intermediate Version

The editorial emendations for the **Intermediate Version** essays 'Nathaniel Hawthorne (II.)', 'Dana' and 'Whitman' have been included in the Variorum apparatus (see below, pp. 619–27, 629–31).

Herman Melville (1)

The order of texts is *MS2*, *TS4*, *TS4C*, *TCC7*, *TCC7C*, *E2*. (*E2* follows *TS4* and *TS4C* unless otherwise indicated.)

334:3   Herman Melville (1)]
        HERMAN MELVILLE'S
        "TYPEE" AND "OMOO"/
        BY D. H. LAWRENCE *TS4*
        HERMAN MELVILLE'S
        "TYPEE" AND "OMOO."
        TCC7C Herman Melville's
        Typee and *Omoo E2*
334:5   far] *Om. TS4*
334:6   far] *Om. TS4*
334:9   sea] ocean *TS4*
334:10 pure] *Om. TS4*
334:11 untranslateable]
        untranslatable *TS4*
334:13 creative] central *TS4*
334:13 life, into ... It is] life into an
        order of lower degree, or of
        external importance: moving
        towards the inanimate in *TS4*
334:17 Vikings: those] *Om. TS4*
334:19 mystery,] ~ *TS4*

334:22 south] South *TS4*
334:25 mystery] principle *TS4*
334:26 beings,] being, *TS4* being [sic]
        E2
334:28 a living consummation] the
        sun which will perfect them
        TS4
334:29 too] *Om. TS4*
334:29 at last] *Om. TS4*
334:29 seas, carrying ... with them]
        seas from whence they were
        derived, fire being the death-
        flame *TS4*
334:31 flame] flames *TS4*
334:31 sea.] sea. But also he seeks the
        Southern sun. *TS4*
335:17 ocean] Ocean *TCC7C*, *E2*
335:25 an aftermath. Of] echoes of
        TS4, *E2* echoes. Of *TCC7*
335:26 we] [about which] we *E2*
335:28 must] *Om. TS4*

335:31 and re-forgotten] *Om. TS4*

335:38 inter-communication] intercommunication *E2*

335:39 as, potentially,] as potentially, as *E2*

336:4 for ever *MS2, TCC7*] forever *TS4*

336:9 these] the *TCC7*

336:16 peasant. We] ~. *P* We *TCC7*

336:18 divine] impersonal *TS4*

336:19 a divine] an *TS4*

336:20 of infinitude] *Om. TS4*

336:21 infinite] *Om. TS4*

336:21 infinitude itself] the gesture of new creation *TS4*

336:22 experience,] ~ *TCC7*

336:24 become *MS2, TCC7*] becomes *TS4*

336:24 —The *MS2, TCC7*] ~ *TS4*

336:28 Mediaeval] mediaeval *TS4*

336:28 christian] Christian *TS4*

336:31 products] idealists *TS4*

336:35 This] The *TCC7*

336:38 has] *Om. TS4*

336:38 Its] The *TCC7*

337:3 Islands.] Islands: the centre of the seas, under the sun. *TS4, TCC7, E2* Islands: the center . . . sun. *TS4C*

337:15 And to this] To which *TS4*

337:16 *Typee.*] "Typee." *TCC7C*

337:20 or in some cloacal apprehension,] *Om. TS4*

337:21 savages] Savages *TCC7*

337:22 dreadful] *Om. TS4*

337:25 children," *MS2, E2*] ~", *TS4*

337:29 splendour *MS2, TCC7, E2*] splendor *TS4C*

337:31 most plainly] at its conclusion *TS4*

337:32 we] one *TCC7*

337:32 north] North *TS4*

337:37 degeneration. No *MS2, TCC7*] ~. *P* No *TS4C*

338:3 back] *Om. TS4*

338:5 Folk-Lore] folk-lore *E2*

338:7 distortions] contractions *TS4*

338:15 untranslateably] untranslatably *TS4*

338:17 image] images *E2*

338:20 savage."] ~". *TCC7*

338:21 look] *Om. TS4*

338:22 subjectively] ~, *E2*

338:23 nothing,] ~ *E2*

338:26 me unaccountable.] unaccountable degree. *TS4* an unaccountable degree. *TS4C*

338:26 have *TS4*] has *MS2*

338:27 words *MS2, TCC7*] ~, *TS4C, TCC7C*

338:28 all, *MS2, E2*] ~ *TS4*

338:31 thy] they *TCC7*

338:31 thee *TS4*] the *MS2*

338:31 eat," *MS2, TS4C*] ~". *TS4 TCC7*

338:32 pride] might *TS4*

338:34 not nearly] even then not *TS4*

338:38 *Oneing*] *oneing TCC7, E2*

339:1 says "all] ~: "All *TS4*

339:2 flesh and,] ~, ~ *TS4*

339:5 'eat] ~ *TS4*

339:6 us.'] ~? *TS4* ~. *E2*

339:22 became a] became *TS4*

339:23 was a] was *E2*

339:29 always had *TS4*] always *MS2* had always *TCC7*

339:30 increasing] ~, *TS4*

339:31 survival of the fittest] idealism which was rooted in unbridled commercialism *TS4*

339:31 It] it *E2*

339:33 sensual] spontaneious *TS4* spontaneous *TS4C*

339:38 cutting himself in two] striving after some fixed, external goal, which is no goal when

he gets there *TS4* striving... fixed, eternal goal...
there *TCC7*
340:2 *forcing*] forcing *TS4*
340:4 arm] leg *TS4*
340:10 Omoo,] "~," *TCC7C*
340:12 joined] gone over to *TS4*
340:12 utterly] *Om. TS4*
340:13 Us he... of forerunner] The
white way of life, ideal and
transcendent, was to him
the only way *TS4* The...
transcendent was... way
TCC7
340:15 But] *Om. TS4*
340:16 races,] ~ *TCC7*
340:16 submission] submission and
spiritual transcendence *TS4*
340:19 submission] meekness *TS4*
340:21 Life] Human life *TS4*
340:21 conquered.] conquered, and
the old world. *TS4*
340:22 death] the far-off savages *TS4*
340:22 conquered: the... indestructible Matter.] reduced to the
same term of the upper consciousness, the great oceans
must be brought under. *TS4*
340:25 utterly finish. It... loved it.]
finish: the conquest of the sea.
TS4
340:27 stay, any... another tree.] remain in the Eden of Nukuheva.
He must strain away, after a
new conquest in spiritual consciousness. *TS4*
340:29 arm] [...] *TS4* leg *TS4C*

340:29 proved to... to depart.] is a
clear indication of his true destiny. He must go on. *TS4*
340:34 way:] ~; *TCC7*
340:38 strive, strive, strive] strive,
strict, strive *E2*
340:39 arm] [...] *TS4* leg *TS4C*
341:1 great] ~, *TS4*
341:3 death,] the universe, *TS4* the
universe *TCC7*
341:8 quite] *Om. TS4*
341:9 really] *Om. TS4*
341:12 rather] *Om. TS4*
341:14 He must... *on.*] *Om. TS4*
341:21 man] vivid man *TS4*
341:21 life. But when] life. When *TS4*
life. *P* When *TCC7*
341:22 say, *MS2, TCC7*] ~ *TS4C*
341:24 goal] goal or some mechanistic
vision *TS4*
341:27 Melville] he *TS4*
341:31 Your] Lowe *TCC7*
341:36 time,] ~ *TS4*
341:39 christian] Christian *TS4*
341:40 love] the spirit *TS4*
342:1 non-moral; *MS2, TCC7*]
non-normal: *TS4*
342:4 be; *MS2, TCC7*] ~: *TS4*
342:4 first-consciousness] first consciousness *TS4*
342:15 effected] affected *TS4*
342:17 infinitude,] ~ *TCC7*
342:18 mastery] automatic mastery
TS4
342:24 processes *MS2, E2*] processess
TS4 process *TCC7*
342:26 triumphs," *MS2, E2*] ~", *TS4*

Herman Melville (2)

The order of texts is *MS2, TS5, TCC5, TS5C, TCC5C, E2, TCC7, TCC7C.* (*TCC5*
was the basis for *E2*, but the latter must have been set from a marked copy of *A1* or
E1: cf. such entries as 348:28, 351:12, 352:15 with *A1*.) *TCC7* and its corrections are
recorded only when they vary from *TS5*.

343:1 Studies... (XII)/ Herman
Melville (2)] STUDIES IN
CLASSIC AMERICAN LIT-
ERATURE (XII)/HERMAN
MELVILLE'S/"MOBY
DICK" / BY D. H.
LAWRENCE *TS5* HERMAN
MELVILLE'S/ "MOBY
DICK" / BY D. H.
LAWRENCE *TCC5* 12.
Herman Melville's *Moby Dick*
E2 XII / HERMAN
MELVILLE'S "MOBY
DICK" *TCC7C*

343:4 *or*] or *TS5*

343:5 a] the *E2*

343:7 Before we... [345:24] still
ahead.] *Om. TCC5 see also following entries to* 345:24

343:16 recipient or negative poles] the
poles union and love *TS5*

343:18 positive] separating *TS5*

343:20 perception] apprehending *TS5*

343:21 absorption] *Om. TS5*

343:26 Anaximenes] Anaxumenes
TCC7

343:32 a term... order. He] the indicator of a new great direction
of consciousness, a great fulfilment in the upper spiritual being of man, a complete escape
from the lower sensual being.
St. John *TS5*

343:34 alongside] within *TS5*

343:37 died *MS2, TS5C*] dies *TS5*

344:10 intelligence] consciousness
TS5

344:18 peace, which... human heart.]
and glowing unification with
that which is beyond us, the
glowing extension of our being,
giving the sense of peace and
fulfilment. The Creator is the
living All: the universe is the
created or material All. *TS5*

344:21 this] the *TS5*

344:23 esoterics] esoteric *TCC7*

344:29 mental] spiritual and mental
TS5

344:31 horizontally. *MS2, TCC7*] ~,
TS5

344:35 then] *Om. TS5*

344:38 ganglia:] ganglia, to *TS5*

344:40 hypogastric] hypogastic *TCC7*

345:6 the negative] as the negative
TS5

345:14 seen] *Om. TS5*

345:15 —The] ~ *TCC7*

345:20 been *MS2, TCC7*] being *TS5*

345:20 full] the full *TS5*

345:21 height. After *MS2, TCC7*] ~.
P After *TS5*

345:24 single] *Om. TS5*

345:28 worship-through-contumely
MS2, TS5C] worship—
through-contumely *TS5*
worship—through—contu-
mely *TCC7*

345:31 material] ~, *E2*

345:34 said] ~, *E2*

345:35 Sea] sea *TCC7*

345:35 Waters] waters *TCC7*

345:36 Material] material *E2*

345:38 his *MS2, TCC7*] this *TS5*

345:39 overthrown *MS2, TCC7*]
over-thrown *TS5*

346:3 monstrous, *MS2, TCC7*] ~
TS5

346:7 go] be conquered *TS5*

346:9 Shark] shark *TS5*

346:9 Crocodile] crocodile *TS5*

346:13 —In] ~ *TS5*

346:14 mantis] Mantis *TS5*

346:18 now.] ~? *E2, TCC7C*

346:22 deliberate attempt... [346:38]
last word.] violence native

to the American Continent,
where force is more powerful than consciousness, and so
is never gracefully expressed.
The life-force itself is so strong
that it tends to come forth lurid
and clumsy, obscure also. It
causes also a savage desire to
go to extremes, to hasten to extremes, whether of idealism or
of violent action. *TS5*

347:1   material unreality] falsity *TS5*
347:2   *water*] water *E2*
347:5   bald] cold *TS5*
347:7   spurious,] *Om. TS5*
347:8   But it is not] Not *TS5*
347:9   It] Yet it *TS5*
347:10 musty] dank *TS5* dark *E2*
347:11 values;] ~: *TS5*
347:13 creature] Yankee creature *TS5*
347:15 rotten rubbish heaps] the un-
        couth incoherence of a self-
        conscious adolescent *TS5*
347:15 out of . . . under-sea stuff]
        from the adolescent, the un-
        couth, unformed creature, not
        from the idealist *TS5*
347:19 last] extreme *TS5*
347:22 *substance*] substance *TS5*
347:24 our] a *TS5*
347:24 A good . . . kow-tow.] The au-
        thor is never quite himself.
        He is always at the mercy of
        the rank, self-conscious ide-
        alism which still rules white
        America, he always has to han-
        dle artificial values. *TS5*
347:29 meanings."] ~". *TCC7*
347:31 behaviour] behavior *TS5C*
347:33 almost] an *TS5*
348:1   In] For *TCC7*
348:8   harpooneer *TS5C*] harpoo-
        ner *MS2, E2*

348:9   almost] *Om. TS5*
348:13 room;] ~, *TS5*
348:14 mild] wild *TCC7*
348:16 twain;] ~: *E2, TCC7*
348:22 —So] ~ *E2*
348:28 thought I . . . is worship?—]
        Om. E2
348:30 fellow-man . . . fellow-man]
        fellow man . . . fellow man *E2*
348:31 fellow-man] fellow man *E2*
349:3   pair—" *P* Elsewhere . . .
        Queequeg that] pair—" The
        sophistry with which he justi-
        fies his act of idolatry is amus-
        ing, and very characteristic of
        Melville. He continually spins
        an ideal logic to fit his new acts.
        The ideal logic is apt to be bor-
        ing. Plainly, he cared nothing
        about worship, and he loved
        Queequeg. Elsewhere he says
        TS5
349:4   him for his] the savage's *TS5*
349:10 voyage as *MS2, TCC7*] ~, ~
        TS5
349:10 Yet] Sometimes its forced fan-
        tasy is irritating. And yet, after
        all, *TS5*
349:12 experience.] experience. The
        blemish is the self-conscious
        posturing about it. *TS5*
349:16 to a] to *E2, TCC7*
349:20 symbolism] symbolisms *E2*
349:20 book.—] ~ *TCC7*
349:24 —But he inclines to supersti-
        tion.] *Om. TS5*
349:31 moreover. *P* Flask *MS2*,
        TCC7] ~. Flask *TS5*
349:33 him] ~, *E2*
349:34 ———This *MS2, TCC7*] —
        —~ *TS5* —~ *E2*
349:36 it—.] ~— *TS5*
349:36 less, *MS2, TCC7*] ~ *TS5*

349:39 monomania] monomaniac
TS5, TCC7C

350:1 have] always have TS5

350:1 Yet he] He TS5

350:3 actuality] ~, TS5

350:5 harpooneers MS2, TS5C]
harpooners TS5, E2

350:6 great] ~, TS5

350:8 boat's-crew] boat's crew TS5

350:8 fire-worshipping, sun worship-
ping] fire-worshipping TS5

350:17 speculation:] ~; TCC7

350:19 taste.—] ~— E2

350:21 below] ~, E2

350:22 overclouded] overcrowded TS5

350:23 feathery] feathered TS5

350:23 hooked,] ~ TS5

350:25 wings— —. Wondrous Ed.] ~
— —. Wonderous MS2 ~—.
wonderous TS5 ~—. Won-
drous TS5C ~.—Wondrous
E2 ~—. Wonderous TCC7

350:26 king's] King's TS5

350:27 inexpressible,] ~ TS5

350:27 methought MS2, E2, TCC7]
me thought TS5

350:28 heavens— —] ~— TS5

350:29 for ever MS2, E2, TCC7]
forever TS5

350:33 —We] ~ TS5

350:35 Chapter] chapter TS5

350:35 *Whiteness.*] whiteness. E2
"Whiteness." TCC7C

350:38 fusion of] reaction between
TS5

350:38 Matter . . . Matter] matter . . .
matter TCC7

351:4 *Pequod TCC7C*] Pequod MS2

351:12 air,] ~ TS5

351:12 resolved] reselved E2

351:13 self—] ~.— TS5

351:15 She blows! She] she TS5 She
E2, TCC7

351:18 earth— MS2, E2] ~,— TS5

351:19 "Give] "~ TS5 " '~ E2

351:19 men,"] ~,' E2

351:20 "there] '~ E2

351:21 Spring!"] '~!' E2

351:24 "Stand up!"] '~ ~!' E2 " ~ ~!
TCC7

351:25 sprang] sprung E2

351:30 curling] curbing TS5

351:32 ' "That's Ed.] "~ MS2 " '~ E2

351:32 *There!*] ~, E2

351:32 there, give E2] *there,* Give MS2
There, give TS5

351:32 him!"] ~!' E2

351:33 —A] ~ E2

351:36 vapour MS2, E2] vapor TS5C

351:38 half suffocated] half-
suffocated TS5

351:39 curdling] curling TCC7

351:40 escaped—'] ~—" TS5 ~.—"
TS5C

352:3 St] ~. TS5

352:5 and] ~, E2

352:8 bow.—] ~— E2

352:9 Brit] brit E2

352:10 Crozetts,] Crozells TS5
Crozello TCC7

352:11 whale] Whale E2

352:12 undulated] modulated TCC7

352:14 whales] Whales E2

352:14 Sperm whaler] sperm whaler
TS5 sperm-whaler E2

352:15 *Pequod,* with] Pequod. With
TS5 Pequod, with E2 *Pequod.*
With TCC7C

352:15 jaws MS2, E2] jaws they TS5

352:18 morning] moving E2, TCC7

352:18 mowers] ~, E2

352:23 mast-heads] mast heads TS5

352:25 else—] ~. E2

352:27 *Pequod TCC7C*] Pequod MS2

352:29 tall,] ~ TS5

352:31 intervals MS2, E2] ~, TS5

352:31 that lonely, *MS2, E2, TCC7*]
       that lonely, that lonely, *TS5*
352:33 "But *TS5C, TCC7C*] ~ *MS2*
352:35 sunglade *MS2, E2, TCC7*]
       sunglare *TS5*
352:37 on *MS2, E2, TCC7*] in *TS5*
352:37 visible *MS2, E2, TCC7*] risible
       TS5
352:39 "In *TS5C, TCC7C*] ~ *MS2*
353:4 Daggoo— —] ~— *TS5*
353:15 sound] *Om. TS5*
353:16 again.—] ~. *E2*
353:19 *Jeroboam*] Jeroboam *E2*
353:25 back-bone] backbone *E2*
353:26 are—.] ~— *TS5, E2* ~.—
       TS5C
353:26 adds— "For] ~: "For *E2* ~: *P*
       "For *TCC7*
353:34 thought,] ~ *TS5*
353:37 agony!—"] ~!"— *TS5* ~!"
       E2, TCC7
353:38 The] the *E2*
353:39 Armada," *MS2, TS5C*] ~",
       TS5
353:39 Volume] volume *TS5*
353:39 *Pequod Ed.*] Pequod *MS2*
354:4 air—"—] ~." *TS5*
354:4 Straits *MS2, TCC7*] straits
       TS5
354:7 whales *MS2, E2, TCC7C*]
       whalers *TS5*
354:8 array,] ~ *TS5*
354:10 Leviathan *TS5*] leviathan *MS2*
354:13 There,] ~ *TS5*
354:15 sea-men] seamen *TS5*
354:18 eyes] ~, *TS5*
354:19 nursing-mothers] nursing
       mothers *TS5*
354:23 time;] ~: *E2*
354:28 us.— — —] ~. — *TS5* ~. —
       — *TCC7*
354:32 fearlessly *MS2, E2, TCC7*]
       fearless *TS5*

354:33 delight.—] ~— *E2*
354:37 The] the *TS5* "The *E2*,
       TCC7C
354:37 Cassock] ~" *E2, TCC7C*
354:39 Try-works] try-works *E2*
354:40 a] the *TS5*
355:9 was, *MS2, TCC7*] ~ *TS5*
355:9 'My] ~ *TS5*
355:10 me!'] ~? *TS5* ~. *TCC7*
355:10 thought I!—] thought I. *E2* I
       thought! *TCC7*
355:13 ghastly.] ghastly. It seems to
       him that his gazing on fire had
       cooked this horror of rever-
       sion, undoing. *TS5, TCC5*
       ghastly. It...had evoked this
       ...undoing. *TS5C, TCC7C*
355:17 tattooing *MS2, E2, TCC7*]
       tatooing *TS5*
355:21 die,] ~ *E2*
355:24 this] the *E2*
355:25 *Pequod MS2, TCC7C*] Pequod
       TS5
355:28 midmost] utmost *TS5*
355:29 fights go] fight goes *E2*
355:31 then,] ~ *TS5*
356:1 a] *Om. TCC7*
356:1 'He *MS2, E2*] "~ *TS5* ~
       TCC7
356:1 it;—] ~; *TS5*
356:2 homage-rendering *MS2*,
       TS5C] homage—rendering
       TS5
356:3 fire';— — — *Ed.*] ~;— — —
       MS2, TCC7 ~;— — *TS5* ~;
       ...*E2 see notes*
356:7 worships:] ~; *TCC7*
356:8 —It] ~, *E2*
356:8 on] of *TS5*
356:8 *Pequod*] Pequod *E2*
356:9 mast-heads] mast-head *TCC7*
356:19 small,] ~ *TS5*
356:19 unspeckled] unspecked *TCC7*

356:23 —On] ~ *TS5*
356:24 "—But] "~ *TS5*
356:25 Starbuck?] ~: *E2*
356:27 It *MS2, E2, TCC7*] —~ *TS5*
356:35 unsuspecting] unsuspectful *TS5*
356:38 vast] ~, *E2*
356:39 Turkish-rugged] Turkish rugged *E2, TCC7*
357:11 "A *TS5C, TCC7C*] ~ *MS2*
357:12 whale— — *MS2, TCC7*] ~— *TS5*
357:15 harpooneer *MS2, TS5C*] harpooner *TS5, E2*
357:20 cry] ~, *E2* ~. *TCC7*

357:20 "'The ship] "~ ship *TS5* "'~ ship *E2, TCC7*
357:21 ship?' *MS2, E2, TCC7*] ~?" *TS5*
357:24 harpooneers *MS2, TS5C*] harpooners *TS5, E2*
357:25 look-outs] lookouts *E2*
357:28 *Pequod*] Pequod *E2*
357:28 sight—] ~. — *TCC5C*
357:30 Indian] American Indian *TS5*
357.32 beat] boat *E2*
357:36 esoteric] exoteric *TS5*
357:37 significance.] significance, and of considerable tiresomeness. *TS5*

APPENDIXES

Foreword to Studies in Classic American Literature (1920)

MS = E382.5a
TS = E382.5c
Per = *New Republic*
A1 = *Phoenix*

The order of texts is as listed above. Corrections in *TS* are recorded only when they affect the transmission of the text.

381:1 Foreword...Literature. *Ed.*] Foreword to Studies in Classic American Literature./ D.H. Lawrence *MS* Foreword... D. H. Lawrence. *TS* Foreword ...Literature./ By D.H. Lawrence. *TSC* America, Listen to Your Own *Per* AMERICA, LISTEN TO YOUR OWN *A1*
381:4 —usually] ~ *TS*
381:9 their] this *TS*
381:13 Cinquecento] Cinquecents *TS* Cinquescents *Per*
381:14 *How*] How *TS*
381:14 to *MS, A1*] Om. *TS*

381:25 However ..] ~..... *TS* ~... *TSC*
381:27 cathedral] Cathedral *TS*
381:28 *Corriere della Sera MS, A1*] Corriere della Sera *Per*
381:30 admiration—"]—] ~[...]" *TS* ~"— *TSC*
381:30 The] the *TS*
381:31 *i Cavalieri di Colombo] i Cavaliere di Colombo TS, A1* i Cavaliere di Colombo *Per*
382:3 temple. Until] ~. until *TS* ~, until *TSC*
382:13 grey *MS, A1*] gray *Per*
382:17 for ever *MS, A1*] forever *Per*
382:19 cathedral] Cathedral *TS*

382:19 Oh] O *TSC*
382:20 Columbus.] ~! *TSC*
382:20 la mer ... ô ... de Colombe] la
mer ... o ... Colombe *Per la
mer, c'est moi. La mer, c'est aussi
vous, o Chevaliers de Colombe A1*
382:25 beauty etc.] ~, etc., *TSC*
382:27 for ever *MS, A1*] forever
TSC
382:28 a] *Om. TS*
382:28 Ghirlandaio] Ghirlandajo *A1*
382:32 cathedrals *Ed.*] Cathedrals *MS*
382:32 coliseums] Coliseums *TS*
382:32 Ghirlandaios] Ghirlandajos *A1*
382:35 Marks] Mark's *TSC*
382:37 limits] limit *Per*
382:39 Year] year *TS*
382:39 Grace] grace *A1*
382:40 Tintoret.] ~? *TSC*
383:2 cathedral] Cathedral *TS*
383:3 soaring] *Om. Per*
383:6 Marks] Mark's *TSC*
383:7 Marks] Mark's *TSC*
383:9 cathedral] Cathedral *A1*
383:10 yesterdays!] ~ ⟨.⟩⟨⌈?⌉⟩⌈⌈!⌉⌉
TSC ~? *Per*
383:12 tomorrows.] to-morrows. *TS*
tomorrows! *Per*
383:14 civilisation] civilization *TS*
383:14 can," we] ~." We *A1*
383:15 American,] Americans, *A1*
383:17 barbarian.] ~! *Per*

383:18 smithereens *MS, A1*] Smithereens *Per*
383:21 Aquileia,] ~ *TS*
383:23 course] ~, *A1*
383:23 simpler] simple *TS*
383:28 sea-bear *MS, A1*] sea-/ bear
TS seabear *Per*
383:32 tradition,] ~ *TS*
383:39 wistful,] ~ *TS*
384:4 cathedral or] Cathedral ~ *TS*
384:4 Ghirlandaio] Ghirlandajo *A1*
384:4 cathedral but] Cathedral ~ *Per*
384:15 fulfilment *MS, A1*] fulfillment
Per
384:31 recognise] recognize *TS*
384:31 recognise,] recognise *TS* recognize *Per*
384:37 Cortes] Cortés *A1*
384:37 continuity—] ~ *TS* ~: *A1*
385:4 responsibility. *P* It] ~. It *Per*
385:8 crystallised] crystallized *Per*
385:8 forever] for ever *A1*
385:9 laws,] ~ *TS*
385:13 Americans] America *TS*
385:13 great,] ~ *TS*
385:18 conscious:] ~; *Per*
385:19 fully, *MS, TSC*] ~ *TS, Per*
385:22 Israel] America *Per*
385:23 Florence. 1920.] ~ ~. *TS* ~,
~. *TSC* D. H. LAWRENCE/
Florence, 1920. *Per Om. A1 see
notes*

Foreword (1922)

Only the corrections in *TCC7* of possible textual significance are recorded.

389:30 Melville, *Ed.*] ~/ *TCC7*   390:15 *vrai Ed.*] vra⌈i⌉ *TCC7C*
390:3 shy] show *TCC7C*

Nathaniel Hawthorne's *Blithedale Romance* (1920–1)

The order of texts is *TS3, TS3C, E2, TCC7, TCC7C. TCC7* follows *TS3* unless
otherwise indicated.

393:1 Nathaniel Hawthorne's
Blithedale Romance Ed.]
NATHANIEL HAWTH-
ORNE'S / "BLITHEDALE
ROMANCE" / By D. H.
LAWRENCE. *TS3* "The
Scarlet Letter" / By D. H.
LAWRENCE. *TS3C*
Nathaniel Hawthorne II *E2*
VIII. / NATHANIEL
HAWTHORNE'S
"BLITHEDALE
ROMANCE" *TCC7* VIII /
NATHANIEL HAWTH-
ORNE'S "BLITHEDALE
ROMANCE" *TCC7C*

393:2 The character . . . *The Scarlet
Letter* . . . not mentioned.] *Om.
TS3C* The character . . . *The
Scarlet Letter* have not mentioned. *TCC7* One character . . . "The Scarlet Letter" we
have not mentioned. *TCC7C*

393:3 is] in the allegory of *The Scarlet
Letter TS3C* in the . . . *Letter,
E2*

393:3 Hester; he] Hester *TS3C* Hester, *E2* Hester: he *TCC7*

393:6 herbs,] ~ *E2*

393:10 science—] ~: *TCC7*

393:11 science] Science *TCC7*

393:15 there indeed] ~, ~, *E2*

393:17 an *E2, TCC7*] and *TS3*

393:19 analyse *E2, TCC7*] analyze
TS3

393:20 our *TS3C, TCC7*] our own
TS3

393:29 Alchemy . . . Astrology]
alchemy . . . astrology *TS3C*

393:30 science] Science *TCC7*

393:32 Alchemist] alchemist *TS3C*

394:1 *not*] not *TCC7*

394:10 moment] ~, *TCC7*

394:11 mechanistic *E2, TCC7*]
anechanistic *TS3*

394:14 eternal] external *TCC7*

394:30 Matter] matter *TCC7*

394:31 water] ~, *E2*

394:34 independent] dependent *E2*

394:37 owing] owning *E2*

395:7 And,] ~ *TCC7*

395:17 But] —~ *TCC7*

395:19 have] *have TCC7*

395:19 Old-Testament] Old Testament *TCC7C*

395:35 an *E2, TCC7*] and *TS3*

395:36 our] one *TCC7*

395:40 Christians] Christians [it be-
came] *E2*

395:40 was the sin *TCC7*] *Om. TS3*

396:1 Naturally. Therefore] ~,
therefore, *E2*

396:5 Creation] creation *TCC7*

396:8 second] Second *TCC7*

396:12 mother] Mother *TCC7*

396:16 me— — —] ~?— *E2*

396:17 round] around *E2*

396:17 not] *Om. E2*

396:23 doctrine] ~, *E2*

396:23 mundus] Mundus *E2*

396:30 sun of *TS3C, TCC7*] sun *TS3*

396:36 has had *TS3C, TCC7*] had
TS3

397:8 "Shall *TS3, TCC7C*] " '~ *E2*
' "~ *TCC7*

397:8 again?"] ~?' *E2* ~?", *TCC7*

397:9 "Shall] '~ *E2*

397:11 Tell] Then, tell *E2*

397:12 seest!"] ~!' *E2*

397:13 "Hush] " '~ *E2*

397:13 Hester—] ~, *E2*

397:13 hush,"] ~, '*E2*

397:13 "The] '~ *E2*

397:14 let] —~ *E2*

397:15 fear!"] ~!' " *E2*

397:26 fact] ~, *E2*

397:35 simultaneous] simultaneously *TCC7*

397:38 No] The Scarlet Leter is a profound & wonderful book, an eternal revelation. No *TS3C The Scarlet Letter* ... profound and ... revelation. No *E2*

398:12 Crèvecoeur *TCC7C*] Crevecoeur *TS3* Crêvecœur *TS3C* Crèvecoeur *E2*

398:14 work] ~, *TCC7*

398:19 labor] labour *E2, TCC7*

398:19 the beast] beast *TCC7*

398:19 herd] ~, *E2*

398:29 too-much] too much *E2, TCC7*

398:33 laborers] labourers *E2*

398:35 the *Scarlet Letter Ed.*] the Scarlet Letter *TS3 The Scarlet Letter TS3C* The Scarlet Letter *TCC7*

398:38 group—] ~ *TCC7*

399:19 Hephaestos *TCC7*] Hephaestor *TS3* Hephaestus *E2*

399:19 underworld] Underworld *TCC7*

399:35 white veil] White Veil *TCC7*

400:4 however. P That *TS3C, TCC7*] ~. That *TS3*

400:8 exist,] ~ *E2*

400:9 impression] impressions *E2*

400:9 souls *TS3C, TCC7*] soul *TS3*

400:14 and] *Om. E2*

400:16 *direct*, within us, as] direct, with us: and *TCC7 direct*, within us: as *TCC7C*

400:23 what] is what *E2*

400:28 cause-and-effect] cause and effect *TCC7*

400:29 cause and effect] cause-and-effect *TCC7*

400:34 enquiry *TCC7*] inquiry *TS3*

400:36 phenomenon] phenomena *E2*

XIII. Whitman (1921–2)

TCC6 E382d
Per1   *Nation and Athenaeum* xxix (23 July 1921), 616–18
Per2   *New York Call* (21 August 1921), 3–4

The order of texts is *TCC7, TCC7C, TCC6, Per1, Per2, E2. TCC6* follows *TCC7* – not *TCC7C* – and *Per2* and *E2* follow *Per1*, unless otherwise indicated. *MS2* as the original source for poetry quotations is used to correct *TCC7*.

403:1 XIII./Whitman. *Ed.*] XIII./ WHITMAN. *TCC7* XIII/ WHITMAN *TCC7C* Whitman:/ By D. H. Lawrence. *TCC6* WHITMAN. *Per1 Walt Whitman/ By D. H. LAWRENCE Per2* 13. Whitman *E2 see notes*

403:3 the last and] *Om. Per1*

403:5 wrong: *TCC7, E2*] ~; *Per1*

403:5 *quite*] quite *TCC6*

403:7 Whitman:] ~; *Per1*

403:30 Christian religious *TCC7, Per1*] christian religion *TCC6*

403:32 esoterics] ~, *Per1*

403:34 prides. P The ... [404:27] Jerusalem." P Now] prides. P Now, *TCC6* prides. # *** # P Now, Per2*

404:34 *returns upon*] returns upon *TCC6*

404:35 centres,] centers *Per2*

404:36 the] *Om. Per2*

404:36 Crêvecoeur,] *Om. TCC6*
Crêvecœur, *Per1* Crèvecoeur,
E2
405:1 motive] ~, *TCC6*
405:2 the] *Om. Per2*
405:2 aesthetes *TCC7, E2*] æsthetes
Per1
405:3 French,] ~ *Per2*
405:9 alike:] ~; *Per1*
405:10 spontaneous. *P* And] ~. # ***
P And *Per2*
405:19 underground,] ~ *TCC6*
405:24 *centres*] centers *Per2*
405:27 Dana *TCC7, Per1*] David
TCC6
405:29 immemorial] ~, *Per1*
405:29 Pacific] *Om. Per2*
405:30 *Typee. E2*] Typee. *TCC7* the
Typee. *TCC6* "Typee." *Per1*
405:32 externals *TCC7, Per1*] exter-
nall *TCC6*
405:37 find his] find the *TCC6*
405:37 extension] ~, *TCC6*
405:39 paeans *TCC6, E2*] paens
TCC7 pæans *Per1*
405:40 All embracing] All-embracing *Per1*
405:40 indiscriminate] ~, *Per1*
406:1 acceptance:] ~; *Per1*
406:2 to you *MS2*] to *TCC7*
406:3 announcements—"—] ~. . . ."
Per1
406:4 myself"—] ~." *Per1*
406:5 I am] "~ ~ *E2*
406:6 consciousness:] ~; *Per1*
406:6 rejected.] ~:— *Per1* ~: *Per2*
406:7 love; *TCC7, E2*] ~: *TCC6*
406:8 gravitate? *MS2, TCC6*] ~,
TCC7
406:15 *everything*] everything *TCC6*
406:16 accomplished. *P* It] ~. # ***
P It *Per2*
406:18 himself,] ~ *Per1*

406:32 on. With . . . [407:17] And this]
on. *P* With . . . And this *TCC6*
on. *P* But this *Per1 see also en-*
tries to 407:9
406:34 an *Ed.*] and *TCC6*
406:38 knew] new *TCC6*
407:8 those] these *TCC6*
407:9 *both*] both *TCC6*
407:17 truth. Always] truth, *Per1*
407:23 himself, he] ~, ~ *Per1*
407:24 Plato. *P* Which] ~. # *** # *P*
Which *Per2*
407:26 infinites] ~, *Per1*
407:26 Masses] ~, *Per1*
407:26 Democracies] ~, *Per1*
407:26 Almightinesses *TCC7C*]
Almightiness *TCC7*
Almightynesses *TCC6*
407:28 and extensions] *Om. Per2*
407:31 half-truth,] ~— *Per1*
407:32 Sennacherib:] ~; *Per2*
407:34 his] *Om. Per1*
407:35 *merging*] merging *TCC6*
407:35 *away*] away *TCC6*
407:39 *right-about-turn?*] right-about-
turnsy *TCC6* right-about-
turn? *Per1*
408:4 systole *TCC7, Per1*] Zystole
TCC6
408:6 poles, and . . . between these]
Om. Per1
408:8 tyranny,] ~ *Per1*
408:8 One Identity *TCC7, Per1*] one
identity *TCC6*
408:12 Even Whitman . . . later days.
TCC7C] *Om. TCC7*
408:14 into] from *Per1*
408:17 Dostoevsky. *P* And *TCC7,*
Per1] Dostoersky. *P* And
TCC6 Dostoevsky. # *** #
P And *Per2*
408:20 universality,] ~ *Per1*
408:20 vaporish] ~, *Per1*

408:13 yourself; *TCC7, Per1*] ~,
        TCC6

408:29 life,] ~ *Per1*

408:33 White Whale] white whale
        Per2

408:38 *himself.*] ~: *TCC6* himself:
        Per2

408:39 body,] ~— *Per1*

408:39 take,] ~ *Per2*

409:2   gratification] ~, *Per1*

409:2   triumph.] ~. # *** # *Per2*

409:3   Whitman's is . . . [409:25]
        trait.] *Om. TCC6*

409:26 beside *TCC7C, TCC6*] besides
        TCC7

409:26 Woman . . . Woman] woman . . .
        woman *TCC6*

409:27 much. She] ~? She *Per1* ~: she
        E2

409:28 States] states *Per2*

409:29 creatures:] ~— *Per1*

409:30 my soul *MS2*] myself *TCC7,*
        TCC6

409:30 Nature *MS2*] ~, *TCC7,*
        TCC6 nature, *Per2*

409:31 One] one *Per2*

409:32 sanity *TCC7, Per1*] Sanity
        TCC6

409:32 beauty, *TCC7, Per1*] ~ *TCC6*

409:34 see." / That] ~." *P* That
        TCC6

409:36 being,] ~ *Per1*

410:1   This *TCC7, E2*] This, *Per1*

410:3   this *MS2*] the *TCC7*

410:5   / So, man . . . [412:16] males
        alone.] *Om. TCC6*

413:1   mover *TCC7, Per2*] ~, *Per1*

413:4   this,] ~ *Per1*

413:5   *épater TCC7, Per1*] *epater*
        TCC6 épater *Per2*

413:6   perfectness,] ~ *Per2*

413:6   fatality. *P* Even] ~. # *** # *P*
        Even *Per2*

413:8   hesitates; *TCC7, Per2*] ~:
        TCC6

413:16 Democracy] democracy *Per2*

413:17 *Drum-Taps. Ed.*] Drum-Taps
        MS2 Drum Taps. *TCC7*
        "Drum Taps." *TCC7C,*
        Per1

413:23 Yet] ~ *TCC6*

413:24 death, *MS2, TCC6*] ~ *TCC7*
        ~. *TCC7C* ~; *Per1*

413:25 what indeed] ~, ~, *Per1*

413:26 except *TCC7, Per1*] *Om.*
        TCC6

413:26 love?)/ I *MS2, TCC6*] ~?) I
        TCC7 ~?)./ I *Per1*

413:28 death,] ~. *Per*

413:30 lovers,] ~; *Per1*

413:31 or] of *E2*

413:31 prefer, / (I *MS2*] ~/ (I *TCC7*
        ~ (I *TCC6* ~, (I *E2*

413:32 most)] ~), *Per1*

413:33 now] *Om. Per2*

413:36 near] *Om. Per2*

414:4   him,] ~ *Per1*

414:5   Great Sea] great sea *Per1*

414:5   lost] last *Per1*

414:7   hurrying not, *MS2, Per1*] ~~
        TCC7, TCC6

414:8   Whisper'd *MS2*] Whispered
        TCC7, TCC6

414:8   and *MS2, E2*] *Om. TCC7,*
        TCC6

414:9   day-break] daybreak *Per1*

414:11 death, / *MS2, Per1*] ~/
        TCC7, TCC6

414:12 Hissing] Hissing the *Per2*

414:12 arous'd] aroused *TCC6*

414:20 responsibility. *P* And] ~. And
        TCC6

414:23 vital] vial *Per2*

414:24 family and clan and nation
        TCC7, Per2] ~, ~ ~, ~ ~,
        Per1

414:25 Next] ~, *Per1*
414:26 And finally] ~, ~, *Per1*
414:29 state however] ~, ~, *Per1*
414:29 other:] ~; *Per2*
414:30 friendship and family] ~, ~ ~,
　　　　Per1
414:36 *d'être TCC7, Per1*] *d'etre*
　　　　TCC6 d'être *Per2*
414:37 marriage,] ~; *Per1*
415:2 life,] ~ *Per1*
415:2 of the] *Om. TCC6*
415:2 life, when...down. *P* The
　　　　TCC7C] life. The *TCC7* life.
　　　　P The *TCC6*
415:6 life. We...[415:11] prosti-
　　　　tuted! *P* If] life. *P* If *TCC6* life.
　　　　# *** # *P* If *Per2*
415:14 should] is *TCC6*
415:15 be] *Om. TCC6*
415:16 sacred] the sacred *TCC6*
415:17 upon the] on the *TCC6*
415:17 way] way in which *TCC6*
415:19 polarity. In ...[417:31] up
　　　　splendour.] polarity. *P* The last
　　　　phase is entered upon, shakily,
　　　　by Whitman. It will take us an
　　　　epoch to establish the new, per-
　　　　fect circuit of our being. It will
　　　　take an epoch to establish the
　　　　love of comrades, as marriage is
　　　　really established now. For fear
　　　　of going on, forwards, we turn
　　　　round and destroy, or try to de-
　　　　stroy, what lies behind. We are
　　　　trying to destroy marriage, be-
　　　　cause we have not the courage
　　　　to go forward from marriage to
　　　　the new issue. Marriage must
　　　　never be wantonly attacked.
　　　　True {True *Per2*} marriage is
　　　　eternal, {eternal; *Per1*} in it we
　　　　have our consummation and
　　　　being. But the final consummation lies in that which in beyond marriage. *P* And when
the bond, or circuit of perfect
comrades is established, what
then, when we are on the brink
of death, fulfilled in the vastness of life? Then, at last, we
shall know a starry maturity. *P*
Whitman put us on the track
years ago. Why has no one
gone on from him? The great
poet, why does no one accept
his greatest word? The Americans are not worthy of their
Whitman. They take him like
a cocktail, for fun. Miracle that
they have not annihilated every
word of him. But these miracles happen. *P* The {happen.
*** # *P* The *Per2*} great-
est modern poet! Whitman, at
his best, is purely himself. His
verse springs sheer from the
spontaneous sources of his being. Hence its lovely, lovely
form and rhythm: at the best.
It is sheer, perfect, {perfect
E2} *human* {human *Per2*}
spontaneity, spontaneous as a
nightingale throbbing, but still
controlled, the highest loveliness of human spontaneity,
undecorated, unclothed. The
whole being is there, sensually
throbbing, spiritually quivering, mentally, ideally speaking. It is not, like Swinburne,
an exaggeration of the one
part of being. It is perfect and
whole. The whole soul speaks
at once, and is too pure for mechanical assistance of rhyme
and measure. The perfect

utterance of a concentrated, {concentrated *E2*} spontaneous soul. The unforgettable loveliness of Whitman's lines! *TCC6*

417:32 rocking—"] rocking." *P Ave America!* *TCC6* rocking." *P Ave America!* D. H. LAWRENCE. *Per1* rocking." / *Ave America! E2*

VARIORUM APPARATUS
(MANUSCRIPT AND TYPESCRIPT
VARIANTS)

Where there is no ⌡ bracket, the final reading of the text can be deduced from the material not in ⟨ ⟩ brackets, e.g. at 14:24 'to point' and at 24:26 'his grandfather, or wiser.'

All revisions are recorded, except for false starts of one or two letters, and '[. . .]' indicates an illegible deletion.

Final Version
Foreword

11:2 struck⟨.⟩⌜!⌝
11:3 ⟨America⟩ ⌜The U. S. A.⌝
11:3 ⟨they⟩ ⌜we⌝
11:9 Toad⌜-⌝in ⌜-⌝the⌜-⌝Hole

11:15 asserting ⌜[underlining added]⌝
12:8 trying ⌜[underlining added]⌝
12:17 c⟨a⟩⌜o(type)⌝me⌜s (type)⌝

The Spirit of Place

13:9 ⌜or later⌝
13:11 ⟨Lybia⟩ ⌜Libya [type]⌝
13:13 it⌜, [type] ⌝ ⟨all, [type]⟩
13:17 ⟨just⟩ declined
13:19 ⌜—⌝Out
14:24 to ⟨to [type]⟩ point
14:25 ⟨⟨The tale, however, points quite a different moral⟨,⟩ ⌜by itself, [type]⌝⟩⟩ ⌜⌜The tail . . . way,⌝⌝
14:29 ⟨functio [type]⟩ business
14:35 ⟨a lie.⟩ ⌜it.⌝
14:38 ⟨and⟩ ⌜at⌝
15:16 ⟨dangerous⟩ ⌜simple⌝
15:24 of course they are A1] they positively want⟨ed⟩ to be MS8
15:25 made or in the making. A1] which is a sign of ⟨absolute⟩

failure to live⌜.⌝ ⟨, to be anything in living.⟩ MS8
15:33 master⌜.⌝ ⟨of men's destinies.⟩
15:34 ⟨real⟩ ⌜true⌝
15:34 ⟨undertook⟩ ⌜bore⌝
16:1 ⟨to/⟩ ⌜to a⌝
16:4 ⌜to [type]⌝ the
16:6 ⟨perhaps always⟩ been the ⟨most⟩
16:7 ⟨is this which⟩ has
16:8 ⟨obedient or⟩ servile
16:9 outlast⟨s⟩⌜ing⌝
16:10 ⌜Like a parent.⌝
16:11 ⟨mastery⟩ ⌜parenthood⌝
16:12 ⟨really [type]⟩ feels
16:12 ⟨from this⟩ ⌜its⌝
16:36 "humanity" A1] free⌜-⌝and ⌜-⌝easiness MS8

16:38 free⌜ ⌝and⌐ ⌝easy
17:33 ⌜living⌝
17:39 ⌜Men are ... always was.⌝
18:4 And there ... [18:6] be sure.
    A1] ⟨It? What is it? [type]⟩
    IT? What is IT? *P* IT is many
    things, more than I know. But
    for one thing, IT is the spirit
    of place. The spirit of the
    continent of America. Amer-
icans will be free when they
are doing what IT likes, and
not what they themselves like.
MS8
18:15 ⟨domination.⟩ ⌜dominion.⌝
18:23 deciders ⟨that⟩
18:37 desire⌜,⌝
18:39 ⟨an illusion [type]⟩ nothing
19:12 ⟨art,⟩ ⌜utterance,⌝

Benjamin Franklin

21:39 fenced ⟨off⟩
21:40 forsooth⟨.⟩⌜!⌝
22:4 trotted inside ... a paddock.
    A1] ⟨practised like people
    do dumb-bells today.⟩ ⌜trotted
    round inside ... a paddock.⌝
    MS8
22:14 Let ⟨each [type]⟩
22:22 ⟨ot⟩ ⌜to⌝ do
23:10 ⟨Rarely use venery but for
    health and offspring, never
    to dulness, weakness, or in-
    jury to your own or an-
    other's peace or reputation.⟩
    ⌜Be not ... unavoidable.⌝
23:18 Socrates./ ⌜_____⌝
23:19 he⌜, Benjamin,⌝
23:29 ⟨horror⟩ ⌜man⌝
24:11 ⟨first momentous Council of
    the⟩ American
24:25 ha⟨d⟩⌜s⌝
24:26 ⟨an old⟩ ⌜his⌝ grandfath⟨r⟩⌜e⌝r⟨.⟩
    ⌜, or wiser.⌝
24:34 ⟨little⟩ ⌜scrubby⌝
25:4 are thorns in young flesh *A1*]
    did me ⟨inestimable⟩ harm
    MS8
25:8 ⌜and [type]⌝
25:15 ⌜And I ... American corrall.⌝
25:16 Moral America ... Benjamin!
    Sound ... to go *Ed.*] ⟨He was
so dreadfully all-of-a-piece,
his attitude is always so consistent and urbane. He has to go⟩
⌜Moral America! Most moral
Benjamin! *P* He had to go⌝
MS8
25:19 ⟨And o⟩⌜O⌝n
25:35 with.⟨"⟩⌜"⌝
26:2 Almost too ... [26:10] give it
    up.] ⟨But this is what a Prov-
    idence must lead to. A Prov-
    idence is a Provider for the
    universe, and the business of
    the provider is to get rid of ev-
    ery waster, even if this waster
    happen to be a part of the self-
    same created universe. When
    man sets out to have all things
    his own way he is bound to run
    up against a great many men.
    Even to establish the idea of
    equality he has to reckon with
    the men who do really feel the
    force of inequality. And then
    equality sharpens⟩ ⌜Almost
    too ... [26:5] ⌜⌜He even ... of
    seed.⌝⌝ ... give it up.⌝
26:17 ⟨turn on the good tap,"⟩ ⌜let
    the good tap flow,"⌝
26:19 tap." *A1*] tap." *P* Damn you,
    Benjamin. ⟨I'll see whether I

let you extirpate me. Perhaps
the Indians have let you put it
over them. More fool them.⟩
MS8

26:35 ⟨in⟩ ⌜the gods in⌝ other
27:8   ⟨even if it is cruel things.⟩ ⌜and
       say it hot.⌝
27:11 to the gods... Recognise...
       all order. *Ed.*] for your own
       soul, and ⟨try to fulfil the
       responsibility⟩ ⌜don't let any-
       body be it for you.⌝ *MS8*
       to... Recognize... order. *A1*
27:17 ⟨submit⟩ ⌜be killed⌝
27:18 same: the... inside you, or
       from... Holy Ghost. *A1*]
       same⟨.⟩ ⌜: the... inside you.⌝
27:26 ⟨the gods⟩ ⌜ideals⌝
27:32 ⟨7⟩⌜8⌝/ The... never just.
       [marked in *MS8* to follow
       l. 31]
28:10 ⟨desire⟩ ⌜issue⌝
28:10 that⌜.⌝ ⟨deepest desire.⟩
28:15 ⟨true⟩ passional ⟨desire,⟩
       ⌜impulse,⌝
28:16 being⟨,⟩⌜;⌝
28:18 ⌜Only know... nothing else.⌝
28:22 See all... the barren *A1*]
       Recognise the ⟨gods⟩

⌜changes⌝ in yourself, and in
other men or women *MS8*

28:24 ⟨follow⟩ ⌜realise⌝
28:28 ⟨real⟩ freedom
28:30 barbed⌜-⌝wire
28:31 Chicagoes. ⟨And how⟩ ⌜*P* And
       how⌝
28:36 -tails. ⟨And how⟩ ⌜*P* And how⌝
29:2   ⟨And⟩ ⌜But⌝
29:6   SOMEOFUS⟨mmanages⟩
       ⌜, manages⌝
29:9   do ⟨not [?]⟩ NEVI'
29:10 ⟨But⟩ ⌜And⌝
29:10 little ⟨little⟩
29:14 ⟨get them⟩ ⌜round them up⌝
29:17 ⟨slave⟩ ⌜servant⌝
29:17 ⌜own⌝
29:28 broken⌜,⌝
29:30 ⟨revolution.⌝ [type]⟩ rebel-
       lion.
29:34 ⟨whole⟩ nature
30:2   ⌜same⌝
30:17 steps ⟨in⟩ ⌜of⌝
30:20 the inner gods, should *A1*]
       IT⟨,⟩⌜,⌝ will *MS8*
30:23 ⌜for this⌝
30:27 ⟨an ide [type]⟩ a pattern
30:35 heaped⌜-⌝up
31:6   strangled ⟨i⟩⌜o [type]⌝n

Henry St. John de Crèvecoeur

32:4   ⟨he came⟩ ⌜he was sent⌝
32:4   ⟨Europe [type]⟩ ⌜England
       [type]⌝
32:5   Canada⟨,⟩ ⌜as a young man,⌝
32:9   wrote ⟨his⟩ ⌜the⌝
32:10 ⌜especially⌝
32:19 ⟨this⟩ ⌜the⌝
32:21 litte⌜'⌝rateur Child⌜-⌝of⌜-⌝
       Nature⌜-⌝sweet⌜-⌝and⌜-⌝pure
32:23 d⟨e⟩⌜'⌝Houdetot
32:25 *Letters... Farmer. A1*]
       ⌜"⌝Letters... Farmer.⌜"⌝
32:31 Cooper⟨.⟩⌜, as a boy.⌝

32:32 practical ⌜*underlining added*⌝
32:34 dollar⌜-⌝fiend
33:2   ⟨[...]y⟩ they
33:10 NATURE. ⟨Cheap too.⟩
33:29 N⟨O⟩ ⌜o⌝
33:31 ⟨might⟩ ⌜may⌝
34:8   she ⌜*underlining added*⌝
34:20 ⟨H⟩⌜h⌝uman
34:26 ⟨so [?] (type)⟩ she
34:29 sweet⌜-⌝and⌜-⌝pure
34:38 isn't⟨.⟩ ⌜anything.⌝
35:10 sweet⌜-⌝and⌜-⌝pureness
35:11 ⟨romantic⟩ ⌜ideal⌝

35:24 ⟨respectable⟩ ⌜decent⌝
36:2 triumph⟨.⟩ ⌜, in the usurped home.⌝
36:8 sun⟨,⟩
36:9 wing⌜s⌝
36:31 ⌜Lions no ... spots!⌝
36:32 read ⟨often⟩
36:32 ⌜elsewhere,⌝,
36:32 W.H.Hudson⟨.⟩⌜, for example.⌝
36:34 ⟨tartar.⟩ ⌜raging lion.⌝
36:36 ⌜like [type]⌝
36:39 ⟨when⟩ ⌜where⌝
37:4 cold⌜-⌝/ cleaving
37:10 ⟨marvellous⟩ ⌜fine⌝
37:28 ⟨benevolence⟩ ⌜sweet-and-pureness⌝
37:30 ophiolat⟨o⟩ry
38:6 sophisticated⟨,⟩ and⟨,⟩ therefore⟨,⟩
38:13 ⟨⟨unde⟨n[?]⟩⌜fil [Mountsier]⌝ed⟩⟩ ⌜⌜undefiled [DHL]⌝⌝
38:26 ⟨know⟩ ⌜imagine⌝
38:26 ⟨within the unlimited sensual impulse.⟩ ⌜to get ... head.⌝
38:27 ⟨But this desire in him was very strictly kept down by a fixed will. For⟩ ⌜He was ... same time⌝
38:34 ⌜But yet ... wish-fulfilment.⌝
39:5 But comfortably ... [39:22] you like.] ⟨⟨But to have it he must forfeit all his fraternity and equality, his belief in a world of pure, sweet goodness, ⟨in⟩ the oneness of all things, and, above all, he must forfeit his own will, which insists that the world shall be so, because it is easiest so. And he will die rather than forfeit his fixed will and his fixed intention. He will {will TCC7C} have life, according to his own prescription, come what may. And life actually is not {is not TCC7C} according to his prescription. So he eschews life, and goes off into sentimental, idyllic fancy, and into practical commerce, both of which he can {can TCC7C} have as he likes it. For though he has a hankering after the wild, sensual life, he so hates the true, sensual mystery of otherness, and of proud culmination, that he will do anything to deny this mystery, and to down it. So he is divided against himself, which makes for madness.⟩⟩ ⌜But comfortably ... [39:9] ⟨of a world⟩ ⟨⟨⌜⌜of a⟩⟩ wor⌜⌜⌜l⌝⌝⌝d⌝⌝ ... you like.⌝
39:23 ⌜staying away and⌝
39:27 ⟨a taste.⟩ ⌜self-provoked.⌝
40:4 The hunter is a killer.] ⟨The hunter, like the soldier, is engaged in the effort to win the fatal ascendancy, the last, over the enemy or the prey. This is the sensual passion in its overweening, destructive activity, the terrible consummation in death.⟩ ⌜The hunter is a killer.⌝
40:5 ⟨sensual⟩ birth
40:8 ⟨strange⟩ ⌜heavy⌝
40:9 humility. The toiling ... [40:13] the doing.] humility⟨, no ecstasy of selfless communing in oneness. It is the dark reality of blood-mastery and blood-sympathy.⟩ ⌜. The

toiling... ⌜⌜For⌝⌝ ⟨Which is⟩ which[?]⟩⟩ ⌜⌜this reason⌝⌝ ... the doing.⌝

40:29 Indians⌜'⌝

40:33 Our cat... thousands of] ⟨Crevecoeur's ⌜Crêvecoeur's *TCC7C*⌝ thousands of instances against not even one instance remind us of our cat and another. Some children may have refused to return to their European parents—but the thought of thousands of these⟩ ⌜Our cat... thousands of⌝

40:35 ⌜white⌝

40:35 turning resolutely... [41:8] ye gods!] ⟨is too good a picture to be true. Also we know that some Indian brides of white men became very good civilised matrons. *P* The truth remains the same, as another century has proved it—it is easier to turn white men into Indians than Indians into white men. Crevecoeur

{Crêvecoeur *TCC7C*} exulted in the thought. He disliked civilisation even whilst he continued one of the most civilised of all beings. He knew the awful barrenness even of emotional self-gratification. He knew the dreariness of living from the pre-determined will, admitting no otherness, only the mechanical oneness, as of two buttons from the same machine. He wanted equality and fraternity, and he would allow nothing else. At the same time he wanted to know the thing {know the mystery of the essential being. He wanted to know the thing *TCC7C*} which he determinedly excluded from knowledge. Which cannot be done. He wanted to have his cake and eat it— the very nice⟩ ⌜turning resolutely... ye gods!⌝

Fenimore Cooper's White Novels

42:6 ⟨that way.⟩ ⌜if you kept on.⌝

42:12 ⌜wherever they are,⌝

42:19 ⟨dispossed [type]⟩ ⌜dispossessed [type]⌝

42:19 ⟨⟨li⟨[...] [type]⟩⌜e [type]⌝e⟩⟩ ⌜⌜life⌝⌝

42:34 of the ⟨old⟩ demon

43:10 ⟨A⟩ white

43:16 soil.⌜'⌝

43:28 ⟨o⟩⌜i [type]⌝f

43:32 ⟨lea [type]⟩ makes

44:2 ⟨They⟩ ⌜The two⌝

44:6 on⟨[...]⟩ ⌜.—⌝ Malice⟨.⟩⌜!⌝

44:7 ⌜It may... unconscious.⌝

44:27 ⟨stuff [type]⟩ thing

44:28 ⟨started as⟩ ⌜was⌝

44:29 His] H⟨e⟩⌜is [type]⌝

44:29 Coopers⌜-⌝Town

44:32 ⟨eighteenth century w[type]⟩ ⌜It is amazing how [type]⌝

44:33 ⟨were⟩ ⌜are⌝

44:35 ⟨old⟩ ⌜elderly⌝

44:36 hoydenish ⟨in comparison.⟩ ⌜, judged... standards.⌝

44:38 America⟨,⟩⌜;⌝

45:1 are. Cooper *Ed.*] are./ ⟨In this matter of refined material culture, external and disillusioned, the Americans were ahead even of the French.) Cooper *MS8* are./ Cooper *MS8R* are. *P* Cooper *A1*

45:2 *"L'Amérique... mûre." Per, A1*] "L'Ame⌐´⌐rique... mu⌐ᐧ⌐re." *MS8R*

45:5 ⌐Cooper's novels... novels first.⌐

45:17 ⟨public⟩ ⌐ideal⌐

45:17 ⟨a dreadful, self-determined thing, cold and mechanical and factitious.⟩ ⌐We have... admired.⌐

45:20 Oh Septimus... [45:34] Spat on!] ⟨No European writer has ever given us such a completely detestable picture of an American as did the American Cooper. Septimus Dodge is the object of loathing and contempt to the Effinghams. Yet they cannot get away from him—neither on ship-board nor even when they reach their own estates. He is the bugbear of their lives—but he is the inevitable negative pole of their Americanism. *P* Mr. Dodge, the democrat, of Dodgetown, alternately fawns and⟩ ⌐Oh Septimus... [45:29] ⟨ashes⟩ ⌐⌐scum⌐⌐... Vandal⟨s⟩⌐⌐ism.⌐⌐... [45:32] ⟨Venus⟩ ⌐⌐dame⌐⌐... [45:34] who⌐⌐m⌐⌐... ⟨spit⟩ ⌐⌐spat⌐⌐ on⌐⌐.⌐⌐ ⟨her.⟩ Spat on!⌐

45:39 down, ⟨don't⟩

45:39 ⟨in⟩upside down

46:7 ⌐the⌐

46:8 ha⟨d⟩s

46:20 ⟨a⟩⌐A⌐merican

46:41 ⟨mi⟩ right

47:6 ⟨is⟩ equal ⟨to⟩ ten

47:13 ⌐to the chin⌐

47:18 ⟨And t⟩⌐T⌐hey

47:23 ⟨But⟩ ⌐For⌐

47:34 ⟨and⟩ since

48:24 Say, couldn't... nearer. *A1*] ⟨Had you nothing nearer at hand to admire, then?⟩ ⌐Say, could nt... nearer.⌐ *MS8*

48:29 superior ⟨then⟩,

48:31 ⟨all⟩ the Dodges

49:4 ⟨Supposing Septimus came to the Court of King Arthur, and said pleasantly: "Good morning⟩ ⌐Septimus at... Hello⌐

49:7 Th⟨at⟩is

49:11 ⟨That is so.⟩ ⌐Yes.⌐

49:12 ⌐about⌐

49:12 ⟨those few yards⟩ ⌐that yard-and-a-half⌐

49:13 ⟨about⟩ with.

49:14 ⟨all this time.⟩ ⌐for quite a while.⌐

49:15 ⟨e⟩⌐E⌐xcalibur

50:1 ⌐"Naked to... [50:4] spear—"⌐

50:22 ⌐in⌐

50:28 is ⟨just⟩ a

50:31 ⟨godly⟩ than

50:32 ⟨do⟩ ⌐give⌐

Fenimore Cooper's Leatherstocking Novels

52:5 ⟨flies⟩ ⌐Americans⌐

52:6 ⟨against⟩ ⌐except⌐

52:18 word⌐.⌐ ⟨: i⟩⌐I⌐n

52:31 ⟨he⟩ ⌐it⌐

52:31 ⟨think⟩ ⌐know⌐

53:16 ⟨spite of⟩ ⌐through⌐

53:18 ⟨a⟩⌐A⌐mericans

53:25 ⌐being⌐

53:26   went home to his WIFE. *A1*]
⟨didn't want on[e.]⟩ ⌜went
home.⌝ *MS8*
53:30   ⟨a⟩ ⌜his⌝
53:32   ⟨and⟩ ⌜while⌝
53:33   ⌜was⌝
53:34   ⌜was⌝
54:7   coat⟨s⟩
54:18   ⌜The coarser . . . to see.⌝
54:25   way. ⟨Have aboriginal
America all his own wa[y.]⟩
54:27   ⟨you⟩ ⌜he⌝
54:28   an⟨d⟩y
55:4   ⟨nineteenth⟩ ⌜eighteenth⌝
55:7   ⟨Englis⟩ ⌜British⌝
55:8   ⟨Indians,⟩ ⌜with Indians . . .
sides,⌝
55:10   ⌜conducted by . . . of life;⌝
55:14   in a chair on *Ed.*] ⌜a chair on⌝
on
55:17   ⟨niece of a sea-faring man.⟩
⌜daughter . . . Fort.⌝
55:19   ⟨Chingachgook, his Indian
blood brother, are both
youth/ virgin in the⟩ ⌜Hurry
Harry . . . hunting in the⌝
55:23   ⟨the Scout⟩, Pathfinder
55:24   ⟨bitterness⟩ ⌜impatience⌝
55:27   ⟨reality,⟩ ⌜actuality,⌝
55:31   ⟨a⟩America
55:33   often⟨.⟩ ⌜, than . . . there.⌝
55:40   it⟨.⟩ ⌜, and . . . common-
sensical.⌝
56:5   ⌜in actuality⌝
56:14   ⌜Renegade.⌝
56:15   ⟨The r⟩⌜R⌝enegade
57:4   ⟨just⟩ a

57:22   ⟨psyche⟩ monster
57:29   t⟨oo⟩o you
59:4   ⌜ridiculous,⌝
59:10   romantic. ⟨Sugar-plums.⟩
59:14   ⟨gorgeous⟩ ⌜resplendent⌝
59:30   ⟨realises⟩ ⌜finds⌝
59:39   ⟨really⟩ ⌜quite⌝
59:40   a ⟨lie.⟩
60:1   ⟨inevitably⟩ ⌜surely⌝
60:1   ⟨one day.⟩ some
60:31   ⟨P⟩⌜p⌝rairies
60:37   ⟨evil,⟩ ⌜crime,⌝
61:2   ⌜beneath him are⌝
61:4   ⟨But i⟩⌜I⌝n
61:7   ⟨P⟩⌜p⌝rairie
61:33   ⟨the⟩ her
61:38   ⟨a little stupid or dull.⟩
⌜limited . . . *borné.*⌝
62:7   passionate⟨,⟩
62:8   ⟨some⟩ ⌜a⌝
62:18   ⟨⟨wom⟨e [?]⟩⌜a⌝nless⟩⟩
⌜⌜womanless⌝⌝
62:29   in *Deerslayer Ed.*] ⌜in
Deerslayer⌝ *MS8*
62:34   ⟨g⟩⌜G⌝reat
62:38   ⟨I'll bet⟩ ⌜No doubt⌝
63:10   ⟨higher⟩ ⌜diffcrent⌝ things.
⟨Or for other things.⟩
63:41   ⌜coarse,⌝
64:13   ⟨H⟩ Thomas
64:20   qui⟨t⟩⌜e⌝t
64:38   Being ⟨the⟩
64:40   meat-fly⌜.⌝ ⟨, Harry.⟩
65:7   life": with . . . and spite. *Ed.*]
life⟨.⟩⌜:⌝" ⌜with . . . ⟨sin⟩ sin
and spite.⌝ life," with . . . and
spite. *A1*

Edgar Allan Poe

66:11   ⟨Hence he is⟩ ⌜This makes
him⌝
66:16   ⟨disintegrated⟩ ⌜broken down⌝
66:26   ⟨metal⟩ ⌜salt⌝

66:32   ⟨disintegrative⟩ ⌜disruptive⌝
67:29   ⟨blood,⟩ love
68:2   itself⟨.⟩ ⌜, it . . . isolation.⌝
68:35   ⟨But⟩ Poe

69:9 ⌜sympathetic⌝
69:20 ⟨to an extreme.⟩ ⌜over a ⟨⟨ver⟩⟩
   verge.⌝
69:20 ⟨an⟩ extreme⌜s⌝
69:22 ⟨now⟩ ⌜become⌝
69:25 ⟨lo⟩ will
69:28 ⟨so⟩ tall
69:34 a ⟨met⟩
69:40 ⟨p⟩⌜P⌝oe's
70:14 was ⟨of⟩
70:23 ⟨summer⟩⌜midsummer⌝
70:38 ⟨of⟩ oh wom⟨e⟩⌜a⌝n⟨,⟩⌜,⌝
70:40 ⌜to *get* you,⌝
71:2 and ⌜of⌝
71:33 ⟨⟨ma ⟨<t>nner⟩⟩ ⌜manner⌝
72:3 "Vultures] ⟨"Stern⟩ ⌜"⌝vultures
72:3 ⌜stern⌝
72:20 confessions⟨."⟩⌜"⌝
72:32 from ⟨them⟩ ⌜him⌝
73:23 ⟨the⟩ ⌜its⌝
73:28 forgiven? ⟨A⟩
73:29 ⟨voice⟩ ⌜thing⌝
73:33 ⌜particularly at ourselves,⌝
74:7 ⟨comes⟩ ⌜goes⌝
74:13 ⌜Poor Poe!⌝
74:31 she ⌜too⌝
74:32 as ⟨an⟩
74:36 ⟨from⟩ through
74:39 For it . . . [75:6] of America.]
   ⟨are one, and neither exists. They are consumed into
   an instrutable {inscrutable
   TCC7C} oneness.⟩ ⌜For
   it . . . of America.⌝
75:11 own images [*underlining
   added*]
75:12 wave: out of . . . that is. *A1*]
   wave⟨.⟩ ⌜: of . . . that is.⌝
75:17 ⟨The symbolism of Poe's
   parables is easy, too easy,
   almost mechanical.⟩ ⌜Every-
   thing . . . [75:21] sex-palaver.⌝
75:23 ⟨take⟩ ⌜pull out⌝

75:31 ⟨somewhat connected⟩⌜linking
   up⌝
75:37 But it . . . [76:8] bitter end.]
   ⟨But this will not do. The
   incest-desire is only one of
   the manifestations of the selfless desire for merging. It
   is obvious that this desire
   for merging, or unification,
   {unification *TCC7*} or identification of the man with the
   woman, or the woman with
   the man, finds its gratification
   most readily in the merging
   of those things which are already near—mother with son,
   brother with sister, father with
   dau{g *MS8R*}ther. But it is
   not enough to say, as Jung
   does, that all life is a matter of
   lapsing towards, or struggling
   away from, mother-incest. It
   is necessary to see what lies
   at the back of this helpless
   craving for utter merging or
   identification with a beloved.⟩
   ⌜But it . . . [75:38] get the⌜⌜ir⌝⌝
   . . . [76:5] g⟨l⟩⌜⌜r⌝⌝ass, even
   . . . bitter end.⌝
76:10 from ⟨De⟩
76:14 overdone⌜,⌝
76:36 ⟨rich⟩ ⌜true⌝
76:39 ⟨It is probably that even
   t⟩⌜T⌝he
77:4 ⟨dissolution.⟩ ⌜material
   existence.⌝
77:17 form[*underlining added*]
77:28 ⌜But while . . . ⟨they had>
   ⌜⌜having⌝⌝ lost their integral
   souls.⌝
77:36 this process . . . [78:1] be
   sucked.] ⟨where human creatures are absorbed away from

themselves, into a unification in death. So Madeline
was gradually absorbed into
her brother; the one life
absorbed the other in a
long anguish of love.) ⌜this
process ... [77:37] extreme
exa⟨[...]⟩⌜⌜lta⌝tion ... be
sucked.⌝

78:13 ⟨again the⟩ ⌜the same⌝
78:24 ⟨really is a symbolic truth⟩ ⌜is
true ... truth⌝
78:25 ⟨inordinate⟩ ⌜beloved⌝
78:25 cannot be ... [78:36] another
being.] ⟨can recognise none
of the sacred mystery of
otherness, but must unite into
unspeakable identification,
oneness in death. Brother
and sister go down together,
made one in the unspeakable
mystery of death. It is the
world-long incest problem,
arising inevitably when man,
through insistence of his will
in one passion or aspiration,
breaks the polarity of himself.⟩
⌜cannot be ... [78:30] listening ⌜⌜in⌝⌝ ... [78:34] dragged
⟨it⟩ ... another being.⌝
79:18 ⌜Becomes a monster.⌝
79:31 ⟨utterly to possess the soul of
the murdered⟩ ⌜to get ... kill
it⌝
80:1 ⟨Inquis⟩ition ⌜Inquisition⌝
80:2 between ⟨conqueror⟩
⌜inquisitor⌝
80:2 as to ... [80:11] and more.]
⟨for the possession of the soul
after death. A soul can be conquered only when it is forced
to abdicate from its own being. A heretic may be burned

at the stake, his ashes scattered
on the winds as a symbol that
his soul is now broken by torture and dissolved. And yet, as
often as not, the brave heretic
dies integral in being, his
soul re-enters into the bosom
of the living, indestructible.⟩
⌜as to ... [80:5] as ⟨today⟩ the
... and more.⌝

80:15 ⟨incalculable influence⟩
⌜yearning⌝
80:15 ⟨of⟩ ⌜the burning of⌝
80:17 But he ... [80:36] particular.]
⟨The necessity to love is probably the source of all our unhappiness; but since it is the
source of everything it is foolish to particularise. Probably even gravitation is only
one of the lowest manifestations of the mystic force
of love. But the triumph of
love, which is the triumph of
life and creation, does not lie
in merging, mingling, in absolute identification of the
lover with the beloved. It
lies in the communion of beings, who, in the very perfection of communion, recognise
and allow the mutual oth-
erness. There is no desire
to transgress the bounds of
being. Each self remains utterly itself—becomes, indeed,
most burningly and transcendently itself in the uttermost
embrace or communion with
the other. One self may yield
honourable precedence to the
other, may pledge itself to
undying service, and in so

doing become fulfilled in its own nature. For the highest achievement of some souls lies in perfect service. But the giving and the taking of service does not obliterate the mystery of otherness, the being-in-singleness, either in master or servant. On the other hand, slavery is an avowed obliteration of the singleness of being.) ⌜P But he... [80:19] to the ⟨h⟩⌜H⌝oly... [80:24] ⟨saw⟩ ⌜knew⌝ only... particular.⌝

Nathaniel Hawthorne and *The Scarlet Letter*

81:5   ⟨What do we mean by⟩ ⌜And what's⌝
81:5   ⟨we mean⟩ a
81:8   *Morte D' Arthur. A1*] ⌜Morte D'Arthur.⌝ *MS8R*
81:10 ⟨ever⟩ has
81:13 ⟨a⟩⌜A⌝merican
81:26 *Destroy*⟨,⟩⌜!⌝ *destroy*⟨,⟩⌜!⌝ *destroy*⟨,⟩⌜!⌝
81:33 ⟨a⟩ the growing
82:8   *The A1*] ⟨t⟩⌜T⌝he *MS8R*
82:12 "sin"] ⟨sun⟩ "sin"
83:13 mind-consciousness⌜.⌝ ⟨and⟩
83:20 ⌜That is our cross.⌝
83:21 ⟨I [...]⟩ it
83:25 ⟨with⟩ heavy
83:32 ⟨They⟩ ⌜Her sons⌝
84:1   ⟨isn't participating. It is left out, co[a?]nnulled. *P* When⟩ ⌜is chemically... [84:4] ponderously. *P*⌝ Americans
84:6   ⟨them.⟩ ⌜it.⌝
84:7   ⟨mindlessly,⟩ with
84:7   blood-consciousness ⌜active,⌝,
84:14 mind⟨:⟩ ⌜(⌝you
84:17 ⟨in⟩ ⌜with⌝
85:3   ⟨All a trick.⟩ ⌜⌜Then t⌝⌝⟨⟨⌜T⟩⟩he prettiest... self-conceit.⌝
85:11 ⟨second⟩ ⌜*first*⌝
85:13 it⟨.⟩ ⌜, and try to understand.⌝
85:16 ⟨s⟩⌜S⌝in

85:27 ⌜pure⌝
85:28 pure] ⌜pure⌝
87:2   ⟨parsons⟩ ⌜clergymen⌝
87:21 ⌜with the mind,⌝—
87:21 for⟨.⟩ ⌜, with whips.⌝
87:22 ⟨spirit⟩ shall
87:27 ⌜*Lash!* I... Hurray!⌝
87:32 He⟨l⟩⌜e⌝l
88:16 ⟨a⟩ the
88:17 when⌜, as men,⌝
88:18 ⟨as⟩ whole ⟨men⟩
88:18 just crawl, and] ⟨are⟩ just ⟨dished,⟩ ⌜crawl,⌝ and ⟨they⟩
88:19 ⌜the⌝ females
89:5   ⟨i⟩⌜a⌝n
89:9   Letter. ⟨That's how things are!⟩
89:11 ⟨lie,⟩ ⌜man,⌝
89:15 ⟨thought⟩ ⌜kept on thinking⌝
89:17 ⟨kept,⟩ ⌜held,⌝
89:23 ⟨united⟩ ⟨⟨⌜muted [?]⌝⟩⟩ ⌜⌜united⌝⌝
89:23 ⟨and⟩ ⌜or American woman or⌝
89:28 h⟨is⟩⌜e⌝
89:31 bec⟨a⟩omes
89:38 ⟨inf⟩ invisible
90:24 ⟨He⟩ ⌜If he⌝
90:38 ⟨Eve to his bosom, she either bites him time after time with repeated poison, or⟩ ⌜sugarplum in... so loving,⌝
91:3   ⟨never,⟩ never

91:10 ⟨this⟩ ⌜the above⌝
91:11 ⟨fi⟩ laboring
91:20 ⟨an infinite⟩ ⌜a whole new⌝
91:21 ⟨male⟩ principle
91:24 ⟨fa⟩ more
91:24 ⟨fathomlessly⟩ ⌜newly⌝
91:25 ⟨break⟩ ⌜have at last broken⌝
91:27 ⟨pal⟩ phallic
91:32 ⟨my⟩ martyr
92:6   ⟨The next mo⟩ ⌜The next⌝
92:17 ⟨never⟩ ⌜not⌝
92:19 ⟨we⟩ ⌜the outcast woman and I⌝
92:19 ⟨tame⟩ ⌜meek-looking⌝
92:25 seduced⟨. And⟩ ⌜, and ... dear. And⌝
92:38 still. ⟨And⟩
93.4   ⟨Evil⟩ ⌜Malevolence⌝

93:5   ⟨good⟩ benevolence
93:26 ⌜Hits ... own mother.⌝
93:32 ⟨an⌝ ⟨a dis⟩order
93:34 ⟨dis⟩order ⟨was⟩ ⌜is⌝
93:35 ⟨here:⟩ ⌜this:⌝
94:5   ⟨"⟩A
94:5   ⟨false⟩ ⌜saintly⌝
94:8   ⟨moke.⟩ ⌜fraud. And⌝ ⟨S⟩⌜s⌝he
94:31 ⌜It was ... Victoria.⌝
94:33 ⌜He is ... tradition.⌝
95:14 ⌜And the ... triumph⌜⌜.⌝⌝ ⟨was. [?]⟩ ... still.⌝
95:20 ⟨triumph⟩ ⌜"coup"⌝
95:25 ⟨the⟩ be
95:26 ⌜And Hester ... rebelling.⌝
95:29 literature, ⟨is⟩
95:32 ⟨its⟩ ⌜his⌝

Hawthorne's *Blithedale Romance*

96:5   ⟨perfect⟩ ⌜complete⌝
96:9   ⟨were⟩ did
96:10 ⟨bel⟩ be
96:14 ⟨at⟩ ⌜of⌝
96:16 invent⌜s⌝
96:19 ⟨he⟩⌜Man⌝
96:28 ⟨eig [eag?]⟩ either
96:28 ⟨profoundly,⟩ ⌜sincerely,⌝
97:32 ⟨the⟩ ⌜her⌝ game, ⟨being cast before swine.⟩ ⌜part of her pearldom⌝
97:35 ⟨n⟩⌜N⌝emesis
98:2   Son *A1*] Beloved ⟨s⟩⌜S⌝on *MS8*
98:7   ⟨H⟩⌜h⌝*im*
98:36 dark ⟨, aboriginal⟩
98:39 ⟨dark⟩ old
99:2   ⟨A⟩ ⌜No⌝
99:19 ⟨reality⟩ ⌜actuality⌝
99:20 ⟨famous⟩ ⌜notorious⌝
99:21 ⌜of America⌝
99:24 ⟨spr⟩ strings
99:31 bookfarming *A1*] ⟨inventing machines, to do the work for them.⟩ ⌜bookfarming. Those that didn't turn to the inventing of machines that should settle hard work, break its back for ever.⌝ *MS8*
100:1 other⟨.⟩ ⌜, turn and about.⌝
100:31 ⟨Mary Davis [?], the famous American feminist.⟩ ⌜Margaret Fuller, ⌜⌜in⌝⌝ ... nature."⌝
100:32 ⟨saw her⟩ ⌜was more ... Zenobia's⌝
100:33 ⟨rather⟩ than ⌜of⌝
101:4 ⟨Scene⟩ ⌜Plot⌝
101:11 ⟨that⟩ Hephaestos
101:11 ⌜Hates him ... monomaniac.⌝
101:32 ⟨meeth⟩ meets
101:39 expensive⟨.⟩ ⌜, lurid with money.⌝
102:1 ⌜the imitation pearl,⌝
102:4 ⟨ghost⟩ ⌜degenerate⌝
102:16 ⟨canary⟩ ⌜hen⌝
102:19 ⟨Your⟩ ⌜A⌝

102:21 ⟨sol [?]⟩ soul
102:30 ⌜dead⌝
103:23 ⟨fact⟩ acceptance
103:26 Ghost⟨s⟩

103:27 ⟨h⟩⌜H⌝oly
103:28 fe⟨els⟩⌜ll⌝
103:29 by this time ⟨sti⟩ he stinketh
103:37 ⟨b⟩⌜B⌝lack

Dana's *Two Years Before the Mast*

105:11 ⟨rolling⟩ ⌜coming⌝
105:22 ⟨Ah no.⟩ None.
105:31 ⟨makes⟩ ⌜has made⌝
106:1 ⟨⟨len⟨se⟩⌜s⌝⟩⟩ lens
106:5 ⟨and become a universal/⟩ ⌜exalt the...universal idea,⌝
106:7 ⟨a⟩⌜A⌝merican
106:7 ⟨national⟩ ⌜local⌝
106:21 Absolutely fail⟨s⟩
106:23 ⌜The most vivid failure.⌝
106:37 ⟨know,⟩ ⌜KNOW,⌝
106:38 ⟨know⟩ ⌜KNOW⌝
107:9 ⟨It is Dan's first days out at sea, winter, the Atlantic.⟩ ⌜And so...the Atlantic:⌝
107:29 The best Americans...instinct. *A1*] ⌜The Americans...instinct.⌝ *MS8*
108:6 death⟨.⟩ ⌜, in KNOWLEDGE ...Cross.⌝
109:33 ⟨h⟩⌜H⌝arry
110:5 ⟨evolution⟩ evolution
110:13 we⟨a⟩⌜e⌝ks
110:36 ⟨There is some⟩ ⌜You have a⌝
110:37 we⟨a⟩⌜e⌝ks
110:39 ⟨i⟩⌜o⌝n
112:35 was ⟨the⟩
113:11 ⟨true passional⟩ ⌜ordinary⌝
113:11 ⟨There was no vindinctiveness, even no violation.⟩ ⌜Sam got...event.⌝
113:15 respect⌜ed⌝
113:37 The case...[114:4] idealism!] ⟨It is the Johns of this world who stultify life, swathe it and strangle it with false emotions, dictated from a theory. And it is the Danas who, fixing the

⟨eht⟩ {the *TCC7C*} ry and the moral deduction, are ten times damnable. In this case, however, owing to conventional ethics, it was upon the captain that the stigma remained. He should have remembered the awful powers of public opinion: particularly Dana.⟩ ⌜The case...idealism!⌝

114:21 ⟨again⟩ ⌜almost⌝
114:30 ⌜Think of...guns.⌝
114:31 ⟨real passion⟩ ⌜strong human emotion⌝
115:13 ⌜saviour-like⌝
115:14 ⟨to⟩ ⌜for a moment to⌝
115:16 ⟨But in life he is barely more than a moment to Dana: a living being, and therefore far more ephemeral than a moral judgment.⟩ ⌜But only...being.⌝
115:22 ⌜He is...forgetting.⌝
117:4 ⌜conscious⌝
117:9 He KNOWS...[117:16] The ship] ⟨He has entered into a new state of mind, a new field of consciousness is awake in him, he has won to a freer ideal self. He is victorious over the vast primordial element, the one-half of the world of death. Now he can continue in a further progressive social life, a higher idealism. *P* So t⟩ ⌜He KNOWS...and——*P* T⌝he ship
117:26 ⟨great⟩ elements

118:9 ⟨⟨Shan⟨ys⟩⌐go⌐⟩⟩ ⌐⌐Shango⌐⌐
120:27 ⟨effect⟩ ⌐result⌐
120:28 We are ... [121:18] don't know.] ⟨Certain substances seem active against the life-principle itself, thus providing, in small quantities, a stimulus. Salt, sulphur, the acids, are instances. They all seem to have a mysterious power for driving asunder the fire and water which are in vital combination in a living organism, preventing any further conjunction of fire and water, so that growth and decay—which after all depends on life—are alike arrested. Salt is one of the elements in which water seems predominant and vindictive. It has a curious power to penetrate into all living tissue, liberating the water from its conjunction with fire. Hence the dropsy-like symptoms of scurvy. Any substance which is in the grip of salt seems to be in the grip of the overweening watery principle, and procreant fire is excluded. It is strange to try to think what effect the salt seas must have upon the atmosphere of the world. [*page removed from MS8*] these acts upon the body, in small quantities, as a stimulus. In large quantities, they cause death. The reason is obvious. *P* Science, to whom the material-dynamic world is given over, knows none of the great secrets of matter or of *dunamis*. ⌐We are ... don't know.⌐

Herman Melville's *Typee* and *Omoo*

122:15 ⟨real⟩ ⌐modern⌐ vi⟨c[?]⟩ ⌐k⌐ing
122:24 ⌐too⌐
122:30 dead⟨.⟩ ⌐, and by this time he stinketh.⌐
122:31 fall⟨.⟩ ⌐into water.⌐
123:26 ⟨o⟩⌐O⌐cean
123:27 ⟨o⟩⌐O⌐ceans
123:32 ⟨pa⟩ Pacific
124:20 ghost⟨e [?]⟩⌐l⌐y
124:21 the/ ⟨the⟩ end
124:24 it⟨.⟩ ⌐, more than Melville did.⌐
125:2 ⟨consciously. Consciously,⟩ ⌐choosingly. Choosingly,⌐ ... ⟨Unconsciously⟩ ⌐Unchoosingly,⌐
125:15 ⟨m⟩Melville's
125:19 ⟨then⟩ is
125:22 ⟨discovered⟩ ⌐called upon and found⌐
125:26 ⟨savagest⟩ ⌐ugliest⌐

125:30 ⟨it.⟩ ⌐this.⌐
125:31 ⟨ceremonious⟩ ⌐fiercely reserved⌐
125:37 in ⟨the⟩
126:1 ⟨equivocation⟩ ⌐side-tracking⌐
126:16 ⟨like a lamplighter.⟩ ⌐as fast ... carry him.⌐
126:31 peoples⟨'⟩
127:19 ⌐Back to their uncreate condition.⌐
127:25 ⟨warm⟩ ⌐uncreate⌐
128:15 ⟨face⟩ ⌐throat⌐
128:18 ⟨keep⟩ ⌐detain⌐
128:22 ⟨in sight now.⟩ ⌐at the ... voyage.⌐
128:24 ⟨had *got*.⟩ ⌐really was⌐ Home ⟨and⟩ ⌐with⌐
128:24 ⟨them⟩ ⌐it⌐
128:26 ⟨almost⟩ murderous

128:26 ⟨with which he made his escape.⟩ ⌜which possessed him, to escape.⌝
128:29 ⟨frenzy.⟩ ⌜fever.⌝
128:30 ⟨that⟩ Paradise
128:30 ⌜was⌝ always ⟨found himself⟩
128:32 ⟨nature.⟩ ⌜destiny.⌝
128:34 ⟨silently⟩ ⌜slowly⌝
129:12 ⟨grind⟩ ⌜ground⌝
129:23 ⌜of the⌝
130:10 ⟨the Long Doctor.⟩ ⌜Doctor Long Ghost.⌝
130:19 ⟨Long⟩ Doctor ⌜Long⌝
130:21 ⟨revulsions⟩ ⌜bilious bouts⌝
130:24 ⟨really⟩ do
130:33 ⟨his⟩ ⌜Herman's⌝
130:37 ⟨Long⟩ Doctor ⌜Long⌝

130:39 ⟨thing⟩ thin
130:39 ⟨his⟩ ⌜Melville's⌝
131:4 ⟨away⟩ ⌜a long way⌝
131:6 ⌜same⌝
131:6 doorstep⌜.⌝ ⟨again.⟩
131:9 ⟨made⟩ ⌜furnished⌝ his home ⟨in⟩ ⌜with⌝ disillusion⟨.⟩ ⌜s.⌝
131:12 ⟨a⟩ being
131:32 ⟨against life.⟩ ⌜and rotten.⌝
131:33 ⟨a⟩ ⌜an impure⌝
131:34 ⟨evil,⟩ ⌜pernicious,⌝
131:34 ⟨evil.⟩ ⌜foul.⌝
131:35 ⟨evil,⟩ ⌜base,⌝
132:13 ⟨sh⟩ soul
132:14 ⌜"*Tous ... seuls.*"⌝
132:32 ⟨each,⟩ ⌜the other,⌝

Herman Melville's *Moby Dick*

133:9 O⟨h⟩⌜f⌝
133:11 ⟨m⟩Melville
133:15 worship⟨s⟩
133:24 ⟨one is⟩ ⌜you are⌝
133:24 journal⟨ism⟩⌜ese⌝
134:3 ⟨so weary⟩ ⌜the solemn ass⌝
134:15 cease⟨d⟩s
134:19 ⟨beings⟩ ⌜contacts⌝
134:24 ⟨even⟩ found
134:26 ⟨al [?]⟩ over
134:28 ⟨old⟩ ⌜old-fashioned⌝ ... ⟨old⟩ ⌜old-fashioned⌝
134:30 ⌜hugged⌝
134:31 ⟨with⟩ ⌜by⌝
134:32 ⟨incense⟩ ⌜burnt offering⌝
135:1 ⟨human connection⟩ ⌜any real human contact⌝
135:4 ⟨at all enters into the soul of⟩ ⌜really enters ... namely⌝
135:4 ⟨This is⟩ ⌜And then ... hearts-brother,⌝
135:28 ⌜"Which ... ⟨⟨thol⟩⟩ theology ... logic.— "Now⌝ ⟨Now⟩
136:13 ⟨for⟩ ⌜to⌝

136:14 ⟨Yet is it unreal?⟩ ⌜The voyage ... whaling-voyage too.⌝
136:16 ⟨It is a mythical, mystical voyage as any Argonaut voyage ever was. ⟨⟨⌜and prevents us from seeing his bare posterior, and his ethical silk hat sits most correctly over his brow.⌝ ⌜⌜The Argonauts ... [136:19] white whale.⌝⌝
136:25 beyond feeling *A1*⌝ ⟨like the Old Testament.⟩ ⌜beyond words.⌝ *MS8R*
137:5 ⟨now.⟩ ⌜by this.⌝
137:8 ⟨steadfast⟩ ⌜good responsible⌝
137:35 ⟨private⟩ ⌜own⌝
138:7 ⟨officered.⟩ ⌜handled.⌝
138:15 ⟨lapses.⟩ ⌜jolts.⌝
138:19 the overclouded *MS2*] ⟨a crowded⟩ the overcrowded
138:21 whiteness, / ⟨whiteness,⟩ and
138:30 ⟨We must remember that⟩ Melville's
139:1 ⟨[...]n⟩ ⌜up⌝

139:5 ⟨on [?]⟩ ⌜to⌝
143:11 ⟨makes a great impression on
him⟩ ⌜is a real soul-experience⌝
143:15 ⌜Perhaps it ... water-born.⌝
144:9 ⌜sundering⌝
145:16 ⟨described⟩ ⌜quoted⌝
145:35 ⌜The eagle ... Spirit. Sunk!⌝
146:13 if ⟨something⟩

146:27 ⟨spiritual⟩ ⌜white⌝
146:28 ⟨consciousness.⟩ ⌜will.⌝
146:33 ⟨upper control.⟩ ⌜the ideal
will.⌝
146:34 will. Our ... ideal consciousness. *A1*] will⟨.⟩⌜,Which is
slow but fatal suicide.⌝

Whitman

148:21 line⟨s⟩rs
149:3 ⟨an isolated⟩ ⌜a limited⌝
149:6 ⟨amorous love that⟩ stays
149:6 ⟨modester⟩ ⌜milder⌝
149:13 ⟨amorous love.⟩ ⌜AMOROUS
LOVE.⌝
149:18 ⟨amorous love⟩ ⌜AMOROUS
LOVE⌝
149:21 |They talk ... for animality.|
149:29 ⟨all⟩ ⌜most⌝
149:33 smell⟨,⟩
149:34 ⌜Even bees ... of bees.⌝
150:8 does⌜n't⌝ ⟨anything but⟩ ⌜by
any means⌝
150:9 ⟨dont want⟩ ⌜wouldn't⌝
150:21 ⌜It's a ... Self.⌝
150:33 Walt. ⟨If⟩
151:4 This ⟨al⟩
151:9 ⟨would⟩ ⌜will⌝
151:9 ha⟨s⟩d ... ha⟨s⟩d
151:11 ⟨could never have assumed⟩
⌜was not able to assume⌝
151:13 Chant⟨,⟩⌜s,⌝
151:16 ⟨But a⟩⌜A⌝s
152:25 ⟨s⟩⌜S⌝tates
153:30 ⟨for⟩ ⌜of⌝ comradeship
154:12 ⟨ined [?]⟩ inadequate
154:25 ⟨a⟩ ⌜the⌝ great poet ⌜he is⌝
155:24 ⟨great,⟩ ⌜wide,⌝
155:25 ground⟨.⟩ ⌜now.⌝
155:26 ⟨edge⟩ ⌜end⌝
155:38 moral⌜ist.⌝ ⟨artist.⟩
155:38 ⟨moral⟩ leader

155:38 ⟨In that, a true American.⟩ ⌜He
was ... of men.⌝
156:1 ⟨The same is true of all
American art. It⟩ ⌜Surely it
i⟨t⟩s ... that it⌝
156:7 ⟨all/ all American art:⟩ ⌜them:⌝
156:10 ⟨discard⟩ ⌜break⌝
156:31 ⟨by⟩ through Charity
156:31 ⌜Not through sacrifice.⌝
156:32 No⟨t⟩⌜r⌝
156:36 c⟨a⟩⌜o⌝me⌜s⌝
156:37 drift⟨ed⟩
156:39 ⟨a direction, however.⟩ ⌜no
known ... her going.⌝
157:1 ⟨And how shall we meet all
the other wayfarers? With⟩
⌜Meeting all ... With⌝
157:7 got ⟨the⟩
157:11 ⟨its⟩ ⌜her⌝ ... ⟨itself.⟩ ⌜herself.⌝
157:14 ⟨its⟩ ⌜her⌝
157:16 ⌜This was ... ⟨spoke⟩
⌜⌜speaking⌝⌝ ... aboriginal.⌝
157:22 ⟨a great⟩ ⌜the American⌝
157:25 ⟨step by step, in the⟩ ⌜as the
... opens⟨⟨,⟩⟩ ... keeping⌝
157:26 ⟨of⟩ ⌜with⌝
157:26 ⌜them⌝
157:28 ⟨of sympathy,⟩ ⌜into the
unknown,⌝
157:31 ⌜American|
157:38 ⟨to a certain extent, he
wanted to make⟩ ⌜because
he ... carried on⌝

157:39 ⌜as⌝
158:3 ⟨The same with⟩ ⌜He didn't follow⌝
158:3 ⟨s⟩⌜S⌝ympathy
158:6 ⟨a⟩ carrying
158:6 of ⟨L⟩love
158:11 ⟨or⟩ ⌜the Christian⌝ Love
158:12 ⌜The highroad ... compulsions.⌝
158:15 Whitman wanted ... [158:20] him his] ⟨He tried to do this, and failed through his inability to escape from the old mode and way of salvation. His Sympathy he only interpreted as a further extension of Love and Charity, an extension almost to madness and soul-death. This gives him his hectic,⟩ ⌜Whitman wanted ... [158:18] ⟨⟨s⟩⟩⌜⌜S⌝⌝ympathy ... him his⌝
158:21 ⌜really⌝
158:24 ⟨the⟩ ⟨⟨⌜his⌝⟩⟩⌜⌜the⌝⌝ soul
158:25 ⟨the⟩ ⌜his⌝ fate to ⌜her and to⌝
158:28 ⟨could n't quite bring it off.⟩ ⌜didn't ... out.⌝
159:11 Th⟨y[?]⟩⌜is⌝
159:11 ⟨love⟩ ⌜merging,⌝
159:17 ⌜help him⌝
159:19 free⟨.⟩ ⌜, if he ... help.⌝
159:20 ⟨wants⟩ ⌜needs⌝
159:24 ⟨I see⟩ ⌜Look at⌝
159:24 ⟨⟨I see⟩ ⌜H⌝⟨h⟩er soul has fallen under the lust of⟩⟩ ⌜⌜Her nature ... lust for⌝⌝
159:26 like⌜s⌝
159:27 ⟨might⟩ ⌜would⌝
159:30 soul.⟨"⟩
159:33 ⟨If I could I would⟩ ⌜We ought to⌝
160:1 body⟨. W⟩⌜: w⌝hen
160:3 syphilis⟨. W⟩⌜: w⌝hen

160:9 ⌜Her feeling ... hatred.⌝
160:12 ⟨the⟩ ⌜your⌝
160:14 ⟨the⟩ ⌜your⌝ soul
160:17 ⟨But⟩ ⌜And⌝
160:18 ⟨To force⟩ ⌜Because it ... to force⌝
160:21 ⌜The soul's ... forces.⌝
160:24 tr⟨y⟩ies
160:33 creed⟨.⟩ ⌜: the ... Sympathy.⌝
161:2 tread. ⟨P Whitman's great message. The message of America. The message of American democracy.⟩ ⌜Therefore I ... ⟨fac⟩ phallus ... ⟨great⟩ message ... [162:6] democracy.⌝
161:8 ⟨But⟩ ⌜And⌝ where a ⟨great⟩
161:9 ⟨riches and pomp.⟩ ⌜clothes or appearance.⌝
161:11 ⟨But in its simple passing, [?] recognised⟩ ⌜Not by a ... by works⌝
161:12 ⟨The great⟩ ⌜Not by anything ... The⌝
161:14 ⟨welcomed, and worshipped, as a lesser soul worships a greater.⟩ ⌜passed by ... the road.⌝
161:17 ⟨an act⟩ ⌜a communion⌝
161:19 ⟨and the worship of the⟩ ⌜all down ... and a⌝
161:20 ⌜seen⌝
161:21 ⟨the open road of life.⟩ ⌜the common ... living.⌝
161:22 ⟨the⟩ great and ⟨the⟩
161:22 ⟨as they pass variously down the road.⟩ ⌜because they ... riches.⌝
161:26 ⟨⟨ ⟨m⟩⌜M⌝erging⟩⟩ ⌜⌜MERGING⌝⌝
161:27 ⟨Myself,⟩ ⌜MYSELF,⌝
161:28 ⟨o⟩Open
161:29 ⟨sweetness⟩ ⌜joy⌝
161:29 ⟨greets⟩ ⌜sees⌝

First Version

The pagination for *TS1* is given, with editorial (final) numbering in square brackets.

Nathaniel Hawthorne

241:3 ⟨we can begin⟩ ⌐beginning⌐

241:3 ⟨we must again examine⟩ ⌐it is . . . to consider⌐

241:7 ⟨body,⟩ ⌐nervous system,⌐

241:8 ideal *Per*] ⟨full⟩ ⌐ordinary⌐ *TS1*

241:9 ⟨recognise⟩ ⌐conceive of⌐

241:11 ⟨self⟩ ⟨⟨⌐darkly⌐ conscious⌐.⌐⟩⟩⟨ness.⟩ ⌐⌐self-conscious.⌐⌐

241:12 ⟨consciousness.⟩ ⌐cognition.⌐

241:15 ⟨⟨self⟩⟩ ⟨conscious.⟩ ⌐aware.⌐

241:16 ⟨conscious, and⟩ ⌐awake,⌐

241:16 ⌐primal⌐

241:21 ⌐whole⌐ primary ⟨consciousness.⟩ ⌐or dynamic mind.⌐

241:25 [p. 2 begins] the primary

241:27 ⟨reasoning⟩ ⌐association⌐

241:28 ⟨where⟩ ⌐equivalent . . . reasoning;⌐

241:29 ⟨association⟩ ⌐su⟨⟨n⌐⟩⟩⌐⌐m⌐⌐

241:31 great ⟨body of⟩

241:32 ⟨body⟩ ⌐physique,⌐

242:1 reason⟨s⟩⌐ing⌐

242:3 ⟨body⟩ ⌐first-mind⌐ ⟨still⟩

242:8 communication⌐⌐.⌐⌐ ⟨⟨of ⟨great primary, sensual⟩ ⌐primal, sensual⌐ conclusions.⟩⟩

242:11 ⟨express⟩ ⌐deal with⌐

242:12 ⌐The great . . . utterance.⌐

242:13 myth⌐s⌐;

242:16 Myth, legend . . . [242:21] inception of the] ⟨⟨If we examine what we mean by romance, we shall find that we mean the expression of the individual ⟨primary⟩ ⌐physical⌐ mind more or less in defiance of ⟨the higher⟩ reason. The magic weapons of heroes, such as the sword Excalibur, symbolise some primal, dynamic power of the heroic psyche over the ordinary psyche. The limitation⟩⟩ ⌐⌐Myth, legend . . . inception of the⌐⌐

242:22 [p. 3 begins] human ⟨race.⟩ ⌐species.⌐

242:23 ⟨primary⟩ genesis

242:28 ⟨But t⟩⌐T⌐he

242:29 ⌐sensual⌐

242:31 ⟨red⟩ bring down⟨, say,⟩

242:34 ⟨great⟩ primary

243:2 ⟨is⟩ lies

243:13 [p. 4 begins] In

243:14 ⟨comprehendable⟩ evident

243:18 great⟨, vague⟩

243:24 ⟨of⟩ ⟨towa [?]⟩ towards

243:28 ⟨soul⟩ psyche

243:29 science⟨, at last,⟩

243:32 fulness. ⟨*P* To return⟩

244:1 [p. 5 begins] his passional

244:10 ⟨most⟩ ⌐some⌐

244:16 ⌐presented⌐ ⟨acting⟩

244:20 mystery, ⟨moral,⟩

244:28 ⟨conne⟩ helpless

244:31 [p. 5 [6] begins] of the flood

244:34 ⟨abstract⟩ ⌐upper⌐

244:35 ⟨mind.⟩ ⌐being.⌐

244:39 ⟨it⟩ ⌐comes the⌐ fa⟨i⟩⌐l⌐l⟨s⟩

244:40 ⟨scientific⟩ ⌐dynamically logical⌐

245:1 ⟨does not⟩ ⌐scarcely⌐ belong⌐s⌐

245:4 ⟨We have seen, in Cooper, the mysterious fascination which sin and adultery exerted over the American mind, the glamour of sensual sin. In Hawthorne this mystery is fully expounded.⟩ It

245:9 Christian *Per*] ⟨C⟩⌐c⌐hristian *TS1*

245:12 b⟨eing⟩⌐ody⌐

245:12 ⟨mystic and actual⟩ sensual

245:15 heart, ⟨and the ⌐seven⌐sword w⟩

245:18 ⟨And [?]⟩ Hester

245:24 This is... [245:35] acutely enough.] ⟨This is the [p. ⟨-18-⟩ ⟨⟨⌐7⌐⟩⟩ ⌐⌐6⌐⌐ [7]] symbol of the sensual mystery, the mystery of division, and division into creation used in the occult books of the ages long preceding Christianity. This is the Magna Mater, with her fiery insignia, presented for worship upon the scaffold, worship in contumely and blame. The revelation is subtle. The almost insane malice of the whole situation and attitude, so subtle, so double, so self-frustrating, so delighting in the Judas principal of betrayal in subtleties, is perfectly conveyed by Hawthorne.⟩ ⌐This is... now ⟨its [?]⟩ ⌐⌐the⌐⌐ ... serpent, ⟨when⟩ ⌐⌐as⌐⌐ ... [245:27] ⟨then[?] it⟩ turns... ⟨takes its revenge. She⟩ ⌐⌐bites back. Woman⌐⌐ ... [245:33] almost ⟨mal⟩ insane... ⟨subtly⟩ ⌐⌐acutely⌐⌐ enough.⌐

246:7 ⟨longs,⟩ ⌐longs,⌐

246:8 for revenge... [246:12] outward self.] ⟨for the darkness of the hot, sensual world, he longs for the world to be lost, utterly.⟩ ⌐for revenge⌐⌐,⌐⌐ even... outward self.⌐

246:13 [p. 7 [8] begins] Hester

246:15 ⌐spirit-worshipping or⌐

246:17 ⟨first⟩ ⌐primary⌐

246:21 ⟨the⟩ ⌐her⌐

246:22 ⟨sou [?]⟩ or mental ⟨being.⟩ ⌐ego.⌐

246:27 ⟨being⟩ ⌐self⌐

247:1 ⟨it⟩ ⌐he⌐ becomes

247:4 ⟨of⟩ ⌐from⌐

247:5 ⟨primary⟩ being

247:6 [p. 8 [9] begins] in

247:9 ⟨undefiled⟩ ⌐virgin⌐

247:11 ghastly *Per*] ⟨ghastly⟩ ⌐nasty⌐ *TS1*

247:13 ⟨trodden⟩ ⌐held⌐

247:13 ⌐long enough⌐

247:14 ⟨vile⟩ spiritual ⟨eloquence⟩ ⌐effulgence⌐

247:15 ⌐and⌐

247:20 ⌐back at⌐

247:20 serpent, secretly, from an *Per*] serpent ⟨from the⟩ ⌐, like an⌐ *TS1*

247:22 ⌐years⌐

247:28 ⟨lead.⟩ ⌐take the... suggestion.⌐

247:30 ⟨falsehood⟩ ⌐prostitution⌐

247:31 ⟨falsity⟩ ⌐vampiredom⌐

247:32 ⟨⌐or⌐⟩ ⌐⌐or intellectual⌐⌐

247:33 ⟨mind⟩ ⌐self⌐

247:34 ⟨sheer⟩ ⌐secret⌐

247:35 ⟨subconscious, unconscious.⟩ ⌐serpent-like, outwardly submissive.⌐

247:37 ⟨lead in mystic destruction. The woman ascendant is always mystically destructive.⟩ ⌐destroy by... [247:38] [p. 9 [10] begins] woman isolate... mystically destructive.⌐

247:40 ⟨lead, she leads⟩ ⌜become alone . . . she goes⌝

248:2 ⟨first⟩ ⌜responsible⌝

248:5 ⟨positive⟩ ⌜leader⌝

248:6 ⟨then⟩ ⟨or⟩ ⌜and⌝ in

248:7 And it . . . impulse of the undoing. *Per*] ⌜And yet it . . . impulse of the new life. But with her it can never be more than a suggestion, a vague, blind gesture. Man must make it sure and definite.⌝ *TS1*

248:21 lead, she can . . . [248:28] old creed.] lead⟨. When she recoils it is in mystic destruction. She cannot make a beginning. She can only make an end. In her hands lies the terrible force of retributive justice. When she tries to lead on creatively, she can only follow the old initative.⟩ ⌜, she can . . . old creed.⌝

248:31 ⟨follow the old line of⟩ ⌜exaggerate the old life of⌝

248:33 ⟨terrible⟩ ⟨⟨⌜awful⌝ and⟩⟩ puzzling

248:36 [p. 10 [11] begins] She cannot

249:2 ⟨What s⟩ ⌜What she . . . matter. S⌝he

249:11 ⟨herself.⟩ ⌜he takes.⌝

249:12 ⟨selfish,⟩ reactionary

249:26 ⟨this⟩ ⌜for⌝

249:31 witchcraft. [p. ⟨10⟩ ⌜11⌝ [12] begins with an earlier version of 248:36–249:31] ⟨She⟩ ⟨⟨⟨⌜*P* She cannot . . . in ⟨service. For she can no other.⟩ ⌜⌜selflessness. To this she . . . condemned.⌝⌝ . . . her profound, potent soul . . . this service. ⌜⌜Secretly she bites the heel of sacred humanity. ⟨⟨And thus the⌝⌝ ⟨So the⟩ Scarlet Woman goes as a grey nurse.⟩⟩ ⌜⌜⌜It is doubtful whether Hester herself was ready for the step to which she prompted Dimmesdale, in begging him to go away with her. When a man accepts and acts upon the prompting of a new spirit in woman he has ⟨ . . . ⟩ inevitably to face a great reaction in the woman, towards the old.⌝⌝⌝ *P* ⟨This gives⟩ Hester ⟨her⟩ ⌜⌜has a⌝⌝ witch-like, sinister quality. Hawthorne gives the picture in all its detail.⟩⟩⟩

249:33 ⟨sub [?]⟩ subconscious

249:34 ⌜exert⌝ ⟨become⟩

249:35 ⟨female⟩ ⌜malevolent⌝

249:37 ⟨base.⟩ ⌜sources.⌝

249:38 ⟨female⟩ ⌜human⌝

249:38 soul, ⟨which can fasten vampire-like⟩ ⌜and this . . . electricity⌝

249:39 ⟨being⟩ ⌜life⌝

249:40 ⟨all being, all life⟩ ⌜the flow, the very life itself

250:2 ⟨woman⟩ ⌜agent⌝

250:3 ⟨thus⟩ harried

250:4 woman⟨,⟩ or ⟨a⟩ man, ⌜wh⟨en⟩⌜⌜o⌝⌝ ⟨he⟩ is⌝

250:5 th⟨e⟩⌜is⌝ ⟨recoil from⟩ ⌜reaction against⌝

250:8 ⌜And the . . . a witch.⌝

250:10 rich⟨,⟩

250:17 [p. ⟨-27-⟩ ⟨⟨⌜16⌝⟩⟩ ⌜⌜1⟨⟨⟨1⌝⌝⟩⟩⟩⌜⌜⌜2⌝⌝⌝ [13] begins] ⟨yet, a⟩⌜A⌝ll

250:18 ⟨and⟩ of ⌜his white⌝

250:19 ⟨the⟩ ⌜his⌝ spiritual ⟨righteousness;⟩ ⌜effulgence;⌝

250:20 ⟨the⟩ ⌜a⌝ centre of ⟨ruthless⟩ ⌜mystic⌝ obstruction

⟨, destruction to the lives⟩ ⌜to the creative activity⌝ ⟨⟨around her.⟩⟩ ⌜⌜of all life.⌝⌝

250:21 ⟨them⟩ ⌜the Puritan being⌝

250:24 ⟨a form of⟩ ⌜her helpless . . . cover her⌝

250:29 Yet she . . . [250:33] rays.] ⟨⟨It is a strange and frightening anomaly, this duplicity in a woman—quite unconscious and helpless. We have Hester, whose heart is a ⟨black⟩ centre of malediction, a ⟨great⟩ source of the destructive, Hecate electricity, going round as a Sister of Mercy, humbly tending the poor ⟨She⟩ ⌜Yet she⌝ is not a hypocrite: she is sternly darkly sincere. Only the ⟨serpent has gained dominion over her, and⟩ ⌜poison has entered her soul, and though⌝ with unthinkable subtlety, ⟨invests her⟩ ⌜she invests herself⌝ in the darkest, sternest righteousness, that she may most perfectly, at the very quick, destroy the body of life, and all the time remain an example of holy humility. Hester cannot help it— she cannot alter it. As far as she know, and wills, she [p. ⟨-28-⟩ ⟨⟨⌜17⌝⟩⟩ ⟨⟨⟨⌜⌜12⌝⌝⟩⟩⟩ ⌜⌜⌜13⌝⌝⌝ [14] begins] *is* good and charitable. But all her goodness and charity are only instrumental to the dark Hecate principle which is primal now in her.⟩⟩ ⌜⌜Yet she . . . [250:29] ⟨struck⟩ ⌜⌜⌜turned⌝⌝⌝ in her⟨.⟩ ⌜⌜⌜soul.⌝⌝⌝ She . . . rays.⌝⌝

250:39 ⟨at its first issuing:⟩ ⌜itself, the . . . life:⌝

251:1 ⟨But t⟩⌜T⌝he

251:3 ⟨caused⟩ ⌜reached⌝

251:10 alone⟨.⟩⌜?⌝

251:13 [p. ⟨-29-⟩ ⟨⟨⌜18⌝⟩⟩ ⌜⌜12⌝⌝ [15] begins] passion

251:19 ⟨The⟩ ⌜After his death, ⟨⟨the⟩⟩⌝ ⌜⌜it comes . . . that the⌝⌝

251:27 ⟨anomaly⟩ ⌜division⌝

251:34 ⟨can⟩ ⌜may⌝

251:35 [p. ⟨-30-⟩ ⟨⟨⌜19⌝⟩⟩ ⌜⌜13⌝⌝ [16] begins] with a

251:37 ⟨hellish⟩ ⌜deadly⌝

251:38 ⟨devil⟩ ⌜demon⌝

252:3 ⟨devilish⟩ triumph

252:3 ⟨shrill⟩ jeering

252:5 ⟨cleverness.⟩ ⌜opposition.⌝

252:6 ⟨the thing⟩ ⌜something that⌝

252:6 ⟨She *hates* the ⌜some⌝thing she has spawned.⟩ And ⟨yet⟩ ⌜as well⌝

252:7 ⟨her⟩ ⌜the child⌝

252:14 ⟨⟨We might apply it ⟨to almost any child;⟩ ⌜nowadays to many children;⌝ though few children are such perfect exemplars as Pearl. And again⟩⟩ ⌜He did . . . to describe⌝

252:17 [p. ⟨-31-⟩ ⟨⟨⌜20⌝⟩⟩ ⌜⌜14⌝⌝ [17] begins] accompanied

252:19 child"—To . . . [252:22] downright that *Ed.*] child"— ⟨Who has not seen such a look, nowadays, in the eyes of a child? — a look of pure perversity, frustration into nought. Pearl might well say⟩ ⌜But to . . . downright that⌝ *TS1* child." To . . . downright that *Per*

252:22 ha⟨d⟩⌜s⌝

252:24 ⌜But even . . . being. We⌝ ⟨She⟩

252:26 amazement⟨.⟩ ⌜, and respect.⌝

252:30 ⌜sensual⌝

252:33 dangerous⌜.⌝ ⟨; or the rat, swift, sly, sure, subterranean.⟩

252:38 ⟨But he is more skilled in the art of the Golden Hermes, the Hermes of the underworld, than in pure [p. ⟨-32-⟩ ⟨⟨⌜21⌝⟩⟩ ⌜⌜15⌝⌝ [18] begins] or modern science.⟩ ⌜The physician is the dead⌜⌜ly⌝⌝ ... [253:1] the undoer.⌝

253:3 underworld⟨.⟩ ⌜, and diabolic there.⌝

253:4 ⟨Only, he is subject⟩ ⌜Still ... subjected⌝

253:4 ⟨in fact, dominated by⟩ ⌜he is ... dominion of⌝

253:7 prototype. ⟨⌜He is again the serpent in recoil.⌝⟩

253:8 Outwardly she ... [253:31] other half.] ⟨⟨But, because he is really enslaved, cringing and subjected in himself, his taking of her is a kind of theft. He pilfers her, really, in marriage. Because she is a free, indomitable being, seeking her completion in marriage. She seeks to balance herself in an equilibrium of pure polarity. From his learning, and his profession of scholarly wisdom in darkness, she takes him for the representative of the true sensual mystery. Whereas she is only a malevolent slave to the spiritual mystery. Hence he *knows* she will inevitably repudiate him. He accepts it as a law, and is even grateful. P ⟨She⟩ ⌜When Hester⌝ turns to Dimmesdale⌜,⌝ ⟨. But now⟩ the triangle of destruction is established. Hester loves Dimmesdale, because he is pure and pre-eminent in spiritual being. But it is an inevitable law of her nature, that she must make him fall⟨;⟩ because ⟨the secret of the sensual mystery has been implanted in her by Chillingworth.⟩ ⌜it is more than time it fell; and because her nature in itself is his doom.⌝ She loves⟩⟩ ⌜⌜⌜Outwardly s⌝⌝⌝⟨⌜⌜S⟩he ... theft. ⟨But it is also an unconscious⟩ ⌜⌜⌜⌜But inwardly ... a tacit⌝⌝⌝⌝ conspiracy a ⟨sp⟩ conspiracy ... [253:14] me⟨—⟩⌜⌜⌜,⌝⌝⌝ — — Art ... other half. [p. 16 [19] begins]⌝⌝

253:32 ⟨admit that⟩ conceive

253:36 h⟨e⟩⌜o⌝ld⌜s⌝

253:40 ⟨sublimation⟩ ⌜transmutation⌝

254:9 ⟨For h⟩⌜H⌝is

254:10 ⟨self⟩ preservation⟨.⟩ ⌜of his appearances.⌝

254:12 ⟨at⟩ ⌜to⌝

254:12 ⟨last flourish.⟩ ⌜saintly triumphs.⌝

254:14 ⟨triumph.⟩ ⌜applause.⌝

254:17 England⟨, meeting⟩ ⌜meets⌝

254:24 [p. ⟨-36-⟩ ⟨⟨⌜25⌝⟩⟩ ⌜⌜17⌝⌝ [20] begins] a girl

254:29 It is ... progress of futility.] ⟨Sin, the act of sin, may have brought him to this terrible state of insanity. But the sin was rendered inevitable by the fatal *pure* halfness of his being. The fatal breach was made when the spiritual being triumphed over the sensual.⟩ ⌜It is ... ⟨⟨jaring [?]⟩⟩ ⌜⌜malignant⌝⌝ progress of ⟨⟨malignant⟩⟩ futility.⌝

254:32 ⟨he⟩ ⌜Dimmesdale⌝
255:2 ⟨one⟩ way⟨,⟩
255:3 ⟨dream-⟩⌜double⟨⟨-⟩⟩⌝
255:3 even marvellous . . . [255:8] praised.] ⟨but rather detestable symbolism, so serpent-like in its duplicity of [p. ⟨-37-⟩ ⌜26⌝ ⌜⌜18⌝⌝ [21] begins] meaning, is almost unbearable. This man reveals us more than all the philosophies of the modern world, if we but read him.) ⌜even marvellous exposition⟨,⟩ . . . [255:6] preaching of ⌜⌜the⌝⌝ conventional ⟨morality,⟩ ⌜⌜creed,⌝⌝ on . . . praised.⌝
255:9 ⟨dream-reality.⟩ ⌜their two-faced reality.⌝
255:10 ⟨in the same class, but less perfect. Only The Blithedale Romance is different.⟩ ⌜again a . . . ⟨⟨soulless.⟩⟩ ⌜⌜vulgar.⌝⌝ . . . personal.⌝
255:13 ⟨only⟩ touched
255:22 The] ⟨It is the old romantic idyllicism, pastoralism, of a decadent age, blossoming forth once more: an elegant, ultra-refined philosopher writing Daphnis and Chloe, or Marie Antoinette in her dairy maid costume.⟩ The
255:24 ⟨is clumsy.⟩ ⌜never works.⌝
255:27 and perfection . . . [256:3] a failure.] and ⟨P The other half of the Brook Farm story is the story of the particular human relationships. The charm of the book lies in the opening, the description of the first days at the farm. The sense of joyful anticipation shows that a Brook Farm life is humanly possible and might be beautiful and full in the extreme. Given individuals grounded in the dark sensual knowledge of the reality of otherness, the reality of being-in-separation, and filled also with the happy breath of spiritual communion, we might live a perfect life at Brook Farm. But with a group of individuals all mutually abjuring the being-in-separation, and yet insanely resenting the imputation of being-in-common, there is nothing but speedy dissolution possible. They neutralised the one half of being against the other half. Whereas success depended on the full duality of their living.⟩ ⌜perfection. The . . . toil. [255:30] [p. ⟨-41-⟩ ⟨⟨⌜27⌝⟩⟩ ⌜⌜19⌝⌝ [22] begins] But . . . a failure.⌝
256:4 of the *Blithedale Romance Ed.*] ⌜of the Blithedale Romance⌝ *TS1* of *The Blithedale Romance E2*
256:8 Hutter ⟨or like Ligeia⟩
256:10 ⟨Priscilla.⟩ ⌜Zenobia, just . . . Cora.⌝
256:13 ⌜secretly⌝
256:13 [p. ⟨-42-⟩ ⌜28⌝ [23] begins] Hawthorne
256:14 ⟨like the⟩ ⌜the⌝ next
256:22 intellect⟨.⟩ ⌜: Chillingworth . . . polarised.⌝
256:24 ⟨subjected⟩ ⌜abject⌝
256:26 it⟨.⟩ ⌜and ⟨⟨cut[?]⟩⟩ mutilate it.⌝
256:27 ⌜ultra-⌝social
256:35 [p. ⟨-43-⟩ ⟨⟨⌜29⌝⟩⟩ ⌜⌜20⌝⌝ [24] begins] strong

256:39 Hollingsworth wants ... [257:2] other man.] ⟨He finds out what Hollingworth is. He hates him for a destructive monomaniac. The subjected, enchained, but overweening sensual self in Hollingworth *needs* to destroy, he needs the activity of destruction, or consuming, in the sensual self.) ⌜Hollingsworth wants ... [257:2] to ⟨bully or⟩ consume ... other man⌝⌝.⌝⌝ ⟨merely for his own will and purposes.⌝⟩

257:5 ⌜admires, even⌝

257:9 ⟨be the positive pole in the circuit of sensual passion between them, he the passive or negative pole, obedient.⟩ ⌜beat him ... in him.⌝

257:12 being⟨.⟩⌜, and ... arrogate.⌝

257:14 Hollingsworth almost ... drowns herself.] ⟨But she needs the triumph in the sensual self, over the dark sensual being in Hollingsworth. It is the process of Hester Prynne reversed. It is as if Hester first married Dimmesdale, the fallen Dimmesdale, and wearied of him, because, in his fallen state, like Hawthorne, he had no [p. ⟨-44-⟩ ⌜30⌝ ⌜⌜21⌝⌝ [25] begins] further power of passional relationship. Then she leaves Dimmesdale, to seek the subject sensual reality in Chillingworth. And she *needs* this victory in the sensual conflict. She *needs* to assert herself the sensual dominant, with the man for the sensual passive or obedient or dominated correspondent. And because she is thwarted in this need, and so trammelled between the sensual necessities and the spiritual domination, she drowns herself.) ⌜Hollingsworth almost ... drowns herself.⌝

257:19 then ⟨all⟩

257:24 like ⟨the⟩ ⌜a⌝

257:26 love. ⟨But in Poe, the spiritual being is overweening. He works to *destroy* the very defines, the very reality of Ligeia.⟩

257:30 ⌜a mystic prostitute,⌝ [p. ⟨-45-⟩ ⟨⟨⌜31⌝⟩⟩ ⌜⌜22⌝⌝ [26] begins]

258:4 ⟨submitted to the will of another⟩ ⌜abstracted from conscious being⌝

258:6 sensory⌜-⌝conscious

258:11 [p. ⟨-46-⟩ ⟨⟨⌜32⌝⟩⟩ ⌜⌜23⌝⌝ [27] begins] spiritualism

258:17 ⟨casual⟩ ⌜causal⌝

258:19 things, ⟨obscene⟩

258:26 body⟨.⟩ ⌜, pure prostitution.⌝

258:27 ⟨passive,⟩ ⌜passive, mediumistic, almost imbecile,⌝

258:33 [p. ⟨-47-⟩ ⟨⟨⌜33⌝⟩⟩ ⌜⌜24⌝⌝ [28] begins] correspondent

259:1 ⟨old⟩ were-wolf

259:7 Holling⌜s⌝worth

259:8 ⟨not⌜-⌝being.⟩ ⌜⌜nought.⌝⌝

259:15 wolf⌜.⌝ ⟨: and hence the⟩ [end of *TS1*]

Dana

272:3 ⟨Two Americans, Dana and Herman Melville show us the move to the sea.⟩ Richard

272:3 lit⌜t⌝e⌜r⌝rateur

272:6 ⟨we derive⟩ ⌜came⌝

272:6 ⟨A⟩⌜a⌝uthor

272:6   *Two ... Mast. Ed.*] "Two
Years Before the Mast."

272:8   eye⌜s⌝

272:11 California. *Ed.*] ~ /

272:17 *Two ... Mast. Ed.*] ⌜"⌝Two
Years Before the Mast.⌜"⌝

272:18 is a simple ... [274:14] unconsciously symbolised] is
⟨⟨astonishing for its ⟨veracity⟩
⌜bareness⌝ and ⟨plainness⟩
⌜directness⌝ of statement,
and for the powerful im-
pression it makes upon the
mind. There is no marvel
or gusto of adventure: just
bare⟩⟩ ⌜a simple ... [272:21]
[p. 2 begins] Fen⟨n⟩imore
Cooper ... [273:20] [p. 3
begins] life. It ... [274:12]
[p. -5- [4] begins] mystic
loneliness ... unconsciously
symbolised⌝ *see also entries to*
274:1

272:29 ⟨a purpose or a desire⟩ ⌜⌜the desire of⌝⌝

272:35 ⟨instinct⟩ ⌜⌜intention⌝⌝

273:4   to ⌜⌜the⌝⌝

273:9   ⟨is⟩ ⌜⌜surges⌝⌝

273:9   him⟨.⟩ ⌜⌜, out of control.⌝⌝

273:9   ⟨great⟩ conquest

273:10 sea⟨.⟩ ⌜⌜, he pits ... sensual
deeps.⌝⌝

273:23 ⟨of⟩ one

273:26 ⟨treading⟩ ⌜⌜existence on⌝⌝
⟨e⟩the

273:26 ⟨the bottomless pit.⟩
⌜⌜oblivion.⌝⌝

273:27 ⟨the bottomless pit,⟩ ⌜⌜human
oblivion,⌝⌝

273:37 t⟨o⟩⌜⌜wo⌝⌝

274:1   ⟨o⟩⌜⌜i⌝⌝n

274:31 flight.⌜"⌝

274:33 ⟨appears from⟩ ⌜flies between⌝

274:34 waters. ⟨It is the creature of
the first mystic principle of
the waters, as it enters⟩ ⌜It is
... [274:35] [p. 6 [5] begins] the
two ... [275:22] the South-⌝
[275:22] [p. -7- [6] begins]
west; and *see also entries to*
275:12

274:38 life, ⟨or being,⟩

275:12 moun⟨d⟩⌜t⌝ [*or* moun⟨t⟩ ⌜d⌝]

275:16 ⟨sail⟩ sailed

275:33 ⟨lowest⟩ ⌜remoter⌝

275:38 dispassionate *Ed.*] dispassion-
/ are *TS1*

276:2   earth. ⟨But the strain of the
long sea-voyage is too much for
these creatures of earth, none
the less. The sea is too strong
for them.⟩ ⌜P Day after ... for
them.⌝

276:6   [p. -8- [7] begins]

276:7   ⌜He is ... the sailors.⌝

276:18 ⟨sensual⟩ passion

276:20 isolation. In ... [278:2] Every
man] isolation. ⟨⟨P Dana could
allow any amount of spiritual
torture—but this flame of sensual passion made him sick.
It shows his strength and his
weakness: his strength in the
spiritual self, his weakness in
the sensual self. For the very
passion that ran between the
Captain and his victim, Sam,
is a justification of the act.
Every truly passional act is jus-
tified as an emanation from the
⟨sensual⟩ ⌜life⌝ mystery. It is
only the *deliberate* or *vindictive* ⌜or hurtful [?]⌝ acts of violence or cruelty which⟩⟩ ⌜In
the ... [276:26] [p. 9 [8] begins]
he lives ... [277:16] [p. 10 [9]

begins] each their . . .
[278:2] readjust it.⌉ [p. ⟨-10-⟩
⌜11⌝ [10] begins] Every man *see
also entries to* 277:34

276:23 ⟨sensual and spiritual⟩ sympathetic

276:24 ⟨d⟩corresponding

276:34 ⟨o⟩in the ⟨back⟩ ⌜⌜nape⌝⌝

276:36 ⟨lowest centres⟩ ⌜⌜extreme
ganglia⌝⌝

276:37 act⟨, very often, out of⟩
⌜⌜before and⌝⌝

277:1 sea-m⟨a [?]⟩⌜⌜e⌝⌝⟩n

277:2 ⟨established in the⟩ ⌜⌜a circuit
of⌝⌝

277:8 o⟨f⟩⌜⌜r⌝⌝

277:21 ⟨an⟩ a

277:34 ⌜⌜spiritual⌝⌝

278:4 ⟨naked⟩ ⌜exposed⌝

278:4 ⌜When John . . . up too.⌝

278:19 all. ⟨Any man who has exposed himself as plainly as
the Captain, has taken his full
share of the effect. If Sam was
unformed, a loose, straggling
character, the Captain also was
unformed, without sense of
his own nakedness and singleness of soul. The two were
complements in passion—
each, no doubt, purified and
improved the other.⟩ ⌜Sam
was . . . [278:26] was ashamed

278:31 [p. 11 begins] delicacy

278:39 ⟨pure and⟩ ⟨⟨⌜normal⌝⟩⟩ impulsive

278:40 Sam. *Ed.*] ~ ⟨.⟩⌜,⌝

278:40 Men should . . . [279:9] him
morose.] ⟨⟨As for the widemouthed Sam,⟩⟩ ⟨his flogging
was even appreciated by him.
A negative, loose, over-passion
sensual being, he *needed* the

concentration of passionately
inflicted pain and anger, to
complete him. And the rest
of the men left the sensual
mystery to adjust itself. They
were too much *of* the sensual world, to talk about
it. Dana was alone in his
sick horrors.⟩ ⟨⟨⌜he should
have been in his measure
grateful, as animals and children are really grateful for a
whipping that is *passionally*
just, if not theoretically so. No
doubt Sam *was* unconsciously
grateful. And intuitively, the
rest of the men understood.
except Dana, who was alone in
his sick horrors. — The painful
mistake was made by the overcharitable John. But it is the
Captain who suffers most, in
the end. He is ashamed, and it
makes him morose.⌝⟩⟩ ⌜⌜Men
should . . . [279:3]
seam⟨a⟩⌜⌜⌜e⌝⌝⌝n . . . ⟨sh [?]⟩
passional . . . [279:8]
second⌜⌜⌜ly⌝⌝⌝ . . . him morose.⌝⌝

279:14 [p. 12 begins] of *substance*

279:15 ⟨Picaesa⟩ ⌜Matisse or Picasso⌝

279:15 ⟨watery⟩ mystery

279:16 ⟨the mystic presence of the
waters, in all substance.⟩
⌜naked substance . . . it down.⌝

279:36 [p. 13 begins] natural

280:3 ⟨in the true mystic⟩ ⌜virgin in
the⌝

280:5 ⟨yet⟩ ⌜really⌝

280:5 ⟨good measure⟩ ⌜the last resort⌝

280:8 ⟨s⟩⌜S⌝ea

280:18 [p. 14 begins] sick

280:31 moment. ⟨⟨Dana is barely ⟨a
person⟩ ⌜an impulsive being⌝

any more. He is a wandering impersonal consciousness.⟩⟩

280:32 ⌜from the western shore⌝

280:33 conveyed⟨, however⟩

280:33 finality⌜, of⌝ ⟨and⟩ fatal ⟨with⟩

280:35 ⟨is given strongest in the description of the leaving California. ⟩ ⌜tears us . . . leaves California.⌝

280:38 [p. 15 begins] cloud

281:1 ⟨The description of the voyage home is wonderful.⟩ ⌜The voyage . . . the waters.⌝

281:4 ⟨our own⟩ earthly

281:19 [p. 16 begins] of

281:29 ⟨is more or less laid up.⟩ ⌜falls sick.⌝

281:40 [p. 17 begins] to

282:6 "In *Ed.*] ~ *TS1*

282:13 ⟨heaven⟩ ⌜confusion⌝

282:21 [p. 18 begins] ⟨spiritual⟩ ⌜triumphant⌝

282:24 self⟨.⟩ ⌜, fulfilled by mystic disintegration.⌝

282:25 ⟨automatically,⟩ ⌜deliberately,⌝

282:25 principle⟨.⟩ He lives from the upper spiritual centres of abstract life, having conquered, through living in, the lower sacral centres. *P* But⟩ ⌜, free again . . . disintegration. *P*⌝ Dana

282:30 delight. *Ed.*] ~ *TS1*

282:37 and ⟨in a perfect reaction from these, takes her way But she is one with them, like a creature, not like a thing.⟩ ⌜as a perfect . . . [283:2] perfectly accepts.⌝

283:6 [p. 19 begins] could

283:22 ⟨adjusting of ourselves to⟩ ⌜equipoising of the s⟨ou⟩⌜e⌝l⌜f⌝ in the midst of⌝

283:23 ⟨And⟩ ⌜Machines depend . . . so that⌝

283:25 ⟨this⟩ ⌜the purest⌝

283:26 ⟨insensible⟩ ⌜⟨⟨du[?]⟩⟩ numb⌝

283:28 life. The . . . [284:23] the mystery.] [p. 21 [20] begins] ⌜life. The . . . [284:15] ⟨shaken.⟩ ⌜⌜between them entangled.⌝⌝ . . . [284:21] play with⌝ [284:21] [p. 22 [21] begins] ⟨*P* This we feel powerfully in Dana's description of a tropical thunderstorm.⟩ ⌜the weapons . . . the mystery.⌝

284:39 "In *Ed.*] ~ *TS1*

285:5 [p. -23- [22] begins] few

285:16 "During *Ed.*] ~ *TS1*

285:28 ⌜Thunderer is . . . from ⟨its⟩ ⌜⌜their⌝⌝ prison in space.⌝

285:29 [p. ⟨-25-⟩ ⌜24⌝ [23] begins] ⟨the process⟩ ⌜Another curious . . . the process⌝

285:30 ⟨mysterious⟩ ⌜material⌝

285:32 ⌜salty⌝

286:10 [p. ⟨-26-⟩ ⌜25⌝ [24] begins] dozen

286:17 potatoes *Ed.*] potatoe

286:27 ⟨effect⟩ ⌜account⌝

286:31 [p. ⟨-27-⟩ ⌜26⌝ [25] begins] creative bond

286:35 ⟨an excess⟩ ⌜a triumph⌝

286:35 ⟨mystery⟩ ⌜principle⌝

286:36 ⟨negative⟩ ⌜static⌝.

286:39 watery ⟨triumph,⟩

286:40 substance⟨. *P* On the other hand, naturally, salt is a disintegrative principle to the living organic being, a direct disintegrative stimulus, if it be in excess.⟩ ⌜: just as . . . [287:5] of water.⌝

287:13 [p. ⟨-28-⟩ ⌜27⌝ [26] begins] or the onions

287:16 scurvy⌐-¬stricken
287:18 earth⌐-¬darkness

287:22 Gea⟨c [?]⟩⌐e¬a
287:23 ⟨wholeness.⟩ ⌐creation.¬

Herman Melville

288:4 ⟨greater⟩ ⌐wider¬
288:5 ⟨far⟩ more
288:10 that ⟨strange⟩
288:10 sea-creatures⌐.¬ ⟨, the untranslateable speech.⟩
288:12 ⌐pagan¬
288:12 who ⟨must have⟩
288:16 ⟨lands.⟩ ⌐earth.¬
288:19 the North ... [p. 2 begins] ⌐the North ... [290:23] man can hear unmoved.] [289:10] [p. 3 begins] root-utterance ... [289:37] [p. 4 begins] pure idea ... [290:23] man can¬ [p. ⟨-9-⟩ ⌐5¬ begins] ⟨⟨"⟨T⟩⌐t¬railing Clouds of glory do we come." Tahiti, Samoa, Nukaheva, the very names are like clouds of glory⟩⟩ ⌐hear unmoved¬. They *see also entries to* 290:17
288:20 form ⟨a⟩
288:21 true⌐⌐st¬¬
288:23 h⟨is [?]⟩⌐⌐as¬¬
288:33 ⟨new⟩ land-root f⟨ew [?]⟩ ⌐⌐use¬¬
289:5 er⟨[...]⟩⌐⌐as¬¬
289:8 ⟨of⟩ established
289:13 scientific-⟨[...]⟩ ⟨⟨⌐⌐social¬¬⟩⟩⌐⌐⌐social¬¬¬
289:16 ⟨whose last⟩ ⟨⟨⌐⌐of profound¬¬⟩⟩ ⌐⌐⌐embodied in deep¬¬¬
289:16 ⟨but⟩ ⟨⟨⌐⌐whose¬¬⟩⟩ symbol⌐⌐s¬¬ ⌐⌐⌐that¬¬¬
289:30 ⟨t⟩⌐⌐T¬¬ree whose
289:31 ⟨t⟩⌐⌐T¬¬ree
289:33 ⟨Rood—Tau⟩ Cross.
290:3 ⟨o⟩⌐O¬cean
290:13 ⟨vast,⟩ ⌐⌐wide,¬¬
290:17 heaven-under-the-wa⟨[...]⟩⌐⌐v¬¬e

290:24 ⟨sensual mystery⟩ ⌐the other wisdom¬
290:29 amazing⌐,¬
290:31 horrible⟨,⟩
291:2 ⟨mystery.⟩ ⌐way.¬
291:4 ⟨mystery.⟩ ⌐understanding.¬
291:4 [p. ⟨-10-⟩ ⌐6¬ begins] children
291:8 Folk-Lo⌐r¬e
291:11 ⌐do¬ ⟨can⟩not
291:14 timelessly⌐-¬repeated
291:15 images. ⟨⌐—Yet of course, the era of sensual-civilisation was only an era of half-civilisation, horrible in its halfness. But is not our half just as mutilated and horrible? All halfness is horrible.¬⟩
291:21 but *Ed.*] bu/
291:21 ⟨forgetfulness⟩ ⌐afterwards¬
291:28 our own ... [292:14] if a negro has human *Ed.*] our [p. 7 begins] ⌐our own ... if a negro¬ [p. ⟨-12-⟩ ⌐8¬ begins] ⟨negro⟩ has human *see also entries to* 292:13
291:35 ⟨B⟩⌐⌐b¬¬eloved,
291:40 ⟨form which⟩ ⌐⌐statement of¬¬
292:1 sacrament⌐⌐.¬¬ ⟨takes.⟩
292:4 ⟨app⟩ implied
292:13 ⟨—⟩This
292:27 Omoo⟨p [?]⟩,
292:31 tossed ⟨in the⟩
292:38 substantial *Ed.*] substantia/
292:38 depart⟨.⟩ ⌐: the sign ... the waters.¬
293:1 [p. ⟨-13-⟩ ⌐9¬ begins]
293:8 ⟨He is not finished in his white civilised self.⟩ ⌐He belongs ... other way.¬

293:13 ⌈He must ... death-process.⌉
293:16 And ⌈in⌉
293:16 end⌈,⌉
293:17 *Moby Dick. Ed*] "Moby Dick"
293:18 ⟨In Omoo, however, the book which succeeds Typee, he continues his wanderings about the southern isles.⟩ No
293:18 magnificent *Ed.*] magnificient
293:19 ⟨p⟩⌈P⌉acific
293:22 ⟨a practical⟩ ⌈an exoteric⌉
293:23 ⟨abstract⟩ ⌈esoteric⌉
293:24 record of ... [296:32] to be] ⌈record of the Apocalypse. [293:25] [p. 1⟨4⟩⌈0⌉ begins] *P* In ... [294:10] [p. ⟨15⟩ ⌈11⌉ begins] with all ... [294:35] [p. ⟨16⟩ ⌈12⌉ begins] ⟨will⟩ have conquered ... [295:20] [p. ⟨17⟩ ⌈13⌉ begins] of the ... [296:8] [p. 1⟨8⟩⌈4⌉ begins] The fault ... [296:33] began⌉ [p. ⟨-25-⟩ ⟨⟨⌈19⌉⟩⟩ ⌈⌈15⌉⌉ begins] to be *see also entries to* 296:32
293:26 ⌈⌈in⌉⌉ ⟨in⟩spite
293:30 *Moby Dick, Ed.*] "Moby Dick, "
294:10 ⟨forces.⟩ one
294:20 ⟨sea-going⟩ ⌈⌈water-born⌉⌉
294:25 ⟨p⟩⌈⌈P⌉⌉rinciple
295:4 ⟨Vineyard⟩ Quaker
295:7 ⟨Ahab's⟩ ⌈⌈his⌉⌉ legs
295:8 ⟨as it were⟩ a symbol of ⟨pure,⟩ ⌈⌈sheer⌉⌉
295:12 ⟨of⟩ ⌈⌈from⌉⌉
295:14 ⟨one⟩ ⌈⌈both⌉⌉ f⟨oo⟩⌈⌈ee⌉⌉t
295:14 god⟨,⟩ in
295:22 is ⟨doomed to the process of undoing, the process of breaking the mystic integrity of being. And the symbolic lame-

ness refers to this lamed or crippled activity of undoing a⟩ ⌈⌈doomed, there ... [295:24] to this⌉⌉
295:41 ⟨and⟩ courage
296:10 ⟨work.⟩ ⌈⌈creation.⌉⌉
296:12 ⟨mal [or mat]⟩ metaphysical
296:13 ⟨in metaphysics⟩ wildly
296:17 *Moby Dick Ed.*] "Moby Dick"
296:32 ⟨a [?]⟩ ⌈⌈us⌉⌉ ⟨i⟩silent
296:37 hypocrisies *Ed.*] hypocrocies
297:2 ⟨O [or Q]⟩ ⌈Y⌉ogo
297:17 "How *Ed.*] [p. ⟨-26-⟩ ⌈16⌉ begins] How
297:23 ⟨[...]⟩⌈P⌉equod
297:24 ⟨so⟩ real, ⟨so⟩
297:28 ⟨host of⟩ ⌈cruise of⌉ ⟨Charon's in the Underworld.⟩ ⌈the Argonauts.⌉
297:28 all ⟨purely⟩
297:29 ⟨anomaly⟩ ⌈beauty⌉
297:31 begins⟨,⟩
297:32 ⟨voyage⟩ ⌈travel⌉
297:36 apothe⌈o⌉sis
297:37 whale⟨r⟩⌈s⌉
297:37 begins. When] begins. ⟨Ishmael dreams at the masthead—" lulled [p. ⟨-30-⟩ ⌈17⌉ begins] *P* I assert, then, that in the wondrous bodily whiteness of the bird chiefly lurks the secret of the spell.—" *P* In spite of the self-conscious manner, and the lapses into bad taste, we get some impression of the albatross. But we must remember the bird was a caught prisoner, detained on the deck of the ship. *P* The pure whiteness of things cold and snowy, is owing to the vanquishing and rejection of *all*

light, the trumph of the watery element over the fiery, as the snow-crystals, in sharp vindictive assertion, entrap and vanquish the enclosed air of the heavens, and reveal the pure refracted, vanquished *corpse* of light. So the first snowdrops show the last triumph of the watery element, the pure white of the triumph over the light or fire: but the crocuses show the first signal of the flame-rush of spring. *P* But it is w)⌐W⌐hen

297:39 ⟨that⟩ Melville is ⌐at his⌐
298:8 [p. ⟨-31-⟩ ⌐18⌐ begins] ⟨Only a master of creative utterance could write this.⟩—And
298:13 ⌐¹⌐"G⟨[. . .]⟩¹i¹ve
298:28 'A *Ed.*] [p. ⟨-32-⟩ ⌐19⌐ begins] Λ *TS1*
298:35 escaped—⟨[. . .]⟩⌐'⌐
298:37 ⟨effort⟩ ⌐waking⌐
298:38 (a) ⟨sea-picture.⟩ ⌐stillness.⌐
299:9 "As *Ed.* [p. ⟨-33-⟩ ⌐20⌐ begins] As
299:30 [p. ⟨-34-⟩ ⌐21⌐ begins] higher and
299:37 Almos⌐t⌐ [*TS1C*, in pencil]
299:38 th⟨r⟩oughts [*deletion stroke could be typed*]
300:8 ⟨pure⟩ account
300:9 ⟨supreme⟩ ⌐accurate⌐
300:9 rendering⌐.⌐ ⟨⟨of ⟨sheer⟩ sea-reality. Then there is the

strange tale of the Jeroboam, a whaler met at sea, and under the domination of a religious maniac, one of the ship's hands. Then t)⟩⌐T⌐here

300:11 [p. ⟨-35-⟩ ⌐22⌐ begins] In
300:17 cord.⟨'⟩⌐"⌐ [*TS1C*, in pencil]
300:31 Sunda⌐,⌐
300:33 stationary. *P* Starbuck's *Ed.*] stationery./ [p. ⟨-36-⟩ ⌐23⌐ begins] Starbuck's
301:16 [p. ⟨-37-⟩ ⌐24⌐ begins]
301:18 ambergris⌐.⌐ ⟨: yet so inevitably human.⟩
301:19 unparalleled *Ed.*] unparallelled
301:21 ⟨"Tyworks"⟩ ⌐"Tryworks"⌐
301:25 'Uppermost *Ed.*] "~ *TS1*
301:31 ' "My *Ed.*] '~ *TS1*
301:33 compass —' *Ed.*] ~—" *TS1*
301:37 [p. ⟨-38-⟩ ⌐25⌐ begins]
302:18 land— [p. ⟨3–9-⟩ ⌐26⌐ begins] breeze
302:26 "He *Ed.*] '~ *TS1*
302:27 homage-rendering *Ed.*] homage⟨—⟩rendering
302:39 ⌐It is . . . latter dominant.⌐
303:1 [p. ⟨-40-⟩ ⌐27⌐ begins]
303:12 Geths⟨s[?]⟩⌐e⌐mane
303:13 ⟨fight⟩ ⌐destroy⌐
303:20 [p. ⟨-41-⟩ ⌐28⌐ begins] prey
304:32 whale's *Ed.*] Whales *TS1*
304:1 [p. ⟨-42-⟩ ⌐29⌐ begins] whale by
304:6 medium⟨s⟩
304:15 Tashtego's *Ed.*] Tashtigo's

Intermediate Version
Nathaniel Hawthorne (II.)

The order of texts from 314:20, where *Per* proofs begin in *MS2* (see Introduction), to the end of the essay is *TS1*, *MS2*.

309:1 Literature (VIII) *Ed.*] ~⌜(⌜VIII⌜)⌝

309:3 Hawthorne (II.) *Ed.*]
~⌜(⌜II.⌜)⌝

309:8 ⌜an influence⌝

309:36 being. It . . . Life *Ed.*] being ⟨It⟩
⌜It is life itself. Life⌝

310:3 ⟨inert,⟩ ⌜material,⌝

310:3 ha⟨s⟩ve

310:6 ⟨inert⟩ ⌜material⌝

310:9 ⟨use this⟩ ⌜master the
dynamic⌝

310:10 ⟨the [?]⟩ ⌜that⌝

310:11 ⟨them, applying them.⟩ ⌜the
laws . . . apply them.⌝

310:12 ⟨use⟩ ⌜master⌝

310:14 ⟨it⟩ ⌜these laws⌝

310:14 *nolentem* ⟨d⟩

312:6 ⟨will⟩ ⌜soul⌝

312:15 ⟨[. . .]⟩ ⌜or⌝

312:16 ⟨[. . .]⟩ ⌜In⌝

312:17 ⌜in⌝

312:18 ⌜it⌝

312:25 ⟨main [?]⟩ maintains

312:26 w⟨as [?]⟩ ⌜in⌝

312:30 ⟨de[. . .]n⟩ deacons

312:31 ⌜self-⌝control

313:5 ⟨do⟩ cause

313:6 again⟨,"⟩⌜?⌝"

313:6 ⟨publi⟩ pulpit

313:32 will⟨, with⟩⌜.⌝

313:35 ⟨perfect.⟩ ⌜personal.⌝

313:38 ⟨New⟩ real

313:39 ⟨advanced⟩ ⌜spiritual⌝

314:3 ⟨of⟩ over

314:5 ⟨o⟩⌜O⌝versoul

314:20 But it] It *MS2C*

314:25 primary] ~, *MS2*

314:29 disintegration *TS1*, *MS2C*]
dis⟨-[?]⟩integration *MS2*

314:31 For the . . . and separative.
MS2R] *Om. TS1*

314:34 the *Blithedale Romance Ed.*]
the Blithedale Romance *TS1*

314:34 *The Blithedale Romance
MS2*

314:37 deep-voiced,] ~ *MS2*

314:38 and fourthly] ~, ~, *MS2*

315:3 nominal *MS2R*] *Om. TS1*

315:13 state] State *MS2*

315:16 Criminal] criminal *MS2*

315:17 down-trodden] downtrodden
MS2

315:20 Quincey] ~, *MS2*

315:20 "Murder . . . Art," *Ed.*]
~ . . . ~, *TS1*

315:21 Hollingsworth's *MS2*]
Hollingworth's *TS1*

315:27 Hollingsworth *MS2*]
Hollingworth *TS1*

315:27 nurses *MS2R*] nursed *TS1 see
notes*

315:29 strong,] ~ *MS2*

315:30 It is . . . himself up. *MS2R*]
Om. TS1

315:31 absolute,] ~ *MS2*

315:33 the passive or spiritual soul
MS2R] he *TS1*

315:36 Hollingsworth *MS2R*] He *TS1*

315:36 in healing consumes *MS2R*]
heals in order to consume *TS1*

315:39 loves] ~, *MS2*

315:40 He fears . . . and freedom.
MS2R] *Om. TS1*

316:1 Hollingsworth *MS2C*]
Hollingworth *TS1*

316:4 at *TS1*, *MS2C*] ai *MS2*

316:4 sensual being . . . [316:8] the
power. *MS2R*] serpent in her
is stronger than the serpent
in him. And for this he hates
her. He needs to be predominant, because, actually, he is the
sensual-subjugate being, and
he craves to arrogate. *TS1*

316:9 She wants to possess him.
MS2R] *Om. TS1*

316:11 her,] ~ *MS2*

316:17 person] ~, *MS2*

316:19 medium". *Ed.*] ~" *TS1* ~."
MS2

316:20 like] *Om. MS2C*

316:23 passivity,] ~ *MS2*

316:24 submission,] ~ *MS2*

316:25 medium",] ~," *MS2*

317:1 creative living *MS2R*] conscious *TS1*

317:1 instance ... existence *Ed.*] passive medium *TS1* instance of ⟨the⟩ materio–dynamic existence *MS2R*

317:5 thought-transmission *MS2R*] thought transmission *TS1*

317:11 thought-transmission *MS2R*] thought transmission *TS1*

317:12 show—]~. *MS2*

317:12 moreover, even *MS2R*] however, can *TS1*

317:13 can *MS2R*] *Om. TS1*

317:14 *material dynamic* or *MS2R*] *Om. TS1*

317:15 cause-and-effect, *Ed.*] cause and effect, *TS1* cause and effect *MS2* cause-and-effect *MS2R*

317:15 dynamic *MS2R*] mechanical *TS1*

317:16 world,] ~ *MS2*

317:16 exist—] ~; *MS2*

317:17 things,—] ~— *MS2*

317:17 What is ... no power. *Ed.*] *Om. TS1* What is ... *never* ⟨the [?]⟩ ⌐of⌐ ... no power. *MS2R*

317:23 him:] ~, *MS2*

317:26 them,] ~ *MS2*

317:29 has a demon ... nullity *MS2R*] is profoundly strong *TS1*

318:3 were-wolf,] ~ *MS2*

318:3 Apuleius *E2*] Apulieus

318:4 *Satyricon Ed.*] Satyricon *TS1*

318:5 metamorphosis *MS2R*] metamorphoses *TS1*

318:7 explicitly] explicit *E2*

Dana

The order of texts is *MS2, TCC7. TCC7* corrections only given when they did affect or might have affected text.

319:1 Studies in Classic American Literature. (X) / Dana.] X. / DANA'S "TWO YEARS BE-   FORE THE MAST" *TCC7* X / DANA'S ... MAST" *TCC7C*

319:4 Richard Henry ... [321:4] whole relationship.]

Life, and the habitable worlds, poise mid-way between the poles of the stark elements. Man, central in all, is the clue to all. In his own way he must become all-conscious. In his own way, he must become universal in consciousness. That is his destiny. *P* And man moves on in degrees, in widening circles of consciousness. True there are two modes of consciousness. But we are fixed in one mode: the mode of pure devotion, or of pure attention, submission to impression from without. We submit ourselves impressively to the outer universe till at last, through the process we call love, imagination, or knowledge, we do become in our own way universal, our consciousness becomes a consciousness of the extensive universe, in one of its aspects of totality. *P* As a matter of fact, we ourselves are plumb-central in the universe, we have our being in our integral centrality. But we forget this. Yearning forever after the extension of consciousness, we at last yearn away from ourselves. We wish to break the bonds of our own integral being. We wish to pass into the air like birds, into the ether as pure universal spirit. We forget that this is loss, not gain. For the living soul itself is the quick of the universe, and the infinite universe itself is nothing, once the quick is not there. *P* None the less it is necessary for us to conquer, to know the infinite universe, in our own mode of consciousness. The Brook Farmers wanted to know, to be at one with all men, through labour: to know and to be at one with the beast of the field, and the fertile earth itself. All this they wanted to translate into terms of the upper, selfless, spiritual consciousness. They wanted the immediate contact, the immediate knowledge, the pure translation into ideal or heavenly terms. It was the same in Europe: Tolstoi, Millet the painter, Wagner, Thomas Hardy: the same yearning of the consciousness to grasp the pure element of earth and place and atmosphere and physical contact, supreme in love. Individuals no longer wish to be individuals. They wish to extend themselves: some into universal love, some into universal light, like the great Turner: a passing out from the confines of individuality into the space around, a returning to the elements. This has got to be. But none of it alters the fact that the individual soul itself, because it is life itself, is the intrinsic quick of the universe, the rest being extrinsic. And because the individual soul *is* the very quick of life, it is *specific* and not by extension universal or infinite. The soul is more than the infinite, this is obvious. *P* But the human soul has none the less to find its extension in the infinite. When the Pilgrim Fathers left Europe, the supreme *soul* experience was finished. Man departed from his own living self. The soul soon ceased to count. God soon degenerated into Providence. Men started the great undoing process, the process of vital katabolism, destructive metabolism. It is necessary in humanity as in plants. Humanity has its autumn and winter. American art, like ⟨frost-[?]⟩ {post- *TCC7C*} Renaissance European art, is autumnal and wintry: tragic: the undoing of the soul. *P* For *being* man substitutes, in these periods of autumn, either sensation or pure elemental consciousness. Franklin seeks a perfect Social State, Crevecoeur {Crêvecoeur *TCC7C*} seeks Nature, ideal Nature, Cooper the ideal aboriginal America, Poe is a sensationalist, Hawthorne tells the story of the breaking of the psyche. Each one thinks that a big thing is more important that a little thing. Each one thinks, for example, that the infinite is greater than a single soul. Whereas it is manifestly much less, less intrinsic. The same with Humanity, or Nature, or the Universe.

All these big things are less than one soul. The oversoul is a tin trumpet compared with the soul of one living man: a m<o>{e *TCC7C*}re abstraction. *P* Dana went beyond Hawthorne. The elements of the human psyche no longer attract him. The elemental, fertile earth no longer holds him. It is all, in some strange way, known, ⟨*common,*⟩ {*commu*, *TCC7C*} explored, sublimated into the ideal or spiritual consciousness. The land, and the peasant on the land, these have no more secret for him. This knowledge is born in him, inherent. *P* What then? What remains. The sea! Suddenly, his eyes failing him at Harvard, he goes to sea as a common sailor. This is what he wants: the naked fighting experience with the sea, the universal consciousness of the sea. He must be one with the common sailors before the mast. *P* Now the sea is the last element in the going asunder, the passing from central being out into universality. The sea is much nearer to the stark universal. It is, on the watery side, what cold light is on the fiery side. *P* In the going asunder, water, in its arrogance over fire produces salt. For the loveliest life, there is a pure conjunction of sweet water and fire. But life passes out in widening circles. The air, shadowless, possessed by the sun of light, brings forth the birds. The birds that sing have their homes on earth, near the quick of life. Strange and mystic birds, like the swan, live in the outer circle of life, songless, between the sweet water and the sky, the two naked elements. *P* But water in its fierce moon-influenced preponderance produces salt, and the salt waters are the "waters under the earth." By under the earth we mean more remote from life, apart from life, savagely apart: an outer circle still. *P* The strange, savage, recalcitrant element of the seas. It produces its life too. But how dumb, awful, and unintelligible: the phosphorescent, fireless fish, dumb. *P* So the human soul must venture into the recalcitrant fastnesses of the sea, and conquer these also: sublimate these also into the perfect consciousness. Matter, the primal movements of Matter, the first Matter of all, Water, salt and recalcitrant, as it slides in its great inorganic motions—this must be conquered into the ideal consciousness. For the sea is also within us. It is part of our own tissue and nature: and we must conquer our own nature. Dana's soul is now a stark, mateless ocean, recalcitrant also, away from the life-union. We move away from land into the salt deeps, in our epoch of destructive undoing. *P* In the very first pages we get the clue—in the first pages of ⟨*Two Years Before the Mast.*⟩ {"Two Years Before the Mast." *TCC7C*} It is curious, by the way, that *all* the great classic American books, except Poe and Whitman, should be regarded as children's books: we do not speak of didactic works, though Emerson is usually given to adolescents, and Prescott to school-boys.—Perhaps, as a matter of fact, only children are sufficiently direct and impersonal to "get" the wonderful quality of these classics, which surely are more profound, if less "cunning," than Dostoevsky or Villier de l'Isle Adam. *P* It is Dan's {Dana's *TCC7C*} first days out at sea, winter, the Atlantic. *TCC7 See also entries to* 320:35

319:6 ⟨c⟩Chief

319:11 ⟨trading ship⟩ ⌜sailing vessel⌝

319:12 ⌜—He ... 1836.⌝

319:16 ⟨s⟩⌜S⌝enate

319:17 bare⌜st⌝⟨F⟩ facts

319:22 ⟨He was not so deliberate.⟩ ⌜In the ... soul union.⌝

319:23 ⟨⟨impulsive⟨.⟩ ⌜, almost an appetite⌝⟩⟩ ⌜⌜a material attraction.⌝⌝

319:29 ⟨the⟩ ⌜a⌝ working m⟨e⟩⌜a⌝n, ⟨but not⟩ ⌜not in order⌝ to

320:2 ⌜concrete⌝

320:14 ⟨e⟩⌜a⌝ffect

320:20 the end ... the human] ⟨⟨sort of ⌜scientific⌝ martyrdom. It was an act of ⟨lonely still⟩ ⌜almost scientific⌝ heroism, whereby the human⟩⟩ ⌜⌜the end ... the human⌝⌝

320:29 ⟨an interesting⟩ ⌜a pleasant⌝

320:29 ⟨"⟩ *Two*

320:35 ⌜His adventure ... universe.⌝

321:6 eastern] Eastern *TCC7*

321:9 give." So] ~. " *P* So *TCC7*

321:9 the human soul] he *TCC7*

321:10 aware] alone *TCC7*

321:11 twilighty] twilight *TCC7*

321:11 ceases, where] lapses, and warm *TCC7*

321:12 gives] begins to give *TCC7*

321:12 life in ... [321:23] the wing.] life in ... [321:12] ⟨of⟩ ⌜which is⌝ ... ⟨life⟩ ⌜individuality⌝ ⟨is surpassed⟩ ⌜is spent and universality supervenes,⌝ ... [321:16] ⟨c⟩ ⌜C⌝ape ... [321:19] ⌜at all⌝ ... ⟨on a shil⟩ ⌜upon a⌝ ... [321:23] the wing. *MS2R* man moving on into the face of death, the great adventure, the great undoing, the strange extension of the consciousness. The same in his vision of the albatross. *TCC7*

321:22 But] "—~ *TCC7*

321:23 during a calm,] *Om. TCC7*

321:30 him, when,] ~; ~ *TCC7*

321:32 It might ... of himself,] We must give Dana credit for a profound mystic vision. Simple and bare as his narrative is, it is deep with profound emotion and stark comprehension. He sees *TCC7*

321:32 last,] ~ *TCC7*

321:33 upon ⟨the edge of⟩ the

321:33 waters. It ... of life,] waters: a speck, solitary *TCC7*

321:34 ⟨the⟩ aerial and ⟨the⟩

321:35 Between the ... [321:39] his consummation.] And his own soul is as the soul of the albatross. *P* It is a storm-bird. And so is Dana. He has gone down to fight with the sea. *TCC7*

321:40 a] the *TCC7*

322:1 He must ... ⟨worships,⟩ ⌜accepts,⌝ he does not master.] If Hawthorne was a spectre on the land, how much more is Dana a spectre at sea. But he must watch, he must know, he must conquer the sea in his consciousness. This is the poignant difference between him and the common sailor. The common sailor lapses from consciousness, becomes elemental like a seal, a creature. *TCC7*

322:3 Tiny ⟨al⟩

322:7 ⟨infinitude.⟩ ⌜mastery over life
and death. This is....*the
waters.*⌝] mastery over life and
death. *TCC7*

322:10 ⟨like the style of Thucydides:
the⟩ the style of a perfect scientist.] the style of a perfect tragic
recorder. *TCC7*

322:15 light sails] lightsails *TCC7*

322:15 tackle⟨d⟩⌜s⌝

322:21 physical] material *TCC7*

322:23 ⟨our⟩ being *TCC7C*

322:23 —not *TCC7*] ~ *MS2*

322:23 passional–emotional] passional
emotional *TCC7*

322:27 Out] *Om. TCC7*

322:28 Crusoe's *TCC7*] Carusoe's *MS2*

322:32 disintegrative force] disintegration force *TCC7*

322:33 ⟨But⟩ ⌜And⌝

322:38 to] to human and ideal *TCC7*

323:10 being⟨.⟩ ⌜, a *knowing* thing.'⌝]
being, an ideal reality. *TCC7*⌝

323:11 ungodlike,] *Om. TCC7*

323:12 nature⟨.⟩⌜, a...the Logos in
him.⌝] nature, a...the ideal in
him. *TCC7*

323:14 nakedness⟨.⟩ ⌜, not to be
known.⌝] nakedness, the wall of
the *will. TCC7*

323:17 perfected⟨.⟩ ⌜, a Logos.—⌝]
perfected, a Logos. *TCC7*

323:21 ⟨Man⟩ ⟨⟨⌜A man⌝⟩⟩ ⌜⌜He is too
much a scientist, a...logician.
—As...fact,⌜⌜⌜a⌝⌝⌝ man⌝⌝]He
is too much an idealist, a...
logician. As...man *TCC7*

323:25 ⌜a⌝

323:26 God,"] ~", *TCC7*

323:29 ⟨an unchangeable⟩ ⌜a physical,
dynamic⌝

323:37 and so] and *TCC7*

323:38 *nolentem*] *nolen tem TCC7*

324:1 ⟨the⟩ polarity

324:2 obedience.]obedience: the perfected vital circuit like a circuit
of electricity between individual and individual. *TCC7*

324:3 circumstance] circumstances
TCC7

324:4 former as...the latter as positive pole of command *Ed.*]
former as...the former as positive pole of command *MS2*
latter as dominant, the former
as subordinate *TCC7*

324:18 mal-adjustment] maladjust-
ment *TCC7*

324:21 Captain] captain *TCC7*

324:22 not *MS2, TCC7C*] no *TCC7*

324:30 It is a ver⟨y⟩itable...[321:37]
positive pole.] Whipping upon
the back will rouse the centres of volition in an individual, make him capable of
alert activity, and of refreshing
passion. It will release a certain turgidity, set up a quick
life-flow and bring about a
higher state of intelligence in
a sluggish or torpid or uncon-
trolled nature. *P* Let us guard
against tyranny and cruelty.
But let us guard even more
against our present negative
mode of tyranny, when millions of loose, formless natures,
degenerating from their own
control and limits, run amok in
like and imperil all free, high
being. Our idealism threatens
us with worse dangers than a
little sporadic cruelty. *TCC7*

324:38 ⟨He⟩ ⌜Afterwards, he⌝

325:5 —because] —Because *TCC7*

325:6 what] why *TCC7*

325:7 "The *TCC7C*] ~ *MS2*
325:7 ran] run *TCC7*
325:8 sick,] ~ *TCC7*
325:8 horror-struck]
horror-stricken *TCC7*
325:13 Captain] captain *TCC7*
325:13 down—] ~. *TCC7*
325:17 theorists] theoretic idealists *TCC7*
325:18 understand the passional] understood spontaneous *passional TCC7*
325:19 ethical] artificial ethical *TCC7*
325:19 force.] force, in man as in nature. *TCC7*
325:20 ever⟨,⟩] ~, *TCC7*
325:23 subject⟨.⟩] ~. *TCC7*
325:24 elder] the elder *TCC7*
325:25 whilst] while *TCC7*
325:25 ⟨hi [?]⟩ ⟨⟨⌜John⌝⟩⟩ John
325:26 Captain] captain *TCC7*
325:26 shouts] ~, *TCC7C*
325:36 ⟨by⟩ that it
325:40 ⟨s[wale [?]] it and bleed [?] it⟩ ⌜swathe it and⌝
326:1 ⟨In [?]⟩) ⌜And it . . . damnable. In⌝
326:3 Captain] captain *TCC7*
326:4 ⟨ . . . ⟩ awful
326:7 dreary] weary *TCC7*
326:13 th⟨is⟩⌜e⌝ coast] the coast, *TCC7*
326:16 —I] ~*TCC7*
326:17 ⟨were not⟩ ⌜had not been entirely⌝
326:23 ⟨robust⟩ ⌜scientific⌝
326:23 self.—He] ~. *P* He *TCC7*
326:32 ⟨love⟩ hate
326:32 Captain] captain *TCC7*
326:33 S⟨[. . .]⟩ ⌜South⌝ *TCC7C*
326:34 phthisis or *TCC7*]
⟨presumably⟩ ⌜pthisis or⌝ *MS2*
326:34 "—but] —"~ *TCC7*
327:1 no-one] no one *TCC7*

327:1 ⟨c⟩kanakas] Kanakas *TCC7*
327:7 said⟨,⟩
327:9 Captain] captain *TCC7*
327:11 Captain] captain *TCC7*
327:14 ⌜But in life ⟨he⟩ ⟨⟨⌜⌜Dana⌝⌝⟩⟩ ⌜⌜⌜he⌝⌝⌝ . . . judgment.⌝
327:17 mad] made *TCC7*
327:21 had] has *TCC7*
327:25 seas] sea *TCC7*
327:26 ⟨defend⟩ ⌜prevent⌝
327:26 ⟨this [their?] wanderer.⟩ ⌜this subtle explorer.⌝
327:35 to—] ~. *TCC7*
328:1 ⟨indigo⟩ ⌜blue⌝
328:6 to] or *TCC7*
328:8 sank] sunk *TCC7*
328:9 dashing] lashing *TCC7*
328:13 fear⟨.⟩—
328:16 pain] pains *TCC7*
328:23 Captain] captain *TCC7*
328:23 all] the *TCC7*
328:31 —In] ~ *TCC7*
328:32 spend—.] ~. *TCC7*
328:34 material] *Om. TCC7*
328:35 ⟨being,⟩ ⌜ratification,⌝
328:35 further] further ideal *TCC7*
328:36 ⟨land⟩ ⌜sea⌝
329:7 ⟨being,⟩ ⌜mind,⌝
329:8 fuller] freer ideal *TCC7*
329:9 further,] ~ *TCC7*
329:10 life:] ~, *TCC7*
329:10 materialist] idealism *TCC7*
329:11 skirts] strikes *TCC7*
329:18 nodalises] moralises *TCC7*
329:23 forces,] ~ *TCC7*
329:26 water,] ~ *TCC7*
329:27 mistresses] mistress *TCC7*
329:27 who⟨se [?]⟩m we heave
329:34 ⟨far [?]⟩ much
329:35 tha⟨t⟩n
329:37 Gods] gods *TCC7*
329:40 an originator of *life*] the source of life *TCC7*

330:1 essential] elemental *TCC7*
330:5 Shango] Shanys *TCC7*
330:6 Father,] ~ *TCC7*
330:8 destruction] force *TCC7*
330:13 ⟨combining⟩ ⌐enchaining⌐
330:14 mixed] clogged *TCC7*
330:16 air: the . . . nonsense.] air.
      TCC7
330:21 ⟨prison.⟩ ⌐hopeless
      conjunction.⌐
330:23 mystery] ~, *TCC7*
330:30 and *TCC7*] an *MS2*
330:31 jib— —] ~. —*TCC7*
330:39 "In *TCC7*] ~ *MS2*
331:8 appeared⟨,⟩
331:10 stupified] stupefied *TCC7*
331:16 "During *TCC7*] ~ *MS2*
331:23 quantity] quality *TCC7*
331:23 ⟨over her⟩ ⌐in various⌐
331:28 *forces*] forces *TCC7*
331:29 de-creation] re-creation *TCC7*
331:33 scurv⟨e⟩y
331:40 him, ⟨he⟩
332:1 ⟨he was going on at.⟩ at which

332:10 in] on *TCC7*
332:15 drink] suck *TCC7*
332:16 ⟨caused a⟩ produced
332:23 Solon] *Solon TCC7*
332:31 conjunction] conjunction with
      fire *TCC7*
332:35 ⟨scurvy⟩ ⌐dropsy⌐-like] dropsy
      —like *TCC7*
332:36 scurv⟨e⟩y
333:3 do] do so *TCC7*
333:9 Geaea] Geaca *TCC7*
333:10 world⟨,⟩ ⌐s,⌐
333:14 sundering] sundering, perhaps
      also of pure combining,
      TCC7
333:15 ⟨certain⟩ ⌐various⌐
333:17 element *MS2, TCC7C*] ele-
      ments *TCC7*
333:17 sundering,] severing, *TCC7*
333:19 ⌐No . . . live.⌐ . . .
333:20 ⟨spell⟩ ⌐advent⌐
333:25 acts⟨,⟩ ⌐upon the body,⌐
333:28 the ⟨ph⟩
333:29 Matter] matter *TCC7*

Herman Melville (1)

334:3 Herman Melville ⟨.⟩ ⌐(1)⌐]
      HERMAN MELVILLE'S
      "TYPEE" AND "OMOO" /
      BY D. H. LAWRENCE *TS4*
      HERMAN MELVILLE'S
      ⌐"⌐TYPEE⌐"⌐ AND
      ⌐"⌐OMOO.⌐"⌐ *TCC7C*
334:27 ⟨at last⟩ ⌐in death⌐
334:28 ⟨gradually⟩ ⌐either⌐
334:32 ⟨it⟩ him
334:35 ⟨gravitating to the sun.⟩
      ⌐sun-children.⌐
336:1 ⟨in [?]⟩ of
336:21 ⟨infinite⟩ ⌐infinite⌐
336:28 ⟨passes⟩ ⌐is beyond⌐

336:39 ⟨dre [?]⟩ end
337:10 glory⟨.⟩")
337:16 ⟨"⟩ *Typee.*⟨"⟩
338:3 ⟨[. . .]⟩a . . . slow, ⟨infl⟩
338:8 ⟨their⟩ ⌐its⌐
338:23 ⟨this [?] absence⟩ ⌐their lack⌐
338:25 a⟨, to me, unaccountable fear
      and horror.⟩ ⌐fear and . . . For
      surely.⌐
338:38 *Oneing*⟨,⟩
338:38 ⟨ta[k]⟩ partakes
339:29 ⟨had⟩ ⌐been driven⌐
339:30 ⟨mad,⟩ ⌐insane,⌐
340:11 ⟨let a⟩ ⌐the⌐ blue
340:17 desire, ⟨i [?]⟩ this

341:12 ⟨mechanical⟩ ⌜arbitrary⌝
341:21 life⟨.⟩⌜,⌝ ⟨Melville⟩ without ⌜imposing⌝

341:27 ⟨who has⟩ ⌜that have⌝
341:28 ⟨men⟩ ⌜individuals⌝
341:34 ⟨life⟩ mind

Herman Melville (2)

343:1 Studies... (⟨12[?]⟩ ⌜XII⌝)/ Herman Melville (2)] XII / HERMAN MELVILLE'S ⌜"⌝MOBY DICK⟨.⟩⌜"⌝ *TCC7C*

343:4 *Whale.(")*

343:21 ⟨centres⟩ ⌜ganglia⌝ below

343:21 call ⟨the ganglia below the diaphragm⟩

343:27 Manich⟨[...]⟩⌜ea⌝ns

343:32 a term...order. He] the indicator {indication *TCC7*} of ...St. John *TS5*

344:1 ⟨b⟩⌜B⌝ook

344:8 ⟨per⟩ reached

344:11 ⟨Henry⟩ ⌜William⌝

344:13 ⟨re [?]⟩ true

344:18 peace, which...human heart.] and glowing unification... Creator {creator *TCC7*}... material All. *TS5*

344:31 ⟨lower⟩ body

344:39 i⟨s [?]⟩⌜ts⌝

345:6 positive⟨.⟩ ⌜and the lumbar ganglion the negative.⌝

345:7 ⟨conscious⟩ ⌜voluntary⌝

345:7 appetit⟨e.⟩⌜es.⌝

345:9 ⟨grea [?]⟩ cervical

345:19 ⟨the trees,⟩ ⌜human beings,⌝

345:20 ⟨⌜one⌝⟩ have ⟨⌜on [?]⌝⟩ each ⌜one⌝

345:23 ⟨p [?]⟩ season

345:27 ⟨are⟩ ⌜show⌝

345:28 Melville ⟨of⟩

345:30 ⟨sacral⟩ ⌜same⌝

345:31 home⟨,⟩ ⌜of its existence,⌝

345:34 esoteri⟨[...]⟩⌜c⌝

346:8 ⟨s⟩⌜S⌝outh

346:13 ⟨true⟩ found

346:22 deliberate attempt...[346:38] last word.] violence native... Continent, {continent, *TCC7*} ...violent action. *TS5 see also following entries* to 346:33

346:25 ⟨reason,⟩ ⌜reason,⌝

346:31 ⟨aspect⟩ ⌜quality⌝

346:33 ⟨of⟩ over

346:40 ⟨la [?]⟩ lurid

347:7 amateur⌜,⌝ ⟨at that,⟩

347:13 ⟨m⟩⌜M⌝elville

347:13 creature] ⟨y⟩⌜Y⌝ankee creature *TS5C*

347:18 ⟨proud⟩ ⌜whole⌝

347:36 ⟨make⟩ ⌜he is⌝

347:39 ⟨m[...]⟩ aggregation

348:8 harpoone⟨e⟩r

348:8 who⟨[...]⟩⌜m⌝

348:11 open⟨s⟩ [?]⟩ed

348:30 to do ⟨do [?]⟩⌜to⌝

348:39 for ⟨a⟩

349:3 pair—" *P* Elsewhere... Queequeg that] pair—" The {pair—"*P* The *TCC7*} sophistry...Elsewhere he says *TS5*

349:15 ⟨young Ahab⟩ ⌜Quaker⌝ Ahab

349:18 ⟨from⟩ ⌜at⌝

349:25 ⟨great⟩ sense

349:29 ⟨experience⟩ ⌜sensation⌝

349:35 w⟨h [?]⟩aggish

349:37 ⟨halv⟩ parts

349:37 ⟨reasoning, impulsive and passional, and⟩ ⌜reason, impulsive passion, and blind will.⌝

350:13 out⌐.⌐ ⟨in the book.⟩
350:22 overc⟨r⟩⌐l⌐ou⟨w⟩⌐d⌐ed
350:25 ⟨At intervals⟩ Though
351:8 ⟨lazily⟩ ⌐vacantly⌐
351:9 ⟨laz⟩ mildly
351:18 ⟨all⟩ ⌐pure⌐
351:24 Stand ⟨" [?]⟩up
351:32 ⟨T⟩⌐t⌐here⌐,⌐⟨!⟩ Give
351:37 us⟨[...]⟩⌐.⌐
351:39 ⟨iron⟩ harpoon
351:40 escaped—⟨"⟩⌐'⌐
352:7 ⟨wa⟩ was
352:10 ⟨B⟩⟨⟨⌐b⌐rit⟩⟩ brit
352:28 ⟨that [?]⟩ ⌐who⌐
352:38 ⟨of⟩ by
353:3 an⟨y⟩d
353:17 ⟨accounts⟩ ⌐records⌐

353:20 ⟨are⟩ ⌐were⌐
353:20 ⟨mani⟩ religious
353:24 ⟨feel⟩ believe
353:40 ⌐vast⌐
354:10 ⟨how⟩ this
354:30 ⟨But thus,⟩ And
354:35 ⟨and⟩ ⌐or⌐
355:2 sea⌐,⌐ ⟨in a great calm,⟩
355:10 me ⟨?⟩⌐!⌐
355:21 ⟨that⟩ ⌐which⌐
356:2 ⟨his homage-rendering⟩ his
357:4 ⟨un or inn [?]⟩ hundreds
357:17 ⟨is⟩ ⌐has⌐
357:20 "⌐‹⌐The
357:21 ⟨s⟩Soon
357:32 ⟨and⟩ then

Whitman

358:7 exemplified⟨.⟩ ⌐than here.⌐
358:9 ⟨Whitman⟩ ⌐he⌐
358:13 ⟨become⟩ ⌐are⌐
358:16 ⟨force:⟩ ⌐energy:⌐
358:21 ⌐corresponding⌐
359:3 ⟨stage⟩ goal
359:10 ⟨a⟩⌐A⌐llness
359:37 eve⟨r⟩⌐n⌐
360:16 stupefied⟨. For each⟩ ⌐,⌐
360:32 ⌐and dissemination⌐
360:35 or ⌐the⌐
361:3 state ⟨like⟩
361:31 The ⟨cy⟩
362:3 ⟨t[?]⟩fusing
362:14 ⟨the⟩ ⌐his⌐
362:16 infinit⟨[...]⟩⌐e⌐
362:29 ⟨affe⟩ emotions
362:30 ⟨care[?]⟩ impulses
362:34 control⟨,⟩ ⌐is set up,⌐
362:38 ⟨the⟩ sexual ⟨appetite, or⟩
363:5 ⟨being⟩ ⌐consciousness⌐
363:21 ⌐and⌐
363:33 to ⌐a⌐
364:33 ⟨save⟩ short

364:37 ⟨submission⟩ ⌐debâcle⌐
365:5 ⟨truel⟩ truly
365:24 ⟨of⟩ and
365:32 l⟨y⟩ie
365:32 ⟨dee⟩ orifice t⟨oo⟩⌐o⌐
366:5 who⟨se⟩⌐m⌐
366:29 ⟨de [?]⟩ almost
366:32 ⟨Here,⟩ ⌐About this reality,⌐
366:33 ⌐He knew the death ... life.⌐
366:35 ⟨life.⟩ ⌐being.⌐
366:35 ⟨death.⟩ ⌐pure loss.⌐
367:4 ⟨mere⟩ gratification⟨-purposes⟩
       ⌐and increase⌐
367:5 ⟨pure relation, pure⟩ ⌐true
       duality, true⌐
367:12 *Calamus Ed.*] Calamus *MS2*
367:14 *Drum-Taps Ed.*] Drum-Taps *MS2*
367:16 ⟨sheer⟩ ⌐great⌐
367:31 ⟨Truly⟩ ⌐At last⌐
367:33 *Sea-Drift Ed.*] Sea-Drift *MS2*
368:1 again⟨,⟩
368:8 *Memories ... Wilson Ed.*]
       Memories of President
       Wilson *MS2*

368:20 ⟨the⟩ second
368:20 ⟨gone⟩ ⌜led us⌝
368:21 ⟨always⟩ ⌜only⌝
368:24 ⌜in America now⌝
368:24 ⟨little⟩ Paul Fort⟨[. . .]⟩
368:26 ⟨Certainly⟩ ⌜Truly⌝
368:26 Americans⟨.⟩ ⌜that have been.⌝
368:28 Whitman's   *Ed.*] Whitmans *MS2*
368:29 ⟨spur⟩ purely
368:31 ⟨gurglings⟩ ⌜strokes⌝
368:31 ⟨strokes⟩ ⌜throbs⌝
368:32 ⌜They follow . . . ⟨t [?]⟩ line after . . . unforeseeable.⌝
368:34 ⟨The whole soul speaks at once:⟩ ⌜Such are . . . at once:⌝
368:36 ⟨listening,⟩ ⌜serving,⌝
369:1 any *Ed.*] any/an *MS2*
369:7 ⟨immanence⟩ ⌜quick⌝ itself. ⟨This is the greatest of poetry.⟩

⌜And each . . . [369:9] greatest poetry.⌝
369:10 ⟨matter,⟩ ⌜material,⌝
369:11 ⟨arbitrary and⟩ ⌜shovelled out⌝
369:12 ⟨such stuff as⟩ *A*
369:12 example⟨[. . .]⟩!
369:13 Yet there . . . great America.] ⟨Yet there we are! It seems to me—and ⌜surely⌝ I have read most of the important books, the front shelf books of the world—that Whitman is the greatest man since Shakspeare.⟩ ⌜Yet there . . . Whitman, ⟨⟨ for what you are, first of all men.⟩⟩ ⌜⌜before any other ⟨⟨⟨man, because I owe the last⌝⟩⟩⟩ ⟨⟨And in saluting you, I salute the great America.⌝⟩⟩ ⌜⌜⌜man, because . . . freedom ⟨⟨⟨⟨,⟩⟩⟩⟩ to . . . great America.⌝⌝⌝

Appendix

Foreword (1920)

The following are revisions in MS (E382.5a).

381:5 ⟨and⟩ usually
381:8 ⟨They⟩ ⌜Which they⌝
381:8 for⌜,⌝ ⟨⟨it: and they ought⟩⟩ ⟨to say so.⟩ ⟨⟨⌜boldly to proclaim their thankfulness.⌝⟩⟩ ⌜⌜boldly proclaiming their thankfulness.⌝⌝
381:11 ⟨excused.⟩ ⌜forgiven.⌝
381:14 ⟨Again, she ought to be thankful.⟩ ⌜*How* . . . to be!⌝
381:17 ⟨poked before⟩ ⌜between⌝
381:19 ⟨enraptured kneeling.⟩ ⌜dropping knees.⌝
381:22 ⟨pronoun⟩ ⌜adjective⌝
381:23 ⟨ours⟩ ⌜mine⌝
381:30 ⟨overwhelmed⟩ ⌜overcome⌝
382:7 *had* ⟨got⟩

382:17 beauty ⟨no doubt⟩
382:19 ⟨sea-urchin⟩/ sea-urchin
382:23 ⌜the⌝ Coliseum or ⌜the⌝
382:29 done⟨.⟩⌜?⌝
383:3 ⟨highest⟩ ⌜pitch of⌝
383:6 ⟨But⟩ ⌜Therefore⌝
383:25 ⟨mer [?]⟩ can
383:32 ⟨culture⟩ tradition
383:33 ⌜How g⌝⟨G⟩ay
383:35 ⟨whl⟩/ whilst
383:35 ⟨her⟩ ⌜a⌝
384:2 ⟨the⟩ fallen
384:5 off ⟨of⟩
384:9 ⟨through effort and lapse of time.⟩ ⌜by going . . . growing old.⌝
384:11 faith⟨, n⟩⌜. N⌝ot

384:18 ⟨it⟩ ⌜they⌝
384:20 t⟨o⟩urn
383:37 ⟨c⟩Cortes
385:1 fell ⟨unproduced⟩
385:9 laws⟨.⟩ ⌜, outside of life.⌝
385:14 ⟨perilous⟩ ⌜delicate⌝
385:19 ⟨self-responsibly⟩ ⌜self–
reliantly⌝

385:20 ⟨issue.⟩ ⌜inner responsibility.⌝
385:20 ⟨morality, a new social *geste*, a
new act. And they must re-
alise finally that it is useless to
look to Europe for that which
is and must be purely, aborig-
inally American.⟩ ⌜act, a . . . to
Europe.⌝

Line-end hyphenation

Of the compound words which are hyphenated at the end of a line in this
edition, only the following hyphenated forms should be retained in quotation:

24:17	122:30	199:33	269:20	336:1
30:26	122:32	203:34	272:31	338:10
33:30	127:15	204:13	279:22	338:16
35:28	128:4	205:2	279:33	342:20
37:4	128:36	205:6	282:30	343:11
37:8	131:19	205:31	288:17	345:38
46:7	133:21	209:31	291:8	346:23
56:9	133:27	211:13	295:33	346:32
61:30	134:28	214:15	297:35	351:9
74:36	136:14	215:9	298:3	354:26
75:9	139:8	223:26	298:10	355:15
75:20	142:26	225:38	300:28	355:34
83:13	143:17	229:31	301:21	356:9
91:19	143:36	230:4	303:24	356:39
100:25	145:2	235:35	309:18	363:10
101:16	148:20	241:33	312:21	363:18
106:3	151:36	243:1	316:30	363:20
112:28	153:25	255:4	317:5	389:21
117:24	155:20	257:34	324:28	394:26
119:3	172:34	258:40	329:19	399:10
119:6	187:34	260:17	329:33	399:22
120:39	197:29	263:1	331:1	400:28
122:13	198:12	265:9	331:4	407:31
122:15	199:21	267:30	334:32	

A note on pounds, shillings and pence

Before decimalisation in 1971, the pound sterling (£) was the equivalent of 20 shillings (20/- or 20s). The shilling was the equivalent of 12 pence (12d). A price could therefore have three elements: pounds, shillings and pence (£, s, d). (The apparently anomalous 'd' is an abbreviation of the Latin *denarius*, but the other two terms were also originally Latin: the pound was *libra*; the shilling *solidus*.) Such a price might be written as £1 2s 6d or £1/2/6; this was spoken as 'one pound, two shillings and sixpence', or 'one pound two-and-six', or 'twenty-two and six'.

Prices below a pound were written (for example) as 19s 6d, or 19/6, and spoken as 'nineteen shillings and sixpence' or 'nineteen and six'. Prices up to £5 were sometimes spoken in terms of shillings: so 'ninety-nine and six'was £4/19/6.

The penny was divided into two half-pence (pronounced 'ha'pence') and further divided into four farthings, but the farthing had minimal value and was mainly a tradesman's device for indicating a price fractionally below a shilling or pound. So 19/11¾ (nineteen and elevenpence three farthings) produced a farthing's change from a pound, this change sometimes given as a tiny item of trade, such as a packet of pins.

The guinea was £1/1/- (one pound, one shilling) and was a professional man's unit for fees. A doctor would charge in guineas (so £5/5/- = 5 gns). Half a guinea was 10s 6d or 10/6 (ten and six).

The coins used were originally of silver (later cupro-nickel) and copper, though gold coins for £1 (a sovereign) and 10s (half-sovereign) were still in use in Lawrence's time. The largest 'silver' coin in common use was the half-crown (two shillings and sixpence, or 2/6). A two-shilling piece was called a florin. Shillings, sixpences and threepences were the smaller sizes. The copper coins were pennies, half-pence and farthings.

Common everyday terms for money were 'quid' for a pound, 'half a crown', 'two bob' for a florin, 'bob' for a shilling (or shilling piece), 'tanner' for a sixpence (or sixpenny piece), 'threepenny-bit' (pronounced 'thripenny-bit'), and 'coppers' for pennies, half-pence or farthings.